Introduction to
Computer Law

Fourth Edition

David I Bainbridge

Barrister, BSc, LLB, PhD, C Eng, MBCS, MICE

Longman

An imprint of **Pearson Education**

Harlow, England · London · New York · Reading, Massachusetts · San Francisco · Toronto · Don Mills, Ontario · Sydney
Tokyo · Singapore · Hong Kong · Seoul · Taipei · Cape Town · Madrid · Mexico City · Amsterdam · Munich · Paris · Milan

Pearson Education Limited
· Edinburgh Gate
Harlow
Essex CM20 2JE
England

and Associated Companies throughout the world

Visit us on the World Wide Web at
http://www.pearsoneduc.com

———————————

First published in Great Britain as *Computers and the Law* in 1990
Second edition published in 1993
Third edition published in 1996
Fourth edition published in 2000

Copyright © David Bainbridge 1990, 2000

ISBN 0 582 42334 1

British Library Cataloguing in Publication Data
A catalogue record for this book can be obtained from the British Library

10 9 8 7 6 5 4
06 05 04 03 02

Typeset by 7 in 10/12.5 pt Sabon
Printed and bound in Great Britain by
Ashford Colour Press Ltd, Gosport

Contents

iii

A Companion Web Site accompanies
Introduction to Computer Law
by David Bainbridge

Visit the *Introduction to Computer Law* Companion Web Site at
www.booksites.net/bainbridge for:

- Regular updates to keep your teaching and learning in tune with legal changes occurring during the lifetime of the book
- Links to useful resources on the World Wide Web
- A Syllabus Manager allowing lecturers to build their own course home page

The first edition of this book was published in 1990 when computer law was still very much in its childhood, if not infancy. It has developed in giant strides since that time, in many ways. Much that remained speculative in 1990 has become settled and well-defined. Nevertheless, there are still many difficulties. It seems that just as the law catches up with one aspect of computer technology, new problems appear as a result of the phenomenal rate of technological development. A good example of this is the growing significance of the Internet and communications technology, which raises numerous issues ranging from the difficulty in controlling the use of copyright works to the impact of the Internet on the law relating to commerce, criminal activity, data protection and defamation.

This fourth edition contains a substantial amount of updating to take account of recent legislation and case law. The part on data protection law has been completely rewritten to take account of the Data Protection Act 1998 and other data privacy legislation. The changes to this area of law are considerable and of great significance to anyone involved in the processing of personal data. It even extends to some manual files and the impact on policies and procedures relating to information processing are most profound. There has also been some important case law which, while decided under the 1984 Act, will remain important in the context of the new law. The meaning of 'fair processing' has been considered further by the Data Protection Tribunal, and in R v *Brown* the House of Lords highlighted a serious weakness in the previous law which will be overcome by the new law.

Intellectual property rights are particularly important in the development and use of computer technology and there have been numerous significant changes since the last edition. We now have a new right in databases and some changes to the copyright protection of databases. The *Shetland Times* case categorises at least part of an Internet service as a cable programme service and the Court of Appeal has ruled further on the patentability of software inventions. There has been a flurry of cases on Internet domain names and an action for groundless threats of trade mark infringement proceedings involving a domain name.

The part on computer contracts takes account of case law such as *Beta* v *Adobe* on the contractual status of a shrink-wrap licence and there is a section on the Directive on the protection of consumers in respect of distance contracts which is particularly relevant to electronic commerce. There is also more coverage of liability for defective software, including the Millennium bug, and the position regarding employees using computers and RSI (repetitive strain injury). Defamation on the Internet is also dealt with, including the 'publishers' defence' under the Defamation Act 1996, which is particularly relevant for Web site operators and Internet service providers. There is also mention of the first case on this defence, involving a service provider.

The section on computer crime takes account of relevant legislative changes including the new section 15A of the Theft Act 1968, which is relevant to electronic funds transfers obtained by deception, and the impact of the Protection from Harassment Act 1997 on electronic messaging systems such as e-mail. Important cases are included in this edition: *DPP* v *Bignall* where the court held, incredibly, that having authorisation to use a computer prevented an unauthorised use of that computer from being a computer hacking offence; and the first important case on pornography and the Internet. There has also been an important House of Lords decision on the admissibility of computer evidence in criminal proceedings.

The style and structure of the book have been retained and it is the author's intention to make the law relating to computers accessible to a wide audience. No prior knowledge of law or computer technology is assumed apart, perhaps, from the superficial knowledge that comes with using computers, whether it be simply for word processing or on-line access. The book has been written primarily for students undertaking computer science studies, managerial or business studies. It should be useful also for managers and computer professionals. Law students too should find the book of interest, especially as computer law seems to becoming even more pervasive in legal disputes. In addition to the description and critical anlaysis of computer law, there is an emphasis on the practicalities of computer use.

Much of the content of the book is of general application throughout the United Kingdom but it should be noted that there are some differences between Scots law and the law of England and Wales, particularly with respect to contracts and evidence. This difference should be borne in mind when looking at a case such as *Beta* v *Adobe*, as indicated in the text. However, many of the statutory provisions discussed in the book have direct or equivalent effect in Scotland and Northern Ireland. For example, most of the law discussed in the intellectual property section is directly relevant to all the United Kingdom.

Researching this new edition has been enjoyable. This continues to be a very fast moving area of law and it is surprising just how much has happened since the third edition was published in 1996. As always, I am indebted to a number of people who have helped improve my understanding of computer law in many ways. Students and practitioners alike have kindly made suggestions and been free with their time to discuss this exciting area of law. Finally, I would like to thank all those who have helped with the preparation for and publication of this edition.

I have endeavoured to state the law as it was at 1 July 1999.

David I Bainbridge

Table of cases

Table of legislation

Proposals for Directives

International legislation

Glossary of computer terms

Algorithm A structured set of rules or operations defining a logical solution to a problem or a methodology to achieve some end result. An algorithm may be expressed in a flow chart.

Chip Sometimes referred to as 'silicon chip' or, more correctly, integrated circuit. A small piece of semiconducting material, such as silicon, which, with layers of conducting and insulating materials, makes up a micro-electronic circuit incorporating numerous semiconductor devices (such as transistors, resistors and diodes). The contents of some chips are permanently fixed (called ROM chips – Read Only Memory) while the contents of others are volatile and can be changed (called RAM chips – Random Access Memory). Another form of chip is the EPROM – erasable programmable memory. The central processing unit (CPU) of a computer is contained on an integrated circuit; this chip is the 'brains' of the computer and carries out the machine language instructions derived from computer programs.

Compiler A program which converts a computer program written in a high-level language (source code) into machine language code (object code). The operation is known as compiling and the reverse operation, converting machine language code into a higher level language code, is known as decompiling.

Computer A programmable machine which can store, retrieve or process data automatically, usually electronically. Section 5(6) of the Civil Evidence Act 1968, now repealed, gave a statutory definition of a computer as 'any device for storing or processing information'.

Computer program A series of instructions which control or condition the operation of a computer. Programs may be contained permanently in the computer, on integrated circuits, or stored on magnetic disks or tapes, or punched cards, etc. and are loaded into the computer's memory as and when required. A legal definition of 'computer program' is given in the Export of Goods (Control) Order (S.I. 1989 No. 2376) as 'a sequence of instructions to carry out a process in, or convertible into, a form executable by an electronic computer and includes a microprogramme'. However, this definition should not be taken to be of general application. Most statutes having a direct bearing on computer law, such as the Computer Misuse Act 1990, the Copyright, Designs and Patents Act 1988 and the Data Protection Act 1998, do not attempt to define 'computer program'.

Data and database Data comprises information which may be stored in a computer or on computer storage media such as magnetic disks. A database is a structured set of data – for example, a list of clients' names and addresses, or a list of employees and their details – typically stored in a computer file. A database is usually operated on by using a computer program to access, manipulate or retrieve the data contained in it. In terms of copyright and data protection, databases may also include manual systems such as a card index or set of structured paper files. A data warehouse is a massive collection of data, often obtained from various sources and pooled together to form a rich repository of information.

Expert system   A computer system designed to provide advice at or approaching the level of an expert. Expert systems (and other similar systems known as KBS – knowledge-based systems) contain knowledge in a database of rules and facts and details of the internal structure of the knowledge, an inference engine which manipulates and resolves an enquiry from a user, together with a user interface to control interaction with the user including the ability to provide justifications for any advice suggested by the system.

Facilities management   This is where a contractor takes responsibility for a particular set of operations or functions for the client. It is common in respect of information technology and data processing. For example, a contractor may be appointed to run the client's IT systems. This may require the contractor to develop the IT systems, designing new systems and making recommendations for IT policies and strategies. The facilities management work may be carried out on the client's premises, using the client's equipment and software or it may be carried on off-site at the contractor's premises. Often, when a client first awards a facilities management contract to a contractor, there will be a transfer of staff, equipment and software.

Firmware   Computer programs which are permanently 'wired' into the computer are often referred to as firmware or as being 'hard-wired'. These programs are permanently stored on integrated circuits ('silicon chips').

Fourth-generation language (4GL)   A programming and system development environment. Often used to create and develop applications which include one or more databases. Several databases may be linked together or cross-referenced, being described as relational databases. A fourth-generation language often speeds development time because many routines and procedures (for example, to append and edit records or to print reports) are already built in or may be quickly specified. 4GLs usually have a built-in query language, allowing the user to query the database direct. There is a standard query language known as SQL, sometimes referred to as structured query language.

Hacker   A computer hacker now means a person who gains access to a computer system without permission, usually by guessing or surreptitiously discovering which passwords will allow him access. A hacker may simply inspect the contents of the system he has 'broken into' or may go on to alter or erase information stored in the system. 'Computer hacker' used to mean a person who was very enthusiastic about computers and who would spend most of his waking hours at a computer terminal.

Hardware   The physical pieces of equipment in a computer system; for example, a computer, printer, monitor and disk drive. Hardware devices often incorporate software.

High-level language   A programming language which is relatively remote from the computer's machine language. A high-level language statement is equivalent to several machine language instructions. High-level languages often resemble a mixture of written English and conventional mathematical notation and are easier to use for writing and developing computer programs than are low-level languages or machine language. A program in a high-level language is often referred to as a source code program. Examples of high-level languages are BASIC, COBOL, FORTRAN, PASCAL and C.

Low-level language A programming language which is very close to the computer's machine language. Each instruction in a low-level language has a direct equivalent in machine language.

Machine language The set of instructions and statements which control the computer directly. Many computer programs are written in high-level languages and have to be converted into machine language code by the use of an interpreter or compiler program. An interpreter produces a temporary translation while a compiler produces a permanent translation into machine language which can be used on its own without the presence of the original program.

Object code and source code A program which must be converted into a different form, such as machine language, before it will operate a computer is known as a source code program. Source code is the version of the program as it is written by the programmer and must be converted, temporarily or permanently, into object code before it can be executed by a computer. Most commercially available computer programs are distributed in object code form only.

Operating system A program or set of programs which control and organise the operation of applications programs in addition to managing memory and providing certain facilities such as loading, saving, deleting files, etc. An operating system sets up the computer so that applications programs, such as word processing and spreadsheet programs, can be used.

Software Software includes computer programs and data stored in a computer, preparatory design materials and also associated documentation such as user guides and manuals. Software may be obtained 'off-the-shelf', as in the case of popular word processing and spreadsheet packages, or it may be specially written or adapted for a client ('bespoke' software). Applications software is software designed to perform a particular applied function required by the user such as word processing, the preparation of accounts, the design and use of a database or the preparation of a drawing. In contrast, operating system software provides the basic platform upon which applications software can operate.

New Civil Procedure terminology

The new Civil Procedure Rules came into effect on 26 April 1999 and make sweeping changes to civil procedure with the aims of removing differences in procedure between the High Court and the county courts, reducing costs, encouraging the settlement of disputes (with litigation seen as a last resort) and giving the courts more powers of case management. Although a detailed knowledge of civil procedure is not relevant to this book, it might be useful if readers are aware of a few of the changes in terminology which are relevant to the subject matter of this book. Cases commenced on or after 26 April 1999 will be reported making use of the new terminology. The changes do not affect Scotland where, for example, the person bringing an action is known as the pursuer and the person defending is known as the defender.

New term	Old term
claimant	plaintiff
claim form	writ or summons
interim injunction	interlocutory injunction
search order	Anton Piller order
freezing injunction	Mareva injunction

Thus, instead of plaintiff and defendant, it will be claimant and defendant.

The following list gives the full name of the law reports for which abbreviated references are used in the text of the book, in line with the usual convention.

AC	Appeal Cases
AIPC	Australian Intellectual Property Cases
ALR	Australian Law Reports
All ER	All England Reports
Ch	Chancery
CMLR	Common Market Law Reports
Const LJ	Construction Law Journal
Cr App R	Criminal Appeal Reports
Crim LR	Criminal Law Review
EHRR	European Human Rights Reports
EIPR	European Intellectual Property Review
EPOR	European Patent Office Report
FCA	Federal Court of Australia
FSR	Fleet Street Reports
IRLR	Industrial Relations Law Reports
ITCLR	IT & Communications Law Reports
KB	King's Bench
Lloyd's Rep	Lloyd's Reports
Med LR	Medical Law Reports
QB	Queen's Bench
RPC	Reports of Patent, Design and Trade Mark Cases
RTR	Road Traffic Reports
S Ct	Supreme Court (US)
TLR	Times Law Reports
USPQ	United States Patents Quarterly
WLR	Weekly Law Reports

Chapter 1

Introduction

Computer technology is having an ever-growing impact upon society and the way that society conducts its affairs. Computers have permeated almost every professional, commercial and industrial activity and many organisations would find it difficult, if not impossible, to function without relying heavily on computers. As far as the law is concerned, computers have been a mixed blessing. They have become useful tools, allowing the use of massive legal information retrieval systems, and are of increasing benefit to lawyers in the context of the preparation of documents, administration, accounting and conveyancing and in terms of decision support. Furthermore, the growth of the Internet has brought with it the possibility of accessing a tremendous amount of legal material, including legislation, judgments and *Hansard*. On the other hand, computer technology, by virtue of its unique and volatile nature, has posed novel and complex legal problems. Frequently, the law has been found wanting when dealing with the issues raised by computers and the efforts of the legislators and the courts to come to terms with the technology have sometimes appeared clumsy.

An understanding of the legal issues involved remains of key importance to persons and organisations concerned with computing, and it is only armed with such understanding that they can satisfactorily address and cater for the legal problems raised by the development and use of computers and computer software. For example, when drawing up a contract for the acquisition of computer hardware or software, the legal implications associated with the technology require careful consideration by lawyers and computer professionals alike. One of the purposes of this book is to bridge the gap between law and computers so that effective legal arrangements can be made for the use and exploitation of computer technology, providing an equitable framework within which the various persons and organisations involved can operate fairly and efficiently. It is hoped that this book can help by indicating various ways of avoiding expensive and lengthy litigation by suggesting suitable legal measures, using the law constructively, as a tool. A practical approach is adopted in the book, giving advice of a preventative nature. If litigation is inevitable, however, such as when it is suspected that the copyright subsisting in a computer program has been infringed, a knowledge of the legal implications should point the way to the most appropriate legal remedies and improve the likelihood of a successful outcome.

Four areas of law of special importance to computer professionals are emphasised in this book: intellectual property (which includes copyright, patents and trade marks), contract, criminal law and data protection law. Other areas of law are brought into the discussion where appropriate. For example, in negotiating a contract for the writing of software it is important to address the issue of liability for defects and an understanding of the law of negligence is important in this respect. When discussing the practical implications of computer crime the admissibility of computer documents as evidence in a criminal trial must be taken into account.

Intellectual property law is important because it is the key to protecting innovation in computer hardware and software. Intellectual property rights, which include copyright, the law of confidence, design rights, trade marks, patents and regulations to protect integrated circuits, are first described in general terms in Chapter 2. These rights provide a basic framework of protection from piracy and plagiarism for computer programs and works created using a computer. The enormous scale of computer software piracy resulted in a general recognition of the desirability of effective laws in this area. Special attention is paid to computer software and copyright, the growing problems associated with electronic publishing and the patentability of software inventions. Intellectual property law has striven to adapt and keep pace with technology to provide the protection necessary but there remain some difficulties which are discussed in detail in Part One, together with suggestions as to how their effects may be mitigated.

Much of the impetus for changes to and the strengthening of intellectual property law comes from the European Community (EC) and the need for harmonised law throughout Europe is very real in the context of rights such as copyright and patent law. This is also true on a wider international scale. The European and international aspects of intellectual property law are described as appropriate, including likely future changes as they will affect the subsistence and exploitation of rights associated with computer technology.

Part Two of the book is concerned primarily with computer contracts. In terms of the acquisition or modification of computer hardware and software, satisfactory contractual provisions are important to deal with problems which may arise both during the performance of the contract and subsequently. A well considered contract can provide effective machinery for determining responsibilities and resolving disputes without recourse to the courts. The special nature of contracts for the writing of computer software (bespoke software) or for the purchase of software 'off-the-shelf' is discussed together with a description of the implications of licensing agreements and the scope and effectiveness of statutory controls on such agreements. Licence agreements between software authors and publishers and contracts for the acquisition of computer hardware are also discussed. There is a chapter on electronic contracting in recognition of the increasing use of information technology as the environment in which contracts may be negotiated and made. The utility and content of terms in various forms of licence agreement are described in the context of computer contracts.

Computer crime is dealt with in Part Three. It is a major concern to computer professionals, especially when the high incidence of computer-related crime is considered and related to the apparently poor security record of computer systems. The criminal law was perceived by many computer professionals and financial institutions as lacking teeth and being largely ineffective in the face of some very worrying threats and dangers which could seriously compromise the security of computer systems and undermine confidence in the use of computer technology. Activities which attracted a great deal of attention were hacking (that is, gaining access to a computer system without permission), computer fraud and damaging or erasing computer programs or data. The spread of computer viruses has been alarming and relatively few organisations running large computer systems can claim to have been unaffected. The Computer Misuse Act 1990 was enacted specifically to deal with these problems and to tighten up the law in other areas where computer crime was involved. Three offences were created by the Act and these are described in detail together with the related practical issues in Part Three. Other areas of law which are still useful in the fight against computer crime are also discussed such as the law of conspiracy to defraud, theft and blackmail. Jurisdictional issues are discussed, bearing in mind the international nature of some computer crime, and there is a chapter on the admissibility of computer documents as evidence in criminal trials.

Part Four deals with privacy and computer data and, in particular, with the provisions of the Data Protection Act 1998. It imposes considerable regulation on the processing of personal data on those who decide the means and purposes of the processing (data controllers). The 1998 Act marks a significant change in data protection law in the United Kingdom and gives individuals more rights than they had under the previous legislation, the Data Protection Act 1984; and the rights that individuals had under that Act have been beefed up somewhat. As well as a right of access, individuals have rights to prevent processing of personal data relating to them in certain circumstances, and rights in respect of automated decision taking, for example where computer software is used to make decisions as to whether the individual will be given credit, or other decisions which significantly affect the individual. Data controllers also have to provide individuals with more information than was previously the case. It is obviously important for organisations and individuals processing personal data to know how the new data protection law impacts upon their processing activity, especially as there are a number of criminal penalties in the Act, and the Data Protection Commissioner (the new title for the Data Protection Registrar) has strong powers of enforcement. A further issue is that the new law, which is the United Kingdom's response to the EC Directive on data protection, has particular provisions to deal with transfers of personal data to countries outside the European Economic Area which do not have an adequate level of protection for personal data. Particular controls have also been brought in to deal with the right to privacy in respect of public telecommunications systems to give individuals rights including in respect of 'cold-calling', 'junk faxes' and capture of telephone numbers.

Data protection is an area where good security is vitally important and obligations are placed on data controllers and those who process data for them such as a computer bureau or company providing IT facilities management. Indeed, a common thread running throughout the subject matter of this book is the need for good security and good housekeeping systems, the application of which will prevent or minimise many of the legal problems which can result from the use of computers.

Although the four main areas covered in this book appear to be quite distinct, it should be noted that there is considerable overlap. Contractual provisions can affect copyright issues and vice versa. Computer hackers can interfere with information which is confidential and which may be subject to copyright protection; additionally, hackers can cause difficulties for the owners and managers of computer systems with respect to their responsibilities and duties under the Data Protection Act. Employees, working under a contract of employment, may commit computer fraud, commit offences under data protection law and make pirate copies of computer programs, thereby infringing copyright, and so on.

A common theme in this book is the manner in which computer technology affects relationships between individuals in terms of rights and duties. Intellectual property endows rights on the owners of works of copyright or proprietors of patents to exploit their works or inventions while imposing a correlative duty on others not to do certain acts in relation to the subject matter of the rights. Contracts are all about reciprocal rights and duties. The criminal law governing computer misuse imperfectly provides rights to computer owners not to have certain acts carried out in relation to the hardware or software while punishing those who fail in their duty to abide by this arm of criminal law. Data protection law imposes obligations on data users and grants rights to individuals who have their personal data stored on computer by others. Thus, an employed computer programmer has a duty not to copy his employer's software without permission, and has duties and rights flowing from his contract of employment. He has a duty not to engage in computer hacking, fraud, or similar activities and a right to process personal data stored on his employer's computer in accordance with his contract of employment.

Another theme of a more practical nature is that this book demonstrates the importance of organisations developing policies with respect to the use of computer technology. For example, systems of auditing should be drawn up to check for unauthorised software, to check for computer viruses and fraud and to verify that the use of personal data is lawful and in accordance with data protection law. Policies and procedures should also be drawn up to deal with the acquisition and use of computer software, and educating users and employees should be a priority. Effective and responsible use of computer technology can only come through an understanding of the legal setting in which it takes place.

Checklists, flowcharts and tables are included in this book at appropriate places to help with the identification and summarisation of the legal position and to give practical suggestions as to how the effects of the law's shortcomings may be overcome or reduced. In line with standard legislative practice, as confirmed by section 6 of the Interpretation Act 1978, the masculine form, used throughout this book, should be taken to include the feminine form unless the contrary is stated.

PART ONE

Computers and intellectual property

This part deals with the branch of law known as 'intellectual property', which includes copyright law, patent law, trade marks, designs and related areas. The rights associated with intellectual property are of immense importance to those involved in the development, exploitation and use of computer hardware and software. Legal remedies are available against those who unfairly seek to take advantage of the efforts and investment of someone else. However, the law strives to balance competing interests and the rights given by intellectual property law are not absolute.

Computer programs, databases and other works created using computers or stored in computers are protected by copyright law. Amending legislation passed in 1985 made it clear that computer programs were protected by copyright law and the current legislation, the Copyright, Designs and Patents Act 1988, confirms that computer programs, preparatory design material for computer programs and databases are literary works for copyright purposes. This Act also uses wide and flexible definitions to make sure, hopefully, that future technological development will not defeat copyright protection.

The law of confidence is a very useful supplement to other areas of intellectual property law and is particularly important in the context of research and development and in matters relating to employees, consultants and freelance workers.

New forms of computer hardware, large or small, usually fall within the province of patent law. Computer programs, as such, are specifically excluded from the grant of a patent but it appears that a program can still be part of a patent application if there is some technical effect which is more than just a software implementation of 'mental steps'. As a patent is generally considered to be a more desirable form of intellectual property than copyright, there have been several attempts to protect computer programs, algorithms and expert systems by patent law, with varying degrees of success.

Trade mark law, the law of passing off and design law are very important in terms of the commercial exploitation of products, including computer hardware and software. Integrated circuits have their own form of protection by virtue of regulations passed in 1989 which apply an amended form of the design right to semiconductor products.

Chapter 2

Overview of intellectual property rights

Introduction

'Intellectual property' is the name given to legal rights which protect creative works, inventions and commercial goodwill. Basically, intellectual property rights are designed to provide remedies against those who steal the fruits of another person's ideas or work. For example, if a person writes a novel, a piece of music or a computer program, he will be able to take legal action to obtain an injunction and/or damages against anyone who copies the novel, music or program without his permission. In view of the large investment required to finance research, design and development in respect of computer hardware and software, these intellectual property rights are of crucial importance to the computer world. Without such protection, there would be little incentive to invest in the development of new products.

What are these intellectual property rights? Some will sound familiar – for example, *copyright, patents* and *trade marks* – while others will be less familiar – for example, the *law of confidence, design rights* and *passing off*. The scope of these rights differs but sometimes overlaps. Different rights may be appropriate at different times during the lifespan of a product from inception through development to marketing and subsequent modification and updating. Sometimes infringement of intellectual property rights gives rise to criminal penalties (described in Part Three) but, primarily, this area of law falls within the bounds of civil law and it is the civil law with which this Part of the book is concerned. At this stage, by way of introduction, it will be useful to describe briefly the various intellectual property rights.

Copyright law

As its name suggests, copyright protects works from being copied without permission. Copyright goes beyond mere copying, however, and extends to other activities such as making an adaptation of the work in question, performing or showing the work in public, broadcasting the work and dealing with infringing copies of the work. The types of works protected by copyright are literary works (including computer programs, preparatory design material for computer programs and databases), dramatic, musical and artistic works, sound recordings, films, broadcasts, cable programmes and typographical arrangements of published editions. Copyright protection has a long duration, the general yardstick being the life of the author (creator) plus 70 years or, depending on the type of work, 50 or 70 years from the end of the year during which the work was created or published. The major attractions of copyright as a form of protection are that it is free and that no formalities are required; it is automatic upon the creation of the work in question. Additionally, copyright law is practical in nature and has developed to take account of technological changes and advances. In short, most things, if they have been recorded in some tangible form (for example, by writing or printing or by storing the work on a magnetic disk), are protected by copyright, subject to some basic requirements being satisfied. Copyright law is of vital importance to the computer software industry and to people who prepare, record or transmit all sorts of works (for example, literary works such as books, reports, letters, or musical works) using computer technology. Copyright law is governed by the Copyright, Designs and Patents Act 1988, the main provisions of which came into force on 1 August 1989, and subsequent amendments, together with a wealth of case law.

Until the Copyright and Rights in Database Regulations 1997 came into force on 1 January 1998, databases were protected as compilations, being a form of literary work. Now, there are two forms of protection for databases. Those that are 'intellectual creations' have copyright protection as databases, while databases that are the result of a substantial investment are protected by a 'database right' which is of shorter duration than copyright. In many cases, databases will be subject to both rights.

Patent law

Patent law is concerned with new inventions such as a new type of computer hardware, or a new process for use in the manufacture of integrated circuits. For an invention to be protected by a patent, an application must be made to the Patent Office, an expensive and lengthy process and, if granted, the patent can be renewed for a total period of up to 20 years. Three routes are open to the potential patentee: a United Kingdom patent; a European Patent Convention (EPC) patent applying in respect of three or more of the member states; or a Patent Co-operation Treaty (PCT) patent designating some or all of the countries covered by the treaty. The choice of countries in which to obtain protection is obviously of fundamental importance and requires careful planning and timing. The relevant statute dealing with patent law is the Patents Act 1977. To be patentable, an invention must be new, involve an inventive step, be capable of industrial application and not be excluded. Most things which are protected directly by copyright law such as a literary work are excluded from patentability; therefore, a new computer program cannot normally be protected by a patent. If there is an associated technical effect, however, a patent may be a possibility. For example, a new computer-controlled industrial process may be patentable even though the inventive step resides in the computer program. A patent is the form of intellectual property *par excellence* giving the nearest thing to an outright monopoly although there are provisions in United Kingdom law and European Community law (and United States law) to prevent abuse of patents and other intellectual property rights.

The law of confidence

The law of confidence protects information. Unlike copyright and patent law, the law of confidence is not defined by statute and derives almost entirely from case law. The scope of this branch of intellectual property is considerable and it protects trade secrets, business know-how and information such as lists of clients and contacts, information of a personal nature and even ideas which have not yet been expressed in a tangible form (for example, an idea for a new dramatic play or an idea for a new computer program). The contents of many databases will be protected by the law of confidence. However, the major limitation is that the information concerned must be of a confidential nature and the effectiveness of the law of confidence is largely or completely destroyed if the information concerned falls into the public domain; that is, if it becomes available to the public at large or becomes common knowledge to a particular group of the public such as computer software companies. Nevertheless, the law of confidence can be a useful supplement to copyright and patent law as it can protect ideas before they are sufficiently developed to attract copyright protection or to enable an application for a patent to be made. Being rooted in equity, the law of confidence is very flexible and has proved capable of taking new technological developments in its stride.

The law relating to designs

The statutory provisions covering rights in new designs are complicated. Essentially, there are two types of right: *registered designs* and a *design right* which is not registrable. The former is available for features of articles which appeal to the eye while the latter is intended to protect any aspect of the shape or configuration of articles without any requirement for visual attractiveness. The complexity of this area of law is compounded by the fact that the distinction between the rights is not easy to draw as there is considerable overlap as regards the rights *inter se* and with respect to copyright law. The durations of the rights are different, being a maximum of 25 years for registered designs and a maximum of 15 years for the design right (but limited to

11

10 years of commercial exploitation). These rights in designs might be appropriate for items such as a new design for a computer 'mouse' or an aesthetically pleasing monitor case, keyboard or a printer casing. Design rights and the exceptions to them also have implications for the manufacturers of spare parts, where the design is dictated by the shape of the article with which the spare part must fit or match, as we shall see. The appropriate statutes are the Registered Designs Act 1949 (as amended) and Part III of the Copyright, Designs and Patents Act 1988.

Trade marks and passing off

Everyone is familiar with trade marks; they are very common and there are many examples in the computer industry: for example, the Apple logo, the words Microsoft and Lotus 1–2–3 and the IBM monogram. Trade marks are often in the form of a name or a symbol and registration is provided for by the Trade Marks Act 1994. Marks may be registered in respect of goods or services. To be registrable, the mark must be distinctive and capable of being represented graphically. Trade marks are very important as they become associated with successful products and purchasers will often buy or order goods or services by reference to the mark. Marks such as 'Hoover' and 'Hovis' are examples of marks which have become very closely associated with the products concerned. However, trade marks are in danger of being revoked if they become a generic name (common name) for goods or services as a result of the acts or inactivity of the proprietor. The main purpose of trade mark law is to serve as an indicator of trade origin. Thus business goodwill and reputation is protected but this has a secondary effect of also protecting the buying public from deceptive practices.

A related area of law is passing off. This derives from the common law and gives a right of action against anyone who 'passes off' his goods or services as being those of someone else. If a trader uses a particular name or mark or has a particularly unusual method of doing business, he can obtain legal redress against others who use similar names or marks or business methods, especially if there is a serious possibility that the buying public will be deceived and the trader's business goodwill damaged as a result. The law of passing off is independent of trade mark law and will often be useful where a mark has not been registered as a trade mark. For the law of passing off to be effective, however, the trader concerned must have established a goodwill associated with the name or mark or business method. An example is afforded by the agreeable alcoholic drink known as champagne. The French producers of champagne were able to prevent products called 'Spanish Champagne' and 'Elderflower Champagne' from being marketed under those names. In some respects, the law of passing off is wider than trade mark law where, to be registrable, the mark must conform to the requirements of the Trade Marks Act

1994. There is no such restriction with passing off, which can apply to marks which fall outside the scope of trade mark law and can also apply to other aspects of business and marketing.

Semiconductor Regulations

Integrated circuits, commonly called 'chips' or 'silicon chips', are protected by virtue of the Design Right (Semiconductor) Regulations 1989 which apply a modified version of the design right to semiconductors. They are given 15 years' maximum protection (15 years from creation or 10 years from commercial exploitation). As with the design right generally, there is no requirement for registration in the United Kingdom and there are a number of similarities with copyright law. It is the 'topography' of the chip which is protected, that is, the patterns fixed in or upon the layers of the semiconductor or the arrangement of the layers of the semiconductor product.

Before looking at each of the intellectual property rights in more detail in the following chapters, Table 2.1 summarises the scope, duration and formalities associated with the various intellectual property rights.

Table 2.1 Intellectual property rights – summary

Right	Types of works protected	Examples with respect to computers	Duration	Formalities (UK only)
Copyright	• Original literary, dramatic, musical or artistic works • Sound recordings, films, broadcasts or cable programmes • Typographical arrangement of published editions (Computer programs and preparatory design material for computer programs are literary works)	Computer programs and preparatory design material. Databases, other types of work made using a computer or generated by a computer; e.g. a weather forecast automatically made by a computer linked to weather satellites or a computer-aided design or music made using a computer. Almost any form of work stored digitally	Generally 70 years after the death of the 'author' for the original works. For most of the other works the period is 50 years	None Copyright is automatic upon the work being created
Patent	New inventions including products and industrial processes	New type of printer or computer, new method of making computer 'chips', software controlled industrial process	Renewable up to a maximum of 20 years	Application to the Patent Office to be placed on the register of patents
Confidence	Almost anything of a confidential nature (whether or not stored on computer)	Idea for a new computer program or for a new invention (prior to patent), secret algorithm, lists of customers, business methods	Until subject matter falls into the 'public domain'	None
Designs • Registered design	New designs, being feature of shape, configuration, pattern or ornament applied to an article by an industrial process and having 'eye-appeal'	Aesthetically pleasing designs for computer hardware including surface decoration, e.g. notebook computer, mouse, computer accessories	Initially 5 years renewable by 5-year periods up to a maximum of 25 years	Registration by application to the Design Registry
• Design right	Original designs, being any aspect of shape or configuration (external or internal) of the whole or part of an article. Applies to functional and aesthetic designs. Spare parts and surface decoration excluded	Diskette case (partly), template for drawing computer symbols, keyboard design, mouse, internal components if not commonplace	15 years from creation or 10 years from first marketing	None – automatic as with copyright
Registered trade marks	Any sign capable of being represented graphically which is capable of distinguishing goods or services of one undertaking from those of other undertakings	'IBM', 'Microsoft', 'Oracle', the Apple logo	Initially for 10 years and renewable in 10-year periods indefinitely	Application to the Trade Marks Registry
Passing off	Trade names and marks, product 'get-up' or style	Software names which have not been registered as trade marks but around which a reputation associated with goodwill has been acquired	Indefinite as long as the name, get-up or style still associated with goodwill, e.g. by continued use	None
Semiconductor Regulations (modified design right)	Topography (patterns or arrangements of layers in 'chips')	New design of integrated circuit	15 years from creation or 10 years from commercial exploitation	None

Note: As far as periods for protection are concerned, for copyright, the design right and the semiconductor regulations, these periods are measured from the end of the calendar year during which the relevant event occurred, e.g. the creation of the work or the death of the author.

Chapter 3

Copyright basics

Note: in Chapters 3 to 7, unless otherwise stated, section numbers quoted refer to the Copyright, Designs and Patents Act 1988.

Fundamentals

Copyright protects a wide range of works and has developed enormously since its early beginnings as a form of controlling printing in the early sixteenth century. Copyright has a pragmatic approach and it extends to all manner of works regardless of quality, subject to some basic requirements, which are usually easily satisfied. Since the end of the nineteenth century, tables, compilations and even codebooks have been the subject matter of copyright law. During the twentieth century, copyright has flourished and now includes under its umbrella the following: photographs, films, broadcasts, sound recordings, cable programmes as well as computer programs, preparatory design material for computer programs, databases and works stored in or produced by or with the aid of a computer. The practical development of copyright has been supported by the judges who have usually been sympathetic to the principle of protecting the results of a person's skill, effort or judgment. As Mr Justice Peterson said in *University of London Press Ltd* v *University Tutorial Press Ltd* [1916] 2 Ch 601:

> ... what is worth copying is *prima facie* worth protecting.

Copyright is declared to subsist (that is, 'exist') in the following works by virtue of section 1 of the Copyright, Designs and Patents Act 1988:

(a) original literary, dramatic, musical or artistic works,
(b) sound recordings, films, broadcasts or cable programmes, and
(c) the typographical arrangement of published editions

providing that the requirements for qualification are met: for example, that the author of an original literary work is a British citizen or has certain other nationality or residential qualifications, or that the work was first published in the United Kingdom.

The owner of the copyright in a work is then given the exclusive right to do certain specified *restricted acts* in relation to the work, described below. It is important to appreciate that copyright is a property right and it can be dealt with just as any other form of property. The owner of a copyright is usually the author of the work (the person creating it), except when the work is made by an employee in the course of his employment, in which case his employer will be the first owner, unless otherwise agreed (section 11). There are other exceptions to the basic rule, such as in the case of Crown copyright. The Copyright, Designs and Patents Act 1988 usually refers to the creator of a work as the 'author' of the work, thus a person writing a piece of music is the author of the music and a photographer is the author of his photographs. For sound recordings and computer-generated works, the author is the person who makes the arrangements necessary for the making or creation of the work (section 9), so the author of a report produced automatically by a computer will normally be the person who operates the computer or who manages the computer facilities. In many cases, ownership, as distinct from authorship, will reside with an employer.

The identity of the author is important because the duration of copyright in original literary, dramatic, musical or artistic works (not being computer-generated) is determined by the life of the author, irrespective of ownership. The copyright in such works lasts for 70 years from the end of the calendar year during which the author dies (recently increased from the life of the author plus 50 years as a result of a European Community Directive on the term of copyright, OJ [1993] L290/9).

If the work is one of joint authorship (a collaborative work in which the contribution of each author is not distinct from that of the other authors), as many computer programs and other computer works will be, the 70-year period starts to run from the end of the calendar year during which the last surviving author dies. This generosity in terms of duration of copyright might seem disproportionate in a fast-moving technology but can be justified on the basis that copyright does not give a true monopoly; it does not protect ideas, merely the expression of an idea. For other works, except films where the 70-year period is used, the duration is set at 50 years from the end of the calendar year during which the work was created, broadcast, included in a cable programme service or released, as appropriate. There are exceptions and copyright in typographical arrangements and certain commercially exploited artistic works lasts for 25 years only. The author's identity may also be important for determining whether a work qualifies for protection. It should be noted, however, that there are two international conventions affording reciprocal protection to foreign works of copyright and which also protect United Kingdom works in other countries (see Chapter 13).

The acts restricted by copyright, and which only the owner of the copyright has the right to do or authorise, are set out in section 16. They are:

(a) to copy the work;
(b) to issue copies of the work to the public;
(ba) to rent or lend the work to the public;

(c) to perform, show or play the work in public;

(d) to broadcast the work or include it in a cable programme service;

(e) to make an adaptation of the work or do any of the above in relation to an adaptation.

Section 16(ba) was inserted by the Copyright and Related Rights Regulations 1996 to comply with a European Community Directive on rental right and lending right (OJ [1992] L346/61). Section 16(b) was also modified to cover all forms of copyright work.

Infringement

A person infringes the copyright in a work if he does one of these restricted acts or authorises another to do one of the acts in relation to a substantial part of the work without the permission of the copyright owner and such a person may be sued by the copyright owner (or an exclusive licensee of the owner) for the infringement. There are certain exceptions to infringement contained in sections 28–77. Copyright is not infringed by 'fair dealing' with a work for the purposes of research or private study or for criticism, review or news reporting or any of the other limited exceptions concerning, *inter alia*, educational and library use. There are also some important exceptions relating to computer programs introduced by the Copyright (Computer Programs) Regulations 1992. These allow for a 'decompilation exception', making back-up copies of computer programs and use of a program including error correction. Further specific exceptions relate to databases. There are additional ways of infringing copyright, some of which also carry criminal penalties, known as secondary infringements. In broad terms, these apply where the infringer has been dealing commercially with infringing copies, such as by importing, distributing or selling them, and, unlike the infringing acts described above, some form of knowledge is required; that is, that the person involved knew or had reason to believe that he was dealing with infringing copies. The equivalent criminal offences under copyright law are dealt with separately in Part Three of this book.

Remedies for infringement

If the owner of a copyright successfully sues a person for infringement of that copyright, there are several remedies available. In particular, an injunction, damages or an account of profits might be appropriate and these are provided for by section 96. Copyright damages may be assessed as the estimated loss resulting from the infringement: for example, the licence fee or royalties that the copyright owner would have expected to receive had he given permission for the acts complained of. For example, if a computer software pirate makes and sells 100 copies of a computer program, and associated documentation, each valued at £500, the copyright owner might expect damages equivalent to a 10 per cent royalty: that is, 10% x 100 x £500 = £5000. Damages are not available if the defendant did not know or had no reason to believe that the work was protected by copyright. The meaning of 'having no reason to believe that copyright subsisted in a work' requires an objective test: that is, whether the reasonable man, having knowledge of the facts known to the defendant, would have believed that copyright subsisted in the work (see *LA Gear Inc* v *Hi-Tec Sports plc* [1992] FSR 121). An infringer of computer software copyright cannot escape an award of damages merely by turning a blind eye to the question of whether the software is protected by copyright or being indifferent to the possibility. In any case, an account of profits, as an alternative to damages, may be available regardless of the defendant's knowledge and could be awarded even where the person infringing copyright has done so innocently. Of course, software piracy can attract criminal penalties also (see Chapter 27).

Injunctions are very important because they prevent continued or anticipated infringement of copyright. An injunction is a court order requiring the defendant to do something or to refrain from doing something. For example, an injunction would be appropriate to stop a computer software pirate continuing to sell unauthorised copies of computer programs. A particularly useful type of injunction is an interlocutory injunction. If a person is sued for infringing copyright, it may be a considerable time before the case comes to trial and, in the meantime, considerable damage can be done to the copyright owner's business. This is very relevant in the context of a fast-moving technology like computer technology and, to deal with this problem, the court may be willing to accede to a request for an interlocutory injunction (that is, an interim injunction) pending the full trial. However, an interlocutory injunction will be granted to a plaintiff only if there is a serious question to be tried and the claim does not appear to the court to be frivolous or vexatious. Additionally, the balance of convenience must be satisfied, meaning that the damage likely to be done to the plaintiff if the alleged infringement continues is greater than the harm that will be done to the defendant if the injunction is granted (see *NWL Ltd* v *Woods* [1979] 1 WLR 1294). This balance of convenience is of particular importance if the granting or refusal of an interlocutory injunction would have very serious consequences for either party. In any case, an interlocutory injunction will not be granted if the payment of damages by the defendant at the full trial would be an adequate remedy.

For an interlocutory injunction to be a possibility, the courts used to require that the plaintiff showed a serious issue. However, since the case of *Series 5 Software Ltd* v *Clarke* [1996] FSR 273, the courts have been more willing to consider the relative strengths of the parties' cases as they appear at that stage. In *Series 5 Software*, the defendant removed software belonging to the plaintiff allegedly in order to encourage the latter to make payment owing to the defendant. The injunctions sought were refused but the judge continued an order for the defendant to deliver up any materials he had which belonged to the plaintiff. If the defendant had any such materials in his possession and failed to deliver them, he would be in contempt of court.

The courts also have a discretion to award additional damages under section 97(2), having regard to the flagrancy of the infringement and the benefit accruing to the defendant. This is akin to punitive damages. Additional damages are suitable in cases where normal damages would not be appropriate: for example, where the defendant has blatantly infringed copyright thinking that he can make a profit far in excess of any normal damages he might have to pay. Another possible use for additional damages is where the plaintiff has not suffered purely economic loss. This might be the case if the infringement concerned some material which the plaintiff did not want to publish such as the contents of his diary. In *Williams* v *Settle* [1960] 1 WLR 1072, additional damages were considered suitable when a professional photographer, without permission of the copyright owner, supplied the press with a wedding photograph showing a man who had been murdered.

Recently, plaintiffs seem more prepared to ask for additional damages. In relation to computer software, such damages may be relevant in the case of blatant infringment, for example, by deliberately using someone else's specialised computer software to gain a competitive edge over that other person. Another example is where a person deliberately makes use of another person's database of highly sensitive information. It has been confirmed that additional damages may only be awarded alongside ordinary damages and not an account of profits. A plaintiff has to elect between damages and an account of profits and cannot ask for both.

In addition to the remedies mentioned above, the plaintiff may apply to the court for an order for the infringing copies to be delivered up to him or for those copies to be destroyed.

Moral rights

Moral rights are a relatively new concept in the United Kingdom, and were introduced by sections 77–89 of the Copyright, Designs and Patents Act 1988. These rights, which have long been recognised in some European countries, are independent and distinct from ownership of copyright and give the author of a literary, dramatic, musical or artistic work and the director of a film the right:

- to be identified as the author (or director) of the work,
- to object to a derogatory treatment of the work (for example, if someone

19

rewrites a serious play in the form of a farce without the author's permission), and

● to not have a work falsely attributed to him (this right previously existed under the Copyright Act 1956).

There is also a right to privacy with respect to photographs and films made for private and domestic purposes.

These moral rights last as long as the copyright in the work, with the exception of the false attribution right which lasts for 20 years after the death of the person falsely attributed. The rights are designed to give the creator of the work, who may no longer be the owner of the copyright itself, a degree of control and recognition in respect of the work. By section 103, infringements of moral rights are treated as a breach of statutory duty, injunctions and damages being appropriate remedies. Strangely, there is no provision for additional damages and, presumably, damages will be based on economic loss only. However, the plaintiff may also have a claim in defamation, particularly in respect of a derogatory treatment of his work or the false attribution of a work.

As computer programs are considered to be literary works, it is surprising that the first two of the moral rights mentioned above are stated not to apply to computer programs. Less surprisingly, nor do they apply to computer-generated works. These exceptions may be justified because of the commercial nature of most computer programs and other software and because of the need to prevent ex-employees attempting to interfere with any future changes to the software they had previously developed. Problems could arise if computer programmers and systems analysts demanded to be recognised as authors, as many computer programs are the result of teamwork, involving many individuals, both in the development of the original program and in subsequent alterations and upgrades.

Moral rights will exist in relation to other forms of original works created using a computer, such as a report or computer-aided design, and in respect of many other types of work stored in a computer in digital form, for example, in a database of artistic works. However, employee-created works are excepted in relation to things done by or with the licence of the copyright owner and the author must positively assert his moral right to be identified. Furthermore, an author may waive his moral rights.

Dealing with copyright

We have already seen that authorship and ownership of copyright are two distinct concepts and that, normally, an employee writing a computer program will be the author of that program but his employer will own the copyright unless they agree otherwise. Frequently, the owner of a copyright will want to use a third party to exploit that copyright for him. It might be more attractive financially to use a publisher to market and sell copies of the work, because the latter will have the marketing expertise and distribution facilities necessary to sell the work in large numbers. The usual way is for the copyright owner to grant a licence to the publisher. In terms of copyright, a licence is a permission to do one or more of the acts restricted by copyright and licences are usually contractual in nature: that is, the publisher will pay a licence fee or royalties in return for the permission. In many cases, the licence will be exclusive, which means that permission will be granted to one publisher only. In the case of marketing computer programs, the copyright owner might grant an exclusive licence to a software publisher who will then grant non-exclusive user licences to 'purchasers' of copies of the program. The users will need licences because loading a program onto a hard disk or into computer memory involves making a copy or adaptation of the program, acts restricted by the copyright. By section 92(1), an exclusive licence must be in writing and signed by or on behalf of the owner of the copyright. No formalities are required for non-exclusive licences but it is sensible to make a written record of the agreement.

Non-exclusive software licences are very common and are used where the copyright owner wishes to retain ownership but wants to allow several or many other persons to use the software. This is the way a great deal of 'off-the-shelf' software is made available. Each person acquiring a copy of the software obtains a licence permitting certain uses. Of course, a licence is only required in as much as the use of software is controlled by copyright but the agreement will include additional terms dealing with other issues such as liability for defects.

Alternatively, the owner of a copyright may *assign* the copyright (that is, transfer ownership of the copyright) to another person and an assignment must be distinguished from a licence. With an assignment, the copyright owner transfers all or part of his rights to another person, whereas a licence is a permission given to another person authorising him to do certain specified things in relation to the copyright work. Furthermore, ownership in copyright can pass under a will or by way of intestacy or as a result of the bankruptcy of the copyright owner. Moral rights cannot be assigned (section 94) but may pass under a will or intestacy (by section 95).

Assignments and exclusive licences, to be effective at law, must be in writing and signed by or on behalf of the assignor (person making the assignment) or licensor (person granting the licence) as the case may be. If these requirements are not complied with the courts may be prepared to use the concept of beneficial ownership or to imply a licence giving the acquirer the right to do what, in the view of the court, was intended by the parties. Nevertheless, it is obviously more satisfactory to make sure that the formalities are complied with.

It is possible to deal with a future copyright; that is, copyright in a work yet to be created (section 91). The prospective owner can assign the future copyright or grant licences in respect of it. These provisions are useful where a self-employed consultant is engaged to create a new item of software. The agreement under which he is engaged should contain a term to the effect that he assigns the future copyright in any work created under the agreement to the person engaging him. This agreement must then be signed by or on behalf of the consultant and, on the work coming into existence, the assignment will automatically take effect. This simple expedient is very important in the software industry, where many persons are self-employed or freelance, and can prevent a bitter dispute later as to ownership of copyright.

Chapter 4

Computer software and copyright

Introduction

Now that the basic principles of copyright law have been described in Chapter 3, the relevance of copyright to computer software can be examined. There are two main areas: the first concerns the protection of computer software and, in particular, computer programs and databases from unauthorised copying; the second area concerns works of various types which have been created *by* or *with the aid of* a computer or are stored and accessed or made available electronically. This chapter concentrates on computer programs and the following chapters are concerned with databases, computer-generated works and electronic publishing.

Copyright law protects computer software, whether it be programs, databases, computer files or printed documentation, whereas patent law protects new and inventive forms of computer hardware bearing in mind, of course, that items of hardware often incorporate software. The distinction between hardware and software is sometimes difficult to determine. For example, does a 'dongle' contain a computer program? A dongle is a device which is inserted into a computer port enabling certain programs to be used and is employed as a form of copy protection, limiting the use of a program to one computer at any given time. In the Australian case of *Dyason* v *Autodesk Inc* (1990) 96 ALR 57 it was held that the dongle together with the program used to write digital information into it were, in combination, a computer program for copyright purposes. Some confusion as to whether a single word in a computer program was itself a program was resolved in the Federal Court of Australia which held that a single statement in a high-level programming language was not a program but was merely the cipher or key to access a set of instructions: *Powerflux* v *Data Access Corp* [1997] FCA 490. In the United Kingdom there has been some judicial confusion as to whether 'hard-wiring' a computer program in a ROM chip allows the algorithm it represents to be patented (see *Gale's Application* [1991] RPC 305).

Although it is clear that computer software is protected by copyright, current issues concern the scope of that protection and the need to preserve a balance between the rights of the copyright owner and the interests of competitors and what should constitute fair use of existing software. It has already been felt necessary to amend the 1988 Act to achieve that balance (as part of the wider goal of harmonising copyright protection for computer programs throughout the European Community). Although the legal protection of computer software has been radically improved in recent years, there remain areas of doubt and uncertainty even now that there have been two important High Court cases on the infringement of copyright in computer programs. An awareness of these areas will be important for those developing, using and exploiting computer software.

Computer programs

The term computer software includes computer programs, databases, computer files, preparatory design materials, all manner of works stored digitally to be accessed by computer and associated printed documentation such as manuals for users. There has never been any difficulty with regard to printed materials as these have been and continue to be protected by copyright. The protection of computer programs has been less certain and before 1985 it was unclear whether they were protected by copyright. One view was that listings of source code programs were protected as literary works by analogy with codebooks or because they resembled written English to some extent. On the whole, the courts appeared to be sympathetic towards the notion that computer programs were protected. For example, in *Sega Enterprises Ltd* v *Richards* [1983] FSR 73, which concerned alleged copies of the computer game 'FROGGER' (the object of which was to get a frog across a busy road without it being squashed by a lorry), the trial judge was of the opinion that the source code program was protected by copyright and the object code program was protected indirectly as an adaptation of the source code version. However, this was an interlocutory hearing only and the case did not go to a full trial, so the point was not finally decided. Indeed, cases involving copying of computer programs did not seem to get beyond the interim stage, probably because the relief granted by the court at that stage, usually an interlocutory injunction, was sufficient to satisfy the plaintiff.

There remained serious doubts about computer programs in object code form and these doubts were brought to a head by the Australian case of *Apple Computer Inc* v *Computer Edge Pty Ltd* [1984] FSR 481. In that case, the defendant imported clones of the Apple II personal computer into Australia. His initial claim that his computers, appropriately called 'Wombats', did not contain the Apple operating system and start-up programs was rejected when it was discovered that the programs in the 'Wombat' chips had the names of the Apple programmers embedded within them. The defendant's second line of defence was that the programs were not literary works in the copyright sense, being object code programs. This was accepted by the trial judge but rejected by a 2:1 majority in the Federal Court of New South Wales. However, this decision was unsatisfactory in many respects and the Australian Parliament acted very quickly, passing amending legislation (the Australian Copyright

Amendment Act 1984) to put the matter beyond doubt. This did little to assuage concerns in the United Kingdom; it merely highlighted the uncertainty concerning object code programs.

Following considerable pressure from the computer industry, notably from the lobby group FAST (the Federation Against Software Theft), the Copyright (Computer Software) Amendment Act 1985 was passed which made it clear that computer programs were protected as literary works. The Copyright, Designs and Patents Act 1988 follows this approach and places computer programs firmly within the literary work category for the purposes of copyright (section 3). It also protects implicitly other forms of works created using a computer or stored in or on computer media. Neither the word 'computer' nor the phrase 'computer program' is defined in the Act. This is sensible in view of the rapid rate of change in the computer industry as attempts to offer precise definitions would probably prove to be unduly restrictive in the light of technological development. It is better to allow the judges to use their discretion sensibly, permitting a degree of flexibility in this respect. There should be no difficulty in a court deciding that copyright subsists in a program written in assembler language or in a computer program in object code form.

On a European Community scale, it has proved necessary to spell out in detail the scope of exceptions to copyright infringement in relation to computer programs and, to this end, the 1988 Act has been amended by the Copyright (Computer Programs) Regulations 1992, as described later in this chapter. The regulations also specifically place preparatory design material for computer programs in the literary work category. Concerns about the protection of databases by copyright law led to another European initiative, resulting in the Directive on the legal protection of databases (OJ [1996] L77/20). This was implemented in the United Kingdom by the Copyright and Rights in Databases Regulations 1997 which further modified the 1988 Act, adding databases to the literary works category. Databases are considered in more depth in the following chapter.

Originality and storage

By section 3 of the Copyright, Designs and Patents Act 1988, for copyright to subsist in a computer program it must be 'original' and it must be 'recorded'. For the meaning of 'original', we must turn to case law prior to the Act and section 172(3) confirms that this practice is permissible (this is standard procedure unless it is clear that previous cases no longer represent the law). The requirement of originality is not an onerous one and does not mean that the computer program must be novel or unique in some respect. It merely means that the program has been the result of a modest amount of skill, labour or judgment and that it 'originates from the author' (Peterson J in *University of London Press Ltd* v *University Tutorial Press Ltd* [1916] 2 Ch 601).

Compilations of existing information as in a street directory have been afforded copyright protection. In *Macmillan & Co Ltd v K & J Cooper* (1923) 40 TLR 186, it was held that, although many compilations have nothing original in their parts, the sum total of a compilation may be original for the purposes of copyright. However, the courts will draw a line somewhere and in *G A Cramp & Sons Ltd v Frank Smythson Ltd* [1944] AC 329, a diary which contained the usual information contained in diaries, such as a calendar, tables of weights and measures, postal information and the like, failed to attract copyright protection. The reason given was that the commonplace nature of the information left no room for taste or judgment in the selection and organisation of the material. In the light of these cases, virtually all computer programs will meet the requirement of originality, even if the program comprises little more than an arrangement of commonly used sub-routines, because the selection and arrangement of those sub-routines requires a reasonable amount of skill and expertise.

In the United States, the expenditure of labour alone is unlikely, without more, to confer copyright protection on a work (the 'sweat of the brow' doctrine put to rest in *Feist Publications Inc v Rural Telephone Service Co Inc* (1991) 111 S Ct 1282). It is difficult to conceive of a computer program which does not involve skill and judgment in its creation, in addition to effort. However, standards vary internationally and in Germany it was said that a computer program, to be protected by copyright, must be the result of creative achievement exceeding the average skills used in the development of computer programs (*Sudwestdeutsche Inkasse KG v Bappert und Burker Computer GmbH* (1985) Case 5483, BGHZ94, 276). In other words, a computer program which simply automated an existing process would be unlikely to be the subject of copyright. In the light of the European Community Directive on the legal protection of computer programs, this case must now be viewed as laying down too stringent a test and, indeed, this was confirmed by the Federal Supreme Court of Germany in the *Buchhaltungsprogram* case (unreported) 14 July 1993 which concerned an accounts program.

In the United Kingdom, another requirement for computer programs, and other literary, dramatic and musical works, is that they must be recorded in writing or otherwise (section 3(2)). This has a very wide meaning and 'writing' is defined by section 178 as including:

... any form of notation or code, whether by hand or otherwise and regardless of the method by which, or medium in or on which, it is recorded.

Storage of a computer program in a computer memory or on computer storage media such as magnetic disks should present no problems as the above definition in section 178 is sufficiently wide to cover any existing form of storage and any new forms which might be invented in the future. Furthermore, given the spirit of the Act, it is unlikely that the courts will attempt to narrow the concept of 'recording'. It must be noted, however, that the House of Lords has decided that a password held transiently in a computer system was not recorded for the purposes of the Forgery and Counterfeiting Act 1981 (see the discussion of *R* v *Gold* in Chapter 25). If the only form of existence of a computer program is in a computer's volatile memory, there may be a possibility that, following the *Gold* case, the program will not be considered to be 'recorded'. Nevertheless, because the program will be saved on to a disk or tape before very long, this is unlikely to cause problems in practice. Of course, the program may have been written down by the programmer before entry into the computer or a printout of the program listing may have been taken, in which case the program will be protected anyway. As a matter of interest, the scope of the Copyright (Computer Software) Amendment Act 1985 (now repealed) was possibly wider in that it specifically covered storage in a computer memory.

Preparatory and ancillary materials

Copyright protection extends beyond the computer program itself and will cover written or printed listings of programs, flowcharts, specifications and notes. Section 3(1)(c) includes preparatory design material for a computer program in the literary work category. Prior to the Copyright (Computer Programs) Regulations 1992, these materials would generally be protected as literary works although flow charts and diagrams would have been protected as artistic works. The artistic work category of copyright includes paintings, drawings, diagrams, maps, charts and plans which are all protected irrespective of artistic quality. As a result of the regulations, however, preparatory design materials are deemed to be literary works, irrespective of whether they would have qualified previously as graphic works and, hence, artistic works. In practice, this should not be of any significance although there are some differences in the provisions for literary and artistic works. All these preparatory and other ancillary materials must be original in the sense already discussed. Because copying includes copying by indirect means, it is possible that making an unauthorised copy of a computer program (or screen display) infringes the copyright subsisting in ancillary or preparatory materials in addition to any question of infringement of the program itself or of the screen display.

Of course, manuals and other documentation distributed with computer programs will be protected by copyright, independently of the program itself, as original literary or artistic works, as appropriate.

Restricted acts for computer programs

Of the acts restricted by copyright, three are worthy of special mention as far as computer programs are concerned. These are:

- copying,
- issuing copies to the public, and
- making an adaptation.

All of these restricted acts have a particular meaning which is only partly explained by the language of the Act. Copying and making an adaptation have fairly technical meanings and both of these acts have been extended to take account of computer technology. Copying now has to include electronic copying and also has to countenance the situation where a person copies a computer program but uses a different programming language with the result that the original and the copy bear little, if any, literal similarity when the program listings are compared. If copyright law was unable to control such 'non-literal' copying, it would be too easy to circumvent the protection afforded by copyright. The restricted act of making an adaptation, concerned originally with translations of literary works and arrangements of musical works, now has to deal with the process of converting source code into object code and vice versa.

Copying

Copying in relation to a literary, dramatic, musical or artistic work means, by section 17(2), reproducing the work in any material form which includes storage in any medium by electronic means – for example, by making a copy of a computer program on a magnetic disk. Additionally, in relation to all forms of copyright work, copying includes making copies which are transient or incidental to some other use of the work (section 17(6)). This implies that the act of loading a computer program into a computer only for the purpose of running the program will be considered to be making a copy of the program, even though this 'copy' will be lost as soon as the computer is switched off. In this way, any unauthorised use of a computer program will infringe the copyright in that program. This is why a licence is required in order to use another person's computer program or database.

Literal copying

An unauthorised copy of a computer program may be an exact duplicate of such where a disk-to-disk copy is made. The original and copy will be identical. The question of infringement of copyright will be an easy one to deal with and will be limited to an inquiry as to whether the first program is protected by copyright. Almost all computer programs will be subject to copyright as the basic requirements for copyright subsistence usually will be present. As long as the first program is original in the sense that it originates from its author and is non-trivial and the qualification provisions are satisfied (or reciprocal protection is afforded through the international conventions) then the program will be protected. Identical copies of computer programs made without the permission of the copyright owner are, apart from difficulties associated with detection, fairly easy to deal with in terms of the law, both civil and criminal. Software piracy usually falls into this category of copying as does making working copies of computer programs by a licensee in excess of the number permitted by the licence agreement.

Sometimes a person copying a computer program will do further work on the program. This might be to disguise the origin of the program or to improve it, or both. Where this happens, proving copying may be more difficult and requires a consideration of three questions.

- Does copyright subsist in the plaintiff's program?
- Has the defendant copied parts of the plaintiff's program?
- Do the parts copied represent a substantial part of the plaintiff's program?

In practice, the answer to the first question will rarely be in the negative. The second question is more difficult and depends, *inter alia*, on objective similarities and inferences that can be drawn from them. It is further complicated if the same person has been involved in the writing of both programs. The third question, as we have seen, is concerned with the quality of the part taken rather than its overall size relative to the whole. A small but important part of a program will be deemed to be substantial. Indeed, it is arguable that even a tiny part of a computer program could be significant as the program may 'crash' without it! However, in *Cantor Fitzgerald International* v *Tradition (UK) Ltd*, *The Times*, 19 May 1999, the court held that substantiality must be judged against the program or programs as a whole in the light of the skill and labour expended in the design and coding which went into the piece of code in respect of which the allegation of copying was made. In that case, the defendant admitted copying some 2952 lines of code from the plaintiff's programs which comprised 77 000 lines of code. The judge found the plaintiff's case made out in part but Mr Justice Pumfrey went on to say that substantiality was not to be determined by whether the system would work without the part copied nor by the amount of use made of the code in question. These and other issues are considered further in the following important case.

In *IBCOS Computers Ltd* v *Barclays Mercantile Highland Finance Ltd* [1994] FSR 275, one of the defendants, a programmer, wrote a suite of programs and files to handle accounts and payroll for agricultural machinery dealers. He further developed this software for the plaintiff and when he left the plaintiff's company, the programmer signed a note agreeing to the fact the company owned the copyright in the software and agreeing not to write competing software for two years. The programmer then wrote another software package, which performed similar functions, for the other defendant. This was not marketed until the two-year period in restraint of trade had expired. Nevertheless, the plaintiff sued for copyright infringement and breach of confidence. Both suites of programs were written in similar programming languages, being variants of COBOL.

When the code of the two suites of programs was examined, common errors were noticed. These were primarily to do with spelling and punctuation in the comment lines in the programs. The same mistakes tended to occur in the same places. The same piece of redundant code was also present in both suites of programs. The judge, therefore, had little difficulty in finding that there had been copying, showing the usefulness of including deliberate mistakes or redundant elements in copyright works. He also held that copyright subsisted not only in the individual programs but in the whole suite of programs as a compilation because the selection and arrangement of the programs required skill and judgment. On this latter point the judge, Mr Justice Jacob, disagreed with Judge Paul Baker who said, in *Total Information Processing Systems Ltd v Daman Ltd* [1992] FSR 171, that linking several programs together could not constitute an original compilation. In view of the increasing structural complexity of software products, Jacob J's approach should be welcomed by the software industry as strengthening the copyright protection of computer programs.

In the *IBCOS* case, it was held that the defendant had infringed copyright in a number of individual programs in addition to an infringement of the copyright subsisting in the overall structure of the software comprising 335 programs, 171 record layout files and 46 screen layouts. The defendant had argued that similarities were the result of programming style and the reuse of well-known routines but was unable to convince the judge on these points. In other words, the defendant was unable to offer a satisfactory explanation for the similarities. It was also held that the defendant programmer was guilty of a breach of confidence in respect of the plaintiff's source code programs.

In his judgment, Mr Justice Jacob discussed previous case law and was critical of some aspects of it (see the section on non-literal copying later in this chapter). Some other important points made by Jacob J included:

- Modifying a computer program could give rise to a fresh copyright.
- The fact that the program, or parts of it, were constrained by the program's function did not weaken or compromise copyright protection.
- The data division of a COBOL program (being the part defining the variables and database structures) can be a substantial part of a program and a file record, though not a program, could be a compilation.
- Where the evidence clearly indicates copying but this is denied by the defendant, the court should infer that similarities are the result of copying and not due to programming style unless independent evidence suggests otherwise.

The *IBCOS* case is an important step in the application of copyright law to computer programs. Bearing in mind that preparatory design material is now expressly (and independently) subject to copyright, the width of protection afforded to software is quite strong. Figure 4.1 shows this in relation to a typical software package including a suite of programs and data files.

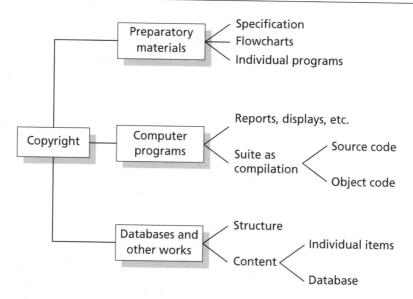

Fig. 4.1 Copyright protection of software package

The concept of non-literal copying can strengthen copyright even more. Whether copying is literal or non-literal, however, it should be remembered that infringement of copyright requires use of the first work and creating a similar work independently will not infringe. Writing new accounts software will not infringe any copyrights in existing software packages provided they have not been used in a way that falls within the restricted acts.

Non-literal copying

Copyright does not give a monopoly in ideas; what it does is to prevent a person from copying or otherwise using the tangible expressions of ideas made by others in accordance with the acts restricted by copyright. In this way, copyright protects expression not idea. Therefore, in principle, it is quite acceptable to write a novel about a secret agent in the style of Ian Fleming as long as it does not contain copies of parts of James Bond novels. The late Ian Fleming did not have a monopoly in tongue-in-cheek, humorous adventures about secret agents licensed to kill, but a novelist might commit the tort of passing off if he changes his name to Ian Fleming or uses the name James Bond or the 007 code in his novel. Copyright protection does not extend, however, to ephemeral things such as skeletal plots for novels or ideas for computer programs unless and until they are recorded in some form or another and, even then, it is the ideas as expressed that are protected, not the underlying concepts. This is a direct consequence of the nature of copyright as set out in the Act.

A literal copy of a computer program infringes copyright if made without the consent of the copyright owner. However, copying is not necessarily limited to duplication of substantial parts and it is possible to copy a computer program in a wider sense. For example, the structure, flow and sequence of operations expressed in a computer program may be copied and, if a different computer programming language is used, a printout of the second program will look dissimilar to a printout of the first program. Should the use of one program to assist with the writing of a second program in such a way be within the ambit of copyright protection even though the codes of the two programs look dissimilar? In other words, should copyright extend to non-literal elements which are not directly perceivable? This question is of such fundamental importance because, if answered in the negative, copyright protection for computer programs would be considerably weakened.

The United States of America progressed much faster than the United Kingdom in determining this question but the basic legal principles are broadly similar: copyright protects expression but not idea. Nevertheless, expression goes beyond the immediate literal form. For example, in the United Kingdom case of *Glyn* v *Weston Feature Film Co* [1916] 1 Ch 261, in which it was argued (unsuccessfully) that a film infringed the copyright in a novel, it was acknowledged that copyright can extend beyond the literal text of a book to the dramatic scenes and incidents contained within it.

Because expression may exist at various levels of abstraction (for example, in the program's structure) the courts have to be able to distinguish between idea and expression. This has not proved easy and the following United States cases give an indication of the development of tests that may be appropriate. (United States law has no binding effect on the United Kingdom courts but it may be of persuasive authority, particularly in the field of computer technology.)

In *Whelan Associates Inc* v *Jaslow Dental Laboratory Inc* [1987] FSR 1, the programs being compared were designed to assist with the administration of dental laboratories. The same person was involved in the development of each program but they were written in different computer languages: the first was written in EDL and the second, attempting to infiltrate the microcomputer market, was written in BASIC. Thus, there was no substantial literal similarity between the listings of the two programs. The United States Court of Appeals (3rd Circuit) distinguished between idea and expression by reference to the purpose of the program. The purpose of a utilitarian work is the idea of the work whereas everything pertaining to the work which is not necessary to the purpose is expression. If there are several ways of achieving the desired purpose, none of which is necessary to the purpose, then the way chosen is expression and, consequently, protected by copyright.

The purpose of the original program in *Whelan* v *Jaslow* was to assist in the running of dental laboratories. There were several different methods which could be employed to achieve that same purpose, and therefore the structure of that original program was not essential to the purpose and, hence, the structure was expression and not idea. The purpose itself, being the idea, was not protected by copyright; it is quite acceptable for others to write programs to help with the running of dental laboratories. In this case the structures of the two programs were similar, the programs had a similar look and feel even though written in different computer programming languages and this, coupled with the fact that the same person had been involved in the two programs, raised a strong presumption that there had been copying and, hence, an infringement of copyright. The distinction between idea and expression has been applied in the context of screen displays. In the 'Pac-Man' computer games the maze and dots were deemed to be idea, being necessarily dictated by the program function, but the 'Pac-Man' and 'ghost monsters' characters were considered to be expression as different graphical representations could have been used.

Another important case involved the spreadsheet program Lotus 1-2-3 and a compatible spreadsheet program called VP-Planner. In *Lotus Development Corp v Paperback Software International* 740 F Supp 37 (D Mass 1990), the defendant claimed that he had not copied the Lotus program code but had used a similar menu system to achieve compatibility (especially with respect to spreadsheet files and macros) and to enable people to change to VP-Planner from Lotus 1-2-3 without requiring retraining. The similarities between the programs were the menu command system (two-line moving cursor menu) and the grid system (letters and numbers arranged in a 'rotated L'). It was held by Judge Keeton that the defendant had infringed copyright by copying the two-line moving cursor menu. Various spreadsheet programs used different menu systems showing that the system used by Lotus was expression and not idea. He confirmed, however, that there was no infringement of the rotated 'L' grid as this was idea, it being almost inevitable that a spreadsheet program would use such a system.

In a later spreadsheet case, *Lotus Development Corp v Borland International Inc* [1997] FSR 61, in the 1st Circuit Court of Appeals, the decision of Judge Keeton along the lines of his *Lotus* v *Paperback* judgment was reversed by the Court of Appeals which found that the menu command hierarchy in the Lotus 1-2-3 spreadsheet was not a work of copyright. Therefore, by using the 1-2-3 menu command system in its Quattro spreadsheet, Borland had not infringed copyright. The rationale was that the menu command system was a method of operation which is excluded from copyright protection by section 102(b) of the United States Copyright Act. The court likened the menu system to the buttons on a video recorder. The distinction in *Whelan* between idea and expression was considered unhelpful by the court which confirmed that the fact that the Lotus designers could have designed the system differently was immaterial to the question of whether it was a method of operation. The case was then appealed to the Supreme Court but there was no substantive judgment as the court reached a split decision, and the finding of the Court of Appeals stands.

The *Lotus* v *Borland* case can be seen as a further weakening of copyright protection for interfaces (in this case, the interface with the user) and facilitates the pursuit of compatibility in software from an operational point of view. However, it could discourage investment in novel forms of software and major software companies may be encouraged to allow someone else to make the investment in developing innovative software in the knowledge that they can copy the ideas and interfaces to produce similar competing software providing that they do not copy the program code or other protected non-literal elements.

Prior to the *Lotus* v *Borland* case, the authority of *Whelan* v *Jaslow* was already looking shaky and that case had been strongly disapproved of by the United States Court of Appeals, 2nd Circuit, in *Computer Associates International Inc* v *Altai* (1992) 20 USPQ 2d 1641. The defendant had produced a program called 'Oscar', a job-scheduling program for controlling the order in which tasks are carried out by a computer. It incorporated a common interface component allowing the use of different operating systems and this part had been added by a former employee of the plaintiff who had a similar program and interface. The plaintiff's former employee was very familiar with the interface element (known as 'Adapter') which was part of the plaintiff's 'CA-Scheduler' program and had even been allowed to take a copy of the 'Adapter' source code home while working on it. When the plaintiff issued a summons and complaint, the defendant rewrote 'Oscar', using different programmers in an effort to avoid infringing the plaintiff's copyright in 'Adapter'. The plaintiff still proceeded even though the defendant had agreed not to challenge an award of $364 444 damages in respect of the earlier version of 'Oscar'. The trial judge held that the later version of 'Oscar' did not infringe the 'Adapter' copyright and the plaintiff appealed to the Court of Appeals which confirmed the decision of the trial judge.

In a far-reaching judgment, the Court of Appeals laid down a new test for the determination of the question of non-literal copyright infringement, that is, whether there has been an infringement of copyright in non-literal elements such as program structure. The test requires a three-step procedure as follows:

- *Abstraction* – discovering the non-literal elements by a process akin to reverse engineering, beginning with the code and ending with the program's ultimate function. The designer's steps are retraced and mapped. This produces structures of different detail at varying levels of abstraction.
- *Filtration* – the separation of protectable expression from non-protectable material. Some elements will be unprotected being idea, dictated by considerations of efficiency (therefore necessarily incidental to idea), required by external factors (*scènes à faire* doctrine), or taken from the public domain. These elements are filtered out leaving a core of protectable material (this is the program's 'golden nugget').
- *Comparison* – a determination of whether the defendant has copied a sub-

stantial part of the protected expression, that is, ascertaining whether any aspect has been copied and, if so, assessing the copied portion's relative importance in respect of the plaintiff's overall program.

Of course, this test only applies to non-literal copying and the actual code remains fully protected against direct (literal) copying. However, this test is likely to reduce significantly the strength of protection for program structure, menu command systems and interfaces. In many cases, it is possible that, after the process of filtration, there will be no 'golden nuggets' left, that is, no protectable expression, to take forward to the process of comparison. It remains to be seen what effect this case will have on copyright litigation in the United States (the judges in the Court of Appeals recognised that their test would be difficult to apply and would need further case law before its application could be predicted with any certainty). Even more interesting is its effect on copyright law in the United Kingdom, discussed below, although it should be noted that the previous test in *Whelan* v *Jaslow* did not achieve any notable successes in the United Kingdom even though it was used in argument on a number of occasions.

Non-literal copying in the United Kingdom

It was not too long after the *Computer Associates* case that a suitable example of alleged non-literal copying came before the High Court. The facts of *John Richardson Computers Ltd* v *Flanders* [1993] FSR 497 are difficult and provide an object lesson in how not to manage the development of computer software, with scant regard being paid to record-keeping and ownership of copyright. Essentially, the plaintiff had a computer program for use by pharmacists to print labels for drug prescriptions and to monitor stock levels. The driving force behind the plaintiff company was Mr Richardson who had originally written a rudimentary program in BASIC and had later engaged computer programmers, both on an employee and consultancy basis and including the defendant, to refine and enhance the program. Eventually it was rewritten in assembly language for the BBC computer (and is referred to below as the BBC program).

The defendant wrote a program called 'Chemtec' to perform the same functions written in QUICK-BASIC for the IBM personal computer. The plaintiff sued for copyright infringement and breach of confidence though the latter claim was not pursued at the trial. The judge, Mr Justice Ferris, had to consider the claim for copyright infringement in the context of two computer programs written in different languages and bearing no significant literal similarities and with very little English case law to assist him. He identified the following issues raised by the case:

- Does copyright subsist in a computer program?
- If it does, does the copyright in the BBC program belong to the plaintiff?

- If the above questions are answered in the affirmative, what should the court's approach be to a claim of 'non-literal' copying?
- Are there any objective similarities between the BBC program and the Chemtec program enabling the Chemtec program to be regarded in any respect as a copy of the BBC program?
- Were any such similarities in fact copied from the BBC program?
- Is any copying thus found copying of a substantial part of the BBC program?

The issue of copyright subsistence was easily dealt with by the judge and ownership of copyright in the BBC program was resolved in favour of the plaintiff. Although the defendant may have been the legal owner of parts of the program he had written as a self-employed consultant, the plaintiff was the owner in equity and, as the plaintiff had joined the legal owner in the action (by suing him), the full range of remedies was available to the plaintiff should infringement be proved.

After reviewing the English and United States authorities on non-literal copying and discussing the *Computer Associates* case at length, Mr Justice Ferris said that there was nothing in any English decision which conflicted with the general approach adopted in that case. However, he said that, in preference to seeking the 'core of protectable expression' in the plaintiff's program, an English court will:

- decide whether the plaintiff's program as a whole is entitled to copyright protection, and then
- decide whether any similarity in the defendant's program resulting from copying amounts to copying a substantial part of the plaintiff's program.

Ferris J went on to say that the approach to separation of idea and expression as expounded in *Computer Associates* was appropriate and a similar approach should be adopted in England. This would be relevant to issues of substantiality of copying and originality. Thus, the non-literal elements of a computer program are to be taken into account. In testing for infringement, the judge concentrated on objective similarities in the non-literal elements of the programs and he classified them in four ways:

- similarities that were the result of copying a substantial part of the plaintiff's program, being the line editor, amendment routines and dose codes;
- similarities that were the result of copying but not in relation to a substantial part of the plaintiff's program – for example, the date option, operation successful, message, etc.;
- similarities which may have been the result of copying but which, in any case, did not involve copying substantial parts of the plaintiff's program – for example, the vertical arrangement of entry prompts;
- similarities that were not the result of copying including the use of the escape key, position of label on screen, etc.

It was held that the defendant had infringed copyright in respect of three non-literal elements. This would mean that it might be a relatively simple matter for the defendant to rewrite the offending parts of his program, notwithstanding any award in damages in respect of the infringement.

The judgment in *Richardson* v *Flanders* attracted a fair amount of criticism. In particular, Mr Justice Jacob in his judgment in *IBCOS* v *Barclays* (a case on literal copying) was particularly critical of a blind allegiance to the United States approach, pointing out that United Kingdom copyright law is different, being based on a different statute. He said that the United States approach was not helpful. It must be noted, however, that Jacob J was dealing with a more straightforward case of copying and the two cases are distinguishable, one being on literal copying (*IBCOS*), the other on non-literal copying (*Richardson*). Consequently, it is possible to reconcile the two cases and the judgments can be seen as complementary. Where *Richardson* is weak is, arguably, in the abstraction to non-literal expression. Furthermore, there was no serious attempt to filter out unprotected elements but this is more likely to be due to differences between United Kingdom and United States law than a failure on the part of the judge.

Finally, it should be noted that the defendant in *Richardson* v *Flanders* had made significant additions and enhancements to his program, which was substantially larger than the plaintiff's program and had more features. Nevertheless, when comparing programs for copyright infringement it was confirmed that more attention should be paid to the parts claimed to be the same or similar than the other parts of the program. As a result of the *Richardson* and *IBCOS* cases, it would appear that copyright protection for computer programs is at least adequate and there is a reasonable balance between strength of protection and the development of competing programs by others, as is investigated below.

Copying in practice

Has copyright law been developed by the courts to prevent the marketing of lookalike computer programs? Obviously, if a company makes a new type of computer program which proves to be very successful, other companies will want to bring out their own versions in order to gain a share in the market created or stimulated by the first program. Essentially, copyright law does not prevent this as long as the first program is not copied or adapted. Although copying now extends to the structure and other non-literal elements of a program this should not prevent competitors bringing out programs to perform similar functions. A line must be drawn somewhere and the following hypothetical examples, involving two software companies Acme and Zenith, indicate where it might be drawn. Acme developed a program to record and monitor drug dosages to hospital patients and Zenith, shortly afterwards, brought out a similar program.

1 Zenith did not know of the existence of Acme's program. (*No infringement of copyright.*)

2 Zenith knew of the existence of Acme's program but had not seen it in use. (*No infringement of copyright; the function of the program is idea, not expression.*)

3 Zenith had seen Acme's program in use and decided to write a program to fulfil the same purpose, that is, to monitor drug dosages. Zenith did not refer to Acme's program further than this and Zenith developed its own methods of performing the purpose. The structures of the two programs are different in many respects and where they are similar this is the result of coincidence only or because they are constrained by the function. (*No infringement of copyright.*)

4 Zenith buys a copy of Acme's program. Zenith cannot see the source code because the copy is compiled (in object code), but by using the program extensively, Zenith gets a good insight into the workings and structure of Acme's program and, based on this insight, Zenith writes its program (obviously without using a source code listing of Acme's program). Zenith's knowledge of Acme's program is no more than a competent user would achieve. (*Possible infringement of copyright because the structure of Zenith's program is determined by Zenith's familiarity with the structure of Acme's program which Zenith copies indirectly. Copying menu systems, screen displays and other non-literal elements may also infringe Acme's copyright.*)

5 Zenith decompiles Acme's program and rewrites parts of it to make its program, perhaps using a different computer language. (*Definite infringement of copyright; the act of decompilation itself will constitute an infringement of copyright. The 'decompilation' exception to infringement is unlikely to apply here (see later).*)

6 Zenith employs an ex-programmer of Acme who is familiar with the program; this person writes a program for Zenith using copies of listings and flowcharts that he retained. Qualitatively substantial parts of the program code are incorporated in the new program. (*Definite infringement of copyright and possible breach of confidence.*)

7 As 6 above but the ex-programmer of Acme has not retained any materials from his previous employment; he simply uses what he can remember. (*Possible infringement of copyright.*)

The last example lies in a difficult area and is tied up with questions relating to the law of confidence and restraint of trade. Ex-employees frequently cause problems because of the difficulty in reconciling their continuing duty to their ex-employer with the need to be able to obtain other employment. If the ex-employee is not allowed to make use of anything at all from his past experience, he may well be virtually unemployable because what he has done previously is an integral part of his skill and expertise. This question will be considered further in Chapter 8 on the law of confidence; at this stage it needs to be noted that an ex-employee will be able to make use of his skills and what he remembers as long as these are not genuine trade secrets. In terms of writing computer software, a program to automate an existing manual process probably will not be considered a trade secret.

If company B writes a program independently and, by chance, it turns out to be very similar to a program written by company A, there is no infringement of copyright because there has been neither copying nor the making of an adaptation of A's program and both A and B will have a copyright in their respective programs. A substantial similarity between programs, however, can suggest that one has been copied from the other and this can shift the burden of proof to the defendant, especially if there is something else to support the view that copying may have taken place, such as access to the original by the defendant (see *LB Plastics Ltd* v *Swish Products Ltd* [1979] RPC 551). This means that instead of requiring the plaintiff to show that copying has taken place, the defendant will have to show that he did not, in fact, copy the plaintiff's work and such a shift in the burden of proof can be exceedingly onerous to the defendant.

One approach to the question of copying was suggested by the Court of Appeal in *Francis, Day & Hunter Ltd* v *Bron* [1963] Ch 587, a case concerning an alleged infringement of an old song entitled 'In a Little Spanish Town'. For copying to be proved, the test is as follows:

- there must be sufficient objective similarity between the two works (an objective issue – would the 'reasonable man' consider the two works sufficiently similar?), and
- there must also be some causal connection between the two works (a subjective question but not to be presumed as a matter of law merely upon proof of access).

It is possible to infringe copyright by subconsciously copying a work, although this is probably more relevant to the music industry than the computer industry. Thus George Harrison's song 'My Sweet Lord' was alleged to have infringed an earlier song 'He's So Fine', but it is thought that the evidence required to support this proposition would have to be quite strong. Taken to its logical conclusion this might encourage software developers to adopt a 'clean-room' approach, denying access to existing software by the programmers and analysts in an effort to try to prevent accusations of copying. In most cases, this would not be realistic given the likelihood that any skilled programmer would already have a wide knowledge of other software products. Even if it is feasible, there is no guarantee that this would provide a defence to an infringement action. In the New Zealand case of *Plix Products Ltd* v *Frank M Whinstone (Merchants)* [1986] FSR 63, the defendant asked his designer to design a kiwifruit pack without talking to others in this field and without looking at existing packs. Although there was no direct copying it was held that the copyright in the plaintiff's packs had been infringed through the medium of the New Zealand Kiwifruit Authority's specification for packs, and the court also seemed to accept the possibility that copyright can be infringed through a verbal description. New Zealand copyright law is very similar to United Kingdom law; but, in the United States, it would be likely that the design features indicated in the specification would be considered to be an unprotectable idea.

The implications of indirect copying (expressly covered by the Copyright, Designs and Patents Act 1988, section 16) are serious for the software industry and care must be taken to avoid such a claim. There is even a case for deliberately making elements in a computer program (including non-literal elements) different from the equivalent part of competing programs if this does not compromise the functionality, usability and attractiveness of the program.

If copyright protection of computer programs is developed by the courts to become too strong, the Act contains safeguards. By section 144(1), as a result of a report of the Monopolies and Mergers Commission (renamed the Competition Commission by the Competition Act 1998), the Secretary of State may grant a licence as of right if the public interest would be prejudiced: for example, if the owner of the copyright in a unique computer program refuses to grant licences on reasonable terms. Therefore, if a company has a virtual monopoly in a particular type of computer system, charges an exorbitant price for it and the Commission prepares a report to the effect that this situation is against the public interest, anyone will be able to apply for a compulsory licence to use the software. The licence fee and other terms of the licence will be decided by the Copyright Tribunal, a body set up to administer licensing schemes. Under section 66, the Secretary of State may order that lending of copies to the public shall be treated as licensed subject to payment of a reasonable royalty of other payments as may be agreed or, failing agreement, as determined by the Copyright Tribunal. Section 66 was amended by the Copyright and Related Rights Regulations 1996. Previously, it was framed in terms of rental rather than lending.

Issuing copies to the public

Under section 18, issuing copies of a work to the public is a restricted act and will infringe copyright if done without the permission of the owner of the copyright. However, the right to control the issue of copies to the public only applies to the first issue of individual copies. Thus, once a particular copy of a computer program has been issued to the public by or with the consent of the copyright owner, he can no longer use that right to control subsequent dealings with that particular copy, apart from rental. The right still applies in relation to unissued copies. This principle accords with the doctrine of exhaustion of rights in European Community law. Exhaustion would apply where, for example, a software company has sold copies of its programs to one dealer in Germany and, at a lower price, to another dealer in France. A third party would be able to buy copies in France and import them into Germany in order to resell them, undercutting the German dealer. The software company would not be able to use its public issue right to prevent this.

Rental or lending copies to the public

By virtue of section 18A (which was inserted by the Copyright and Related Rights Regulations 1996) the rental or lending of copies of a work to the public is an act restricted by the copyright. This provision applies to literary, dramatic and musical works, to artistic works (except works of architecture and works of applied art) and films and sound recordings.

Making an adaptation

Making an adaptation of a literary, dramatic or musical work is a restricted act. In terms of a musical work, a new arrangement of a song is an adaptation of the original. Changing a cartoon strip into a story told by words only is also an adaptation, as is a translation of a literary or dramatic work. Additionally, for a computer program, making an arrangement or altered version comes within this restricted act. 'Translation' has a special meaning for computer programs, by section 21(4), and includes:

> ... a version of the program in which it is converted into or out of a computer language or code or into a different computer language or code.

If a high-level, source code computer program is compiled (converted) into an object code program, this will be an adaptation of the source code program and, therefore, a restricted act. This provision is aimed at controlling the compilation, decompilation, assembly and disassembly of computer programs – that is, the conversion of source code programs into object code and vice versa as shown in Fig. 4.2. This would seem to be a reasonable activity to be controlled by copyright, especially as reverse-engineering an object code program will make the techniques, ideas and principles underlying a computer program more accessible. As we shall see later, however, under certain circumstances this is expressly permitted under copyright law.

Source code programs are protected by copyright provided they are 'original' – that is, they are the result of skill, labour or judgment. The position is less clear as far as object code programs are concerned because they may not be original in the sense described above. In most cases, an object code program will have been created by submitting the source code program to a compiler program or assembler program. This process may require little effort or skill on the part of the person creating the object code unless there are several errors detected which need correction before a suitable executable version of the object code is obtained. Even if an object code program is not

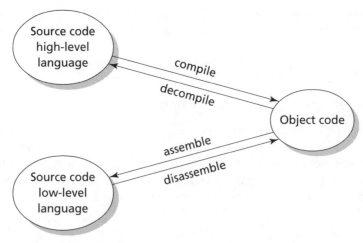

Fig. 4.2 Making an adaptation of a computer program

an original literary work, it will be protected by copyright as an adaptation of such a work and the restricted acts extend to an adaptation as they do to the original work. Thus, it is an infringement of copyright to copy an adaptation of a program or even to make an adaptation of an adaptation.

It could be argued that the meaning of translation is too wide as it seems to catch a version of a source code program written in a different high-level language from that used for the original program, that is, a manual conversion. If a computer program is written using BASIC and someone then rewrites the program in COBOL, the latter will be an adaptation of the BASIC program because it has been converted into a different computer language. To produce a program in a different high-level language, however, is not merely a question of translating the program instructions from one language to another as with spoken languages. The programmer would have to reduce the original program to its underlying concepts and ideas and from those concepts and ideas (not from the computer program itself) develop a new version of the program in another high-level language, as shown in Fig. 4.3.

The differences between the two programs could be as those between Romeo and Juliet and West Side Story and, as a basic principle, copyright should not protect ideas as such, only the expression or recording of those

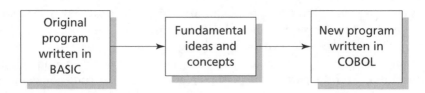

Fig. 4.3 Conversion of a computer program

ideas. However, it seems that the new version of a program in a different high-level language will be an adaptation, regardless of the quite considerable amount of skill and effort required to 'translate' the program in such a way.

Restricted acts apply to a work as a whole or to any substantial part of it (section 16(3)). What is substantial is a matter of fact and the courts will look to quality as well as quantity (see *Hawkes & Sons (London) Ltd* v *Paramount Film Service Ltd* [1934] Ch 593). Therefore, a computer program which includes parts (such as sub-routines) copied from another program will infringe the copyright in that other program if the copied parts represent a substantial part of the original program and they may be substantial if they go to the root of the other program or capture its essence, even though they are small in terms of quantity. Theoretically, it is possible to increase copyright protection by modularising a single program into a number of separate sub-programs which, if each individually is the result of skill, labour and effort, will all be independently protected in addition to any copyright in the suite of programs as a compilation. Substantiality, in terms of infringement, will be measured by comparison with a sub-program rather than the unified whole.

Exceptions to copyright infringement

When it was decided to classify computer programs as literary works for copyright purposes, the usual exceptions to copyright infringement applied. The Act contains a great many exceptions, called the 'permitted acts': for example, fair dealing for research or private study or for criticism, review or news reporting. In order to provide for uniform protection of computer programs throughout the European Community, a Council Directive on the legal protection of computer programs was published in 1991 (91/250/EEC, OJ [1991] L122/42). United Kingdom law was already well developed and complied with most of the Directive's provisions. However, because some aspects of United Kingdom law were somewhat vague and ill-defined (for example, the meaning of fair dealing) it was decided to tighten up some of the exceptions to copyright infringement, the necessary changes to the 1988 Act being made by the Copyright (Computer Programs) Regulations 1992. In terms of the permitted acts, three particular issues were addressed:

- 'decompiling' an existing computer program for interoperability;
- making necessary back-up copies;
- copying and adapting including error correction.

These three important exceptions to copyright infringement are described and examined below. It should be pointed out that the previous law probably covered the above acts in most circumstances. For example, fair dealing for research purposes might have allowed decompilation to achieve interoperability and implied licences might have been appropriate in some cases involving error correction and back-up copies. One further point is that, in addition to statutory defences to copyright infringement, there is a defence of public interest – for example, if it is in the public interest that a program listing is published. This might apply to code used by 'hackers' to penetrate computer systems because publication would assist managers of computer installations in their attempts to combat computer hacking.

Decompilation of computer programs

'Decompilation' is used in a wide sense and defined in section 50B as converting a copy of a computer program expressed in a low-level language into a version expressed in a higher-level language and extends to copying incidental to such conversion. The restricted act of making an adaptation includes decompilation and infringes copyright unless allowed by the new decompilation permitted act. The normal fair-dealing provisions apply otherwise. By section 50B(1), a lawful user (being a person having a right under a licence or otherwise to use the program: section 50A(2)) may decompile the program if necessary to obtain the information necessary to achieve the interoperability of any independently created program with the decompiled program or other program. In other words, it is permissible for a lawful user to decompile or disassemble a computer program to determine its interfaces if this is a necessary step in creating a new program which will interoperate (interact) with that or some other program.

Typically, a software developer might want to write a word processing program which will be compatible with another company's spreadsheet program so that data and files can be passed between the two programs (see Fig. 4.4). This form of compatibility is certainly desirable and should not cause any great concerns, unless the spreadsheet company was hoping to make its own compatible word processor in the future. Once the compatible interoperable program has been created there seems no reason why the interface details cannot be used subsequently to create competing, replacement programs as long as there is not a substantial copy made of the code in the original program, as indicated in the figure.

The Act, as amended, attempts to deal with this situation by making the use or supply of the information for any other objective, or in the development, production or marketing of any computer program substantially similar in its expression to the original program, an infringement of copyright (section 50B(2)). However, reuse of interface details will not necessarily result in a substantially similar expression and, in the example in Fig. 4.4, the expression (program listings and structure) may be quite different. Interface details may be qualitatively insubstantial; after all the program is a spreadsheet program, not an interface program, and may be written in different

that it can exploit the resultant program itself, or it may simply want to prevent its competitors from obtaining a copy of it. In either of these situations the contract should specifically state that the ownership of the copyright belongs to the organisation and not to the programmer and, furthermore, there should be a written assignment of copyright, signed by the freelance programmer. Of course, the fee charged will probably be greater as a result because the freelance programmer might have envisaged making use of the program elsewhere; he may know of other businesses which would be interested in what he produces. On the other hand, if the commissioning organisation does not itself contemplate commercially exploiting the software or preventing others from using it, then it is important that a term is included in the contract granting a licence for the continued use of the program.

If the contract is silent on such matters, the freelance programmer may later decide to test his ownership of the program by offering it to others or, worse still, claim that, as owner, he will permit the continued use of the program only on payment of a licence fee. These difficulties may arise especially when the program in question turns out to be more useful and successful than the parties originally envisaged. There is a danger that a freelance programmer will try to hold his client to ransom if he later realises that the value of the software he has produced is out of all proportion to the payment he received for writing it.

Unfortunately, not all 'freelance staff' are self-employed and some are employed by an agency. In this case the same precautions apply and it is even more important to deal with ownership of copyright, otherwise the agency (as employer) could turn out to be the first owner of the copyright.

The employee and the course of employment

As regards persons who can safely be classified as employees, their employers cannot safely assume that they will own the copyright in everything produced by those employees. For example, if an employee writes a computer program to help with his work but he is not employed as a computer programmer, his job is not to write computer programs and an employer cannot necessarily assume that he owns the copyright in that particular program. A lecturer normally owns the copyright in any book or article he writes because he is primarily employed as a teacher and not as a writer of books and articles, even though his employer may encourage this. A person employed as an accountant who writes a computer program to help with the production of financial accounts will own the copyright in that program if he wrote it in his own time, using his own equipment. Initially, this may create no problems because the accountant may have been motivated by interest and a desire to improve his own efficiency at work but problems could arise later if the accountant moves to another firm or discovers that his program is commercially viable. If an employer is faced with the situation where an employee has, in his own time and using his own equipment, developed a useful computer program, then the employer should immediately try to reach agreement as regards questions of ownership and use of the program with the employee concerned, rather than allowing the program to be used without such agreement.

If an employee has produced a computer program outside the normal course of his duties, but has used his employer's equipment or done it during the hours of his employment, the ownership of copyright is more difficult to predict, although it is more likely that the employer will be treated as owner. Even here, however, it is wiser to seek agreement at the outset rather than leave matters until there is some disagreement about the continued use or exploitation of the program. Employers should consider the introduction of, or extension of, a 'suggestions' scheme to include computer programs or systems written by staff who are not employed to do this, with effective rewards and suitable provisions as regards ultimate ownership.

Programming languages and instruction sets

A computer program is written using a specific computer programming language. Languages vary enormously from the basic instruction set of the central processing unit to 'fourth-generation' languages and languages used for programming logic. A great deal of skill, imagination and effort goes into the design of a new programming language and the development of new languages will be encouraged if some form of protection is afforded to them. However, the exercise of rights in languages could seriously interfere with the licensing and distribution of computer programs and databases. In principle, there is a strong argument for saying that programming languages are ideas and, as such, cannot be protected by copyright. Therefore a person who writes an original program in COBOL infringes no copyright in the process of writing the program. There is an analogy with natural language and it would be ridiculous to suggest that writing an article or report using 'Esperanto' infringed any copyright subsisting in the language. Of course, making an unauthorised copy of an Esperanto–English dictionary would infringe copyright, if only that subsisting in the typographical arrangement.

The European Council Directive on the legal protection of computer programs recognises that programming languages, at least to the extent that they comprise ideas and principles, should not be protected by copyright. Given that this is so one might wonder wherein lies the incentive to create a new language. The answer lies in the fact that, usually, the program, once written, can only be run on a computer if it is converted into object code whether temporarily, using an interpreter program, or permanently, using a compiler program. The licensing of these interpreter and compiler programs, together with appropriate documentation describing the syntax, semantics and use of the language, is the method by which financial reward is usually sought. These programs are, of course, protected by copyright. However, the obsession in the United States of withholding copyright protection from ideas including features of programs dictated by function might have the drastic effect, if taken to its logical conclusion, of robbing interpreter and compiler programs of copyright protection.

Some languages and program development tools (languages in a wide sense including expert system shells) require 'run-time' licences to be acquired before application programs and systems may be distributed. These generally permit the copying and distribution of a cut-down version of the language, tool or shell sufficient to run the application.

A computer's instruction set represents a language at its most basic level and, at this level, it is nearest to idea and, when used to write small programs, it has been argued that there is a merger of idea and expression – in which case protection will be denied. This happened in the United States case of *NEC Corp* v *Intel Corp* (1989) 10 USPQ 2d where it was held that Intel's microcode programs were dictated by the instruction set of the microprocessors and, as there were no alternative ways of expressing the ideas incorporated, reverse analysis of the microcode programs did not infringe copyright. However, it was also accepted that such programs could be protected if not dictated by idea.

In the United Kingdom, the question of copyright protection for an instruction set was considered in *Microsense Systems Ltd* v *Control Systems Technology Ltd* (unreported) 17 June 1991, Chancery Division. The plaintiff made traffic control systems and controllers for pelican crossings, which were programmed using a set of mnemonics (a set of three-letter symbols) which were in turn used to monitor the controllers. The defendant made similar controllers and used a total of 49 of the plaintiff's mnemonics arguing that there was no copyright in them because, once the functions had been decided, there was no room for skill and labour in devising the mnemonics. This was an interlocutory hearing so no final decision was taken but the judge thought that there was an arguable case that the list of mnemonics was protected by copyright because of the work in designing the controller in the first place. This seems to contradict the *NEC* v *Intel* case although, being an American case, it is not binding on the United Kingdom courts. However, the defendant's argument that the list was effectively idea reflects the desirability of standardisation in traffic controllers as, otherwise, there could be catastrophic mistakes.

Devices to overcome copy-protection

Some computer programs were marketed in a form that makes them difficult to copy. Almost inevitably, devices and software designed to overcome these attempts at copy-protection soon appeared on the market, to the intense irritation of the software industry. A distinction must be made at this stage between things that can be used to make unauthorised copies of programs, but which also have legitimate uses (for example, computers with two disk drives and cassette players with twin tape decks) and things specifically designed to overcome copy-protection, such as software to be used to copy other software which has been copy-protected. Where a device or software has lawful uses, it would obviously be unsatisfactory to ban its sale. The music industry tried to interfere with the sale of twin-cassette music centres in *CBS Songs Ltd* v *Amstrad Consumer Electronics plc* [1988] AC 1013, on the basis that, by the sale and advertising of these machines, Amstrad was inciting the public to infringe copyright. The fact that the machines made by Amstrad had other legitimate uses, such as making copies of the purchasers' own music or of works not protected by copyright, was important, even though it was obvious that the largest use would involve copyright infringement. Nor was Amstrad authorising infringement.

There can be little sympathy, however, for firms who make devices or software deliberately designed to permit the copying of works which are copy-protected. The sole purpose of these devices and software is to enable copy-protection to be overcome. By section 296 of the Copyright, Designs and Patents Act, devices or means specifically designed or adapted to circumvent copy-protection of works issued to the public in electronic form are controlled by treating the making, importation, sale or hire, possession in the course of business, etc. of the devices or means as an infringement of copyright. Furthermore, publishing information to enable or assist the circumvention of copy-protection is similarly treated. The use of the phrase 'devices or means' should be wide enough to cover both hardware devices and software methods designed to overcome copy-protection. Computers with dual disk drives and twin tape cassette machines are not caught by these provisions because they are not 'specifically designed or adapted to circumvent copy-protection'. Similarly, normal copying programs which come with a computer operating system are within the law because they are designed to be used legitimately, to take back-up copies of programs and data files. Indeed, such programs will usually fail to copy computer programs that are copy-protected. A difficulty with this provision is that it is enforceable only by the person issuing copies of the copy-protected work in question to the public, and if the person making, importing, selling or hiring, etc. the device, means or information knows or has reason to believe that it will be used to make infringing copies.

It is arguable that the opportunity should have been taken to deal with this matter by way of criminal penalties as the making, importing, selling or hiring of unauthorised decoders for encrypted broadcasts or cable programmes has been criminalised by section 297A of the Copyright, Designs and Patents Act 1988 (inserted by section 197 of the Broadcasting Act 1990). However, there has been a move away from copy-protection because it is troublesome to customers who, not unreasonably, wish to take back-up copies of important programs. Indeed, the Copyright Designs and Patents Act 1988 now contains a specific right to make a back-up copy if necessary for the lawful use of the program concerned (section 50A).

Implications of software copyright law

The scope of copyright law in relation to computer software in general and computer programs in particular has become more certain in the last couple of years or so. Consequently, a number of practical recommendations can be made to software developers.

- Do not copy screen displays, menus, program structure, database structure or other non-literal elements of software.
- Even if some element of new software is likely to be 'dictated by function', create it independently and retain all the preparatory materials in respect of it.
- Prepare, date and keep preparatory materials for all items of software.
- Insert deliberate mistakes or redundant code or entries into programs, databases and other works.
- Be aware that copyright extends to a compilation of individual programs and/or data files.
- Make sure employees do not use materials or confidential information belonging to previous employers.
- Obtain a signed written assignment of copyright in respect of works to be created by self-employed programmers or consultants.
- Check licence agreements for void terms in respect of decompilation and making back-up copies.
- Make sensible arrangements for error correction of computer programs.

In general terms, copyright law does not protect the function of a program. It will be perfectly legal to write a program that performs the same function as an existing program provided the function itself is not protected by the law of breach of confidence and the first program is not used in a manner which falls within the acts restricted by the copyright. However, where the same person is involved in writing the first and second programs a great deal of care must be taken to be able to rebut any presumption of copying that is likely to be raised in any action for infringement of copyright.

Chapter 5

Copyright and databases

Introduction

Until recently, it was generally accepted that computer databases were protected by copyright as literary works as they could be considered to be compilations. This was, of course, without prejudice to any individual copyrights subsisting in the individual items or works contained within the database. For example, consider a database of modern romantic poems. Each poem would be protected by copyright as an original literary work and, providing sufficient skill, labour or judgment was expended in selecting and arranging, indexing or annotating the poems, there would be a separate copyright in the database as a whole. There could be other copyrights also, such as in respect of any index, cross-referencing system or annotations. Some of these elements could be protected as non-literal elements such as, for example, any hypertext links or the indexing system itself.

There was some doubt about whether a database of artistic works could be a compilation as literary works are defined in section 3(1) in terms of works which are written, spoken or sung. It is arguable that this does not apply to most forms of artistic works. An exception is a circuit diagram which, according to Mr Justice Jacob in *Anacon Corp Ltd* v *Environmental Research Technology Ltd* [1994] FSR 659, was also a literary work because it was intended to be read by the person making a circuit board in accordance with the diagram. Mr Justice Laddie agreed with this in *Electronic Techniques (Anglia) Ltd* v *Critchley Components Ltd* [1997] FSR 401. However, he said that, when considering a circuit diagram as a literary work, the graphic elements must be ignored and, that being so, the work could not be a literary work as it was little more than a list of five or six components. In other words, the circuit diagram was not sufficiently substantial for copyright as a literary work.

The legal protection of databases was significantly changed by the Copyright and Rights in Databases Regulations 1997 which came into force on 1 January 1998. The Regulations were made in order to comply with a European Directive on the legal protection of databases (OJ [1996] L77/20). A particular concern, following developments in the United States in the *Feist* v *Rural Telephone* case (discussed below), was that some databases that might be commercially valuable would fail to attract copyright protection in some member states of the European Community. Thus, a dual approach to protection was taken in the Directive. First, providing a database can be regarded as an intellectual creation, it will have copyright protection. If the database can be regarded as the result of a substantial investment, it will attract a new right, referred to in the Regulations as a 'database right'. Of course, in many cases, databases will enjoy both a copyright and a database right (as well as separate rights in the constituent parts in some cases) but the database right was designed specifically for valuable databases which failed to reach the requirements for copyright protection.

In this chapter, the new provisions for databases are described. However, first it will be useful to look at the basic position before the changes brought about by the Regulations and the position in the United States.

Copyright in a database before 1 January 1998

Databases were not expressly mentioned in the Copyright, Designs and Patents Act 1988 but were potentially protected by copyright as compilations, provided they were original. Copyright might have subsisted at two levels if the database was a collection of individual works, as mentioned earlier. Each work may be subject to copyright but, on a higher level, there may be a separate copyright in the database as a whole if the selection and arrangement of materials contained within it is the result of a modicum of skill or judgment. This is similar to the copyrights found in the *IBCOS* case discussed in Chapter 4. It appeared that most databases would have had copyright protection providing they were the result of a minimum amount of skill, labour or judgment. Traditionally, the threshold for copyright protection in the United Kingdom has been relatively low in comparison, for example, to German copyright law which requires a work to be a personal intellectual creation (German Copyright Act 1965, section 2(2), as amended). This appeared to be a higher standard than that required in the United Kingdom where copyright developed in a very pragmatic manner.

Consider a database comprising details of a company's customers. Say that the information stored includes names and addresses of existing and potential customers together with details of the customers' operations and views on the customers' creditworthiness, payment facilities, discounts, etc. This database would have been protected by copyright in the United Kingdom because it required skill and judgment in the design of the structure of the database (that is, the design of the number and type of fields and their length) and in the selection of the information to be entered. Thus the structure and the information would have been forms of expression for copyright purposes.

This should be contrasted with a database containing simply the names and addresses of all a company's customers because there is no selectivity or judgment (or very little) in the decision as to what should be included and relatively little skill in designing the structure of the database. This would be similar in principle to *G A Cramp & Sons Ltd* v *Frank Smythson Ltd* [1944] AC 329, discussed in Chapter 4, in which copyright was denied to a simple diary because the commonplace nature of the information left little room for judgment in the selection and organisation of the information. If the creation of a database was the result of a great deal of effort alone, with little judgment in the design of the database or in the selection of material (for example, a telephone directory stored in a computer database or a directory of postcodes), it was debatable whether it would attract copyright protection. However, the United Kingdom law traditionally has been generous and compilations of non-original matter have been protected providing that some judgment at least has been expended in their making (see *Macmillan & Co Ltd* v *K & J Cooper* (1923) 40 TLR 186). In reported cases on copyright and databases, including some on the copyright in a database of lawyers, the question of whether the databases were protected by copyright was not put into issue; see for example, *Waterlow Directories Ltd* v *Reed Information Services Ltd* [1992] FSR 409.

The United States and the sweat of the brow principle

The 'sweat of the brow' principle, affording copyright protection to works which are the result of labour only, was roundly rejected in the United States Supreme Court in *Feist Publications Inc* v *Rural Telephone Service Co Inc* (1991) 111 S Ct 1282. In that case, it was held that the 'white pages' in a typical telephone directory were not protected by copyright because of a lack of creativity, as they did not owe their origin to an act of authorship. The court did recognise, however, that a compilation of facts could be the subject of copyright because the author has to choose which facts to include and in what order to place them. The court went on to suggest that the 'yellow pages' section of a telephone directory was protected because of the presence of original material such as drawings in advertisements. There is also some skill in devising the classification system used. Subsequently, however, it was held in the United States that taking a large amount of data from a classified directory did not infringe copyright (see *Bell South Advertising & Publishing Corp* v *Donnelley Information Publishing Inc* (unreported) 2 September 1993, 11th Cir. It is fair to say that the position in the United Kingdom has probably been more generous to database compilers and it has been accepted that headings in a trade catalogue are protected by copyright. The United States Constitution gives a clue to the more rigorous approach there as it states the object of copyright is 'to promote the progress of science and the useful arts' (Article 1, Section 8, clause 8). This would appear to be incompatible with rewarding acts of labour only.

Protection of databases on or after 1 January 1998

In view of problems such as that highlighted in *Feist* v *Rural Telephone* and bearing in mind even telephone directories and directories of postcodes can be commercially valuable – for example, by being sold on CD-ROM – it was considered important to improve the protection of databases on a European scale. Another factor was that standards of protection varied throughout Europe and there was a need for harmonisation of national laws. The model of protection adopted was to provide for a standard copyright treatment for databases requiring skill or judgment in their making but, in addition, to introduce a new *sui generis* right specifically aimed at providing shorter-term protection for databases that might not meet this standard but which were, nevertheless, the result of a substantial investment which would be prejudiced if such databases had no protection.

The new copyright and the database right apply equally to both electronic and non-electronic databases, in line with the general approach of the European Commission not to distinguish between electronic and manual databases. Both of the new rights are without prejudice to copyright in the contents. Thus, where a database contains individual works of copyright, those works will retain their own copyright in addition to any copyright or database right in the database as a whole. For example, consider a database of recipes. If a person copies one of the recipes without permission, he will infringe the copyright in it. If he copies several recipes without permission, he will infringe the copyright in each individual recipe as well as infringing the copyright in the database and/or the database right, depending on whether one or both subsist.

It should also be noted that the moral rights have not been affected by the changes and, consequently, an author of a copyright database may have moral rights in respect of it although there are no moral rights in respect of a database only protected by the database right (ignoring any copyrights in the constituent parts) and music collections on CD-ROM are expressly excluded from these new provisions. They will continue to be treated as compilations for copyright purposes.

First, the copyright protection of databases is considered, followed by an examination of the new database right.

Copyright in databases

Section 3(1) of the Copyright, Designs and Patents Act 1988 is amended and 'database' is added to the non-exhaustive list of works that are literary works. Databases are then excluded from compilations and there are now some differences as to how databases and compilations are treated by copyright law. Of course, many of the provisions are the same for both but it should be noted that there is a difference in the fair dealing provisions and there is a special non-derogation from grant provision, preventing undue interference with the rights of lawful users of databases.

The precise nature of the original works of copyright are not expressly defined in the Act but there is now a detailed definition of 'database', following that in the Directive. A new section 3A is inserted into the Act which defines 'database' as a collection of independent works, data or other materials which (a) are arranged in a systematic or methodical way, and (b) are individually accessible by electronic or other means. The use of the phrase 'other means' shows that the provisions apply equally to non-electronic databases and this is confirmed in the recitals to the Directive. A card index will be a database for copyright purposes. Although the Act, as modified, is silent on the point, the Directive makes it clear that the copyright protection for a database does not extend to any program used in the making or operation of an electronic database. Of course, computer programs are separately protected as another form of literary work.

Unlike the other original works, a gloss is added to the test of originality and a database is original for copyright purposes if and only if, by reason of the selection or arrangement of its contents, the database constitutes the author's own intellectual creation. This is equivalent to the German approach to copyright and seems to be a much stricter requirement than that which existed before 1 January 1998. However, this is not to prejudice pre-existing databases and, where a database was created on or before 27 March 1996 (which was the date on which the Directive as adopted was published) and was protected by copyright immediately before 1 January 1998, that copyright will continue for its full term (that is, 'life plus 70 years'), even if it does not qualify for copyright protection under this new test for originality.

The usual restricted acts apply to databases as they do for literary works generally except that the restricted act of making an adaptation is redefined for databases in terms of an adaptation being an arrangement or altered version or a translation of the database. Examples of these acts are:

- a version in which the information contained in the database has been sorted into a different order (arrangement);
- a version in which some of the information is suppressed (either records or fields or both) (arrangement or altered version);
- the database is converted to be used with a different program to access the contents or it is converted from 8-bit to 7-bit code or it is imported into a word processing or spreadsheet program (altered version or translation).

The Directive left member states with some discretion as to which permitted acts they applied to copyright databases. The approach in the United Kingdom was to apply the traditional permitted acts that apply to literary works, with the exception of fair dealing for research and private study where two specific changes were implemented for databases. A new subsection (1A) was inserted into section 29 which, in respect of fair dealing for research or private study, requires the source to be indicated. Furthermore, under section 29(5), it is not fair dealing to do anything in relation to a database for a commercial purpose.

Section 50D was inserted into the Copyright, Designs and Patents Act 1988. This applies to any person having a right to use a database or part of a database. Such a person does not infringe copyright if, in the exercise of that right, he does anything which is necessary for the purposes of his access to and use of the contents of the database (or part of the database). This prevents a person licensing a database to another including terms in the licence agreement which purport to hinder access to and use of the database. It is essentially a non-derogation from grant provision. It is clear from this provision that a database may be made available in such a way that a licensee may be restricted to part only of the database. The restriction may be in terms of certain records or certain fields. For example, in a database of potential customers, a licensed user may be restricted to customers living in the South of England only or it may be that the user can retrieve names and addresses only and not data relating to individuals' financial standing. The right under section 50D cannot be prohibited or restricted and section 296B makes void any term or condition in an agreement in so far as it purports to prohibit or restrict those acts permitted under section 50D or any act necessary for the exercise of the rights granted by the agreement.

The database right

The Copyright, Designs and Patents Act 1988 was not amended to include the provisions relating to the database right. Instead it is provided for separately in Part III of the Copyright and Rights in Databases Regulations 1997.

The database right, described in the Directive as a right *sui generis*, was designed to protect the investment in obtaining, verifying or presenting the contents of a database. It is of limited duration compared to copyright but the right is not restricted to non-copyright databases and many databases will be subject to both copyright and the database right. As with the copyright provisions, the database right is unaffected if the database contains works which are themselves subject to copyright. Take, for example, a database of original maps or charts which required the exercise of skill and judgment (assuming that this test is the same as 'author's intellectual creation') and which was also a substantial investment, for example, in the presentation of its contents. The individual maps or charts will be works of copyright; the database as a whole will be a work of copyright and it will also be subject to the database right.

Definitions

The database right is a right given to the maker of a database to prevent the unauthorised extraction or reutilisation of the contents of a database. To understand this basic right, it is important to look at the definitions in the Regulations which are set out below. However, it must be noted that the meaning of 'database' is the same as applies to databases subject to copyright. The definitions are contained in regulation 12, although the fine detail of some of them occur in other parts of the Regulations as indicated:

- 'database right' is defined in regulation 13(1) as a property right which subsists in a database if there has been a substantial investment in obtaining, verifying or presenting the contents of the database;
- 'investment' includes any investment, whether of financial, human or technical resources;
- 'substantial', in relation to any investment, extraction or reutilisation, means substantial in terms of quantity or quality or a combination of both;
- 'insubstantial' is relevant to infringement and, under regulation 16(2), the repeated and systematic extraction or reutilisation of insubstantial parts of the contents of a database may amount to the extraction or reutilisation of a substantial part of those contents;
- 'extraction', in relation to any contents of a database, means the permanent or temporary transfer of those contents to another medium by any means or in any form;
- 'reutilisation', in relation to any contents of a database, means making those contents available to the public by any means;
- 'maker' is defined in regulation 14(1) as the person who takes the initiative in obtaining, verifying or presenting the contents of a database and assumes the risk of investing in that obtaining, verification or presentation, such acts constituting the act of making the database. The basic rule is that the maker will be the first owner of the database right. Where a database is made by an employee in the course of his employment, the employer is regarded as the maker of the database and there is provision for Her Majesty to be regarded as the maker of a database where it is made by an officer or servant of the Crown in the course of his duties (Parliamentary database right is also provided for);
- 'jointly' in relation to the making of a database is defined in regulation 16(2) in terms of two or more persons who act in collaboration in taking the initiative and assuming the risk of investing; however, unlike the case in copyright law, there is no requirement that the contribution of each is not distinct.
- 'lawful user', in relation to a database, means any person who (whether under a licence to do any of the acts restricted by any database right in the database or otherwise) has a right to use the database.

A few points can be made about these definitions. First, the fact that the right is a property right (as is copyright, of course) should come as no surprise. The meaning of 'substantial' is slightly different from that generally accepted (though not defined) for copyright purposes, because quality, quantity or both are factors, whereas for copyright purposes attention tends to focus on quality rather than quantity. However, that is not to say that the proportion of the work taken can never be a factor in determining infringement. A curious provision is that continuing to take or make available insubstantial parts may amount to a substantial taking or making available. This is to prevent any doubt as to whether such action would infringe the database right. There is some doubt under copyright law as to whether the repeated taking of insubstantial parts can infringe although it would seem sensible to view such taking as a connected series of takings and view them cumulatively, in the round.

The meanings of 'extraction' and 'investment' are quite wide. In particular, the latter is not restricted to financial investment and covers a situation where a person spends time and effort in making a database or simply where technical resources are tied up. This could be the situation where a central computer is dedicated to receiving information from remote users who submit information to the computer which is automatically collated and entered into a database. As quality of investment is a factor in the investment, it is possible that the skill of any person involved or the power or technical advancement of equipment used could be relevant in determining whether the right subsists. The meaning of 'reutilisation' is directed to making the contents available to the public rather than simply making use of the contents. Thus, making use of the contents for one's own benefit without authorisation does not, *per se*, infringe the database right. However, it is likely that the person concerned will have previously infringed by extracting those contents and there may also be infringements of any copyright in the underlying works included in the database, where such copyright exists.

Lending a copy of a database (not for direct or indirect commercial advantage) by an establishment accessible to the public does not constitute extraction or reutilisation of the contents of a database but this exception does not extend to making available for on-the-spot reference use which could, therefore, fall within the meaning of extraction or reutilisation.

The doctrine of exhaustion of rights within the European Economic Area (EEA) applies to copies sold within the EEA by or with the consent of the owner of the database right to the extent that further sale of such copies does not constitute extraction or reutilisation of the contents of the database. Therefore, if a person lawfully buys a copy of a database, that person can resell that copy elsewhere in the EEA without infringing the database right. The fact that a database has been made available on-line for consultation by members of the public does not, however, exhaust the maker's right of reutilisation. It is only sale of copies that exhausts any right to control resale.

Qualification

For the database right to subsist, it must satisfy the qualification requirements. These are set out in regulation 18, and require that, at the 'material time', the maker (or at least one of them where there are joint makers) is:

- a national of an EEA state (or habitually resident in the state),
- a body incorporated in an EEA state, having its central administration or principal place of business in an EEA state or registered office in the EEA and the body's operations linked on an ongoing basis with the economy of an EEA state, or
- a partnership or other unincorporated body formed under the law of an EEA state, having at that time its central administration or principal place of business within the EEA.

The 'material time' is the time when the database is made or, if this extended over a period of time, a substantial part of that period. The qualification requirements do not apply in the case of Parliamentary database right although there is no express exception for Crown database right.

Duration

The Directive emphasised that the right is to be limited in time, subject to a new right arising if a database undergoes substantial change, and the term of protection afforded by the database right is stated in regulation 17 as 15 years from the end of the calendar year during which the making of the database is completed; although, if it is made available to the public before the end of that period, the right will continue to endure for 15 years from the end of the calendar year during which it was first made available. Of course, many databases are subject to continuing or periodic modification. Thus, a new period of protection arises if changes to the database are substantial and this includes any substantial change resulting from an accumulation of successive additions, deletions or alterations, provided the database would be considered to be a substantial new investment.

The definitions should again be reflected upon. It could be, for example, that a new database right arises simply because the maker has redesigned his software to improve the presentation of the contents of the database, or has put resources into checking the accuracy of the contents. For example, in the case of a database of customers, the owner has sent out a mailing asking for confirmation of the details of individuals and made corrections to the database as appropriate.

If the database in question was made on or before 1 January 1983 and the database right subsisted in the database immediately on 1 January 1998, the database right will last for 15 years beginning with 1 January 1998.

Infringement and exceptions

Infringing acts are defined in regulation 16 in terms of the extraction or re-utilisation of all or a substantial part of the contents of the database without the consent of the owner. Reflecting the special nature of databases and the damage that may be done to the owner's interests by a systematic course of unauthorised use of small parts of the database, the repeated and systematic extraction or reutilisation of insubstantial parts of the contents of a database *may* amount to the extraction or reutilisation of a substantial part of those contents. In terms of 'insubstantial infringement', the Directive stated that the repeated and systematic extraction or reutilisation must imply acts conflicting with a normal exploitation of the database or be unreasonably prejudicial to the legitimate interests of the maker of the database.

One way of looking at repeated insubstantial takings is to view them as a continuing act and as equivalent to a substantial taking by accumulating them. However, it is clear that what is intended is that an accumulation of insubstantial takings could infringe even if, when accumulated, they still do not amount to a substantial part of the database.

There are a number of exceptions to infringement. Regulation 19 contains a 'non-derogation from grant' provision which prevents the owner of the database right interfering with the subsequent use of insubstantial parts by a lawful user such as a person having access under a licence agreement. A lawful user of a database, which has been made available to the public, cannot be prevented from extracting or reutilising insubstantial parts of the database for any purpose. Any term in an agreement, under which the right to use a database or part of a database has been granted, which attempts to prevent this is void. Regulation 20 contains a fair dealing exception to infringement. Where the database has been made available to the public in any manner, fair dealing with a substantial part of the contents does not infringe if:

- the part is extracted by a person who is otherwise a lawful user,
- it is extracted for the purposes of illustration for teaching or research (but not for a commercial purpose), and
- the source is indicated.

Further exceptions are set out in Schedule 1 to the Regulations and relate to parliamentary and judicial proceedings, Royal Commissions and statutory inquiries, material open to public inspection or on official register, material communicated to the Crown in the course of public business, public records and acts done under statutory authority. These mirror the equivalent permitted acts for copyright. However, apart from these exceptions and those mentioned above, none of the other permitted acts that apply generally to literary works under copyright apply to the database right. For example, there is no provision for fair dealing for criticism or review or for reporting current events.

Where it is reasonable to assume that the database right has expired and the identity of the maker (or makers in the case of a database made jointly) cannot by reasonable enquiry be ascertained, the right will not be infringed by the extraction or reutilisation of a substantial part of the contents: regulation 21. It is important, therefore, for the owner of databases to indicate the identity of the maker on copies of the database and the year during which it was first published. If the database is made available on-line, this information should appear on the title screen or other appropriate place. This is also worth doing so as to raise useful presumptions as discussed below.

It should be noted that it is the identity of the maker which is important, not that of the owner, where the maker and owner are not the same person. This is similar to copyright where it is the identity of the author which is crucial. However, unlike copyright, the duration of the database right is not dependent on the life of the maker and is fixed by the act of making or first publication. Of course, it may be dangerous to rely on this and other permitted acts which relate to the database right, as the database and/or its contents may be subject to copyright. Such copyright, where it subsists, is independent of and not prejudiced by the database right. Where copyright subsists in the database or its contents, a person using a database must ensure that the agreement under which he is using it extends to the appropriate use of copyright materials. A person relying on the exceptions to infringement of the database right must also check to make sure that his intended use is also covered by the exceptions to copyright infringement. For example, if a person who has the right to use a database wants to extract any part for the purpose of illustration for teaching, he should confirm that he can rely on the equivalent permitted acts in relation to teaching which apply to copyright works if the part extracted is protected by copyright unless, of course, his right to use the database covers this.

Presumptions

There are some presumptions which apply to the database right and which may be helpful to the owner in an action for infringement. They are not dissimilar to the equivalent presumptions which apply in relation to copyright works. Under regulation 22, where a name purporting to be that of the maker of the database appears on copies of the database as published, it is presumed that that person is the maker and the database was not made in circumstances where the employer would be the first owner and is not Crown or parliamentary database right. Where copies of a database as published bear a label or mark stating that a named person was the maker and that it was first published in a specified year, the label or mark shall be admissible as evidence of those facts and presumed correct until the contrary be proved.

Where a database has been made jointly, these provisions apply in relation to each person alleged to be one of the makers. Under copyright law, the usefulness of the equivalent presumptions was seen in the case of *Microsoft Corp v Electro-wide Ltd* [1997] FSR 580 where, in the absence of any evidence submitted by the defendant, the Microsoft Corporation did not have to prove that it owned the copyrights subsisting in software such as 'Windows 95'.

Other provisions

The provisions which apply to dealing with rights in copyright works, the rights and remedies of the owner of copyright and of an exclusive licensee under the copyright are all applied without modification to the database right. Thus, assignment of the database right must be in writing and be signed by or on behalf of the assignor and exclusive licences are required to be in writing and be signed by or on behalf of the owner of the database right. This is helpful and where the database and/or its contents are also protected by copyright a simple form of words can be used. For example, an assignment may use the phrase 'I hereby assign the copyright and database right subsisting in [the database] and the copyright subsisting in its contents' or, more simply, 'I hereby assign all the rights subsisting in [the database] and its contents'.

Remedies are the same as for copyright and include damages, injunctions, accounts or otherwise as is available for infringement of any other property right, and additional damages are also possible in the case of flagrant infringement. Exclusive licensees have rights concurrent to those of the owner and may bring an action themselves. As is usual, the owner would be expected to be joined in the action, for example, as co-plaintiff.

Schedule 2 to the Regulations contains provisions for licensing the database right and deals with licensing schemes, licensing bodies and referral of licensing schemes to the Copyright Tribunal. These provisions are equivalent to those in sections 116–129 and 144 of the Copyright, Designs and Patents Act 1988 which apply to copyright works. The jurisdiction of the Copyright Tribunal is enlarged accordingly to give it jurisdiction over the database right.

Database structure

As the non-literal elements of a computer program, including its structure, can be protected by copyright, it would seem sensible to assume that the structure of a database can also be protected by copyright. However, in *Total Information Processing Systems Ltd v Daman Ltd* [1992] FSR 171, it was held that the field and record specifications as expressed in the data division of a COBOL program were not protected because, in this form, the information did not form a substantial part of the computer program as a whole. This part of the program defines the structure of the database in addition to setting out the variables and their nature and format. In the second edition of this book the author submitted that this approach was wrong and that it would be better to consider the database structure as a form of expression in its own right and not as part of the computer program. This would accord with common sense because, in many cases, a great deal of work involving skill and judgment is expended in the design of database structure. Indeed, subsequently in *IBCOS Computers Ltd v Barclays Highland Mercantile Finance Ltd* [1994] FSR 275, Mr Justice Jacob made a number of criticisms of the judgment in the *Total Information Processing Systems* case and he said that there may well be a considerable degree of skill in devising the data division of a program and so it would be considered to be a substantial part of a program as a whole.

In an earlier case, *Computer-Aided Systems (UK) Ltd* v *Bolwell* (unreported) 23 August 1989, Chancery Division, the mere fact that a new program had file compatibility with an earlier program written by the same people failed to impress the judge who considered the plaintiff's application for inspection of the defendant's program to be nothing more than a 'fishing expedition'. There was no evidence of copying and the two programs were written in different languages, the original being written in COBOL, the latter one being written in a fourth-generation language called PROGRESS. The structure of the databases in terms of input and output formats must have been identical or similar but this did not seem to be sufficiently argued; instead the plaintiff concentrated on an argument that the structure of the two programs must have been similar. Alternatively, the fact of file compatibility could have been the result of a 'filter', a program which converted the file structure from one format to another.

Although the Copyright and Rights in Databases Regulations 1997 make no mention of the structure of a database, recital 15 to the European Directive on the legal protection of databases states that copyright protection should cover the structure of a database. The only major requirement for protection, apart from qualification, therefore, is that the database is an 'intellectual creation'. If it is and someone copies the database structure but not its contents without the permission of the owner, this will infringe the copyright if the database structure represents a substantial part of the database. It should not be necessary to demonstrate that the database structure, as opposed to the database as a whole, is an intellectual creation. It would seem that if a database is subject to the database right only, its structure is not protected by that right. In order to further strengthen protection of databases, whether protected by copyright or the database right or both, the author or maker should retain copies of preparatory design materials such as diagrams, layouts and specifications. It is possible that anyone copying the structure of a database will indirectly infringe the copyright subsisting in such materials.

Chapter 6

Computer-generated works

Introduction

The Copyright, Designs and Patents Act 1988 expressly recognises that works produced by or with the aid of a computer are worthy of copyright protection. Such works were protected before the 1988 Act but there were difficulties in determining the identity of the author of the work for copyright purposes. Grids of random numbers selected by computer for a newspaper competition called 'Millionaire of the Month' were held to be protected by copyright in *Express Newspapers plc v Liverpool Daily Post & Echo plc* [1985] 1 WLR 1089. Arguments that there was no human author and, consequently, the lists of numbers drawn by the computer were not protected by copyright were rejected by Whitford J who said that such a claim was as silly as saying that a pen could be the author of a literary work. The human expertise in computer-derived works could be found to reside in the programs which, in this case, produced the lists of random numbers.

In works produced by or with the aid of a computer, human skill can reside in the person who enters information into the computer to produce the output or in the programmer who writes the program used or a combination of them both. Section 178 of the Act defines a work as 'computer-generated' when it is generated by a computer in circumstances such that there is no human author of the work. Section 9(3) states that, in the case of a literary, dramatic, musical or artistic work which is computer-generated, the author is the person by whom the arrangements necessary for the creation of the work are undertaken. This will generally mean that the person who has control of the computer will be the author of any computer-generated work. These two definitions are tautologous when taken together: a computer-generated work is one created in circumstances such that there is no human author but if we attribute authorship to a human it cannot be computer-generated. The only way round this dilemma is to determine authorship *after* the creation of the work but this seems illogical. Normally, creation and attribution of authorship are coincident in time.

The approach taken in the Act can lead to difficulties because in many cases of works produced *with the aid of a computer* it will not be possible to say with any certainty whether the work has a human author. At one end of the spectrum a work will be produced using a computer as a tool, just as a writer uses a pen or a typewriter, while, at the other end, the computer will produce its works with little or no direct human effort. Neither of these situations should cause any great difficulty, but in between these two extremes lie a great many types of work which are the result of a modest amount of direct human input and classifying such works will not be easy. In order to consider this question further, works which involve computers in their production will be categorised as follows:

- works created using a computer,
- works created by a computer, and
- intermediate works.

In these cases 'computer' means a programmed computer.

Works created using a computer

Examples of works which fall into this category are: documents produced using a word processing system; CAD (computer-aided designs) such as plans for a house or a new car body panel; music written using a program designed to assist with the composition of the music (as opposed to a program designed to write music); and an accounts report created using a spreadsheet program. In all these cases, the person operating the system is using the computer to achieve the results that he wishes to obtain. The programmed computer is merely a tool that allows the operator to use his creativity and imagination to the fullest extent and efficiency. Such works are not computer-generated; the skill and expertise (or at least the greatest part of these) derives from the user of the system. Word-processed documents, drawings, music and reports produced using packages which facilitate the making of these works are protected by copyright as original literary, dramatic, musical or artistic works in their own right. Indeed, section 51 of the Act recognises that copyright can subsist in data stored in a computer representing a design as a form of design document.

The person using the computer to create the work provides the expertise necessary for the making of the work and is, for copyright purposes, the author of the work. That expertise may be applied directly or indirectly: for example, a person writing a report may draft it out on paper and then hand it to a word processor operator who enters it into the computer. In these circumstances, the author is not the operator but the person writing the report. It is similar to the process of amanuensis in which a person dictating a letter will be the author of that letter; the person who writes the dictation down is merely his agent.

The person who wrote the computer program used to assist in the creation of the types of works described above has no rights in the work because, although the programmer may control or influence the *format* of the finished work, he has no control or influence on the *content*. The fact that many works in this category may be produced directly using a computer before any other tangible form exists presents no serious problems because these works will exist, in terms of copyright protection, the instant they are recorded; that is, as soon as they are stored on a computer disk or printed out on paper.

Works created by a computer

These works, which may be literary, dramatic, musical or artistic, are those in which there is 'no human author' (section 178). This implies that the direct degree of human intervention in the making of the work is lacking or minimal. Examples include:

● the automatic generation of weather forecasts by a computer communicating with satellites;
● the selection of lists of random numbers for a competition or for the Premium Bond draw;
● programs which produce artistic designs or music automatically, being based upon a set of rules or algorithms built into the program;
● a program designed to simulate some particular environment, such as climate, monetary systems, battle scenarios, etc. and to produce reports based on that simulation.

Many of these systems operate with no human effort or skill apart from switching the equipment on and checking that there is sufficient paper in the computer printer or plotter and so on. The human operator has very little or no control over the *format* or *content* of the output produced by the computer. The author of such a work is the person who makes the arrangements for the work to be created. Therefore, if a business organisation buys and installs computer equipment and software to produce such works, that business organisation will be regarded as the author and, as a result, the first owner of the copyright in the work. The Act contemplates non-human authors as, by section 154, an author can be a qualifying person if, *inter alia*, it is a body incorporated in the United Kingdom, such as a limited company. In the case of an unincorporated body, such as a partnership, the partners will be considered to be the joint authors of the work. If a company can be an author of a computer-generated work, there has to be a special rule for determining the duration of copyright in such works: the copyright expires at the end of the period of 50 years from the end of the calendar year in which the work was made (section 12(7)).

Interestingly, and controversially, the Act appears to ignore the skill and expertise of the person or persons who wrote the computer program used to generate these works. It could be argued that the computer programmer whose skill lies behind the computer output should have some recognition of authorship. However, this could cause difficulties because a person obtaining a computer program would expect to own the copyright in anything produced using the program, and any provisions sharing the ownership of the copyright between the user and the programmer could result in an undesirable fetter on the subsequent use of information and reports generated by the computer. The owner of the copyright in the computer program, suddenly realising that he has rights with respect to the output generated from using the program, might attempt to interfere with the subsequent use of that output in the hope that he will be able to negotiate a fee for his permission.

A concept, as yet untested in the courts, is that there is no such thing as a computer-generated work; that is, a work without a human author. After all, the argument that a list of numbers drawn at random by a programmed computer had no human author was rejected, as we have seen, in the *Express Newspapers* case. The approach adopted by the Copyright, Designs and Patents Act is a utilitarian one but it does not reflect the reality of the situation as it fails to recognise that all computer output is the result, albeit in many cases the indirect result, of human skill and effort. It would have been better if the programmer's skill was recognised making him the author or joint author of 'computer-generated' works. The practical difficulties resulting from this could be assuaged by raising a presumption that ownership of copyright would lie with the licensee, the ultimate user, of the computer program, subject to any agreement to the contrary.

Intermediate works

These works lie in the area between computer-generated works and works made using the programmed computer as a tool. The *content* of the output produced is the result of the skill and effort of the person using the computer *and* the skill and effort of the person who wrote the computer program and/or the person who produced any database used. There are many examples of these intermediate works, such as a specialised accounting system for a particular type of business, builders' estimating systems, or a music synthesiser designed to produce music from a basic framework of notes entered by the user and expert systems.

A great deal of specialised software falls into this category where the skill required to produce the finished results is contained partly within the program, the remainder being provided by the user of the computer system. In some systems, the skill may come from more than two sources. For example, consider a computer system designed to be used to estimate the cost of building work. The system itself will comprise a suite of computer programs, which include routines to provide analyses and breakdowns of the costs derived, and a database of standard prices, based on sets of resources and labour outputs. The person using the system to work out the cost of a building brings a substantial degree of skill by deciding whether the standard

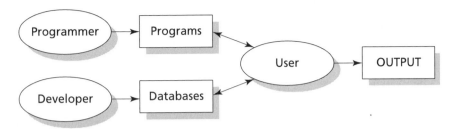

Fig. 6.1 Authorship of intermediate works

prices are applicable and, if not, by building up new prices and entering them into the database. As Fig. 6.1 shows, the resulting computer output has three sources of expertise: that of the programmer, of the persons responsible for developing the database of standard prices, and of the person using the system. Who is the author of the finished work? Because the person using the system brings an amount of skill to the task, it would not be unreasonable to suggest that he is the author. Indeed, the user has the most direct link with the finished product and has ultimate control but may, nevertheless, rely to a great extent on the programs and information contained in the database. It could be argued that the finished work is partly created by human author and partly computer-generated. Alternatively, all three persons – programmer, database developer and user – might be considered to be joint authors. In the absence of any clear guidance in the Act and until we have a judicial precedent which clarifies the meaning of 'computer-generated', it is important that contractual provisions are made to cover the ownership of rights in the output of such intermediate works. In some cases, because all the persons involved are employees of the company developing and using the software, there will be little difficulty, but if outsiders are involved at any stage, terms should be inserted in contractual agreements dealing with ownership and use of the computer output.

The same considerations apply to expert systems. These computer systems, which are intended to emulate the thought processes, analytical reasoning and advice of experts, contain a great deal of skill and expertise within the systems themselves. An expert system, in basic terms, contains three main elements: a knowledge base (rules and facts provided by experts), an inference engine (a computer program which manipulates the knowledge base and applies it to a particular problem) and a user interface to make the system 'user-friendly' and to provide explanations of the reasoning adopted and advice given by the expert system. When an expert system is used to produce some advice or a report, the expertise underlying the output comes from the following sources:

● the experts who provided the knowledge;

- the persons (sometimes called 'knowledge engineers') who refined the knowledge and formalised it so that it could be installed in the knowledge base;
- the persons who wrote the inference engine and the user interface (or adapted existing ones); and
- the user of the system.

The user of the system provides expertise because he will have to understand and respond to the system, and he will have to interpret the questions asked by the system and know what the scope and limitations of the system are. At this stage, most if not all expert systems cannot be used by naive users; a reasonable general knowledge of the area of expertise covered by the system (its knowledge domain) is essential if the output produced is to be taken seriously, just as the scope, limitations and difficulties presented by a new piece of legislation can only be predicted with any certainty by a lawyer and, even then, not always correctly.

What will the law make of the output of expert systems when it comes to deciding the authorship and ownership of the copyright in that output? To argue that it is computer-generated and has no human author runs counter to common sense. To say that the user of this system is its sole author might be convenient but is unrealistic. To attribute authorship to the experts and knowledge engineers who developed the knowledge base is unsatisfactory because they cannot predict how the system will be used and what responses will be made by the user; they have no control over its use. In reality, all the persons listed above are the joint authors, in differing proportions, of the output resulting from the use of the system. It must be said, however, that, if the courts follow this interpretation, it will lead to all manner of complications regarding the commercial use of expert systems and other 'intermediate' systems. Although the courts might be willing to imply terms – for example, that the licensee or 'purchaser' of such systems owns the copyright in any output – it is obviously more sensible to recognise the difficulties associated with this part of the Act and to make suitable contractual provision for ownership (as opposed to authorship) of computer output. Better still, the provisions relating to computer-generated works ought to be repealed.

Chapter 7

Copyright and electronic publishing

Introduction

All manner of works can be stored and made available electronically. Literature, music, works of art, audio-visual works, industrial designs can all be represented in digital form. Even three-dimensional works and moving images can be expressed digitally and, using appropriate software, displayed on screens, copied, manipulated or transmitted anywhere in the world 'at the touch of a button'.

The ease with which all forms of creative expression can be exploited digitally has far-reaching consequences as regards the dissemination of information and has opened up the exciting prospect of a global information village. Al Gore's term 'The Information Super-Highway' is very apt to describe the technology, and the rate at which the largely unregulated Internet has grown and continues to grow is impressive. Another recent phenomenon is the growth of multimedia (CD-ROM) technology offering large storage of a wide variety of works on a single disk. Typically, a CD-ROM may contain film, music, photographs, text and the spoken word, a collection of disparate works, each of which may be subject to copyright and may incorporate other rights such as rights in performances.

It is unsurprising that these new technologies pose considerable challenges to copyright law and the traditional role of copyright, which has only recently come to terms with the computer program and database. Already there are serious issues relating to balancing controls over the access and use of works and freedom of speech.

In the United States, a corporation which owns the copyright in certain works created by L Ron Hubbard, the founder of the Church of Scientology, sued a former member who placed extracts of the works on the Internet for infringement of copyright and trade secret violations (BBC2, *The Net*, 15 May 1995). It seems that the access provider was also threatened with legal action and that members of the Church sent cancel messages on the Internet to delete previously posted messages about the Church. The former member of the Church responsible for placing the works on the Internet, Dennis Erlich, said, 'We're using 18th and 17th century law to define what goes on in a 21st and 22nd century medium.' As a matter of note the defences of fair dealing and public interest were available to a defendant who had reproduced extracts of Mr Hubbard's writings in the United Kingdom in paper form (see *Hubbard* v *Vosper* [1972] 2 QB 84).

Before looking at the copyright implications of these new forms of information dissemination, it is worth looking at what is meant by electronic publishing.

What is electronic publishing?

The term 'electronic publishing' is lacking in precision and it is by no means clear what it encompasses. For example, it could include publication by one of the following methods:

- sale, rental or lending of a physical carrier containing a copy of the work or works in question – for example, CD-ROM, magnetic disk or magnetic tape;
- by means of communications networks – for example, the Internet or on-line facilities; or
- by means of a broadcast, whether or not encrypted and whether or not in digital form – for example, Prestel and CEEFAX.

All these three forms of electronic publishing are capable of copyright subsistence. In all cases, the individual works so made available may be subject to copyright and, in some cases, there will be other copyrights, such as that in the broadcast or cable programme. Additionally, there may be a further copyright in the form of a compilation.

It should be noted that, for copyright purposes, the word 'electronic' has a particularly wide meaning, by section 178 of the Copyright, Designs and Patents Act 1988, as being 'actuated by electric, magnetic, electro-magnetic, electro-chemical or electro-mechanical energy' and the term 'in electronic form' means in a form usable only by electronic means. However, even this width of definition may be incapable of keeping up with technological change. Would the above definitions be appropriate in relation to a liquid DNA computer described by Alexander (Alexander, G, 'DNA holds key to explosion in computer power', *The Sunday Times*, 30 April 1995, p 29)? Nevertheless, it is clear that the definitions of 'electronic' and 'in electronic form' apply to CD-ROM, laser disk and magnetic disk technology and this is important as, under section 17(2), copying includes storage in any medium by electronic means. The Act has specific provisions for broadcasts and cable programmes and some forms of on-line publishing would be deemed to be cable programme services. Information made available over the Internet has been considered to be a cable programme or part of a cable programme.

This chapter concentrates on publication by means of multimedia and the Internet. It also looks at the potential liability of Internet Service Providers for copyright infringement.

Multimedia

A CD-ROM typically may contain a whole range of works. For example, a multimedia product on the topic of romantic poems may include among other things:

- the text of poems to be displayed on screen;
- the sound of poems being recited;
- a commentary comprising an oral and/or textual description of material relating to the poets and their poems;
- film sequences showing the poets at work or meditating, for example, while walking a dog or smoking a pipe;
- photographs of the poets' birthplaces, homes, relatives and acquaintances; and
- introductory and background music.

A feature of multimedia is that the person using the product can move about it at will. The information is, therefore, structured and may have hypertext links. In terms of copyright subsistence, all the works above may be subject to copyright in addition to the whole as a compilation or database. The following example gives some idea of the complexity of rights in such a work.

MultiMega, a multimedia publisher, decides to produce a CD-ROM containing selected poems written by Andrew, Belinda and Clarence. Andrew is still alive, Belinda died some 20 years ago and Clarence has been dead for 80 years. Diana, a famous self-employed literary critic has been commissioned by MultiMega to select the poems to include in the CD-ROM and to write some material giving a critical appraisal of each poem. MultiMega's editing manager, Edward, selects some music written by Frances, who died 57 years ago, to use as background music. George, an actor, is commissioned to recite the poems in front of a studio audience. A selection of modern photographs of the poets' homes and favourite haunts, taken by Harriet, is to be included in the work. There is also some old footage of Belinda being interviewed live on ICE television. MultiMega has created its own computer programs to access and display the works and has also created hypertext links.

Assuming that there has been no subsequent transfer of the various copyrights except on the death of a copyright owner, the following permissions will be required by MultiMega:

- a licence from Andrew and from Belinda's estate (as she is now deceased) allowing for the copying, performance and issue to the public of their poems;
- an assignment (or exclusive licence) from Diana in respect of the compilation copyright and the material she has written;
- an exclusive licence from George in respect of his live performance (this is protected as a right in a performance, a right analogous to copyright); and
- a licence from ICE in respect of the broadcast.

No permission is required in respect of Clarence's poems which are now out of copyright but care must be taken as far as Frances's music is concerned as the copyright in it might be revived as a result of the extension of the term of copyright to life plus 70 years (this will be so if her music is still protected in any member state of the European Community). As Edward presumably is an employee, none of his efforts will result in a copyright that belongs to him rather than MultiMega. Another problem for MultiMega is that some of the persons involved will have moral rights (in particular, Andrew, Diana and Harriet), and it must take account of moral rights, either by acknowledging the authors or seeking a waiver in respect of the right to be identified. It is clear that, in most cases, obtaining the necessary permissions for a work of multimedia will be difficult, drawn out and, probably, expensive!

The changes to copyright in relation to databases result in the ensuing multimedia product probably being considered to be a database rather than a compilation. The definition of a database is a collection of independent works, data or other materials which are arranged in a systematic or methodical way and are individually accessible by electronic or other means. This would certainly seem to be the case with MultiMega's CD-ROM. However, one proviso is that it may be that not all the works included are 'individually accessible'. For example, a particular piece of music may be played only when a specific film sequence is accessed and it may not be possible to access that music entirely on its own. This may seem overly pedantic but, if the CD-ROM does not qualify as a database, it almost certainly will as a compilation. As far as copyright is concerned, there is very little difference between copyright in a database and copyright in a compilation. But, databases must be personal intellectual creations to attract copyright whereas the requirement for originality for compilations is not further qualified. The other main difference is that fair dealing for the purposes of research or private study in respect of databases requires an indication of the source and does not extend to research for a commercial purpose. There is also a provision protecting the carrying out of any act necessary for access and use of the contents of a database by a person having a right to use it.

On balance, it seems most likely that CD-ROM products will be classified as databases, except CD-ROMS of music compilations which are excluded by the Directive on the legal protection of databases: these will be protected as compilations. If a CD-ROM like that made by MultiMega is a database, the next question is whether it is a copyright database or whether it is only subject to the database right. As seen in the preceding chapter, this is a question as to whether its making was the result of a personal intellectual creation and/or whether it required a substantial investment. In the above example, it is possible that both of these rights subsist.

A further issue is whether the hypertext links built into the software are protected by copyright. These may be considered to be a structural element of the database protected as a non-literal element. As the Directive on the legal protection of databases makes clear, the protection of copyright databases extends to their structure. It seems entirely reasonable to assume that a person copying the structure of hypertext links from one multimedia product to another, different, product may infringe the copyright in the first if those parts taken represent a substantial part of the first, providing it is a copyright database. Of course, it would be rare that much would be gained simply by copying the structure of hypertext works alone.

The Internet

Publishing works on the Internet looks very attractive at first sight. It is a really effective way of making a work available to a wide audience at minimal expense. Many academic writers have been quick to seize the opportunity to spread their work on a world-wide scale. A number of academic journals are now appearing on the Internet and while many authors may be happy to distribute their work in this way, without recompense, there are large numbers of authors who depend on the income they receive from publishing their work. There is a view, held by many, that the Internet is equivalent to the public domain and anything available there should be freely copied and used. This view is misguided.

Typically, individuals gain access to works on the Internet, which are stored on host computers, via an access provider (see Fig. 7.1.)

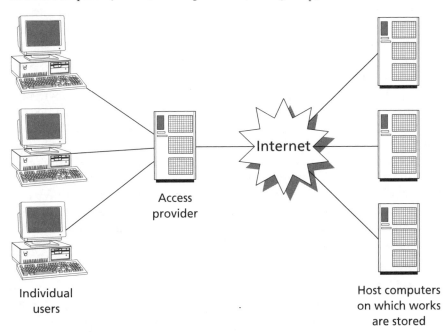

Individual
users

Access
provider

Internet

Host computers
on which works
are stored

Fig. 7.1 The Internet

The Internet itself is, basically, made up of public telecommunications systems which are used to carry information from host computers. The technology makes use of the most effective path through the system at the time of transmission, rerouting to avoid busy lines. No one is in overall control of the Internet.

Individual works available on the Internet will normally have their own copyright which may well be a foreign copyright. Contrary to the view that the Internet is equivalent to the public domain, this does not affect the fact of subsistence of copyright. A copyright owner may choose to make his work available freely but it will remain a work of copyright and will not affect the copyright position of other works. It is advisable for owners of copyright works to make it clear whether the work can be printed or downloaded or used in other ways. While it is almost impossible to police the use of works on the Internet the copyright position, including moral rights, should be spelt out.

There are proposals for harmonisation of certain aspects of copyright and related rights in the Information Society. This results from the Copyright and Performing Rights Treaties of the World Intellectual Property Organisation which will modify the Berne Copyright Convention. Apart from a communication right and controls over the circumvention of technological measures to prevent unauthorised copying (both of which already exist under United Kingdom copyright law), a particular feature is the protection of electronic 'rights management information'. This is information which identifies the work, the author, the owner of any right in the work, or information about terms and conditions of use. Remedies will be available also against any person who, without consent, disseminates any works in respect of which such information has been removed or altered with express knowledge of this. Compliance is likely to be required by 30 June 2000. The utility of protecting rights management information is obvious.

If information such as the name of the author or owner of the copyright in a work or any conditions as to its use is removed and a work is placed on a Web site, anyone accessing it might think they can do with it as they wish. They may think that they can download it, make copies of it, modify it or distribute it freely. In view of this, and the forthcoming protection afforded to rights management information, it is doubly important for owners of copyright works to clearly mark them with the name of the author and owner, if different, the year of creation and any conditions as to its use. For example, if Fred Smith decides to make his new musical composition available on his Web site, he may decide to add the following information:

Copyright F Smith 1999. The right of F Smith to be identified as the author of this music is hereby asserted. This music may be listened to in private and a single copy may be downloaded for your personal and domestic use only. Any further use may infringe copyright and moral rights and may attract civil remedies and criminal penalties.

Under United Kingdom law, apart from any copyright in the individual works, databases or compilations of works, there may be separate copyrights as cable programmes included in a cable programme service. This is defined by section 7(1) of the Copyright, Designs and Patents Act 1988 as a service consisting wholly or mainly in sending visual images, sounds or other information by means of a telecommunications system, otherwise than by wireless telegraphy, for reception:

(a) at two or more places (whether for simultaneous reception or at different times in response to requests by different users), or
(b) for presentation to members of the public.

It seems clear that information available via the Internet falls within (a) above. There are a number of exceptions (including systems which are predominantly interactive such as electronic mail). There are difficulties, however, with applying cable programme copyright to the Internet. This form of copyright was intended to be the equivalent to the broadcast copyright for providers of cable television. In this sense it works well but, by section 9(2)(c), the author of a cable programme is the person providing the cable programme service in which the programme is included. The question here is: who is the person providing the service? As no one person is in overall control this is not easily answered. The access provider who arranges connection to the Internet does not, in reality, provide the service in which the programmes (or works) are included. Rather, the service provider is a facilitator rather than a provider.

The first case on the copyright nature of the Internet was heard in Scotland. It involved Web pages of the *Shetland Times* on which extracts of news items appearing in printed editions of its newspapers were placed. It was hoped that advertisers would want to advertise on the front page of the Web site. The defender, Dr Jonathan Wills, had a Web site called 'The Shetland News' on which he had placed verbatim headlines from the *Shetland Times*. Anyone accessing these headlines could, by clicking the mouse button on them, gain access to the news items on the *Shetland Times* Web site, by-passing the front page with its advertisements. It was claimed that the copyright in the headlines had been infringed. In *Shetland Times Ltd* v *Dr Jonathan Wills* [1997] FSR 604, in the Outer House of the Court of Session, Scotland, Lord Hamilton granted an interim interdict (injunction). He said that it was arguable that the copyright in the headlines had been infringed by including them in a cable programme service. He also said it was at least arguable that operating a Web site was operating a cable programme service within section 7(1) of the Copyright, Designs and Patents Act 1988 (see above).

There is an exception in section 7(2)(a), where an essential feature of the service is that it is interactive. However, Lord Hamilton did not accept that this provision applied to save the defender as, although persons accessing the Web site could send messages and communicate with the *Shetland Times* via the Internet, this was not an essential feature of the service. Alternatively, that part of the service was severable, leaving the remainder of the service to be classed as a cable programme service. An appeal was lodged but the parties settled the dispute before the appeal got properly under way. That being so, it is not beyond doubt whether operating a Web site is within the meaning of operating a cable programme service, although that does seem to be the most appropriate form of copyright.

If operating a Web site is operating a cable programme service, this has important consequences. A cable programme is defined as 'any item included in a cable programme service' by section 7(1) of the Copyright, Designs and Patents Act 1988. As a cable programme service consists wholly or mainly in sending visual images, sounds or other information and infringement extends to including a cable programme in a cable programme service, this could mean even very small items, normally regarded as too small or trivial to attract copyright protection otherwise, could be protected. In particular, an item of 'information' could be quite small. It should be sufficient to convey something (a dictionary definition of 'information' is 'something told, knowledge, items of knowledge') and it is likely that even a small newspaper headline could do this. Somewhat controversially, in the *Shetland Times* case, Lord Hamilton considered that the headlines were literary works in their own right. Normally these would be considered too small for copyright protection and, in the past, phrases such as 'Beauty is a social necessity, not a luxury' and 'The man who broke the bank at Monte Carlo' and words such as 'EXXON', 'Kojak' and 'Elvis' have been held not to be works of copyright. However, if a generous view is taken of 'information', very trivial things could be protected by virtue of cable programme copyright. Apart from continuing doubts as to the copyright status of the Internet as a service (notwithstanding that individual works placed on Web pages will, in most cases, have their own independent copyright) there are other serious problems for copyright in 'cyberspace' such as:

- powerful copyright owners may use 'bully-boy tactics', obtaining or threatening injunctions against individuals and, more seriously, against access providers,
- it becomes impossible to control copying and unauthorised use of works (copies can be made on disk virtually instantaneously – much cheaper and quicker than photocopying), and
- the international dimension is a nightmare in terms of policing, jurisdiction and acting against infringers.

Until recently, there has been an emphasis on the medium on which a work is stored with too little appreciation of the nature of copyright. For example, a book comprises two separate and distinct property rights. The paper, ink and binding together make an item of tangible property as a 'good'. The work contained within the book and expressed therein is subject to a copyright which is a form of intangible property. There has been insufficient focus on the existence of the intangible right that is copyright and, with the advent of the Internet, freeing the copyright from its medium, like releasing the genie from the bottle, will have interesting and probably unexpected consequences.

Licensing

When it is required to commercially exploit works published electronically (whether by cable, broadcast or in multimedia products) it is usual for access to be provided by means of a licence agreement. A licence is necessary because accessing the works will involve an act restricted by copyright. For example, retrieving a document from a database of documents will require a copy to be made in the computer's memory and the copyright owner's permission to do this must be obtained. This is not so with traditional paper materials. Taking a book from a library shelf and reading it does not require any acts to be done which are restricted by copyright. Any use of a work involving computer technology will usually require copies to be made even if they are only transient. By section 17(6) of the Copyright, Designs and Patents Act 1988, it is an infringement of copyright to make a transient copy.

The use of licence agreements brings contract law into play in addition to copyright law. A licence agreement will contain terms concerning the use of the work and may impose restrictions going beyond copyright. Typically, a licence may specify the acts that may be done in a negative way by stating what may not be done. For example, a licence for the use of a multimedia product such as a CD-ROM may state that the licensee shall not duplicate the CD-ROM or print out any of the works contained in it or download any of those works apart from viewing on a screen. If the product is available with an updating service there may be a term requiring that old copies are destroyed or returned to the licensor. The licence may also require that the licensee place notices near computer terminals warning of copyright infringement. Failure to abide by the terms of the licence will be a breach of contract and, in many cases, also an infringement of copyright.

There are important international differences in the protection of creative works. For example, the United Kingdom does not yet provide for an artist's resale right as applies in France. This can make the identification of rights and obtaining the permissions required very difficult, especially with a product such as multimedia. The person acquiring a multimedia product should satisfy himself that all the relevant permissions have been obtained and provided for in the licence and should check that the licence agreement also contains an indemnity. If it turns out that a relevant permission has not been obtained, the licensor should indemnify the licensee against any claims arising and which are directed at the licensee. An example of the difficulty that might be experienced is whether a consent that had been obtained 40 years ago in respect of playing music from a vinyl sound recording in public would now extend to incorporating the music in a multimedia product. Peggy Lee obtained some $3.8 million in an award of damages resulting from an action against Walt Disney. She claimed that her original agreement with Walt Disney for her work on *Lady and the Tramp* did not extend to selling videos of the film. Video had not been invented at the time! (*The Times*, 7 October 1992, p 16.)

On-line databases are already well established and, usually, made available through a subscription in the form of a licence agreement. In addition to paying an annual fee, it is common for each search of the database to be charged individually. An interesting feature of an on-line database is that the provider can keep an exact record of the use of the database and can charge a sum reflecting the precise use that has been made of the database by the subscriber. The ability to monitor use in this way will have increasingly significant implications in the future.

An on-line database may comprise a number of copyrights as is the case with CD-ROM products. Taking LEXIS as an example, a database containing the full text of legislation and cases, the legislation is, in the United Kingdom, a work of copyright which belongs to Her Majesty (Crown copyright). The cases contain court judgments each of which comprise catchwords, a headnote and the judgment itself. The copyright in the catchwords and headnote will belong in the first instance to the organisation employing the law reporter but the judgment will be Crown copyright on the basis that a judge is probably a servant of the Crown who writes the judgment in the course of his duties (section 163). The database maker will have a copyright in the whole database as a compilation and will have been permitted to enter the individual materials into the database under licence agreements. The licence under which the subscriber is permitted to use the database will restrict that use, particularly in terms of downloading and copying.

Other questions are raised in relation to databases. For example, is a particular database protected by copyright or by the database right or both? How is substantiality determined in relation to a database? Is the copyright in a database refreshed from time to time as it evolves and undergoes changes? At what stage does an aggregation of incremental changes give rise to a fresh copyright or database right?

Collecting societies such as the Performing Right Society and the Copyright Licensing Agency assist in the exploitation of copyright by increasing the accessibility of works and allowing a certain amount of copying while providing copyright owners with income. However, most collecting societies do not, at the moment in the United Kingdom, cover electronic publishing with their blanket licence schemes. The disparate nature of works available electronically makes the establishment of a workable and equitable set of rules governing the use of works very difficult.

Special copyright problems posed by electronic publishing

Apart from the issues identified above, there are a number of specific problems that may result from the widespread use of electronic storage and publishing of works. These problems relate to digitisation, typographical arrangements, electronic publication of old works and the liability of 'facilitators', persons or organisations (such as libraries) which make electronically published works available to end users and, especially, Internet Service Providers. These are considered below.

Digitisation

Some doubts have been expressed as to whether digitising (storing in digital form) is within the restricted act of copying for copyright purposes. In *Anacon Corp Ltd* v *Environmental Research Technology Ltd* [1994] FSR 659, the defendant had used the plaintiff's circuit diagram to create a printed circuit board. As an intermediate step, the defendant made a net list (a list of the electronic components with details of their interconnection) from the circuit diagram. Although a circuit diagram is, *prima facie*, an artistic work, the judge held that it was not an infringement of the copyright in the circuit diagram as an artistic work because the circuit board did not look like an artistic work. He said that it was the visual significance of an artistic work that mattered.

On this basis, making a digital copy of an artistic work will not infringe as the digital copy will not look like the original work or, for that matter, any artistic work. Previous case law under the Copyright Act 1956 supports this view but the Copyright, Designs and Patents Act 1988 contains a provision that clearly contradicts this approach. Section 17(2) states that copying a literary, dramatic, musical or artistic work 'includes storing the work in any medium by electronic means' – a phrase that was not mentioned by the judge, Mr Justice Jacob. Of course, the words of the statute, if they are clear and unambiguous, which they are, prevail. Therefore, that part of the judgment dealing with infringement of copyright in artistic works must be read with caution.

Jacob J overcame this apparent (and mistaken) limitation by holding that the circuit diagram was also a literary work because it was intended to be read. A person making a circuit board would have to read the information contained in the diagram, which also included written information such as the rating of components. By doing so and creating a net list, the defendant had reproduced the literary work in a material form.

The definitions of sound recordings, films, broadcasts and cable programmes are very wide and, for these works, converting or storing the work in digital form should present no particular problems. For example, by section 5(1) a 'film' means 'a recording on any medium from which a moving image may by any means be produced'. Of course reproducing a work from a digital recording will normally infringe copyright if done without the copyright owner's licence and this is so even if any intervening act does not infringe (see section 16(3)). For example, say that Mary in London buys an LS Lowry print. Mary converts this into digital form and then transmits it to Thomas in Cardiff who then reproduces the work on screen and prints it out on paper. Neither Mary nor Thomas has the permission of LS Lowry's estate to do any act restricted by copyright. By section 17(2), by storing the work electronically, Mary has infringed copyright. Transmitting the work digitally does not infringe (assuming that act does not fall within the restricted acts of broadcasting, inclusion in a cable programme service or issuing to the public). However, storage in Thomas's computer probably infringes because, by section 17(6), copying includes making copies which are transient or are incidental to some other use of the work. Furthermore, by printing the work out on paper, Thomas has reproduced the Lowry print in a material form. The fact that an intervening act (transmission) did not infringe does not break the chain as far as Thomas is concerned. Mary will probably be liable also for the infringing acts of Thomas because infringement includes authorising another to do any of the acts restricted by copyright. This is shown diagrammatically in Fig. 7.2.

It is arguable that because of the weak link in the above acts (transmission other than by way of a broadcast or cable programme service) there should be a strengthening of the Copyright, Designs and Patents Act 1988 in this respect. Though it should cause no particular difficulties within the United Kingdom, it could if a copy of the work is obtained already in digital form (e.g. CD-ROM) and it is then transmitted to another country. On the face of

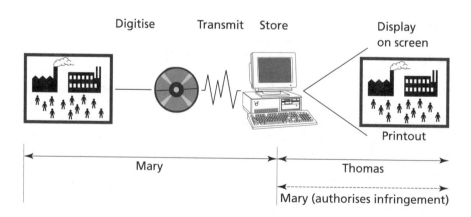

Fig. 7.2 Infringement of copyright in a digital work

it, the person transmitting the work from the United Kingdom does not himself infringe copyright. Liability might still accrue, however, on the basis that he has authorised the infringement by facilitating it and this form of liability is considered later in this chapter.

Typographical arrangements of published editions

Typographical arrangements of published editions are protected as a distinct form of copyright (section 1(1)(c) of the Copyright, Designs and Patents Act 1988). This copyright gives protection to publishers of literary, dramatic and musical works irrespective of the copyright subsisting in those works as such. Thus a new publication of a new play will have two copyrights: the play which, as a dramatic work, will be protected for the life of the author plus 70 years and the typographical arrangement, the copyright of which will endure for 25 years from the end of the calendar year during which it was first published (section 15).

The typographical arrangement copyright is particularly useful to a publisher of a work which is itself out of copyright. For example, if a publisher decides to publish a document containing the writings of Charles Babbage (1791–1871) he will be able to sue someone who photocopies the document without permission on the basis of the copyright in the typographical arrangement even though the copyright in the writings as literary works expired some time ago. If the publisher engages an author to select and arrange Babbage's writings and to add a commentary there will arise additional new copyrights in the commentary, providing it is more than trivial and, potentially, in the work expended on the selection and arrangement resulting in a compilation copyright.

The purpose of copyright in typographical arrangements is to protect the publisher's work in selecting the typeface, margins, headings, spacing and other typographical details; in other words, the layout of the print on the page. This is all well and good in the context of print on paper but what is the position where the work in question is published electronically? To take an example, say that Charles decides to store the entire known works of William Shakespeare (1564–1616) on computer disk. Copyright in Shakespeare's works expired some centuries ago and, as the entire known works are to be stored, it is unlikely that there is any copyright in the whole as a database because, on the basis of *G A Cramp & Sons Ltd v Frank Smythson Ltd* [1944] AC 329, there is no room for skill and judgment in selecting the materials to include. For the sake of this example, it is assumed that the individual works are not entered in any particular order or subject to a newly devised classification system.

For copyright to subsist in a typographical arrangement, the following requirements must be met:

- the arrangement must qualify for United Kingdom copyright (this will not usually be an issue),
- it must not simply be a reproduction of the typographical arrangement of a previous edition, and
- it must be applied to a published edition of the whole or part of one or more literary, dramatic or musical works (section 8).

The last point is doubtful in terms of electronic publishing. The phrase 'published edition' is not defined in the Act other than as above although it is reasonable to suppose that the meaning of 'publication' will be relevant. This is defined in section 175 as issuing copies to the public and includes, in the case of a literary, dramatic, musical or artistic work, making it available to the public by means of an electronic retrieval system. Thus, electronic publishing of the original works of copyright is specifically covered, but typographical arrangements are not mentioned. Even if it does extend to typographical arrangements, there may be further difficulty with the word 'edition'. This reflects traditional publishing but may be inappropriate in the context of, say, a database which is continually being updated. Certainly, when a database is first made available to the public that could be said to be its first edition. But when does a second or subsequent edition exist? Does the owner of the database have to change the font, point size, margins, etc. to obtain a new typographical arrangement copyright? 'Typographic arrangement' is not defined in the Act and this may allow the courts to take a flexible view and to confirm, if the need should arise, that it applies to the layout of text or musical notation on a screen and/or the details of font, spacing, page and style setting, etc. embedded within the relevant computer file containing the work. That there are doubts about typographical arrangements of published editions in the context of electronic publishing is regrettable. Perhaps there should be a new electronic document format copyright which would extend not only to the choice of fonts, margins, page settings and such like but also to protect the work involved in creating hypertext links and other structural or indexing systems used in computer documents. Electronic publishers should not be disadvantaged compared to traditional paper publishers.

Returning to our example, if Charles sells CD-ROM disks containing the works of Shakespeare, even if his electronic arrangement is deemed to be a typographical arrangement of a published edition, this will not enable him to take legal action to prevent someone copying out the works in a different form, for example, by handwriting. Converting the format by changing details such as font, point size, margins, etc. to produce a different format will not infringe copyright as the restricted act of making an adaptation does not apply to typographical arrangements of published editions. Thus Charles may have limited protection only and the situation should be the same if he makes the works available to the public on-line.

It has already been noted that a copyright might arise if Charles has to expend skill or judgment in selecting what to include and in arranging the individual works, perhaps using a classification system based on type of work: tragedy, love sonnet, etc. Certainly, if he adds commentary and criticism that itself should attract copyright. The position is less clear where Charles has carried out extensive research in an effort to get to the precise wording of Shakespeare's works as written, correcting errors in known texts. Can there be a copyright in correcting mistakes in old works? It would seem reasonable to reward the skill, effort and judgment expended by Charles but if he succeeds in recreating the true text as written by Shakespeare that would produce the anomaly of resurrecting a long extinct copyright!

Clearly, there are problems with typographical arrangements in electronic publishing. Although it is entirely reasonable to accept that the provisions protecting typographical arrangements also ought to apply to the format of electronically published works it is far too easy to copy the work without the format. For example, a word processed document which has been carefully set out and formatted to look attractive on a computer screen or as printed and has numerous font changes, indents, headings, etc. can simply be converted to ASCII code to avoid infringing the copyright in the typographical arrangement. Some word processors have 'style sheets' which determine the format and layout of the document. Could these be deemed to be typographical arrangements? The difficulties are amplified where the copyright in the work itself has expired because of its age.

Legal liability of Internet Service Providers

Internet Service Providers (ISPs) facilitate access to material on the Internet. Through their agreements with persons to whom they provide access, ISPs have some measure of control, for example, by requiring the client to adhere to copyright law and not to make infringing material available to others, whether on a Web page or by transmitting by e-mail. ISPs may even seek indemnities from their clients for copyright infringement attributable to their actions. Nevertheless, ISPs may be vulnerable for copyright infringement in a number of ways:

- by being secondary infringers,
- by authorising infringement, or
- by joint infringement.

These are considered below.

Secondary infringement

Under section 24(2) of the Copyright, Designs and Patents Act 1988 it is an infringement of copyright to transmit a work, without the licence of the copyright owner, by a telecommunications system knowing or having reason to believe that infringing copies will be made by means of the reception of the transmission in the United Kingdom or elsewhere. Although it matters not where the reception takes place, the definition of 'infringing copy' provides territorial constraint as, in relation to infringing copies made outside the United Kingdom, the copy must either have been imported or is proposed to be imported into the United Kingdom. Also, had it been made in the United Kingdom that would have been an infringement of the copyright in the work or a breach of an exclusive licence agreement relating to the work.

A serious limitation is that the transmission must be otherwise than by broadcasting or inclusion in a cable programme service. As discussed above, the *Shetland Times* case is authority for the view that operating a Web site is within the meaning of operating a cable programme service. If this is confirmed, then this form of infringement does not apply to those parts of the service deemed to be cable programme services. However, parts of the service intended to be interactive, such as e-mail or bulletin boards, may still be caught by section 24(2) as these will fall within the express exception to cable programme services.

If a person who subscribes to an ISP gains access to an infringing work of copyright, that person will infringe copyright by making a copy, whether transient or otherwise. Innocent copying still infringes, although innocence may be a factor in whether damages are available. However, an ISP will infringe under section 24(2) only if he has reason to believe that infringing copies will be made by means of the reception of the transmission in the United Kingdom or elsewhere. This is an objective test. Would a reasonable person, with knowledge of the facts known to the alleged infringer, have reason to believe infringing copies would be made?

Authorising infringement

Section 16(2) of the Copyright, Designs and Patents Act 1988 states that copyright in a work is infringed by a person who without the licence of the copyright owner does, or *authorises another to do*, any of the acts restricted by the copyright. If the act which infringes is done in the United Kingdom, it does not matter if the authorisation comes from elsewhere. In *ABKCO Music & Records Inc* v *Music Collection International Ltd* [1995] RPC 657 a Danish company granted a licence to an English company to make and issue to the public recordings of the plaintiff's sound recordings in the United Kingdom and Eire. It was held that it did not matter where the authorisation was given as long as the restricted act was carried out within the jurisdiction of the United Kingdom courts. Thus, if an Australian ISP authorises someone in the United Kingdom to make infringing material available on the Internet, the ISP is caught by section 16(2) and is liable for the infringement together with the person responsible for making the material available.

It is important to understand what is meant by authorisation. It has been construed by the courts in a fairly wide sense and turning a blind eye can amount to authorisation. Indifference or even failing to inform persons of the implications of copyright law may suffice. In *Moorhouse* v *University of New South Wales* [1976] RPC 151 a failure to inform users of a library with photocopying facilities as to copyright law and to supervise the use of the copiers was held to be authorising infringement of copyright. In the United Kingdom, judges have equated authorisation with '... the grant or purported grant, which may be express or implied, of the right to do the act complained of'.

An ISP could be said to authorise infringement if it fails to inform its clients of copyright law and the need to avoid infringement of copyright. It is possible that an even stronger duty could be placed on an ISP, for example, a positive duty to check material made available through its service. This may require spot checks or sampling of material made available through its service by its clients.

Joint infringement

It is possible that an ISP could be claimed to be a joint infringer along with the client responsible for making infringing material available through its service. Joint infringement occurs where two or more persons act in concert pursuant to a common design to infringe. In terms of stereo equipment having dual cassette tape players, in *Amstrad Consumer Electronics plc* v *The British Phonograph Industry Ltd* [1986] FSR 159, it was held that supplying machines which would be likely to be used to unlawfully copy pre-recorded cassettes subject to copyright protection was not authorising infringement of copyright. The supplier had no control over the way the machines were used once sold.

In the case of ISPs, things are different. They do have some control. They can monitor and check what is being made available through their service. They can erase or block infringing material. The problem they have is that the sheer volume of material involved makes effective control and policing almost impossible. The best they can do is to warn their clients about the dangers of copyright infringement. But if they encourage, even implicitly, a disregard for copyright laws, this could be seen as authorisation or even joint infringement. A sensible approach for an ISP is to inform their clients and to carry out a reasonable level of policing and checks on what material is being made available and transmitted through their service, the only difficulty being that they may then be accused of invasion of privacy.

What has been said above in relation to ISPs also applies to others who facilitate access to material over the Internet. Thus, libraries with on-line facilities or employers who allow or encourage employees to make use of the Internet should be careful as regards copyright infringement by their clients or employees. Education and vigilance seem to be the key words in respect of the Internet.

The future

It is arguable that the mass storage of all manner of works on electronic media will create insuperable problems for copyright law. Until recently copies of copyright works were only available as stored in or on some tangible item, for example, a book, disk, oil on canvas, magnetic tape and so on. Now, as we are entering an information 'Cyberspace', these tangible items are no longer necessary to the distribution or use of copyright works and there are unprecedented challenges ahead for copyright law. This gloomy view of copyright, however, takes no account of future development and refinement of the law. In the past, copyright law has proved itself to be capable of adapting to protect new forms of technological expression such as the photograph, sound recordings, broadcasts, cable programmes and computer programs. Technology is both a threat to copyright law and its potential saviour. For example, developments in cryptography, the increasing power of computers to monitor and record the use and copying of copyright works and to extract payment by electronic funds transfer and to precisely distribute that income among the plethora of right holders must not be underrated. Authors and copyright owners will be reimbursed for the actual use made of their work. This could diminish the role of the traditional publisher. Authors of works of copyright instead may deal directly with the providers of electronic databases and Internet access providers. Agents may become more important, being persons who will negotiate the best deals for authors to enable the work to be made available by the most effective providers.

Collecting societies such as the Copyright Licensing Agency may have a role to play in the above developments. One danger of the technological control of works of copyright is that the permitted acts under copyright law may be reduced to vanishing point as access may be denied without the appropriate licence fee being paid. Because of this we can expect that compulsory licensing provisions will be extended more and more into the copyright field. The mechanism already exists in the United Kingdom Copyright, Designs and Patents Act 1988 for provision to be made for compulsory licensing in respect of rental of sound recordings, films and computer programs by section 66, and the Commission of the European Communities has not entirely ruled out the need for compulsory licensing in the copyright field. One thing that is certain is that copyright law is facing unprecedented challenges and it will be interesting to see how it develops. At the end of the day, however, given the power of technology to make works available anywhere at any time, the main issues may be concerned more with policing copyright and bringing pressure to bear on countries with weak or unenforced copyright laws.

Chapter 8

The law of confidence

Introduction

The law of confidence is concerned with the protection of secrets whether they be trade secrets, secrets of a personal nature or concerning the government of the country. The fundamental rationale underlying the law of confidence is that it can prevent a person divulging information which has been given to him in confidence, on an express or implicit understanding that the information should not be disclosed to others or otherwise used by the recipient of the information. Alternatively, if the information has already been disclosed or used in breach of confidence, damages may be awarded against the person divulging or using the information. The roots of the law of confidence lie in equity and it is almost entirely based on case law. It is given statutory recognition in the Copyright, Designs and Patents Act 1988, section 171, which states:

> ... nothing in this Part [the part dealing with copyright] affects ... the operation of any rule of equity relating to breaches of trust or confidence ...

Although of older pedigree, the modern law of confidence developed in the nineteenth century and then lay relatively dormant until the middle of the twentieth century. It soon became clear that breach of confidence was actionable *per se*, and did not require a contractual relationship between the parties. An important case, *Prince Albert* v *Strange* [1849] 1 Mac & G 25, helped to establish this area of law and concerned etchings made by Queen Victoria and her consort, Prince Albert. The Queen and Prince made etchings for their own amusement, intended only for their own private entertainment, although they sometimes had prints made to give to friends. Etchings were sent to a printer to make some impressions and someone surreptitiously made copies which he passed on to the defendant who intended to display them in an exhibition which the public could attend on payment of an admission charge. It was held that relief would be given against the defendant even though he was a third party. He had argued that the prints were not improperly taken but it was said that his possession must have originated in breach of trust, confidence or contract and, therefore, an injunction was granted preventing the exhibition.

The law of confidence can be a very useful adjunct to other intellectual property rights. Copyright protects the expression of an idea, but the law of confidence is wider and can protect the idea itself. In *Andersen Consulting* v *CHP Consulting Ltd* (unreported) 26 July 1991, Chancery Division, a case concerning a dispute about maintenance of computer software by third parties, it was said that confidence is frequently used in connection with copyright material as it is:

> ... of course notorious that copyright protects only the expression of ideas and does not protect the idea itself ...

The law of breach of confidence can supplement copyright and patent protection especially in the early stages when there is nothing tangible or substantial enough for copyright law or patent law to protect. Additionally, the law of confidence can be useful for certain types of secrets for which other rights are inappropriate such as the recipe for Coca-Cola or a secret research technique or industrial process.

Basic requirements

A good working formula for the application of the law of confidence was laid down in *Coco* v *AN Clark (Engineers) Ltd* [1969] RPC 41, by Megarry J (as he then was). This involved a moped engine designed by the plaintiff who entered into informal negotiations with the defendant; no contract was executed. Megarry J held that the defendant owed the plaintiff an obligation of confidence (although he doubted the confidential quality of the information) and said that, apart from contract, an action for breach of confidence will require three elements:

1 The information must have the necessary quality of confidence about it.
2 The information must have been imparted in circumstances importing an obligation of confidence.
3 There must be an unauthorised use of that information to the detriment of the party communicating it.

The third of these elements is self-evident, but the first two require further discussion.

Quality of confidence

To be protected by the law of confidence, the information must have a quality of confidence about it. If the information is commonplace or is common knowledge to a group of persons (for example, it is well known to computer programmers) or to the public at large, it cannot be confidential; instead, it will be considered to be in the public domain. Often, it will be obvious whether the information is or is not confidential. The concept of confidentiality was considered in the case of *Thomas Marshall (Exports) Ltd* v *Guinle*

[1976] FSR 345, in which the defendant, who was the managing director of the plaintiff company, resigned half-way through his 10-year service contract to set up a rival business. The information involved sources of supply and the names of officials and other contacts in Europe and the Far East. Megarry VC found for the plaintiff and he said that four elements were necessary in testing for confidential quality.

1 Release of the information would injure the owner of the information or benefit others.
2 The owner must believe the information to be secret and not already in the public domain.
3 The owner's belief in 1 and 2 above must be reasonable.
4 The information must be judged in the light of usages and practices of the particular trade or industry concerned.

To come within the scope of the law of confidence, the information does not have to be particularly special and, as in the above case, ordinary and mundane information can be the proper subject matter of confidence as long as it is private to the person who has compiled the information, even though others could gather similar information if they took the trouble to do so. In this way, the law of confidence prevents others from gaining benefit from the work of the person who accumulated the information in the first place. As a result, a great deal of material related to the running of a business will fall within the ambit of the law of confidence. Examples of information relevant to computers which may be the subject matter of confidence include:

- ideas for a new or improved computer system, hardware and software, and research and development work generally;
- details of existing computer systems as would be known by computer analysts or programmers or even users of the system (in terms of users, the system would have to be uncommon in some respect);
- lists of customers or sub-contractors and associated information – for example, what services they perform, what their credit rating is. Information stored in computer databases is often confidential;
- a company's strategy for future research and development, production and marketing.

Obligation of confidence

An obligation of confidence will not be imposed on everyone. A person who is given confidential information and is unaware of its confidential nature (and has no reason to be aware) will be able to use the information freely. This is a major weakness of the law of confidence as it is largely ineffective against innocent third-party recipients of the information. For example, if A tells B something in confidence and B (without A's permission) passes the information on to C, who has not been told that it is confidential and the circumstances are such that an obligation of confidence cannot be imputed to C, then C will be able to use the information freely although B himself can be prevented from using the information or divulging it further. However, it may still be possible for A to obtain an injunction against C in respect of future disclosure or use by C if the information has not yet entered the public domain. C will not, of course, be liable for any acts that he may have carried out innocently before notification that B had divulged the information in breach of his obligation of confidence to A.

Obviously, an obligation of confidence can arise by express agreement: for example, where a freelance computer programmer is engaged to carry out some work under a contract which contains a term stating that the programmer will not use or divulge details of the client's business. An obligation of confidence may also be implied by the courts where there is a duty of good faith as in the relationship between a client and a solicitor, patent agent or bank manager. Another situation where the obligation will be imposed is where a person discusses his ideas with business organisations with a view to the commercial exploitation of those ideas: for example, if a computer analyst has an idea for a new computer system and discusses that idea with software houses interested in developing and marketing the system.

Employees

The employee–employer relationship is a special case and may be governed by express terms, as incorporated in the contract of employment, or implied terms or both. Generally, the duty of confidence owed by ex-employees will be less than for current employees who should always act in their employer's best interests. A present employee must respect the confidentiality of his employer's information even to the extent that he should not pry into information he has been told not to look at. In *Denco Ltd* v *Joinson* [1991] IRLR 63, an employee who had a right of access to certain information in his employer's computer system used another employee's password to gain access to other parts of the computer system – something he was not entitled to do. It was held that the employer was entitled to dismiss the employee summarily for his unauthorised use of the password.

Ex-employees have to make a living and much of the ex-employee's skill will involve what he learnt while in his previous employment, thus providing the courts with a dilemma. In many cases, to complicate matters, there may be an overlap with copyright law. However, the courts have developed rules for resolving the conflict which strike a reasonable balance between the interests of employee and employer alike.

When there are no express terms, the employer will not be protected to any great extent. If the ex-employee remembers details of some of the previous employer's customers, there is nothing to stop him using this information. Of course, it would be different if he deliberately memorised the customers' names or made a copy of them. In the absence of an express term in the contract of employment dealing with confidentiality, it was said, in *Printers and Finishers Ltd v Holloway* [1965] RPC 239, that there would be nothing improper in the employee putting his memory of particular features of his previous employer's plant at the disposal of his new employer. Even if there is an express term the employer would have to show that the information was over and above the employee's normal skill in the job and amounted to a trade secret. The nature of a trade secret was considered in *Lansing Linde Ltd v Kerr* [1991] 1 WLR 251, in which it was recognised that it was not confined to secret formulae or processes but could, in appropriate cases, extend to names of customers and the goods which they buy.

In *Northern Office Microcomputer (Pty) Ltd v Rosenstein* [1982] FSR 124, a South African case, the problem of where to draw the line between the employer's and employee's interests was considered. In this case, a computer programmer developed a computer program which was similar to one he had written for his previous employer. The case involved copyright matters in addition to the law of confidence and is notable in that the court recognised that computer programs were protected by South African copyright law as literary works. The trial judge agreed that the computer programs were protected by confidence but said that the protection should be of a limited nature. Although the defendant programmer would not be allowed simply to copy the programs in question, he would not be required to 'wipe clean the slate of his memory' because to do so would unduly restrict his use of his own training, skill and experience. There would be nothing, in principle, to prevent an ex-employee computer programmer writing a similar program by the exercise of his own mental effort provided he did not simply plagiarise his previous employer's program. To some extent, an important factor is the computer program itself, whether it is a commonplace program, carrying out mundane operations, or whether it is designed to do something novel, that is, whether the purpose of the program can be said to be in the nature of a trade secret.

In many cases, the employer's 'trade secrets' may be no more than the result of the application by an employee of his own skill and judgment, but if the employee was engaged specifically to produce that information then it can still amount to a trade secret. If the material is commonplace, however, there would be nothing to stop an ex-employee deriving the same or similar material again as long as he did not simply copy his employer's material. In such circumstances, all that would be protected would be the employer's 'lead time', the advantage of getting his product to the market place first.

An important case laying down principles which can be applied to the employer–employee relationship was *Faccenda Chicken Ltd v Fowler* [1986] 1 All ER 617. The employer's business was supplying fresh chickens and it was alleged that the employee had made wrongful use of sales information such as customers' names and addresses. The employer's action failed, but the following guidelines were laid down in the Court of Appeal.

1 If there is a contract of employment, the employee's obligations were to be determined from the contract.

2 If there were no express terms, the employee's obligations would be implied.

3 While still in employment, there was an implied term imposing a duty of good faith. This duty might vary according to the nature of the contract of employment but would be broken if the employee copied or deliberately memorised a list of customers.

4 The implied term imposing an obligation on the employee after the termination of his employment was more restricted. It might cover secret processes and trade secrets.

5 Whether information fell within this implied term to prevent its use or disclosure by an ex-employee depended on the circumstances, and attention should be given to the following:

- the nature of the employment;
- the nature of the information;
- whether the employer stressed the confidential nature of the material;
- whether the information could be easily isolated from other material the employee was free to use.

An ex-employee is thus allowed to make use of his own memory of the work he has carried out in his previous employment unless it involves genuine secrets or is covered by an express term in the contract of employment. Computer programmers and analysts will be allowed to make use of programming techniques and skills which they have learnt and which have become part of their own skill and experience, unless there is something very special about them or they have expressly agreed not to make further use of them. However, a very restrictive express term which tries to prevent an ex-employee making use of mundane skills will be struck out by the courts as being in restraint of trade. The same fate will await any terms which restrict the ex-employee's future employment prospects to any great extent – for example, a term which states that a computer programmer cannot work for computer software companies in the United Kingdom for five years following the termination of his employment. Such restrictive terms will be upheld by the courts only if they are reasonable, such as when a computer programmer working for a bank agrees not to work for another similar bank within a five-mile radius for the first year following the termination of his employment. The purpose of a covenant in restraint of trade should be to protect the employer's legitimate interests rather than simply preventing competition. Essentially, to be enforceable, the term should be aimed at protecting the employer's genuine business interests rather than trying to prevent lawful competition.

It is not easy to lay down an all-purpose formula based on time and geographical area as each case will turn on its own facts. For example, in *Office*

Angels Ltd v *Rainer-Thomas* [1991] IRLR 214, it was held that a covenant precluding an ex-employee from opening an employment agency anywhere in an area only within a 1000-metre radius of the previous employer's agency for a period of only six months was inappropriate and would do little to protect the employer's interests because clients usually placed orders over the telephone and the geographical location of the office was of no consequence to them. In that case, the Court of Appeal also confirmed that, where a covenant in restraint of trade was ambiguous, the narrower construction would be taken.

Computer hackers

A computer hacker is a person who gains access to a computer system without permission. Computer hackers pose a serious threat to the security of computer systems and some of the activities in which they engage are potentially criminal in nature. These activities are fully discussed in Chapter 25. However, computer hackers also might be liable under the law of confidence, depending on the circumstances. If a hacker gains access to confidential files stored on a computer, it is just possible that the law of confidence might be used to prevent the hacker from making use of the information assuming, of course, that the hacker can be identified. In many cases, information stored in computer systems is highly confidential. It might, for example, concern medical records, creditworthiness, employment or lifestyle details. But will an obligation of confidence attach to a computer hacker? The case of *Prince Albert* v *Strange*, discussed above, suggests that an action might lie in breach of confidence even if the information was obtained surreptitiously. The court in that case was quite happy to imply an obligation of confidence even though it was not possible to say how the confidential information (that is, the prints taken from the engravings) came into the defendant's hands. It could only be assumed that the prints had been obtained in a clandestine manner. In principle, this is very similar to the position of a computer hacker. A hacker must know that there is a strong possibility that the information he accesses will be confidential and, therefore, he will be fixed with an obligation of confidence. If the information turns out to have a quality of confidence, then there is no reason in principle why the hacker should not be sued for breach of confidence if he uses that information or discloses it to others.

If the information is accidentally overheard or intercepted in circumstances where the owner of the information utters it or transmits it by insecure means (for example, by telling it to someone in a crowded room or by transmitting the information by a public telecommunications system) an obligation of confidence might not be imposed on the person obtaining the information in this manner. In *Malone* v *Metropolitan Police Commissioner* [1979] Ch 344, information overheard during an authorised telephone tapping operation by the police was held not to have been disclosed in confidence. However, the law on the matter of unauthorised interception of information is not clear.

The Law Commission recommended codifying the law of confidence and its report, *Breach of Confidence* (Cmnd 8388, HMSO 1980), contains a draft breach of confidence Bill. Clause 5 of the Bill would impose an obligation of confidence on a person who improperly acquires information by using or interfering with any computer or data retrieval mechanism – a welcome clarification. However, there has been no resulting legislation along these lines and it is unlikely that such action will be taken in the foreseeable future.

Remedies for breach of confidence

The most important remedy for breach of confidence is an injunction preventing the use or disclosure of the information. If the information has been divulged to sufficient people so that it can be said to be no longer confidential, an injunction will not be of any help; it would be like locking the stable door after the horse has bolted. If this has happened and the information has been used to the detriment of the person to whom it 'belongs', however, damages will be available against the person responsible and a limited injunction may be granted against that person.

As an alternative to damages, an account of profits may be available and this may be more advantageous to the plaintiff, especially if the defendant has made substantial profit from his use of the information. Being an equitable remedy it is discretionary and the plaintiff must have 'clean hands' and have acted promptly in enforcing his rights. An example of the use of this remedy is the case of *Peter Pan Manufacturing Corp* v *Corsets Silhouette Ltd* [1963] RPC 45, which involved the use of confidential information, after the expiry of a licence agreement, in the manufacture of brassières. The plaintiff asked for the whole of the profits on the brassières but the defendant said that the account of profits should only be based on the profit resulting from the wrongful use of the confidential information; that is, the profit relating to the parts of the brassières incorporating the confidential information. The difference between the two sums was substantial and the plaintiff was awarded the higher sum because the defendants would not have been able to make the brassières at all without using the confidential information.

It can be seen that the law of confidence is very useful at an early stage when ideas are being formulated and discussed. Although the law of copyright gives some protection at this stage by protecting plans, specifications and notes, the protection does not extend to the ideas behind them. Confidence is particularly important during the development of inventions before they are granted patents because a patent will be refused if details of the invention have been made available to the public, as we shall see. In the computer industry, as with any other, ideas have to be discussed with various persons and organisations with a view to raising finance and granting licences to use or reproduce the resulting invention or copyright work. Many licences for the use of patented inventions include permission to use 'know-how', the confidential information needed to work the invention to best effect. Some licences may be purely for know-how where there is no patent involved. In most circumstances, during negotiations, an obligation of confidence will be implied but it is sensible to stress confidentiality – for example, by stating that the information is confidential and must not be disclosed to anyone else without permission.

Chapter 9

Patent law

Introduction

A patent is a very desirable form of intellectual property because it gives to the owner a monopoly in his invention, enabling him to exploit the invention for a number of years to the exclusion of all others (subject to provisions designed to prevent abuse of the monopoly granted). Patent law has a long history and has developed as a means of protecting innovation which has a benefit to innovator and public alike. Inventors are encouraged to invent and investors are more likely to risk money in the development of new inventions if a monopoly right is available for inventions. Society reaps a benefit because the invention will eventually fall into the public domain and because, in the meantime, commercial enterprise is stimulated.

There are two types of patentable invention – a product invention and a process invention – and it has been said that an invention is a new way of making something old or an old way of making something new. A patentable invention could relate to a new piece of computer hardware such as a new interface device, a new type of output device such as a more efficient flat screen display or a new form of storage medium or it could be a new way of making integrated circuits or flat screens. There have been many patent applications for computer hardware and other electronic materials: for example, the invention of the printed circuit board, the transistor and the integrated circuit have all been patented. Sometimes, other forms of protection may be available such as design law or copyright. If the invention fails to meet the rigorous standards required for patentability, these and other forms of protection may still be available. For example, a new layout of components on a printed circuit board may be protected by the design right even if there is no inventive step for patent purposes.

Fundamentally, the inventor (or more usually, the employer of the inventor) applies for a patent to the Patent Office in London, whether the inventor wants a United Kingdom patent or one which extends to other countries as well. If the application is successful, a patent will be granted for four years initially and may be renewed, annually, up to a maximum of 20 years from the date the application is first filed (the priority date). The renewal fees become progressively steeper throughout the life of the patent and most patents do not run the full 20 years. Obtaining a patent is a complex, expensive and lengthy process and the services of a patent agent are desirable because the drafting of the patent specification and claims is extremely important as regards the future scope of the patent. Until the Copyright, Designs and Patents Act 1988, only a registered patent agent or a solicitor could act for gain as an agent for persons seeking patents, but now anyone can do this as long as he does not describe himself as, or hold himself out to be, a 'patent agent' or 'patent attorney'. In view of the complicated nature of the process, however, the person applying for a patent would be well advised to satisfy himself as to the ability of his agent. In some circumstances, it may be preferable simply to keep the idea secret and rely on the law of confidence; this costs nothing and there is no requirement that the invention must eventually fall into the public domain. Examples of the effectiveness of this approach are the recipes and processes used in many familiar drinks and foodstuffs such as Coca-Cola and Kentucky Fried Chicken. In many cases, however, the invention cannot be kept secret, especially if articles made to the invention are to be marketed commercially or if a large number of employees know of the invention, in which case a patent is the only realistic solution.

Procedure

The ponderous patent application process seems to be unsuited to a fast-moving technology as it can take several years from initial application before a patent is finally granted. The procedure for obtaining a patent in the United Kingdom is as follows.

1 The application is filed together with a specification describing the invention, an abstract (the title for the invention and concise summary) and the claims (defining the scope of the monopoly claimed). Drawings will usually be included in the specification.
2 The Patent Office will carry out a search for patents and other documents which may be relevant to the invention. Typically, this will find previous patents in the same field which might have a bearing on the patentability of the invention. It is common for the application to be amended following the search.
3 Eighteen months following the first filing of the patent it is published. This is referred to as 'A' publication.
4 The Patent Office examiners then carry out an extensive examination of the patent application to check for conformity with the requirements of the Patents Act 1977. Again, some amendments may be necessary at this stage, though it should be noted that the monopoly claimed cannot be widened.
5 Finally, the patent will be granted (all being well) and it will be published again – 'B' publication.

The procedure is shown in Fig. 9.1. It is greatly simplified and assumes no problems are encountered. Since 1995, the United Kingdom Patent Office has

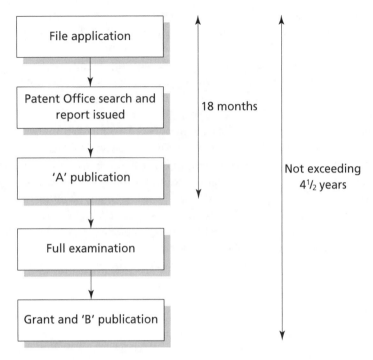

Fig. 9.1 Patent procedure (simplified)

offered a speedier procedure whereby the applicant can request a combined search and examination and earlier publication. This procedure may be suitable for straightforward applications. It is unlikely to be appropriate for software patents.

The proprietor's monopoly dates back, effectively, to the date of 'A' publication. Although he cannot sue until the patent is granted, he will be entitled to damages in respect of any infringement carried out after publication.

The date when the patent application is first filed becomes its priority date. As a result of international conventions, the applicant may make further applications in convention countries within the next 12 months and the novelty of the invention will still be judged as at its priority date. Thus, the applicant has 12 months to decide in which other countries he wishes to obtain a patent. Two international conventions – the European Patent Convention and the Patent Co-operation Treaty – facilitate the obtaining of patents in a number of other countries.

The main legislation governing patents is the Patents Act 1977 and the Patents Rules 1995. The 1977 Act was passed to bring United Kingdom patent law in line with the European Patent Convention (EPC) to which the United Kingdom is a signatory in addition to other European countries such as Belgium, France, Germany, Holland, Italy, Sweden and Spain. A number of non-EC countries also belong to the EPC, including Norway and Switzerland. The EPC is not a European Community institution although the European Patent Office (EPO) will administer the proposed Community Patent Convention, providing a Community-wide patent system, when it comes into force. In addition to the Patents Act 1977, there are a number of rules and regulations dealing with details such as registration procedure, fees and the Patents County Court in London. The Comptroller of Patents also has jurisdiction to hear certain patent disputes if the parties are willing and to hear other matters, such as determining who should be the true proprietor or whether an employee inventor should be awarded compensation for an invention belonging to his employer which is of outstanding benefit to the employer.

Not all inventions are capable of supporting a patent. The Patents Act 1977 lays down several requirements which must be satisfied before a patent can be granted and, furthermore, certain things are specifically excluded from patentability. The basic requirements for the grant of a patent will now be explained, followed by a consideration of the exclusions and their impact, especially with respect to computer software.

Basic requirements

The basic requirements for the grant of a patent are stated in section 1(1) of the Patents Act 1977 as follows:

> A patent may be granted only for an invention in respect of which the following conditions are satisfied, that is to say:
>
> (a) the invention is new;
> (b) it involves an inventive step;
> (c) it is capable of industrial application;
> (d) the grant of a patent for it is not excluded by subsections (2) and (3) below ...

The exclusions referred to in (d), which include computer programs, will be considered later but first the interpretation of the first three conditions will be examined.

New invention

The word 'invention' is not defined in the Act but its meaning is really a matter of common sense and it can be used in a fairly wide sense. It is obvious that a patent should not be granted for anything which is not new, which is already in the public domain, otherwise the grant of the patent could make illegal an act which was previously legal. For example, if a company has been making integrated circuits by a special process for several years but has failed to apply for a patent, a second company, wishing to do the same type of work, will be refused a patent on the grounds that the invention is not new. The first company could set up such prior use as a defence against a patent infringement action under section 64. The prior use could invalidate the patent unless such use had not made the invention available to the public. This might be the case where the prior use was in secret until after the priority date of the patent. The prior use must have occurred before the priority date or serious and effective preparations must have been made in respect of such use before that date.

Section 2 of the Act expands on the meaning of 'new' and says that an invention is new if it does not form part of the 'state of the art'; this expression comprises all matter which has been made available to the public in the United Kingdom or elsewhere, by written or oral description, by use or in any other way. Matters contained in prior patent applications are also included. There is no need for the invention to have been made widely available to the public and, in *Windsurfing International Inc* v *Tabur Marine (GB) Ltd* [1985] RPC 59, it was held that a 12-year-old boy, who had made his own sailboard which he used at Hayling Island on summer weekends, had made the invention available to the public with the effect that a patent later granted to the plaintiff for a sailboard was declared invalid after the defendant had challenged its validity on the grounds of lack of novelty and lack of inventive step.

The inventor must resist any temptation he might have to publish details of his invention before the first filing date (the priority date), otherwise he could inadvertently add his invention to the state of the art and anticipate his own invention. Similarly, the inventor must be careful when discussing his invention with potential manufacturers and the like and the law of confidence is very important at this stage. However, if details of the invention are disclosed by a person acting in breach of confidence or who has obtained details unlawfully, that disclosure will be disregarded in determining the state of the art if such breach occurs no earlier than six months preceding the filing of the patent.

As technology advances and the pool of knowledge in the public domain grows, it is increasingly difficult to devise something which is absolutely 'new'. Indeed, it is not an easy task to find out if the invention has been anticipated and is already part of the state of the art, given the massive world-wide volume of published work, and it is possible that a publication which anticipates the invention will not be discovered. If that material is subsequently found and shows that the invention was not new when the patent was applied for, the patent is in danger of being revoked. A number of patents may be on shaky ground as far as novelty is concerned if sufficient time and effort were expended on trying to trace anticipatory materials or prior use. A person who is being sued for infringing a patent will try to find such material.

Inventive step

By section 3 of the Patents Act 1977 an invention involves an inventive step if it is not obvious to a person skilled in the art. This test, known as the 'notional skilled worker test', takes account of the complexity of technology, hence the reference to a skilled person rather than the ubiquitous 'reasonable man', so often used as a benchmark by judges. The reason is that a great many 'inventions' would not be obvious to a layman but would be to someone who knew something of the technology involved. It has been accepted that the 'skilled person' may be a team of highly qualified research workers such as a team of analysts and computer programmers. When it comes to applying the test, the skilled person is not endowed with any inventive faculties himself, a somewhat artificial premise, but to hold otherwise would mean that virtually all inventions would be obvious and not patentable.

'Obvious' has no special meaning but is judged by looking at the invention as a whole and considering the entire state of the art. Whether the invention is obvious is a question of fact. In the *Windsurfing* case discussed earlier in connection with novelty, Lord Justice Oliver suggested the following four-stage test for determining whether an invention is obvious.

1 Identify the inventive concept embodied in the patent.
2 The court then assumes the mantle of the normally skilled but unimaginative person in the art at the priority date of the patent and imputes to him what was, at that date, common general knowledge in the art.
3 Identify what, if any, differences exist between that knowledge and the patented invention.
4 Consider whether, without knowledge of the invention, those differences constitute steps which would have been obvious to the person skilled in the art or whether they require any degree of invention.

Commercial success is a factor which can be taken into account in determining obviousness though it is not conclusive. In *Technograph Printed Circuits Ltd* v *Mills & Rockley (Electronics) Ltd* [1969] RPC 395, a case involving a patent for a method of making printed circuits, Harman J said:

> It was objected that in fact it was not until ten years after the invention was published that it was commercially adopted ... and it was argued from this that it was not a case of filling a long felt want. I do not accept this argument. In the years immediately following the war, manufacturers could sell all the machines they wanted using the old point-to-point wiring and had no need to trouble themselves with anything better.

Computer technology spreads into all kinds of other technologies and this may lead to patentable inventions, even though the computer technology itself is not new, if the application of the technology is new. In principle there is nothing to prevent the application of well-known technology to a particular problem being the proper subject matter of a patent. This may not be obvious if there has been a major problem and a solution has evaded many attempts to reach it. Again, the commercial success of the invention is a useful guide. In *Parks-Cramer Co* v *G W Thornton & Sons Ltd* [1966] RPC 407, the invention was a method of cleaning floors between rows of textile machines. There had been many unsuccessful attempts to find a satisfactory solution but none of them, unlike the present invention, actually worked. Essentially, all the invention consisted of was an overhead vacuum cleaner which moved back and forth between the textile machines and which had attached to it a long vertical tube, reaching almost to the floor. It was argued that this was obvious because every competent housewife knows that dust can be removed from a floor by the passage of a vacuum cleaner. This argument was rejected and the patent was held to be valid as the many unsuccessful attempts by inventors to find a solution coupled with the immediate commercial success of the present invention denied the possibility of a finding of obviousness.

The courts have to draw a line somewhere when it comes to obviousness although it is difficult to lay down hard and fast rules. It is clear, however, that there must be a sufficient inventive step and merely taking two older inventions and sticking them together will not necessarily be regarded as an inventive step.

Industrial application

Another requirement for the grant of a patent is that the invention must have an industrial application but this is widely defined by section 4 of the Patents Act 1977 which states that the invention must be capable of being made or used in any kind of industry, including agriculture. However, a method of treatment of the human or animal body by surgery or therapy or a method of diagnosis practised on the human or animal body is not capable of industrial application although this does not prevent the patenting of drugs to be used in any such treatment or diagnosis.

The need for industrial application shows the practical nature of patent law, which requires that the invention should be something which can be produced or that it relates to some sort of industrial process.

Examples of refusal on the grounds that the invention does not have an industrial application are rare, but one example is provided by *Hiller's Application* [1969] RPC 267. This case concerned an improved plan for underground service distribution schemes for housing estates; that is, the layout of the gas, sewerage and water pipes and electricity cables. It was held that this could not constitute a 'manner of manufacture' (the phrase used instead of 'industrial application' prior to the 1977 Act). Therefore, if someone develops a new form of layout for the components in a computer or a new configuration for printed circuit boards, these are unlikely to be granted patents. However, the layout of components and the configuration of a printed circuit board may be protected by copyright through any drawings which have been made indicating the layout or by the design right. Methods or principles of construction are excluded from the design right. A new form of layout cannot, without more, be said to be capable of industrial application.

Exclusions from patentability

Several things are excluded from the scope of patent law. Section 1(2) of the Patents Act 1977 contains those which can generally be classified as coming within the scope of copyright law or the law of confidence and, in that context, computer programs are of particular interest. (Section 1(3) concerns things which might encourage offensive, immoral or antisocial behaviour or new varieties of animals or plants.) Section 1(2) of the Act states that the following are not inventions for the purposes of the Act:

(a) a discovery, scientific theory or mathematical method;
(b) a literary, dramatic, musical or artistic work or any other aesthetic creation whatsoever;
(c) a scheme, rule or method for performing any mental act, playing a game or doing business, or a program for a computer;
(d) the presentation of information;

but the foregoing provision shall prevent anything from being treated as an invention for the purposes of this Act only to the extent that a patent or application for a patent relates to that thing *as such* [emphasis added].

Note that the above exceptions only apply to the extent that a *patent relates to that thing as such*. This means that these particular things mentioned in the above list of exclusions can be protected by patent indirectly if they are part of a patent application which includes other elements which are patentable in their own right. For example, a computer program *as such* to control the temperature of a furnace cannot be patented (it will, of course, be protected by copyright). If an application is made to patent a computer-controlled furnace, however, it may well succeed and be granted a patent.

Computer programs

The exclusion from patent of computer programs reflects international trends. Copyright is seen as the proper vehicle for the protection of computer programs although, when the current Patents Act was passed in 1977, it was far from clear whether copyright did protect computer programs. Even before the 1977 Act, computer programs were not generally patentable *per se*, but there have been cases, ~~both in the~~ United Kingdom and in the United States, where computer programs have been granted patents indirectly, usually as being part of a piece of machinery or an industrial process. For example, in *Diamond* v *Diehr* [1981] 209 USPQ 1, the United States Supreme Court confirmed that a computer-controlled process used in rubber curing was patentable.

In *Gever's Application* [1970] RPC 91, data processing apparatus was arranged to work in a certain way associated with punched cards inserted into it. The purpose of the apparatus was to file world trade marks in such a way that they could be easily produced to check for similarity and prior registration. The patent application, which concerned a piece of machinery which functioned in a certain way because of the punched cards, was allowed to proceed. The cards were described by the judge as a 'manner of manufacture' because he thought that a punched card was analogous to a cam for controlling the cutting path of a lathe. This was distinguished from a card which merely had written or printed material on it, intended to convey information to the human eye or mind, and not meant to be ancillary to some machine by being specially shaped for that purpose. However, because of subsequent technological developments, integrated circuits, magnetic disks and tapes and optical character readers now are used to enter information into a computer or to store the programs which control the computer. The analogy with a mechanical process no longer rings true and it is unlikely that this case will be followed.

In another case, *Burrough's Corporation (Perkin's) Application* [1974] RPC 147, computer programs controlled the transmission of data to terminals from a central computer (a communications system). The system, including the computer programs, was held to be the proper subject matter of a patent because the programs were embodied in physical form; they were 'hard-wired' – permanently embedded in the electronic circuits of the equipment. In many respects the significance of the physical form of a program, whether hard-wired on a silicon chip or stored on magnetic disks, is an irrelevance and should not affect patentability.

The distinction between modes of storage and their effect on patentability was considered more recently in *Gale's Application* [1991] RPC 305, concerning an application for a method of calculating square roots by program instructions contained in a ROM chip. The Comptroller of Patents, Designs and Trade Marks rejected the application but the applicant's appeal to the Patents Court was allowed by Aldous J who said that the claimed invention related to a product (the ROM chip) and was, therefore, patentable. He then said that the program would not have been patentable had it been stored on a floppy disk. This decision would have had the effect of making a software designer's choice of storage medium crucial to the question of patentability but it was, fortunately, quickly overruled in the Court of Appeal where Lord Justice Nicholls said:

It would equally be nonsense if a floppy disc containing a computer program was not patentable that a ROM characterised only by the instructions in that program should be patentable.

The Court of Appeal's decision conforms with common sense and the simple expedient of hard-wiring a computer program should not, *per se*, make the program patentable. Something else must be present such as a technical effect.

Technical effect

Two alternative approaches have been made to the question of the patent protection of inventions which include a computer program. The first is that the patent application should be considered without the contribution of the excepted thing. For example, if a machine includes a computer program it is then a question of whether the machine, without taking the computer program into account, adds anything to the state of the art. Does the machine, ignoring the computer program, meet the requirements for patentability? If the only novel and inventive step concerns the computer program itself, then the machine as a whole is not patentable. The case of *Re Merrill Lynch, Pierce Fenner & Smith Incorporated's Application* [1988] RPC 1, illustrates this approach. The invention related to an improved data processing system for implementing an automatic trading market for securities. The system received and stored the best current bids, qualified customer buy and sell orders, executed orders as well as monitoring stock inventory and profit. The Principal Examiner of the Patent Office rejected the application for a patent and the appeal against his decision was dismissed. On appeal to the Patents Court, it was held that where an invention involves any of the excluded materials in section 1(2), the proper construction of the qualification in that subsection requires that the Patent Office inquires into whether the inventive step resides in the contribution of the excluded matter alone. If the inventive step comes only from the excluded material, then the invention is not patentable because of section 1(2). The judge, Falconer J, said that the novel and inventive effect must reside outside the computer program even though it may be defined by the program.

In a further appeal to the Court of Appeal (*Merrill Lynch's Application* [1989] RPC 561), the approach of Falconer J was qualified and that taken by the European Patent Office, as described below, was approved. However, the Court of Appeal still confirmed that the invention in *Merrill Lynch* was not patentable but on the grounds that there was no technical effect, the operation being entirely software based.

In *Vicom Systems Incorporated's Patent Application* [1987] OJ EPO 14, a different approach to that of Falconer J was taken. This case concerned an application to the European Patent Office (EPO) and the invention was a new digital image processing system, the process steps being expressed mathematically in the form of an algorithm. It was held that this claim was allowable. It was said that if a claim is directed to a technical process which is carried out under the control of a program (whether implemented in the hardware or the software), then the claim cannot be regarded as related to a computer program as such. It is an application of the program for determining the sequence of steps in the process and it is the process for which protection is sought. In the present case, the subject matter of the invention was the practical application of a computer program, the technical effect resulting from the operation of the programmed computer and not the computer program itself. The EPO's approach has been followed and approved subsequently by the English courts. In *Genentech Inc's Patent* [1989] RPC 147, it was held, *inter alia*, in the Court of Appeal that a patent which claimed the practical application of a discovery did not relate to the discovery as such and was not excluded by section 1(2) of the Patents Act 1977 even if the practical application might be obvious once the discovery had been made. *Gale's Application* [1991] RPC 305, discussed above, confirms this as the correct approach.

It would seem that the technical effect does not have to be external to the computer and, in principle, operating systems are patentable because they determine how a computer operates technically. Indeed, there are patents in the United Kingdom and the United States in respect of operating systems including the recently litigated data compression software. With applications programs it is more difficult to achieve a technical advance and, in *Wang Laboratories Inc's Application* [1991] RPC 463, an application for a patent for an expert system shell was rejected because there was no new technical effect. Aldous J said that the computer (being a conventional machine) and the program combined do not produce a new computer. In *Hitachi Ltd's Application* [1991] RPC 415, an application in respect of a compiler program was rejected by the Patent Office as being no more than an application for a computer program as such.

While a patent will be refused for a computer program *simpliciter* (or any of the other exceptions in section 1(2) for that matter) it will be allowed if the purpose of the program is to bring about some technical effect and it is that effect which is the subject matter of the patent application. The subject matter should make a technical contribution to the state of the art.

Commercial effect

The emphasis on technical effect applies to most countries, but in Australia following *IBM* v *Commissioner of Patents* (1992) AIPC 90-853, a case where a method of creating a visual representation of a curve by a series of calculations was allowed, it seems that an effect which is commercially useful may be patentable even though it is entirely software based. Some commentators argue that patents will be allowed eventually in Australia and, perhaps, in the United States for computer programs as such.

The European Patent Office remains steadfastly loyal to the technical effect approach and in *IBM/Card Reader* [1994] EPOR 89, the Technical Board of Appeal dismissed an appeal against a refusal to grant a patent in relation to an invention whereby an automatic card-reading machine could read any card. This would allow the use of any bank card with a machine such as an automated teller machine (ATM or cashpoint machine) to carry out a transaction. The Board of Appeal confirmed that the subject matter of a patent must have a technical character and be industrially applicable. It also went on to say that applying technical means to perform a business activity does not mean that the business activity has a technical character and is thus an invention. It should be noted that a method of doing business is also excluded according to section 1(2) of the Patents Act 1977.

It is submitted that the approach of the EPO is correct and accords with the basic historical nature of a patent. England's first patent legislation was the Statute of Monopolies 1623 which allowed patents for new manners of manufacture, a phrase which was used right up to the 1977 Act. Insisting on a new technical effect whether inside or outside the computer is entirely consistent with that phrase and its replacement 'industrial application'.

Mental steps

The operation of a novel computer program may produce a technical effect which is itself caught by the exceptions to patentability as in the *IBM/Card Reader* case above. Another exception is a scheme, rule or method of performing a mental act and it seems that simply programming a computer to carry out something that can be performed by the human intellect will not be patentable. For example, in *Re The Computer Generation of Chinese Characters* [1993] FSR 315, an application for a patent in respect of a method of storing, processing, displaying and printing Chinese characters was turned down in Germany. It was said that the subject matter neither solved a technical problem by a technical method nor did it make a technical contribution to the state of the art.

Similarly, in the United Kingdom, a patent was refused for a software means of identifying ships by comparing the silhouette of an unknown ship with a database of ship's silhouettes in *Raytheon Co's Application* [1993] RPC 427. The fact that the equivalent mental act in the human mind would not be a deliberate conscious process did not bring the application out of the exception. Recognition of shapes by humans is almost instantaneous, whereas a computer program doing this would be based on algorithms that may operate quite differently, in logical terms, to the human brain. The deputy judge was not prepared to read the exception in a narrow sense. Thus, it appears that a computer program that simply does something that can be done by mental acts in the human brain will not be patentable even though the program may do it differently and in a totally new way. The same must apply to the other exceptions such as methods of doing business.

The mental steps doctrine has become even more ingrained in United Kingdom patent law. *Fujitsu Ltd's Application* [1997] RPC 610 involved an application for a patent in relation to software which was developed to help chemists design new chemical compounds. A computer screen displayed the crystalline structure of two known chemicals and these images could be rotated and manipulated so as to align one face of one crystal to be aligned with the complementary face of the other crystal. This then formed the blueprint for a new hybrid 'designer' chemical.

It was held that the application was for a method of performing a mental act as such. In the Court of Appeal, Lord Justice Aldous rejected the submission that, as it was not possible to perform a mental act using a computer, a claim for a method of using a computer could not be a claim to a method of performing a mental act. He stressed that it was important to look at the substance of an application. Thus, a claim for a computer program operating in a particular way is no more than a claim to a computer program. Furthermore, a claim to a method of carrying out a calculation, which is a method of performing a mental act, can never become more patentable simply because the calculation is being performed by a computer rather than being done manually on a piece of paper.

It was also accepted by the Court of Appeal that the application was for a computer program as such and not patentable on this ground also. The invention used a conventional computer to do what was previously done using plastic models. The only advance was that of using a computer to enable the result to be portrayed more quickly. Mr Justice Aldous said that this was just the sort of advantage to be obtained by the application of a computer program. In other words, there was nothing special in it.

In the context of computers, the exception for methods of performing a mental act is potentially very wide. Many programs automate what used to be done by the human mind, even if a computer does it on the basis of a completely different algorithm. Although not really discussed, it was highly arguable that the application would also have failed for lack of novelty (the exercise was done before but by using physical models) or through lack of inventive step. It is fairly obvious that advantages can be achieved by automating existing processes. This is why most computer programs would fail to be patentable. However, there are some programs that make new and effective technical contributions and it is for these that the patent system is important. Incidentally, the Fujitsu patent appears to have been granted in Japan.

To summarise, if a patent application includes excluded matter, such as a computer program, there must be an associated technical effect which does not result in something which is itself excluded (see Fig. 9.2).

It has been argued that a special, hybrid type of right should be introduced

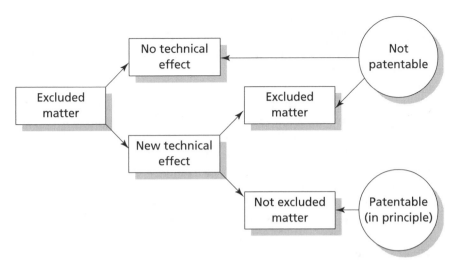

Fig. 9.2 Patentability of excluded matter such as computer programs

for computer programs – something between a patent and copyright. Such a right would give a monopoly in the program, thus protecting the underlying ideas more effectively than copyright, but the right would last for a shorter period than a patent, say five or seven years maximum. Given the developments both in the United Kingdom and elsewhere over the last few years, however, it is now unlikely that this course will be taken. The Copyright, Designs and Patents Act 1988 confirms this forcibly by its clear inclusion of computer programs in the literary work category of works protected by copyright.

Infringement, defences and remedies

A patent is infringed if a person does one of certain things in relation to the invention in the United Kingdom without the permission of the proprietor (owner) of the patent. Section 60 of the Patents Act 1977 defines what does and what does not constitute infringement. The nature of the infringement depends on whether the invention is a product (for example, a new type of computer printer) or a process (for example, a new method of making integrated circuits). If the invention is a product, the patent is infringed by making, disposing of or offering to dispose of, using, importing or keeping the product. Similar provisions apply to a process: for example, using the process infringes but, additionally, the patented process may be infringed by using or disposing of, etc. any product obtained directly from that process. Another difference between products and processes relates to the knowledge of the infringer. For a process, knowledge that a patent is being infringed is required. However, 'knowledge' is used in a special way and a person can still be deemed to have the requisite knowledge if it would be obvious to a reasonable man that a patent was being infringed. There is no requirement for knowledge as regards a product and, therefore, in the absence of a defence, liability for infringement is strict.

A patent is also infringed if a person supplies or offers to supply some other person with any of the means, relating to an essential element of the invention, for putting the invention into effect. Knowledge is required in that the person supplying knows, or it is obvious to a reasonable man, that those means are suitable for putting the invention into effect and that person so intends. This 'supplying the means' infringement is useful as it applies to persons who supply products in kit form. For example, if a person supplies a computer in kit form which, when assembled, infringes a patent, then the supplier of the computer kit infringes the patent even if he is just a middleman as long as he has the requisite knowledge. This prevents a possible loophole in patent law such as where a person imports components made in a foreign country to be sold as a kit. The person assembling the kit computer will not be liable under patent law, however, if he assembles and uses the computer privately and for non-commercial purposes. To give a practical example of infringement, consider the following situation:

An inventor **A** has invented a new type of computer 'chip' and a new process which will be used for making those chips. He has taken out patents for the process and for the chips. **B** finds out about the process and decides to build a similar process for making these computer chips. **B** asks **C** to supply equipment which is essential to the process. **B** then makes some computer chips and sells them to **D**, a trade supplier.

The position is:

B, if he knows, or it would be obvious to a reasonable man, that the process was patented, has infringed the patent for the process. Even if **B** had no actual knowledge it would be most likely that he would be fixed with knowledge on the basis of the reasonable man test. (Patent specifications are available for public inspection – would a reasonable man check first?)

B has infringed the patent for the computer chips even if he did not know or could not be expected to know of the patent.

C has infringed the patent for the process if he knows, or it would be obvious to a reasonable man, that the equipment he supplied was suitable for putting the process into effect and the equipment was intended to do so.

D infringes the patent for the computer chips, regardless of knowledge.

The fact that some infringements do not require any form of knowledge may seem unduly harsh, but knowledge is required for some of the remedies and the situation is not as inequitable as it might appear, bearing in mind the need to protect the patent.

There are certain defences or exceptions to infringement: for example, if the act is done privately and for non-commercial purposes or for experimental purposes (on the basis that the proprietor's interests are not harmed by such use). There are other, unusual defences, but these are outside the scope of this book. Of more importance is whether, if someone has 'copied' an invention but has introduced some minor changes, the patent has been infringed. What is the scope of the patent? To determine whether there has been an infringement, the specification and, in particular, the claims for the patent must be looked at and interpreted to find the limits of the patent. Although judges tend to interpret Acts of Parliament and legal documents literally (unless this leads to an absurd result), patent specifications are interpreted purposively; that is, in line with the presumed intention of the person who wrote it. In *Catnic Components Ltd* v *Hill & Smith Ltd* [1982] RPC 183, the plaintiff obtained a patent for a load bearing lintel, the main strength of which came from a vertical metal rear face. The specification and claims in the patent referred to the rear face as being vertical. Claim 1 described the rear face as '... a second rigid support member extending vertically from or from near the rear edge of the first horizontal plate ...'. The defendant made a similar lintel but with a rear face inclined at 6 degrees from the vertical. The House of Lords, by interpreting the word 'vertical' to mean, in effect, 'vertical or nearly vertical' held that the patent had been infringed. The important feature was the metal face, the purpose of which was to support the load. This approach is in line with both common sense and the European Patent Convention and prevents others from flouting patent law by making minor changes to details of an invention while retaining the underlying principles involved, and is justified on the basis that patent specifications and claims are directed to technical people, not lawyers. It also shows the different scope of patent law compared with copyright law, because patent law can protect purpose and principle whereas, generally, copyright law cannot. The so-called 'Catnic Test' has recently survived an attack upon its validity and it has been confirmed by the Court of Appeal that it is still useful.

A patent, once granted, can be revoked if it is subsequently shown to fail to meet the requirements for patentability: for example, it was not novel at the priority date or does not involve an inventive step, or if it was not granted to the person entitled to it. The fact that a patent has been granted by the Patent Office is not conclusive proof that the invention has satisfied all the requirements and the discovery of a prior publication disclosing the invention can result in the patent being revoked. Often, a person sued for infringement of patent will attack the validity of the patent. As far as the alleged infringer is concerned, this can be a useful ploy as the proceedings will be drawn out and the proprietor of the patent will be put to extra expense in defending his patent. Although the validity of patents is frequently brought into issue by defendants, only a handful of patents are revoked each year.

The remedies available for infringement of a patent are injunctions, delivery up or destruction of infringing articles, damages or an account of profits and a declaration that the patent is valid and infringed by the defendant. Damages and accounts of profits are alternatives. If the defendant proves that he was not aware and had no reasonable grounds for supposing that the patent existed, then neither damages nor accounts of profits are available. If a product carries the word 'patent' or 'patented' or similar, this does not automatically mean that the defendant knows of the patent unless the number of the patent also appears on the product concerned. This enables anyone to look up and inspect the patent specification to determine its scope.

The proprietor of a patent must be careful how he warns alleged infringers. There is a remedy under section 70 in respect of groundless threats of infringement proceedings. A person aggrieved by the threat may bring an action, unless the person making the threat can show that the acts in respect of which the threats were made were or would constitute an infringement of the patent, and the patent is not shown to be invalid by the person bringing the action. The remedies available are a declaration that the threats are unjustified, an injunction against a continuance of the threats, and damages for any loss sustained by the person aggrieved who has brought the action. Groundless threats actions do not apply to all forms of infringement (making or importing a product or using a process) and simply notifying any person of the existence of the patent does not constitute a groundless threat.

An example where a groundless threats action might be appropriate is where it is alleged that a computer imported into the United Kingdom by Acme Importers Ltd and is alleged to infringe a United Kingdom patent belonging to Esoteric Computers plc. The computers are sold by Acme to Krafty Computer Sales Ltd, a retail outlet. Esoteric send a letter to Krafty threatening to sue Krafty unless it ceases selling the computers forthwith. Krafty will be 'a person aggrieved' and so may Acme, if Krafty stops buying computers from Acme. Either should be able to bring an action for groundless threats and will be entitled to remedies unless Esoteric can show that the sale of the computers infringes the patent and, if a challenge has been made on the validity of the patent, or any relevant part of it, that it is valid.

Miscellaneous

Certain other provisions contained in the Patents Act 1977 are worthy of brief mention. An invention may be potentially very beneficial but might also destroy or seriously undermine an existing business: for example, a car engine that does 200 miles to a gallon, or an everlasting light bulb. To prevent the proprietor sitting on his patent, deliberately failing to use it, section 48 of the Act allows any person to apply for a compulsory licence under the patent, after the expiry of three years from grant if, for example, the patent is not being worked or some abuse is being made of the patent monopoly such as if the product is not being made available at reasonable terms.

An employee who, in the course of his employment, has made an invention which belongs to his employer may be awarded compensation to be paid by the employer if the patent is of outstanding benefit to the employer (section 40). This provision is seldom used, perhaps because reasonable employers reward such employees sufficiently well so that they do not apply for compensation. However, it is clear that the benefit must be truly outstanding if the employee is to stand any chance of obtaining compensation. The author is not aware of any examples of compensation awarded under section 40.

Utility model

There are plans for a new form of protection in the United Kingdom which is called the utility model and is like a lesser version of a patent, sometimes referred to as a 'petty patent'. This new right will come about through moves to harmonise this form of protection throughout the EC; Proposal for a Directive for the protection of inventions by a utility model, COM (97) 691, OJ [1998] C36/13. At the present time, only three member states do not have any equivalent form of protection, these being the United Kingdom, Luxembourg and Sweden. In its original form, computer programs were excluded from protection by the utility model, but as a result of an amended proposal in June 1999, computer programs will be appropriate subject matter for protection, providing they are new, involve an inventive step and are suitable for industrial application. Protection will be for up to 10 years and the harmonised utility model is intended to be implemented some time during 2001.

Chapter 10

Trade marks and passing off

Trade marks

Marks have been used to identify the makers of goods for thousands of years. Individual marks become associated with a particular product and with the quality of that product. As regards the value of a trade mark to a manufacturer, two factors are important: the buying public's familiarity with the mark and their experience of reasonable quality or value for money in the past associated with the mark. A trade mark which is used with a successful product is of tremendous value to the owner of the mark and he will want to prevent others from using the mark or a similar one to capture some of his trade. Trade marks law serves two main purposes: first it protects the goodwill and reputation which a trader has built up around the mark involved and, second, it prevents the public from being deceived as to the origin of goods or services. By doing so, it establishes a property right in the mark in question and requires that the mark be used (failure to use a mark may result in it being revoked).

A manufacturer, trader or person who makes goods or provides a service may register a mark for one or more classes of goods or services. This will give the owner of the mark a monopoly in the use of that mark in the classes under which the mark has been registered. There are a total of 34 classes of marks for goods (for example, chemicals, electrical goods and scientific apparatus, vehicles, clothing, fancy goods and smokers' articles) and a further eight classes for services (for example, advertising and business, insurance and financial, communications and miscellaneous). Software trade marks may be registered in Class 9 which includes data processing equipment and computers. A person providing services by writing software would register a mark in Class 42 which includes computer programming.

If anyone else uses the mark, or one deceptively similar, in the course of trade without the owner's permission, that person can be sued for infringement of the trade mark. Depending on the circumstances, a criminal offence may also be committed, as mentioned in Chapter 27. The remedies available to the owner of the trade mark are as usual: injunctions, damages or an account of profits as an alternative to damages, plus removal of offending marks. The infringing articles may be ordered to be destroyed if the offending marks cannot be removed.

In the computer industry, the power of trade marks can readily be seen as, in a relatively short space of time, names such as Apple computer, IBM, WordPerfect, Lotus 1-2-3 and Microsoft became household names. Trade marks are especially important in a fast-moving industry and it is very comforting to buy goods with familiar names when so many products and businesses come and go in rapid succession, as happened with microcomputers in the early 1980s. A familiar name or mark is very influential as many who buy computer hardware and software will look for a product which is likely to be of reasonable quality and will be supported in years to come. There have been few examples of trade mark infringement in the world of computers and most counterfeiters have used different names or marks: for example, copies of the Apple computer imported into Australia were called 'Wombats'. Other Apple lookalikes have been called 'Pineapples' and 'Microprofessors'. Perhaps this is a testimony to the effectiveness of trade mark law.

Until 1994 trade mark law was provided for by the Trade Marks Act 1938 which was widely recognised as being difficult and outdated. The new law is contained in the Trade Marks Act 1994 which is a result of a European Directive harmonising trade mark law (OJ [1989] L40/1), though some of the old case law is still relevant. The new Act is a welcome and much awaited improvement of trade mark law.

What is a trade mark?

By section 1 of the Trade Marks Act 1994, a trade mark is:

> ... any sign capable of being represented graphically which is capable of distinguishing goods or services of one undertaking from those of other undertakings.

It goes on to say that a trade mark may, in particular, consist of words (including personal names), designs, letters, numerals or the shape of goods or their packaging. This definition is much wider than that in the 1938 Act, under which an application to register the Coca-Cola bottle as a trade mark failed in *Re Coca-Cola Co's Application* [1986] 2 All ER 274. The new definition allows the registration, potentially, of music and even smells (represented by chemical formulae or a written description of the fragrance perhaps). There should be little difficulty for software companies to register marks embedded in software such as a moving image produced on a screen when a computer game is being loaded together with any associated distinctive musical motif.

Even the threshold for registration has been eased by the new law. Under the 1938 Act, there were two parts to the register of trade marks. Part A was for marks adapted to distinguish the goods of one trader from those of other traders while Part B was for marks which were capable of distinguishing, a lower standard which offered less protection. Now the lower requirement 'capable of distinguishing' applies to all marks and the nonsense of a two-part register has been abolished. In *Davies* v *Sussex Rubber Co* (1927) 44 RPC 412, a case involving 'Ustikon' for stick-on rubber soles for shoes, it was said that a mark was capable of distinguishing if it would become distinctive through use; in other words, if it was not incapable of becoming distinctively associated with the goods of the trade mark proprietor.

This approach was accepted as also being appropriate under the 1994 Act in *AD2000 Trade Mark* [1997] RPC 168. In that case an application to register AD2000 as a trade mark failed. A combination of two letters and four numbers could be capable of distinguishing if it was idiosyncratic. However, that was not the case here as AD2000 naturally referred to the year 2000 and was not idiosyncratic. Mr Geoffrey Hobbs QC, hearing the case, refused to be swayed by the fact that the word 'MILLENNIUM' had previously been accepted for registration as a trade mark.

Unregistrable marks

The fundamental purpose of a trade mark is to distinguish goods or services of one undertaking from those of other undertakings. In other words the mark must serve as an indicator of trade origin. If it does not do this, it is not registrable. For example, 'TARZAN', 'ELVIS' and 'ELVIS PRESLEY' were held to be unregistrable. By the time the applications were received, these names were so well known as 'household' words that they could not serve the function of indicating a connection in the course of trade between a trader and his goods. Although 'three-dimensional' signs are now potentially registrable, the same principle applies. In *Philips Electronics NV* v *Remington Consumer Products* [1998] RPC 283, a registration as a trade mark of a representation of a three-headed electric razor was declared invalid because it denoted function rather than trade origin.

Apart from the basic requirement that a trade mark must serve as a badge of origin, there are two types of grounds for refusal of registration – absolute grounds and relative grounds – the latter being so called because refusal depends on the mark's similarity with other marks. The absolute grounds for refusal are, by section 3 of the Trade Marks Act 1994, where the mark is:

- not capable of graphical representation or not capable of distinguishing;
- devoid of any distinctive character;
- exclusively descriptive or laudatory (words of praise) – for example, 'Superb Computers';
- in *bona fide* use in the trade – for example, 'Software Bug';
- of a shape necessary to achieve a technical result which gives substantial value to the goods; or
- contrary to public policy, accepted principles of morality or deceptive – for example, where a dating agency that does not possess or use a computer wishes to register the mark 'ComputaDate'.

Also excluded are certain flags and emblems; nor will a mark be registered if it was applied for in bad faith, such as where a tobacco company registered 'Nerit' to try to protect its 'Merit' mark. 'Merit' is a laudatory word and not registrable. The 'Nerit' mark was ordered to be removed from the register of trade marks.

The meaning of 'bad faith' under the 1994 Act is not entirely clear. In *Road Tech Computer Systems Ltd* v *Unison Software (UK) Ltd* [1996] FSR 805, the plaintiff traded in computer software for the transportation business and was the registered proprietor of the trade mark 'Roadrunner', which was registered in respect of 'computer software and programs; all included in Class 9 but not including any such goods relating to birds'. The reason for the latter exception was that an American bird, the paisano, is also known as a road-runner. The defendant claimed that the registration was not *bona fide* as the plaintiff had no intention of using the mark. The plaintiff argued that bad faith was more restrictive and required dishonesty. The judge pointed to the difficulty of determining the meaning of bad faith under the 1994 Act, which was not helped by looking at the Directive. Accordingly, he granted the defendant leave to defend the plaintiff's action for infringement as he considered that the plaintiff's argument was not sufficiently clear to allow it summary judgment against the defendant. He added that if the hearing had been a full trial, he would have considered referring this issue to the European Court of Justice for a preliminary ruling.

A mark will be refused on relative grounds if it is identical to an earlier mark or sufficiently similar as to be likely to cause confusion on the part of the public (section 5). This also applies where the earlier mark is used for different goods or services but has achieved such a reputation that the later use of a similar mark would take unfair advantage of it or would be detrimental to it. Thus, attempts by companies other than the Microsoft Corporation to register the word Microsoft for software, computer hardware or even bicycles will all fail. Indeed, use of the word in those circumstances without permission would undoubtedly infringe the Microsoft trade mark. Not only will similarity to earlier registered trade marks be grounds for refusal but similarity with works of copyright, designs or unregistered marks will also be likely to lead to a refusal to register the later mark.

Examples of marks turned down on the basis of a similarity with an earlier mark (under the 1938 Act) are:

- 'Huntsman' – earlier mark 'Sportsman' (both cherry brandy), and
- an application showing a picture of three pigs was refused because of a prior word mark 'Three Pigs Brand' (bacon).

In *Coca-Cola Co of Canada Ltd* v *Pepsi-Cola Co of Canada Ltd* (1942) 59 RPC 127, however, it was held that 'Pepsi-Cola' was not too close to 'Coca-Cola' because the suffix 'Cola' was a word that had become common and descriptive of a type of beverage – that is, a generic word.

Rights and infringement

The registered proprietor of a trade mark has, by section 9 of the Trade Marks Act 1994, the exclusive right to use the mark in the United Kingdom. Use by another without the proprietor's consent will infringe if within section 10. This states that use of an identical mark for identical goods or services infringes *per se*. Otherwise use of identical or similar marks for similar or identical goods or services infringes only where there exists a likelihood of confusion. Well-known marks may be infringed if an identical or similar mark is used for different goods. However, in this case it still appears that confusion is required. Use must be in the course of trade and extends to signs under which goods are sold, business stationery and advertising.

In respect of whether goods or services are similar, Mr Justice Jacob laid down some guidelines based on an old test under the 1938 Act which he said was still applicable under the 1994 Act. In *British Sugar plc v James Robertson & Sons Ltd* [1996] RPC 281, he said that respective uses and users, the physical nature of the goods or services, the respective trade channels, whether goods are sold alongside each other in supermarkets and the extent to which the goods compete are all useful factors to consider.

Practice as developed at the Trade Mark Registry may also be a factor. In *Avnet Inc v Isoact Ltd* [1998] FSR 16, the defendant used the word 'Avnet' for his Internet service for the aviation industry. This service also allowed subscribers to place advertisements on their own Web pages. The plaintiff had registered 'AVNET' for advertising and promotional services and complained of the defendant's use of the word. However, summary judgment was refused. An important factor was that, at the time, Registry practice was to classify the plaintiff's and defendant's activities in different classes of the trade marks register.

Comparative advertising occurs where a trader advertises his goods or services in comparison with those of another trader in a way which includes a reference to that other trader's registered trade mark. It used to infringe under the 1938 Act and may still do so under the 1994 Act. However, under section 10(6) of the 1994 Act comparative advertising will not infringe if it is in accordance with honest practices in industrial or commercial matters and the use without due cause does not takes unfair advantage of, and is not detrimental to, the distinctive character or repute of the trade mark.

Under the 1938 Act the case of *Compaq Computer Corp v Dell Computer Corp Ltd* [1992] FSR 93 gives an example of comparative advertising. Dell advertised its computers with a photograph showing its computer and a Compaq computer with both makers' names (including the word 'Compaq', a registered trade mark) and the price of the machines. The plaintiff, Compaq, sued for trade mark infringement, passing off and trade libel. The court granted an interlocutory injunction to Compaq. It was at least highly arguable that Dell infringed the Compaq mark through its advertising.

However, there was some doubt as to whether the Compaq mark should have been accepted for registration because of its phonetic similarity with 'Compact', an everyday word.

The 1994 Act marked a sea change in legal responses to comparative advertising and it was not long before traders were exploring the boundaries of what was permissible. In *Barclays Bank plc* v *RBS Advanta* [1996] RPC 307, the defendant advertised its new credit card by reference to the Barclaycard trade mark with a list of features comparing both cards. Of course, the features selected were designed to show the defendant's card in the best light. The judge said that it was for the proprietor of the trade mark to show that the use was not in accordance with honest practices. Further, persons reading the advertisement would realise that the advertiser would be selective in choosing which features to compare and would also expect a certain amount of hyperbole. What an advertiser can get away with would depend to some extent on the nature of the goods or services concerned.

In *Vodafone Group plc* v *Orange Personal Communications Ltd* [1997] FSR 34, where the defendant advertised by stating that on average subscribers would save £20 per month by switching to its service, the judge accepted that the public would expect some elasticity of price and usage in relation to the quoted average saving. However, if the information is clearly untrue or misleading, comparative advertising is likely to infringe as in *Emaco & Aktiebolaget Electrolux* v *Dyson Appliances*, *The Times*, 8 February 1999.

Remedies for trade mark infringement are, by section 14, damages, injunctions, accounts or otherwise. There are also orders for delivery-up, erasure or destruction.

Exceptions to infringement

There are a number of exceptions to trade mark infringement which may be set up as a defence. They include, by section 11:

- use by a person of his own name or address;
- use of indications of the kind, quality, quantity, intended purpose, value, geographical origin, the time of production of goods or rendering of services, or other characteristics of goods or services;
- use, where it is necessary, to indicate the intended purpose of a product or service, in particular, as accessories or spare parts (for this and the exceptions above to apply, the use must be in accordance with honest practices in industrial or commercial matters); or
- use of an earlier right (such as an unregistered mark protected by the law of passing off) in a particular locality.

The third exception (actually, its equivalent under section 4(3) of the Trade Marks Act 1938) was considered in *IBM Corp* v *Phoenix International*

(Computers) Ltd [1994] RPC 251. Phoenix supplied computer equipment including 'reworked' memory cards which contained IBM components. Phoenix advertised these cards as 'IBM manufactured' and IBM sued for trade mark infringement and for passing off. Phoenix argued, as far as the trade mark infringement was concerned, that it had IBM's implied consent or that the use indicated that the boards were adapted from IBM components. The judge refused to strike out this defence. However, this does not mean that the defence would succeed at a full trial. The wording of section 11 in the 1994 Act is much simpler and, provided the use of the mark in such cases is necessary to indicate the intended purpose (for example, that the cards will work in IBM mainframe computers) and such use accords with honest practices, the defence ought to succeed. It is submitted that the use of the phrase 'manufactured from IBM components' would be more likely to be acceptable than simply 'IBM manufactured'.

As with patents (and designs) there is a remedy in respect of groundless threats of infringement proceedings. This was introduced into trade mark law by the 1994 Act. An example of a successful action was *Prince plc* v *Prince Sports Group Inc* [1998] FSR 21 in which the defendant, a United States company with a United Kingdom registration in respect of the word 'Prince', threatened the plaintiff, which had registered 'prince.com' as its Internet name, with litigation if it did not transfer the domain name to the defendant. The court held that the threats were unjustified and granted an injunction against their continuance.

Licensing of trade marks

The 1938 Act and previous trade mark legislation were very concerned with protecting the public from deceptive practices and one consequence was that an owner of a mark could not register the mark if he intended to allow other persons to use it unless he maintained a link with the other persons' business operations. One way this was done was to register a user of the mark and maintain quality control over the goods to which it was applied. However, if the owner of the mark simply wished to grant licences to others allowing them to use the mark on their own goods in return for a royalty this would result in any application to register the mark being refused. This happened in *Holly Hobbie Trade Mark* [1984] FSR 199 where the applicant to register the mark (a drawing of a little girl in an old-fashioned dress) wished to grant licences to companies in the United Kingdom so that they could apply the drawing to their own products. The House of Lords remarked on how this ban on 'trafficking' in registered trade marks was out of touch with commercial reality. Thankfully, it has now been repealed by the 1994 Act.

The Trade Marks Act 1994 contains much improved provisions for the licensing and sub-licensing of trade marks and takes due account of the existence of character merchandising. Licences may be exclusive or non-exclusive and, in some circumstances, licensees can sue in their own right for infringement of the trade mark.

For example, say a computer manufacturer, A, owns the trade mark 'Comquik' which is registered in relation to Class 9 (computers and data processing equipment) and Class 41 (education and training, etc.). Another hardware company, B, making accessories has devised an optical character reader. Company A grants company B an exclusive licence, in respect of the Class 9 mark, to apply the 'Comquik' mark to the OCR equipment it makes in return for a 5 per cent royalty on net sales. A number of organisations providing training in the use of computers, C, D and E, each have non-exclusive licences from company A allowing them to provide computer training under the name 'Comquik' on the basis of the Class 41 mark. Each pays a small annual fee to Company A. All the organisations B, C, D and E may call upon A to sue in respect of any infringement of the marks and, unless the licence agreement states otherwise, sue in their own name if A refuses to take action or fails to do so within two months of the request. The licence agreements must be in writing, signed by the licensor, and the licences must be noted on the register of trade marks.

Registration of a trade mark

Initial registration of a trade mark is for ten years and the renewal period is also ten years (under the old law the periods were seven years and 14 years respectively). There is no upper limit to the duration of a trade mark, which can be renewed again and again providing it has not suffered a period of non-use of five or more years. Many of the trade marks first registered under the Trade Marks Registration Act 1875 (the first Act allowing registration of trade marks) are still registered and in use today, demonstrating the importance of trade marks, including Britain's No. 1 trade mark, the BASS 'red triangle' mark.

The fee for registration, which has recently been reduced, is £200 against one class of goods or services. For each additional class the fee is £50. The renewal fee is £200 plus £50 for each additional class.

The Trade Marks Act 1994 is important in that it paves the way for the European Community Trade Mark (CTM) and provides for the accession of the United Kingdom to the Protocol to the Madrid Agreement which allows for international registration of trade marks. The CTM has a unitary nature and applies throughout the European Community. It is already proving popular and should be a serious consideration for any software company hoping to trade in Europe.

Passing off

In many ways, the law of passing off is a common law version of trade mark law although of older pedigree. Passing off protects business goodwill and safeguards the public from deception by giving a right of action against anyone who tries to pass off his goods or services as those of someone else. One trader might try to 'cash in' on the goodwill and reputation of another trader by dressing up his goods in such a way that they look like those of that other trader. There is a large overlap between trade marks and passing off and it is not unusual for a legal action to involve both passing off and trade marks. The law of passing off is particularly useful if there is no registered mark to be infringed; perhaps a trader or manufacturer has used a mark for several years without registering it as a trade mark. The mark may fail to qualify for registration or the act complained of might fall outside the scope of trade marks – for example, if it relates to the format of an advertising campaign.

The following example shows the application of passing off. A computer retailer has been operating for three years under the name of 'Computer Equipment Sales' and has a chain of stores in the South of England. The retailer has acquired a reputation for low prices and efficient service. Recently, another retailer has opened a store in the South of England and uses the name of 'Computer Equipment Sales and Service'. Neither name is registered as a trade mark; in fact the names would be refused registration because they are too descriptive of computer retailing generally and would make it difficult for other traders to describe their business activities. As there is a danger that people will be confused and might buy from the second retailer thinking that they are buying from the first, the first should be able to obtain an injunction preventing the second retailer from continuing to use the name he has chosen. If the first retailer has only been in business a short time before the second retailer opens his store then it is unlikely that anything can be done. This is because there has not been sufficient time to build up goodwill connected with the name and, hence, there is little danger that the public will be confused. Similarly, if the second trader's store was in North Wales, it would be unlikely that the first trader's business would be affected, unless his goodwill extends to that location, for example, because he advertises nationally.

Basic requirements for a passing-off action

Before the plaintiff can suffer the type of damage caused by passing off, he must have a reputation associated with goodwill. He must be able to show that his name, mark, get-up or something else which is distinctive about his business will be associated with his goods by the public. If a trader has just started in business he will not succeed in a passing-off action but a newly registered trade mark has immediate protection. However, the necessary reputation could be obtained relatively quickly by an intensive advertising campaign on a national scale.

The ingredients necessary to a successful passing-off action were described in *Erven Warnink Besloten Vennootschap* v *J Townend & Sons (Hull) Ltd* [1979] AC 731. The plaintiffs made a liqueur called advocaat which came to be well known. It was made from brandewijn, egg yolks and sugar. The defendants decided to enter this market and they made a drink called 'Keeling's Old English Advocaat' which was made from Cyprus sherry and dried egg powder, an inferior but cheaper drink. This captured a large part of the plaintiff's market in the United Kingdom. It was held that, because of the reputation the plaintiff's product had gained, it should be protected from deceptive use of its name by competitors even though the goodwill was shared by several traders. There was a misrepresentation made by the defendant calculated to injure the plaintiff's business or goodwill and an injunction was granted in favour of the plaintiffs. Lord Diplock laid down the essentials for a passing-off action as:

- a misrepresentation,
- made by a trader in the course of trade,
- to prospective customers of his or ultimate consumers of goods or services supplied by him,
- which is calculated to injure the business or goodwill of another trader, and
- which causes actual damage to a business or goodwill of the trader by whom the action is brought.

Lord Oliver, in *Reckitt & Colman Products Ltd* v *Borden Inc* [1990] 1 All ER 873 (which involved the Jif Lemon and a competing lemon-shaped container for lemon juice), usefully condensed the test for passing off into the presence of the plaintiff's goodwill, a misrepresentation as to the goods or services offered by the defendant and damage or likely damage to the plaintiff's goodwill.

Normally, one would expect damage in the form of lost sales as a result of the defendant's misrepresentation. However, it also extends to damage to the plaintiff's goodwill itself such as where its unique character is eroded. This happened in *Taittinger SA* v *Allbev Ltd* [1993] FSR 641, in which the defendant produced a sparkling non-alcoholic drink which he called 'Elderflower Champagne'. It was sold in green bottles which resembled champagne bottles for £3.50. It was held that this was passing off. Although it was unlikely that many would be deceived in fact, the use of the name champagne in this way would reduce its distinctiveness and, hence, injure the champagne manufacturer's goodwill. Although this case has not been overturned, doubts have been expressed about it as it could be perceived to be an undesirable extension of passing off.

The misrepresentation

The misrepresentation is not necessarily limited to an exact copy of the name or get-up. It may be sufficient if it unfairly imputes a quality into some product or service, such as where a new trader uses another, established, trader's name or mark. An important factor is whether the buying public will be deceived by this unauthorised use of another's name. In deciding this it is not necessary to consider whether members of the public who are knowledgeable about the product are deceived; it may be sufficient if members of the public who have very little knowledge of the product concerned are likely to be deceived (see *J Bollinger* v *Costa Bravo Wine Co Ltd (No. 2)* [1961] 1 All ER 561, where an injunction was granted to prevent the use of the name 'Spanish Champagne').

As mentioned earlier, a misrepresentation does not have to be confined to a name or mark. The tort of passing off is wide enough to encompass other descriptive material such as slogans and visual images associated with an advertising campaign if this material has become part of the goodwill of the plaintiff's product. The test is whether the plaintiff has acquired an intangible property right for his product deriving from the distinctive nature of this material which is recognised by the market. In applying the test, the courts have to bear in mind the balance between the plaintiff's investment in the product and the protection of free competition.

In one respect, Lord Diplock's judgment is misleading. He spoke of the misrepresentation being calculated to injure. This suggests that passing off must be deliberate. However, this is not necessary and innocence is not an absolute defence although it may influence the remedies granted.

Common fields of activity

If the traders in a passing-off action operate in different fields of activity, it will usually be assumed that there is less danger of confusion and thus less danger of damage to the plaintiff. For example, in *Granada Group Ltd* v *Ford Motor Company Ltd* [1973] RPC 49, the Granada television group could not prevent the Ford Motor Company calling one of their cars a Ford Granada; the court held that there was no danger of confusion because of the different fields of activity – namely television and cars. However, in *Lego UK Ltd* v *Lego M Lemelstrich Ltd* [1983] FSR 155, the Lego company, which makes children's construction kits comprising coloured plastic bricks, was granted an injunction against the manufacturers of coloured plastic irrigation material preventing them using the name 'Lego' as part of the description of the material. The plaintiff was able to show that there was a real danger of confusion and damage to its goodwill.

The plaintiff in *Silicon Graphics Inc* v *Indigo Graphic Systems (UK) Ltd* [1994] FSR 403 supplied computer work-stations for computer-aided design under the 'Indigo' mark and had 3 to 5 per cent of the top end of the pre-press market, that is the market for all stages in the printing process prior to actual printing. The defendant made printing equipment under the Indigo name and although the plaintiff did not make printers it sued for trade mark infringement and passing off and applied for an interlocutory injunction. As far as passing off was concerned the plaintiff based its claim on a natural future extension of its business into the manufacture of printers. The judge accepted that there was a triable issue on passing off but, on the balance of convenience, refused the injunction requested.

There is no copyright in a fictitious name and an action in passing off is unlikely to be of much help if the defendant uses that name in relation to different goods or services. The test, as always, is whether the public is likely to be deceived by the use of the name, and in applying this test it is important to consider the fields of activity involved: do the two parties operate in the same or different fields? In the past, judges have not assumed that the public has a detailed knowledge of character merchandising. An example is provided by the case of *Wombles Ltd* v *Wombles Skips Ltd* [1977] RPC 99. Wombles were fictitious animals from a TV series noted for their cleanliness, and for cleaning up litter and putting it to good use. The plaintiff company owned the copyright in the books and drawings of the Wombles, and their main business was granting licences so that manufacturers, in return for a fee, could use the Womble characters to promote their goods. They granted one such licence for waste-paper baskets. The defendant formed a company to lease builders' skips for rubbish. After considerable thought, and remembering the Wombles' clean habits, he decided to call his company Wombles Skips Ltd. In finding for the defendant, the court held that there was no common field of activity and, therefore, no danger of confusion. However, some judges do seem prepared to accept that the public are now more aware of character merchandising and there may be a change in this aspect of passing off before too long.

As technology moves on, sometimes two distinct fields of activity may converge. In *Nad Electronics Inc* v *Nad Computer Systems Ltd* [1997] FSR 380, the plaintiff sold high quality hi-fi systems and the defendant sold computers. Developments in computer technology have resulted in modern personal computers being equipped with compact disc drives capable of playing music CDs. As the fields of audio entertainment and computers are converging, the judge held that the defendant was liable in passing off. An important factor was that the parties' respective goods were similarly advertised and were sold alongside each other in retail outlets.

Internet domain names

Every Internet domain name must be different to every other one. However, computers can distinguish the smallest changes, so changing a hyphen to an underscore or a full stop will result in two potentially usable and distinct domain names: for example, smith-jones.com and smith_jones.com. If such close names are registered by different persons, it is highly likely there will be confusion on the part of persons accessing the relevant internet addresses. There is a distinct possibility of passing off where traders are using similar domain names.

Although a dispute resolution procedure is taking shape, in the past, names have been registered on a first-come, first-served basis without any consideration as to whether the applicant had the right to register the name. Individuals have registered names such as 'mcdonalds.com', 'mtv.com' and 'harrods.com'. Such registrations may have been made in order to sell the addresses to the relevant organisations but, in the United Kingdom, the law of passing off has proved valuable in respect of such practices.

In *Pitman Training Ltd* v *Nominet UK* [1997] FSR 797 two companies, now distinct but sharing a common origin, had similar names: Pitman Training Ltd and Pitman Publishing. The case concerned the right to the domain name 'pitman.co.uk'. Pitman Publishing, which was the second defendant, successfully applied to register that name but did not make use of it for a period of time. Due to an error, the name was re-allocated to Pitman Training Ltd. Pitman Publishing complained when it found out and the name was re-allocated to Pitman Publishing. Pitman Training Ltd commenced proceedings, wanting the name transferred back to it, claiming, *inter alia*, that its use by Pitman Publishing was passing off. However, this failed to impress the judge who thought it highly unlikely that the public would associate the domain name with Pitman Training Ltd. Rather, it was more likely to think it belonged to Pitman Publishing as it had been trading under that name for nearly 150 years. An additional factor was that, when the Pitman companies were sold off in 1985, there was an express agreement that Pitman Training Ltd would not use the word Pitman without the word 'Training'.

In another case, a company with no connection to Harrods (the famous store in Knightsbridge) registered 'harrods.com' as a domain name. Use of the name was suspended pending the outcome of the dispute resolution procedure provided by the registration body in the United States but, in the meantime, Harrods launched an action in England for passing off and trade mark infringement: *Harrods Ltd* v *UK Network Services Ltd* [1997] EIPR D-106. Summary judgment was granted and the defendant was ordered to release the domain name to the plaintiff.

In a subsequent case, *Marks & Spencer plc* v *One in a Million Ltd* [1998] FSR 265, five actions were brought by well-known organisations, each of which had substantial goodwill, against the defendant which was a dealer in Internet domain names. It had registered names such as 'bt.org', 'sainsbury.com', 'marksandspencer.co.uk'. The defendant wrote to the organisations offering to sell the domain names. The judge considered that threats of passing off and trade mark infringement were made out and he granted injunctions ordering the defendant to transfer the domain names to the plaintiffs. Similar activities in relation to company names have been described by one judge as a 'scam'.

It is clear that the courts will not look sympathetically at persons who register famous names as domain names with the intention of selling them for large sums of money. The law of passing off is appropriate, though at the time there may not have been any actual use of the name. The threat of passing off if the intended buyer does not accede is very real where someone registers a name in bad faith. However, real difficulties still may arise, for example, because of the international nature of the Internet. What if an American company, having a Web site in the United States but which can be accessed in the United Kingdom, has a very similar name for its Internet address to that of an English company having an established goodwill? Furthermore, what if a sole trader whose name happens to be John Sainsbury wishes to register john-sainsbury.com as his domain name?

The problems of Internet domain names are taken very seriously by organisations such as the Commission to the European Communities and the World Intellectual Property Organisation, which are looking at ways of regulating the allocation of domain names and resolving disputes.

Remedies for passing off

The available remedies are injunctions, including interlocutory injunctions, and damages. An account of profits may be available as an alternative to damages. The damages are assessed by considering the harm done to the plaintiff's goodwill and the lost sales of the plaintiff's product as a result of the passing off. The most desirable remedy is an injunction, preventing the other person or business from continuing to use the plaintiff's established name, get-up or style.

Trade libel

An action related to passing off is trade libel, sometimes referred to as malicious falsehood. This is the commercial equivalent of defamation and an example is where a person publishes untrue information concerning the quality of a trader's goods. In terms of computer technology, trade libel would occur if someone falsely claimed that a particular software dealer was trading in pirated software or was in financial difficulties or that a software house's products were defective or would not operate on a particular make of computer. Of course, the information must be false and must be published or stated maliciously. This means made without good cause or excuse and could extend to a reckless statement. In *Compaq Computer Corp* v *Dell Computer Corp Ltd* [1992] FSR 93, discussed earlier in this chapter, it was held that there was an arguable case of trade libel because the computer systems compared were materially different and the representations as to price were misleading and not justified. However, the requirement to prove malice reduces the frequency with which trade libel actions are brought.

In *Joyce* v *Sengupta* [1993] 1 All ER 897, the Vice Chancellor said that essential ingredients for an action in trade libel were falsity and malice. Proof of financial loss was also required, subject to the relaxation in section 3 of the Defamation Act 1952 (that is, where the offending words are calculated to cause pecuniary damage and are published in writing or other permanent form).

Chapter 11

Designs

Introduction and background

Designs are relevant to computer hardware and semiconductor products (discussed in the following chapter). Computer equipment may be designed in such a way that it is aesthetically pleasing as well as functional or there may be something novel about the design which falls short of the scope of patents. Examples of these are an attractive outer case for a computer monitor, a useful case for computer disks with built-in carrying handle, a desk for a computer or a new shape for a portable computer. A considerable amount of effort may have been expended on the design of such items and their components so that they perform their intended function efficiently or are visually attractive. It is right that such effort should be rewarded and this is the purpose of design law which applies to new or original shapes or decorative features.

Unfortunately, this area of law is far from straightforward and the Copyright, Designs and Patents Act 1988 has done little to simplify matters. To add to the confusion, there are now two forms of right relating to designs; one is subject to registration, the other not. Registered designs are provided for by the Registered Designs Act 1949, amended by the Copyright, Designs and Patents Act 1988. The design right was introduced by the 1988 Act. The history of designs and their relationship with copyright is an interesting study in its own right and in many cases an original design was capable of dual protection under the 1949 Act as a registered design and, through any drawings of the design, under the Copyright Act 1956 (as amended) as an artistic work. The duration of copyright protection was limited to 15 years if the design was registrable; that is, if it was new and had eye-appeal. However, many functional designs were protected through the artistic copyright subsisting in drawings of the design for the full term of life of author plus 50 years.

Drawings are prepared for most designs and drawings are protected by copyright as artistic works, irrespective of artistic quality. Before the 1988 Act, anyone copying a design would infringe the copyright in a drawing made for the design even though that person had never seen the drawing, because making a three-dimensional copy of a two-dimensional work infringed the copyright in the latter and vice versa. For example, in *Valeo Vision SA v Flexible Lamps Ltd* [1995] RPC 205, it was held that the defendant had infringed the copyright in the plaintiff's drawings by making the rear light clusters for lorries represented in the drawings. The only proviso to indirect copying of drawings was that a layman would be able to recognise the one from the other. For example, in *British Leyland Motor Corp Ltd* v *Armstrong Patents Co Ltd* [1986] 2 WLR 400, the defendant made replacement exhaust pipes for the plaintiff's cars by copying the shape and dimensions of the original pipes – a process known as 'reverse engineering'. The plaintiff claimed that the exhaust pipes made by the defendant infringed the copyright in the original drawings of the exhaust systems, although the defendant had not seen the drawings. This argument was accepted by the House of Lords but their lordships refused to allow the plaintiff to assert its rights under copyright law. They said that car owners have an inherent right to repair their cars in the most economical way possible and, for that purpose, are to have access to a free market in spare parts. The same principle ought to apply to software maintenance and is discussed in this context in Chapter 17.

Before the 1988 Act, all a person had to do to gain copyright protection for a design was to make a drawing of the design in such a way that the design could be recognised from the drawing (as long as the design did not relate to a spare part). However, the overlap between designs and copyright has been eroded by section 51 of the Copyright, Designs and Patents Act 1988 which states that it is not an infringement of any copyright in a design document or model recording or embodying a design for anything other than an artistic work (or a typeface), to make an article to the design or to copy an article made to the design. In this context, 'design' has the same definition as it does for the purposes of the design right and a design document includes a drawing or other documents such as specifications, photographs and data stored in a computer. This means that industrial designs must fall either within the design right or be registered as a design to be protected unless they are copies of artistic works – for example, sculptures. It is no longer possible, in most cases, to rely on copyright in any drawings or computer data relating to the design. In the case of designs created before 1 August 1989, however, under the transitional provisions in the 1988 Act, a limited copyright protection existed until no later than 1 August 1999. The *Valeo Vision* case mentioned above is an example of the workings of these transitional provisions. It should be noted that the unregistered design right does not subsist in designs created before 1 August 1989.

Many of the intricacies of the law of designs have little relevance to computer technology and a complete discussion of the rights is outside the scope of this book. The following description of the two forms of right is thus necessarily brief and the emphasis is on computer equipment rather than attempting to give a detailed account of design law. Nevertheless, computer equipment manufacturers may find that design law gives valuable protection, either in its own right or as a supplement to other intellectual property rights.

Registered designs

Section 1 of the Registered Designs Act 1949, as amended, defines registrable designs as being:

> ... features of shape, configuration or ornament applied to an article by any industrial process, being features which in the finished article appeal to and are judged by the eye.

The design must be one intended to be applied to an article. By section 44(1), 'article' means any article of manufacture and includes any part of an article if that part is made and sold separately. In *Ford Motor Co Ltd's Design Applications* [1995] RPC 167, the House of Lords held that the phrase should include the words 'to be' because it was the design that was protected rather than the article. The House suggested the phrase should read '... if that part is to be made and sold separately'. This requires that the article should have an independent life as an article of commerce and be not merely an adjunct to some larger article of which it is a part. Thus, spare parts which are simply replacements for worn or damaged components are not registrable.

Does this mean that the design of a new computer keyboard or a new computer mouse is not registrable? This is probably going too far as new shapes of such articles are likely to be made to enhance the overall eye-appeal rather than simply be acquired to replace existing components.

Registered design law is concerned primarily with aesthetic aspects and it is not sufficient that the article simply looks pretty or pleasing but the eye-appeal of the article should be such that persons acquiring or using the article do so because of the appearance of articles made to the design. By section 1(3), a design shall not be registered if the appearance of the article is not material; that is, if aesthetic considerations are not normally taken into account to a material extent by persons acquiring or using articles made to the design. In addition, to be registrable, the design must be new (section 1(2)). Examples are a new shape of coffee cup or a new transfer pattern applied to plates or attractive and novel computer furniture and, with such articles, the appearance is important to a person buying it. Even if a person is buying desks for computers or word processors for an office, the appearance of the furniture is a major factor influencing choice. Although, at first sight, an attractively designed computer is less likely to be registrable as a design because the person acquiring one will be primarily influenced by performance rather than appearance, it may still be registrable as the appearance of an item of hardware is not without aesthetic impact, as the current range of Apple computers demonstrate.

Certain things are excluded from registration, such as a method or principle of construction or features of shape or configuration dictated solely by the function the article has to perform, or which depend upon the appearance of another article of which the former article is intended to form an integral part. Methods or principles of construction are verging on patent law, while eye-appeal resulting from function, or from having to match another article, is excluded because it is an indirect effect and would severely restrict spare part manufacturers. The proprietor (owner) of a design is the author, the person who created it, unless the author is acting in the course of employment or has been commissioned, for money or money's worth, to create the design. If the design has been generated by a computer in circumstances where there is no human author, the person making the arrangements necessary for its creation is treated as the proprietor of the design. The right lasts for five years initially from the date of registration but may be renewed in five-year stages up to a maximum of 25 years. Registration fees are relatively inexpensive.

There are some transitional arrangements to cope with designs which had been registered on or after 12 January 1988 but prior to the more rigorous standards now applicable (that is, prior to 1 August 1989) and which would fail to be registrable subsequently. Those design registrations are limited to a maximum of ten years. Examples are designs which depend upon the appearance of another article of which the article is intended by the author of the design to form an integral part. This exception was introduced by the 1988 Act and does not apply to pre-1 August 1989 designs. Other designs registered prior to 1 August 1989 are limited to 15 years maximum.

The proprietor of a design is given certain exclusive rights in relation to articles embodying the design (for example, making or importing such articles for trade or business purposes or selling or hiring them). A person infringes a registered design by doing any of these acts without the licence of the registered proprietor. Infringement is judged through the eyes of the interested person (typically a consumer) and an infringing design is one which, when applied to the type of article for which the design is registered, is not substantially different. There are other infringements such as making anything to enable articles to be made or doing anything in relation to a kit. Remedies available include injunctions, damages and orders for delivery up or destruction of infringing articles.

The design right

Like copyright, this right is automatic and does not depend on registration but, unlike registered designs, there is no requirement for the design to have eye-appeal, although if it does, it is not barred from protection by the design right. The result is that the design right will apply to both functional and aesthetic articles and, hence, there is an overlap with registered designs. The potentially longer duration of registered designs is the main reason why a design which lies in this overlap should be registered. Another reason is that a registered design gives a monopoly right while infringement of a design right depends on proof of copying. The design right does not apply to designs recorded (or having articles made in respect of them) prior to 1 August 1989.

A 'design' in the context of the design right is, by section 213 of the Copyright, Designs and Patents Act 1988:

... the design of any aspect of the shape or configuration (whether external or internal) of the whole or part of the article.

This definition is not too dissimilar to that relating to registered designs. The design right applies to all manner of industrial designs whether functional or not. A design must be original and section 213(4) states that a design is not original if it is commonplace in the design field in question at the time of its creation. It has been held, in *C & H Engineering* v *F Klucznik & Sons Ltd* [1992] FSR 421, that this requires a two-stage test. First, is the design original in a copyright sense; that is, did the design originate from the author? If the answer is 'yes', then it must be determined whether the design is commonplace (at the time of its creation). The design, therefore, must be the independent work of the designer which was not commonplace in the relevant field when created.

The test for originality was once more considered in *Ocular Sciences Ltd* v *Aspect Vision Care Ltd* [1997] RPC 289. Mr Justice Laddie pointed out that the word 'commonplace' is new to English law and could be traced back to the EC Directive on the legal protection of semiconductor topographies, discussed in the next chapter. He accepted as plausible a defintion that any design which is 'trite, trivial, common-or-garden, hackneyed or of the type which would excite no peculiar attention in those in the relevant art is likely to be commonplace'. Nevertheless, that did not mean that a design which is made up of such commonplace features must necessarily itself be commonplace. A new and exciting design could be produced from the most trite of ingredients providing the combination itself is not commonplace.

The *Ocular Sciences* case is also authority for the view that detail differences, which may be too small to be readily distinguished by the naked eye, could be protected by the design right. In that case, it was accepted that, in principle, the design right could apply to details of a range of soft contact lenses, although, in the event, Mr Justice Laddie decided that the designs, as a whole, were commonplace.

As with registered designs, there are exceptions to design right protection. The first exception, a method or principle of construction, is common to both rights. The second exception is subdivided into features of shape or configuration of an article which:

- enable the article to be connected to, or placed in, around or against, another article so that either article may perform its function (the 'must-fit' exception); or
- are dependent upon the appearance of another article of which the article

is intended by the designer to form an integral part (the 'must-match' exception).

These exceptions are significant for manufacturers and suppliers of spare parts. The former part of the exception applies to 'functional' spare parts which have to be a particular shape to fit another article. An exhaust pipe for a car will fall into this exception. Any piece of computer equipment which has to be fitted to some other equipment, such as a replacement 'card' (printed circuit board containing integrated circuits) which has to be a certain shape, or have a certain type of connector, in order to fit into a computer, will also fall into the first part of the exception. This exception is directed at rationalising the *British Leyland* case and it allows for the fact that persons who buy items of equipment which eventually may need replacement or additional parts should be able to obtain those parts in a free market at reasonable cost. If a design right monopoly were to be granted to spare parts, manufacturers of cars, washing machines, computers, etc. would be able to control the supply and price of spare parts and might be tempted to charge exorbitant prices for them.

The second part of the exception (which is, in effect, identical to the equivalent exception for registered designs) would apply to spare parts such as replacement body panels for cars where the design is dictated by the appearance of the car, but it is unlikely that many computer spare parts will fall into this category.

It could apply in respect of replacement parts for items of computer equipment such as a replacement paper feed tray or some other part, having visual significance, intended to replace some worn out or damaged part. A further exception to design right protection is surface decoration, being more appropriately protected by registration as a design.

The surface decoration exception was considered in *Mark Wilkson Furniture Ltd* v *Woodcraft Designs (Radcliffe) Ltd* [1998] FSR 63, a case concerning fitted kitchen furniture. It was said, in that context, that the exclusion was not restricted to features lying on the surface which were essentially two-dimensional such as a painted finish but could extend to other features such as small grooves. However, other features might not be excepted where, for example, they themselves were subject to surface decoration. A cornice or recessed door panels might be subject to the right.

With registered designs, the person creating the design is known as the author but, and for no explicable reason, the person creating a design which is subject to a design right is known as its designer. The owner of a design right is the designer unless he creates the design in the course of his employment or has been commissioned to create it. A computer-generated design belongs to the person making the arrangements necessary for the creation of the design. Design right lasts for 15 years from the end of the calendar year in which it was first recorded in a design document (which includes storage in a computer) or an article was made to the design, unless articles have been made available for sale or hire within the first five years, in which case the right lasts only a further ten years.

The result of the provisions relating to duration is that the owner of the right can only have a maximum of ten years to exploit the design commercially. This period will be reduced if the owner fails to market articles made to the design within the first five years. Effectively, and in a commercial sense, the right lasts for ten years with the owner being given a five-year breathing space within which to bring articles made to the design to the market place. The right is further diluted because licences are available as of right during the last five years. This means that anyone can exploit the design during its last five years subject to the payment of a royalty to the design right owner. Failing agreement of the terms of the licence, the Comptroller-General of Patents, Designs and Trade Marks will settle the terms.

Infringement occurs when a person makes articles to the design or makes a design document recording the design for the purpose of enabling such articles to be made. This covers identical articles and articles made to substantially the same design. There are also secondary infringements where a person 'deals' with infringing articles, for example, by importing, selling or hiring. Remedies for infringement are as for copyright but there are no criminal penalties for dealing with infringing articles. In *C & H Engineering* v *F Klucznik & Sons Ltd* [1992] FSR 421, the defendant claimed his design right in a pig fender, a three-sided box structure, had been infringed. The 'original' part of the design was a round bar welded around the top. Aldous J said the question of infringement involved an objective test through the eyes of a person to whom the design is directed (in this case, a pig farmer). There was no infringement here because the plaintiff's and defendant's articles were not exactly or substantially the same. Although a design can relate to a part of an article, it seems that the whole article must be looked at when deciding infringement.

Apart from the appearance of computer hardware, the design right is important for the computer industry because a variant of it is used to protect the layout of circuitry within semiconductor products, particularly silicon chips. This is examined in Chapter 12.

European Community developments

There are proposals for harmonising design rights throughout the European Community and for Community-wide design rights. A proposal for a harmonising Directive has been published (OJ [1993] C345/14). This proposes a two-tier system of rights – one based on registration, the other coming into existence automatically, not unlike the present mechanisms for design protection in the United Kingdom. The registered design will last for up to 25 years though there will be no requirement for eye-appeal. The unregistered informal right will endure for three years only but will, in other respects, apply to designs that are registrable.

A one-year period of grace is proposed so that the owner of the design can test the market by selling articles made to the design without compromising the novelty of the design. The informal design right will afford protection during this period and will also be useful for designs with a short commercial life, in fields where fashions change regularly.

A Directive on harmonising registered design systems was adopted by the European Parliament and the Council on 13 October 1998 (OJ [1998] L289/28). This affects only the registered design system. There are some similarities to the present United Kingdom registered design law system but the Directive does not have any specific requirement for eye-appeal apart from being focused on the appearance of the whole or part of a product.

The design must be new and have an individual character and component parts are registrable only if they remain visible in normal use and it is those visible features which are new and have an individual character. A design is not new if it has been made available to the public before the date of the filing (or priority date) of the application. As with the proposed Community design there is a 12-month period of grace, something new to United Kingdom intellectual property law.

The right will last for five years initially and be renewable in five-year periods up to a maximum of 25 years. It is due to come into effect by 28 October 2001.

Chapter 12

Semiconductor products

Introduction

Integrated circuits, commonly known as 'silicon chips' or, simply, 'chips', are of tremendous importance to the computer industry and to other areas of industry and commerce which rely heavily on information technology. Without the miniaturisation that they bring, the powerful personal computer of today would have remained an impossibility. Integrated circuits are made from layers of materials by a process which includes etching using various 'masks' (templates) which are made photographically. Alternatively, electron beam machines are used. The simplest integrated circuit consists of three layers, one of which is made of semiconductor material. A semiconducting material, in terms of its ability to conduct electricity, is one which lies between a conductor such as copper and an insulator such as rubber. Examples of semiconducting materials include silicon, germanium, selenium and gallium arsenide. A wafer of semiconductor material is coated with a layer of silicon oxide (an insulator) and the electronic components (for example, transistors) are made by chemically doping the semiconductor material with impurities through holes etched through the oxide. Finally, an aluminium coating is applied which is partly evaporated using a mask, leaving behind the interconnections between components formed in the semiconductor layer.

The patterns formed by the processes of etching and/or evaporation of the conductor make the electrical circuitry of the integrated circuit. These patterns represent the circuit design. The processes involved in the making of integrated circuits fall within the province of patent law and the first patents for integrated circuits were filed in the late 1950s, the most important one being developed by Noyce of the Fairchild Semiconductor Corporation in 1959. Licences were readily available and in 1961 the first chips were available commercially. Now that the early patents have expired and much of the know-how lies in the public domain, it is essential that the considerable effort that goes into the design and development of new integrated circuits is protected. New types of integrated circuits are unlikely to be patentable for lack of novelty because many are simply more efficient or miniaturised forms of well-known electronic circuits or because, even if new, they do not involve an inventive step, being obvious to persons skilled in the art.

Semiconductor design right

One view was that integrated circuits were protected by copyright through drawings or photographs as most of the masks used in the manufacturing process were produced photographically and would be protected as photographs. This was uncertain, however, because of the requirement in the Copyright Act 1956 for a non-expert to recognise the circuit as being a three-dimensional reproduction of the drawings or photographs. As a result of a European Community Directive (Legal Protection of Topographies of Semiconductor Products (87/54/EEC, OJ [1987] L24/36)), the Semiconductor Products (Protection of Topography) Regulations 1987 were laid before Parliament and came into force on 7 November 1987. These regulations gave a right (called a topography right) in the layout of an integrated circuit. With the advent of the Copyright, Designs and Patents Act 1988, however, it was decided to replace these regulations with an amended version of the new design right by the Design Right (Semiconductor Regulations) 1989, which came into force on 1 August 1989. The new right, referred to hereinafter as the 'semiconductor design right', draws heavily from Part III of the Copyright, Designs and Patents Act 1988 which deals with the unregistered design right but with some differences as far as semiconductor topographies are concerned (see Chapter 11 for a general description of the design right). The manner in which this has been done is most inept and we now have the situation where some sections of the 1988 Act are different depending on whether they are being applied to semiconductors or other designs. References below to the 1988 Act are to the Copyright, Designs and Patents Act 1988 as it applies to the semiconductor design right.

The 1989 regulations are similar to the 1987 regulations in several respects: for example, it is the topography of a semiconductor which is protected, being, by regulation 2, a design which is either:

(a) the pattern fixed, or intended to be fixed, in or upon
    (i) a layer of a semiconductor product, or
    (ii) a layer of material in the course of and for the purpose of the manufacture of a semiconductor product, or
(b) the arrangement of the patterns fixed, or intended to be fixed, in or upon the layers of a semiconductor product in relation to one another.

A semiconductor product is defined as:

> ... an article the purpose, or one of the purposes, of which is the performance of an electronic function and which consists of two or more layers, at least one of which is composed of semiconducting material and in or upon one or more of which is fixed a pattern appertaining to that or another function.

These definitions are not very helpful being somewhat tautologous but despite that it is fairly plain that all original integrated circuits will be covered by the regulations. If the description of integrated circuits given earlier is now considered, it can be seen that the requirements are met: there are two or more layers (usually three), one layer is made of a semiconducting material and a pattern is fixed upon it for the purpose of performing an electronic function. Normally, the ingenuity which requires protection is in the circuitry represented by the patterns formed by the conducting materials, but the regulations are wider in the sense that they will apply in situations where the ingenuity lies not so much in the horizontal patterns themselves but in the vertical arrangement of layers.

Incidentally, the printed circuit boards commonly found inside most electronic equipment, ranging from transistor radios to computers, are not protected by these regulations because, although composed of layers (usually two), neither layer is made from semiconductor material. The board is made of insulating material and a conductor which is etched away leaving the circuitry to which electronic components are later attached by solder. Generally, however, printed circuit boards will be protected, through their preparatory drawings, by copyright as artistic works and, as they are intended to be read by the person making the printed circuit board, as literary works. Alternatively, they could be considered to be protected by the design right as a configuration when all the components are mounted onto the board. A single electronic component such as a silicon diode or a transistor is not protected because it possesses no topography within the meaning of the regulations. A novel electronic device or component might be patentable in its own right if the other requirements for a patent are satisfied, as may be a new process for manufacturing integrated circuits and other electronic devices.

Subsistence and ownership

To be protected, the semiconductor topography must be original and it is not original if it is commonplace in the design field in question at the time of its creation (section 213 of the 1988 Act). 'Original' is liberally interpreted in copyright law, but the requirement that the topography is not commonplace is likely to lead to a much narrower interpretation (see the discussion of *C & H Engineering* v *F Klucznik & Sons Ltd* in Chapter 11). The two-stage test of originality and not being commonplace derives directly from the European Directive on the legal protection of topographies of semiconductor products, Article 2(2), which states:

> **The topography of a semiconductor topography shall be protected in so far as it satisfies the conditions that it is the result of its creator's own intellectual effort and is not commonplace in the semiconductor industry.**

Note the preferred European definition of originality being the creator's own intellectual effort, a similar test to that used in respect of copyright databases and, although not expressly stated in the Copyright, Designs and Patents Act 1988, computer programs. It is arguable that the United Kingdom model of protection for semiconductor topographies is unsatisfactory as the first part of the test remains that of originality not intellectual effort. The traditional United Kingdom approach to originality has been fairly generous, as discussed in Chapter 6 in relation to databases.

Article 2(2) goes on to confirm that where a topography comprises commonplace elements, it may still be protected if, taken as whole, the conditions of originality and not being commonplace are satisfied. The modified version of the design right which applies to semiconductor topographies, like the Directive, does not attempt to define 'commonplace'. In *Ocular Sciences Ltd v Aspect Vision Care Ltd* [1997] RPC 289, Mr Justice Laddie accepted counsel's submission that it would be likely to cover designs which were 'trite, trivial, common-or-garden, hackneyed or of a type which would excite no peculiar attention in those in the relevant art'. Although this seems to be a good working definition, equally applicable to semiconductor topographies and other designs protected by the design right, it must be noted that this part of Laddie J's judgment can only be regarded as a helpful guideline as he had already decided that the defendant had not copied the plaintiff's designs.

Apart from being required to be original (and not commonplace), the design has to qualify for protection. These requirements differ somewhat from those that apply to copyright. Qualification is based on the citizenship or domicile of the creator of the topography (or his employer or commissioner) or the person by whom and country in which semiconductors containing the topography are first marketed.

The qualification requirements are similar to those that apply in respect of the design right but there are a number of differences. In particular, the rule that a commissioned design qualifies by virtue of the commissioner (if he is a qualifying person) is subject to any agreement in writing to the contrary. This proviso is missing from the basic design right model. The same applies to designs created in the course of employment. There is also a change with respect to semiconductor designs which qualify by virtue of the first marketing, in that the person must be exclusively authorised to put the semiconductor products on the market in every member state of the EU, whereas for other designs the exclusivity relates to the United Kingdom only. There are a number of other differences concerning territorial scope for qualification purposes. Protection is also afforded to semiconductor topography designs to persons from the Isle of Man, the Channel Islands and any colony and to firms or companies formed under the law of Gibraltar and to firms or companies having a substantial business activity in a number of other countries including Iceland, Japan, Liechtenstein, Norway, Switzerland and the United States of America.

One reason the 1989 regulations were passed was to satisfy the United States as to the protection offered in the United Kingdom, otherwise there might have been some doubt as to whether topographies derived from the United Kingdom would have been afforded protection in the United States.

Ownership of the semiconductor design right is dealt with by amending section 215 of the 1988 Act. The first owner of the right is the designer unless the design is created in pursuance of a commission or in the course of employment in which cases the commissioner or the employer respectively is the first owner of the right, subject to any written agreement to the contrary. If the right arises by reference to the first marketing of the article, such as where a semiconductor topography is designed by a Brazilian in Brazil but is marketed in the United Kingdom by an importer who is exclusively authorised to put articles made to the design on the market in every member state of the EC, then the importer will be deemed to own the semiconductor design right. By section 214 of the 1988 Act, the designer is the person who creates the design and in the case of a computer-generated design, the designer is the person by whom the arrangements necessary for the creation of the design are undertaken. The recognition of computer-generated topographies was added by the 1989 regulations.

Duration

The duration of the semiconductor design right depends on if and when the topography is commercially exploited. Normally, by section 216 of the 1988 Act, the right endures for ten years from the end of the year in which it was first commercially exploited (anywhere in the world). If the right is not commercially exploited within 15 years of the creation of the topography, however, the right expires 15 years from the time the topography was first recorded in a design document or the time when an article was first made to the design, whichever is the earlier. These rules mean that it might benefit the owner of a topography right for him to sit on that right until such a time as it can be exploited to its full potential as long as this is done a reasonable period before the 15 years have expired. Given the speed of development in the industry, however, this is unlikely to be a great advantage as there is a danger that the product will be obsolete before it has been exploited. As with the unregistered design right as it applies to other articles, the semiconductor design right is automatic and does not require registration. Bearing this in mind (and the same applies to the unregistered design right generally and to copyright works) it is worthwhile keeping good records of the development of the topography so that the date it was created can be proved in a court of law. This is to prevent a copier claiming that he was the first to develop the topography in question. By regulation 9 of the 1989 regulations, licences of right are not available in relation to semiconductors as they are with other designs (such licences are normally available in the last five years of a design right).

Rights and infringement

The semiconductor design right is, by section 226(1) of the 1988 Act as substituted for semiconductor topographies, the exclusive right to reproduce the design by making articles to that design or by making a design document (which includes data stored in a computer) recording the design for the purpose of enabling such articles to be made. A person doing either of the above infringes the right whether he does it in relation to the whole or a substantial part of the topography. There are important exceptions to infringement connected with research, non-commercial or educational purposes. The regulations have one very unusual effect in that it is permissible to make a reproduction of a topography for the purpose of analysing or evaluating that topography or the concepts, processes, systems or techniques embodied in it by section 226(1A) of the 1988 Act as substituted. Furthermore, by regulation 8(4), it is not an infringement of the semiconductor design right to create another original topography as a result of such analysis or evaluation or to reproduce that other topography. Therefore, a form of 'reverse engineering' is positively encouraged allowing the knowledge gained from an inspection of an existing topography to be used in the design of a new topography. In practice, a limiting factor will be the requirement for the new topography to be original and not commonplace. On reflection, this exception is probably justified on the grounds that to provide otherwise might inhibit innovation in this very fast-moving field where the existing technology is being built upon all the time while property rights still subsist in that existing technology. However, this runs counter to basic principles of intellectual property rights; such an activity with respect to a copyright work would probably infringe copyright because any derivative work would contain a copy of a substantial part of the first work. It will really depend on how the word 'substantial' is interpreted in terms of the semiconductor design right. For the reverse engineering provisions to have any real effect, the word 'substantial' would have to be interpreted in a quantitative sense which would run counter to copyright law.

If an infringement of a topography right also infringes copyright, the semiconductor design right is suppressed leaving remedies to be pursued under copyright law only, by section 236 of the 1988 Act. This is the same as with other designs. Regard must be had to section 51 of the Copyright, Designs and Patents Act 1988, however, which removes from the scope of copyright infringement the making of articles to designs recorded in design documents (or embodied in models) unless the design is for an artistic work. It is highly unlikely that semiconductor designs will be considered to be artistic works. Design documents include drawings, photographs and computer data and the effect of section 51 is to remove copyright protection from semiconductor topographies leaving the modified design right with its limited duration as the only form of legal protection, apart from the law of confidence which will protect until, at least, the semiconductor products are made available to the public. Compliance with the European Directive, following pressure from the United States, has had the opposite effect to that intended: it has significantly reduced protection in the United Kingdom from what was potentially available under copyright law.

Remedies for infringement

Remedies for infringement are as for the design right generally and are injunctions, damages and accounts of profits 'or otherwise' (section 229 of the 1988 Act). Additional damages are also provided for as they are for copyright infringement and the unregistered design right generally. Orders for delivery up and destruction are also available. In the case of innocent infringement (if the defendant did not know and had no reason to believe that the semiconductor design right subsisted in the article) damages are not available although other remedies may be, such as an account of profits.

Secondary infringement – for example, where a person imports or deals with infringing copies of semiconductors – does not apply if they have already been marketed in the United Kingdom or any member state of the European Community by or with the licence of the owner of the right or other person entitled to do so.

Chapter 13

International implications and summary

International implications

Bearing in mind the international nature of business, the territorial scope of intellectual property rights is a serious issue to those creating and developing computer hardware and software. Some forms of intellectual property rights fare better than others when it comes to their subsistence and enforcement in other countries. With the United Kingdom's membership of the European Community, it is to be expected that there should be some degree of harmonisation with our European trading partners and recent legislation in the United Kingdom has been influenced by this. For example, the Patents Act 1977 went some way towards achieving compatibility, and the consolidation of moral rights in copyright law, which is a traditional European concept, reinforces the move towards European trading unity. A steady flow of European Community Directives harmonising intellectual property rights confirms the important role of intellectual property in commercial activity within the Community.

On a world-wide scale there are many difficulties, and some countries fail to appreciate the significance of intellectual property. World-wide legal protection of invention and innovation is still a long way from being realised, although countries which include the major producers and users of intellectual property have strong laws protecting the same. There are also signs of growing international co-operation in harmonising and enforcing intellectual property laws.

The GATT TRIPs Agreement (General Agreement on Tariffs and Trade, Trade-Related Aspects of Intellectual Property Rights, 15 December 1993) now administered by the World Trade Organisation goes some way towards establishing a level playing field and will assist in the international protection of intellectual property rights. In particular, countries which are parties to the agreement must be committed to providing national treatment: that is, nationals of other parties must be given treatment no less favourable than that afforded to the party's own nationals. Parties to the TRIPs agreement, *inter alia*, must comply with the major international conventions protecting intellectual property.

Copyright is subject to two international conventions by which reciprocal protection is granted between members. The conventions are the Berne Convention and the Universal Copyright Convention and the United Kingdom is a signatory to both. This means that most works of copyright protected under the Copyright, Designs and Patents Act 1988 are also protected in the countries which are members of these conventions, which include most of the major developed countries. In some of these countries, a copyright notice is required and it is for this reason that the familiar copyright symbol © is used. To be valid the symbol must be shown with the name of the copyright owner and the year the work was created though alternatives to the symbol are allowed such as the unabbreviated word 'copyright'.

The territorial scope of patent protection is determined by the application procedure. The applicant may apply for a United Kingdom patent, a European patent to be granted for three or more countries under the European Patent Convention or a 'world-wide' patent for one or more of the member countries under the Patent Co-operation Treaty. Whichever route is chosen, if successful, the applicant will acquire a bundle of national patents. For example, if a person applies through the European Patent Convention for a patent in respect of the United Kingdom, France, Spain and Germany, that person will end up with four separate, though identical, national patents. There is not, as yet, a single patent which is valid and enforceable in a number of countries. However, there are plans to introduce a Community-wide patent which will have a unitary nature and be effective throughout the European Community.

The more countries for which patent protection is sought the more expensive the operation becomes but the expense may be worthwhile if it is intended to exploit the invention internationally. There is an international agreement, the Madrid Agreement, for the international registration of trade marks and a protocol to this agreement has been ratified by the United Kingdom, with the result that United Kingdom persons should no longer have to make separate application to each country covered by the protocol in which they wish to gain registration of their mark. The first countries to ratify the protocol, which runs alongside to and separate from the Madrid Convention, were China, Cuba, Denmark, Finland, Germany, Norway, Spain, Sweden and the United Kingdom. Furthermore, a European Community trade mark system is now under way. This gives a single trade mark registration which is valid throughout the European Community.

Generally, intellectual property rights are territorial in nature. However, the Brussels and Lugano Conventions on jurisdiction and enforcement of judgments in civil and commercial matters have a significant impact on jurisdiction, that is, the country in which a legal action can be brought. These Conventions were implemented by the Civil Jurisdiction and Judgments Acts of 1982 and 1991 and the rules apply to the member states of the European Community and the European Economic Area (Norway, Liechtenstein and Iceland).

The basic rule is that a defendant is sued in his home country. However, where a breach of contract or an infringement of an intellectual property right, such as a patent or copyright, is concerned, the action can be brought where the harmful event occurred. Where there is more than one defendant having joint liability in respect of the same action, litigation can be pursued in the country in which any of the defendants is based. Where a German citizen has a German copyright in a literary work, by virtue of the Berne Convention and the Copyright (Application to Other Countries) Order 1993, he will also qualify for copyright protection in the United Kingdom. If his copyright is infringed by an English company, he can sue in England. If the English company is a joint infringer with a French company and infringing copies of his work are sold in Germany, he can sue in England, Germany or France.

An exception applies in relation to rights that are subject to formalities such as patents. Where the validity of the right is in issue, as it almost certainly will be in an action for infringement of a patent, the action can only be brought in the country in which the patent is registered. This can lead to a very unsatisfactory situation. It means that if a person holds a number of European patents for the same invention and it is being infringed in some of the countries where the patents are registered, that person may have to embark upon a number of separate actions, one in each country, to enforce his patent. This is very unsatisfactory and is compounded by the fact that some countries take a different view of the application of the Conventions. Furthermore, it exposes the owner of a bundle of patents to additional expense and the possibility of conflicting decisions in different countries. A potential defendant may even be able to bring a pre-emptive strike by commencing an action in a country in which an action may take a long time to come to trial.

Some areas of intellectual property discussed in this Part of the book have little, if any, international scope and are restricted to the United Kingdom. Prime examples are the law of confidence, as demonstrated by the failure to prevent the publication of the *Spycatcher* book in Australia (and, eventually, also in the United Kingdom), the tort of passing off and, as yet, the new design right. Other countries have other laws to deal with these rights such as a law of unfair competition.

European Community law and intellectual property

Computer technology and its use has attracted much interest from the European Community (EC). There have been a number of harmonising Directives including those dealing with copyright in computer programs and databases, term of copyright, semiconductor products, rental and lending rights, data protection, safety and product liability. In the field of intellectual property the EC has plans for further harmonisation of rights throughout the

Community and, ultimately, the development of more Community-wide rights such as the Community Patent. In these respects, the EC has taken a very proactive role, guided by the importance of the Single Market which cannot effectively exist if intellectual property rights vary from one member state to another or if they can be used to restrict the free movement of goods or services. The EC has also taken on the role of policing the exercise of these rights through the Commission and the European Court of Justice, taking its brief from the provisions of the Treaty of Rome 1957 concerning the free movement of goods and services, restrictive trade agreements and abuses of dominant trading positions.

There remain significant differences in the intellectual property law of member states of the EC. However, where these differences operate so as to discriminate against persons on the grounds of nationality, they are likely to offend against Article 12 of the EC Treaty (formerly Article 6) which states that, within the scope of the Treaty, any discrimination on grounds of nationality is prohibited. In *Collins* v *Imtrat Handelsgesellschaft mbH* [1994] FSR 166, bootleg recordings of performances by Phil Collins and Cliff Richard were being distributed in Germany. The recordings had been made at performances in the United States and the United Kingdom. German copyright law gave protection to German nationals wherever the recording was made but refused protection to non-Germans. The European Court of Justice held that this was contrary to Article 6 and the discrimination offended Community law. The implications of this case are wide-ranging. Provisions in national legislation which deny protection to nationals of member states which are not parties to an international convention providing for reciprocal protection must now be viewed with extreme suspicion.

A full description of the work of the EC in relation to intellectual property is outside the scope of this book but the main provisions and effects are summarised below, including mention of the future implications.

Harmonisation and Community-wide rights

Copyright

Directives on the legal protection of computer programs, the legal protection of databases, the term of copyright, rental and lending right, satellite broadcasting and cable retransmission have all been implemented in the United Kingdom. There is a proposal for a Directive on artists' resale right and a proposal for a Directive on copyright and related rights in the Information Society.

Patent law

There has been, for some time, a proposal for a Community Patent (CPC). Unlike the European Patent Convention, which effectively gives a bundle of national rights, the CPC will introduce a unitary system applying throughout the EC. It is likely to be administered by the European Patent Office and is likely to come into effect in the near future. There is also a proposal for harmonisation of a utility model form of protection. This will introduce this right into the United Kingdom.

Trade marks

Community Trade Mark (CTM): the Office for the Harmonisation of the Internal Market (Trade Marks and Designs) began accepting applications to register CTMs on 1 January 1996. It appears to have been quite successful with a good deal of interest being shown in acquiring a CTM. The CTM exists alongside national trade mark systems.

Design law

Law in individual member states is quite different, apart from protection of semiconductor topographies which has already been harmonised. The EC intends a two-pronged effort: first to harmonise national laws and then to introduce Community-wide design rights. Two forms of design right are proposed: one subject to registration, the other right being unregistered but only lasting for three years. At the time of writing a harmonising Directive for registered designs has been adopted though not yet implemented and a proposal for a Community Design Regulation has been published.

EC competition law

One of the main aims of the EC is to remove internal barriers to trade. The EC Treaty (Treaty of Rome 1957, as amended) imposes obligations and provides rights effective upon and in the United Kingdom by virtue of its membership of the EC. The EC Treaties are given direct legal effect in the United Kingdom by section 2 of the European Communities Act 1972. In terms of the exercise of intellectual property rights, the following provisions of the Treaty of Rome are important. (*Note*: most of the Articles of this Treaty have been renumbered as a result of the Amsterdam Treaty; the new numbers and old numbers are indicated):

- Article 12, prohibiting discrimination on grounds of nationality (previously Article 6).
- Articles 28–30, promoting the free movement of goods (previously Articles 30–36).
- Article 81, prohibiting restrictive trade practices (previously Article 85).
- Article 82, preventing the abuse of a dominant market position (previously Article 86).

These provisions apply only in as much as trade between member states is affected. Although EC law recognises the *existence* of intellectual property rights it may interfere with the *exercise* of those rights if this offends against the Treaty. For example, the proprietor of a patent may wish to be selective about markets and grant licences to work the patent to different organisations in different member states under different conditions. This would have the effect of segregating and splitting the market and would be likely to attract the attention of the Commission, particularly if one of the licensees objects (perhaps the one having the least advantageous terms in its licence agreement).

The application of the Treaty provisions to actual cases has led to the development of the following principles (the second is a direct consequence of the first):

- *Exhaustion of rights* – where the right owner has put articles into circulation (directly or with his consent) he cannot subsequently use his rights to prevent further sale or distribution in respect of those particular articles.
- *Parallel importing* – where articles have been put into circulation by or with the consent of the right owner, he cannot use his rights to prevent the subsequent import into another EC country even though he may be selling those articles himself in that other country. This removes any temptation to sell articles at different prices in different member states.

The restrictive trade practices provisions obviously control price-fixing agreements and other abuses by cartels but they also control licensing agreements – for example, where the proprietor of a patent attempts to impose onerous terms on the licensee. Also covered are agreements to 'pool' (share) intellectual property rights such as patents and know-how. There are exemptions under Article 81(3), either block exemptions (several have been promulgated) or individual exemptions.

Abuses of dominant positions might include demanding excessively high royalty rates or a refusal to grant licences. However, being in a dominant position, *per se*, does not conflict with Article 82. In *Volvo AB v Erik Veng (UK) Ltd* [1989] 4 CMLR 122, the plaintiff claimed that the defendant had infringed its registered design for front wings for Volvo 200 series cars. It was held that, although refusal to grant licences did not amount to an abuse as such, it could so do if refusal was arbitrary or if prices were fixed at unfair levels or if the right owner stopped making spare parts. However, this would be so only if trade between member states was liable to be affected.

In the absence of full harmonisation of intellectual property rights, determination of the scope of the rights was a matter for national laws but, in exceptional circumstances, the exercise of a national right could amount to an abuse under Article 82. So it was held in *RTE & ITP v Commission of the European Communities* [1995] FSR 530, a case in which the plaintiffs were refusing to grant licences to others to publish listings of television programmes.

Summary

The law has developed, somewhat slowly it might be claimed, to take account of computer technology and to protect ideas and innovation concerning the technology. However, the importance of such protection has been recognised by United Kingdom and EC legislators and the judiciary and, as a result, computers and computer software are reasonably well protected from counterfeiting and piracy. The civil remedies available to owners of intellectual property rights have been supplemented by criminal sanctions, showing the seriousness with which Parliament views these matters. Certainly, without strong protection, the computer industry would seem a poor area in which to invest, and foreign investment and the resulting jobs created would be lost to the United Kingdom.

Although this area of law is diverse and complex, it should be noted that, frequently, these various rights overlap and several different rights may each serve a purpose during the life of a product from inception to marketing. For example, in the case of a new piece of computer equipment, the law of confidence is all important in the early stages as it is being developed and evaluated. Then, as specifications and drawings are produced, the law of copyright comes into play and gives parallel protection. When a patent is granted in respect of the equipment, the law of confidence drops from the scene to be replaced by patent law and, possibly, trade mark law if a registered mark is to be used with the equipment. Design law also may be relevant at this stage.

This parallel and overlapping protection is all the more important in the computer industry. For example, imagine that a new computer has been designed. It is to be sold with and includes software which is hard-wired (firmware), resident on integrated circuits inside the computer in addition to software on magnetic disk. The computer has a new type of keyboard and an attractive design embossed on the monitor case which also carries the manufacturer's stylised name. The following rights may be relevant to this computer system:

Patent	Being new, the computer may incorporate some new and patentable inventions.
Copyright	The software on disk and the programs stored on the integrated circuits (firmware) and all accompanying documentation are protected under copyright law.
Semiconductor regulations	The topography of the integrated circuits containing the firmware.
Trade marks	The stylised name may be registered as a trade mark.

Registered design   The embossed pattern and the overall shape of the equipment may be registered as designs.

Design right   The new type of keyboard and any other new shapes may fall within the scope of the new design right.

Key aspects to be remembered with respect to intellectual property rights are:

- the importance of confidence, especially concerning employees and potential business partners,
- the usefulness of keeping a documented record of the development of an idea or invention so that its origin can be verified, and
- the value, sometimes unexpected, of making drawings.

Finally, although the legal enforcement of intellectual property rights is an expensive business, delay or dalliance can be disastrous and the possibility of obtaining some legal remedies, such as interlocutory injunctions, may be prejudiced. There follows a list of practical suggestions concerning ways in which the protection of intellectual property rights can be maximised.

Practical suggestions

Copyright

1 Those writing and developing computer software should distribute the computer programs in object code form only. Consider embedding the names of programmers or the company name within the program code; this can be extremely useful evidentially if a software pirate denies copying. The same applies to deliberate mistakes and redundant code. Software, as it is written and developed, can be deposited with an independent person (for example, a solicitor or the Stationers' Company) who can verify important dates such as when the software was first written and when it was modified. Written and signed contractual arrangements should be made with freelance workers and consultants dealing with the ownership of the copyright in anything they produce.

2 Lawful users of software may now make back-up copies of any programs they have acquired if necessary to the lawful use of the programs. If the programs are transferred later to another person, all back-up copies must also be transferred. Licensees of software should not assign or transfer their rights if the licence agreement prohibits this. If the agreement allows assignment conditional upon certain matters being complied with, it is essential to make sure that these conditions are met. Software users should operate secure and efficient housekeeping systems to reduce the danger of unauthorised copies of programs being made.

155

3 Software developers and users of software should clarify any doubts concerning the ownership of any output produced by the use of the computer system in question. The scope of the permitted act of decompilation must be fully understood if decompilation is envisaged. The position as regards error correction of software must be examined and clarified.

Confidence

4 An air of confidence must be maintained during negotiations between those with new ideas for software, computer systems, etc. and potential manufacturers, investors and the like.
5 Confidence can be reinforced by contractual provision in respect of employees and freelance workers. This may entail a reasonable covenant in restraint of trade.
6 It is essential that any ideas and development work concerning a possible future patent application are kept absolutely secret and confidential.

Patent

7 The use of an experienced patent agent is highly recommended if a patent application is being considered.
8 Although a patent is a very powerful form of intellectual property, it is worth considering whether the invention involved can be kept secret indefinitely as an alternative to seeking a patent.
9 It may be possible to obtain a patent for an invention which includes a computer program despite the apparent exception of computer programs from the scope of patent law providing there is some technical effect which is not itself excepted. It needs to be borne in mind that the computer program will be protected by copyright law regardless of the patent situation.

Trade marks and passing off

10 Distinctive names or marks are very powerful marketing devices. Those manufacturing or marketing computer software or hardware are advised to register a distinctive name or mark as a trade mark and not to rely on the law of passing off which requires an established goodwill. Computer bureaux and other persons providing computer services for payment can register a trade mark.

Design law

11 Although this is a complex area of the law and subject to much speculation as regards the various overlaps between artistic, aesthetic and

functional designs, if a design has been made which has some degree of eye-appeal, however small, an application for registration should be made.

12 Manufacturers and distributors of spare parts for computer equipment must familiarise themselves with the 'must-fit' and 'must-match' exceptions and their scope. The law of non-derogation from grant also must be considered.

13 Design law can be a useful supplement to other intellectual property rights.

PART TWO

Computer contracts

Contracts for the acquisition and use of computer hardware and software are dealt with in this Part of the book. Many such contracts are not sale contracts as such but are licence agreements; this is particularly so with respect to computer software where the owner of the rights subsisting in the software grants licences to customers, giving them permission to use the software in return for a licence fee. For these agreements, the existence and scope of intellectual property rights is of fundamental importance. The acts restricted by copyright may form a substantial part of the licence's subject matter. Contracts for the acquisition of hardware and software are subject to many of the legal constraints on contracts such as the Unfair Contract Terms Act 1977 and those provided for by copyright law.

Following the introductory chapter, the fundamentals of the law of contract are discussed and related to computer technology. Liability issues related to defective hardware and software are discussed next and it should be noted that, in some cases, liability is not dependent upon the existence of a contractual relationship and, where appropriate, liability for negligence and product liability is discussed. An employer's liability in relation to RSI (repetitive strain injury) caused by long periods of work at a keyboard is also discussed. In subsequent chapters, particular types of computer contracts are described: contracts for the writing of computer software, 'off-the-shelf' software licences, agreements between software authors and publishers, and hardware contracts. There is a separate chapter looking at the implications of electronic contracting, an area which is growing in importance at an exponential rate. The summary chapter includes a checklist of terms normally to be found in contracts concerning computer hardware and software.

Chapter 14

Introduction to computer contracts

Contracts for the acquisition of computer equipment and software present special problems, many of which flow from the unique nature of computer technology. For example, we cannot see or touch a computer program running in a computer; all we can do is experience its effects through a peripheral device such as a screen or a printer. It may be possible to read a listing of a computer program and perhaps make some sense of it but, certainly to many of us who have to use computer programs, they take on a quasi-mystical nature as they are, after all, intangible. It is the difficulty in coming to terms with the nature, effects and implications of computer equipment and software that is a direct cause of many of the contractual and other problems associated with computers.

The case of *Brownton Ltd* v *Edward Moore Inbucon Ltd* [1985] 3 All ER 499 provides an example of the financial implications of misunderstandings between the parties to a contract involving computer systems. A firm of commodity brokers sought advice from a computer consultant on the installation of a computer system. The consultant recommended a particular system which was installed in 1978. Unfortunately, the system never worked properly, was quite inadequate for the broker's needs and was eventually scrapped. The consultant had charged over £66 000 for his work and the computer system had cost in the region of £75 000. The broker claimed damages, for breach of contract, of over £250 000 based on the wasted expense and the difference in price between the system obtained and a new system that would be capable of doing the work. Later, the broker submitted better particulars and claimed that an alternative computer system capable of carrying out the work would cost in excess of £1.1 million. Eventually, a settlement of around £300 000 was reached.

In another case, discussed in detail in Chapter 16, a lack of understanding of the ORACLE fourth-generation computer language on the part of the client and software developer during the feasibility study for and initial development stages of complex accounting software led to the inevitable result. The software was delivered late and, because it contained a large number of errors, it was unusable. The client was awarded £662 962 in damages (see *The Salvage Association* v *CAP Financial Services Ltd* [1995] FSR 654). The software developer was unable to avail itself of a clause in the contract limiting liability for defects to £25 000.

A hypothetical example can further illustrate the difficulties. A company wants to install a computer system in one of its departments which has previously had to use slow, laborious (but reliable) manual methods. The initial decision to do this is probably based on some vague notion that a computer system will increase efficiency, or perhaps because all its competitors have installed computer systems. The company already may have a mainframe computer and the IT manager might suggest that some potentially suitable software packages be evaluated and that obtaining a ready-made package should be considerably less expensive than writing one from scratch. The first problem is to decide how the available packages should be evaluated and by whom. The people in the company who will use the proposed system ought to be involved in the selection process, but such people are unlikely to have much knowledge of computers and computer software although they may be familiar with word processing and spreadsheet systems running on their desktop computers.

The IT manager and other computer professionals, either within the company or brought in from outside as consultants, will have an important contribution to make to the decision. Although they will have an intimate knowledge of computers, they will probably not have a deep knowledge of the particular application of the proposed software. Their priorities will differ. The computer people will want to know how the software will fit in with their portfolio of software, whether it will require additional computer equipment, how well it will be maintained, how portable it is and so on. There may follow a lack of communication and understanding between the computer professionals, the legal advisers, the ultimate users and the supplier of the software resulting in the purchase of a system which is cumbersome, does not provide all the information the users now realise they would have liked and which runs far too slowly to be of any practical use. The software company which supplied the package is not unsympathetic but claims that it was just not given clear and sufficient guidance as to what was expected of the software. The software company may even suggest that the problems will be overcome if new and more powerful equipment is obtained. An allegation that the problem lies with the client's own computer installation might be difficult to refute. It is at this stage that the contract is carefully examined, perhaps for the first time, and the company obtaining the software realises, too late, that as far as it is concerned, the contract is little more than worthless and does not provide adequately for the situation. The client might refuse to make the final payments and the ensuing legal struggle is both predictable and inevitable. IT personnel and independent computer consultants must educate department heads and legal advisers as to the implications and dangers involved in acquiring computer equipment and software. Departmental heads and legal advisers, for their part, must be prepared to ask questions of their computer advisers and, even more importantly, to listen to the answers.

The point of the above story is to demonstrate the importance of the parties to a computer contract knowing precisely what is to be expected in terms of performance and the standards required. The role that the equipment or software is intended to fulfil must be clearly identified and quantified, a comprehensive and precise specification must be drawn up. The lack of, or defects in, specification is probably at the heart of most disputes resulting from the acquisition of computer equipment and software.

The importance of choosing the most appropriate hardware and software should not be underestimated and, as a corollary, a contract which provides a reasonable and fair machinery for identifying responsibilities and resolving disputes needs to be negotiated. A mistake in the choice of equipment or software coupled with a poor contract can be disastrous for a purchasing company. The problems are not all one-sided, however, as it may be that a supplier of equipment or software has to fall back on contractual remedies. If the acquiring company refuses to provide, or is incapable of providing, clear instructions, if it refuses to accept and/or pay for the equipment or software, if it tampers with the programs, misuses them and allows employees to copy them freely, the supplier will need to take action. The company making the acquisition will need to decide: how the contract can protect it if the equipment or software fails to perform as it should; how it should be maintained and how its staff should be trained; and what to do if the software or hardware infringes a third party's copyright or patent. Other decisions will concern the selection of the software developer or hardware supplier, the form of contract and whether a feasibility study or prototyping work is to be undertaken.

One thing is clear, whatever form of contract is used, and that is that great care must be taken in drafting the contract. Judges interpret contracts strictly and will use certain principles of construction when it comes to resolving inconsistencies and ambiguities. If a contract is silent on a particular matter, judges may if necessary imply terms to give the contract business efficacy on the basis of the presumed intention of the parties. A judge will not, however, write the contract for the parties. There must be, at least, something resembling a concrete agreement between the parties. It is certainly very unwise to use a form of contract designed for one jurisdiction in another, even though both have similar legal systems. In *Andersen Consulting* v *CHP Consulting Ltd* (unreported) 26 July 1991, ex-employees of the plaintiff set up in business on their own account, providing maintenance for the plaintiff's computer programs. The plaintiff argued that a term in their licence agreements prevented maintenance by third parties. Mr Justice Harman refused to grant an injunction in favour of the plaintiff and strongly criticised the use of an American contract which he described as having odd and inept phrasing. The contract should have been drafted to take account of United Kingdom law; it was simply not good enough to make a few modifications to an American form of contract.

In Chapters 15 and 16, the basic legal consequences of computer contracts will be described. The nature of the contract, contractual and tortious liabilities and the use of exclusion clauses will be considered. Individual terms which may be found in various types of computer contracts will then be discussed in subsequent chapters with a view to avoiding the disasters that await the unwary. Balanced, fair and thorough negotiation is the key to a smooth-running contract and all the relevant contractual terms and mechanisms should be considered and agreed before the parties become committed to the contract. The final chapter in this part of the book contains a summary and checklist of terms commonly found in computer contracts.

Chapter 15

Fundamentals of computer contracts

Terms of the contract

It is important to know precisely what the terms of a contract are. Of course, in many situations where the whole contract is in writing, this should be an easy matter. Providing one is skilled in 'legalese', the technical legal jargon is still commonly found in legal documents. But even here, things are not necessarily that straightforward and the law may insert additional terms into the contract or strike out some of the terms apparently agreed upon by the parties to the contract. This is notwithstanding the English tradition of freedom of contract – to the effect that the parties should be free to agree precisely what terms they want in their contract. Another problem may be where the contract is not in writing or is only partly in writing. An example of the latter is where a signed note or memorandum indicates that a contract exists but clearly does not contain all the terms on the face of it. For example, the note may state that Ace Software Ltd agrees to write process control software for Boris Boring and Drilling Co Ltd for the sum of £45 000. On its own such a note would be unenforceable because it lacks certainty. Apart from other missing information, there is no specification or other description of what is required of the software nor any time for delivery. In relation to oral contracts and contracts partly in writing, it will be a matter of submitting evidence of the other terms to give the contract sufficient certainty. To overcome some of these difficulties, the law may imply terms into the contract.

The first task is to look at what has been expressly agreed by the parties. The *express terms*, whether oral or in writing, may be the only terms of the contract, although this would be rare. In many cases, the law will imply terms into the contract, particularly as a result of statute. These *implied terms*, such as those implied into certain contracts by the Sale of Goods Act 1979 or the Supply of Goods or Services Act 1982 are particularly important and are discussed later in this and subsequent chapters. Sometimes, the courts may imply terms into a contract. However, this will only be done in limited circumstances as indicated by Lord Pearson in *Trollope & Colls Ltd* v *North West Metropolitan Regional Hospital Board* [1973] 1 WLR 602 where he said (at 609):

> An unexpressed term can be implied if and only if the court finds that the parties must have intended that the term form part of their contract: it is not enough for the court to find that such a term would have been adopted by the parties as reasonable men if it had been suggested to them: it must have been a term that went without saying, a term necessary to give business efficacy to the contract, a term which although tacit, formed part of the contract which the parties made for themselves.

In other words the term must be such as is necessary to make the contract effective and must be a term which the parties would clearly have agreed must be included had it been mentioned to them at the time. It is not enough for the term to be one which would be reasonable to include. The above sentiment was agreed with in the Court of Appeal by Sir Iain Glidewell in *St Albans City & District Council* v *International Computers Ltd* [1997] FSR 251 where he held that, in a contract for writing computer software without involving the transfer of property in tangible items such as magnetic disks, the court could imply a term to the effect that the software was reasonably fit for its purpose. This important case of liability for defective software and the scope of exclusion clauses is discussed in more depth in the following chapter.

As well as implying terms into a contract, the law may impact upon the express terms. It may make a term, agreed by the parties, void and unenforceable. Normally, this will be the result of a statutory provision. For example, a term in a software licence which prohibits or restricts the making of a necessary back-up copy of a computer program by a person having the right to use it under an agreement is declared void and unenforceable by section 296A(1) of the Copyright, Designs and Patents Act 1988. The Unfair Contract Terms Act 1977 is important in controlling the use of terms which try to exclude or limit liability for negligence and breach of contract, among other things. Another way the courts will control contract terms is by using the common law: for example, by declining to enforce a term which is in restraint of trade such as where a computer programmer's contract of employment prevents him working for a competitor of his employer for a period of five years without any geographical limitation. A common ploy in some contracts is where the party in the stronger bargaining position inserts some draconian terms and, knowing that the courts may interfere with them, seeks to save as many of them as he can. A 'saving' clause, sometimes referred to as a 'blue pencil' clause, may be worded as follows:

> In the event that any provision of this agreement is unenforceable but would be enforceable if part of the wording of the provision were to be deleted, it shall apply with the minimum of such deletions being made as required to make the provision enforceable.

Such terms are unlikely to be met with judicial favour. Judges will not write the contract for the parties and draconian terms may be consigned to the court's waste bin rather than the judge striking out the offending parts. The general rule, however, is that if a term is severable, that is, the contract can stand without it, the term will be deleted, leaving the rest of the contract in force. If the term in question is of fundamental importance to the contract, then the entire contract will be in jeopardy. Of course, the ploy of having draconian terms which may be unenforceable is that they may be accepted at face value by the other party and not tested in the courts. Nevertheless, great care must be taken not to attempt to take away certain statutory rights as to do so may result in criminal prosecution.

Nature of the contract

It is not always easy to separate hardware and software and this fact has been demonstrated on several occasions in the courts. For example, in *Dyason* v *Autodesk Inc* (1990) 96 ALR 57, there was much confusion as to whether a 'dongle', a device required to be inserted into a computer before a program would operate, contained a computer program and in *Gale's Application* [1991] RPC 305, the trial judge (erroneously) drew a distinction between a program on disk and one hard-wired into a ROM chip. Such confusion is largely a result of the difficulty many lawyers have when dealing with a highly technical field such as computer science but it does not stop there. Even if the technological aspects are fully understood, the application of the law to them may still perplex.

Although there is some common ground and some similarity in other provisions, contracts for hardware and software are governed by different legal rules. Computer hardware, if it is sold, will be subject to the Sale of Goods Act 1979 whereas an agreement to write software ('bespoke' software) will be within the scope of the Supply of Goods and Services Act 1982. There are other differences, for example, as regards the statutory controls over exclusion clauses. This simple distinction is not always easy to apply in practice because hardware equipment often incorporates software and the contractual position of 'off-the-shelf' software is far from clear. Nevertheless, the classification in terms of the legal nature of the transaction is important and the author's suggested approach is to look at the predominant purpose of the transaction. In other words, did the person acquiring the subject matter think that he was obtaining hardware or software?

Consider a person purchasing a new motor car. This is a 'good' and the transaction is clearly subject to the Sale of Goods Act 1979, section 2(1), which states:

> ... a contract of sale of goods is a contract by which the seller transfers or agrees to transfer the property in goods to the buyer for a money consideration called the price.

The whole purpose of the transaction is to transfer ownership in the car. Suppose the car is faulty, however, and that fault is traced to a computer program installed in the electronic ignition system. The purchaser would still expect, rightly, to be able to obtain a remedy from the seller under the Sale of Goods Act even though he has not obtained ownership of the copyright subsisting in the computer program. After all, the buyer wanted to acquire a car not a computer program. Therefore, a contract to purchase a computer is a sale of goods contract notwithstanding the inclusion of computer software embodied within the computer. If other software is provided (often referred to as 'bundled') that will usually be subject to a separate, collateral licence agreement.

Contracts for the acquisition of software alone cannot be sale of goods contracts; the title to the software is not normally transferred nor is a computer program or database a good. The only proviso is that, as far as manuals, disks and packaging are concerned, we might have a collateral sale of goods contract. However, the predominant nature of the contract is the provision of a service, the function of the software being the service in question. This is so even if the copyright ownership is transferred, that is, if the agreement is an assignment and not simply a licence.

The nature of software contracts has long puzzled judges and legal writers. Certainly, in the case of software which is specifically written for a client, it must be a service contract as opposed to a sale of goods contract. Although some writers have focused on the fact that tangible items such as magnetic disks may be provided, suggesting a sale of goods contract, where software is delivered on-line or by loading it onto the client's computer, the nature of the arrangement becomes clearer. The delivery of tangible items in addition to the software has only served to cloud the reality of the transaction.

A case which involved a book gave an indication of the approach preferred by the author of this book. In *Ashley v Sutton London Borough Council* (unreported) 8 December 1994, the appellant, Ashley, brought an appeal against his conviction for an offence under section 14 of the Trade Descriptions Act 1968. The charge was that he had made a statement which he knew to be false as to the nature of services he provided in the course of a trade or business.

Ashley had supplied books by mail order which described a winning strategy to be used with fixed odds gambling and he guaranteed to refund the purchase price if customers were not satisfied. It was argued on his behalf that he had supplied books, not services, and, consequently, could not be guilty under section 14 which only concerns services not goods. The Divisional Court of the Queen's Bench Division held that, although goods were supplied (that is, the books), the essential nature of the contract was the provision of a service – the service of providing information. The book was merely the medium through which the information was imparted and the contract was, therefore, predominantly a contract for services and the appeal against conviction was dismissed. The same can be said in terms of software even more forcefully. It is a copy of the programs and/or data that the customer wants. As in the *Ashley* case, the high price of the information relative to the tangible items delivered confirms this. The fact that software can be transmitted without the need for a tangible carrier reinforces the view that software contracts are service contracts. At best, any tangible items delivered with the software give rise to a collateral sale of goods contract in respect of those items only. To return to the analogy with a book, sale of goods law will give a remedy if the book is physically defective: for example, if it falls apart or has pages missing. It will not give a remedy simply because the plot is not very good or if there are grammatical errors. Such defects relate to the information not the good itself.

Two software cases have reinforced the deceptive simplicity of that approach. In *St Albans City & District Council* v *International Computers Ltd* [1997] FSR 251, Sir Iain Glidewell said that a computer program is clearly not within the meaning of 'good' for the purposes of the Sale of Goods Act 1979 nor the Supply of Goods and Services Act 1982. However, at first instance, Mr Justice Scott-Baker accepted that software was goods within the Sale of Goods Act 1979 (although he did not have to decide the point) because '… it is difficult to see what it can be other than something to which no statutory rules apply …'. Not a very convincing argument!

As has often been the case, it was a Scots judge who most ably defined the nature of a software contract in the context of a licence for off-the-shelf software. In *Beta Computers (Europe) Ltd* v *Adobe Systems (Europe) Ltd* [1996] FSR 367, Lord Penrose in the Outer House of the Court of Session in Edinburgh had to determine the nature of an agreement to acquire off-the-shelf software. He decided that the supply of such software for a price is a *sui generis* (unique) contract rather than a sale of goods contract or a hybrid contract. He considered the Copyright, Designs and Patents Act 1988 and concluded that the supply of the medium on which the program is stored must be accompanied by an appropriate licence conferred directly or by implication from the acquisition of the software. An essential feature of the arrangement was that the supplier undertook to make available to the purchaser both the medium and the right of access and use of the software.

There are some differences between English and Scots contract law and, under the latter, it is possible to grant third parties rights under a contract. Nevertheless, the judgment is an excellent analysis of the nature of a software contract and an important feature of the case was that the predominant purpose of the contract – that is, to acquire the right to use the software – would be subjugated if it were classed as a sale of goods contract.

Software acquisition

The most common method of acquiring computer software is by way of a licence which is granted by the copyright owner to the person or company acquiring a copy of the software, giving permission to use the software in return for the licence fee – the 'price'. The licence may be for a fixed, perhaps renewable, period of time or there may be no mention of duration, in which case it can be assumed that the licence will last as long as the software is subject to copyright protection. The copyright owner will prefer to grant a licence because he will want to retain the copyright in the software and be free to grant licences to others. The licence may be exclusive, however, which means that the copyright owner cannot grant licences to others in respect of that software. More usually, the licence will be non-exclusive so that the copyright owner will be free to grant licences to anyone else he wishes to. An exclusive licence will be appropriate between an independent software writer and a software publisher who undertakes to market the programs on behalf of the writer (this type of arrangement and its contractual implications will be examined in Chapter 19). Sometimes, ownership of copyright will be transferred and this form of transaction is called an assignment of copyright.

The special nature of computer software and the fact that a copy of software is usually acquired by means of a licence have several legal implications. To begin with, the Sale of Goods Act 1979 does not apply to computer software as such. This Act is very important in the commercial world; in addition to being a very comprehensive regulator of contracts of sale it implies important terms into contracts such as requirements that the goods must match their description, be of satisfactory quality and that the seller has the right to sell the goods. However, 'goods' are defined by section 61(1) of the Act as including:

... all personal chattels other than things in action and money.

It seems unlikely, even if the copyright is transferred with the computer programs, that an intangible computer program resident on a magnetic disk or in a computer chip is a personal chattel (as opposed to the disk or chip), because copyright is a 'thing in action' like company shares or a money order, to be contrasted with the more tangible 'things in possession' such as motor cars or computers. Copyright is thus excluded from the definition of goods. In any case, a licence cannot be a sale of goods contract as there is no transfer of property. The result of all this is that the terms contained in the Sale of Goods Act which are implied into a contract for the sale of goods will not apply to a computer software contract at least as far as the software is concerned. Any tangible items such as magnetic disks transferred with the software may be subject to a collateral contract (a subsidiary or parallel contract). This may seem unfortunate as these implied terms are a very useful weapon for the buyer and, in the case of consumer sales, the implied terms cannot be excluded or modified at all. In non-consumer sales the implied terms can only be so excluded or modified if the terms purporting to do this are reasonable in accordance with the Unfair Contract Terms Act 1977, sections 5 to 7. Service contracts are also subject to implied terms, however.

Supply of Goods and Services Act 1982

The Supply of Goods and Services Act 1982 implies terms into contracts under which the property (ownership) in goods passes, and also into contracts for the hire of goods and contracts for services. Some of the terms implied are similar to those implied by the Sale of Goods Act. Examples of contracts governed by the Supply of Goods and Services Act are hybrid contracts: that is, those which involve part services and part goods such as a contract for the painting of a portrait. In this particular instance the service is the actual act of painting; the goods are the canvas, frame and paint. The Act also governs a contract purely for services, such as a contract for a haircut. Has the Supply of Goods and Services Act any relevance for computer software contracts? As far as 'goods' are concerned, the situation is the same as with a sale of goods contract because the definition of goods excludes things in action of which copyright is an example. The 1982 Act will be particularly relevant, however, if an independent computer firm or a programmer is engaged to write a computer program as this should come within the meaning of 'service'. The draftsmen of the Supply of Goods and Services Act elected not to attempt to define 'service', probably in deference to the very wide variety of services offered both to consumers and to businesses. There is good reason to believe, therefore, that a contract for writing a computer program will fall within that part of the Act dealing with the supply of services – sections 12 to 16. The fact that goods such as manuals and floppy disks may also be transferred does not prevent the contract from being a contract for the supply of services (section 12(3)).

Expert systems and other types of software, including databases, which provide information or advice could, arguably, be construed as supplying a service and thus fall within the ambit of the Supply of Goods and Services Act 1982. If this view is taken by the courts, bearing in mind that 'service' is not defined in the Act, it will result in the appropriate terms from the Act being implied into a contract for the supply of such computer software systems. The dealer who supplies an expert system may be deemed to be supplying a service (that is, providing the advice available from the system) even though others, such as the experts who provided the knowledge used in the system and the makers of the system, are responsible (in a non-legal sense) for how the system operates. This is because section 12(1) of the Supply of Goods and Services Act 1982 states that a 'contract for the supply of a service means':

... a contract under which a person (the supplier) agrees to carry out a service.

It may sometimes be difficult to determine the identity of the supplier where computer software is obtained off-the-shelf. For example, if an expert system is obtained from a dealer, is he the supplier or is it the company which made the expert system? In other words, who is the contracting party? Two possibilities exist: either the contract is between the person acquiring a copy of the system (the 'acquirer') and the dealer or it is between the acquirer and the software company, in which case the dealer acts as the company's agent. The answer to this is of crucial importance because of the doctrine of privity of contract: only the parties to a contract can sue on it. If the expert system turns out to be defective the acquirer will need to know who is liable. Apart from contract law there may be liability in negligence which does not depend on a contractual relationship and may even extend to others involved in the development of the system such as the experts who provided the knowledge contained in the system.

If a dealer has been asked to supply a suitable expert system it is possible that, by doing so, he carried out a service. By supplying expert systems, the dealer has enabled the advice-giving service to be performed and in some respects it is similar to the position where a supplier sub-contracts all or part of the work. The customer relies on the dealer to provide a suitable and effective system and, consequently, there is a duty on the dealer to select and recommend an adequate system (see *Stewart* v *Reavell's Garage* [1952] 2 QB 545). Therefore, dealers marketing expert systems should satisfy themselves as to the veracity and reliability of these systems and their suitability for particular customers. Dealers may also wish to consider including appropriate and reasonable exemption clauses in their supply contracts with respect to advice-giving computer systems.

The dealer as agent for the software company is a more likely interpretation if the acquirer specifies the system he wants. Of course, the fact that there will, invariably, be a licence agreement with the software company reinforces the view that the dealer acts as an agent to bring about the contract between the software company and the acquirer. The legal position is far from clear, however, and there is a lack of authority on this point. The situation is much simpler where software is written for and at the request of a client. This is a straightforward service contract between the client and the software developer and is covered by the Supply of Goods and Services Act 1982. This has been confirmed in *The Salvage Association* v *CAP Financial Services Ltd* [1995] FSR 654 in which the Official Referee in the High Court confirmed that a contract to develop new accounting software for a client was a service contract. He went on to imply into that contract section 13 of the Supply of Goods and Services Act 1982.

Section 13 implies a term that the supplier, if acting in the course of business, will carry out the service with reasonable care and skill. This restates the previous position at common law, that a person who holds himself out as being prepared to carry out a service is expected to exercise a level of skill that could be expected of a reasonably competent member of the relevant trade or profession. Therefore, if a firm engaged to write a computer program fails to measure up to the standards that would normally be expected from able computer programmers and the program turns out to be sub-standard then, *prima facie*, the firm will be liable in contract. It does not matter that the firm's employees tried their best; the question is: does the program meet this objective standard?

In the *Salvage Association* case it was held that there was a breach of section 13 and also a breach of an express term in the contract that the software developer would assign suitably qualified staff to perform the work. The staff originally assigned to write the software were insufficiently experienced in the use of ORACLE, the language in which the software was to be written.

Another term implied by the Supply of Goods and Services Act 1982 concerns the time for performance. Again, this only applies to suppliers acting in the course of business, although a similar term might be implied at common law. Section 14 states that, in the absence of an agreed time for performance or an agreed formula to determine the time for performance, the supplier will carry out the service in a reasonable time. The Act also says that what is reasonable is a question of fact; that is, it depends on the facts of the case. The case of *Charnock* v *Liverpool Corporation* [1968] 1 WLR 1498 gives an example of an unreasonable time. The defendant garage was liable in damages because it took eight weeks to repair a motor vehicle when a normally competent garage would have taken about five weeks. A contract for the writing of computer programs should have detailed provisions about completion times and all section 14 does is to provide a net to catch those instances where there has been an oversight. What is a reasonable time will depend on the nature of the programs and their complexity, taking into account the time required for testing and acceptance.

Section 15 of the Act states that, unless the contract fixes the payment or a method of calculating payment, the supplier will be paid a reasonable amount. Usually, the contract will mention the fee, but this provision might be useful if the supplier takes on additional work at the request of the other party and no mention is made at the time of agreement of the charge for this extra work. It means that the supplier cannot, much as he might like to, charge an unreasonably high price. Comparative fees and prices for writing similar software would provide a good indicator of what is reasonable.

Hardware acquisition

As far as computer equipment (hardware) is concerned, this may be purchased outright or hired. If purchased then the Sale of Goods Act 1979 will apply and terms as to quality, complying with description, satisfactory quality, etc. will be implied into the contract, subject to any valid exemption clauses. There have been some important changes to this Act. The Sale and Supply of Goods Act 1994 replaces the old section 14(2) of the Sale of Goods Act 1979 (which required that goods were of merchantable quality) with a new requirement that goods must be of satisfactory quality. This is stated by section 14(2A) to apply if the goods meet the standard that a reasonable person would regard as satisfactory. Account is to be taken of the description of the goods, the price (if relevant) and all other relevant circumstances. In a welcome tightening of the implied term, section 14(2B) defines the aspects of quality to be taken into account, being:

(a) fitness for all the purposes for which goods of the kind in question are commonly supplied (this is simply a restatement of the previous law);
(b) appearance and finish;
(c) freedom from minor defects;
(d) safety; and
(e) durability.

This implied term is a condition in England, Wales and Northern Ireland and applies where goods are sold in the course of business. In Scotland, it is simply a term, the remedies depending on whether the breach is a material one. For a breach of condition (or a material breach in Scotland), the buyer may reject the goods without prejudice to any claim for damages.

The old requirement that goods must be of merchantable quality caused injustice in a number of cases. It did not appear that the goods had to be durable and the presence of minor defects did not necessarily render goods unmerchantable. For example, in *Millars of Falkirk Ltd* v *Turpie*, 1987 SLT 66, it was held that an oil leak from the power-steering unit of a new car did not make the car unmerchantable and, in *Bernstein* v *Pamson Motors* [1987] 2 All ER 220, an engine seizure in a three-week-old car that had only covered 140 miles did not render the car unmerchantable. Only occasionally did the courts seem to take a sympathetic view of the buyer's position: for example, in *Rogers* v *Parish (Scarborough) Ltd* [1987] QB 933 the Court of Appeal recognised that the buyer of a luxury car such as a Range Rover had a right to expect a vehicle that did not continually break down and suffer from rust.

In the context of computers, the courts also took a fairly narrow view of unmerchantability and in *Micron Computer Systems Ltd* v *Wang (UK) Ltd* (unreported) 9 May 1990, the High Court considered that the failure of a computer's hard disk was a perfectly normal teething problem and did not give the buyer the right to reject the computer. Of course, the buyer may still have a claim to damages in respect of such a defect. Now, because of the test of satisfactory quality, it is more likely that the buyer of a computer with a faulty hard disk would be able to reject the computer and insist on a refund of the purchase price. The same should apply if the computer has an intermittent but troublesome fault.

If the supplier goes beyond the mere supply of the equipment and carries out some work such as assembling and installing the equipment, the Supply of Goods and Services Act 1982 will apply, as discussed above. If the contract is for the hire of the equipment, then the Supply of Goods and Services Act will apply, whether or not installation or other services are also provided by the supplier. An agreement which is described as a lease or a rental is essentially a contract of hire, and a hire agreement is one under which the possession of the goods passes to the other party but the property in the goods (the ownership) remains with the supplier. 'Hire' does not include hire-purchase agreements, which are covered by the Supply of Goods (Implied Terms) Act 1973 – this Act implies similar terms into the contract as under the Sale of Goods Act 1979. The relevant provisions in the Supply of Goods and Services Act 1982 regarding hire agreements include implied terms about the right of the supplier to transfer possession of the goods, that the goods must correspond with their description and implied terms about quality and fitness for purpose (sections 7 to 10). These terms are equivalent to those in the Sale of Goods Act.

Breach of contract

If a party to a contract is in breach of one or more of its terms, the remedy depends on the status of the particular term or terms which have been broken. The aggrieved party may want to repudiate the contract, treat the contract as discharged by reason of the other party's breach and recover any money he has paid out as well as any other expenses. In the *Salvage Association* case it was held that the client was entitled to repudiate the contract when it became clear that the software developer would fail to meet the extended deadline for delivery of the software. The client was entitled to £662 926 in damages being made up of:

- £291 388 paid under the contract;
- £231 866 wasted expenditure; and
- £139 672 wasted management time.

Alternatively, the injured party might prefer to hold the other party to the contract but would like some compensation for the breach and if the breach concerns a minor term this is usually the better solution. However, the injured

175

party does not always have a free choice as the law lays down rules determining and limiting the scope of remedies.

Traditionally there are two types of terms in contracts: 'conditions' and 'warranties'. The distinction is important because breach of a condition gives the other party the right to repudiate the contract and claim damages. For example, consider a contract to deliver a computer by '1 June at the latest'. If the machine has not been delivered by that date, the buyer can treat the failure to deliver as a breach of a condition and he can cancel the contract as time for delivery is usually construed as being a condition (see *Hartley* v *Hyams* [1920] 3 KB 475). Furthermore, the buyer can claim damages that would be equivalent to the difference in cost of buying another similar computer elsewhere and any other expenses and losses he has been put to as a direct consequence of the breach, with the proviso that he mitigates his losses – that is, he keeps them to a minimum. The buyer may have wanted the computer to expand his business and he will be able to claim the resulting loss in profits, provided the seller knew or should have known of this – that is, it was in the reasonable contemplation of the parties.

On the other hand, a breach of warranty allows the aggrieved party to claim damages only. The contract is still in force and must be completed by both parties. They must both perform the remainder of their agreed duties under the contract. For example, if a supplier has agreed to deliver a computer system and the contract states that the terminals are to be a deep yellow colour but, instead, he delivers a computer with lemon coloured terminals, this will amount to a breach of warranty unless there is some special reason why the deep yellow colour was specified. The buyer will be entitled to damages only and he will still have to pay the purchase price of the computer, although he may be able to set off a sum representing the damages. Damages are assessed on the basis of the damage naturally arising from the breach and in the contemplation of the parties. In the example given, the damages would be little more than nominal.

In *Koufos* v *C Czarnikow Ltd* [1969] 1 AC 350, a ship was chartered by sugar merchants to transport a cargo of sugar. The shipowners knew that there was a sugar market at the port of destination but did not know that the merchants wanted to sell the sugar immediately on its arrival. The ship deviated from the agreed voyage and arrived about ten days late; in the meantime the price of sugar had fallen and the merchants lost over £4000. It was held that this loss should be recoverable from the shipowners because they should reasonably have contemplated that the delay would have resulted in a loss. The shipowners knew there was a commodity market at the destination and that prices would be liable to fluctuate, so that any delay could lead to a diminution of the value of the cargo. Unfortunately, this does not appear to work the other way – the shipowners would not be entitled to any share in a windfall profit if the market value of the cargo increased dramatically and was sold for much more than it would have done had it arrived on time.

How does the basic principle that damages are based on the losses that were within the contemplation of the parties when the contract was made work in the context of computers? Suppose that you run a computer bureau and carry out ordinary data processing work. You decide to expand the business and buy a more powerful computer to be delivered by a certain date. You tell the supplier that you need the computer to carry out some additional data processing but neglect to inform him that you are negotiating a very lucrative top secret government contract on the basis of having the new computer. If the computer is delivered late, then you would be entitled to damages based on the loss in profits in the normal course of business but you would not be entitled to anything should you lose the government contract. This is simply because the supplier did not know, and could not reasonably be expected to know, of this potential contract. A buyer should therefore consider informing a supplier of all the uses to which the equipment or programs will be put, especially if they are unusual.

The distinction between conditions and warranties is not always clear. Sometimes a contractual term lies in a grey area between the two. If the term is broken, then it will be classified in the light of the facts surrounding the breach and it will depend on the facts as to whether the breach goes to the root of the contract. If it does, then the term will be effectively promoted to the rank of condition with all that that entails; otherwise it will be classed as a warranty. These intermediate terms are called innominate terms and their nature is determined retrospectively, after a breach. The case which paved the way for this approach was *Hong Kong Fir Shipping Co Ltd* v *Kawasaki Kisen Kaisha* [1962] QB 26, in which it was held that a term implied in a hire contract for a ship that it must be seaworthy was such an innominate term. The nature of the breach determined the nature of the contractual term. For example, if the ship had a 5 degree list and was badly leaking it would be totally unseaworthy and this would be a breach of a condition enabling the hirer to repudiate the contract. However, if the breach concerned some trifling defect, perhaps a mere technicality, which could be put right very quickly and easily, the term would be classed as a warranty. For example, if a word processing program is acquired which is claimed by the supplier to be a 'professional package' and it does not have a built-in thesaurus, this might be considered to be a breach of warranty. It cannot be truly said that the breach goes to the root of the contract if the program has all the other usual features normally found in powerful word processing systems. However, if the package does not include features such as right-justification, a spelling checker and cut-and-paste facilities this would be more serious and could make the system virtually useless in a business environment. Such a breach would go to the root of the contract and would be a breach of a condition, giving the person acquiring the program the right to cancel the contract and recover the cost of the system plus any direct losses.

This way of looking at terms and not deciding their status until there has been a breach is very useful as it gives a welcome degree of flexibility to contracts, although it could be criticised for introducing uncertainty. There may be some terms, however, which are obviously conditions: for example, if the contract is for the delivery of a particular make of computer, and the seller attempts to deliver a different make altogether, this would clearly be a breach of condition.

What sort of terms in computer contracts could be described as innominate terms? Suppose that a contract is made for the provision of a network to link individual computers together, a term in the contract stating that the network will support at least 16 personal computers. If there is a small degradation of performance when 15 or more machines are in use but otherwise the network is fine, this might be regarded as a breach of warranty. On the other hand, if it turns out that the network fails when more than seven machines are in use, the term would be regarded as a condition. Sometimes a term can start as a condition, become a warranty and then revert to a condition. In *Rickards* v *Oppenheim* [1950] 1 KB 616, the defendant wanted a body built on his Rolls-Royce chassis and he agreed that the plaintiffs (from whom he had purchased the chassis) could use a sub-contractor to do this specialised work, which should have been completed in March 1948. The work was not complete by that time and, although time for delivery is usually a condition, the defendant did not cancel the contract as he was entitled to do, but continued to press for delivery, thereby waiving his right to cancel. In the end the defendant gave an ultimatum. He said that the car must be ready by 25 July 1948 and that he would refuse to take delivery after that date. The car was not ready by that date, so the defendant bought another car elsewhere and claimed back the price he had paid for the chassis. It was held that when time for delivery is of the essence of a contract for the sale of goods (that is, a condition) and, after the stipulated time has elapsed, the buyer waives his right to cancel by pressing for delivery, converting the term into a warranty, he may later give notice setting a reasonable deadline, once again making the time for delivery a condition of the contract.

It is not unusual for new software to be delivered late. In this case, the client must be careful when granting extensions of time and should bear in mind that he will hope to avoid fudging the issue of the date at which he can repudiate the contract on the grounds of the software developer's late delivery. It is essential that any extensions be agreed in writing with the new date being firmly stated as a condition. If this is not done, the client must allow a reasonable time when delivering an ultimatum to the software developer. It is not satisfactory to allow work to drag on for months and then to suddenly state that the contract will be repudiated if the software is not completed 'by the end of this week'.

It is common to find provisions for late delivery and late payment included in contracts. The contract might state that the supplier will pay £150 per week if he delivers late, or that the buyer will pay interest at 0.75 per cent above the current base bank rate, should he be late in making payment. Predetermined damages, known as liquidated damages, are frequently found in contracts. 'Liquidated' simply means that the damages or the method of calculating them are fixed and agreed. Liquidated damages are to be distinguished from a penalty. Liquidated damages are a genuine pre-estimate of the loss resulting from the breach, whereas a penalty, which might be out of all proportion to the loss suffered, will not be enforced by the courts. The stipulation of liquidated damages for breach of a particular term contradicts the possibility of that term being a condition. Terms backed by liquidated damages will usually not be regarded as conditions, therefore, unless the scale of the breach is considerable.

In practice, many terms will be innominate terms, in which case it will only be possible to determine whether breach of the term allows a party to repudiate the contract in the light of the actual facts of the breach. This accords with Scots practice where the question is whether the breach is a material one. Provisions concerning the performance of a computer system, how fast the programs work in practice and the degree of compatibility with other equipment are likely to be innominate terms. Terms which will probably be classed as conditions from the beginning deal with aspects such as the time for delivery and the description of the actual computer concerned. Time for payment is usually treated as being a warranty unless the contract states otherwise or the circumstances suggest a different interpretation (see, for example, section 10(1) of the Sale of Goods Act 1979).

By its very nature, when delivered, bespoke software often contains errors and it may be some time before they can all be traced and corrected. It is a brave software producer who claims that his software is error-free. The contractual position was considered in *Saphena Computing* v *Allied Collection Agencies* [1995] FSR 616. A contract for writing a number of programs was terminated while there were still errors in the programs. The Court of Appeal accepted that software was not a commodity that was handed over once and for all and that it would usually require testing and further modification. It would not, therefore, be a breach of contract to deliver software that might, initially, have a defect in it. Usually, the supplier would have a right and a duty to correct the errors within a reasonable time. In this particular case the client, who had a copy of the source code, could carry out error correction himself but, because he had brought the contract to an end, the supplier would cease to be liable for the remaining errors.

Misrepresentation

If you are negotiating with a salesman with a view to acquiring computer software, he may make statements regarding the software and its performance. It is not unknown for a salesman to describe the product in glowing terms and you would expect him to highlight the best features. Sometimes, he can go too far; he may be anxious to make a sale and may make statements which are simply untrue in an effort to try to induce you to buy the product. Some statements are so wild that no one is expected to take them seriously; these are sometimes referred to as salesman's 'puff'. Examples abound from the second-hand motor trade: for example, an ageing car may be described as being 'immaculate'. Such statements are not to be taken seriously and the courts would not support a case brought on them. Less extravagant statements, however, if untrue, may give rise to remedies. The standing of the statement needs initially to be determined and it may be elevated to the rank of contractual term if the courts consider on the facts that this was the intention of the parties. If this happens then normal contractual remedies are available to the aggrieved party if the statement turns out to be untrue.

If the statement does not become incorporated into the contract, it is said to be a representation – something said in the course of the negotiations leading up to the contract itself. It may well induce the other party to conclude the contract, in which case a remedy may be available on the basis of misrepresentation if the statement turns out to be untrue. Obviously, if the party, to whom the representation is made, knows that the statement is untrue he will not have any remedy. He has entered into the contract with his eyes open to the true facts; the statement itself will not have influenced him.

There are three forms of misrepresentation: fraudulent, negligent and innocent. If the representation has been made fraudulently (or recklessly, not caring whether or not it is true), then at common law the remedy of rescission is available (setting the contract aside as if it had never been made at all), together with a right to recover any money laid out. Fraud may be difficult to prove; the person making the statement may simply say that he honestly believed, at the time he made it, that it was true. The Misrepresentation Act 1967, as amended by the Unfair Contract Terms Act 1977, made the situation more satisfactory. Rescission is the standard remedy for misrepresentation but this may cause hardship; therefore, in the case of negligent or innocent misrepresentation, a court may award damages in lieu of rescission by section 2 of the Misrepresentation Act. This is important because rescission is an equitable remedy and as such will only be ordered by the courts if the aggrieved party has acted promptly. Formerly, if the aggrieved party had already accepted the goods, the very fact of acceptance would mean that rescission would not be available. Imagine that a company buys a computer. It is important that this computer is directly compatible with its existing equipment and the supplier confirms in good faith, before the contract is made, that the computer is compatible although the contract itself is silent on the matter. Some weeks after accepting delivery and paying for the computer, it is found that, although the computer works well in every other respect, it is not compatible with the company's other machines and cannot reasonably be made so. Before the 1967 Act, the company acquiring the computer would have no remedy for this innocent misrepresentation, unless it was deemed to be a contractual term, as it would be too late to have the contract set aside. Now the courts would be likely to award damages instead, which might be considerable in our example. The better approach would have been for the company to insist that an express term was inserted into the contract to the effect that the computer to be acquired must be compatible with the existing equipment.

Summary

In this chapter the basic implications of computer contracts have been discussed. Apart from the difficulties arising from classifying software contracts the law is relatively well settled. One remaining difficulty is to apply that law to computer technology. For example, how do we set the standards for reasonable care and skill and quality in relation to computer hardware and software? Fortunately, to date, judges have shown themselves reasonably well equipped to do this, though some doubts remain.

Of greater uncertainty is the potential for liability for defective software and this is something which is examined in the following chapter together with a consideration of the effectiveness of exemption clauses, limiting or excluding liability for defective software or, indeed, for breach of contract. Case law has amply demonstrated the care that must be taken in this respect when drafting computer contracts.

Chapter 16

Liability for defective hardware or software

Introduction

There have been a number of occasions when defects in software have had very serious implications. The term 'safety-critical' is applied to software (and hardware) which is used in situations involving risk to life and limb. For example, in 1992 it was discovered that around 1000 patients at a North Staffordshire hospital had received incorrect dosages of radiation therapy because of an alleged fault in a computer program. Later that same year the London Ambulance's new computer system failed dramatically throwing the ambulance service into chaos and, possibly, resulting in a number of deaths caused by the consequential delays in getting ambulances to their call-out destinations.

Defects in computer equipment and software can cause all manner of damage. The failure of flight control systems, nuclear power station systems and defence systems could result in major loss of life. The same could be true of software used to design buildings and vehicles. Defects in other systems might result in financial loss only such as where an expert system is used to provide financial advice. The fact that organisations developing or supplying software or manufacturing and distributing hardware could be liable for the consequences of failure requires them to consider means of reducing or limiting liability and, while practical measures such as quality control and testing are of vital importance, regard must be had to the legal position regarding defects.

The 'Millennium Bug' has focused minds recently as regards the potential for disaster caused by 'computer error'. That particular problem is caused by the old (and now clearly perceived to be foolish) convention of only using two digits to store the year of a date. Thus, the date 4 August 1999 would be stored in a form equivalent to 04/08/99. Where a calculation is performed which involves dates, such as in determining the duration of some computer controlled process or operation, it is obvious that things can quickly go wrong on or after 1 January 2000. The convention of using two digits for the year was a result of a desire to save what was then very expensive computer storage. Additionally, most programmers working in the 1960s and 1970s thought the programs they were working on would become redundant long before the Millennium. In those days, in terms of the pace of development of computer technology, the turn of the century seemed an awful long way off.

If a person suffers loss or damage as a result of defective hardware or software, one or more of the following areas of law might provide a remedy:

- contract;
- law of negligence;
- negligent misstatement; or
- product liability.

The basic principles of contractual liability have already been discussed in Chapter 15 and often can provide the simplest route to a satisfactory remedy. However, because of the doctrine of privity of contract, only the parties to a contract can sue upon it. If the aggrieved person is not in a contractual relationship with the person responsible for the loss or damage, other areas of law must be looked to for a remedy.

Once the risks and liabilities have been identified, the contract should provide a suitable mechanism for apportioning liability between the parties. Insurance can then be obtained to cover the potential losses resulting from defects and from issues relating to the performance of the contract. This is important as recent case law has amply demonstrated that reliance on contract terms, limiting liability to a relatively small sum, is misplaced.

In this chapter, forms of liability for defects, other than contractual, are examined. The focus is upon the law of negligence, negligent misstatement and product liability. These areas are of particular concern because they impose liability in respect of loss or damage sustained by third parties. Finally, the legal control of exemption clauses and notices, which attempt to exclude or limit liability, is considered.

Negligence

Negligence is part of an area of law known as tort. Basically, a tort is a civil wrong, independent of contract. It imposes legal liabilities on a person who has acted carelessly or unreasonably omits to do something. Under certain circumstances a person will be liable to another for failing to exercise a required duty of care. In the case of consumer goods, such as a table lamp or television set, if the negligence of the manufacturer causes them to be defective, then the person injured as a result will be entitled to damages. A claim in negligence does not depend on the presence of a contract, so if the person injured is someone other than the buyer, that person can still sue. The buyer also should be able to sue, but on the basis of breach of contract if the item is defective and fails to comply with implied terms such as that concerning satisfactory quality. To be able to sue in negligence, three essential ingredients must be present:

- a duty of care owed to the injured party;
- a breach of that duty of care; and
- consequential loss – that is, loss which is a direct and natural result of the breach of duty of care.

The landmark case on negligence is *Donoghue* v *Stevenson* [1932] AC 562, in which the plaintiff had been bought a bottle of ginger beer by a friend in a café. The bottle was made of opaque glass and so the contents could not be seen. The café owner poured part of the contents into a glass which the plaintiff drank. The plaintiff's friend then poured out the rest of the contents and the decomposed remains of a snail came out of the bottle. The plaintiff suffered shock and severe gastroenteritis as a result of the revolting sight and the fact that she had already swallowed some of the ginger beer. The plaintiff could not sue in contract because she was not a party to the contract – it had been her friend who had bought the drink. Nevertheless, the House of Lords held that a manufacturer who sold food or medicine or the like in containers of a nature that the distributor or ultimate purchasers or consumers could not discover the defect by inspection is under a legal duty to the ultimate purchaser or consumer to take reasonable care that the article is free from any defect likely to cause injury to health. This duty of care is owed to any person who might be contemplated to be injured by the act or omission of the manufacturer (the 'neighbour' or proximity test). Negligence can be thought of as an early form of product liability and has developed over the years to its present wide scope, although this is tempered to some extent by the growth of insurance. It is also limited, to some extent, by policy considerations. This is particularly so where the loss is purely economic or the claim is in respect of nervous shock.

What is the significance of the tort of negligence as far as computers and software are concerned? Although it is unlikely that decomposing snails will be found within the workings of computers, it is possible to come across computer 'bugs' and there may still be some further nasty surprises. At first sight it may seem unlikely that computers and computer software could kill or cause serious injury; however, negligent liability does not stop at personal injury but extends to damage to property. Computer equipment runs on electricity so there is always the danger of electrical shock and, if this results from negligence, there is a strong possibility of an action in negligence. But what if a large passenger aircraft has to be fuelled ready for flight? A computer program is used to calculate the amount of fuel required. This is based on information such as the number of passengers, the weight of baggage, the flight distance and prevailing winds, etc. Then, because of a hitherto undiscovered bug in the computer program, less fuel is loaded than required, with the result that the aircraft runs out of fuel over the mid-Atlantic. It is possible that the company writing the computer program was negligent in its testing of the program. The total size of the claims resulting from such an incident might well be enormous, even though the copy of the computer program may have cost only a few hundred pounds.

Other nightmare scenarios include where an air traffic control system contains a software error which incorrectly records the location of an aircraft or where a railway signalling system contains a fault or where guidance software directs a missile with a warhead to the wrong location. Of course, although most software errors do not have catastrophic effects, they can have very costly consequences if they are not spotted. A simple error in software to assist self-employed persons calculate their tax liability for the purposes of self-assessment of tax resulted in many people underestimating their tax liability bringing the possibility of fines from the Inland Revenue (*The Times*, 13 August 1997, p 5). The error was a mistake where pounds and pence were confused. In this case, most of the persons affected would have contractual remedies had they fined on the basis of the licence agreement with the software developer (subject to any valid exclusion or limitation clauses).

The fact that an action in negligence lies without the need for a contract is important both for computer program writers and manufacturers of computer equipment. If a program is licensed by a publisher, the program author could be liable in negligence even though he is not a party to the licence agreement. In the case of computer hardware, a person suffering loss or injury as a result of the negligence of the manufacturer will have a claim in negligence against the manufacturer regardless of the fact that the equipment was bought from a dealer.

There are limitations, however, to the scope of the law of negligence and, as mentioned above, certain ingredients must be present. A person writing a computer program, or a company manufacturing computer equipment will not necessarily be potentially liable to the world at large in negligence; they will be liable, however, to those whom they could contemplate being adversely affected by any negligent act or omission by them. A further limiting factor is that the plaintiff bears the burden of proof; he has to show that the defendant was negligent and this is not always easy to do. There may be an exception if the event causing the injury or damage could only be reasonably explained by assuming there had been negligence. This is known to lawyers as *res ipsa loquitur*, that is, 'the thing speaks for itself'. If you are hit on the head by a pot of paint while walking under a ladder you would not be asked to show the precise act of negligence that caused the paint to fall; it goes without saying that someone had been negligent. This is the exception, however, and normally the plaintiff must prove the negligent act or omission.

Even if negligence is proved, the amount of damages awarded may be reduced if the plaintiff has contributed in a causal sense to the negligence. If a computer has been badly made and is an electrical hazard then, if the person who has been electrocuted had tampered with the machine, the damages awarded may be reduced in proportion to the extent of his contribution to the accident. Fortunately, death or personal injury resulting from the use of a

185

computer has been a rare occurrence, but other forms of loss or damage might be more common: for example, in a business context where a computer may be used to assist with decision-making, there is a strong probability that a financial loss will be blamed on the computer. However, an action based solely on economic loss is unlikely to succeed under the normal law of negligence due to policy considerations. It may be possible in such a case to base an action on negligent misstatement instead, as described later.

Negligence and RSI

Typists, word processor operators and data entry operators spend long periods of time at a keyboard. By doing so, they may risk acquiring some form of cramp or painful condition in their wrists and fingers which is often described as repetitive strain injury or RSI. That is not, however, a medical term of precision, but for some time the Department of Health has recognised a condition known simply as PDA4 which is on a list of prescribed diseases for the purposes of industrial injury benefit. It is defined as cramp of the hand or forearm due to repetitive movements, such as writer's cramp. The types of occupations where it is possible are those which involve prolonged periods of handwriting, typing or other repetitive movements of the fingers, hand or arm.

The most important case to date on RSI (or PDA4) in the context of a word processor operator was *Pickford* v *Imperial Chemical Industries Ltd* (unreported) 25 June 1998. The plaintiff worked for the defendant for a number of years as a secretary and spent around 50 per cent of her time using a word processor. She claimed that, at times, that went up to 75 per cent. Eventually, she complained of pain in both hands and, after consulting a number of doctors and specialists, she commenced proceedings against her employer alleging negligence. She claimed that it was reasonably foreseeable that operating the word processor for long periods without breaks or rest periods would cause the condition and that the employer was negligent in failing to warn her of it and the need to take rest breaks. At the trial, the judge found that the plaintiff failed to establish the case against her employer but the Court of Appeal overturned that decision by a 2:1 majority. The employer appealed to the House of Lords which allowed the appeal by a 4:1 majority.

The majority in the House of Lords considered that the Court of Appeal was wrong to overturn the decision of the trial judge. All the relevant issues related to findings of fact and an appeal court will interfere with such a finding only in exceptional circumstances as it is the trial judge who has the benefit of seeing and hearing the witnesses including, in this case, a number of expert and lay witnesses. Lord Hope of Craighead made a number of observations as follows:

- PDA4 has two possible causes: one is organic and the other is that its basis is psychogenic (that is, 'it is all in the mind'), the product of conversion hysteria whereby the mind uses the body to escape from an objectionable working situation,
- medical opinion is divided as to the cause,
- the trial judge rightly decided that the plaintiff failed to prove that the cause was organic and the defendant did not have to prove that the cause was psychogenic (the burden of proof lay on the plaintiff),
- the judge was right to hold that PDA4 resulting from typing work was not reasonably foreseeable, in the light of the state of knowledge at the time the plaintiff developed the condition (that is, in 1988–89),
- the nature of the work meant that the plaintiff had ample non-typing work to intersperse with her word processing and, consequently, there was no duty on the employer to prescribe rest periods,
- there was no duty on the employer to warn of the dangers of PDA4 – this was particularly so as issuing such a warning might bring about the condition, given that one possible cause was psychogenic.

Although the plaintiff failed in her claim, that does not mean to say that word processor operators and others who, as part of their work, spend long periods at a keyboard would also fail. In the present case, the plaintiff failed to prove causation – that is, that her injury was caused by the negligence of the employer. Indeed, the dissenting judge, Lord Steyn, said that among the 'tangled words and imperfect scientific insights' the central proved facts established that the plaintiff's work caused her disability and this could, had the employer exercised reasonable care, have avoided the occurrence of the disability.

One point to make is that it appears that an action might lie only if the court accepts that the cause is an organic one. If the court finds that it is a result of the mind (psychogenic), any claim is bound to fail. That is somewhat controversial as to the sufferer the pain and discomfort will probably feel just as real and it might have been brought on by having to work at a keyboard at high speed for intolerable periods. In terms of causation, the injury will be the result of the work.

The case raises the question of what advice an employer should give to an employee about the dangers of working at a keyboard for long periods of time without breaks. To warn specifically of PDA4 might induce it in persons of a nervous disposition. The best approach, as was suggested in the above case, is to tell employees simply to go and see a doctor if unusual pain or discomfort is experienced. To warn word processor operators and the like that if they developed pain they would never work again was, in the words of one expert witness, 'disgraceful'. The defendant had an excellent record with respect to health and safety and gave advice to persons using computers with respect to eye-strain and ensured that work stations were suitably designed and sited.

Computers have been claimed to be harmful to the health of the operator because of radioactive emissions, although at the present time there does not appear to be any conclusive proof that a real danger to health exists. If a definite association were to be found, however, between the occurrence of skin cancers or miscarriages and the continued use of computer monitors, then computer manufacturers and importers who continued to make or sell equipment giving off such dangerous emissions would be liable. There may also be implications under the Health and Safety at Work etc. Act 1974 if an employer persists in requiring his staff to use such machines. The producer would have to consider fitting some device such as an ionisation screen to absorb the rays and, in the absence of a technological way of overcoming the problem, might be forced to withdraw the product until such time as a solution could be found. As regards computer display screens, there is specific legislation dealing with their use and safety and extending to the ergonomic features of the computer equipment and the desk at which the computer operator sits (Health and Safety (Display Screen Equipment) Regulations 1992). These regulations came into force on 1 January 1993. Nowadays, most screen displays are designed to minimise radioactive emissions. Nevertheless, a good employer should ensure that the equipment and the manner in which it is used is not such as to give operators eye-strain or other injuries.

Negligent misstatement

It is in terms of expert systems or other items of computer software designed to provide advice that the potential for liability for negligence takes on special significance. If the system is used to derive advice for a professional to use in the execution of his duties, the ultimate recipient of the advice may find that he has a right of action against the professional or the system developer (or even the independent experts and knowledge engineers engaged by the system developer). The leading case on tortious liability for negligent advice, referred to as negligent misstatement, is *Hedley Byrne & Co Ltd* v *Heller & Partners Ltd* [1964] AC 465. In that case, the House of Lords concluded that a bank giving information as to the liquidity of one of its own customers to another bank so that the latter could show the information to one of its customers could be liable to that customer, even though the first bank did not know the identity of the second bank's customer – the ultimate recipient of the information. The fact was that the bank giving the reference must have appreciated that the information would be shown to a customer of the other bank and this was sufficient to satisfy the 'neighbour test'. Therefore, the required relationship exists where one person holds himself out as an expert and gives advice which is intended to be taken seriously and acted upon even though no contractual relationship exists.

This could have the effect of making the persons and organisations responsible for the creation of expert systems liable to the ultimate consumers of the advice generated. The experts who provided the rules and facts used by the system, the knowledge engineers who formalised the knowledge, the programmers and analysts responsible for designing the inferencing and interface programs could find themselves liable if the advice generated by use of the system is incorrect. There are, however, two factors which might negate or reduce liability. The first is whether a duty of care will be imposed and the second is the status of any disclaimer. Although the people involved in the development of the system are directly responsible for the performance and accuracy of the system, they have little control over the way the system will be used or interpreted. Unlike a simple bank reference where the significance and use of the information provided is fairly obvious, the advice obtained from an expert system depends on the interaction between the system and its user. As expert systems are designed for use by persons who have some general understanding of the knowledge domain, it is reasonable to assume that the user will take at least some of the responsibility for the output obtained. However, a professional such as a general medical practitioner who has to seek the advice of a specialist consultant will find it difficult to verify and validate the advice of the specialist and this is true also of expert systems which contain knowledge beyond that of the user of the system. Lack of control over the use to which the information will be put does not in itself negate liability. The central issue is whether a duty of care will be imposed by law. In *Caparo Industries plc* v *Dickman* [1990] 2 AC 605, it was held that there are three criteria for imposing a duty of care:

- foreseeability of damage;
- proximity of relationship; and
- the reasonableness or otherwise of imposing a duty of care.

In that case, a company bought additional shares in another company following receipt of audited accounts prepared by the defendant. The House of Lords said that liability for statements, put into general circulation in such circumstances that they might foreseeably be relied on by strangers, would only be imposed when the maker of the statement knew it would be communicated to the person relying on it either as an individual or member of a class and that it would be likely to be relied on for a known purpose. In the present case it was held that an auditor owed no duty of care to the general public nor to individual shareholders who relied on the accounts to buy shares because of a lack of proximity. To hold otherwise would give rise to unlimited liability on the part of the auditor. However, in allowing a claim by the intended beneficiaries of a will which should, but for the negligence of the solicitor acting for the person making the will (the testator), have been prepared before the testator died, the House of Lords, in *White* v *Jones* [1995] 2 AC 207, raised the spectre of widening the scope of persons to whom a duty of care was owed. Two of the five Law Lords dissented on the basis that this could lead to the recognition of an extensive new area of potential liability.

Advice produced using expert systems or other decision-support systems is nearer to the *Hedley Byrne* facts than those of *Caparo* v *Dickman* in which the primary purpose of the information was to comply with a statutory requirement, that is, having the company's accounts audited. Advice flowing from expert systems is intended to be taken seriously and acted upon. If the system is designed to produce advice as to trading in stocks and shares that is precisely the use to which it will be put. Therefore, the law of negligent misstatement ought to apply to such systems.

On the other hand factual software such as a database of vehicle performances lies nearer to the *Caparo* v *Dickman* case. The maker of the database has no clear idea as to the particular uses to which the data will be used, unless it has been sold for a specific purpose. Thus, the maker of the database should not be liable to a third party in respect of a mistake contained within it. He may be contractually liable, however, to the purchaser of a copy of the database. Of course, many computer systems lie between these two extremes.

In the *Hedley Byrne* case, the bank providing the advice was able to escape liability because it had printed a clear disclaimer on the information excluding legal responsibility for the advice. Since the *Hedley Byrne* case, the Unfair Contract Terms Act 1977 was enacted to control, *inter alia*, exclusion or limitation of liability for negligence, whether under contract or tort. As far as business liability for death or personal injury is concerned, it cannot be excluded or limited by a notice or term in a contract. In other cases, the notice or term must satisfy the requirement of reasonableness. Furthermore, the use of a disclaimer will be effective only if it is clear and unambiguous and drawn to the attention of the person relying on the advice. Figure 16.1 shows the potential liability (tortious and contractual) with respect to incorrect advice derived from a defective expert system. It assumes that the experts and knowledge engineers are consultants to the software company and not its employees (this will be a common arrangement in practice).

The person using an expert system to advise a client will be potentially liable under the laws of contract and negligence. Liability will not be avoided simply because the system has a fault and the same principles apply here as in the case of conventional computer software. It might be important to consider whether it would be reasonable for the person using the system for the purpose of advising others to rely on the system's output. In relation to the exercise of a profession such as medicine, the fact that a person has acted in accordance with practice which is recognised as proper by a responsible body of persons skilled in that profession means that there has been no negligence. In *De Freitas* v *O'Brien* [1995] 6 Med LR 108, however, the Court of Appeal stressed that a responsible body of expert opinion does not have to be a substantial body. A small number of specialists could constitute a 'responsible body'.

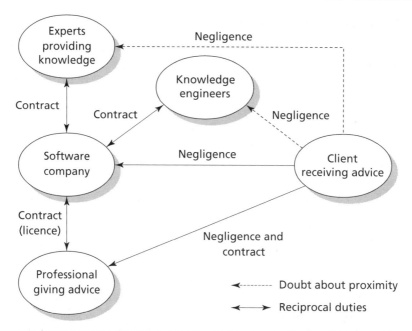

Note: For a duty to arise in negligence, owed to the client by anyone other than the person giving advice, it would have to be shown that the client relied on that person's statement rather than on the statement of the person giving advice.

Fig. 16.1 Liability for defective advice from an expert system

Consider an expert system designed to recommend financial investments which is used by a responsible body of financial advisers. If a particular financial adviser uses the system to recommend an investment to a client, the adviser will not be negligent if the system was used in a reasonable and satisfactory manner, even if the advice turns out to be bad retrospectively. The problem is that, until such time as a particular expert system is used by a sufficient number of skilled practitioners (sufficient to be classed as a responsible body), anyone using an expert system is taking a chance should the advice turn out to be wrong, although it must be stressed that the fact that advice is wrong does not inevitably and conclusively mean that there has been negligence. In *Whitehouse* v *Jordan* [1981] 1 All ER 267, the House of Lords confirmed that an error of judgment does not automatically indicate negligence; it depends whether the error would have been made by a reasonably competent professional man professing to have the standard and type of skill that the defendant held himself out to have. If the person using the expert system does not have the degree of skill and knowledge contained in the system he should make this clear to the client and obtain his agreement prior to using the system. The advantage of negligent misstatement over normal negligence claims is that it can be used where the loss has been economic only, although it is not restricted to this.

Liability for indirect statements

Where the original maker of the statement does not directly communicate it to the person relying on it, it appears that for a duty of care to arise, the latter must realise who is the source of the statement. In *Abbott* v *Strong* (unreported) *The Times*, 9 July 1998, a firm of accountants made statements as to a profits forecast, which were included in a circular sent to shareholders inviting them to subscribe for new shares in a rights issue. It was held that the accountants were not potentially liable for any misstatement to shareholders who subscribed as they had not relied on the accountants' statement. Where a person makes a statement to another person who uses it to advise another but that other does not know of the first person's participation in the advice, then the recipient cannot be said to have relied on the first person. Thus, where a person uses computer software in order to advise a client who believes that the advice comes from the person using the software alone, then any person who has been involved in the development of the software cannot be liable to the client in tort. Of course, this will be different if the client knows that the advice derived from using the software emanates from a person or persons involved in the development of the software, such as in the case of an expert system which contains rules and advice set forward by a particular person.

This approach is based on the concept of reliance. The person originally giving the advice cannot be liable if the ultimate recipient is shown not to have relied on that person but on advice given by another (even if originally given by that person) and can be contrasted with *Hedley Byrne* where it was clear that the recipient of the advice did indeed rely upon the first bank. The recipient's bank was merely the messenger. Thus, if a patient, Tom Cobb, consults a general practitioner, Dr Akerman, in respect of an illness and the doctor uses diagnostic software which includes diagnostic rules and suggested treatment devised by a specialist, Mr Rudge, he will not have a claim against Mr Rudge as he does not rely on him. It is Dr Akerman on whom Tom Cobb relies. It would be different if Dr Akerman first told Tom Cobb that he was going to use a computer system which contained advice from Mr Rudge, a specialist in the field.

The need for reliance does not necessarily require that the recipient of the statement knows the precise identity of the person from whom the advice originated providing that he knew it came from some other person. Reliance as an essential ingredient in an action for negligent misstatement was confirmed by the House of Lords in *Williams* v *Natural Health Foods Ltd* [1998] 2 All ER 577. In that case it was held that a director of a franchisor company (the franchise was in respect of health food shops) was not liable to the franchisees for loss resulting from negligent advice *given by the franchisor company* as there was no evidence that the franchisees believed that the director was undertaking a personal responsibility to them. In the example given in Figure 16.1, if liability for negligent misstatement is to be imposed on anyone other than the professional giving the advice directly to the client, it would be necessary to show that the client relied on any statement made by that person.

Negligent provision of a service and concurrent liability

At first, it was thought that *Hedley Byrne* was limited to negligent statements but it is now apparent that it also applies to the negligent provision of a service. In *Henderson* v *Merrett Syndicates Ltd* [1995] 2 AC 145, discussed later, Lord Goff said that there was no reason why a person should not be liable under the *Hedley Byrne* principle for economic loss which flows from the negligent performance of a service, and this sentiment was approved in *Williams* v *Natural Health Foods Ltd* [1998] 2 All ER 577. The provision of the service must be coupled with a concomitant reliance and will often be set in the context of a contract. This brings into question whether there can be concurrent liability under contract and tort where, for example, a service is provided under a contract.

At one time it was thought that where there was a contract between the parties, that contract would provide the sole basis for the injured party seeking a remedy. At least liability in negligence could not be imposed if it contradicted the express terms of a contract. However, the position was clarified in *Henderson* v *Merrett Syndicates Ltd* [1995] 2 AC 145, where the main issue was whether the defendants (managers of syndicates at Lloyd's) could be liable concurrently in contract and tort to Lloyd's underwriters for the negligent management of syndicates to which the underwriters belonged.

The House of Lords held that such concurrent liability can exist unless the contract itself precludes it. This means that in many cases, the injured party may choose whether to sue on the contract or in tort. Although in many cases the outcome will be the same in practical terms, in some the contractual and tortious duties may be different and the limitation periods may be different. The limitation period is the time within which an action must be commenced, otherwise it will be time-barred. For contract it is six years from the breach (Limitation Act 1980, section 5), while for negligence (and negligent misstatement) generally it is six years from the date the damage occurred (Limitation Act 1980, section 2); although for personal injury cases, the period is three years.

As an example of the above principles, consider a situation whereby Conway Computer Systems Ltd has agreed to maintain for one year the computer system of Willett & Co Ltd, a company with a parcel delivery operation. The contract states that Conway will remedy any defects within 24 hours of being informed by Willett and there is a clause in the contract providing for the payment of £500 per day in liquidated damages by Conway for every 24-hour period in excess of the first such period during which the computer system remains out of action because of a defect. One day, Willett informed Conway of a fault on its computer system. Due to the negligence of its programmers, Conway took 72 hours to remedy the defect. Under the contract Conway is liable to pay £1000 to Willett. However, under the circumstances, Willett's operations were badly disrupted and its total loss was in the order of £15 000. It was reasonably foreseeable that Willett would be so affected by its computer system being inoperable for such a period of time. That being so, the damages arising out of negligence ought to be in the order of £15 000, whereas, under contract, they are only £1000. Although, theoretically, there are concurrent liabilities in contract and tort, it would be highly unlikely that a court would allow Willett to pursue a remedy in tort as the contract has an express limitation on the measure of damages for failure to repair the defect in time. If the limiting clause did not exist, however, it would seem that Willett could be free to chose which route to pursue. This might be advantageous, particularly if the duty of care under the contract is of a lesser standard than that under the tort of negligence.

Product liability

Related to negligence are the product liability provisions contained in the Consumer Protection Act 1987. Under the Act, an ultimate consumer can claim against the producer of a defective product regardless of the lack of a contractual relationship between the consumer and the producer and without having to show the basic requirements for an action in negligence. Part I of the Act deals with product liability and stems from the Council of European Communities Directive on product liability (Directive on the approximation of the laws, regulations and administrative provisions of member states concerning liability for defective products 85/374/EEC, OJ [1985] L210/29). A 'product' is defined by the Consumer Protection Act as being any goods including electricity and includes a product comprised in another product whether a component part or a raw material. A computer would therefore come within the meaning of product but computer software, *per se*, will be outside the scope of this part of the Act.

Although product liability does not appear to apply to software it will apply to a defective product which incorporates software such as a computer-controlled microwave oven. There would seem to be no reason why liability on the basis of product liability should be avoided even if the defect which causes the damage lies within the software. A defect in software controlling a microwave oven or any other product will result in the microwave oven itself being defective.

The producer of a defective product is liable for damage resulting wholly or partly from that defect. Distributors and retailers selling 'own brand' goods can be liable if they can be said to be holding themselves out to be the producer. If a person imports a product, in the course of business, into a country belonging to the European Community from outside the Community in order to supply the product to another, then that importer will be regarded as the producer for the purposes of determining liability by section 2 of the Act. This might have implications for the many companies which import computers made outside the European Community, especially importers who affix their own name to the equipment. If one of these machines is defective and someone is injured as a result, then the importer/distributor will be liable under the Act, apart from any remedies available against him under contract. The Consumer Protection Act also makes a supplier liable if he fails to identify the producer within a reasonable time, having been asked to do so by the claimant.

A defect is defined by reference to the expectation of safety in the product and this relates to property damage as well as death and personal injury. A computer with an exposed unearthed metal chassis would fall short of the expectation of safety.

State of the art defence

An important defence is the 'state of the art' defence contained in section 4(1) of the Consumer Protection Act 1987. This provides that it is a defence in any civil proceedings to show that 'the state of scientific and technical knowledge at the relevant time was not such that a producer of products of the same description as the product in question might be expected to have discovered the defect if it had existed in his products while they were under his control'. This defence would apply, for example, where a product failed suddenly as a result of a form of material fatigue hitherto not widely known amongst producers of such products. The defence as set out in the Act has been criticised as introducing a subjective element as it is a question of whether the producer might be expected to discover the fault, not whether a reasonable producer would be expected to discover the defect. The Directive seems to imply a more objective test as it requires the state of scientific and technical knowledge to be such as to enable the existence of the defect to be discovered. However, in *Commission of the European Communities* v *United Kingdom*, *The Times*, 23 June 1997, the European Court of Justice concluded that the Act validly implemented that part of the Directive and rejected the Commission's argument that the United Kingdom had widened the defence so that the strict liability imposed by the Directive had been turned into mere liability for negligence. As Part I of the Consumer Protection Act 1987 is stated to be intended to comply with the Directive and shall be construed accordingly, it would appear that the courts in the United Kingdom are likely to interpret the 'state of the art' defence on an objective basis.

A possible application of the defence is in the aeronautical industry, for example, where software companies develop sophisticated software for 'fly-by-wire' aeroplanes. Imagine there are two such companies: one is a very large company, Goliath plc, with enormous resources at its disposal whereas the other company, David Software Ltd, is much smaller, being a new entrant into this field, and having proportionally less resources. As a result of considerable research and testing, Goliath is aware of an inherent danger in such software in that it takes a short period of time for the pilot to override the computer software. Consequently, Goliath has incorporated an emergency override command in its software. David Software is not aware of this problem because it has not been published by Goliath and David Software has not carried out sufficient research to detect the problem. If the test in section 4 of the Consumer Protection Act 1987 is subjective, David Software might be able to avail itself of the defence but is less likely to if, as it appears it should be, the test is objective.

The defence is most likely to be relevant in leading-edge technology where new types of products are being developed. This is particularly so where computer technology is being used in process control, traffic control, guidance systems and the like. Consider, for example, the implications of a car with a computer software designed to apply the brakes in an emergency, say if the traffic in front comes to an abrupt standstill. One day a cat runs across the road in front of the car. The software interprets the image of the cat as a stationary object immediately ahead and brings the car to an emergency stop. A lorry following the car runs into the back of it injuring the occupants. Who is liable? The company making the braking system could be potentially liable subject to the state of the art defence (a product includes a product comprised in another product as a component part). The lorry driver, and his employer, may also be liable in negligence.

Extent of liability

Under section 5 of the 1987 Act, the liability covered by Part I of the Act extends to:

(a) death or personal injury;
(b) damage to or destruction of any item of property (including land) other than the defective product itself (there is a lower threshold of £275 before a claim can be made) provided that the property:
  (i) is the type normally intended for private use and consumption, and
  (ii) it is used mainly for the private use or consumption of the person claiming.

Therefore, in dealings between businesses, the product liability part of the Act will only apply to defective products causing death or personal injury. As far as property damage is concerned, the provisions are really aimed at the consumer market, so, if you buy a computer as a Christmas present for your uncle and because of a fault it catches fire and causes £1500 of damage to his house, your uncle will have a claim under the 1987 Act against the manufacturer of the computer for the damage to the house and furniture. Personally, you may have a separate claim against the retail outlet because the computer was not of satisfactory quality under the Sale of Goods Act 1979.

Criminal liability for defective products

Part I of the Consumer Protection Act 1987 imposes civil liability on producers. However, if a person is killed as a result of a defective product and the defect is attributable to the negligence of any person, that person could be exposed to a prosecution for manslaughter. This could even expose a company to prosecution if the negligence of a senior officer of the company is the root cause of the negligence and this is imputed to the company on the basis that the acts of its senior officers are the acts of the company.

Apart from liability for manslaughter resulting from defects in safety critical systems, there are numerous statutes which impose criminal liability and which may be triggered by a computer defect. Examples include the Health and Safety at Work etc. Act 1974, the Food Safety Act 1990 and the Environmental Protection Act 1990. An offence might be committed under the Food Safety Act where a computer is used to calculate cooking times and underestimates safe times because of a defect. A pollution control system run by a computer may result in an offence under the Environmental Protection Act 1990 if toxic substances are released into a stream without treatment because of a software error. The areas where civil and criminal liability may result from the use of defective computer technology are immense and, with the growth of safety legislation and environmental protection law, these areas are increasing rapidly.

The General Product Safety Regulations 1994 impose criminal liability on producers and distributors in respect of products that are not safe. A 'product' means any product intended for consumers or likely to be used by consumers, whether new, used or reconditioned. A 'safe product' is one which, under normal or reasonably foreseeable conditions of use, including duration, does not present any risk or only the minimum risks compatible with the product's use considered as acceptable and consistent with a high level of protection for the safety and health of persons. Account is to be taken of the product's characteristics, presentation (including information given) and categories of consumers at serious risk (for example, children). There is a defence of due diligence.

These regulations are highly relevant in terms of second-hand computer equipment and any electrical equipment sold to children. In terms of software the same difficulty will apply as identified above – that is, that it is unlikely that software will be deemed to be a product although it is possible that the disks and other tangible items supplied with the software may be so classed.

Exemption clauses

An exemption clause is one which excludes or restricts the liability of a party who is in breach of contract. Exemption clauses can be sub-divided into exclusion clauses and limitation clauses. An exclusion clause gives the party relying on it total exemption for the breach whereas a limitation clause limits liability to a specified amount. An example of an exclusion clause is where a supplier totally excludes his liability under the contract for late delivery if this is caused by circumstances beyond his control such as industrial action. An example of a limitation clause is where a supplier of computer software limits his liability for faulty software to the licence fee he has received for that software.

When people draft contracts they are usually keen to limit or exclude their liabilities and yet wish to ensure that the other party is absolutely bound to perform his part of the contract. Such one-sided contracts were fairly common in the past (they are by no means extinct now), particularly in circumstances where there was an inequality of bargaining power. An ordinary individual buying a product from a supplier who had a monopoly in the product had little choice but to accept the terms imposed on him or manage without it. A golden principle in contract was 'freedom of contract' meaning that the parties should be free to agree whatever terms they wished. This doctrine was acceptable where two powerful companies were negotiating a contract in a free market, but contractually weaker persons suffered. Over the years, however, Parliament and the courts have intervened to mitigate the harshness of the situation and certain terms are now implied into sale of goods and similar contracts, while exclusion clauses have been disapproved of by the courts, especially if such clauses are demonstrably unfair.

The courts developed techniques to limit the effects of exclusion clauses, including the interpretation of an ambiguous clause to the disadvantage of the party seeking to rely on it. For example, in *Andrews Brothers (Bournemouth) Ltd* v *Singer & Co Ltd* [1934] 1 KB 17, the plaintiff ordered a new Singer car from the defendants. When the car was delivered it was found to have done some 550 miles. The defendants sought to rely on an exclusion clause which stated that liability for terms implied by statute was excluded; one of these terms was that goods must comply with their description. The contract, however, repeatedly described the car as a 'new Singer car'. It was held that, because the car was referred to in the contract as a new car, this was an express term and since the exclusion clause sought to exclude liability for implied terms only, the defendants were liable. The exclusion clause was of no effect for this breach of an express term. The plaintiff was awarded £50 in damages.

Exemption clauses are also controlled by statute. The Unfair Contract Terms Act 1977 limits the extent to which liability can be excluded or limited for breach of contract, or for negligence, or under the terms implied by the Sale of Goods Act 1979 and other legislation containing similar provisions, such as the Supply of Goods and Services Act 1982. Sections 2 to 4 of the Unfair Contract Terms Act apply to contractual terms or notices which attempt to exclude or restrict liability for negligence and breach of contract.

A person may seek to exclude or limit his liability for negligence by means of a notice or a term in a contract. Whether the liability arises in tort or contract, the legal controls are the same and mainly result from section 2 of the Unfair Contract Terms Act 1977. This applies to business liability for negligence whether a breach of a contractual obligation to exercise reasonable care and skill in the performance of a contract or a breach of an equivalent common law duty. Section 2 of the Act prohibits the exclusion or limitation of liability for death or personal injury resulting from negligence, while liability for other loss or damage may only be excluded or restricted in so far as the term or notice satisfies the requirement of reasonableness. Section 11 of the Act provides that a term in a contract is reasonable if it is fair and reasonable to have been included in a contract having regard to the circumstances which were, or ought reasonably to have been, known to or in the contemplation of the parties when the contract was made. In relation to a notice, the test is whether it is fair and reasonable to allow reliance on it having regard to the circumstances. By section 11(4), where the term or notice seeks to limit liability to a specified sum of money, regard must be had to the resources available to the person who would have to meet the liability and how far it was open to that person to take out insurance cover. The burden of proof is on the person claiming that the term or notice is reasonable.

In terms of defective hardware, the basic provisions of the Unfair Contract Terms Act work reasonably predictably but it is in respect of software that doubts were expressed as to the reach of the Act, and this has been the source of some speculation. This is because Schedule 1, paragraph 1 to the Act states that:

Sections 2 to 4 of this Act do not extend to – ...

(c) any contract so far as it relates to the creation or transfer of a right or interest in any patent, trade mark, copyright, registered design, technical or commercial information or other intellectual property ...

One view was that the important provisions in section 2 (liability for negligence), section 3 (contractual liability for breach or in relation to performance) and section 4 (unreasonable indemnity clauses) were inapplicable to software contracts because the essence of most software contracts is the granting of a licence to use the software – the creation of a right under copyright law. A number of software companies considered that they could largely ignore the effects of the Unfair Contract Terms Act 1977 and exclude or strictly limit their liability for defects. The courts have taken a more restrictive approach, however, to the scope of paragraph 1 of Schedule 1.

In *The Salvage Association* v *Cap Financial Services Ltd* [1995] FSR 654, the plaintiff invited tenders for the computerisation of its accounts system. The defendant submitted a successful bid for a feasibility study (strategy study and definition stage) and was awarded the contract in the sum of £30 000. Following this, a second contract was awarded to the defendant to develop and implement the software specified in the feasibility study. The date for completion of the second contract was 18 July 1988 and the contract price was £291 654. The system was to be implemented using ORACLE, a fourth-generation language operating as a relational database management system. In July 1988, the software was declared to be ready for user-training but almost immediately it became apparent that it was unusable and contained a large number of errors that would require substantial work to correct. Many of the errors could be attributed to the fact that the defendant's project team was not sufficiently experienced in the use of ORACLE. Nevertheless, the plaintiff persevered and allowed additional time for the defendant to complete the work satisfactorily. Several new dates for delivery were agreed but, eventually, it became clear to the plaintiff that the work was likely never to be completed satisfactorily and, on 13 July 1989, the plaintiff terminated the contract because of the serious breaches of contract on the part of the defendant.

The plaintiff claimed that it was entitled to reject the system and terminate the second contract and claimed damages of £855 550 (being the sum of £291 388 already paid under both contracts and £564 162 for wasted expenditure resulting from the defendant's breaches of contract). The defendant sought to rely on limitation clauses in its standard form contract which formed the basis of the first contract and, in relation to the second contract, terms which purported to exclude liability except as provided for by the contract and, in any case, to limit liability under that contract to £25 000. The limit in the first contract was £250 000 in respect of physical damage and £25 000 for other loss or damage (except for liability for death or physical injury where there was no limit).

Both contracts contained terms to the effect that the defendant would assign appropriately qualified staff to perform the work and the judge in the High Court held that there was a breach of these terms. Furthermore, the judge implied a term under section 13 of the Supply of Goods and Services Act 1982 to the effect that the defendant would exercise reasonable care and skill and held that the defendant was also in breach of this term. The time for completion of the second contract was extended on a number of occasions but the judge held that time was of the essence and the extensions agreed by the plaintiff did not alter that simple fact. The plaintiff's patience had been stretched to the limit and it was entitled to repudiate the contract at the time it did.

If sections 2 and 3 of the Unfair Contract Terms Act 1977 applied to the limitation clauses, they would be upheld only in as much as they met the requirement of reasonableness – otherwise the defendant would probably be able to rely on them. The judge decided that paragraph 1 in Schedule 1 only concerned those provisions in a contract that dealt with the creation or transfer of a right or interest in the relevant intellectual property and did not extend to all the other terms of a service contract simply because the service will result in a 'product' that is subject to intellectual property rights. Thus, terms concerned with aspects of the contract other than those relating to the creation or transfer of an intellectual property right are still subject to sections 2 to 4 of the Unfair Contract Terms Act 1977. In other words, paragraph 1(c) does not create a blanket exception for software contracts.

As mentioned above, the reasonableness test is expressed in section 11 of the Act. Schedule 2 provides guidelines for the application of the reasonableness test and, though not expressed as being applicable to sections 2 and 3 of the Act, the judge accepted the suggestion of Potter J in *Flamar Interocean Ltd* v *Denmac Ltd (The Flamar Pride)* [1990] 1 Lloyd's Rep 434 that it would be sensible to take the guidelines into account in such cases. He referred also to the judgment of Lord Griffiths in *Smith* v *Eric S Bush* [1990] 1 AC 831 where his lordship identified four matters that should always be considered:

- the relative bargaining power of the parties;
- whether it was reasonably practicable to obtain advice from an alternative source;
- the difficulty and dangerousness of the task to be undertaken – that is, the risk; and
- the practical consequences of the court's decision, the ability of the parties to bear the losses involved and the availability of insurance.

In the present case, the parties were of equal bargaining power but it would have been almost impossible for the plaintiff to insure to cover the liability excluded by the defendant. The insurance factor was crucial to this case as the defendant itself had recognised the inadequacy of the £25 000 figure in its standard form contracts and it had been raised to £1 million at around the time of the first contract. Unfortunately for the defendant, it had not been able to explain convincingly why the higher figure had not been used in its contracts with the plaintiff. The judge, therefore, held that the terms limiting liability to £25 000 were unreasonable and awarded a total of £662 926 in damages comprising £291 388 (already paid by the plaintiff), £231 866 for items of wasted expenditure (computer time, wasted computer stationery, payments to consultants and for testing) and £139 672 for wasted management time.

In another important case, *St Albans City & District Council* v *International Computers Ltd* [1995] FSR 686, the judge had to consider the effectiveness of clauses limiting liability in the context of a software 'bug' which caused financial loss to the client. It concerned software used to administer the community charge (poll tax) and has far-reaching implications for software developers, who should look carefully at their standard term contracts and level of insurance cover.

The plaintiff, a local authority, was responsible for setting the level of and collecting the community charge and invited tenders for the supply of suitable hardware and software to keep a register of charge payers and to carry out additional functions such as raising the necessary bills. The contract was awarded to the defendant in 1988. Perhaps exacerbated and compounded by unbelievably tight deadlines, an error in the software resulted in the population being over-estimated by some 2966 persons and the community charge was set at too low a level as a consequence. This had a knock-on effect in terms of money flows to and from central government and the total financial loss to the plaintiff was £1 314 846. The contract was made on the defendant's standard written terms.

Mr Justice Scott Baker accepted that the defendant was under an obligation to provide software that would maintain a reliable database of names entered on to the community charge register, accurately count those names and accurately retrieve and display the population count. Furthermore, the software had to be reasonably fit for its purpose of maintaining and retrieving a reliable register. There was a plain breach of contract because of the erroneous figures produced by the software. Additionally, an assurance made by the defendant's project manager that the figures could be relied upon was a breach of the project manager's contract of service which was part of the overall agreement. This was a negligent misrepresentation and the project manager's obligations were not, as required, exercised with due diligence. A term in the contract that errors had to be notified to the defendant within three months was of no effect because the plaintiff was unaware of the error and had no way of discovering it.

The judge, in awarding the plaintiff the full amount claimed, said that the plaintiff was not at fault in failing to discover the error nor in failing to take different action when it became apparent that there was a problem with the software. He was of the opinion that the defendant had failed to establish that the limitation clauses in the main agreement and the service agreement incorporated in it were reasonable in the circumstances. By section 3 of the Unfair Contract Terms Act 1977, where one party deals as consumer or on the other's written standard terms of business, the other cannot, by reference to any contract term, exclude or restrict any liability for his own breach of contract except in so far as the term satisfies the requirement of reasonableness. The plaintiff was not dealing as consumer but the judge held that the contract was based on the written standard terms of the defendant even though there had been some negotiation between the parties. He said that it was not necessary for all the terms to have been fixed in advance by the supplier for the contract to be deemed to be on the basis of written standard terms. Some terms, such as those dealing with quality or price, would often be the result of negotiation but that did not necessarily take the contract out of the reach of section 3. In any case, the judge held that either section 6 or 7 of the Unfair Contract Terms Act 1977 also applied.

Sections 6 and 7 deal with implied terms in contracts of sale or hire purchase of goods and other contracts under which the title to goods pass and also require that the reasonableness test be satisfied in relation to terms excluding or restricting liability. Scott Baker J followed the approach of Judge Thayne Forbes in *The Salvage Association* v *CAP Financial Services Ltd* and considered that it would be better for the loss to fall on a large international computer company (which was well able to insure itself against such claims) rather than falling on a local authority. Other factors of particular note were the resources of the defendant and its total insurance cover which was claimed to amount to £50 million. The judge decided that the plaintiff was in a slightly weaker bargaining position than the defendant and, although the plaintiff knew of the term (indeed, it had complained about its presence in the contract), had received no inducement, and was unable to enter into a similar contract with another without such a term, the defendant had failed to discharge its burden of establishing that the term was fair and reasonable in the circumstances.

The Court of Appeal confirmed that the limitation clause was unenforceable in *St Albans City & District Council* v *International Computers Ltd* [1997] FSR 251. However, the defendant's appeal was allowed in part in that the award of damages was reduced to £685000. The plaintiff's claim in relation to payments by chargepayers was held not to be recoverable as they were under an obligation to pay (otherwise they would get a bonus) and the plaintiff could simply increase the charge the following year to recoup that loss. This was notwithstanding the fact that some persons would have left the district and some would have moved into the district in the meantime. However, the Court of Appeal confirmed that the plaintiff could recover for the increased precept payments made to the County Council which it was unable to recover.

The *St Albans* case is very instructive and shows the difficulty that a software company may have in convincing a judge that any term excluding or limiting liability for defective software is reasonable. Here, the defendant's term was deemed to be unreasonable even though the plaintiff was aware of the term, other software companies had comparable terms and the software was in use while still under development. However, the judge's view that the plaintiff was in a weaker bargaining position can be criticised. It was a local authority responsible for a population in excess of 100000 persons, employing professional staff and making use of a respected firm of management consultants to advise on the tender process. The plaintiff would certainly be in a stronger bargaining position than most small and medium-sized commercial enterprises dealing with a major computer company. Nevertheless, there are important lessons for computer software companies contained within the judgment.

Before the Unfair Contract Terms Act 1977 came into force, the courts developed, somewhat erratically, the doctrine of 'fundamental breach' as a way of curbing the worst excesses of exclusion clauses. *Pinnock Bros* v *Lewis & Peat Ltd* [1923] 1 KB 690 concerned a contract for the purchase of copra cake. When delivered, it was discovered to be poisonous because it had been contaminated with castor oil. It was held that it was not copra cake at all but a substance quite different to that contracted for and, because of this, the sellers could not rely on an exclusion clause purporting to exempt them from liability. Later, it was said that where there had been a fundamental breach of contract – that is, if one party fails to carry out his part of the bargain at all or attempts to render a performance totally different from that contemplated – then the party in breach could not rely on an exclusion clause (see *Karsales (Harrow) Ltd* v *Wallis* [1956] 2 All ER 61). However, the courts later took a more *laissez-faire* attitude to exclusion clauses and fundamental breach on the basis that the parties should be free to agree that there should be no liability under the contract even for a fundamental breach, if that was their desire: see *Photo Production Ltd* v *Securicor Transport Ltd* [1980] AC 827. This case concerned the law before the implementation of the Unfair Contract Terms Act 1977, but the impact of this Act on exclusion clauses was in the minds of their lordships.

Nevertheless, the doctrine of fundamental breach may still have some utility when it comes to controlling exclusion clauses in contracts which do not come within the scope of the Unfair Contract Terms Act – for example, where the breach concerns the grant of the licence itself such as where the licensor turns out not to be entitled to grant the licence or in the context of liability arising outside the course of business. Of course, where a purported licence for the use of software fails because the licensor does not have the right to grant the licence (for example, if he does not own the copyright and does not have the copyright owner's permission to grant licences) then it could be said that the contract will be void on the basis of a total failure of consideration.

Section 8 of the Unfair Contract Terms Act provides that a clause in a contract which purports to exclude or restrict liability for misrepresentation will only be effective if it satisfies the requirement of reasonableness. The burden of proof is on the person seeking to rely on the clause. If a computer salesman claims that the computer he is selling will run a particular software package and this claim turns out to be untrue, it will be for the company selling the computer to show that any exemption clause it hopes to rely on passes the test of reasonableness. The test is laid out in section 11 of the Unfair Contract Terms Act 1977 which requires that the term be:

> ... fair and reasonable ... having regard to the circumstances which were, or ought reasonably to have been, known to or in the contemplation of the parties when the contract was made ...

This is a nebulous requirement which also applies to some of the other provisions in the Act. It gives the courts scope to be flexible and to take the facts of a particular case into account. Some indication of the court's approach was given by the decision in *George Mitchell (Chesterhall) Ltd* v *Finney Lock Seeds Ltd* [1983] 2 All ER 737. The plaintiff bought cabbage seed from the defendant for £192. The seed was defective and the resulting crop was little better than useless. The loss to the plaintiff, a farmer, was in the order of £61 000. When sued, the defendant claimed to be liable only for the cost of the seed because of a clause in their contract to that effect. Lord Denning (it was his last case) said that the term was not fair and reasonable in the circumstances, although he did say that this was a borderline case. The following were important factors:

- Farmers had no way of knowing or discovering that the seed was defective.
- The defendant seed merchant could have insured against the risk of defective seed but it was unlikely that an individual farmer could so insure.
- The defendants had not relied on the clause but had reached a negotiated settlement in similar prior cases.
- It was likely that the seed merchant or their Dutch suppliers had been negligent.

In a subsequent appeal to the House of Lords, the Court of Appeal's decision was affirmed. It should be noted that, by section 7 of the Unfair Contract Terms Act 1977, liability for defective products under Part I of the Consumer Protection Act 1987 cannot be excluded or limited by any contract term.

Individual consumers making contracts for non-business purposes are given greater protection in relation to standard form contracts as from 1 July 1995, by the Unfair Terms in Consumer Contracts Regulations 1994. This controls terms which are unfair and, being contrary to the requirement of good faith, cause a significant imbalance in the parties' rights and obligations under the contract to the detriment of the consumer. The nature of the goods or services must be taken into account in assessing the unfair nature of the term in question. Schedule 2 to the Regulations gives a list of things to be taken into account when assessing fairness: the strength of bargaining position, whether the consumer received an inducement to agree to the term, whether the goods or services were sold or supplied to the special order of the consumer and whether the seller or supplier has acted fairly and equitably.

Schedule 3 contains a list of terms that are likely to be regarded as unfair. Some of these would not be effective in any case under English law, an example being a term which allows the unilateral alteration of a term in the contract by the seller or supplier. The provisions do not apply to terms which have been individually negotiated or, if written in plain intelligible language, which define the main subject matter of the contract or are concerned with the adequacy of the price or remuneration. The seller or supplier has the burden of proof in showing that a term was individually negotiated. Where there is any doubt as to the meaning of a term, the meaning most favourable to the consumer will be taken. If a contract contains an unfair term, it will not be binding on the consumer but the contract will continue in existence if it is capable of so doing without the unfair term.

Chapter 17

Contracts for writing software

Introduction

If an organisation wishes to obtain some new computer software, there may be several options open to it. Appropriate software may be available as an 'off-the-shelf' package or the organisation may employ its own computer staff who can develop the software. In other circumstances, it may be advantageous to have the software written or adapted by a software development company – a firm specialising in particular types of computer software. The following example is typical of instances when software will be developed under a contractual agreement.

A company owns a mainframe computer and network of personal computers or terminals. It requires software to automate its accounting and invoicing systems. After reviewing software available off-the-shelf, the company comes to the conclusion that none is ideally suited to its methods of operation and it is neither appropriate nor satisfactory for it to change its methods to suit the available software. Although the company employs a number of analysts and programmers, it decides against asking them to write the software as they are not sufficiently experienced in the development software that is likely to be used as a platform to deliver the applications software. The company selects an experienced software company to carry out a comprehensive feasibility study which includes development and strategy studies. The software company produces a detailed plan and specification for the work and is awarded the contract to carry out the work following the submission of bids by it and a number of other experienced software companies. We will now turn to the terms and provisions commonly found in a contract for writing computer software. The company commissioning the development of the software will be referred to as the 'client' and the company writing the software will be called the 'software development company'.

Definitions

The very first clause in the contract is likely to deal with a description of the parties to the contract and appropriate definitions relating to the software and the equipment on which the software will be installed. Apart from being a word-saving provision in that the client's full business name can be abbreviated throughout to CLIENT or CUSTOMER, the definitions clause can usefully describe terms such as software and hardware and thus assist with the interpretation and construction of the agreement. Consequently, any expressions defined here should be defined precisely and comprehensively as they will be the key to understanding the remainder of the contract and the scope of the parties' obligations and liabilities under it.

Licence agreement

What will the software development company deliver to the client in return for the payment? On the face of it a set of programs, data files and associated documentation is what will be provided, but will the software development company really hand over ownership of the programs and other software? This will be unlikely and an important term usually states that the software is being licensed; the contract is, first and foremost, a licence agreement. A licence is a permission to do something; in terms of computer software, a licence is a permission to use the software and, without this permission, using the software would be an infringement of the copyright subsisting in it. This is because loading programs and data into a computer's memory is making a copy and copyright can be infringed even if the copy is transient by section 17(6) of the Copyright, Designs and Patents Act 1988.

The software development company will undoubtedly want to retain the ownership of the intellectual property rights in the programs and the documentation, for its business is licensing software and it will want to grant licences in respect of the software, or variants of it or modules contained within it, to others. If it is especially important for the company acquiring the software that it is not made available to others, it should insist on an exclusive licence, which is likely to be much more expensive. Alternatively, ownership of the copyright subsisting in the software could be transferred to the client under an assignment of copyright. In practical terms, there is little difference between an exclusive licence and an assignment of copyright. Where an exclusive licence or assignment of copyright is granted, however, the software development company would be wise to reserve the right to reuse modules in other software or even in the writing of new software to perform similar functions. The drafting of an appropriate and workable clause to allow for this will require a great deal of care and the implications must be thoroughly considered. On the one hand the client may not want its competitor obtaining similar software from the software development company while, on the other hand, the latter will not want to unduly constrain its future software development activities.

Important points to check in the licence agreement will include the duration of the licence and its scope (sometimes the licence will be silent on the matter of duration). Because a licence is a permission to do something which would otherwise be unlawful, it does not give any proprietary interest in the software. The implications of this are twofold.

1 The licence should be for a fixed duration or there should be some provisions for termination of the licence. If the licence appears, on the face of it, to be perpetual, this contradicts the nature of a licence and it might even be implied that the agreement is not a licence but an assignment of the copyright and other rights in the software, especially if the rights granted appear to be exclusive. It is more likely, however, in the absence of any express reference to duration, that the licence will endure as long as the copyright subsists in the software. The wording of the agreement as a whole should give a clue as to which interpretation is correct.

2 The licence agreement should state whether the software can subsequently be transferred to a third party. In the absence of any provision covering this aspect, it would appear that the benefit of the licence is transferable, depending on the circumstances (see the following section).

The scope of the licence is very important. Is it permissible to run the software on several computers or just one particular computer? If the acquiring company is part of a group of companies, can the programs be used throughout the group or just within the one company? Is the licence a single-user licence (if so, can it be used on any computer by the user)? Is it a site licence, a company licence or group licence? Can the software be transferred to another company? Is transfer subject to approval? All these questions should be considered and discussed with the software development company in the light of the contract and the intended uses to which the software is to be put. The possibility of expanding computing facilities and usage in the future must not be overlooked. In this respect, the client should carry out regular audits to make sure that its licensed software is not being used in excess of the licence agreements and to identify whether existing licences are adequate.

Assignment of agreement

It is common for contracts to contain a term dealing with the assignment of the benefit of the contract. That is, the transfer of the right to use the software. For example, in an agreement for the writing of new software by a software development company for a client, there may be a term stating that neither party shall assign the agreement. Sometimes, assignment is permitted providing the other party consents. Note that in this context, we are talking about the assignment of the benefit of a contract rather than the assignment of the ownership of copyright. Terms dealing with assignment are particularly relevant where the performance of the contract will be carried out over a period of time, such as a building contract or a contract for writing new software.

Both parties to a contract enjoy benefits and suffer burdens emanating from the contract. For example, a client for whom software is to be written under a contract may have the benefits and burdens listed in Table 17.1.

Table 17.1 Benefits and burdens in software contract

Benefits	Burdens
1 The services of the software development company in writing the software	1 The obligation to pay the software development company
2 A copyright licence allowing use of the software	2 Providing facilities and information to the software development company
3 The grant of ownership of the property in disks, manuals, etc.	3 Accepting the software after attending testing
4 The services of the software development company in maintaining the software and correcting errors	

Unless prohibited, a party to a contract may assign (that is, transfer) the benefit of the contract but not the burden. The original parties remain liable for their obligations under the contract. In *Linden Gardens Trust Ltd* v *Lenesta Sludge Disposals Ltd* [1993] 3 WLR 408, a building contract contained a term which stated 'The employer [the client] shall not without the written consent of the contractor assign this contract'. There was a purported assignment of the contract but the House of Lords held that this was void. There was some criticism of the drafting of the above term. Lord Browne-Wilkinson said:

> On any basis, clause 17 is unhappily drafted in that it refers to an assignment of 'the contract'. It is trite law that it is, in any event, impossible to assign 'the contract' as a whole, i.e. including both burden and benefit. The burden of a contract can never be assigned without the consent of the other party to the contract in which event such consent will give rise to a novation.

(A novation is where a new contract is substituted for an old one.) Lord Browne-Wilkinson also said, later:

> ... lawyers frequently use those words ['assign this contract'] inaccurately to describe an assignment of the benefit of a contract since every lawyer knows that the burden of a contract can never be assigned.

The House of Lords confirmed that a party to a contract might have good commercial reasons for refusing to grant consent to an assignment. For example, if a software company is providing continuing maintenance of software it might not want to maintain it if the software is transferred by the client to a third party. As the burden cannot be assigned, the original party remains liable to fulfil his obligations under the contract. For example, if a client transfers the benefit of a software licence to a third party, that original client remains liable for any outstanding payments. Where there is an assignment, the original party, the assignor, might want to consider an indemnity clause to protect himself against any legal action brought by the other party in respect of his obligations under the contract.

It is common for a licence agreement (and the same applies to other forms of agreement such as a maintenance agreement) to state that the benefit of the agreement shall not be assigned without the prior written permission of the other party.

In *Circuit Systems Ltd & Basten* v *Zuken-Redac (UK) Ltd* (1995) 11 Const LJ 201, the defendant rented computer equipment to the first plaintiff (Circuit Systems) and also entered into a maintenance agreement with it. Both agreements prohibited assignment though, in the case of the maintenance agreement, assignment with written consent was possible. The same day that the first plaintiff issued a writ against the defendant alleging, *inter alia*, breach of contract and economic duress, the first plaintiff went into liquidation. The second plaintiff, Basten (who owned at least 98 per cent of the shares in Circuit Systems) took an assignment of Circuit Systems' rights of action for £1 and was granted legal aid to pursue the claim. It was held that the assignments were not valid. However, in *Orion Finance Ltd* v *Crown Financial Management Ltd* (unreported) 30 March 1994, the assignment was subject to consent but the party whose consent was required, Crown, knew that the assignment had been made without consent but failed to draw the other party's attention to this before a lease of computer equipment was registered as a charge under the Companies Act 1985. Crown was estopped from relying on the lack of consent. Crown's lack of activity was, in effect, a representation that it accepted the assignment as valid.

Under what circumstances might an assignment of the benefit of a contract be appropriate? Consider a client, Acme Manufacturing Ltd, which is a member of a group of companies and which makes an agreement with Grotsoft Ltd, a software development company, for the development, installation and maintenance of stock control software. After a while, because of changes in Acme's manufacturing methods, the software is no longer useful but another company in the group, Zenith Fabrications Ltd, would like to use the software. After seeking Grotsoft's permission as required in the contract, Acme assigns the benefit of the agreement to Zenith and Grotsoft will continue to maintain the software at Zenith's offices for the remainder of the maintenance period. Assuming that Grotsoft will be entitled to a final payment at the end of the maintenance period, this will be payable by Acme which remains responsible for this. In the separate agreement between Acme and Zenith in which the benefit of the agreement with Grotsoft is transferred to Zenith, there is provision for Zenith to refund Acme after it has made the final payment. Figure 17.1 shows the effect of the assignment to Zenith.

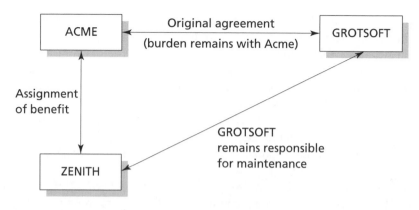

Fig. 17.1 Assignment of benefit of agreement

If, on the other hand, Acme had wished to hand over the entire contract to Zenith, this would result in a novation (providing Grotsoft agreed to this). The original agreement would be set aside and a new contract between Zenith and Grotsoft would come into existence. If Grotsoft refused to agree to this, however, and Acme indicated that it no longer wanted to proceed with the contract, Grotsoft could sue for wrongful repudiation of contract or anticipatory breach. A novation is shown in Fig. 17.2.

The contract price

As the agreement will be almost certainly in the nature of a licence, the sum payable should be termed a licence fee. This fee is often described as the price, however, and often it will include other things such as training and tangible items such as disks and documentation. The word 'price' will be used,

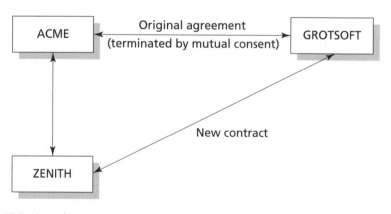

Fig. 17.2 Novation

therefore, bearing in mind that this will include a once and for all licence fee which will usually make up the largest portion of the overall price. In some cases, the agreement will not be a licence but, instead, will provide for the assignment of the copyright subsisting in the completed software to the client. Nevertheless, similar considerations will apply as regards the price and many other aspects of the contract.

Wherever possible, the question of price should be tied down precisely. If it comprises a licence fee, maintenance fee, price for any hardware supplied, etc., there should be a breakdown of the constituent costs. Apart from anything else, this could be important for tax reasons. In addition, the contract should provide some machinery for calculating the cost of any extra work or services provided other than those which the software development company has agreed to provide as its consideration for the contract. There may be unanticipated problems with the computer equipment, for example, or the client may change his mind half-way through the work and require modifications to be made to the specification. Therefore, the contract should include a list of hourly rates for programmers, analysts and others.

If a lump-sum price is agreed, it should be clear from the contract exactly what this includes: whether maintenance and training are included, whether the price includes the documentation and, if so, how many copies. What about the cost of the media such as magnetic disks and tapes? If the payment is to be made in instalments, when are they due? If they become due following the performance of certain stages of the work, can these stages be clearly identified? For example, the contract might provide for payment of two-thirds of the total price when certain specified programs are operational and draft documentation has been provided. If the client is late in paying, does the contract include provision for charging interest? What if the client shows no intention of paying? It is in the interests of both parties that there should be no ambiguity as far as time for payment is concerned.

It may be that the software development company feels unable to quote a firm price from the start. Perhaps the client's computer equipment is unusual or unfamiliar in some respect. A software development company may refuse point blank to be tied down to a fixed price, particularly if the work involves modifying existing software to run on unusual equipment. If the software development company refuses to quote a fixed price the reason should be ascertained. Is it because the software development company is tackling something beyond its capabilities or are there more acceptable reasons? Is it genuinely difficult even for an experienced company to forecast the amount of work and the timescale because of the complexity of the work? One way round this problem is to ask the software development company or, preferably, a competent and independent consultant, to carry out a feasibility study. This will enable the viability of the project to be determined before the parties are committed, and the actual amount of work involved and the price can be more accurately predicted. If carried through to the writing of a detailed specification, it can form the basis for inviting tenders or quotations from a number of software development companies to carry out the work. The cost of the feasibility study, however, can be a considerable addition to the overall cost of implementing the software though it may prove money well spent in the long run.

If the work involved in writing the software is substantial, the possibility of obtaining quotations by competitive tender should be considered but, if this course is chosen, specialist advice should be sought as to the specification and other aspects of the tender documentation. The company inviting tenders is taking upon itself the responsibility for the feasibility of the project and the quality of the documentation provided to the tenderers. If the specification is inadequate, any software development company awarded the contract will be able to point to this in its defence should the programs fail to be satisfactory, or use the deficiencies as a basis for claiming additional payment. Therefore, this approach can only be recommended for companies who have access to the necessary professional expertise. A major problem with comparing quotations and tenders is that it is unlikely that all those submitting will have put their bids together on the same basis. The chances are that some or all will have modified the specification in some way or another in spite of a request not to diverge from the specification. Some of those quoting may be unable to obtain a particular piece of equipment or software tool and will offer an alternative or they may offer an alternative simply because it is cheaper and they hope this will make their quotation appear more attractive. Although it could be argued that initiative should be rewarded, in fairness to the others quoting, all should be asked to reconsider their quotes in the light of the alternative should it appear to be worthwhile considering. The legal position regarding tenders is discussed in Chapter 20 in relation to hardware and the same principles apply to software.

Specification

Whether the company acquiring the software, an independent consultant or the software development company writes the specification, there are several important points to be made in respect of it. The specification is the main provision in the contract which concerns the performance and capabilities of the software. It should be a detailed description of what the software is, what it will do and how quickly it will do it. The specification may well be contained in a separate document or be an appendix to the contract, but it must be noted that it is of crucial importance, being the yardstick by which the software will be measured in the case of a dispute about the character and performance of the software.

Ideally, the specification will be clear, comprehensive and exactly mirror the client's requirements. Alas, this is not always the case and one of the most common problems is that the client moves the goalposts part way through the work, typically asking for changes to be made to the specification. The client may decide that he requires different or additional reports to be generated, links to other software not envisaged at the outset or the inclusion of additional routines, none of which are mentioned in the specification. Alternatively, some parts of the specification may have to be compromised because of operational and other difficulties not envisaged at the time the specification was written and agreed on by the parties to the contract. For example, the client may want to take advantage of a newly available upgrade to his operating system software which will require changes to the application software being written under the agreement. While changes made to the specification during the performance of the contract may result in the completed software being of a higher standard, more powerful or of increased functionality, the contractual implications of such changes must be catered for in the original agreement.

While the law will imply terms, based on reasonableness, dealing with additional payment and extensions to the time for completion, for example, under the Supply of Goods and Services Act 1982, it is better to build mechanisms into the contract for this purpose. A schedule of rates is a useful addition to a contract to be used for the determination of the additional price to be paid for extra work not included in the original contract because of changes to the specification made part-way through the work. Another term dealing with extensions to the time for completion would also be useful, as discussed later. If the changes are required because of unforeseen problems, then it would be useful to provide a term allowing additional payment if, and only if, a reasonably competent software company would not have anticipated the problem. The use of an independent professional contract supervisor, as advocated at the end of this chapter, will be very useful in dealing with the contractual implications of changes to the specification.

It is useful to include a mechanism for variation orders in the agreement. A basic method is for any variation to the specification or work required to be set out in writing and signed by both parties before the changes are implemented or incorporated in the work programme. The additional cost (or reduction to the overall price) should be agreed by the parties as should the impact on the overall time for completion. It is far better to have agreement before any additional work is done or any other changes made to the planned programme of work implemented and for the consequences of any changes to be thoroughly considered and agreed. Trying to agree additional costs and extensions to the time for completion after the event can often result in acrimonious disputes although it has to be admitted that time pressures sometimes force retrospective action on the parties. At least a schedule of rates provides a safety curtain and a wise software development company will ensure that all the additional or modified work is carefully noted in terms of resources and duration.

If the changes made to the specification are considerable, the contracting parties ought to contemplate whether it would be better to terminate the existing contract and substitute it with another after negotiating a new contract and any settlement under the old contract. This is an example of novation. If the changes made are substantial this is probably the best route. Of course, the costs and liabilities under the original contract which had already been incurred must be dealt with by mutual agreement (otherwise there could be an action for breach of contract). An experienced software development company should not get into a situation such that the original contract has to be substituted by a new one. Where the work to be carried out is particularly difficult or covers new ground, it may be better to make an agreement to build a prototype system first backed by a broad specification, with a view to a subsequent contract to build the finished system backed by a much more detailed and explicit specification, written with the benefit of the experience gained in building the prototype.

The specification will have to address all the technical issues associated with the performance of the software. In particular, the three most important items which the specification should discuss are:

- a detailed description of the tasks the software will perform;
- the equipment on which the software will run and other software with which it will interface; and
- how quickly the software will carry out the operations involved, bearing in mind any networking and concurrent use requirements.

The client may have little knowledge of the mysteries of computer science and will hope to receive some guidance on these matters from the experts writing the programs. Here, as elsewhere, however, the client should contemplate seeking independent advice unless he has his own computer professionals to consult. There are real dangers at this stage of over-optimism by both parties, plain misunderstanding or just a difference in emphasis of priorities. A great number of retrospectively ill-founded assumptions can be made about performance; computer programmers and analysts cannot be expected to know all the intricacies of the client's business, the nature of which may call for very fast information processing.

If the client does rely on the software development company to supply a system that will do a particular job, he can expect that it will bring a certain degree of expertise to bear upon the work and will perform its part of the contract in a workmanlike manner, using reasonable care and skill. Companies in the business of writing computer systems are implicitly holding themselves out to possess a minimum level of skill and experience when it comes to writing their particular type of system, and the courts have long been prepared to imply an appropriate duty in contracts for supplying services, such as in the case of hairdressers, garages and the like. A contract to write or modify computer software is analogous to such contracts; indeed it is a service contract. In *Stewart* v *Reavell's Garage* [1952] 2 QB 545, a customer relied on a garage to reline the brakes on his 1929 Bentley. The garage obtained a quotation from a sub-contractor; the quotation was recommended to the customer who agreed to it. The work by the sub-contractor was carried out in a way unsuitable for Bentley cars and because of this the customer crashed the car, causing £362 worth of damage. It was held that, because the customer had relied on the garage to repair the brakes in a suitable and efficient manner and because the garage owed a duty to provide good workmanship and materials of good quality so that the braking system would be reasonably fit for its purpose, the garage was liable for the faulty work, even though the work itself was carried out by a sub-contractor. The garage had a duty to select and recommend a suitable sub-contractor. The implications of this are very appropriate in the field of software development, given that it is very common for sub-contractors and freelance programmers to be used by the main contractor.

An equivalent duty of care and skill is now implied into service contracts, where the supplier of the service is acting in the course of business, by section 13 of the Supply of Goods and Services Act 1982. We have already seen in Chapter 16 that the courts are willing to imply these terms into contracts for writing software and, indeed, into contracts for feasibility studies for software. Liability for loss resulting from failure to exercise reasonable care and skill can be excluded or limited subject to the provisions in the Unfair Contract Terms Act 1977. However, the inclusion of such an exemption clause would be unlikely to add to the client's confidence in the software development company and, in any case, the courts have shown a vigorous reluctance to enforce such terms. The fact that the burden of proof in respect of the reasonableness of an exclusion clause lies with the party seeking to rely on it is another point to bear in mind. Generally, it will be better (and safer) business practice for the software development company to provide a reasonable level of insurance cover against its own negligence and to use that as a basis of any limitation of liability clause. It should be noted that, by section 2(1) of the Unfair Contract Terms Act 1977, business liability for death or personal injury cannot be excluded or restricted at all.

In terms of computers, if you have a particular computer and approach a company to write software for that computer, the company has a duty to bring a reasonable amount of skill to the task and to supply software that will be fit for its purpose. If your computer is particularly demanding about the nature of the software it will run, or it has a strange or outdated operating system, then you can expect the software development company to use its skill in taking such matters into account. If it sub-lets part of the work, it is under a duty also to select a sub-contractor capable of carrying out the work in a like manner. The software development company cannot avoid liability for defective software merely because it has asked you to agree to the particular sub-contractor recommended by it. An example of a sub-contract is where a software development company, contracted to write an accounts package, uses another specialist firm or, perhaps, freelance programmers to carry out part of the work. The software development company owes a duty to the client to choose the specialist firm and the freelance programmers carefully.

Other matters to which the specification should address itself include details of any data files and information to be entered to be used by the programs and how they will be entered. Will entry be by keyboard, optical character reader, from magnetic disk or through a modem? Will the entry be of an interactive nature and can the programs operate quickly enough? What results and reports are expected from the system and is there any likelihood of further reports being required once the programs have become established in use? What files, temporary and permanent, will be created? Is access to be controlled by passwords and, if so, is a hierarchical system of passwords required? With what other software must the new software interact or be interoperable?

The feature of computer systems which lies at the root of many disputes is the speed of operation. Computers work at fantastic speeds, measured in microseconds, but they have a great disadvantage in that the vast majority are designed to process information in serial fashion, a piece at a time. The human brain, because of its massive parallel processing capabilities, can easily outperform a computer and, when given real work to do, computers are anything but fast. Therefore, it is essential that the specification contains information about the speed of the programs in use – for example, response times at the keyboard (two seconds can seem an eternity), the time taken to sort items into ascending or descending order, the time taken to compile and print reports. These timings should indicate the effect of multiple concurrent use of the same files and the fact that the equipment might be carrying out other demanding work at the same time. The specification should also describe the portability of the software – that is, can it be run on other equipment with little effort or will a major 'refit' be needed? The client should ask questions about the effect of a future change of or a modification to his computer equipment or operating system software. Another problem might concern the compatibility of the software with other systems run by the client; can data be easily transferred from the new system to the client's existing computer systems and vice versa?

Time for completion

A contract for writing computer programs and preparing associated documentation is fundamentally different in character from a contract for the sale of goods but is, however, analogous to a building contract. The performance of the contract is not a single event but rather extends over a period of time. This fact alone brings some doubt to any assumption that time is of the essence of the contract. We have already seen that, although time for payment is not usually a condition in a commercial sale of goods contract, time for delivery is. If we enter into a contract with a builder for the construction of a house, however, we would not expect that we could repudiate the contract if the house was completed a day late and the position is similar with contracts for writing computer software. A delay of a few days might give rise to a claim for damages but would be unlikely to give the client the right to cancel the contract altogether, although if completion is very late the client may be entitled to cancel.

Writing computer software carries with it a degree of unpredictability and the client should be aware of this, especially if he is planning his business operations around a particular completion date. Unexpected problems frequently arise which can add considerably to the overall time for performance, just as construction projects are often delayed because of unanticipated problems with the sub-soil which has to support a new building, requiring extensive changes to be made to the design of the foundations. In *The Salvage Association* v *CAP Financial Services Ltd* [1995] FSR 654, however, the judge held that time is of the essence in a contract for writing software, though, in that case, the delay was inordinately long. It is submitted that, if the delivery of the software is late by only a few days, this would not amount to a breach of condition (or a material breach in Scotland) giving the client the option of cancelling the contract. An exception would be where the delivery date was particularly important such as where the software was to be written for some special event such as the launch of a new product at an international exhibition.

In case the software is completed late, it would be sensible to have some contractual provisions to cover this situation rather than arguing about the damages. The usual method of dealing with late completion is to include a term which gives the client a right to liquidated damages. These damages may be quantified as a certain sum of money for every week completion is late – for example, £200 per week. The sum must be a genuine pre-estimate of the financial losses which the client will suffer as a result of the delay and it must not be in the nature of a penalty. The courts will not enforce a 'penalty clause'. An example of acceptable liquidated damages would be an estimate of the loss of profits arising from the late completion. Sometimes, it may be in the client's interests to offer a bonus for early completion.

It is not always easy to determine when completion has taken place. The software might have been installed on the client's computer and be working in a fashion, but it requires some further work to be carried out. Alternatively, the programs may be finished but the documentation is only available in draft form. It is clear that problems might arise in determining when completion takes place and it is advisable to define completion in the contract. Does it include testing and documentation? What, if anything, does the client have to do to signify his acceptance of the software? What is the effect of completion on payment? Do all outstanding moneys become due? The concept of substantial completion could be used whereby upon substantial completion a large percentage of the agreed price becomes due with the moiety retained by the client until the remaining work has been completed. Of course, substantial completion must be defined if this approach is used.

If completion is late, this will not necessarily be the fault of the software development company. The completion of the work could be late as a result of the inaction of the client in providing information necessary to the continuation of the work or the client might fail to provide on time the facilities required by the software development company. The contract should clearly state what information and facilities the client must provide and when he must provide them. The contract should also contain machinery dealing with extensions to the time for completion as a result of the client's default in his duties under the contract and compensation for the additional expenses incurred. Ideally, the contract should include rates or formulae to help determine such additional costs.

Maintenance of and enhancements to the software

No matter how much skill and care have been put into the writing of the software or how much testing has been carried out, the odds are overwhelmingly in favour of it containing errors or, colloquially, 'bugs'. Some of these bugs might not appear for a considerable period of time and they may be discoverable only under a very rare combination of factors. If a bug does appear this will normally be a breach of warranty and the client can expect that the software development company will correct the error. Naturally, the latter will wish to limit responsibility to correct such errors to a specified period of time. It is therefore important that the contract takes account of the maintenance of the software. A compromise might have to be struck: perhaps the software development company will be happy to rectify errors in the programs and manuals free of charge for a period of time and thereafter they will be prepared to offer this service for a fee. The Court of Appeal in *Saphena Computing* v *Allied Collection Agencies* [1995] FSR 616 has recognised that even when software is delivered there will still be some work to be done. The software will almost certainly contain errors and the software development company will normally be expected to test the software to locate errors and make the necessary modifications. This duty will endure for a period of time though it is difficult to predict how long.

A software development company will usually offer an ancillary contract for maintenance for which the client will have to pay. It would be reckless to eschew a maintenance agreement and the cost of it should be allowed for in the overall budget for the work. A maintenance agreement may also provide for enhancements and updates to be made available to the client, which can be very useful because software is continually being developed and having new features added to it. There is likely to be a long-term relationship between the client and the software development company if the software is complex or likely to require ongoing development and enhancement.

Section 50C of the Copyright, Designs and Patents Act 1988 (inserted by the Copyright (Computer Programs) Regulations 1992) allows the lawful user to copy or adapt a computer program for error correction purposes. Terms in a licence agreement prohibiting this are not automatically void under copyright law though they may be subject to other legal controls such as the principle of non-derogation from grant or competition law. Without a copy of the source code (and preparatory materials), however, maintenance of a computer program is, to all intents and purposes, a practical impossibility.

In many cases, the software development company will be unwilling to allow third parties, or even the client himself, to modify the software. The person carrying out the work might do so badly and the software could acquire a bad reputation as a result and this would reflect on the software development company. If the client considers it very important to be allowed to modify the software himself or use the services of a third party providing software maintenance, this should be discussed before the contract is made and a suitable term incorporated. It is highly desirable that the client receives a copy of the source code to facilitate the making of modifications should this be permitted and the contract must clearly provide for this. The contract should also cover questions of copyright ownership in the modifications, the assignment of modifications and whether the software development company has any other rights in respect of them.

Escrow

It is worthwhile considering what happens if the software development company goes out of business. Will the client be able to maintain and modify the software or find another company to do this for him? If the software development company has only supplied the object code this will be very difficult, if not impossible. A receiver or a company taking over the software development company's business may obtain the source code and expect to be paid by the client for a copy. If the software development company is taken over, the new parent company might refuse to support the software yet not be willing to make the source code available. Many licence agreements include an escrow clause which is invaluable in such situations – that is, where the client is not given a copy of the source code.

Source code escrow describes a situation where the software development company deposits, with an independent person, a source code copy of the programs together with copies of all the documentation and preparatory materials essential to the continuing maintenance of the software – in short,

221

all the materials that will enable the client or a third party to take over the maintenance and further development of the software. The independent person (the 'stakeholder') holding these materials is instructed not to divulge them to anyone and to keep them generally secure. If a specified event occurs, such as the software development company going out of business or being unable to continue to support the software, then the stakeholder will release all the materials to the client who will then have all the information he needs to arrange for the software to be supported. Escrow works in the form of a guarantee or as insurance should something unfortunate happen to the software development company. The stakeholder must obviously be someone who can be absolutely trusted in the performance of his duties under the escrow arrangement and the details of the agreement need to be carefully thought out. It should include terms dealing with the following matters:

- definitions of the source code and other materials subject to the escrow;
- confidentiality of the source code imposed on the escrow organisation and the client should the source code be released under the agreement;
- delivery of updates to the escrow organisation;
- payment details and provisions in respect of late payment;
- a detailed description of the eventualities which will bring about the client's right to obtain the source code;
- an indemnity that the software development company owns the rights in the source code or otherwise has the right to deposit the source code and eventually, if the right to obtain the source code comes to fruition, that the client will be able to use the source code without hindrance ('quiet enjoyment');
- a system of formal notices requiring the software development company to carry out maintenance by a given deadline subject to the release of the source code;
- termination of the agreement, for example, because of the failure of the client to pay an outstanding fee after receipt of a written demand; and
- the liability of the escrow organisation for loss of or damage to the source code and other materials.

An organisation which provides an escrow service is the National Computing Centre at Oxford House, Oxford Road, Manchester M1 7ED.

The typical mechanism is that an agreement is signed by the client, the software development company and the organisation offering the escrow service. This is a strange tripartite arrangement as shown in Fig. 17.3. A basic rule of English contract law is that there can only be two parties to a contract. An escrow agreement can thus be seen as two separate contracts: one between the software development company and the escrow organisation, the other between the escrow organisation and the client. The way the service will be paid for reinforces this analysis. Usually, the software development company will pay a fee upon depositing the materials with the escrow organisation and

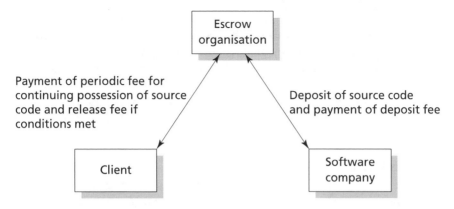

Fig. 17.3 Escrow arrangement

the client will then pay the periodic fees to the escrow organisation and, if it becomes necessary, a release fee.

The implications of mergers and takeovers will need to be carefully dealt with: the new company might want to carry on business as usual, keeping the source code from the client, for reasons connected with confidentiality. The basic test determining whether to pass on the source code and other materials subject to an escrow agreement should be the permanent inability, for whatever reason, of the software development company to continue to support the software.

Copyright and other intellectual property rights

The contract may impose duties on both parties associated with intellectual property rights. The software development company will be anxious to prevent unauthorised copying of the programs and will want its techniques kept secret. The client will want to be able to use the software with impunity, without interfering with the rights of some third party who might seek an injunction preventing continued use of the software. The client will also be worried about the fact that some of the software development company's staff will have gained a detailed insight into his business. The law of copyright and, to some extent, the law of confidence will give some protection to the software development company should the programs or the ideas contained therein be copied or plagiarised, but problems of proof and evidence make it desirable to place a contractual duty on the client to prevent copying or unauthorised disclosure of methods. This duty will run in parallel to any duties imposed by intellectual property law, but the contractual approach will be useful because it will draw the client's attention to the existence of these rights and the importance of making his employees aware of them and the consequences of infringement.

The client's employees may make, surreptitiously, copies of the programs and pass these on to others. If the software development company discovers these copies, it has remedies available under copyright law to prevent the use of these copies by the recipients and their further transmission to others, but it might be difficult to prove that the copies originated from the client. A unique serial or code number could be embedded in the programs identifying the software as being that given to the client and if the client is made aware of this and the consequences he may be more careful. The contract may state that the licence is to be terminated forthwith should copies of the programs find their way into the hands of third parties without the permission of the software development company. This will not preclude the software development company from seeking remedies for infringement of copyright – a fact which is often expressly stated in software licences.

On the subject of confidentiality, the client will want a term included strengthening and extending the common law duty of confidence. He will want to prevent the software development company's employees divulging details of his business methods and techniques and other confidential information such as client accounts, debtors and creditors. It is inevitable, if the contract is for a substantial amount of work, that the employees of the software development company and any freelance staff they use will be exposed to confidential information. Without such a term in the contract, the client may be lacking legal recourse, especially if the confidential nature of materials involved is not otherwise made clear. The software development company, too, may have worries about confidentiality: it may have developed special techniques for writing and testing software which the client's staff might see when the software is installed and tested. A contractual term imposing a two-way duty in respect of confidentiality should be included in the contract.

Warranties and indemnities

It is usual for a licence agreement to contain a section headed 'Warranties and Indemnities'. Warranties normally found include those relating to the fact that the software development company warrants that it has the right to grant the rights to the client provided for by the agreement and that the client will have 'quiet enjoyment' of the software and the client's use of it will be unaffected by any third party rights. Where, instead of licensing the right to use the software, the agreement is one under which the title to the copyright (ownership) is transferred (that is, an assignment of copyright), the Law of Property Act 1925 used to contain a form of words which would automatically include such warranties in the agreement (although that Act was primarily concerned with rights in or over land, it also had some impact on other forms of property transactions). The person granting the rights would use the term 'As beneficial owner'. Now, as a result of the Law of Property

(Miscellaneous Provisions) Act 1994, the phrase used is 'With full title guarantee'. This automatically implies covenants to the effect that the person making the assignment has the right to do so and that the property right transferred is free from all charges and encumbrances and all other rights exercisable by third parties (sections 2 and 3). Other warranties may be given which relate to the performance of the software and its freedom from major defects. This may be tied down to the specification.

Another aspect of intellectual property rights concerns the possibility that the software might infringe a third party's copyright or other right such as a patent or trade mark. Whether or not the infringement is deliberate will not usually be relevant. The client could have been using the software quite happily for a number of years when the software development company is successfully sued for infringement of copyright by some third party. That third party may then decide to pursue all the clients of the software development company who are using the infringing software and seek injunctions to prevent them continuing to use the software. Even if the client is not troubled in this way by the third party, the software development company will be prevented from continuing to support the software. It may be that the third party will be happy to allow the client to continue to use the software in return for a licence fee. In any case, the client should satisfy himself that there is a term in the agreement with the software development company covering the infringement of intellectual property rights belonging to others. The term should give the client an indemnity against the event of legal action being taken against him as a result of the software infringing third party rights. The term should be widely drafted so as to include all forms of intellectual property rights such as copyright, patents, designs and trade marks. The costs and implications of suddenly being unable to use an item of software might be quite enormous and it is likely that the software development company will hope to limit its liability under this head, perhaps to the amount of the licence fee. Any term dealing with an indemnity against third party claims should allow the software development company a reasonable time to modify the software so that it no longer infringes the third party right, if that is a possibility without jeopardising the software's functionality.

Liability

Computer software is widely used to assist in the decision-making processes in business. A decision to engage upon a particular line of action may be based upon an interpretation of the results of running a computer program. For example, a construction company might submit a bid for a motorway contract worth many millions of pounds; the bid total will have been calculated by estimators using computer software. If there is an error in the software, the total might be miscalculated by, say, £1 million; this could mean that the company fails to secure the contract because their bid is too high or, worse still, they win the contract by too great a margin and make a substantial loss.

The software development company will be very keen to limit its liability if the software proves to be defective. The software development company will attempt to limit or exclude its liability for defects by the insertion of a suitably drafted exemption clause – for example, limiting its liability to the cost of replacing the software or remedying the defect. This is unsatisfactory from the client's point of view. Until recently, this way of dealing with liability has been very common but now must be reviewed in the light of recent court decisions such as those in *The Salvage Association* v *CAP Financial Services Ltd* [1995] FSR 654 and *St Albans City & District Council* v *International Computers Ltd* [1997] FSR 251. It is now clear that the controls over exclusion clauses in the Unfair Contract Terms Act 1977 will apply to most terms in software licences, the only major exception being those terms dealing exclusively with the transfer or creation of intellectual property rights. Thus, section 2 of the Act applies to liability for negligence and section 3 controls attempts to exclude liability arising from the performance of the contract. In some cases, liability cannot be excluded or limited at all – for example, in the case of death or personal injury resulting from negligence. In most other cases, the exclusion or limitation of business liability depends upon the reasonableness of the appropriate term.

A software development company should take out professional liability insurance to a reasonable level and limit its liability accordingly. Alternatively, the software development company could offer a minimum level of insurance and offer to increase this if the client is prepared to pay the additional premium. How successful this approach will be is difficult to predict but, above all, the software development company must make sure that its liability under the licence and its insurance are matched as far as it is possible to do this.

It should be noted that a defect in software does not necessarily and inexorably lead to the conclusion that the software development company has been negligent or has failed to exercise reasonable care and skill. The problem may result from the client's use of the software and the question of how much control the software development company has over the use by the client may be a factor. For example, in the case of a spreadsheet, a mistake may be the result of an incorrect formula entered by the client or the client may be using the spreadsheet software to make calculations requiring extreme mathematical precision. If the software development company has exercised the level of care and skill to be expected from responsible software development companies writing equivalent software, there should be no liability. If a financial loss arises because the software development company and the client have both been negligent, the amount of damages awarded will be reduced on the basis of contributory negligence.

Arbitration

It is prudent to include provision in the agreement for arbitration whereby a dispute between the parties will be referred to an arbitrator, an independent expert, who will rule on the dispute. Arbitration is a commonly used method of resolving disputes without having to go to the courts. The parties to the contract appoint an independent third party who will listen to both sides and then make a ruling. Arbitration is less formal than a court hearing, although the basic rules of evidence and procedure are adhered to, and it has the advantage that the arbitrator, unlike a judge, will be an expert in the technical matters involved. In a dispute involving computer software, the arbitrator would be expected to have considerable knowledge of software engineering and be a leading member of the computer profession. Another advantage of arbitration over a normal court hearing is that arbitration should be, in principle, quicker and cheaper, although this is not always so. Arbitration hearings can be fairly formal involving the calling of expert witnesses.

It is common for arbitration clauses to state that the arbitrator's decision shall be final and binding on the parties, and the courts will not interfere with an arbitrator's decision unless he has erred on a point of law. A court will usually accept the arbitrator's evaluation of the facts of the case as being conclusive. If the contract provides for arbitration, neither party will be able to take a short-cut to the courts because a judge will insist that the arbitration procedure is adhered to in the first instance. It must be stressed that the decision of an arbitrator, and any award(s) he makes, is binding upon the parties.

A disadvantage of arbitration is that the arbitrator might not have the depth of legal knowledge of a High Court judge and an arbitrator could be more likely to err on a point of law or procedure. For example, an arbitrator might admit evidence which should be inadmissible. Although a judge will not usually have the technical expertise of an arbitrator, judges by their training and experience have the knack of getting to the kernel of a dispute and are able to concentrate on the important issues without being sidetracked. It must be said, however, that, in practice, arbitration works extremely well and the standard of arbitrators, who belong to the Chartered Institute of Arbitrators, is very high. If an arbitration clause is included in the agreement, the machinery for selecting an arbitrator should also be dealt with, the usual practice being to appoint an arbitrator agreed upon by the parties or, failing such agreement, a person to be nominated by the British Computer Society which holds a register of suitably qualified arbitrators.

Alternative dispute resolution

Taking a dispute to the courts or submitting it to arbitration will plunge the parties into the adversarial contest fundamental to the English legal system.

The outcome usually will be total success or failure; there are no half measures even though the decision of the court may be based on the most slender weight in favour of one party on a balance of probabilities. Occasionally, a more attractive route may be that offered by Alternative Dispute Resolution (ADR) where a mediator is appointed to assist and encourage the parties in the negotiation of a settlement to their mutual satisfaction.

The mediator can take an active role and make suggestions for resolving the conflict. However, there is no legally binding obligation on the parties to continue with the process and they may abandon it at any time. The process itself is based on informality and consent. It is said to be a highly successful means of settling disputes with an estimated settlement rate of 90 per cent (Hayward, D, 'Compromising Positions', *Computing*, 8 June 1995, p 31). One technique which may be used is for both sides to make a presentation before senior members of the organisations who will then attempt to negotiate a settlement with the assistance of the mediator. It would be better if the negotiators were not directly involved in the matters leading to the dispute as they are likely to be more objective and more willing to compromise. The following example shows how ADR might present the best course of action.

Imagine that Pickwick Trading has asked Bardell Software to develop and deliver new accounting software. An appropriate contract was made and a detailed specification annexed to it. When the software was delivered it was found to be slightly slower than allowed by the benchmark tests in the specification. Additionally, one particular feature was missing in that the software would not produce annual VAT summary reports as detailed in the specification. The total price is £85 000, 10 per cent of which was payable upon commencement of the work. The time for delivery is six months.

Pickwick has refused to accept the program and has withheld the final payment of £76 500. Bardell presses for more time to add the VAT report and argues that the speed of the software is so close to that specified as to be of no consequence. The possible outcomes of resolving the dispute by litigation and ADR are discussed below.

Litigation

Bardell sues Pickwick for wrongful repudiation of the contract and seeks damages equivalent to the outstanding sum plus interest and other direct costs. Pickwick submits a defence and counterclaim based on the shortcomings of the program. Pickwick claims the return of the £8500 already paid plus £12 5 00 in wasted management time, etc. At the court action, the judge holds that Bardell is guilty of a breach of condition and that Pickwick's repudiation was lawful. He awards Pickwick £21 000 plus costs, leaving Bardell to pick up the bill for £31 000 in legal costs also.

This result is unsatisfactory from the point of view of both parties. At the end of it all, Pickwick does not have the program it wanted and will now have to engage another software development company. It may be another six months or so before the program is ready. This could seriously handicap Pickwick's business. Bardell is even less happy as six months' work has been wasted and it has a bill for £52 000. Bardell now thinks that it would have been better had it never heard of Pickwick – a view that is reciprocated by the latter.

Alternative Dispute Resolution

The contract between Pickwick and Bardell contains a term providing for ADR and a mediator is appointed. After only two days of negotiation the following settlement is reached:

- Bardell will be given one more month to complete the software so that it will be capable of producing the VAT report (Bardell has also agreed at no extra cost to alter a particular screen display because Pickwick has had second thoughts about it).
- Pickwick will be given a 5 per cent discount on the total price which it will put towards some additional memory for its computer which should increase its speed of operation.

Pickwick and Bardell will share the mediator's fee of £2500. It is left to the reader to reflect on which is the best solution.

Other ADR techniques are adjudication in which a neutral third party gives a non-binding ruling on the case or certain aspects of the case and expert appraisal in which a technical expert assesses each of the parties' cases for the purpose of assisting negotiations.

Alternative Dispute Resolution is not always appropriate; indeed, it may only be a minority of disputes for which it represents a satisfactory method. There are some drawbacks. It is inappropriate where a point of law is involved, where the issues are very complex or where one party seeks an injunction or court declaration. Although any negotiations will have taken place without prejudice to either party's legal rights, there is danger that subsequent litigation could be influenced by what has been said in abortive negotiations. ADR allows the parties to gauge the strengths and weaknesses of each other's case and could even be used, cynically, as a prelude to litigation. It should be noted, however, that the court will not, under normal circumstances, allow evidence to be given of what has been admitted in negotiations which have been conducted 'without prejudice'. Another factor is that getting involved with ADR could compromise any insurance policy that might be relied upon to pay damages and costs awarded in any court action.

Any ADR clause in a contract must make it clear that anything admitted, said or done in connection with ADR is without prejudice to the legal rights of the parties. The clause should make provision for the appointment of a mediator (who should be skilled in resolving disputes by negotiation), payment of his fees (usually these will be borne equally by the parties) and procedures to be adopted. The Centre for Dispute Resolution, at Princes House, 95 Gresham Street, London EC2V 7NA, provides information and advice about ADR and the procedures to be adopted.

The courts are becoming increasingly keen to encourage parties to consider alternative dispute resolution and a Practice Direction has been published to deal with the impact this may have on legal proceedings and directions given by the judge. See, for example, *Practice Statement (Commercial Cases: Alternative Dispute Resolution)* [1994] 1 WLR 14.

Other terms

A contract for the writing or modification of software will undoubtedly contain other terms dealing with matters such as the training of the client's staff, termination of the licence and misrepresentation. These will be dealt with in Chapter 18 which covers 'off-the-shelf' software. It is also usual to include a term stating which is the applicable law; this is essential where there is any doubt – for example, where a Scottish and English company are entering into a contract. Entire agreement clauses are common which attempt to limit the terms of the contract to those expressly contained within the formal agreement, thereby attempting to exclude any representations that may have been made in preliminary negotiations. Notwithstanding this, there may still be a remedy for misrepresentation should one party have entered into the contract on the basis of a promise by the other party which turns out to be untrue. Finally, the question of staff poaching is often addressed. This is where one party offers employment to an employee of the other party. The employees of each party will probably be in close contact for some time – for example, because the software is being developed at the client's premises – and this gives each party the opportunity to spot a 'star performer'. The client may have a vested interest in employing a key member of the software development company's staff who has intimate knowledge of the software written under the contract. Over a period of time, a software development company could find that it has a high turnover of staff. The usual means of countering this threat is for a clause stating that neither party will offer employment (or canvass with a view to offering employment) members of the other party's staff for a period of time, normally six months. In practical terms, there is little to be done beyond this, especially as such terms could be deemed to be in restraint of trade.

Consideration could be given to the use of standard form contracts such as those published by the Institute of Purchasing and Supply, at Easton House, Easton on the Hill, Stamford, Lincolnshire, PE9 3NZ. These contract forms have been developed to provide a fair balance between the parties' interests and incorporate a great deal of experience in this field. Standard form agreements exist for a variety of hardware and software contracts and can be adapted, if necessary, for a specific contract.

Independent professional supervision

In the case of large important contracts for writing software it may be advisable that the performance of the contract is overseen by a professional engineer who is a member of the British Computer Society. This person would be responsible for the following aspects:

- ensuring compliance with the specification;
- general supervision;
- determining whether the software is acceptable;
- certifying payments and completion;
- fixing rates for delays or extra work;
- authorising extensions of time for unavoidable delays or additional work; and
- acting as a first-stop informal mediator.

Although it is normal for such a person to be paid by the client, the contract should give certain powers to him as regards determination of the reciprocal rights and duties of the client and software development company. A chartered engineer will remain neutral as between the parties and will help the parties to resolve difficulties amicably and fairly, being particularly good at dealing with the day-to-day minor problems that are bound to occur. This will prevent small problems turning into full blown disputes with the parties breathing fire at each other. This form of contract supervision has been used to great effect for well over 100 years in the construction industry. Should the engineer be unable to bring the parties to agreement concerning a serious difference, the parties could still have recourse to an independent arbitrator or alternative dispute resolution.

Is there a contract?

It is not unusual for work to begin on a contract for the development of software before the precise details of the contract have been properly agreed and formalised. The modern pressures of business life may make it tempting to commence work before the 'legal stuff' has been sorted out but it is a temptation that should be avoided if at all possible. After committing resources or carrying out work, the other party may claim that there is not a contract. Even if it is accepted that there is a binding contract, there may be some uncertainty as to the precise terms of the contract and there is a limit to how much the courts may be willing to imply. Uncertainty itself can be a factor in making a purported contract void and unenforceable.

The case of *Fraser Williams (Southern) Ltd* v *Prudential Holborn Ltd* (unreported) 22 July 1991 provides an example of the dangers and difficulties which might ensue if work begins before a contract is properly in place

231

although, in the event, it was held that there was a valid contract. The plaintiff submitted a proposal to the defendant to develop software. It was dated 3 March 1989 and was expressed as being 'subject to contract'. Two telephone calls from the defendant on 7 and 9 March 1989 confirmed that the plaintiff had got the job and a letter was sent from the plaintiff to the defendant on 10 March 1989 confirming this, though the letter showed that there were still some things to be resolved, in particular how responsibilities would be shared between the plaintiff and an independent consultant engaged by the defendant in respect of the software. On 13 March 1989 the plaintiff commenced work and on 5 April it sent a draft contract to the plaintiff. Subsequently, the plaintiff raised three invoices which were paid by the defendant, but on 5 May 1989 the defendant informed the plaintiff that it was terminating the relationship and requested that the plaintiff vacate the defendant's premises immediately. The plaintiff complained in writing of the alleged breach of contract by the defendant but the correspondence remained unanswered until, on 27 November 1989, the defendant's solicitor wrote to the plaintiff asserting that there was no contract between them. It was argued that the letter of 10 March 1989 was merely a letter of intent and, even if it were an acceptance, there was still no contract as the plaintiff's offer was expressed to be subject to contract.

It was held that there was a binding contract. A number of factors were important, in particular:

- the plaintiff committed significant resources to the work and this was suggestive that there was a contract – it would hardly have done so otherwise,
- the proposal made it clear that the plaintiff required a contract to be in force before it commenced work,
- the phrase 'subject to contract' was of very limited effect – the proposal indicated that a contract could come into being in a number of ways by using terminology indicating the existence of a contract such as 'signing of the contract', 'signing the order' and placing a 'firm order',
- the letter of 10 March 1989 was a clear acceptance – it was not expressed as being a letter of intent nor was it stated to be 'subject to contract',
- the issue of shared responsibilities yet to be resolved was deemed to be an administrative matter and did not detract from the contract being sufficiently certain to have effect,
- even if the letter of 10 March 1989 did not create a contract, the subsequent conduct of the parties was sufficient – the plaintiff did some work and the defendant paid for it, and at no time during this period did the defendant seek to redefine the functions of the plaintiff.

The dangers inherent in embarking on work without a formal contract in place are fairly obvious. In the above case, if the court had held otherwise, the software developer would have found it difficult to obtain any recompense for the work it carried out. One possibility is under a *quantum meruit* (see below). Another difficulty is determining the precise nature and scope of the contractual terms. If, eventually, in the above case, an administrative decision was taken assigning responsibility between the software developer and the independent consultant, it could have been detrimental to the software developer. It could, for example, reduce the total job value for the software developer or increase the amount of work to be completed in an already tight timescale. However, where there is some uncertainty as to the precise terms of the contract, the terms implied by the Supply of Goods and Services Act 1982 may save the contract and make it valid. Otherwise, if there is a previous course of dealing between the parties, that may provide some clue as to the precise scope of the parties' rights and obligations under the contract.

Where it turns out that there is no valid contract – for example, through a lack of certainty as to the terms of the contract – the software developer may be entitled to payment on the basis of the work he has done in pursuance of what he believed was a valid contract. The law will require that the defendant pays the plaintiff for the 'fruit of his labour'. This is what is termed a *quantum meruit* (roughly translated – as much as he deserves). Of course, the defendant must have agreed to or at the very least acquiesced in the plaintiff carrying out the work. For example, if a software development company is appointed to write some software for a client but the purported contract between them is so vague and uncertain that it is ruled void, then if the software company has done satisfactory work for the client, it ought to be entitled to payment on the basis of a *quantum meruit*. Nevertheless, it is clearly preferable to have a valid and detailed contract containing all the necessary terms in writing and signed by both parties before the work commences. Writing computer software is sufficiently difficult and unpredictable without adding to the problems by having unsatisfactory legal provision for the work.

Chapter 18

Licence agreements for 'off-the-shelf' software

Introduction

This is software which is acquired as a ready-made package; it is mass-produced software usually obtained from a dealer and includes familiar packages such as word processing systems, spreadsheets and databases. It can be described as 'general purpose software'. It may be applications software (word processing, etc.), operating system software (for example, Windows or MS-DOS) or utility software such as disk management software, software for archiving files or anti-virus software. The contractual nature of transactions involving off-the-shelf software is not absolutely clear. Several possibilities exist:

- a licence agreement with the software publisher;
- a sale of goods contract with the dealer;
- a hybrid licence agreement/sale of goods contract with the software publisher (the dealer acting as the software publisher's agent); or
- a *sui generis* (unique) form of contract.

Before looking further at these possibilities, it must be noted that it is the intangible rights which are dominant in the transaction – for example, the right to use the software. This right requires the licence of the copyright owner, otherwise the copyrights subsisting in the software (there are likely to be a number of copyright works) will be infringed. This is confirmed by section 16(2) of the Copyright, Designs and Patents Act 1988 which states that the copyright in a work is infringed by a person who without the licence of the copyright owner does, or authorises another to do, any of the acts restricted by the copyright. As copying a work of copyright extends to making copies which are transient, it is quite clear that simply operating or running software involves making copies, whether transient or not, and this must have the licence of the copyright owner. Of course, in most cases, the software will be copied from the disk or CD-ROM on which it was supplied to the hard disk of the computer of the person acquiring the software. Subsequent copies will be made when the software is used as it will be loaded into the volatile memory (RAM) of the computer.

This simple fact appears to have been overlooked by a number of persons who have considered the nature of a contract for the existence of off-the-shelf software. Another key fact is the method of delivery of the software. It may be handed over in a box which contains disks or a CD-ROM together with printed documentation such as a manual and licence agreement. Increasingly, these days, software may be delivered on-line, with no tangible items being delivered to the person acquiring a copy of the software. Where software is supplied on physical media, in some cases the licence agreement will be exposed on the outside of the package. This is the so-called 'shrink-wrap' licence. The idea is that it enables the person acquiring the software to inspect the terms before opening the package. This is usually backed by a statement to the effect that, if the person acquiring the software does not agree with the terms of the licence, he can return the package unopened to the dealer and recover his payment. Another technique is to have the disks or CD-ROM in a sealed package separate to the licence and with a statement that breaking the seal signifies acceptance of the terms of the licence agreement, again, usually backed by a promise that the software can be returned before the seal is broken and any payment refunded. In the case of software delivered on-line, the person acquiring it will usually be required to signify his acceptance of the terms of the licence before the software can be 'downloaded'. Incidentally, the word 'download' has come in for judicial scrutiny and in *R v City of London Magistrates and the Director of the Serious Fraud Office, ex parte Jeffrey Green* (1998) ITCLR 35, it was held that it meant 'transfer from one storage device or system to another', as in the *Concise Oxford Dictionary* which also suggests it applies especially in relation to it being done remotely.

Licence agreement

Where no tangible items are transferred to the person acquiring the software – for example, where the software is downloaded from the Internet – the only contract is a licence agreement. This would also apply where software is specially written for a client and installed on the client's computer from the software development company's disks which are then retained by the latter. If the software is obtained remotely, it is likely that an opportunity will be given to read the licence agreement before the person wishing to obtain a copy of the software is committed to the transaction. Some software is available without cost over the Internet but it must be stressed that its copying and subsequent use must still be licensed by the copyright owner. Even with 'free' software, there are likely to be terms imposed on the person acquiring it, controlling or limiting its subsequent use and copying. For example, it may state that the software is for personal and private use only and must not be further distributed or sold without the permission of the copyright owner. There may also be other rights in relation to the software such as the author's moral rights to be identified as such and to object to a derogatory treatment of the work (these rights do not apply to computer programs but can apply to other items of software such as a database or document or image in digital form).

The licence agreement is likely to state what the applicable law is and, in many cases, it will be that of one of the United States of America such as California, New York or Florida. Where this is so, it should be noted that the copyright owner may still enforce his rights in the United Kingdom. The Copyright (Application to Other Countries) Order 1993, amended in 1994, extends the qualification provisions for United Kingdom copyright in the original works to persons and incorporated bodies from a considerable number of other countries. This is to give effect to the international conventions on copyright such as the Berne Copyright Convention. Thus, an American company or citizen of the United States can bring an action for copyright infringement occurring within the jurisdiction of the United Kingdom.

As far as the licence agreement itself, this may be enforced subject to the rules of jurisdiction. The licence may state that not only is the licence subject to the law of a particular country or state but that it is also subject to the sole jurisdiction of that country or state. The rules on jurisdiction are complex and, in relation to bringing an action outside the European Economic Area, leave of the court is required before proceedings can be commenced. Within Europe, the Brussels and Lugano Conventions on jurisdiction and enforcement of judgments in civil matters apply.

The licence will often be of indefinite duration, with no fixed period being stated, although there may be some provision for termination, such as if the person acquiring it, the customer, contravenes some term in the licence agreement which is stated to terminate it. A term requiring the customer not to transfer the software to a third party could be an example. Strictly speaking, the licence cannot endure longer than the copyright in the software because, when the copyright expires, the software effectively falls into the public domain and can be used freely without requiring permission. Some licence agreements allow the customer to terminate unilaterally simply by destroying all the copies of the programs and documentation, although why he should want to do this is hard to understand. If he no longer requires the software, he may be able to transfer both it and the licence to a third party in return for a payment unless the licence agreement provides otherwise.

Sale of goods contract

We have already seen in Chapter 15 that a contract for the acquisition of computer software is unlikely to be regarded as a sale of goods contract, especially where the predominant purpose of the transaction is the acquisition of the software. It has also been noted that where the software is incorporated into a good such as a motor car and the predominant purpose is the acquisition of the good rather than the software, then it will be a sale of goods contract. Where off-the-shelf software is obtained, it cannot be a sale of goods contract because to so classify the contract is to trivialise the main purpose of the contract, being the right to use the software. To say it is a sale of goods contract on the basis that some tangible items are handed over is to defy logic and to completely ignore the fact that the use of software requires the licence of the copyright owner. Even so, some writers (and some judges) seem unconvinced and prefer to rely on a familiar and tried and tested area of law to discuss or resolve actual or potential disputes. The convenience of this is that the Sale of Goods Act 1979 implies important terms into sale of goods contracts which give the person acquiring the software some useful rights if it turns out to be defective in some way.

The perceived problem of taking a contract to acquire off-the-shelf software out of the sale of goods arena is not serious as the common law has long since been capable of implying appropriate terms into contracts – indeed, many of the terms implied by the Sale of Goods Act 1979 and the Supply of Goods and Services Act 1982 are derived from terms which were implied under common law. This was recognised by Sir Iain Glidewell in the Court of Appeal in *St Albans City & District Council* v *International Computers Ltd* [1997] FSR 251 where he implied a term into a contract for the transfer of a computer program that the program would be reasonably fit for its purpose, that is, for achieving its intended purpose.

Hybrid contract

This is a possible scenario where the property in tangible items also passes to the person acquiring the software in addition to the right to use it, typically where a person goes into a retail computer shop and buys a software package. There may be two separate contracts: one between the person and the shop owner, being a sale of goods contract; and a licence between the person and the owner of the copyright subsisting in the software.

Consider a situation where George, who wishes to obtain a copy of the ABC spreadsheet software, goes to a computer software dealer, Acme Computers. George goes to Acme Computers and asks for a copy of the ABC spreadsheet software. He pays £200 and is given a sealed box. Inside the box is a CD-ROM on which the software is recorded, a manual and a licence agreement. There must be a contract between George and Acme Computers on the basis of normal sale of goods law. This will relate to the tangible items. Thus, if the CD-ROM is damaged and the software cannot be loaded onto George's computer because of this, he will have a remedy under section 14(2A) of the Sale of Goods Act 1979 as the CD-ROM is not of satisfactory quality. He will be able to obtain a replacement from Acme Computers or he may return the whole package and obtain a refund of the price he paid.

As between George and the owners of the copyright subsisting in ABC, Lemming Software plc, George must have Lemming's licence to use the software. The problem is what the terms of that licence are. It could be that they are those printed on the licence agreement which came with the software but there may be some problems with this as George may not have seen the licence until after he bought the software. A basic rule of English contract law (and many other jurisdictions) is that it is not possible to unilaterally introduce new terms into a contract after it has been made. If the contract is made at the time George hands over the money in return for the box containing the software, then he will not have seen the licence until it is too late.

Software publishers have tried various methods of giving their licence agreements the force of law. One technique used is to have the licence exposed on the outside of the package, the whole being wrapped in clear plastic, so that the licence may be inspected before the package is opened. This is the 'shrink-wrap' licence. Another technique used is for the licence to be printed on a sealed packet containing the disks or CD-ROM with a note to say that breaking the seal signifies acceptance of the terms of the licence. This is usually coupled with a promise that the customer can obtain a refund if he returns the software with the seal unbroken in the event of the customer being unwilling to accept the terms.

Both of the above approaches and variants of them are not without their difficulties as a means of incorporating the terms of the licence into the contract with the customer. The opportunity to read the terms comes after the contract is made because, at the latest, this occurs when the package containing the software is handed over to the customer. In *Olley* v *Marlborough Court Ltd* [1949] 1 All ER 127, a husband and wife went to an hotel and paid for a room. Their room contained a notice excluding liability for articles lost or stolen unless handed to the manageress for safe custody. A fur coat belonging to the wife was stolen and the hotel sought to rely on the exclusion notice. It was held that the notice was not part of the contract which had been completed at the reception desk when the room had been paid for and the hotel was liable for the loss because of its negligence. There had been insufficient supervision at the reception desk and the thief was able to take the key to the room from behind the desk. However, there are two contrasting cases dealing with tickets: one for a railway excursion ticket, *Thompson* v *LMS Railway* [1930] 1 KB 41, and one involving a ticket given after hiring a deck chair, *Chapelton* v *Barry Urban District Council* [1940] 1 All ER 356. In the former, the ticket contained a reference to the conditions in the company's timetable and was held to be validly incorporated into the contract whereas, in the latter case, the exclusion of liability on the reverse of the ticket was deemed to be ineffective as the ticket was considered to be a mere receipt.

The Court of Appeal has suggested that a particularly burdensome term on a delivery note would only be enforced if it had been specifically drawn to the attention of the other party (see *Interfoto Picture Library Ltd* v *Stiletto Visual Programmes Ltd* [1988] 1 All ER 348). Of course, if the term is in a document signed before or at the time the contract was made, the term will be binding on the party signing whether or not he has read it, providing that he has not been misled by the other party as to its effect. Therefore, to be absolutely sure that the terms in the licence are part of the contract the customer should be asked to sign the licence before the package is handed over. In many situations, however, this is impracticable – for example, where software is acquired by mail order.

If the terms do not become part of the contract by means of any of the ways discussed above, one way in which they might do is by virtue of a previous course of dealing – for example, where the customer previously has acquired software produced by the same software publisher. One final possibility is that the courts will imply appropriate terms based on what is reasonable in the circumstances and necessary to give the contract business efficacy. Custom may be very helpful in this respect and the courts would almost certainly look at what terms have become customary in the trade of software publishing.

A further but less likely possibility is that the Acme Computers acts as agent for Lemming Software and, as agent, makes a sale of goods contract and a licence agreement between George and Lemming.

Sui generis contract

This is the fourth mechanism which might be possible and it has a lot to commend it. A Scots judge suggested that contracts for the acquisition of off-the-shelf software of the 'shrink-wrap' licence variety in *Beta Computers (Europe) Ltd* v *Adobe Systems (Europe) Ltd* [1996] FSR 367 were *sui generis*. Beta, the pursuers (plaintiffs), supplied Adobe, defenders (defendants), with computer software produced by Informix Software Inc, a third party. It was accepted that Informix owned the copyright subsisting in the software. It had been ordered by Adobe by telephone and was a standard upgrade package suitable for Adobe's computer. The software was delivered with a 'shrink-wrap' licence and the package bore the words 'Opening the Informix S.I. Software package indicates your acceptance of these terms and conditions'.

Adobe claimed that it had the right to return the software without using it and that it had the right to reject it until such time as the package was opened, which it had not been. Beta sued for the price of the software.

Lord Penrose, in the Outer House of the Court of Session, in Edinburgh, reflected upon the legislative framework of the Copyright, Designs and Patents Act 1988 in the context of computer programs. He concluded that the supply of the medium on which the program is stored must be accompanied by an appropriate licence conferred directly or by implication from the acquisition of the software. An essential feature of the supply of off-the-shelf software is that the supplier undertakes to make available to the purchaser both the medium and the right of access and use of the software. In effect, the supplier undertakes that he has the right to communicate the benefit of the use of the software: in other words, that he transfers the benefit of the copyright owner's licence. Lord Penrose said:

> The supply of proprietary software for a price is a contract *sui generis* ... [it is] unacceptable to analyse the transaction in this case as if it were two separate transactions relating to the same subject matter. There is but one contract ...

The time such a contract is made is when the conditions imposed by the owner of the copyright were tendered to the purchaser of the software and accepted by the purchaser. Otherwise, there could be no *consensus ad idem* (agreement of the same thing) which is essential for a contract to exist. That being so, the purchaser can reject the software at any time before acceptance by performing the stated act – in this case, opening the sealed package.

Lord Penrose said that if the contract was considered to be a sale of goods contract this would produce the odd result that the dominant characteristic of interest to the parties (the right to use the software) was subordinated to the medium by which it was transmitted to the users.

There is one problem with the decision which may prevent it being fully applicable in other jurisdictions. Scots law is based on Roman law, not common law, and it was held that the contract gave rights to the copyright owner as a third party. This is possible under the Scots law of contract but not under English law. However, an alternative way of looking at the transaction is that it does not give rights to the copyright owner. Conversely, it is the copyright owner who gives rights to the purchaser of the software. Where there are restrictions in the licence agreement, they simply constrain the rights given to the purchaser rather than giving rights to the copyright owner.

In the United States, there has been less difficulty with shrink-wrap licences. In the 7th Circuit Court of Appeals, shrink-wrap licences were held to be enforceable; terms did not have to be exposed on the outside of the package containing the software. It was sufficient if there was a notice to the effect that there was a licence agreement inside. Furthermore, the purchaser was entitled to a full refund if, after reading the licence, he did not agree with the terms and conditions (*The Times*, 'Interface Supplement', 10 July 1996, p 6).

Typical terms in licences for off-the-shelf software

Usually, licence agreements for off-the-shelf software are not very lengthy. The copyright owner will want to set out the conditions of use of the software and confirm the fact of copyright subsistence and the grant of a licence to the purchaser. The licence may include some warranties and will have to address the impact of the applicable law on the licence. It may also deal with upgrades, user support and termination. Typically, the use may be limited to a single computer or a stated number of computers or users. A term dealing with whether the software and licence can be transferred to another person is also common.

It has been noted in Part One of this book that the Copyright, Designs and Patents Act 1988 makes void and unenforceable some terms in licence agreements which try to prohibit or restrict the permitted acts of decompilation of computer programs and making necessary back-up copies of computer programs. There some other controls which relate to databases. A form of words which might be used in a licence agreement to restrict decompilation to that permitted under the Act is 'You may not reverse engineer, decompile, disassemble or otherwise modify or alter the software except as provided for by section 50B of the Copyright, Designs and Patents Act 1988.'

The inclusion of warranties is not universal by any means and where they are given by the copyright owner, they are usually very limited. It may be that they are restricted to the return of the price paid for the software if it fails to perform substantially as stated in the documentation. We have seen that terms excluding or restricting liability for defective software are strictly controlled by the Unfair Contract Terms Act 1977 in the context of bespoke software. However, it is possible that much greater restriction or even exclusion is possible with off-the-shelf software, bearing in mind, of course, that liability for death or personal injury caused by negligence cannot be excluded or restricted by a term in a contract or notice by virtue of section 2 of the Unfair Contract Terms Act 1977. In respect of other types of liability, it would seem reasonable that liability can be restricted or excluded. The main reason is that the software is 'general purpose' and has not been written for a particular client's requirements. Furthermore, the company producing the software has no knowledge of the uses to which end users will put the software. If a person using spreadsheet software to perform some complex financial calculation makes a mistake, that is hardly the software company's fault. However, if there is an inherent defect in the software which is not obvious to a reasonable user, it is a moot point as to whether an exclusion clause would be effective. Until such time as exclusion clauses in off-the-shelf software licences come under judicial scrutiny, it is likely that no warranties will be given or, where they are, they will be limited to the price paid for the software.

If there are no warranties (whether the licence expressly states this or is silent on the point), would the courts be likely to imply any warranties? We have seen in the *St Albans* case that one judge thought an implied term of fitness for purpose would be appropriate. This would seem a sensible approach with off-the-shelf software, the purpose being that for which such software is usually obtained.

Finally, the licence is almost certain to contain an applicable law clause and, possibly, a term stating which courts are to have jurisdiction. A typical formula might be 'This licence agreement is governed by the laws of England and Wales and any dispute under it is subject to the sole and exclusive jurisdiction of the courts of England and Wales'.

Misrepresentation and dealers' promises

If we accept that a computer software dealer (or mail order supplier) acts as the agent of the copyright owner (usually the software publisher) in bringing about a licence between the software publisher and the customer, this has certain legal implications. The dealer has the authority, express or implied, to bind the software publisher contractually and this should not lead to problems. The dealer may have misled the customer, however, about the nature and performance of the software; he may, deliberately or otherwise, have made false claims which have induced the customer to obtain the software. A licence agreement is likely to contain a term to the effect that the software company will not be bound by anything which the dealer says in the pre-contractual negotiations and that the licence itself contains the entire agreement between the parties to the exclusion of anything else. Entire agreement terms are subject to the reasonableness test as stated in section 11(1) of the Unfair Contract Terms Act 1977 by virtue of section 3 of the Misrepresentation Act 1967 (as inserted by section 8 of the former Act). In *Mackenzie Patten & Co* v *British Olivetti Ltd* (unreported) 11 January 1984, discussed in more detail in Chapter 20, the buyer of computer hardware claimed, *inter alia*, that he had been induced into entering into the contract on the basis of a salesman's misrepresentation. However, the judge did not need to rule on whether an entire agreement clause in the contract was effective to remove any liability resulting from the misrepresentation as he found for the buyer on the basis of a collateral warranty (a term in a subsidiary contract inducing the party to enter into the main contract).

If the view is taken, contrary to *Adobe* v *Beta*, that a shrink-wrap licence is ineffective and a licence is implied, this could defeat the copyright owner's preferred choice of applicable law. Some licence agreements contain a term stating that the applicable law is other than English law. It is common to see licence agreements for software from the United States with the law of California or New York designated as the applicable law. If the licence supplied with the software can be disregarded and a licence is implied, that implied licence will most likely be subject to English law (or Scots law as the case may be). In any case the legal maxim *caveat emptor* (let the buyer beware) applies. The vast majority of mass-produced software is of a very high standard but, if the customer is uncertain, it is wise to check with some existing users of the software or in some of the many excellent computer journals and publications which carry out comparative tests on these software packages. It should be borne in mind, however, that sometimes magazines fail to be truly objective or may omit to test some particular software.

Back-up copies of programs

Making a back-up copy of a computer program infringes copyright unless its making is:

- permitted by the copyright owner;
- within the scope of an implied term; or
- necessary to the licensed use of the program.

Notwithstanding that there may be some doubt as to the contractual status of the licence agreement, as discussed above, it is sensible to check any provisions concerning back-up copies. If making a back-up copy is necessary to the licensed use of the program then section 50A of the Copyright, Designs and Patents Act 1988 states that any term in a licence agreement which attempts to take this right away is void and unenforceable at law. One way around this would be to prohibit the making of back-up copies while providing a service to replace the licensed copy of the program promptly, thereby making the need to take a back-up copy no longer necessary. Even so, it is unlikely that the word 'necessary' will be interpreted in a strict and narrow sense.

In practical terms, a sensible approach to back-up copies is required by both sides. Licensees should guard against the danger of proliferation of back-up copies which can soon become working copies, exceeding the licensed use. If an organisation requires 12 working copies, it should obtain a licence to cover 12 users, not a single-user licence. Users of software should develop a system of software audits to check and monitor the number of copies in use, and information and advice on how to implement software audits can be obtained from the Federation Against Software Theft (FAST). There are a number of other benefits. Regular auditing is part of good practice and quality management and will encourage a responsible attitude towards the use of software. During an audit, some employees might be found to be using old or defective versions of software and any pirated software brought into work by an employee may be discovered and dealt with. The implementation and enforcement of effective software audits also prevents the embarrassment of being raided by software copyright owners who have obtained an Anton Piller Order (now called a 'search order') giving them powers, accompanied by a solicitor, to enter and inspect the computer equipment and remove unauthorised copies of software to be used in evidence in copyright infringement actions.

Integration and upgrades

A person acquiring software should always check how well, if at all, the software will integrate with other software and whether data can be easily transferred to and from the software. Will the software run satisfactorily on

243

the customer's hardware? What is the position if the customer decides to upgrade his equipment or operating system software: will the software still be usable? What if a better version of the software is made available in due course: can the customer trade in his old software or will he have to pay the full licence fee for the new version? These are the type of questions someone contemplating an off-the-shelf system should consider; even though some of the events described might seem unlikely at the time, they have a nasty habit of becoming relevant later and if a customer is in doubt it is better to err on the side of flexibility. The pace of development in the computer industry shows no signs of slowing down and, as more powerful hardware becomes available, existing software packages will be enhanced in a like fashion and new software applications which were hitherto impossible or impracticable will appear on the market.

Training and support

Training is an aspect which is often overlooked. A computer dealer may offer training under a separate contract between himself and the customer. The quality of the training will obviously be important as will the provision of refresher courses. Many organisations have their own internal training and training videos can usefully supplement this but many organisations will need some external support. Most software publishers provide support, usually by telephone, and it is worth checking with existing users as to the effectiveness of the service. Many such support services leave much to be desired and there seems to be a general inability to deal with anything but the most obvious problems. A typically hard nut to crack is whether the fault is caused by a hardware defect or software fault. A computer dealer may be able to help but, in many cases, a user group may be of more assistance.

A final point concerns 'hotline' support. Will the dealer be prepared to provide an emergency call-out service if there is a problem related to the use of the software, such as trying to interface a word processing package with a new printer? In a case like this, the software itself will not be at fault; it will be a matter of installing the software in the correct manner for the particular printer. A dealer will charge for this type of support and the rate he requires will depend, among other things, on the speed of call-out expected by the customer.

Chapter 19

Contract between software author and publisher

Introduction

Not all software is developed directly by companies marketing the software. A self-employed software author, being the owner of the copyright, may prefer to deal with a software publishing company, already well established, with a good reputation and a high volume of sales. This may prove to be the most satisfactory way of exploiting the software. The software author will therefore consider granting a licence to a software publishing company permitting the latter to market the product on the basis of agreed royalty payments. The licence is likely to be an exclusive licence, which means that the author will grant the publisher the sole rights to deal with the software.

An important side-effect of an exclusive licence is that the licensee, the software publishing company, will have rights under copyright law as if it owned the copyright itself; the software publisher can sue for infringement of copyright directly, usually by joining the author in the action. Thus, if Arnold grants an exclusive licence in respect of his new computer game to Boris, a software publisher, and the game is copied without permission by Carol, Boris can sue Carol after joining Arnold as co-claimant. Any award made by the court will be shared with Arnold, usually on the basis of his royalty. As far as Arnold is concerned, this is an excellent arrangement as he may not have the resources to mount an infringement action himself. The licence agreement between the author and publisher should make provision for legal action taken by the exclusive licensee. For example, it may specify that the licensee will pay all legal costs and pay the author's other expenses in addition to a share in any award of damages or account of profits based on the royalty rate in the agreement. The agreement should also lay down whether the licensee is bound to take action if called upon by the author to do so or whether the licensee has discretion to take action and/or to make a settlement.

Rather than granting an exclusive licence, the author may assign the copyright (that is, transfer the ownership of the copyright) to the publisher. In practical terms, there is little difference between an assignment and an exclusive licence although from the author's point of view an exclusive licence is preferable. If the publisher is granted an assignment of copyright and later

245

reassigns that copyright to a third party, the author may have difficulty enforcing any obligations owed to him under the agreement. He will still be able to sue the first publisher but will not be able to take any action against any subsequent owner due to lack of privity of contract. Thus, if the first publishing company has ceased to exist – for example, because it has been wound up – the author will not be able to take any action in respect of royalties now due or accruing in the future. If the author does assign copyright, he could consider including a term in the agreement to the effect that the benefit of the agreement cannot be subsequently assigned at all or only with his express written approval.

Payment

A very important provision in the agreement will concern payment: how it will be calculated and when it will become due. Usually, the software author will be paid on the basis of royalties; it may be a fixed sum for every unit sold, or it may be expressed as a percentage of the price charged for the software. Less commonly, the author will be paid a lump sum for granting the exclusive licence, although this should be avoided unless there are special circumstances. The quantification of royalty payments must be precisely defined in the licence agreement. If royalties are based on the price of the software, is this the retail price or the payment the software publisher receives from a dealer? The author should look at the agreement and ask questions such as, what happens if the software publisher does not try very hard to market the product? What if the software publisher suddenly decides to distribute the software at a cut price? How does the software author know that the sales figures disclosed by the publisher are correct? Has the author the right of access to the publisher's accounts and sales information? How frequently will payments be made and what is the position if the publisher is consistently late in making payment? What is the position in respect of 'returns' – for example, unsold software that has been returned by a dealer? What if the publisher decides to stop marketing the software package; does this terminate the agreement? Finally, can the author terminate the agreement and, if so, under what circumstances?

Training, maintenance and defects

Other matters that will require the attention of the author and publisher include questions of training and maintenance and who is responsible for doing this. If the author is to be responsible, will he be paid anything for his work or is it included in the royalty payments? If the software publisher has to correct subsequent defects in the software, will the author be charged?

Related to such questions is the need for the licence agreement to state clearly and precisely what the author has to provide and when he has to provide it.

Indemnity

The software publisher will expect to receive an indemnity from the author in case the software or any part of it turns out to infringe a third party's right, such as a copyright or trade mark. An indemnity clause should allow the author the opportunity to make the necessary modifications to the software to remove or substitute the offending part so that the software no longer infringes. The software publisher may wish to recoup the cost of distributing modified copies of the software to existing users and other associated costs from the author.

Some thought needs to be given to the extent of the indemnity required should it not be possible to modify the software so that it does not infringe the third party right. It is reasonable to expect the author to return all payments received under the agreement but is it reasonable to expect him to pay the whole of the software publisher's costs (including legal costs), expenses and lost profits? The relative economic strength and bargaining position of the author and publisher should be a factor, especially if the author is a self-employed individual working on his own with few resources. Whether the author can insure against such an eventuality is another factor. Indemnity clauses are subject to the test of reasonableness by section 4 of the Unfair Contract Terms Act 1977. Where the indemnity granted relates to an intellectual property right or interest, however, paragraph 1(b) of Schedule 1 will apply nullifying the effect of section 4. Thus, if the author does not own the copyright he purports to grant a licence in respect of, any indemnity clause is not controlled by the Unfair Contract terms Act 1977 (it might be controlled in other ways) but, if he does own the copyright and the software displays some third party's trade mark on the screen thereby infringing it, it seems that section 4 will apply because that is outside paragraph 1(b). The usual test for reasonableness in section 11 has been discussed in Chapter 16.

An indemnity might also be sought by the publisher in respect of any defamatory statement contained within the software or if the software is otherwise illegal and the publisher is prevented from exploiting it or has to defend any legal action resulting from use of the software.

Confidentiality

The author should satisfy himself that the software publisher is fully aware of the confidential nature of elements of the software. The author may provide the publisher with the source code and the specification, including flowcharts, for the software. The agreement should spell out the duty of confidentiality in respect of these materials, reinforcing the common law duty. If the author has access to the publisher's information about sales and marketing techniques, a reciprocal duty could be placed on the author.

Liability

The relationship between the author, publisher and ultimate customers is shown in Fig. 19.1.

The author grants an exclusive licence to the publisher giving the publisher the exclusive right to produce copies of the software and to market them. The publisher 'sells' the software through a dealer, granting non-exclusive licences to the customers. The dealer is an agent whose role in this context is to act on behalf of the publisher to bring about the contract (the licence agreement) between the publisher and the customer subject to what has been said about the nature of such transactions in Chapter 18. The dealer having brought this about then effectively drops out of the picture. The author and ultimate customers are not in a contractual relationship but the law of negligence operates without the need for a contract as long as there is a duty of care owed by one person to another. The author will therefore want to be protected against any claims for losses to ultimate customers caused by defects in the software. The publisher will probably protect himself by having a suitably drafted exclusion or limitation clause in his licence agreements with the customers. The author should ask the software publisher to draw up any such term in the licence agreement with the ultimate customers in language wide enough to give some protection to the author, bearing in mind the legal controls on exclusion clauses.

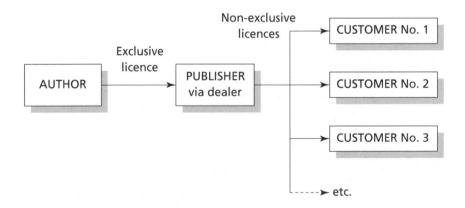

Fig. 19.1 Licence arrangement between author, publisher and customers

Other terms will be relevant in these forms of agreements, dealing with matters such as definitions, items provided, specification, delivery, liquidated damages, copyright and arbitration (or alternative dispute resolution); reference should be made to Chapters 17 and 18 for further details of these aspects.

Internet service providers and defamation

Organisations providing Internet access to authors are potentially liable in a number of ways. Information placed on the Internet (or other electronic publishing medium) by an author may infringe copyright, be defamatory or include a negligent misstatement. The Internet service provider could find himself liable at law as publisher of the information – for example, by implicitly authorising infringement of copyright by persons who download the information or as a publisher of defamatory material. (Note that Scots law on defamation is not identical to that in England and Wales.) The liability under copyright law is described in Chapter 7 in the context of electronic publishing.

Already, there have been a number of cases of defamation on the Internet. For example, in *Rindos* v *Hardwick* (unreported) 31 March 1994, the Western Australian Supreme Court found that a statement made by an academic which seriously denigrated another academic's competence and which also imputed misconduct on his part was defamatory and an award of A$40 000 in damages was made. In *Stratton Oakmont Inc* v *Prodigy Services Co* (unreported) 24 May 1995, the Supreme Court of the State of New York held that the defendant, a service provider, was the publisher of statements on its bulletin board and granted summary judgment against it in respect of libellous statements made on the bulletin board. In the United Kingdom, a lecturer accepted undisclosed damages in an out-of-court settlement for on-line statements that were potentially defamatory (Calow, D, 'Defamation on the Internet', *Computer Law and Security Report* (1995) 11(4), p 199).

A publisher is likely to require a warranty from an author that the material concerned is not defamatory in any way. This applies as much to software as to written statements. The warranty may be backed by an indemnity so that, if the publisher is sued for defamation and has to pay £40 000 in damages to the person defamed, the publisher will be able to recover this from the author. It is important that authors check for the presence of such warranties and indemnities in the agreement as awards in defamation cases can be notoriously high. Defamation is something of a rarity in that it is a civil action in which a jury may be sworn in and, if this is the case, it is the jury which decide whether defamation has been made out and, if so, the jury also decides the award. Under section 8 of the Defamation Act 1996, however, the judge may deal with the case summarily where it appears that the case is very clear cut – for example, where the plaintiff has no real chance of success.

249

One thing an author should be wary of is a term in the agreement which enables the publisher to settle a defamation action out of court at the publisher's discretion and still be able to recoup the money agreed in settlement from the author. There should be, at least, the insertion of the word 'reasonable' – for example, as in '… the reasonable exercise of the publisher's discretion'. The danger is, of course, that a publisher may be prepared to settle out of court simply to avoid the nuisance and publicity of a trial, safe in the knowledge that it will be able to recoup the settlement from the author.

There are two branches of defamation: libel and slander. Generally, libel relates to written statements whereas slander relates to the spoken word. The distinction is important because libel is actionable *per se* – that is, without proof of damage. Except in some cases, slander requires proof of damage. It appears that a defamatory image will be classed as libel rather than slander. In *Yousopouff* v *MGM Pictures Ltd* (1934) 50 TLR 581, the defendant made a film which suggested that the plaintiff was a Russian princess who had been 'ravished' or seduced by Rasputin. This was held to be libel, not slander.

Recently, an image taken from a computer game resulted in a libel action in the House of Lords. In *Charleston* v *News Group Newspapers* [1995] 2 AC 65, a Sunday newspaper carried a photograph which had been taken from a pornographic computer game. It depicted a man and woman who appeared to be engaged in sexual intercourse or other sexual activity. Superimposed on the photographs were images of the heads of the plaintiffs, actors who played Harold and Madge Bishop in the television 'soap' *Neighbours*. The captions ran 'Strewth! What's Harold up to with our Madge?' and 'Porn Shocker for Neighbours Stars'. However, because the text underneath made it clear that the image had been produced as part of a pornographic computer game which had used the images of the plaintiffs without their permission, it was held not to be libellous. The law does not take account of 'a moron in a hurry' – that is, a careless reader who would not read such a 'disclaimer' and might not realise the true nature of the image is ignored in determining whether it is libellous.

The difficulty in which publishers of electronic media containing information and Internet Service Providers could find themselves in respect of defamatory material made available through their service has been eased somewhat by the Defamation Act 1996. Before looking at the defence available to publishers and Internet Service Providers, the basic requirements for defamation are set out briefly.

Basics of defamation

A defamatory statement is one which, when published, tends to lower a person in the esteem of right-thinking members of society generally; or which tends to make them shun or avoid that person. The statement does not have to allege some moral turpitude or wrongdoing on the part of the claimant (plaintiff) and it can be defamation to allege insanity or being the victim of a crime such as rape.

It is common to see disclaimers as to the characters portrayed in a film. It is dangerous to publish something containing, for example, a fictional character with a name that might be the same as a real person. In *Hulton & Co v Jones* [1910] AC 20, an article was published by the defendant which was alleged by the defendant to be fictitious. It contained defamatory statements about one 'Artemus Jones', a churchwarden from Peckham. However, and unfortunately for the defendant, by coincidence there was a person with that name who happened to be a barrister living in North Wales. He successfully sued for libel. It was thought that some of his friends and acquaintances might think the article referred to him.

Publication is required and it must be to at least one person other than the plaintiff. It may be by means of words, pictures, visual images, gestures or any other method of signifying meaning. The defendant must either publish the material himself or be responsible for publication. Every repetition of a defamatory publication is a fresh publication and actionable. Thus, if defamatory material is placed on the Internet, every time it is accessed and read by someone, this constitutes a separate defamation. The potential is that thousands or even millions of causes of action could accrue in respect of placing defamatory material in, say, a Web page. Also, a reasonably foreseeable repetition of a publication by a third party will also bring liability. In *Slipper* v *British Broadcasting Corp* [1991] 1 QB 283, which concerned a film broadcast by the defendant, the claims made by the plaintiff included damages for reviews of the film in the press. The Court of Appeal refused to strike out these additional claims. In respect of republication it was held that this could be a *novus actus interveniens* (a new act breaking the chain of causation) if it was unauthorised. However, where reasonably foreseeable, the chain of causation was not broken.

There are a number of defences to a defamation action including fair comment, justification (that is, that the statement is true), an offer to make amends and privilege. The publisher's defence is described below.

Publisher's defence

Prior to the passing of the Defamation Act 1996, the Lord Chancellor's Department specifically looked at this problem. The 1996 Act has, therefore, a specific defence in which a person can show that he had no responsibility for the publication. The defence came into force on 4 September 1996. Under section 1, the defence applies if a person shows that:

- he was not the author, editor or publisher of the statement complained of,
- he took reasonable care in relation to its publication, and

- he did not know, and had no reason to believe, that what he did caused or contributed to the publication of a defamatory statement.

Under section 1(3) of the Defamation Act 1996, a number of persons are not to be considered authors, editors or publishers if only involved:

(a) in printing, producing, distributing or selling material containing the statement;
(b) in processing, making copies of, distributing, exhibiting or selling a film or sound recording containing the statement;
(c) in processing, making copies of, distributing or selling electronic medium in or on which the statement is recorded, or in operating or providing any equipment, system or service by means of which the statement is retrieved, copied, distributed or made available in electronic form;
(d) as the broadcaster of a live programme containing the statement in circumstances in which he has no effective control over the maker of the statement;
(e) as the operator or provider of access to a communications system by means of which the statement is transmitted, or made available, by a person over whom he has no effective control.

It can be seen that (c) above applies in relation to publishers of computer software on disk or CD-ROM and (e) applies particularly to Internet Service Providers. In other cases, the court may use the above provisions by way of analogy in deciding whether a person is considered to be an author, editor or publisher.

Under section 1(4), employees or agents are in the same position as their employer or principal to the extent that they are responsible for the content of the statement or the decision to publish it.

To determine whether a person took reasonable care, under section 1(5), regard is to be had to:

(a) the extent of his responsibility for the content of the statement or the decision to publish it,
(b) the nature of the circumstances of the publication, and
(c) the previous conduct or character of the author, editor or publisher.

Thus, where an author or publisher has been in trouble before in relation to defamatory material, that is a factor in determining whether he took reasonable care. In other words, a previous history of publishing defamatory material requires the person responsible to exercise greater care to prevent it happening again. This could apply, for example, where a publisher of computer games has previously published games including libellous statements.

The section 1 defence may be vulnerable once an Internet Service Provider has been informed that material which contains a statement alleged to be defamatory has been placed on the Service Provider's server and it is not removed immediately. In *Godfrey* v *Demon Internet Ltd, The Times*, 20 April 1999, a subscriber to an Internet Service Provider, the defendant, made material available through the defendant's service which was alleged by the plaintiff to be defamatory of him. The plaintiff brought the present action to strike out part of the defence as disclosing no sustainable defence to a libel action, based on the publication of the material by the defendant. After the plaintiff informed the defendant of his allegation that the material was defamatory, the defendant did not remove the material (although, eventually, it did so).

It was held that the defence did not apply in this case as, at common law, once the defendant became aware that the material contained defamatory statements it could no longer satisfy two of the requirements in section 1(1) – that is, that reasonable care had been taken in the publication and that the defendant had no knowledge or reason to believe that he caused or contributed to the publication of the defamatory statement. Mr Justice Morland pointed out that section 17 of the Defamation Act 1996 states that 'publication' and 'publish' have the meaning they have generally for the law of defamation but 'publisher' is specially defined in section 1. He did accept, however, that the defendant was not a commercial publisher for the purposes of section 1(2), being a person whose business is issuing material to the public, or a section of the public, who issues material containing the statement in the course of that business. Unfortunately for the defendant, for the section 1(1) defence to apply, all three requirements must be satisfied. The defendant's argument that it had played a passive role was not accepted and the judge thought the situation analogous to that of a bookseller who sold a book containing defamatory material.

The significance of this case is that the special defence may be quite limited in its scope. If a person alleges that defamatory material has been placed on the Service Provider's server, it may no longer be safe to rely on the defence and the Service Provider ought to consider removing the material immediately. This is quite important as each time an individual accesses the material, there will be a fresh libel. Whether a Service Provider has no reason to believe that he causes or contributes to the publication must be an objective test based on the reasonable person having knowledge of the facts known to the Service Provider and which must be coloured by the allegation of defamation.

Consider a situation where an Internet Service Provider is informed by someone that a statement defamatory of him has been placed on the Service Provider's server. If the material is not removed immediately, the issue for the court may become one simply relating to the general law of defamation. If the statement is held by the court to have a defamatory meaning, it is highly unlikely that the section 1 defence can apply. For example, if the matter is being decided by a jury and it finds the statement defamatory, it will almost certainly consider that, after being informed of the allegation of defamation, the Service Provider did indeed 'have reason to believe'. The same probably applies where there is no jury and the case is heard before a judge alone. On the other hand, if the finding is that the statement is not defamatory, that is an end to the matter. Thus, the section 1 defence is likely to be relevant only up to such time as an Internet Service Provider has been informed of the allegation. If that is so, Internet Service Providers would be well advised to remove the material immediately. However, if they respond in that way, that makes freedom of information vulnerable to persons who simply do not like what is said about them over the Internet without the statements necessarily being defamatory. Given the sensitivity of the issue and the potential of numerous actions for defamation, Internet Service Providers are likely to play safe if there is any possibility that the statement complained of may be defamatory.

Chapter 20

Hardware contracts

Introduction

Computer hardware may be purchased outright or hired. Much of what has already been discussed in relation to computer software contracts, in particular contracts for the writing or modification of software, will apply to contracts for the acquisition of hardware. Very often, the purchase of or hire of computer equipment will include software, such as operating system software, computer programming languages, utility programs or applications programs. These items of software usually will be subject to collateral licence agreements.

Computer software is important; the choice of the software best suited to the client's requirements is critical and when it comes to setting up a computer system in a company or business that has not used computers before or where a change in computer equipment is contemplated, the decisions regarding the selection of software are of primary importance. The secondary decision should then be to determine the type of computer equipment which will be most suitable for running this software, not forgetting other important considerations such as future growth, the impact of the computing operations and the future of the software packages and computer equipment. Will the company manufacturing the computer continue to develop and support it in the longer term? Is it an industry standard with a wide range of available software?

If the client already has some computer equipment and software, this will influence any decisions about obtaining new hardware. Compatibility with the existing equipment will be important and some compromises may have to be made. The aim should be that in three or five years' time the decision will still seem to have been a good choice. Long-term planning is essential, not only in terms of computer equipment but also taking into account the client's business strategy and plans for development and how these will prescribe and influence its computer needs.

Performance

The performance of software is directly related to the computer's performance. The speed of operation of the computer will be very important and a contract for the purchase or hire of computer equipment should make reference to this. Information about processing speeds, storage capacities, data transfer and networking capabilities will be paramount. The purchaser must satisfy himself as to the performance of the equipment, bearing in mind the environment in which the equipment will be working.

Simple benchmark speed tests may not provide a very good picture of the computer's performance if it will be used to carry out many different tasks at the same time, with multiple concurrent access to data files. The client should think about the operating system and whether it is a common one able to run a large variety of applications programs. Similar considerations apply to networking hardware and software. Another point which might be relevant is whether there are any limitations on the number of data files the computer will permit to be in use at the same time.

Representations and collateral warranties

A salesperson will usually extol the virtues of the equipment he is trying to sell and he will try to convince the would-be purchaser that it is everything he needs; in other words, it is the answer to a maiden's prayer. If the equipment turns out to be totally unsuited to the client's needs, the supplier will probably point to a term in the contract of sale which states that the printed agreement represents the entire agreement between the parties and nothing said or done in preliminary negotiations is part of the contract. This ploy may not always work, as the case below demonstrates.

In *Mackenzie Patten & Co v British Olivetti Ltd* (unreported) 11 January 1984, the plaintiff was a firm of solicitors which wanted a computer to handle its accounts and the defendant company was approached by the plaintiff with this in mind. Following negotiations with the defendant's salesman, the plaintiff agreed to obtain one of the defendant's computers under a leasing agreement with a third party. The computer proved totally unsuitable for the plaintiff's needs and the plaintiff's staff were incapable of using the computer effectively even following training by the defendant. After hearing expert evidence, the judge decided that the computer was obsolete and not suitable for the defendant's requirements. Indeed, as the plaintiff firm was a small one, it was questionable whether a computer was needed at all. (Things are much different now; even the smallest firm needs computer technology and, preferably, also access to the Internet.)

The judge held that the plaintiff had relied on the salesman's statements when entering the leasing agreement. The statements were a collateral warranty and, as they were not true, there was a breach of this warranty. There was an 'entire agreement' clause in the contract but this was held to be ineffective as it was stated in terms of a contract of sale and, in fact, the contract entered into by the plaintiff was a leasing contract. No sale to the plaintiff took place or was contemplated (the plaintiff could not afford to buy the computer outright). The contract contained an exclusion clause but the judge held that the defendant had failed to prove that it was reasonable, applying the test in section 11 of the Unfair Contract Terms Act 1977. The judge awarded the plaintiff the sum of £16 204 which comprised £2661 for payments made under the lease agreement, £12 692 for payments owing under the agreement and £851 interest. A further claim for wasted time in meetings and the like of £1200 was dismissed by the judge as being too vague and too remote.

If the entire agreement clause had been found to be effective to exclude the salesman's statements, the plaintiff would probably have had a remedy under section 2 of the Misrepresentation Act 1967, any attempt to exclude liability being subject to the reasonableness test in the Unfair Contract Terms Act 1977. Hence, suppliers of computer equipment should make every effort to ensure that the would-be purchaser is fully aware of the equipment's capabilities and limitations. The purchaser would be wise to seek independent advice and the supplier, if there is any doubt about the suitability of a particular piece of equipment, would be wise to suggest that such independent advice is sought. In particular, it is unwise to attempt to sell obsolete or unsuitable equipment to a solicitor, although, in the above case, it appears that the solicitor signed the agreement without first reading it thoroughly!

Maintenance and upgrades

The contract should state exactly who does what in terms of installation and initial testing. Once the equipment is installed, how well will the supplier support it? Maintenance will probably be provided for by a separate contract, renewable annually, and the client should check this contract to see what it has to say on the point of speed of response to a breakdown. If repairs have to be made to the computer equipment, does the client have to pay for parts or labour or both and is there a minimum call-out charge? The maintenance contract may provide for the loan of alternative equipment while repairs are carried out and, if it does not so provide, it could be worth asking why not. The client should also check whether third party maintenance is a possibility.

Sooner or later the computer equipment will become obsolete as faster, more powerful equipment is continually being developed. This can have one of two consequences. First, the new equipment is better in so many respects and so different that there is no possibility of upgrading the old equipment to the new standards. It is then a matter of making do, standing by the existing equipment, consolidating it and adding improvements when they become available with a view to reviewing the situation in a year or two, when the quality and performance of the new equipment has been fully tested by others. The general acceptance of equipment among the computer world is very important. Sometimes, a new computer will catch on and sell in volume and this will then encourage the leading software companies to produce appropriate software for the new machine, making it an even more attractive proposition. Once a new computer attracts the attention of the software companies it is well on its way to becoming established. It is very tempting to stay with the market leaders when buying computer equipment. As the old adage used to go, 'No one was ever fired for buying IBM!'

A second consequence of the announcement of new, improved equipment is that it may be possible to upgrade the existing equipment to those standards, and the new equipment may be in the form of an upgrade. When buying computer equipment, it is worthwhile finding out what the manufacturer's attitude is to his existing customers regarding upgrades or new equipment. Will the improved equipment be sympathetically priced as far as existing customers are concerned? Will a generous trade-in be allowed on the old equipment or is there a good second-hand market for the manufacturer's equipment? Does the manufacturer have a history of upwardly compatible machines or does he bring out new equipment that is totally unlike the old equipment? Does he change operating systems continually? Ideally, the manufacturer should have a policy of building on his past products. It must be borne in mind that there is a dichotomy here for manufacturers. A manufacturer will want to attract new customers and, to do this, the equipment must be up to date and make use of the latest technological developments. On the other hand, the manufacturer will owe a moral duty to his loyal customers to maintain some degree of compatibility. The history of computing is one of change and abandoning out-of-date equipment and the person or company considering purchasing a computer or other computer equipment would do well to bear this in mind. There is little that can be done contractually, apart from insisting that the supplier (it will be the supplier and not the manufacturer who will be a party to the contract unless the supplier and manufacturer are one and the same) will continue to support the equipment for a reasonable period of time, regardless of whether it is later withdrawn from the market place.

If the equipment is hired, problems of obsolescence are less important providing the hirer is not committing himself to an unduly long period of hire. Hiring is often referred to as leasing; there is no particular significance in this because a lease contract and a contract of hire are basically the same thing. The duration of the agreement will be important as will be the presence of any term in the agreement concerning termination and the relevant circumstances. If a much better piece of equipment is suddenly available, the hirer may wish to terminate the agreement quickly so that he can avail himself of the new equipment. The company hiring the equipment out will obviously want some form of compensation should the hirer want to return the computer equipment before the normal time and this requires a sensible compromise.

Legal controls

Statutory safeguards are more in evidence when it comes to hardware contracts. For example, the Sale of Goods Act 1979 will apply because a computer or other related equipment comes within the meaning of 'goods'; a computer is a personal chattel. This means that the important terms such as compliance with description and meeting the requirement of satisfactory quality will be implied into a contract to purchase a computer. Certain terms implied by the Sale of Goods Act 1979 are implied into all contracts of sale while others only apply where the seller sells in the course of business. Compliance with description is an example of the former while satisfactory quality is an example of the latter. Most of the contracts under consideration in this book will be in the course of business. Similar terms will be implied into hire contracts by the Supply of Goods and Services Act 1982. These implied terms can be excluded or limited in the case of a non-consumer sale but only in so far as the exemption clauses purporting to do this meet the requirement of reasonableness as provided for by the Unfair Contract Terms Act 1977, sections 5 to 7.

The fact that the hardware is sold complete with software does not prevent the contract from being a sale of goods contract. For example, in the Australian case of *Toby Constructions Products Pty Ltd* v *Computer Bar Sales Pty Ltd* (1983) 50 ALR 684, the Supreme Court of New South Wales held that the sale of a computer system, comprising both hardware and software, was a sale of goods contract. The contract was primarily one for equipment as the hardware cost was A$12 230 and the software cost was A$2160. This logic was approved of by Scott Baker J in *St Albans City & District Council* v *International Computers Ltd* [1995] FSR 686. Looking at the primary objective of the contract is a sensible approach. After all, the purchaser of a defective washing machine would be surprised to find that the Sale of Goods Act did not apply, even if the defect was traced to the program controlling the washing cycle. Where the balance between hardware and software is more even, however, it is better to make two separate contracts so that the application of statutory controls is predictable.

A final point to consider is that there is a possibility that the computer hardware or the software sold with it infringes some intellectual property right. The hardware itself could infringe a patent, design or trade mark while the software might infringe a copyright or trade mark. The client should make sure that the contract contains a term indemnifying him in case this should happen. If the contract is governed by the Sale of Goods Act 1979, however, there will be remedies available to the buyer if he is prevented from using or hindered in his use of the equipment because it infringes another person's rights. By section 12(1), there is an implied condition that the seller has the right to sell the goods and, by section 12(2), there is an implied warranty that the buyer will enjoy 'quiet possession' of the goods. Section 6 of the Unfair Contract Terms Act 1977 provides that section 12 of the Sale of Goods Act 1979 cannot be excluded or restricted by reference to any contractual term. If a company buys a computer and, at the time of the sale, the computer infringes a trade mark or patent, then the seller is in breach of section 12(1) of the Sale of Goods Act 1979. Because this is a condition, the buyer can repudiate the contract and claim back the purchase price, plus damages for any consequential losses he has suffered (provided they are not too remote). In *Niblett Ltd* v *Confectioners' Materials Co Ltd* [1921] 3 KB 387, it was held that because goods, when sold, infringed a trade mark, this entitled the buyer to repudiate the contract. In Scotland the question is whether the breach is a material one.

It may happen that equipment does not infringe a patent when it is sold but does infringe a patent soon afterwards, perhaps because at the time of sale a patent application, made by a third party, was being processed. When the patent is granted, the third party may commence an infringement action against the buyer of the equipment. This occurred in a case involving road marking machines, *Microbeads AC* v *Vinhurst Road Markings* [1975] 1 WLR 218, where it was held that:

- there was not a breach of section 12(1) because, at the time of the sale, the seller had every right to sell (the patent could not be enforced at that time); and
- the seller was in breach of section 12(2), the implied warranty as to quiet possession, and was liable to the buyer in damages.

There is always a danger that computer equipment or software will infringe a third party's rights (even if it is inadvertent) because of the rapid development of new hardware and software. The remedies in section 12 of the Sale of Goods Act 1979 are useful but it is advisable to make specific contractual provision for the eventuality. For example, in a situation like that in the *Microbeads* case, the buyer may prefer to be able to repudiate the contract rather than being limited to damages only. However, there is a defence to a patent infringement action if a person, in good faith, does the act or makes effective and serious preparations to do the act before the patent's priority date (see Patents Act 1977, section 64).

Tenders

An organisation wishing to obtain computer equipment (the client) may ask a number of suppliers or manufacturers to submit tenders. Each of the companies submitting tenders will be asked for their price to supply the equipment described in a detailed specification. In this way, the bids can be compared on a like for like basis and, usually, the one submitting the lowest bid will be awarded the contract to supply equipment complying with the specification. Letting contracts by means of a tendering process is very common and public authorities and many large private organisations make use of this process. In some cases, the organisation will have no other option as it will be laid down in the constitution or articles of association. In some cases, it may be imposed from elsewhere – for example, where the contract value exceeds a particular value, it will have to be open to tenders because of government or European Community regulations.

The contractual status of a tender is that a company submitting a tender is making an offer which can be rejected or accepted by the client as he thinks fit. Indeed, the client can choose not to accept any unless, for example, he has bound himself to accept the lowest. Consequently, the company submitting a tender bears the cost involved in its preparation such as determining which equipment is suitable and calculating the total price. If the hardware is complex, this cost can be considerable. The use of tendering as a means of letting contracts is very common in the construction industry. The convention that the person submitting the tender bears the costs of preparation of the tender is deeply ingrained; that it also applies in the context of computer contracts was emphatically stated in *Comyn Ching Ltd* v *Radius plc* (unreported) 17 March 1997, which concerned a tender for the supply of computer equipment and software. The judge cited a passage from *Keating on Building Contracts*, 6th edn (a leading practitioner text), to the effect that the contractor preparing a tender may incur considerable cost in doing so but there is no implication that he will be paid for this work. Indeed, ' ... he undertakes this work as a gamble, and its cost ... he hopes will be met out of the profits of such contracts as are made as a result of tenders which prove to be successful!' The judge went on to say 'I see no difference in principle between a building contract and a computer contract.'

Tenders can be requested from a selected list of companies or open tendering can be used – that is, where anyone who wishes may submit a bid. Select list tendering is more usual nowadays and has the advantage that only those companies perceived as being competent are invited to submit bids. However, this may again be subject to rules imposed by government or through the European Community.

The tender process is broadly as follows:

1 A detailed specification is drawn up detailing the functional and performance requirements.
2 If it is to be a select list tender, that list is drawn up and those on it are asked if they are interested in submitting tenders. If open tendering is to be used, an advertisement will be placed in an appropriate newspaper or journal or other publication (for example, the *Official Journal of the European Communities*).
3 To each tenderer, a set of tender documents will be sent comprising the

261

specification (including any drawings and schedules), a form of agreement (so that the tenderer can see what the contractual obligations will be) and, in some cases, a bill of quantities in which the tendering company can write prices or a schedule of rates to be completed or a simple form on which the overall price can be written. The bill, schedule or form will contain a reference to the other documents.

4 A period of time will be allowed and a deadline will be stated for return of the tenders in sealed envelopes – for example 'no later than noon on 28 February 2000'. Tenders received after this deadline must be rejected (to prevent the possibility of corruption).

5 The sealed tenders will be opened after the deadline. This may be before a senior officer and chairman of the appropriate committee in the case of a public authority. Any arithmetic will be checked carefully. (Mistakes can cause all sorts of problems if not picked up and dealt with. If there is a mistake it is usual practice to ask the company submitting that particular tender whether it wishes to stand by its mistake or withdraw the tender.)

6 A letter of acceptance will be sent to the successful company (usually that submitting the lowest bid) and a contract will be executed, typically under seal, as per the original form of agreement.

Tenders can be seen as a very fair means of letting contracts and the system has evolved as a way of reducing the possibility of bribery and corruption. However, tendering is not without difficulties. The client has to make sure that the tender documents are of a high quality, accurately describe the desired equipment and its performance and provide fully for any eventuality. If there are any shortcomings, the successful company may use these as a basis of additional payments and extensions to the time for delivery. A major headache for the client is that the companies submitting tenders, or at least some of them, will wish to make changes to the specification or time for delivery, etc. If this is permitted, it makes comparison of the tenders more difficult. A usual means of trying to maintain some comparability is to ask any company which has expressed a wish to submit on a different basis to submit two tenders, one as per the original tender documents, the other on its preferred specification.

Chapter 21

Electronic contracting

Introduction

Information technology allows and encourages the conduct of many aspects of commercial activity by electronic means, at least in part. Forms of agreement and other contractual documents are likely to be created using a computer and may be transmitted in electronic form anywhere in the world. Standard forms and precedents used by solicitors to draw up agreements, such as a software licence or a will, are now published electronically. Typically, a solicitor acting for a party to a contract will load an appropriate form of agreement into his word processor, make any required modifications and additions, and then either print it out or transmit it to the other party's solicitor. A contractual offer may be made in this way and may be accepted electronically by the other party transmitting his acceptance of the terms of the agreement.

Many transactions are now effected electronically. For example, by the use of automated teller machines (ATMs or cash point dispensers outside banks) and electronic fund transfers (EFTs) transactions are made between financial institutions and even at the point of sale. A growing number of organisations exchange data electronically. For example, a large manufacturing company may order components automatically and electronically from its suppliers when stock levels reach a predetermined lower limit. Electronic data interchange (EDI) has the potential to maximise efficiency by reducing repetition and delays, increasing accuracy and permitting the maintenance of minimum stock levels by placing orders for 'just-in-time' delivery. A large proportion of the information flows between organisations may be handled electronically, including quoting or submitting tenders for work, ordering, scheduling, invoicing and accounting.

All of this sounds very good apart, perhaps, from concerns about security but, as expected, there are a number of legal consequences associated with electronic trading.

- The law requires that some contracts are in a particular form – for example, by deed or in writing.
- There may be doubts as to when the contract was made and, if the parties are in different countries, which country's law will apply to the contract.
- The evidential weight of electronic documents must be considered and assessed.

To take an example, imagine that Karen, who has a large footwear store in London, wishes to buy 1000 pairs of shoes from Luigi in Milan. Both Karen and Luigi have computers and both use electronic mail. All the preliminary negotiations are carried out using electronic mail. Eventually, Karen transmits a contract for Luigi's approval on Monday at 10.00 am GMT. Later that day, at 2.00 pm GMT, Luigi sends a message to say that he accepts Karen's offer. However, Karen does not read that message until Wednesday as she has to make a trip to Scotland in the meantime. There is a term in the contract to the effect that Karen can terminate the contract if she fails to sell more than 50 pairs of shoes in any one week, returning the remaining stock to Luigi and paying only for those that she has sold. After four weeks, Karen has sold 250 pairs of shoes but 175 pairs were sold in the first week following an intensive advertising campaign. Sales have plummeted since and in the fourth week only 12 pairs were sold. Karen wishes to exercise her right to terminate the contract but the only evidence she has of the numbers sold each week is the record of sales on her computer, entered by her various shop assistants as and when they sold shoes.

The questions that arise in the above scenario related to the use of electronic contracting are:

- Is the contract valid – that is, did the electronically transmitted offer and acceptance create a binding contract? (If so, what would the position have been if Luigi, who did not receive confirmation until Wednesday, had sold the shoes to a third party on Tuesday?)
- If there is a valid contract, when was it made and is it subject to English or Italian law?
- Can a printout of the computer record of sales be used as evidence to prove that Karen sold insufficient numbers of shoes so allowing her to invoke the termination clause?

The three main issues relating to electronic contracting concern the legal formalities, the time and place that the contract was made and the admissibility of computer evidence in civil proceedings. These are considered below. At the end of the chapter, we will return to Karen and Luigi and advise them accordingly.

Legal requirement as to form

A contract may be made in a number of different forms. For example, a contract may be made by deed, made in writing, evidenced in writing or it may be oral, or it may be a combination of these. For example, section 4 of the Sale of Goods Act 1979 states that a contract of sale:

... may be made in writing (either with or without seal), or by word of mouth, or partly in writing and partly by word of mouth, or may be implied from the conduct of the parties.

An example of a contract implied from the conduct of the parties is given by the case of *Brogden* v *Metropolitan Rail Co* (1877) 2 App Cas 666 concerning a contract to supply coal. It was held that the conduct of the parties by dealing with each other in accordance with a draft contract could only be explained on the basis that they approved the draft contract and a binding contract came into existence, at the latest, when the plaintiff supplied the first order of coal placed by the defendant.

Although for some contracts the form used does not matter (as in a sale of goods contract above), occasionally the law requires that a particular form be used. Some contracts must be by deed, an example being a lease of real property (land) for more than three years (sections 52 and 54(2) of the Law of Property Act 1925). A deed is a written document that is signed, sealed and delivered and a contract made by deed is referred to as a contract under seal. This requirement can be traced back to the Statute of Frauds 1677 which was intended to prevent lack of documentation being used as a means of fraud. The formality associated with a deed demonstrates a clear intention to be bound and, therefore, in terms of a contract, there is no requirement for consideration (for example, payment or goods) which is a normal prerequisite of legally binding contracts.

In recognition of the fact that some flexibility is now required and the traditional form of deed – originally written in beautiful cursive script on vellum with a wax seal attached (or more recently a red adhesive wafer) – is no longer relevant in today's society, the Law of Property (Miscellaneous Provisions) Act 1989 abolishes some of the old rules that applied to some deeds. Now, to qualify as a deed, the instrument must make it clear on its face that it is intended to be a deed (for example, by using a form of words making it clear that it is a deed) and it must be validly executed – for example, signed in the presence of witnesses and delivered (section 1(2) and (3)). The meaning of 'sign' includes making one's mark. It is possible that this could extend to a digital electronic representation of a signature and, because of the other relaxations in the rules, there seems to be no reason why an electronic deed cannot be valid. Nevertheless, because there is still a degree of uncertainty, it would be wise to print out the deed on paper before it is signed before witnesses, although this would then require physical delivery, losing one of the advantages of using information technology.

Relatively few legal documents are required to be by deed. However, some must be in writing. For example, an assignment of a copyright must be in writing and signed by or on behalf of the assignor (section 90(3) of the Copyright, Designs and Patents Act 1988), and regulated consumer credit agreements must be in documentary form and signed (section 61 of the

Consumer Credit Act 1974). The same applies to contracts for marine insurance, by section 22 of the Marine Insurance Act 1906, and contracts for the sale or other disposition of an interest in land, which must also incorporate all the terms expressly agreed by the parties (section 2(1) of the Law of Property (Miscellaneous Provisions) Act 1989). Yet other contracts must be evidenced in writing, an example being a contract of guarantee by section 4 of the Statute of Frauds 1677.

For contracts where writing is a requirement it is important to determine whether documents stored magnetically in digital form comply. Fortunately, Schedule 1 to the Interpretation Act 1978 contains the following definition:

'Writing' includes typing, printing, lithography, photography and other modes of representing or reproducing words in a visible form, and expressions referring to writing are construed accordingly.

This would appear to include computer storage. Words stored in a computer may be reproduced on screen or printed on paper. In any case, it is unlikely that a judge would take a restrictive view of this, although the preceding words are somewhat narrow.

Where signatures are required, what has been said earlier in respect of deeds should still hold. The matter is not beyond doubt but there is no logical reason why a person's mark cannot be stored in digital form and affixed to a computer file electronically. The purpose of a signature is to identify the signatory's assent to the document or transaction. This can be done effectively by electronic means, particularly if a form of encryption is used. The stylised handwritten name signatures we are so familiar with are of relatively recent origin. Most of us now have one or more PIN numbers so that we can draw cash from the 'hole in the wall' without the need for any signature. However, use of such facilities is founded on a printed contract signed in the usual way!

If the formalities required by law are not complied with then, at law, the contract will be unenforceable. However, equity may still be available. For example, the party denying that there is a legally binding contract may be estopped from denying its existence and may have to perform his obligations nonetheless. This would be appropriate where that person had behaved in some dishonourable way in the knowledge that the other person was acting to his detriment in the belief that the contract would be binding.

When and where is the contract made?

The ability to point to the exact time that a contract is made may be important in a number of cases. For example, a contract for the writing of a new item of software may require that the work is completed no later than three months from the date of creation of the contract. A contractual offer for the sale of computer equipment may be expressed as being open for acceptance for seven days only (though such an offer will be binding only if supported by consideration – for example, where the person to whom the offer has been made has paid a fee for the benefit of the 'option').

Most contracts contain a term, often at the end of the agreement, stating under which country's law the contract is to have effect. For example, the agreement may state that 'this agreement is subject to the laws of England and Wales'. Where the contract is silent about the applicable law, however, pragmatic rules have been developed by the courts to determine this question. In the absence of any statement or indication to the contrary, the basic rule is that the applicable law is that of the country in which the contract is made. This is all well and good where the parties execute the contract in each other's presence but, where they are dealing at arm's length and are based in two different countries, the question becomes more difficult. This problem is not new to computer technology and also arises in connection with the post, telephone, telex and the fax machine as means of communicating offer and acceptance.

The normal way that a contract is made is when an offer made by one party is accepted, unconditionally and on identical terms, by the other. The contract is made the instant that the person to whom the offer is made (the offeree) communicates his acceptance to the person making the offer (the offeror). The first time this rule ran into difficulties was in relation to the use of the postal system which, as a means of communication, inevitably results in a time lag between making the offer or the acceptance and its receipt by the other party. Typically, problems can arise where the person making an offer revokes that offer before receiving the other's acceptance. A revocation of an offer is effective when communicated to the offeree – that is, when it is actually received by him. If, in the meantime, he posts an acceptance of that offer there is likely to be a conflict.

In *Adams* v *Lindsell* (1818) 1 B & Ald 681, the plaintiff was a manufacturer of woollen items located in Bromsgrove. The defendant was a wool merchant in St Ives, now in Cambridgeshire, some distance away. The defendant wrote to the plaintiff making an offer to sell wool to the plaintiff requiring an answer in the course of the post. Due to the defendant's negligence, the letter was delayed by three days but almost immediately upon receiving it, the plaintiff wrote back accepting the offer. In the meantime, not having received a reply by the date he expected, the defendant sold the wool to a third party. The plaintiff successfully sued for breach of contract as the court decided that the contract was made when the letter of acceptance was posted.

This exception to the general rule applies only where it is reasonable to expect communication of acceptance through the post – for example, where the offer is made through the post and there is no stipulation for a different form of communication (see *Byrne* v *Van Tienhoven* (1880) 5 CPD 344). The rule would not apply if the offeror required communication of acceptance by some other method – for example, by telephone or fax.

The postal rule is an exception and where the means of communication being used by the prospective parties is almost instantaneous, the general rule will prevail. Thus, in *Entores Ltd* v *Miles Far East Corp* [1955] 2 QB 327, where offer and acceptance were communicated by telex, it was held that the acceptance took effect not when it was transmitted from Amsterdam but when it was received in London and, accordingly, the contract was subject to English law rather than Dutch law. The House of Lords approved of this decision in *Brinkibon Ltd* v *Stahag Stahl und Stahlwarenhandelsgesellschaft mbH* [1983] 2 AC 34. In that case, the plaintiff, an English company, wished to buy a quantity of steel from the defendant, an Austrian company. The plaintiff sent a telex from London to Vienna, accepting the defendant's offer but the steel was not delivered and the plaintiff claimed damages for breach of contract in England. The House of Lords confirmed that the contract was made in Austria and, therefore, outside the jurisdiction of the English courts. Where the method of communication of acceptance is instantaneous a contract is made when the acceptance is received by the offeror. (This case may have been decided differently had the Brussels Convention on jurisdiction and enforcement in civil trials been applicable – an option is that a defendant can be sued in the state in which the breach of contract occurs).

The House of Lords went on to stress that this is not a universal rule and the circumstances of a particular case might result in a different outcome. There may be all sorts of variations – for example, where the transmission will be received outside office hours and it is expected that it will be read later or where it is sent to a third party's telex machine or to the agent of the offeror. Lord Wilberforce said:

No universal rule can cover all such cases; they must be resolved by reference to the intention of the parties, by sound business practice and in some cases by a judgment where the risks should lie.

Where an offer and acceptance are to be communicated by electronic mail, the basic rule should prevail, that is, that the acceptance is effective when it is received. Confirmation of receipt and reading is available in electronic mail systems and should be used. Difficulties may arise where the message accepting the offer is not read immediately upon receipt, perhaps because it is received during the night (for example, where one party is in Hong Kong and the other is in England) or the person to whom the receipt is addressed is out of the office for some time. It makes sense in such situations for the parties to stipulate their own rules – for example, that the acceptance is not effective until such time as it is read by the offeror or acknowledged by him. Great care must be taken by any person who has made offers to a number of other persons in respect of the same subject matter. However, where a person wishing to sell an item of computer equipment, for example, places details on the Internet, this will not be deemed to be an offer as such. It is more akin to placing an advertisement in a magazine which is an invitation to treat – in other words, an invitation to others to make offers to buy the equipment. In *Partridge v Crittenden* [1968] 2 All ER 421, Partridge placed an advertisement in the Cage and Aviary Birds magazine for the sale of Bramblefinches at £1 5s each. He was prosecuted under section 6(1) of the Protection of Birds Act 1954 for offering for sale a wild bird. His conviction was quashed – he had not offered the birds for sale because the placing of the advertisement was not an offer, merely an invitation to treat.

Bearing in mind the transnational nature of the Internet, any person making offers or advertising goods or services should include a message to the effect that all enquiries, negotiations, offers, acceptances or transactions will be governed by English law unless some other specified legal system is preferred.

Evidential status of electronic documents in civil trials

A court of law will only allow evidence to be placed before it if it is admissible in accordance with what generally can be said to be the complex rules of evidence. The best evidence rule requires that only an original document can be put in evidence. This rule has all but disappeared but remnants of it still remain.

The courts have recognised that a rigid adherence to the best evidence rule is inappropriate in the context of the accuracy with which copies of originals may now be made. Lord Justice Lloyd said in *R v Governor of Pentonville Prison, ex parte Osman* [1989] 3 All ER 701:

> **We accept that it [the best evidence rule] served an important purpose in the days of parchment and quill pens. But, since the invention of carbon paper and, still more, the photocopier and telefacsimile machine, that purpose has largely gone.**

A general exclusion on copies of original documents is no longer fitting. Indeed, in some cases, a document may be unintelligible in its original form without its being converted and displayed on a screen or printed out – for example, in the case of a document stored digitally on a magnetic disk. However, the original must still be produced if it is available. This would not apply where the original had been destroyed or lost.

A long tradition in English law has been the importance of a person giving evidence of what he personally knows or has witnessed with his own eyes. The fact that a witness is confined to matters of which he has personal knowledge and can be examined and cross-examined on those matters is a central plank of the English law of evidence. Second-hand or third-hand evidence is by its nature very unreliable, so much so that it was not allowed to be heard until recently.

There was a rule against admitting hearsay evidence in civil trials (the rule still exists in relation to criminal trials). Hearsay evidence is secondary evidence such as where a witness relates something that was told to him by another person but not directly seen or heard by the witness – for example, where Bill states that Jenny told him that she saw Paul trying to erase a computer program. The rule was quite strict and such evidence would not be admitted at all except in specific circumstances, some of which applied to information stored on computer. Section 5 of the Civil Evidence Act 1968 allowed statements contained in documents produced by a computer to be admitted in civil trials as evidence of any fact stated therein if the evidence would have been admissible as direct oral evidence, but only subject to certain conditions. However, the Civil Evidence Act 1995 has effectively swept aside the old rule against hearsay evidence in civil cases. The relevant provisions came into force on 31 January 1997. The new law applies only in respect of cases where proceedings commenced before this date.

Hearsay evidence is now admissible under section 1 of the Civil Evidence Act 1995 and is defined as a statement made otherwise than by a person giving oral evidence in the proceedings and includes hearsay evidence of whatever degree. There are certain safeguards as regards notice to be given to other parties.

Although hearsay evidence is now admissible, it may not be given much weight. For example, if it is a document stored on computer which has undergone many alterations that have not been properly recorded or logged, it may carry little weight. Under section 4 of the Act, the weight, if any, to be given to hearsay evidence depends on the circumstances and regard shall be had to whether:

- it would be reasonable and practicable to call the original maker of the statement as a witness,
- the original statement was made at the same time as the occurrence or existence of the matters stated,
- the evidence involves multiple hearsay,
- any person involved has any motive to conceal or misrepresent matters,
- the original statement was an edited account or made in collaboration with another for a particular purpose, and
- the circumstances in which the evidence is adduced as hearsay are such as to suggest an attempt to prevent proper evaluation of its weight.

Hearsay may carry little weight unless it would have been admissible under Part I of the Civil Evidence Act 1968, now repealed. Factors included:

- regularity – whether the computer was regularly used to store or process information, for the purposes of any activities regularly carried out, over a period which includes the time when the document was made,
- consistency – during the relevant period information of the kind contained in the document (or of a kind from which such information is derived) was

regularly supplied to the computer in the ordinary course of those activities,

- reliability – the computer was operating properly during the material part of that period (or, if not, any malfunction or breakdown that occurred would not have affected the accuracy of the material contained in the document),
- orthodoxy – the information contained in the document reproduces or is derived from information supplied to the computer in the ordinary course of the activities regularly carried out over the period in question.

Where a number of computers had been used – for example, successively or in a network – all the computers involved were treated as a single computer in determining the purpose of the activities. A person wishing to proffer a computer statement as evidence had to provide a certificate identifying the relevant document and the manner in which it was produced and giving other particulars. The certificate was required to be signed by a person occupying a responsible position in relation to the operation of the relevant device or the management of the relevant activities. It did not matter if the information was supplied or produced without any human intervention by means of appropriate equipment. This covered the situation where a computer was set up to record information and produce documents automatically.

Although the hearsay rule has been relaxed, if not altogether scrapped, the fact that a number of factors determine the weight to be given to such evidence means that it may not always be very influential, if at all. The main advantage flowing from the 1995 Act is that the formal rules under the 1968 Act have gone to be replaced by a welcome degree of flexibility. It will still be important, however, to show that the computer was operating reliably at the time and there is nothing to indicate that the evidence is unreliable. Adherence to the relevant standards applying to security and good computer practice will help in this respect.

Distance selling

Buying goods or services by means of the Internet poses particular dangers for consumers. Credit card fraud is one problem and another is that insufficient information may be provided by the seller. The very nature of the Internet may tempt individuals to buy on impulse without properly thinking through the implications of the obligations they are entering into. As a result of these and other dangers, there is a possibility that individual member states of the European Community may implement very restrictive legislation, while others might encourage contracting over the Internet leaving it largely unregulated. The Commission to the European Communities considered that distance selling, particularly in the light of the introduction of new technologies, ought to be subject to regulation which is harmonised throughout the Community. Eventually a Directive was adopted by the European Parliament and the Council (Directive 97/7/EC on the protection of consumers in respect of distance contracts, OJ L144, 4.6.1997, p 19). It has a number of implications for contracting over the Internet and is due to be implemented by member states no later than 4 June 2000. The main provisions of the Directive are described below.

Definitions and exemptions

A distance contract is one concerning goods or services between a supplier and a consumer under an organised distance sales or service provision scheme run by the supplier who, for the purposes of the contract, makes exclusive use of one or more means of distance communication up to and including the moment the contract is concluded. Thus, right up to and including the time the contract is made, all negotiations and contacts must be by distance communication which includes electronic mail, videotext, videophone, television, radio and fax machines as well as more traditional forms of distance selling such as by post, catalogue and advertising in the press with an order form. The list is not exhaustive and is intended to be indicative only.

A consumer is an individual who does not make the contract in the course of his trade, business or profession and a supplier is a person (an individual or legal person such as a company) who makes the contract in a commercial or professional capacity. An operator of a means of communication is a public or private provider of a method of distance communication to suppliers. This will include, for example, Internet Service Providers, commercial television and radio bodies and postal authorities.

The Directive does not apply to some contracts including certain contracts relating to financial services, automatic vending machines, in relation to land and auction sales. Also exempted are contracts concluded with telecommunications operators through the use of public telecommunications systems. The provisions in the Directive which apply to the giving of information, the right of withdrawal and the obligation to execute an order within 30 days do not apply to certain contracts for the supply of perishables and for the provision of accommodation, transport, catering or leisure.

Provision of information

Certain information must be provided to the consumer before the contract is concluded. This is set out in Article 4 of the Directive and includes information about the identity of the supplier, the main characteristics of the goods or services, the price, delivery costs, payment details and existence of the right of withdrawal. It must be provided in a clear and comprehensible manner, having regard to the principles of good faith in commercial transactions. Where the telephone is used, the supplier must make his identity known at the beginning of any telephone conversation with the supplier. As regards the Internet or electronic mail, the provision of prior information should not be onerous and can be easily incorporated into the supplier's Website or e-mail message.

Article 5 requires that written confirmation must be provided (or confirmation in another durable medium – for example, this might be by downloading a computer file) of much of the information mentioned above. This must be provided in good time. The right of withdrawal must be mentioned as must be the geographical address of the supplier to which the consumer may address complaints. Further information such as that relating to after-sales service and the effect of cancelling the contract must also be given. These provisions do not apply, however, to services performed through the use of means of distance communication where supplied on only one occasion and invoiced by the operator of the means of distance communication, although the geographical address must be divulged nonetheless.

Other aspects

There is a right of withdrawal under Article 6 but this is limited. Bearing in mind the ease with which computer software, video and sound recordings may be duplicated, the right may not be exercised unless otherwise agreed and does not apply in respect of the provision of services after performance has commenced, the supply of personalised goods and the like, and the supply of audio and video recordings and computer software. Other things are included such as periodicals and magazines.

The basic rule is that orders must be executed within 30 days, subject to a refund if the supplier is unable to deliver within that time because of the unavailability of goods and services, though the provision of equivalent goods or services is possible if the consumer was informed of this possibility.

There are provisions dealing with credit card fraud, a major concern when making transactions over the Internet. A consumer will have a right to request payment be cancelled where fraudulent use has been made of his credit card in a distance selling contract and, if this occurs, a right to be re-credited with the sums paid or to have them returned. Inertia selling is also controlled although law in the United Kingdom already deals with this under the Unsolicited Goods and Services Act 1971 and makes this form of selling a criminal offence.

Further provisions relate to the requirement that a supplier must have the prior consent of the consumer to distance communication by automatic calling systems (see also Chapter 33) and fax machines and other forms of distance communication may be used only where there is no clear objection by the consumer. Does this mean that, before too long, we will have an E-mail Preference System?

The rights provided to consumers will be protected by judicial and administrative remedies and the rights cannot be waived nor compromised by a choice of law clause where the applicable law is that of a country outside the European Community. Member states may adopt a higher level of protection and may, in particular, prohibit the marketing of certain goods or services such as medicinal products. Furthermore, member states are required to inform consumers of these rights. As is becoming usual in consumer protection legislation, the burden of proof will lie with the supplier in most cases.

Summary

The law has developed to take account of the use of information technology in commercial activity and, on a number of occasions, judges have had to deal with modern modes of information transmission such as telex, facsimile machines and computers. As has been shown, there are still some grey areas and those wishing to make full use of new technology to conduct their business must be aware of these areas and make appropriate provision. The strictness of the old rules relating to deeds and written documents has been mollified to some extent but the day has not yet arrived when writs can be served by electronic mail. In *Hastie and Jenkerson* v *McMahon* (unreported) 3 April 1990, the Court of Appeal accepted that some documents could be validly served by fax. In this case a list of documents was required to be identified by court order and served by the plaintiff to an action on the defendant. All that was required was a legible copy of the document in question placed in the possession of the party on whom it was served and the fax machine achieved this. However, this does not apply to documents which must be served personally or documents initiating legal proceedings, such as a writ.

To conclude this chapter, it will be useful if we return to consider the position of Karen and Luigi and their contract for shoes. First, is there a valid contract? Karen appears to have made a clear offer by sending a copy of the contract for approval and Luigi has indicated his acceptance of its terms. If the transmission of the contract and Luigi's acceptance have been accurate, there should be a legally binding contract providing all the other requirements are met (for example, that the offer and acceptance were unconditional and that there was clear mutual agreement (*consensus ad idem*)).

The next question to determine is the time that the contract was made. It would seem reasonable to expect that the acceptance became effective when it was first read by Karen on Wednesday, on the basis of the *Brinkibon* case – that is, when it was first communicated to Karen. *Brinkibon* is also authority for the contract being made in England and, providing there was no term in the contract to the contrary, the contract will be subject to English law.

Chapter 22

Summary and checklist

Introduction

Many potential pitfalls in contracts for computer software and hardware have been discussed in Chapters 14 to 21, as were ways in which they can be avoided or at least assuaged by careful consideration of the terms of the contract. The rapid rate of change in the computer industry, while bringing great improvements to computer technology, has contributed to the scale of the problems. Tales of incompatibility and abandoned systems are commonplace and the effect of bad decisions coupled with poor contracts can be quite horrendous, contributing to the downfall of the client's business. Choice of computer equipment and software is a very crucial decision and often is given far too little thought.

When looking at a contract for computer equipment or software, the golden rule is to be suspicious and sceptical. Awkward questions should be asked and their answers sought by reference to the contract. The contract needs to be assessed in the light of such questions as:

- What if the software contains bugs?
- What if the computer breaks down in the middle of the wages run?
- What if the client copies the programs and distributes the copies?
- What if the programs run too slowly to be of any practical use?
- What if the computer becomes obsolete and the manufacturer washes his hands of it?

It is so easy to be over-optimistic when acquiring computers and software and it is essential to have a long hard look at the contract and be a little bit cynical about it. Both parties to a contract for hardware or software should be prepared to look at that contract from the other's point of view and be prepared to negotiate an agreement giving a fair balance of responsibilities, rights and liabilities.

The choice of the correct form of agreement is important as is the recognition that the course of action anticipated may affect third party rights – for example, if third parties suffer loss or damage as a result of defects in the software or the manner in which it is used. Although a contract only gives rights to and imposes duties on the parties to the contract, others may be owed duties under the law of negligence or product liability in addition to having intellectual property or other rights which are affected by the use of the hardware or software.

Summary

The previous chapters in this part of the book have considered software and hardware contracts and related issues, such as liabilities to third parties, in addition to looking at the impact of information technology on the formation of contracts and evidence. By way of summary, the following key points are identified.

General points

- Care must be taken in drafting contracts so that the rights and duties, risks and liabilities are precisely defined and equitably shared.
- The nature of the contract needs to be reflected upon as it will affect the legal controls over the terms in the contract.
- The courts will imply terms into contracts, if necessary, to give effect to the presumed intention of the parties but will not make the bargain for the parties.
- Damages for breach of contract can be high and can include wasted time.
- Liability to third parties can arise through negligence, negligent misstatement or product liability.
- Exclusion clauses are likely to be controlled by the Unfair Contract Terms Act 1977.
- The burden of proof to show that an exclusion clause is reasonable lies on the party seeking to rely on it and the courts usually find exclusion clauses unreasonable.
- Failure of an exclusion clause to be effective can be grave and appropriate provision should be made to insure in respect of defects resulting from negligence.
- Only the benefit of a contract can be assigned (transferred) to a third party; the original party remains liable for any burden.
- Appropriate confidentiality and indemnity clauses should be considered, bearing in mind the law of restraint of trade and controls over unreasonable indemnity clauses.
- Provisions should be made for arbitration or alternative dispute resolution.

Contracts for writing software

- These are service contracts subject to the Supply of Goods and Services Act 1982.

- The basis of the contract is a copyright licence or assignment of copyright (transfer of ownership of copyright).
- The specification is particularly important and will define the software, its performance and quality.
- Maintenance of the software must be catered for and associated with this will be whether the client is to obtain a copy of the source code.
- If the client does not obtain a copy of the source code, an escrow arrangement should be entered into by both parties.
- The contract should have provisions to deal with delays, extensions to the time for completion and payment for additional work.
- Issues relating to liability for defects should be addressed.
- Independent professional supervision of the performance of the contract should be considered.

Contract for off-the-shelf software

- Nature of the agreement is uncertain – may be a hybrid, part licence, part sale of goods, or unique.
- Shrink-wrap licence is inconsistent with the English law of contract and may be ineffective, in which case the terms may be implied by law. Alternatively, the making of the contract may be suspended until the person acquiring the software does an act signifying acceptance, such as by breaking the seal on the package containing the disk or disks on which the software is stored.
- Back-up copies of computer programs may be made if necessary to their lawful use – for example, use by a licensee.
- Training and support must not be overlooked.

Contract between software author and publisher

- Basic mechanism is a copyright licence, normally exclusive.
- Licensor should not grant more rights than are necessary for the exploitation contemplated (he may be able to exploit other rights separately).
- Exclusive licensee can sue infringers, usually after joining the copyright owner in the action as co-plaintiff.
- Payment may be based on a royalty, being a percentage of the net income received by the publisher.
- The publisher may require an indemnity from the author in case the software infringes a third party right or contains defamatory material.
- The liability of both the author and the publisher for defects should be considered: for example, is the author to indemnify the publisher for any claims in respect of defects?
- Who is responsible for maintenance of the software, enhancements to the software and training in respect of it?

Hardware contracts

- These are governed by the Sale of Goods Act 1979 if the title to the hardware is transferred to the buyer, even if software is bundled with the hardware.
- If leased or hired, the contract will be subject to the Supply of Goods and Services Act 1982.
- Misrepresentations by a dealer may be dealt with as a collateral warranty or on the basis of the Misrepresentation Act 1967.
- Entire agreement clauses are common.
- There should be an indemnity should the hardware (or bundled software) infringe a third party right.
- Use of tenders as a means of acquiring hardware is common (and for buying computer supplies).

Electronic contracts

- The requirements as to form in legal documents have been relaxed.
- 'Writing' should extend to electronic forms of storage but there is some doubt as to whether an electronic signature is acceptable as proof of signing.
- If offer and acceptance are communicated by means of electronic mail, a contract will be made when and where the acceptance is received by the party making the offer.
- The 'best evidence' rule is of little relevance now and should not prevent the admissibility of computer printout as evidence.
- The rule against hearsay has been abolished in civil cases and computer evidence will be admissible, but a number of factors may be relevant as to the weight to be attached to such evidence.
- Consider the impact of the Distance Selling Directive.
- Issues such as applicable law and jurisdiction should be addressed.

Checklist

Table 22.1 indicates the purpose and relevance of contractual terms to the four types of agreement specifically covered in this part of the book.

Table 22.1 Checklist of terms normally found in computer contracts

Note: ∗ – indicates that this term will normally be present in the particular form of agreement.

Term	Purpose	Type of contract/agreement			
		Software			Hardware
		Bespoke	Off-the-shelf	Author–publisher	
Definitions	To clarify and assist with the interpretation of the contract	∗	∗	∗	∗
Form of agreement	Describes the nature of the contract, e.g. sale contract licence or lease agreement	∗	∗	∗	∗
Assignment/ Transfer	States whether the benefit of the contract can be assigned or transferred to a third party	∗	∗	∗	(if leased)
Items provided	List of items included in the contract, e.g. disks, manuals, etc. Also, any facilities or information to be provided by the client	∗	∗	∗	∗
Price or licence fee	The price to be paid or the method of calculating the price. Instalment details and when they are due	∗	∗		∗
Royalties	The 'price' paid to an author usually based on a percentage of sales income. The formula for calculating royalties should be clearly stated as should details of the timing of payments			∗	
Specification	Describes in detail the performance, quality and content of the subject matter of the contract	∗		∗	∗
Delivery	Defines the time when the subject matter of the contract will be delivered, completed or made available. Delivery may be made by instalments	∗		∗	∗
Liquidated damages	To quantify the damages payable in the event of late performance of all or part of the contract	∗	(only if expressly provided for)	∗	∗
Acceptance	To define what the client has to do to signify acceptance of the software or hardware. Deemed acceptance may be provided for	∗	∗	∗	∗

Continued overleaf

Table 22.1 cont.

Term	Purpose	Type of contract/agreement			
		Software			Hardware
		Bespoke	Off-the-shelf	Author–publisher	
Use	The scope of the uses to which the client can put the software or hardware. For off-the-shelf software, may limit the number of users	*	*		*
Maintenance	Expresses the duties of the supplier to correct errors in the software or faults in the equipment. May be subject to a separate agreement	*	*	*	*
Enhancements	Outlines whether subsequent improvements to the software or hardware will be available. Enhancements may be available as part of a maintenance contract	*	(upgrades may be available)	*	*
Modifications	States whether the client can modify the software or hardware without recourse to the supplier. If permitted, ownership of rights in any modifications must be dealt with	*	*	*	*
Training	Describes responsibility for training the client's staff in the use of the software. May be a separate agreement with a dealer	*	*	*	
Copyright, etc.	Defines the client's duty to prevent unauthorised copying or transmission of the software or trade secrets relating to the hardware or software	*	*	*	*
Escrow	The machinery for the provision of the source code version of the programs and preparatory materials to the client in the event of the supplier ceasing to support the software	*		*	
Confidentiality	States the supplier's duty not to divulge confidential information concerning the client's business	*		*	*
Liability	To limit the liability of the supplier in the event of defects subject to legal controls such as the Unfair Contract Terms Act 1977	*	*	*	*

Table 22.1 cont.

Term	Purpose	Software			Hardware
		Bespoke	Off-the-shelf	Author–publisher	
Indemnities	To protect the client if the subject matter infringes a third party right such as a copyright or if it contains defamatory material or in respect of claims arising in negligence	*	*	*	*
Staff poaching	To provide contractual remedies should either party offer employment to a member of the other party's staff (taking care that it is not seen as being in restraint of trade)	*			*
Termination	Describes under what circumstances the contract can be terminated. There should be provision for termination by either party. If termination is available for a breach of contract, there should be provision to allow the party in breach an opportunity to remedy the breach	*	*	*	(hire contracts)
Legal action	Provision for the other party to assist in or institute any legal action against a third party, for example, who is infringing copyright	*		*	(if contract includes a patent or copyright licence)
Entire agreement	Ensuring that the formal written agreement contains all the terms of the contract and anything else can be no more than a mere representation	*	*	*	*
Arbitration	The machinery for settling disputes without recourse to the courts by appointing a suitably qualified arbitrator. Instead, provision may be made for alternative dispute resolution to assist in a negotiated settlement	*		*	*
Applicable law	Denotes the country or state whose law and jurisdiction will be used to settle disputes. Bear in mind that Scots law is different to English law. May also restrict jurisdiction, for example, to England and Wales	*	*	*	*

PART THREE

Computers and crime

Computer technology impacts on criminal law in two ways. It facilitates the commission of existing crimes such as fraud and theft but it has also given birth to a new range of activities such as computer hacking and the development and distribution of computer viruses. The criminal law was perceived to be patchy in its application, both to existing and new forms of crime, and this caused considerable concern to the computer industry and financial institutions. Largely as a result of lobbying and pressure from the industry, the Computer Misuse Act 1990 was enacted, having started life as a private member's Bill. The Act closed the loopholes in the prior law and also dealt with questions of jurisdiction and extradition. In particular, it created a new offence of unauthorised access to computer programs or data (hacking), an ulterior intent offence (hacking with intent to commit a further offence) and an offence of unauthorised modification of computer material.

This Part of the book concentrates on three areas of criminal activity associated with the use of computers – computer fraud, hacking, and damage to programs and data. These have all attracted a great deal of media attention and the nature of these offences and the scope of the criminal law in relation to them are discussed in practical terms. Additionally, the criminal offences available to combat piracy and counterfeiting are described. There is also a chapter on evidential issues in criminal proceedings where it is sought to admit computer documents as evidence. One point to be remembered when reading the following chapters is that the actions described will sometimes give rise to liabilities under civil law. For example, if a hacker makes a copy of some of the information stored on a computer system, he may be infringing the copyright subsisting in that information and may also be in breach of confidence if he divulges it to others, depending upon the circumstances. Similarly, a fraudster transferring funds will be guilty of the civil law tort of conversion. If the culprit is an employee who has obtained access to parts of a computer system to which he has no authority to access, then internal action such as a reprimand or dismissal may ensue instead of or as well as a criminal prosecution.

Note that although many criminal offences also apply in Scotland, for example offences under the Computer Misuse Act 1990, there are some significant differences between English and Scots criminal law. Furthermore, where offences do apply in Scotland, there may be differences in their application and scope.

Chapter 23

Nature of computer crime

Introduction

The advent of computer technology has brought many kinds of opportunities and some of these, not surprisingly, are of a criminal nature. Computers may facilitate the commission of 'old-fashioned' crimes such as fraud or counterfeiting or give rise to new mischiefs such as computer hacking and the deliberate erasure of programs or data. Contrary to popular belief, the law is reasonably well equipped to deal with computer crime and has been substantially strengthened by the Computer Misuse Act 1990. The biggest stumbling block, in practical terms, is detection and a considerable amount of thought must be given to the security of any computer system as, in this case, prevention is better than cure.

By far the greatest threat to a computer system comes from within – that is, from employees. One of the largest reported computer frauds ever attempted, which concerned the transfer of $70 million, involved an employee of the First National Bank of Chicago. Even when computer crime is detected and the persons involved are prosecuted and convicted, the penalties imposed seem relatively trivial when compared with other forms of criminal activity. In 1989, a teenage bank cashier who transferred nearly £1 million into his own and a friend's bank account, received only one year's youth custody.

The diversity of criminal activities associated with computers is remarkable and has given rise to a whole new vocabulary. Examples are computer hacking, time-bombs, logic-bombs and computer viruses. These terms will be defined at the appropriate sections of this Part of the book, the purpose of which is to describe the criminal offences associated with computers, what remedies are available at law and to suggest how the threats posed by these activities can be avoided or, at least, minimised. In Chapter 24 the offences popularly described as 'computer fraud' are considered. In Chapter 25 the activity known as hacking is examined followed, in Chapter 26, by a discussion of the legal implications where a person erases programs or data from a computer system or leaves a virus on a system which later corrupts or deletes information. Other forms of criminal activity, such as blackmail, forgery and counterfeiting and piracy offences, are discussed in Chapter 27. Computer evidence in criminal proceedings is dealt with in Chapter 28 and practical suggestions to prevent computer crime are contained in Chapter 29 which concludes with a summary of offences, their maximum penalties and scope, presented in tabular form.

The scale and nature of computer crime

Stories, often unsubstantiated, of massive computer frauds, widespread hacking and chaotic disruption to computer systems caused by viruses are legend. Cinema films such as *Superman III* and *War Games* fuel the imagination, and reporting in the media, warning of the Friday 13th virus, for example, adds to this. Determining the true scale of crime is an impossible task when considering conventional crime because of under-reporting (a great deal of crime goes unreported for a variety of reasons – this is known as the dark figure of crime) and this is even more so when it comes to computer crime. In some cases the crime will remain undetected or it may result in no action or disciplinary action rather than prosecution if the offender is an employee. It has been rumoured that some financial institutions attempt to cover up the fact they have been a victim of computer crime, fearing that publicity will damage their reputation.

Wild, exaggerated figures are sometimes quoted as the total cost of computer crime. In most cases, these can be taken with a pinch of salt because they are purely speculative; there is no foundation for them whatsoever. Of course, computer crime has been and remains a very serious issue and, fortunately, some realistic data is available as the Audit Commission for Local Authorities and the National Health Service in England and Wales carry out surveys triennially (Audit Commission Update, *Ghost in the Machine: An Analysis of IT Fraud and Abuse*, February 1998 and *Opportunity Makes a Thief: An Analysis of Computer Abuse*, Audit Commission, 1998). The latest survey covered the three-year period ending in December 1996 and, as before, involved both the public and the private sector. The survey was based upon responses from 900 organisations, reporting a total of 510 incidents. Table 23.1 shows a summary of the results of the surveys in 1987, 1990 and 1993. Unfortunately, the forms of misuse do not exactly match the legal definitions of offences but the criminal law has changed significantly since the first survey was carried out in 1981. Due to a different format in the latest report, precise statistics are not available but Figure 23.1 shows the results from the latest survey in percentage terms.

There has been a significant increase in the reporting of incidents, particularly in respect of viruses. This may be a reflection of an increase in incidents of computer misuse but could be explained, at least partly, by an increase in awareness of computer crime. Nevertheless, just over half the incidents were detected by accidental means. Confirming that most computer crime comes from within: 85 per cent of reported incidents were perpetrated by internal staff, mainly administrative staff, although a proportion were committed by

Table 23.1 Computer misuse (survey based on three-year periods)

Type of misuse	1993		1990		1987	
	No.	Direct loss (£)	No.	Direct loss (£)	No.	Direct loss (£)
Fraud	108	2 904 430	73	1 102 642	61	2 526 751
Theft[1]	121	196 305	27	1 000	22	34 500
Hacking[2]	47	65 500	26	31 500	35	100
Viruses	261	30 485	54	5 000	0	0
Totals	537	3 196 720	180	1 140 142	118	2 561 351

[1] includes illicit software, private work, theft of data or software
[2] includes invasion of privacy and sabotage

Source of data: Audit Commission, *Opportunity Makes a Thief: An Analysis of Computer Abuse*, HMSO, 1994 and previous reports.

managers. The most common preventative measure taken by organisations was internal auditing followed by the adoption of an information technology security policy.

A report from the National Audit Office (*IT Security in Government Departments*, HMSO, 1995) also confirms a growing threat from computer misuse. Over 100 government departments and agencies were asked to provide information on incidents of computer misuse in the year 1993/4. Compared to the reported figures for 1992/3, the following increases were noted, as shown in Table 23.2. In the National Audit Office study, very little fraud was reported. Indeed, from 1990 to 1994 only 36 cases were reported and the total value was less than £250 000, an average of only £7000 per incident. The average for the Audit Commission study in the three-year period to 31 December 1993 based on direct losses only was around £27 000. In spite of all the publicity, big time computer fraud appears to be relatively

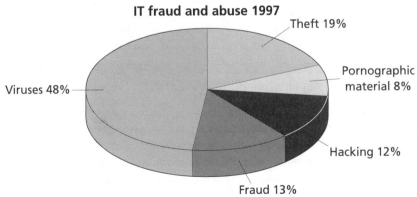

IT fraud and abuse 1997

Theft 19%
Pornographic material 8%
Viruses 48%
Hacking 12%
Fraud 13%

Source of data: Audit Commission Update, *Ghost in the Machine: An Analysis of IT Fraud and Abuse*, February 1998.

Fig. 23.1 Forms of computer abuse

Table 23.2 Computer abuse in government departments

Type of abuse	Increase (%)
Hacking	140
Viruses	86
Theft of IT equipment	60

Source of data: National Audit Office, *IT Security in Government Departments*, HMSO, 1995.

rare! In the three-year period to 31 December 1996, total losses for the 900 organisations responding to the survey was £3.9 million.

One thing that is apparent from the Audit Commission surveys is that a significant proportion of perpetrators are not prosecuted and, in many cases, no action is taken or the perpetrator, if an employee, is reprimanded, transferred to other duties or dismissed. In the case of *Denco Ltd* v *Joinson* [1991] IRLR 63, it was held that an employee who used an unauthorised password to gain access to information stored in a computer and which he knew he was not entitled to see was guilty of gross misconduct and could be summarily dismissed from his employment. The employer's security arrangements were criticised by the Employment Appeal Tribunal and the Industrial Tribunal which heard the case first (the employee had argued that he had been unfairly dismissed).

A disregard for basic control safeguards and ineffective monitoring were highlighted by the Audit Commission as still being prevalent. Recommendations made in the reports, accepting that prevention is better than cure, include:

- carrying out risk analysis reviews;
- developing and implementing secure and controlled environments;
- having rigorously implemented IT security policies;
- giving staff computer awareness training, focusing on risks and precautions to be taken;
- assigning responsibility for security and developing secure access control;
- making sure that the internal audit department has computer audit skills; and
- making the necessary financial commitment to security aspects of an organisation's computer systems.

An awareness of the criminal law and its application to computer technology is an important part of implementing security strategies and it is also important that persons working with computers are aware of the potential seriousness of what might seem to them a trivial matter. Prevention will not, sadly, eliminate computer misuse altogether and the remainder of this Part of the book examines the criminal law in relation to computer crime.

The prosecution of criminal offences

Before specific offences are examined, it will be useful to describe, very briefly, the procedure for prosecuting offences, the classification of offences and the different modes of trial.

When a criminal offence has been committed, the normal procedure is for the police to be informed (the police detect very little crime themselves but depend on the public bringing incidents of crime to their notice). The police will then investigate the crime and, if they suspect a particular person or persons of having committed the crime, they may charge the person or persons and then pass the case over to the Crown Prosecution Service which decides whether to prosecute and what charges to bring. In coming to its decision, the Crown Prosecution Service uses guidelines which include the possibility of securing a conviction and the public interest. If the decision is made to proceed, the accused will appear before a Magistrates' Court where, depending on the nature of the offence and other matters, either his case will be dealt with, or he will be committed for trial in the Crown Court. It is possible to bring a private prosecution if, for example, the Crown Prosecution Service declines to act. However, the Director of Public Prosecutions has the power to take over a private prosecution. Other bodies may bring prosecutions such as local authority trading standards officers, the Department of Social Security, the Data Protection Commissioner and HM Customs & Excise. Bringing a private prosecution is, in most cases, an extreme action, but it may be relevant to computer crime if the official bodies fail to take an interest in prosecuting certain behaviour, due perhaps to a lack of understanding of the problems involved or a feeling that the civil law offers sufficient remedies. Though this latter point may be true, it does not have the deterrent effect that a successful criminal prosecution can have.

Criminal offences are heard in either the Crown Court or Magistrates' Courts. The latter tend to deal with the less serious offences which make up the vast majority of criminal cases. Offences are classified according to how they may be tried. Relatively minor offences, such as exceeding the speed limit, may be tried only in Magistrates' Courts and these offences are described as being *summary* offences. Serious offences such as murder and robbery can only be tried in the Crown Court and these are called *indictable* offences. In between these two types of offence, there is a vast number of intermediate offences which can be tried in either a Magistrates' Court or the Crown Court; these offences, of which theft is an example, are called *triable either way* offences. These may be tried summarily in a Magistrates' Court or, on indictment, in the Crown Court. Many of the offences which will be described in this part of the book fall into this category; they are offences which are triable either way, an example being the unauthorised modification of computer programs or data. On the other hand, computer hacking (unauthorised access to computer material) is triable summarily only.

289

When an offence is classified as being triable either way, the choice of mode of trial initially rests with the magistrates. They may decide that the nature of the case is such that it should be tried in the Crown Court: for example, if it is a serious example of the offence. If the magistrates decide that the case can be heard in their court, the accused person can then decide whether to proceed in the Magistrates' Court, or to elect trial in the Crown Court. Certain other factors are important in deciding on the mode of trial apart from the seriousness of the offence. For example, the magistrates might consider that the accused, if found guilty, is deserving of a punishment greater than they can award (although they can commit a convicted person to the Crown Court for sentence if they feel that their sentencing powers are inadequate in the particular case), or the accused might think he stands a better chance of acquittal before a jury. In one case, a hacker was acquitted by a jury on the basis that he was addicted to hacking even though addiction is not a defence known to English law (see the *Bedworth* case discussed in Chapter 25)!

The maximum penalties available in Magistrates' Courts need to be mentioned. Providing the relevant statute does not contain a lower maximum, for a single offence the magistrates may send a person to prison for a term not exceeding six months and/or impose a fine not exceeding £5000. Other sentencing powers are available to the magistrates such as discharging the offender or imposing a probation order or a community service order. In the context of computer crime, the use of imprisonment and fines are the most likely punishments, although other forms of sentence may be appropriate in some circumstances.

Chapter 24

Computer fraud

Introduction

Computer fraud often makes headline news but it is thought that the number of cases of fraud detected and prosecuted are just the tip of the iceberg. Rumours abound about massive frauds which are not reported by the victims (usually large financial institutions) because of a fear of publicity. It does not help a bank's image of solid dependability to have employees prosecuted for computer fraud at regular intervals. All the major financial institutions throughout the world use computers to carry out their business and vast sums of money are transferred by computer (electronic funds transfer). As far as the criminal is concerned, the creation of an account in his own name, followed by instructions via a computer terminal to the main computer to transfer large sums into that account, is much more attractive than walking into a bank with a shotgun. There seems to be a feeling that to commit fraud by using one's own brains to defeat a computer system is something to be applauded and is not really serious crime. However, this form of crime causes great anxiety in the commercial world and is considered by the authorities to be very serious. The maximum penalties available are quite heavy and computer fraud can be dealt with by prison sentences of up to ten years.

Types of computer fraud

The phrase 'computer fraud' is used to describe stealing money or property by means of a computer: that is, using a computer to obtain dishonestly, property (including money and cheques) or credit or services or to evade dishonestly some debt or liability. It might involve dishonestly giving an instruction to a computer to transfer funds into a bank account or using a forged bank card to obtain money from a cash dispenser (automated teller machine).

The types of activities described as computer fraud can be considered to be of two main types: data frauds and programming frauds. In the first type, unauthorised data is entered into a computer or data that should be entered is altered or suppressed. The main distinguishing factor in this type of fraud is that it is computer data, either input or output data, which is tampered with. Data fraud is probably the most common type of computer fraud (it is the most easily detected) and is relatively easy to carry out. The Audit Commission recognises four types of computer fraud (data fraud is subdivided into three categories):

- input fraud,
- data fraud,
- output fraud, and
- program fraud.

In the latest survey by the Audit Commission (*Ghost in the Machine: An Analysis of IT Fraud and Abuse*, Audit Commission Publications, 1998), fraud was the second most common form of incident reported. Routine auditing procedures should eventually expose most input, data and output frauds but this is not necessarily true of program frauds which may remain undetected for a long period of time. The sub-species of frauds are described below. Unless otherwise indicated, examples are taken from an earlier Audit Commission report (*Survey of Computer Fraud and Abuse*, HMSO, 1991) which, unlike the later reports, contained substantial detail of individual incidents in an informative and entertaining supplement.

Entry of unauthorised instruction (input fraud)

This is the unauthorised alteration of data prior to it being input into a computer. Typically, an employee preparing data to be entered into a computer by another employee will make incorrect entries on the relevant document or form. The employee who enters the data into the computer may be an innocent agent or, in some cases, may be an accomplice of the first person or conspiring with him. It is an easy form of fraud to attempt and requires no particular computer skills. The only intelligence required to succeed is in knowing the organisation's checking and auditing systems thoroughly and matching the fraud up with any shortcomings in those systems. This is a strong argument for organisations to continually review, modify and enhance their auditing systems.

In one case the perpetrator gave incorrect data input forms to a clerk who then entered the data which related to debits to customer accounts. The perpetrator misappropriated the money concerned – £100 000. His actions were detected by internal audit and he was prosecuted under the Theft Acts 1968 and 1978, sentenced to four years' imprisonment and fined £10 000 (Audit Commission Survey, 1991, Supplement, p 12).

Alteration of input data (data fraud)

In one case, a box office supervisor cancelled tickets which had been sold and then later resold them, keeping the cash. The box office supervisor falsified the audit trail but this was detected after problems with the software were investigated. The employee was prosecuted under the Theft Acts 1968 and 1978 and given six months' imprisonment (Audit Commission Survey, 1991, Supplement, p 38). In another case reported in the National Audit Office study a member of staff in an employment department entered false data in relation to a claim made by his brother resulting in the brother receiving girocheques to which he was not entitled for a total of £2933. The employee was dismissed and prosecuted and, on conviction, was sentenced to two months' imprisonment (National Audit Office, *IT Security in Government Departments*, HMSO, 1995, p 17).

Data fraud, as defined by the Audit Commission, differs from input fraud in that with data fraud it is the person entering the data into the computer that makes changes to the data. This form of fraud is also fairly common and is easily carried out, but it will be detected if appropriate checking procedures and auditing are adopted. Most organisations using computers are vulnerable to fraud perpetrated by employees preparing data for entry into a computer or authorised to enter data into a computer system and, consequently, care must be taken in the selection of such employees and an effective way of checking systems for the occurrence of fraud should be used, bearing in mind that an audit trail can be vulnerable.

Suppression of data (output fraud)

This particularly applies to output data – for example, printed reports generated by a computer system. These reports may be suppressed simply by tearing them up or not printing them out or, if printed, they may be altered. In either case, the motive will usually be to hide some criminal activity. For example, a person responsible for collecting money for a club might destroy a computer printout, which would indicate that he had kept some of the money collected. Concealing information can be a criminal offence. For example, in *Adams* v *The Queen* (unreported) 4 November 1994, two company directors by the use of offshore companies and bank accounts concealed information relating to secret profits they had made from the company they worked for. One of the directors brought an appeal to the Judicial Committee of the Privy Council against his conviction in New Zealand for conspiracy to defraud. His appeal was dismissed.

An example of this type of fraud is reported in the Audit Commission survey. A cashier who had taken money from her till destroyed daily audit rolls from each printer at her place of work thinking that this would make it impossible to trace her as the thief. Unfortunately for her, she was unaware that a computer file was also used to keep a record of transactions and this identified her as the culprit. She was sentenced to 18 months' imprisonment (Audit Commission Survey, 1991, Supplement, p 25).

Program frauds

The second form of computer fraud (as opposed to fraud involving data in one way or another) is more sophisticated and dangerous, and this is where someone alters a computer program to effect the fraud. Program fraud is much harder to detect than data fraud and reported examples are few and far between. We have to go back to the Audit Commission survey published in 1988 to find a good example. Two computer programmers wrote some stock accounting software and concealed a routine in the software which suppressed certain details in reports generated, in order to reduce Value Added Tax liability (Audit Commission Survey, 1988, p 58). The software was designed for use in video-hire shops and the routine was activated by a special password. The software was sold to 120 shopkeepers although only 12 had been informed of the secret routine. These 12 had defrauded Customs and Excise of £100 000. Each of the programmers was prosecuted and convicted. They were each imprisoned for nine months and were fined a total of £34 000.

Another example of this form of fraud, which was discovered in West Germany and made famous in the film *Superman III*, involved the alteration of a program to collect decimal fractions of financial transactions, such as half-cents which were normally rounded down and ignored. Instead, these fractions were placed in an account opened by the perpetrator of the fraud. This is known as a 'salami fraud' because it involves thin 'slices' of money.

Computer programmers, analysts and others involved in the commissioning or alteration of software present another source of danger in that many of them will have detailed knowledge about the security and password systems used and could pass such information on to persons intent on committing fraud. As a result of their knowledge of the computer systems, computer staff are also susceptible to involvement with would-be fraudsters.

The computer as an unwitting accomplice

A computer system might be used to detect information which assists the criminal in the commission of his crime. For example, in the case of *R v Sunderland* (unreported) 20 June 1983, Court of Appeal, an employee of Barclay's Bank used the bank's computer to discover a dormant account and then forged the holder's signature to withdraw some £2100. The employee of the bank used the computer in a very simple way to detect an account which had not been used for a long period of time but which had some funds in it, a simple but effective way of stealing money although, eventually, the scheme was discovered when the holder of the dormant account attempted to make a withdrawal and discovered that the account contained less money than it should have done. The employee, who was of previous good character, was sentenced to two years' imprisonment, which was changed on appeal by the Lord Chief Justice who suspended 18 months of the sentence. He said:

... other people like bank clerks and bank officials need very little reminding that if they commit this sort of offence they will lose their job and go to prison, albeit for a comparatively short time.

This case illustrates the vulnerability of some computer systems to criminal activities. Of fundamental importance in the design of any computer system is the attention given to passwords and security, audit trails and the controls placed on employees.

Few of the activities described above require a great deal of computer expertise to carry out; often they will be committed by employees on low income engaged to perform relatively menial tasks such as data preparation and entry. Such frauds are fairly easy to detect by careful scrutiny, audits, spot-checks and occasional manual checks. Strong security measures will also have a major deterrent effect, especially if they are performed in a high-profile manner.

Fraud offences

When discussing computer fraud, the word 'fraud' can be a little misleading, and the activities commonly described as computer fraud can involve criminal offences other than those traditionally described as fraud. Fraud comprises a collection of similar offences such as obtaining property or services by deception, false accounting, false statements made by company directors, suppression of documents and income tax fraud including cheating. Most of these offences are covered by sections 15 to 20 of the Theft Act 1968 and sections 1 and 2 of the Theft Act 1978. Section 15A of the Theft Act 1968, obtaining a money transfer by deception, may also be relevant. Income Tax and Value Added Tax fraud are dealt with by specific legislation such as the Finance Act 1972 although the common law offence of cheating is still available for offences relating to the public revenue. Apart from this exception, cheating was abolished by section 32(1) of the Theft Act 1968. Certainly, some of these offences may be carried out using a computer, but it is with respect to those offences requiring deception that the greatest difficulty lies. Often, the most appropriate offence to charge is theft. Although theft (section 1 of the Theft Act 1968) is not normally considered to fall within the 'fraud' group of offences, there is an overlap between theft and fraud and, depending on the circumstances, a charge of theft might be more likely to lead to a successful prosecution. First, the deception offences will be considered.

Obtaining by deception

At first sight, the offence of obtaining property by deception (section 15 of the Theft Act 1968) seems to be most appropriate to computer fraud as the culprit usually means to obtain someone else's money or other property by a deception or trick – for example, by pretending to have authority to carry out some transaction on the computer such as transferring money. There is no problem stemming from the intangible nature of money, credits or cheques as section 4(1) of the 1968 Act states that property includes money and things in action. Bankers' cheques, money orders and bills of exchange are all examples of 'things in action'. This definition of property applies to the 1968 Act generally and therefore applies to section 15. There are several forms of deception provided for by the Theft Acts of 1968 and 1978 involving the obtaining of property or a pecuniary advantage or services, and the evasion of liability. So far as obtaining property by deception is concerned, section 15(1) of the Theft Act 1968 defines the offence as follows:

> A person who by any deception dishonestly obtains property belonging to another, with the intention of permanently depriving the other of it, shall on conviction on indictment be liable to imprisonment for a term not exceeding ten years.

Dishonesty is an important requirement and this affects the nature of the deception. The Theft Act 1968 further states that the deception can be 'deliberate or reckless', so if a person carelessly causes a computer system to transfer money into his own or a friend's account (an unlikely occurrence if he is no more than careless), he is not guilty of the offence as carelessness is not sufficient in this context, though recklessness is likely to be judged objectively.

In terms of computer fraud, the difficulty with this offence is that it requires a deception and this implies that it is an actual person that is being deceived, not a machine. In *DPP* v *Ray* [1974] AC 370, Lord Morris said:

> For a deception to take place there must be some person or persons who will have been deceived.

Other case law does not help very much and the question was left open in one case involving an automatic car park barrier (*Davies* v *Flackett* [1973] RTR 8). Bearing in mind that *DPP* v *Ray* was decided in the House of Lords, the better view is that the deception must work upon a human mind.

If a person gains access, whether with or without permission, to a bank's computer system and dishonestly instructs the computer system to transfer money from one account into another, then that person is 'deceiving' the computer or computer system: that is, he purports to have the authority to carry out such an act. Even if he has authority to transfer money from one account to another under normal circumstances as an employee would, that authority is nullified by his dishonesty. The main point is that it is the computer which is being 'deceived'. Under normal circumstances, no other human being is involved and, therefore, it would seem that the offence of obtaining property by deception is not made out. It would be different if, before the transfer was made, a message is displayed at someone's terminal requesting confirmation of the transfer. In that case, the other person would be subject to the deception as well as the computer and there should then be no difficulty related to the applicability of the offence of obtaining property by deception or any other offence involving deception.

The notion that a machine cannot be deceived is strengthened by the Theft Act 1978 which defines the offences of obtaining services by deception (services such as hiring a car or providing bed and breakfast) and evasion of liability by deception (such as where a debtor tells a lie to his creditor in order to let him off part or the whole of the debt) because the wording used strongly suggests that the deception must operate on the human mind. For example, section 1(1) states:

> **A person who by any deception dishonestly obtains services from** *another* **shall be guilty of an offence [emphasis added].**

This interpretation is reinforced by other language used in the statute. An example of obtaining services by deception in the context of computers is where a person makes an unauthorised use of a system which is normally paid for, such as PRESTEL. The problem of who has been deceived still exists, but if the person has deceived some other person by saying that he has permission to use the terminal used to access the system, then the offence of deception will have been made out under section 1 of the Theft Act 1978. There is a requirement for the services to be subject to payment, so the same act with respect to a 'free' service does not involve the offence – for example, if a person dishonestly uses a computer system in a library to locate a particular book.

Obtaining a money transfer by deception

A new offence was inserted into the Theft Act 1968 as a result of the case of *R v Preddy* [1996] AC 815. Charges were brought against the accused persons under section 15 of the Theft Act 1968. They had made over 40 applications for mortgages by making false statements. Their plan was to use the money to buy houses with the intention of reselling them at a profit and redeeming the mortgages. They hoped to make a substantial profit as, at the time, property prices were rising quickly and there was something of a property boom. The lenders said that they would not have lent the money to the accused persons had they known the true motive for obtaining a mortgage. Some of the mortgage advances were made telegraphically or electronically, by electronic funds transfer, while others were made by cheque. The accused were convicted and their appeals to the Court of Appeal were dismissed.

The appeals to the House of Lords were allowed and the convictions were quashed. An account in a bank or building society is classed as a 'chose in action' (thing in action). As regards the telegraphic or electronic fund transfers, it was held that when payment was made from one bank or building society account in credit (the lender's account) to another bank account, the chose in action represented by the credit balance in the lender's account was extinguished or reduced and a new chose in action was created in the borrower's account (or the borrower's solicitor's account). Therefore, the borrower did not get the lender's chose in action. Consequently, the borrower did not obtain 'property belonging to another' as required by section 15(1) of the Theft Act 1968. The account itself, the chose in action, was not transferred to the borrower.

As regards the cheques, the chose in action represented by the cheque never belonged to the bank or building society as when it came into existence it belonged to the borrower – it was made out to the borrower or his solicitor who would then transfer the payment to the person selling the house. As the chose in action belonged to the borrower right from the start, no property belonging to another was obtained by the borrower. Although the cheque itself was a physical object (that is, the paper as opposed to the chose in action relating to the amount it was made out for) and was property belonging to another, the borrower did not obtain it permanently as it would be returned to be bank or building society after presentation to the borrower's bank (or his solicitor's bank). Therefore, even charging these persons with theft of the piece of paper on which the cheque was written would have been doomed to failure.

Section 15A of the Theft Act 1968 was inserted by section 1 of the Theft (Amendment) Act 1996. This provides that a person is guilty of an offence if by any deception he dishonestly obtains a money transfer for himself or another. A money transfer occurs when a debit is made to one account and a corresponding credit is made to another account and the credit results from the debit or the debit results from the credit. Both credit and debit relate to an amount of money and it does not matter if the credit and debit are exactly the same amount or whether the transfer results from the presentation of a cheque or by another method or whether there is a delay in the transfer process. Nor does it matter whether either account is overdrawn before or after the transfer. The maximum punishment is imprisonment for a term not exceeding ten years on conviction on indictment. It is reasonable to assume that dishonesty is a matter of satisfying the *Ghosh* test, discussed later under the section on theft.

This new offence is very welcome. In the light of *Preddy*, anyone who carried out a fraudulent electronic fund transfer could possibly have escaped conviction not only for obtaining property by deception but also for theft as that offence also requires that the property which is stolen belongs to another. The diminution of the victim's bank balance and the corresponding increase in the fraudster's bank balance would not be an obtaining (or, for theft, an appropriation) of property *belonging to another*. The importance of plugging this loophole was reflected in the speed with which the new offence was brought into force. Other offences could be relevant such as under the Computer Misuse Act 1990, and, if two or more persons were involved, the common law offence of conspiracy to defraud, as described below, would be appropriate.

To summarise, an essential element for the deception offences contained in the Theft Acts is that a human being has been deceived. In such a case, the deception could be simply a person claiming to have permission to use a computer system to gain access to a terminal or by pretending to be someone else. Some related offences such as false accounting, where 'deception' is not an element of the offence, should cause no additional problems merely because the offence was committed by or facilitated by the use of a computer system.

Conspiracy to defraud

Generally, a conspiracy is an agreement between two or more persons to carry out an unlawful act. Conspiracy may be statutory or common law. A statutory conspiracy is when a person agrees with another or others to embark upon a course of conduct which will necessarily involve a criminal offence by section 1 of the Criminal Law Act 1977 as amended by the Criminal Attempts Act 1981. An example is where two persons agree to steal a computer; both will be guilty of a conspiracy to steal the computer even if they do not go on actually to steal it. Statutory conspiracy requires that the proposed act is itself a criminal offence and, in the case of obtaining by deception, difficulties remain relating to the concept of deceiving a machine, as discussed above.

However, at common law, the offence of conspiracy to defraud may be available. It appears that, in this context, 'deceit' is not an essential element of the offence and in *Scott v Metropolitan Police Commissioner* [1975] AC 819, Viscount Dilhorne said:

> ... 'to defraud' ordinarily means ... to deprive a person dishonestly of something which is his or of something to which he is or would or might but for the perpetration of the fraud be entitled.

In other words, it is not necessary to show that a person has been deceived. In the *Scott* case, the accused made an agreement with cinema projectionists to make copies of films being shown in the cinemas and to sell those copies for profit. The original films were borrowed overnight, copied and then returned the next day. It was held that it did not matter that no person had been deceived and the appeal against conviction was dismissed.

The common law offence of conspiracy to defraud is separate and distinct from the fraud offences in the Theft Acts, although in many cases, such as where two or more persons agree to obtain goods or services by impersonating others, the offence of conspiracy to defraud and offences under the Theft Acts will be committed if the course of action is carried through to its conclusion. The maximum penalty for conspiracy to defraud is ten years' imprisonment.

The consequence is that if two or more persons agree to dishonestly operate a computer, perhaps entering a password they are not entitled to use, to transfer funds to their own accounts, they will be guilty of a conspiracy to defraud even though no human being has been deceived. Of course, a limitation of the scope of this offence is that it requires an agreement between two or more conspirators and it cannot apply when only one person is involved. Nevertheless, the offence is a useful weapon in the fight against computer fraud, especially if the act of transferring the funds in question is not completed and the circumstances are not sufficient to warrant a charge of attempting to steal. In the past, and particularly before the advent of the Computer Misuse Act 1990, the track record of conspiracy to defraud in terms of dealing with computer fraud was very good. Indeed, even now, it may be preferable to use this offence because of its inherent flexibility and freedom from the technicalities of the Computer Misuse Act. In one example, a junior bank clerk was imprisoned for five years after pleading guilty to conspiracy after trying to transfer £31 million to a bank account in Geneva (*Computing*, 2 March 1995, p 1).

At one time it was held that conspiracy to defraud and statutory conspiracy were mutually exclusive – that is, if the carrying out of the agreement would result in some offence being committed, however trivial, then a charge of conspiracy to defraud would be bad for duplicity. Section 12 of the Criminal Justice Act 1987 changed that rule and now it does not matter if carrying out the intended acts involves the commission of some other offence. The activities in the *Scott* case did not entail the commission of another offence. The conspirators were infringing copyright in a film, in those days a civil matter only. Now their activities would be a criminal offence under section 107 of the Copyright, Designs and Patents Act 1988 but this would no longer be fatal to a charge of conspiracy to defraud. Indeed, the conspirators could also be charged with a conspiracy to commit a section 107 offence.

Attempts

To be charged with an attempt, the person involved must have done an act which is 'more than merely preparatory to the commission of the offence' (section 1 of the Criminal Attempts Act 1981). The scope of the law of attempts is uncertain when it comes to computer fraud but it does not apply to conspiracies. It could be argued that a computer fraud which is not completed is an attempt to steal money. However, it depends on how far towards the completion of the theft the fraudster got and whether any of his acts were more than merely preparatory. It has been argued that a criminal attempt occurs when the person concerned carries out an act penultimate to the commission of the offence, that is, the last act before completion. In the end, however, the question is one for the jury to decide being a question of fact.

Consider the case of an employee at a bank who decides, on his own, to transfer money to his own account from a customer's account. First, he switches on a computer terminal. Second, he enters the appropriate password to gain access. Then, he enters the instruction at the keyboard which causes the funds to be transferred. Finally, he draws the money out of the account. The problems arise when the bank employee fails to complete the offence of theft of the money for one reason or another. At what stage in the course of the events described do his actions become more than merely preparatory? A reasonable member of a jury might conclude that the offence of attempting to steal is not made out until the third act has been carried out – that is, the entry of instructions which cause the computer system to transfer the money to the employee's account.

Doubts about the applicability of the law of attempts in the context of uncompleted computer frauds were among the reasons why section 2 of the Computer Misuse Act 1990 was enacted. This creates an 'ulterior intent' offence, where someone commits the basic hacking offence with the intention of proceeding to commit a serious offence. Section 2 is discussed in Chapter 25.

Computer fraud as theft

It might seem from the above that, unless a conspiracy or attempt can be proved, a person who dishonestly convinces a computer that he is authorised to do something when he is not in fact so authorised, and makes the computer transfer money into his own bank account, commits an offence only if some other person has been deceived. Unless a human being has been subjected to the deception, it might seem that a charge of obtaining property by deception would not succeed. However, the criminal law is not so easily defeated. Usually, the offence of theft will be committed, regardless of the interposition of a computer. The offence of theft is defined in sections 1 to 6 of the Theft Act 1968 and section 1(1) states:

A person is guilty of theft if he dishonestly appropriates property belonging to another with the intention of permanently depriving the other of it ...

The words 'dishonestly', 'appropriates', 'property' and the phrases 'belonging to another' and 'with the intention of permanently depriving the other of it' all have special legal meanings which are set out in sections 2 to 6 of the Act.

As far as computer crime is concerned, there is no real difficulty arising from the meanings of these words and phrases although the following points should be noted:

(a) the definition of 'property' is very wide and will cover most things that can be stolen with the aid of a computer, but land does not usually come within the meaning of property nor do wild mushrooms or flowers, fruit or foliage on a wild plant;

(b) property is deemed to 'belong to another' if that person has control of it or has any proprietary right of interest in it;

(c) 'appropriation' is the assumption of the rights of the owner;

(d) the 'thief' must intend to permanently deprive the other of the property; usually a mere 'borrowing' of an article is not theft, although it can be if, for example, it is for a very long period of time or if, when it is returned, there is no 'goodness' left in the property.

Point (d) above is quite interesting. What is the position if a person gains access to a bank's computer system, draws money from various accounts and puts the money in his own account for a few weeks, collecting interest on the money, and then transfers the money back from whence it came, less the interest earned? Although there has been an appropriation (the person involved has assumed the rights of the owners in respect of the money in the accounts), the account holders have not been permanently deprived of their money; it has merely been borrowed for a few weeks and what has been lost is the interest which the capital would have earned. Clearly, there is no theft of the capital which has been returned intact, but what about the interest – has this been stolen?

A case involving the borrowing of cinema films adds weight to the argument that a person who uses the computer to transfer funds temporarily into his own account does not commit the offence of theft. In *R v Lloyd* [1985] 2 All ER 661, a projectionist at a cinema, in association with two others, removed films from the cinema for a few hours so that they could be copied and then returned the films so that no one would know what had occurred. The pirated copies of the films were then sold, making a considerable profit for the pirates. A charge of theft (actually a conspiracy to steal in this case) was held to be inappropriate. As has been seen in the *Scott* case above, where the facts were very similar, a charge of conspiracy to defraud would have been more likely to secure a conviction.

In the *Lloyd* case, it was obvious that there was no intention permanently to deprive the owners of the films, nor was the copyright in the films stolen (it is not altogether clear whether copyright can be stolen). As mentioned earlier, borrowing can be theft if the period and circumstances are equivalent to an outright taking or disposal by section 6(1) of the Theft Act 1968, and this would be when the 'goodness' or 'virtue' in the thing taken had gone from it. Examples would include when a person borrows a radio battery intending to return it when it is exhausted, or borrows a bus pass intending to return it to the rightful owner when it expires. In the case of the films, however, there was still virtue in them when they were returned; they were still capable of being used and shown to paying audiences, so the pirates' convictions were quashed.

The fact that the owner of the copyright in the films had been deprived of potential 'sales' of the films by the circulation of pirate copies was not relevant to the offence of theft, but would it be relevant in a case of the temporary transferral of funds while interest is collected? Although the lawful owner of the money (or other things such as shares and investments) has been deprived of the interest or earnings, it would appear on the basis of *Lloyd* that the law of theft cannot be invoked. Nevertheless, the person borrowing the money could still be deemed to have an intention to permanently deprive the owner by section 6(1) of the Theft Act 1968. This is expressed in terms of treating the thing as one's own to dispose of regardless of the rights of the owner and borrowing or lending may amount to so treating it if, in the circumstances, it is equivalent to an outright taking or disposal. However, it is hard to know whether this would apply to a short-term borrowing without permission as section 6(1) has been described as 'gobbledygook'. Even if it is not equivalent to an outright taking or disposal, the owner may be able to get some relief by obtaining damages for conversion at civil law. Other criminal offences, such as unauthorised access to computer material, discussed in Chapter 25, also may be relevant.

The meaning of 'dishonesty' for the purposes of theft needs also to be considered. The test used, derived from the case of *R v Ghosh* [1982] QB 1053, has two elements: first, was what was done dishonest according to the ordinary standards of reasonable and honest people? Second, did the person involved realise that what he did was dishonest by those standards? In the example above, where money is borrowed for a period of time for the purpose of collecting interest or as capital for a short-term investment, the second limb of the test could be difficult to prove beyond reasonable doubt as regards the obtaining of interest from the bank. Certainly, the actions as a whole are dishonest and should be criminal and it is likely that a jury would convict on the facts.

What if the money is borrowed for a very short period of time, however, and invested in a high-risk speculation which pays off and the borrower returns the capital and an amount to compensate for lost interest? There has been no intention to permanently deprive the owner of the capital. As far as the interest is concerned, that would seem to be a matter between the owner of the capital and his bank which is contractually bound to pay the interest. However, in *Chan Man-sin v Attorney-General for Hong Kong* [1988] 1 All ER 1, an accountant forged cheques drawn on company accounts and was charged with theft of the debt owed by the bank to the companies. The accountant argued that he had not committed theft because the companies had not been deprived of anything as the bank was contractually bound to the companies to replace the money. The Judicial Committee of the Privy Council rejected this argument because the accountant had purported to deal with company property regardless of the rights of the companies and that was within the meaning of an intention to permanently deprive the companies of their property.

Authority and consent

A person committing fraud may have authority to use the computer system concerned. An employee whose duties include entering data into a computer system may alter the data to effect the fraud. Here, the employee is doing no more than carrying out his duties, albeit fraudulently. However, as discussed in the following chapter, in a controversial case (*DPP* v *Bignall*), the court suggested that doing something authorised in an unauthorised way may still be deemed to be authorised.

In other cases, an employee who has permission to use a computer system might do things using the computer in a manner beyond his normal duties. How does the law of theft deal with such cases? The concept of authority or consent is an important one in theft, for how can a person steal something if he has permission to take the thing? In *R* v *Morris* [1984] AC 320, a case involving label-switching in a supermarket (that is, substituting one price tag with another stating a lower price), it was said that an unauthorised act was required for the appropriation necessary to constitute theft. Switching price labels is obviously not authorised by the supermarket. An employee who attempts to commit a fraud using computers will be doing something outside the scope of his authority to use the computer system: for example, the person employed to input data into a computer system does not have authority to enter false data. If the other elements of the offence are present, such as an intention to permanently deprive, then theft will be committed.

Another case which reinforces and expands this approach is *Lawrence* v *Metropolitan Police Commissioner* [1972] AC 626. An Italian visitor to England hired a taxi and at the end of the journey gave the taxi-driver a £1 note for the fare. The taxi-driver said that this was not enough (the correct fare was just over £0.50) and proceeded to help himself to an additional £6 from the visitor's wallet which was still open. The defence argued that the money had been taken with consent but it was held that the prosecution did not have to prove that the taking of the money was without the victim's consent. This is considerably wider than the *Morris* case and it is difficult to reconcile the two. Even if the narrower view is taken, however, it is difficult to think of a case of computer fraud where the person will not be guilty of theft when he exceeds or otherwise compromises his authority to use a computer system. The fact that the computer system 'consents' to the transaction should not be relevant, as in *Lawrence*, because it is consent obtained by deception. The restriction of deception operating on a human mind should not be relevant in these circumstances. In *R v Gomez* [1992] 3 WLR 1067, the House of Lords confirmed that the wider approach in *Lawrence* is the correct one. Therefore, any assumption of the rights of the owner in respect to any property where it is done with consent obtained by deception can amount to an appropriation for the purposes of theft.

Other offences

Other offences which contain an element of fraud are provided for in the Theft Act 1968 – for example, false accounting (section 17), false statements by company directors, etc. (section 19) and the suppression of documents (section 20). There is nothing special about these offences in terms of computers except that their commission may be carried out with the aid of a computer.

The remaining part of the common law fraud-related offence of cheating is of interest. Cheating was abolished by section 32(1) of the Theft Act 1968, with the exception of cheating with respect to offences relating to the public revenue. If a person makes a false declaration concerning his Income Tax or Value Added Tax, whether by using a computer or not, he will be guilty of the offence of cheating in addition to any offence under the Finance Acts. This dual liability is useful because there is a higher ceiling on the penalty available for cheating, which can consequently be used for more serious examples of revenue fraud. For example, in *R v Mavji* [1987] 2 All ER 758, the accused had evaded Value Added Tax of over £1 million and was charged with cheating; he was sentenced to six years' imprisonment and fined. If he had been charged under the Finance Act 1972, the longest sentence of imprisonment he could have received was two years. In the light of this case, it appears that no deception is required; the omission to make a tax return is sufficient. According to the Theft Acts, it appears that the offence of deception requires a human being to be deceived, but in the case of cheating there is no such requirement. This leads to the conclusion that if a person has a computerised accounts system which incorporates a Value Added Tax report generator, then suppressing or altering computer reports, and consequent failure to submit a return or submitting a 'doctored' return, means that the offence of cheating has been committed and the fact that a computer has been used should not cause any difficulty.

A final possibility is that the fraudster may be prosecuted under the Computer Misuse Act 1990. The section 2 offence is particularly appropriate where the fraud has not been completed, with the advantage that, if there is insufficient evidence of intention, the court or jury (if tried in the Crown

Court) can return a verdict of guilty under section 1 (the basic hacking offence). Even the section 3 offence may be applicable (unauthorised modification of computer material) and an example of a conviction for this in relation to fraud is given in the Audit Commission report, 1998. The Computer Misuse Act offences are discussed in the following chapters.

Chapter 25

Hacking – unauthorised access to computer material

The problem in perspective

Computer hacking is the accessing of a computer system without the express or implied permission of the owner of that computer system. A person who engages in this activity is known as a computer hacker and may be motivated by the mere thrill of being able to outwit the security systems contained in a computer. A hacker may gain access remotely, using a computer in his own home or office connected to a telecommunications network.

Hacking can be thought of as a form of mental challenge, not unlike solving a crossword puzzle, and the vast majority of hacking activities have been relatively harmless. Sometimes, the hacker has left a message publicising his feat and this reflects the popular image of a hacker – a young enthusiast who is fascinated by computers and who likes to gain access to secure computer systems to prove his skills to himself or his peers. At worst, this form of hacking is no more than a nuisance although, once it is known that a hacker has entered a computer system, the system manager may have to carry out a significant amount of work to confirm that the hacker has not modified or erased data. Many hackers are motivated by a sense of achievement; the very act of breaking into a computer system using their own mental effort is reward enough for them. There is a danger, however, that such 'innocent' hackers can cause damage to computer systems inadvertently and they may pave the way for other, more malicious, persons.

There is a more sinister side to computer hacking. Many computer systems concern what might be called 'high-risk' activities such as the control of nuclear power stations, defence systems, aircraft flight control and hospital records. These are known as 'safety-critical systems'. The dangers stemming from hacking into these systems are self-evident and the potential for terrorism is worrying. As terrorists are unlikely to be deterred by the criminal law, it is not just a matter of strengthening the law to deal with hackers. The key to overcoming the problems lies with those responsible for computer systems in these high-risk areas and it is essential that they do their utmost to make sure that the systems are as secure as possible. There is something to be said for the view that the enthusiastic young hacker has done the computer industry a great service by highlighting the deficiencies in the security aspects of many computer systems. Rather than subjecting these hackers to criminal proceedings, perhaps the computer industry should consider making use of their skill and expertise. In 1989, the co-founder of the Apple Computer Corporation made a donation to the University of Colorado for a computer hacking scholarship in the belief that it increased knowledge and understanding of computer systems.

Once the hacker has penetrated a computer system he might do one of several different things. He might read or copy information, which may be highly confidential, or he might erase or modify information or programs stored in the computer system, or download programs or data, or he might simply add something, such as a message boasting of his feat. He might be tempted to steal money or direct the computer to have goods sent to him, in which case what has been discussed in Chapter 24 in terms of computer fraud is relevant. By their very nature and relative susceptibility to unauthorised access, computer systems pose different problems to those encountered with information stored on paper. In the days before computers, sensitive information was kept locked away in filing cabinets in locked rooms on the premises of the organisation holding the data. This way the sensitive information was relatively safe from being tampered with or copied. The biggest threat would then come from employees but, burglars and industrial spies apart, persons outside the organisation would find it extremely difficult to gain access to the information. By contrast, information stored on a computer that is linked to a telecommunications system is much more vulnerable. It is analogous to information stored in paper files kept in locked cabinets but left in a public place. It is just a matter of finding the right key to fit the cabinet, and not only can a total stranger try the lock but, often, he can spend as long as he likes trying different keys with impunity until he finds one that turns the lock.

The House of Lords decision in the case of *R v Gold* [1988] 2 WLR 984 highlighted the problem of computer hacking and the ease with which it could be done. After the case, which was taken by many to indicate that computer hacking was not a criminal activity, the computer industry became most dissatisfied with the scope of the criminal law and the perceived lack of haste on the part of Parliament to act. Concern at this position led to the Law Commission Working Paper No. 110, *Computer Misuse* (HMSO, 1988), examining the scope of the law in terms of computer misuse generally and proposing alternative suggestions for legal changes directed at the problem of computer crime.

Emma Nicholson MP introduced a private member's Bill to combat computer hacking in 1989 but withdrew it after a Government promise to legislate in this area. That promise was broken and, in 1990, Michael Colvin MP brought in another private member's Bill on computer misuse, which was successfully steered through Parliament and became the Computer Misuse Act 1990. This Act did not restrict itself to computer hacking but also dealt with some other problems such as the law of attempts, unauthorised modification of computer programs and data, as well as addressing problems of jurisdiction and extradition. This chapter deals specifically with the basic hacking offence and ulterior intent offence following a discussion of the decision in *R* v *Gold*.

The case of *R* v *Gold*

Two computer hackers gained access into the British Telecom Prestel Gold computer network without permission and they altered data. One of the accused also got into the Duke of Edinburgh's personal computer files and left the message:

GOOD AFTERNOON. HRH DUKE OF EDINBURGH

The two accused hackers were journalists who claimed that they had hacked into the network in order to highlight the deficiencies in its security. They were charged under the Forgery and Counterfeiting Act 1981 on the basis that they had made a false instrument within section 1. This states that a person shall be guilty of forgery if he makes a false instrument, with the intention that he or another shall use it to induce somebody to accept it as genuine, and by reason of so accepting it to do or not to do some act to his own or any other person's prejudice.

It was claimed that the false instrument was the CIN (customer identification number) and password. Section 8(1) of the Act states that a false instrument may be 'recorded or stored on disc, tape, sound track or other device'. However, their lordships suggested that 'recorded' or 'stored' connoted a process of a lasting and continuous nature from which the instrument could be retrieved in the future. In this case, the CIN and password were held only temporarily in the computer system while they were checked for validity and, after the check, they were eradicated totally and irretrievably.

The accused had been found guilty at Crown Court – one being fined £750 and the other £600 – but their convictions were quashed by the Court of Appeal and this was confirmed in the House of Lords. In the Court of Appeal, the Lord Chief Justice, Lord Lane, said that the acts of the accused in gaining access to the Telecom Gold files by what amounted to a dishonest trick were not criminal offences. If the defendants' convictions had been upheld, the only rational interpretation of the effect of section 1 in the circumstances was that the defendants had deceived a computer. Bearing in mind that, in terms of the Theft Act offences, it does not appear to be possible to deceive a machine, the decision in the *Gold* case was eminently sensible.

The basic hacking offence

Section 1 of the Computer Misuse Act 1990 is aimed directly at hackers who gain access to computer programs or data without any further intention to carry out any other act. It says that a person is guilty of an offence if:

(a) he causes a computer to perform any function with intent to secure access to any program or data held in any computer;
(b) the access he intends to secure is unauthorised; and
(c) he knows at the time when he causes the computer to perform the function that this is the case.

The intent does not have to be directed at any particular program or data or at programs or data of a particular kind or at programs or data held in any particular computer. The offence is triable summarily only (that is, in a Magistrates' Court) and the maximum penalty is imprisonment for a term not exceeding six months or a fine not exceeding level 5 (presently £5000) or both.

Section 17 of the Act contains definitions and other aids to interpretation but the Act does not define 'computer', 'program' or 'data'. Securing access is widely defined as causing a computer to perform any function, altering or erasing a program or data, copying or moving it to a different location in the storage medium in which it is held, using it or having it output from the computer in which it is held, and access to a program includes access to a part of a program. Note that the offence is made out if the hacker simply intends to make access regardless of whether he succeeds but he must know, at the time, that the access is unauthorised. Careless or reckless access will not suffice. Because copying is within the meaning of securing access, potentially it can be an offence under section 1 to make a pirate copy of a computer program or other software or to download an unauthorised copy of a computer program. However, there may be some difficulty as to whether such an act is unauthorised for the purposes of the Act, as discussed later.

The language of section 1 is rather strange at first sight as it speaks of access to programs or data in *any* computer, presumably including the computer being used by the hacker. This has been subject to judicial scrutiny in *Attorney-General's Reference (No. 1 of 1991)* [1992] 3 WLR 432, in which a former employee went to visit his previous employer, a wholesale locksmith, to purchase some articles. While alone (an assistant had temporarily left the room), the ex-employee entered instructions into the computer effecting a 70 per cent discount on the articles he had bought. There was no need for him to use a password. At the trial, the judge said that the wording of section 1 required that a second computer had to be involved. This was rejected on appeal to the Court of Appeal, where it was held that the wording of section 1, given its plain and ordinary meaning, was not limited to the use of one computer with intent to gain access to another computer. The offence was made out even if only one computer was used.

There have been a number of successful prosecutions under section 1 of the Act, the first being in March 1991 when a man was fined £900 for making unauthorised calls to the United States using Mercury Communications equipment. Because 'computer' is not defined, it is likely to be given a generous meaning by the courts and can include equipment which has computer technology built into it although it would not normally be described as a computer.

A tremendous amount of publicity was generated by the acquittal of Paul Bedworth following his prosecution for conspiracy to commit offences under sections 1 and 3 of the Computer Misuse Act 1990 (for example, see *The Times*, 18 March 1993, p 3). The defence counsel argued that Bedworth was addicted to computer hacking and, as a result, he was not capable of forming the necessary intent to commit the offences charged. Although addiction, *per se*, is not a defence to a criminal charge (although it could be a mitigating factor when it comes to sentencing) the jury acquitted him. This raised concerns that the Act was not doing its job and there were calls for it to be strengthened, presumably by watering down the requirement for intention. This is unnecessary and would cause more problems and could result in the imposition of criminal liability on careless, clumsy or inept computer operators who, without meaning to, gained access to material they were not authorised to. The only sensible explanation of the Bedworth decision is that the jury probably felt some sympathy towards the accused. Perverse jury verdicts are not unknown. Two other hackers who had been charged along with Bedworth pleaded guilty and received six-month prison sentences. Altogether, the activities of the three hackers cost the victims hundreds of thousands of pounds.

It is certainly possible for employees to commit the basic hacking offence when using their own computer terminals at work if they intend to gain access to any program or data in respect of which they know they do not have authority to access. The concept of authority is strangely defined in section 17 in terms of being entitled to control access or having the consent of such a person. If the person is not so entitled and does not have the necessary consent, his intended access is unauthorised. Of course, the hacker must know this and the implication is that employers must make it quite clear to employees which programs and data they are entitled to access. This also applies to others such as pupils or students and self-employed consultants. Ideally, a written statement as to access entitlement should be issued.

Authorised access for an unauthorised purpose

An employee may have authorisation to use a computer system as a normal part of his duties to his employer. If the employee subsequently uses the system for an unauthorised use – for example, for his own purposes such as carrying out private work or retrieving information for other purposes unconnected with his employment – does the access become unauthorised for the purposes of the Computer Misuse Act 1990? An example of this form of unauthorised use is given by the Audit Commission. A nurse at a hospital had authorisation to use the patient administration system but used it to search for medical details relating to friends and relatives. She then discussed these details with other members of her family. The nurse was not prosecuted under the Act but given a written warning for this breach of patient confidentiality (Audit Commission, *Ghost in the Machine: An Analysis of IT Fraud and Abuse*, Audit Commission Publications, 1998, p 18).

Where authorised access is used for an unauthorised purpose, it seems that the access remains authorised. So it was held in a surprising judgment in *DPP v Bignell* [1998] 1 Cr App R 1. Two police officers had used the police national computer to gain access to details of motor cars which they wanted for private purposes unconnected with their duties as police officers. They were charged with the unauthorised access to computer material offence under section 1 of the Computer Misuse Act 1990 and convicted at Bow Street Magistrates' Court but their appeals to Southwark Crown Court were allowed and this was confirmed by the Queen's Bench Divisional Court.

The sole issue was whether the access was authorised. The Divisional Court held that it was, even though the purpose of the access was not authorised. Whether access is unauthorised is defined in section 17(5) of the Computer Misuse Act 1990 in the following terms:

> **Access of any kind by any person to any program or data held in a computer is unauthorised if –**
>
> **(a) he is not himself entitled to control access of the kind in question to the program or data; and**
> **(b) he does not have consent to access by him of the kind in question to the program or data from any person who is so entitled,**
>
> **but this subsection is subject to section 10.**

Section 10 is simply a saving in respect of access carried out for purposes associated with any search warrant, etc.

The Court decided that as the police officers were, in fact, entitled to control access to the material within section 17(5) they were authorised to access the computer data even if this was for an unauthorised purpose. As part of their normal duties, the police officers were entitled to access such computer information. But being entitled to access computer material is not the same as being entitled to control access to such material. This is an important and crucial distinction which the court failed to make. Even so, whether entitled to access the material or entitled to control access, that entitlement is surely subject to it being for police purposes only.

This is clearly a worrying decision and it is probably wrong as to this aspect of the Act. Otherwise, any employee using his employer's computer system to which he has been given access cannot commit the section 1 offence (nor for that matter the section 2 offence) if he uses the system for his own personal or private purposes. For example, if Joe, who is employed by the Mammoth Bank plc and has access to the customer database, uses the database to discover details of famous customers and their accounts at the bank and divulges that information to the media, he will not be guilty of the unauthorised access offence. Of course, as pointed out by the judge in *DPP* v *Bignell*, there could be an offence committed under data protection law (see the offence under section 55(1) of the Data Protection Act 1998 discussed in Chapter 31). However, not all use of computer material for unauthorised purposes will be caught by this and, unless the data relates to a living indiviudal who can be identified from that data, the Data Protection Act 1998 will not apply.

The decision in *DPP* v *Bignell* leaves an unsatisfactory gap in the Computer Misuse Act 1990. The judge drew support for his view of the Act from the Law Commission Working Paper No. 110, *Computer Misuse* (1988), which suggested that it would be undesirable for the hacking offence to extend to an authorised user who is using the computer for an unauthorised purpose. The Working Paper was far from unambiguous and put forward various options for dealing with computer misuse in all its various forms. It went on to give an example of a situation which should not be criminalised: where a word processor operator uses the office computer to produce private correspondence. That is not the type of behaviour at which section 1 of the Computer Misuse Act 1990 was directed and this is confirmed by the White Paper which preceded the Act (Law Com. No. 186, *Criminal Law: Computer Misuse*, 1989). This specifically acknowledged that employees may be liable for the basic hacking offence and stated (para 3.35):

> **The thrust of the basic hacking offence is aimed at the 'remote' hacker, but the offence is apt to cover the employee or insider as well. For that reason it is particularly important ... that (in addition to defining 'access' to exclude merely physical access to the computer itself) the *mens rea* of the offence should catch only the case where the employee consciously and deliberately misbehaves.**

That sentiment is most appropriate in the circumstances of the case before the Divisional Court and would certainly cover the situation where the accused knowingly exceeded the scope of his authorisation intending to access data for his own purposes. From the reported facts of the case, it would seem beyond doubt that the accused police officers had consciously and deliberately misbehaved in the sense suggested in the White Paper by using the police national computer to gain access to information to be used for their own private purposes.

One of the main aims of the Computer Misuse Act 1990 was to deter unauthorised access to computer programs and data. When one contemplates that most computer misuse comes from within an organisation, perpetrated by its own employees, the decision in *DPP* v *Bignell* significantly prejudices the effective operation of the Act. In the Audit Commission Report, *Opportunity Makes a Thief: An Analysis of Computer Abuse*, HMSO, 1994, no less than 85 per cent of reported incidents of computer abuse were carried out by employees.

All three offences in the Computer Misuse Act 1990 are seriously affected by this decision as they all depend on the concept of authorisation. The ulterior intent offence under section 2 requires a section 1 offence to be committed as a precursor to the ulterior intent and section 3 is couched in terms of an unauthorised modification, being defined in section 17(6) in terms of being entitled to determine whether the modification should have been made or having the consent of such a person.

The ulterior intent offence

Apart from hacking pure and simple, other problems were identified by the Law Commission. The law of attempts was of uncertain application to computer fraud and it did not seem that a person who obtained services without permission using a computer committed a significant offence. Of course, if two or more persons were involved a charge of conspiracy might be apposite but, otherwise, there were problems. Section 2 of the Computer Misuse Act 1990 covers these situations and also provides an alternative and, perhaps, better route to conviction where other offences are intended by the hacker. The section 2 offence is described in the Act as unauthorised access with intent to commit or facilitate the commission of further offences. It is a preliminary offence, particularly useful where the offence to which the ulterior intent applies is not completed. Another way of looking at it is to say that it is an aggravated form of the basic hacking offence.

The further offence must be one for which the sentence is fixed by law (for example, murder or high treason) or one for which the maximum sentence is not less than five years. Thus, section 2 applies to theft, blackmail, obtaining property or services by deception, abstracting electricity and a great many other offences, all having maximum punishments of five or more years' imprisonment. If the further offence is completed, then that offence will normally be charged but section 2 is useful where, for one reason or another, this is not the case. An example is where a hacker attempts to gain access to a computer with the intention of sending a blackmail message to someone but is not able to get beyond the log-on screen. It is unlikely that a charge of attempted blackmail will succeed because he has not done an act which is more than merely preparatory, but a charge under section 2 will be more likely to result in a conviction providing the necessary intentions and knowledge can be proved – that is:

- the intention to secure access,
- the knowledge that the access is unauthorised, and
- the intention to commit blackmail.

The ulterior intent offence is triable either way and carries a maximum penalty of five years' imprisonment and/or a fine if tried in the Crown Court. Any person who is tried for a section 2 offence (or a section 3 offence) in the Crown Court can, if found not guilty, be found guilty by a jury of the section 1 offence and sentenced accordingly (section 12). A person can be found guilty of a section 2 offence even if the commission of the further offence is impossible: for example, where a hacker intends to erase details of a debt he owes when the person to whom the debt is owed has already written it off or if the hacker is mistaken about owing the debt in the first place.

Jurisdiction

The international character of some computer crime has caused concern about the possibility of criminals escaping prosecution because of jurisdictional issues. For example, in *R v Tomsett* [1985] Crim LR 369, the accused sent a telex from London intending to divert funds from New York to the accused's account in Geneva. It was held in the Court of Appeal that, had the attempt been successful, the theft would have taken place in New York and the English courts would not have had jurisdiction to try the perpetrator. To prevent this type of problem (making it tempting for fraudsters to set up in England to carry out frauds abroad using computers and telecommunications systems), the Computer Misuse Act contains complex provisions relating to jurisdiction and extradition in sections 4 to 9. All that is required is a link with the home country – England and Wales, Scotland or Northern Ireland, as appropriate. That is, the offence must either originate from the home country or be directed to a computer within it: for example, a person from within England attempts to carry out a computer fraud in Sweden or a person from Italy attempts to hack into a computer located in London.

A final requirement is that of double criminality; that is, if the person operates from within any of the home countries intending to commit a further offence under section 2 in a different country, that offence is indeed a criminal offence in that other country as well as in the home country. Of course, in most cases this will not present any problems – most countries recognise theft and fraud.

Other offences associated with hacking

Although it is to be expected that the Computer Misuse Act 1990 will be the main weapon in the fight against computer hacking (and some other forms of computer misuse), certain other areas of criminal law may be relevant. It is possible that these other offences will apply in situations outside the scope of the 1990 Act: for example, there could be a problem in proving that the hacker knew that his access was unauthorised. In such a case, recourse must be had to the pre-existing law and the possibilities are discussed below.

The law of theft

As we have seen, the offence of theft is defined by section 1 of the Theft Act 1968 as a dishonest appropriation of property belonging to another with the intention to permanently deprive the other of it. If a hacker gains access to a computer system without permission and then makes a printout of some information contained therein, has he committed theft? The fact that the owner of the information has not been deprived of it, because the hacker has only made a copy, is fatal to any charge of theft.

In *Oxford* v *Moss* (1978) 68 Cr App R 183, it was held that confidential information does not come within the definition of property for the purposes of theft. The case concerned the 'borrowing' of an examination paper by a student before the date of the examination. Although the authority of the case is weak, having been decided at first instance only, it is likely that it would be followed because the consequences of the decision are fundamentally sensible. After all, the owner still has the information unless the only copy was taken, but this is different from saying that the information is not property for the purposes of the Theft Act. Property is defined as including 'money and all other property, real or personal, including things in action and other intangible property' and it could fairly be argued that confidential information comes within the meaning of 'other intangible property'. A better construction of *Oxford* v *Moss* is that the taking of the examination paper could not be theft because there was no intention to deprive the owner of it permanently. For this reason a hacker who simply reads or copies information has not committed theft. Similarly, in the Scottish case of *Grant* v *Procurator Fiscal* [1988] RPC 41, an employee who offered copies of his employer's computer printouts to a competitor for £400 was acquitted. It was said that there was no authority for the proposition that the dishonest exploitation of the confidential information was a criminal offence.

If the information concerned is copied onto paper belonging to someone else, such as an employer, there will be an offence of theft committed with respect to the paper. Likewise, if a person copies information from a computer on to a disk which belongs to someone else and takes the disk, this would be theft of the disk if the other elements of theft are present such as the intention to permanently deprive the owner of the disk.

If the hacker goes further and not only makes a copy of the information but then, immediately after, goes on to erase the original from the computer system, is this more likely to be viewed as theft? An act of deliberate erasure will almost certainly be an offence under section 3 of the Computer Misuse Act 1990, as discussed in Chapter 26. In terms of theft, there will be a dishonest appropriation of property belonging to another, but is there an intention to permanently deprive the owner of that information? The difficulty here will be if the hacker believes that the owner has another copy of that information, for, if he does so believe, there is no intention to permanently deprive. In the world of computers, back-up copies of programs and data are the rule and it would be very reasonable for the hacker to believe that back-up copies have been made. Therefore, it would appear that unauthorised copying, even coupled with the subsequent destruction of the original, is unlikely to be theft.

There is an offence in the Theft Act 1968 which holds out some promise and that is the offence of abstracting electricity. The very act of hacking will result in the host computer (the computer hacked into – accessed without permission) performing work as it retrieves information from its store. If that information is stored on magnetic disks, the disk drive heads will physically move, tracking across the disks, locating and then reading the information which will then be moved into the computer's volatile memory by means of tiny electrical currents. More electricity will be consumed in transmitting the information to the hacker's computer terminal. The total amount of electricity used to perform these acts will be small but, nevertheless, a definite amount will have been used as a result of the hacker's actions.

Section 13 of the Theft Act 1968 describes the offence of abstracting electricity as its dishonest use without due authority, or its dishonest waste or diversion. The offence is committed regardless of the amount of electricity so used and the only difficulty concerns the concept of dishonesty. There is no definition of dishonesty in the Theft Act 1968 for the purposes of section 13, but case law provides some guidance. The test of dishonesty which is used for the offences of theft and obtaining by deception derives from the case of *R v Ghosh* [1982] QB 1053, and there is no reason to doubt that the same test would apply to the offence of abstracting electricity. This test has already been described in the context of fraud in Chapter 24. Ultimately, the test must be resolved by the jury and while a jury would probably consider, objectively, that hacking was dishonest, the members of a jury might have more difficulty in deciding whether the accused hacker would realise that what he was doing was dishonest by the ordinary standards of reasonable and honest persons.

Communications offences

Section 1 of the Interception of Communications Act 1985 makes it an offence to intercept a communication intentionally during its transmission through a public telecommunications system. This will only apply to a case where the hacker actually intercepts something (for example, the transmission of computer data over the BT network). In most cases, the hacker will initiate the transmission and will cause the sending of the information. This offence therefore applies only to the situation where the hacker is 'eavesdropping': that is, listening in for interesting communications to intercept.

Section 43 of the Telecommunications Act 1984 makes it a criminal offence to transmit messages which are grossly offensive, indecent, obscene or menacing by means of a public telecommunications system. Similarly, an offence is committed if false messages are sent by a person knowing of their falsity, or persistent use is made of the system for the purpose of causing annoyance, inconvenience or needless anxiety. The Act refers to messages, so if a pornographic diagram or picture is sent by the hacker, the offence might not be applicable. It could be argued, however, that a picture is just another way of conveying a message, in which case section 43 of the 1984 Act would apply. It would seem that the Obscene Publications Acts of 1959 and 1964 do not apply because there must be publication or possession of an obscene article and the definition of article given by section 1(2) of the 1959 Act, as extended by section 2(1) of the 1964 Act, requires some tangible object. It would be different if a person distributes disks containing computer pornography; this would certainly fall within the meaning of the Acts.

Menacing messages could be linked to the offence of blackmail (see Chapter 26) where the threat itself is transmitted by such means. The threat could concern the computer system – for example, where someone threatens to destroy information stored on the computer system. Alternatively, the threat may be of a less technical nature – for example, a threat to inform the IT Manager's wife of his adultery. This offence under the Telecommunications Act will only be committed where a public system is used. It would appear that a hacker who sends just one false message will commit the offence if he knows that the message is false and transmits it for one of the purposes mentioned – for example, to cause annoyance. The same applies if the hacker persistently sends messages, whether true or false, with any of the motives mentioned above. Another possibility is a prosecution under the Protection from Harassment Act 1997, for example, if messages which cause alarm or distress are sent. A course of conduct is required, meaning more than one occasion.

A weakness has been found in the telecommunications statutes in a case concerning evidence of a telephone conversation involving a drug trafficker. In R v Effick (unreported) 22 July 1994, the accused had argued that a recording of the conversation was made in contravention of section 1(1) of the 1985 Act. Section 9 declares that evidence obtained in breach of section 1(1) is inadmissible. However, the House of Lords held that the signals transmitted from a cordless telephone handset to the base unit were not in a public telecommunications system and intercepting the signals by means of a radio receiver was not caught by section 1(1) of the Interception of Communications Act 1985. Unfortunately for the trafficker, this meant that the evidence was correctly admitted in his trial and the conviction was confirmed.

Data Protection Act 1998

This Act is described more fully in Part Four. However, there may be some scope for the Act in terms of computer hacking and therefore this aspect will be discussed here.

The Data Protection Act 1998 regulates the use and storage of personal data – that is, information relating to individuals who can be identified from that information.

A 'data controller' is a person who processes personal data and must notify the Data Protection Commissioner if the processing is carried out by automatic means (some forms of sensitive manual processing may also be required to be notified). Failure to notify is a criminal offence, triable either way, carrying an unlimited fine if tried in the Crown Court, or a fine not exceeding £5000 if tried in a Magistrates' Court.

If a computer hacker gains access to a computer system on which personal data is stored and then makes a copy of that data which he stores in his own computer, the hacker is guilty of the offence of processing personal data without having notified the Commissioner. There are a number of other offences under the Act, for which see Part IV of this book.

Postscript

In R v *Bow Street Magistrates' Court and Allison (A.P.), ex parte Government of the United States of America*, 5 August 1999, the House of Lords considered the concept of authorisation in the context of the Computer Misuse Act 1990. An employee, who was authorised to access customer accounts as part of her duties, accessed them for the purposes of carrying out fraud-related offences.

The House of Lords considered the decision in *DPP* v *Bignell* and the decision in the present case in the Divisional Court, and noted a misunderstanding of the concept of authorisation for the purposes of the section 1 offence. The error was to consider authorisation in relation to programs or data of a particular kind (control of the computer at a particular level) when what the Act required was to consider authorisation in relation to a particular program or to particular data. Lord Hobhouse said:

> Nor is s 1 of the Act concerned with authority to access kinds of data. It is concerned with authority to access the actual data involved.

Although the employee had authority to access the kind of data that she accessed, as part of her normal duties, she did not have authority to access the particular data she did access, as such access was made with a view to conspiring with others to commit theft and forgery.

Chapter 26

Unauthorised modification of computer programs or data

The law before the 1990 Act

Prior to the Computer Misuse Act 1990, damage or erasure of computer programs or data was an offence under the Criminal Damage Act 1971. By section 1(1) of that Act, a person is guilty of an offence if, without lawful excuse, he destroys or damages any property belonging to another. The definition of the offence required that the person intended such consequences to occur or was reckless as to whether property would be so destroyed or damaged. In the case of *R* v *Caldwell* [1982] AC 341, it was held that whether a person had been reckless was an objective test – that is, whether the course of action undertaken by the accused created what would be an obvious risk of damage in the eyes of the ordinary prudent individual.

One potential difficulty with the Act is that property must be destroyed or damaged and property is defined by section 10 as meaning tangible property. This creates an immediate problem when programs or data stored on magnetic media such as a disk are erased. Programs or data are not tangible in this form, although the disk itself certainly is. The first case to tackle this apparent difficulty was *Cox* v *Riley* (1986) 83 Cr App R 54, in which the accused erased programs from a printed circuit card used to control his employer's computerised saw for cutting out timber sections for window frames. He was charged with criminal damage but argued that the programs were not tangible property within the meaning of the Act. Nevertheless, he was found guilty on the basis that the printed circuit card had been damaged and was now useless. It would require some work in reprogramming it before it could be restored to its former condition.

The 'mad hacker'

The Court of Appeal had an opportunity to examine the applicability of criminal damage when it heard the appeal against conviction of the self-styled 'mad hacker'. In *R* v *Whiteley* (1991) 93 Cr App R 381, the accused gained unauthorised access to the Joint Academic Network (JANET) and gave himself the status of Systems Manager. He deleted and added files, changed passwords and deleted audit files recording his activities. He was very skilled and even deleted a special program inserted to trap him. His activities caused serious disruption and he was convicted of damaging computer disks. The Court of Appeal rejected his appeal confirming that the value of the disks had been impaired. The Lord Chief Justice, Lord Lane, said that the Act required that tangible property had been damaged, not that the damage itself should be tangible.

The appeal in R v *Whiteley* had been heard after the Computer Misuse Act 1990 came into force but had to be decided on the basis of the prior law. The 1990 Act provides that, for the purposes of the Criminal Damage Act 1971, a modification of the contents of a computer is not to be regarded as damaging any computer or computer storage medium, unless its effect on that computer or storage medium impaired its physical condition (Computer Misuse Act 1990, section 3(6)). This is to try and remove any overlap between the unauthorised modification offence under the Computer Misuse Act 1990 and the Criminal Damage Act 1971.

Current position under the Criminal Damage Act 1971

It would seem that the 1971 Act no longer applies to damage of programs and data stored in a computer. In R v *Whiteley*, however, the conviction was based on the fact that the state of the magnetic particles on the disks had been altered. These particles, it could be argued, are tangible even if they are not visible. This point may be of academic interest only as it is unlikely that a charge would be brought under the Criminal Damage Act 1971 in respect of damage to programs or data; the 1990 Act would be used instead. There is one occasion, however, when the 1971 Act might be helpful and that is when the accused denies an intention to cause damage because, under the 1971 Act, objective recklessness suffices. It goes without saying that a hacker moving around in a strange computer system without training or the appropriate documentation is being objectively reckless.

Unauthorised modification under the Computer Misuse Act 1990

One of the reasons for the replacement of criminal damage in relation to computer programs and data stored in a computer or on computer storage media was that there were doubts about the logical validity of the approach adopted in *Cox* v *Riley*. Section 3 of the Computer Misuse Act 1990 was intended to put the matter beyond doubt and states that a person commits an offence if:

... **he does any act which causes an unauthorised modification of the con-**

tents of any computer; and at the time when he does the act, he has the requisite intent and the requisite knowledge.

The meaning of 'authority' applies in a way similar to that in relation to the section 1 offence – the modification is unauthorised if the person causing it is not entitled to determine whether the modification should be made and he does not have the consent of any person who is so entitled.

As mentioned in the previous chapter, there is a problem where a person who is authorised to access computer material uses his access for an unauthorised purpose. The same consideration could apply here: for example, where an employee is authorised to enter updated information into a customer database but deliberately changes some information to make it incorrect, he may escape liability as he is deemed to be entitled to determine whether any modification should be made. The better view is that *DPP* v *Bignell* is wrongly decided and an employee would not have *carte blanche* to make any modifications he wanted, only those in the course of his duties. Alternatively, as authority here relates to modification rather than access to programs or data, the concept of authorisation in *DPP* v *Bignell* does not apply in this context. It would be unthinkable if an employee could erase his employer's computer data as an act of revenge and escape liability under the Computer Misuse Act 1990. In practice, there have been a number of successful prosecutions under the Act for such activities. For example, a former operations manager who resigned from his post persuaded an operator on duty to give him access to the master operator terminal and loaded onto the computer system a malicious program which would have caused severe disruption had it not been discovered (Audit Commission, *Ghost in the Machine: An Analysis of IT Fraud and Abuse*, Audit Commission Publications, 1998, p 17).

'Modification' is extensively defined in section 17, the interpretation section, as the alteration or erasure of any program or data or the addition of any program or data to the contents of a computer. The latter covers situations where someone leaves messages on a computer without authority (a form of computer graffiti perhaps) or the situation where a person introduces a computer virus into the system. It clearly covered the activities of the person who distributed disks claiming to contain advice for the prevention of Aids; after using one of these disks, data files on the computer were made inaccessible and a message was displayed asking for money in return for a cure. The culprit was arrested in the United States and convicted of blackmail.

For the purposes of section 3, the requisite intent is an intent to cause a modification to the contents of any computer:

- to impair the operation of any computer,
- to prevent or hinder access to any program or data held in any computer, or
- to impair the operation of any program or the reliability of any data.

It is immaterial whether the intent is directed at any particular computer, program or data or programs or data of a particular kind or at any particular modification or any modification of any particular kind. The requisite knowledge is knowledge that the intended modification is unauthorised.

The section 3 offence is useful in that it deals with the problem with precision and is wide enough to cover viruses, time-bombs and logic-bombs as well as dealing with immediate, direct modification. However, the need for the prosecution to prove that the accused possessed both of two states of mind – that is, having the requisite intent and the requisite knowledge – may make conviction less certain, particularly where employees are concerned. There seems to be no justification for narrowing intention in this way and the objective recklessness approach in criminal damage is preferable in this respect.

The offence is triable either way and the maximum penalties in the Crown Court are the same as for the section 2 offence: that is, imprisonment for a term not exceeding five years and/or a fine. The jurisdiction provisions apply to this offence as they do the section 1 offence.

There have been some successful prosecutions under section 3. For example, in June 1992 a freelance typesetter tampered with a computer owned by a client thereby denying access to the client. He argued that the client owed him £2000 in fees but was, nevertheless, convicted of an offence under section 3 of the Computer Misuse Act 1990 and given two years' conditional discharge and fined £1650. The judge said that his crime was not particularly serious even though the client claimed to have lost £36 000 in lost business as a result (*Computing*, 18 June 1992, p 2). In December 1993, a nurse hacked into the hospital computer and changed patients' drug prescriptions in a way that was potentially lethal. He was found guilty of two offences under section 3 and sentenced to 12 months' imprisonment. It is possible that a charge of attempted murder or manslaughter is appropriate in such circumstances but it might be difficult to prove the required intention. The same applies to the ulterior intent offence in section 2. The section 3 offence is much simpler as the intention only has to be directed towards the computer or programs or data stored in the computer.

If a prosecution is brought under section 3 it is important that there is sound evidence linking the alleged culprit with the unauthorised modification. In *R v Vatsal Patel* (unreported) July 1993 (see *Computers and Law* (1994) 5(2), p 4), strange things started to happen on a project to write bespoke software. Database tables started to disappear and eventually development work was halted. The accused was a freelance programmer and a member of the team writing the software and two 'wrecking programs' were found on his computer. One of the programs was named VAT which was the accused's nickname. A trap was set but nothing further happened – although the wrecking programs had been erased in the meantime. A charge was brought under section 3 of the Computer Misuse Act 1990 but, following a trial lasting six days, the jury acquitted the accused. The total losses to the client were in the order of £90 000 and there was a suspicion that the accused had erased the tables in order to prolong his lucrative contract. However, any number of persons could have been responsible for erasing the data and, in addition, there had been problems with the hardware and the development platform itself had been highly unstable. In other words, there was no real proof that the accused was responsible. It was remarked upon that had he been responsible, he would have been unlikely to use his own nickname for one of the wrecking programs.

A person might modify computer records in order to cover up some other criminal or disreputable activity. In *R v Sinha* [1995] Crim LR 68, a doctor at a medical practice in Cardiff was charged with manslaughter and attempting to pervert the course of justice. A 30-year-old female patient who suffered from asthma consulted the doctor and he prescribed a beta-blocker drug which induced a fatal asthma attack. The doctor later altered the computerised records relating to the patient to remove references to her suffering from asthma. However, although the references were no longer displayed they could still be retrieved from the computer disk. A charge was not brought under section 3 of the Computer Misuse Act 1990. As mentioned previously, because the doctor had authorisation to use the computer and access patient records, there could have been a problem with the issue of whether the modification was unauthorised. The offence of perverting the course of justice is more reliable in this respect and certainly applies to the destruction or concealment of evidence.

Computer viruses

A computer virus is a self-replicating program which spreads throughout a computer system, attaching copies of itself to ordinary programs. Often, by the time the virus is detected, many back-up disks also will have been infected. Rumours abound to the effect that viruses are far more likely to be on disks containing pirated software. There were no reports of computer viruses in the Audit Commission surveys prior to the one undertaken in 1990 where a total of 54 incidents were reported, accounting for some 30 per cent of all reported computer fraud and abuse (Audit Commission, *Survey of Computer Fraud & Abuse*, HMSO, 1991). The next survey showed a massive increase to 261 incidents (Audit Commission, *Opportunity Makes a Thief: An Analysis of Computer Abuse*, HMSO, 1994). In the latest survey, nearly 50 per cent of the organisations surveyed reported problems with viruses (Audit Commission, *Ghost in the Machine: An Analysis of IT Fraud and Abuse*, Audit Commission Publications, 1998).

There are, literally, thousands of viruses and strains of viruses; some are relatively innocuous (though irritating) like the Italian virus which causes a bouncing ball to appear on screen but others are more pernicious and may completely corrupt a hard disk. The 'Aids' disk mentioned earlier was distributed as part of a blackmail scheme to over 30 000 organisations worldwide. Obviously, viruses are going to remain a threat in the future but persons responsible for introducing them deliberately into a computer system are clearly guilty of an offence under section 3 of the Computer Misuse Act 1990. This is so even if the perpetrator does not personally carry out the act causing the infection because section 3 states that the person is guilty if he does any act which causes the unauthorised modification and this will include distributing infected disks.

Publishing details of how to write computer viruses could fall within the law of incitement; that is, the person publishing the details could be inciting others to commit a section 3 offence. However, there must be an intention on the part of the inciter to bring about the criminal consequences and this may be difficult to prove, although, in May 1995, an unemployed man who called himself the 'Black Baron' became the first person to be convicted of incitement in respect of computer viruses (*Computing*, 1 June 1995, p 1). He was also convicted of 11 charges under the Computer Misuse Act 1990 and the judge warned him to expect a custodial sentence.

There is also a possibility of a charge as an accomplice but, again, intention must be proved. Obvious doubts about the applicability of the law of incitement and accomplices were confirmed by police fears concerning the then imminent publication of a book revealing virus techniques in 1992 (*The Times*, 12 June 1992). The same difficulties apply in regard to access providers on the Internet, though individuals responsible for posting details of how to write and spread viruses could be liable to prosecution. Bearing in mind the international nature of the Internet, however, jurisdiction and extradition will be problematic in many cases.

Blackmail

Blackmail is a serious offence and is triable only on indictment: that is, in the Crown Court. The offence is provided for in section 21 of the Theft Act 1968 and carries a maximum penalty of 14 years' imprisonment. Basically, a person is guilty of blackmail if, with a view to gain for himself or another or with intent to cause loss to another, he makes any unwarranted demand with menaces. The menaces are not restricted to threats of violence and include threats of action which is detrimental or unpleasant to the person to whom those threats are directed. An example is where a person threatens to reveal someone's previous financial difficulties unless that other person pays him some money. The 'protection racket' provides another example: that is, a shopkeeper's premises will be destroyed unless he makes certain payments.

So far as computers are concerned, a person would be guilty of blackmail who inserted a 'time-bomb' into a computer system and demanded money in return for details of how to disable the time-bomb. If the owner of the computer system has already discovered and removed the time-bomb when the demand is made, it makes no difference; the offence has still been committed. The offence of blackmail will also have been committed even if the computer owner is not worried about the threat because he has a complete, up-to-date set of back-up copies of everything likely to be affected.

Blackmail may be associated with a virus. The fact a virus is present may focus the victim's mind more wonderfully than would be the case with a time-bomb where no harm would be done until a predetermined date. A virus starts its destructive work by immediately spreading throughout a system. If freelance workers feel inclined to leave a virus or time-bomb behind to be used to pressurise a client into paying the agreed fee promptly, they should think again. A university lecturer carried out some consultancy work but when he was paid the client deducted part to pay for the telephone bill the lecturer had incurred. The lecturer retaliated by placing a virus in the client's computer with a message to the effect that he was owed money and that files were being modified and that the sooner the matter was settled, the less damage would be done. He was convicted of attempted blackmail and fined £500 (*Computing*, 8 October 1992, p 2).

The meaning of the word 'unwarranted' can cause problems. A demand is unwarranted unless the person making the demand does so in the belief that he has reasonable grounds for so doing and that the use of menaces is a proper way of reinforcing the demand. In most cases, the demand will plainly be unwarranted on the basis of this test, but there might be circumstances where this was not so. For example, a freelance programmer has carried out a substantial amount of work for a company which, he believes, has substantially and deliberately underpaid him. In order to encourage the company to pay up, the programmer might tell the company that he has entered a computer virus into the computer system and he will not remove it unless the shortfall in his payment is made up. It appears from case law that the accused must be judged by his own standards when it comes to the interpretation of 'unwarranted' and a jury might acquit the programmer if it feels that the programmer genuinely believes that he has reasonable grounds for making the demand and that the means he employs are proper, in his subjective opinion. Although this is somewhat unsatisfactory in that an accused person is being judged by his own moral standards, this is the current state of the law. However, the case discussed above where a university lecturer used a virus as a means of securing payment shows how a jury is likely to react in practice. If the action threatened is of a very serious nature (for example, if it would result in the commission of a serious offence), a jury should be directed that the means cannot be proper.

Bearing in mind the serious nature of blackmail, any victim should not hesitate to inform the police. As with other forms of blackmail, a payment made to a blackmailer in return for not destroying computer data is likely to be followed by further demands in the future. Good security and comprehensive back-up systems are the best defences against this insidious form of crime. At the same time as committing blackmail, the blackmailer may also commit other offences such as unauthorised modification of computer material, basic hacking, abstracting electricity and offences under section 43 of the Telecommunications Act 1984.

Chapter 27

Piracy and other offences

Copyright law

We have already seen that infringement of copyright can give rise to a wide range of civil law remedies such as injunctions, damages and accounts of profits. Copyright is unique among intellectual property rights in that it is also well served by the criminal law. While patent law and trade mark law contain criminal sanctions, the rights prescribed by those branches of law are almost entirely enforced by the application of the civil law. Although it is true to say that the majority of copyright infringements will be dealt with in a satisfactory manner by the civil law, the criminal penalties available may be more appropriate in some circumstances.

Copyright law contains criminal penalties for many of the activities collectively known as 'secondary infringements'. The common denominator is that these activities can be thought of as being of a commercial nature and include the infringements of copyright commonly known as 'computer software piracy' – an example would be importing or selling copies of computer software without the permission of the owner of the copyright in the software.

The criminal offences under copyright law are not restricted for cases of blatant piracy. In *Thames & Hudson Ltd* v *Design and Artists Copyright Society Ltd* [1995] FSR 153 the Design and Artists Copyright Society Ltd commenced private prosecutions against Thames & Hudson Ltd and its directors for offences under sections 107 and 110 of the Copyright, Designs and Patents Act 1988 on the basis that Thames & Hudson was selling and distributing a book knowing, or having reason to believe, that it contained material infringing copyright. (Section 110 imposes liability on officers of corporate bodies for offences under section 107.) An application by Thames & Hudson for a stay of proceedings until after the civil case had been heard was rejected by the judge who confirmed that section 107 does not differentiate between a reputable firm and a pirate. The activities which attract criminal penalties are listed in Table 27.1 with the appropriate maximum penalties.

As can be seen from Table 27.1, the scope of these criminal offences is fairly wide and will cover most forms of commercial exploitation. Of particular note is the fact that making an article designed to make copies is a criminal offence, as is being in possession of such a device if the intention is to make copies for sale or hire or use in the course of business. This would

Table 27.1 Criminal offences and copyright law

Offence *(Copyright, Designs and Patents Act 1988)*	Classification of offence (see below)
Section 107(1) With respect to an article which the person concerned knows or has reason to believe is an infringing copy of a copyright work:	
(a) making for sale or hire	MC/CC
(b) importing into the UK (not for private or domestic use)	MC/CC
(c) possessing in the course of business with a view to committing any act infringing the copyright	MC
(d) in the course of a business:	
(i) selling or letting for hire	MC
(ii) offering or exposing for sale or hire	MC
(iii) exhibiting in public	MC
(iv) distributing	MC/CC
(e) distributing otherwise than in the course of a business to such an extent as to affect prejudicially the owner of the copyright	MC/CC
Section 107(2) With respect to an article specifically designed or adapted for making copies of a particular copyright work where the person concerned knows or has reason to believe that it is to be used to make infringing copies for sale or hire or for use in the course of a business:	
(a) making such an article	MC
(b) being in possession of such an article	MC

Classification of penalties:

MC/CC – (triable either way). On summary conviction: imprisonment not exceeding 6 months and/or a fine not exceeding £5000. On conviction on indictment: imprisonment not exceeding 2 years and/or a fine (unlimited amount)

MC – (summary trial only, i.e. in Magistrates' Court). Imprisonment not exceeding 6 months and/or a fine not exceeding level 5 (presently £5000)

cover a piece of equipment specifically designed for this purpose but not a computer with a dual disk drive. Although the latter can be used for this purpose, computers are not designed for infringing copyright; they are designed for legitimate uses. The word 'article' is used in section 107(2) but is not defined in the Act in this context. Section 296 of the Act concerns devices and means to circumvent copy protection, but the word 'article' is not used in that section. It would seem unlikely that computer software designed to overcome copy protection, which facilitates the copying of other computer software, would fall within the meaning of 'article' and, therefore, producing such software may not be a criminal offence, although it would give rise to civil remedies. Alternatively, the software and the medium on which it resides might, taken together, be properly described as an article. The lack of clarity in section 107(2) is regrettable, although the primary purpose of this offence is the control of activities such as the making and use of plates for printing processes and the like. In fact, the Copyright Act 1956 talked in terms of a plate for making infringing copies. As discussed later in this chapter, however, the supply of software or devices to assist with the copying of computer software protected by copyright may be caught by the law of incitement.

The reason why the criminal law is relatively strong as regards copyright is the ease with which copyright works can be copied and the scale on which it can be done. In 1998, customs officers in Germany seized £37 million worth of pirated software in two warehouses (*Computing*, 13 August 1998, p 4). Various estimates of the losses due to software piracy have been made: in 1990 the losses in Europe alone were estimated at $4.3 billion (*Computing*, 9 January 1992, p 3). More recent estimates show that the losses may have peaked but world-wide losses stand at an estimated $12.8 billion (*PC Week*, 3 May 1994, p 4). Of course, such figures must be taken with a pinch of salt, but they do give some indication of the scale of the problem. It is a simple matter to copy most computer software, even if it is copy-protected, and, what is more, the investment required to do this and to market and sell the copies is relatively small. In contrast, to copy and sell an invention protected by patent law is likely to involve a substantial investment, requiring the acquisition of factory space, storage, expensive equipment, transport, etc. The scope and magnitude of criminal penalties have been gradually increased and strengthened to cater for the growing ease of copying with the advent of high speed photocopying, video recorders, twin-tape cassette players and computers.

The formula used for liability is that the person concerned 'knows or has reason to believe'. The meaning of this phrase was considered in *LA Gear Inc v Hi-Tec Sports plc* [1992] FSR 121, where the Court of Appeal said that the test to apply was an objective one – that is, whether the reasonable man, having the defendant's knowledge of the facts, would have believed that the copy was an infringing copy. Previously, the High Court had gone further saying that the phrase connoted the allowance of a period of time to allow the reasonable man to evaluate the facts and so form a reasonable belief. Although the Court of Appeal said the test was objective, it is not truly so if it takes into account the facts known to the defendant. What if the defendant deliberately turns a blind eye to the facts; he suspects that copies are infringing copies but does not enquire into this?

The availability of equipment which facilitates copying has not gone unchallenged. In the United States of America, the film industry attempted, unsuccessfully, to prevent the sale of the Sony Betamax video recorder. In the United Kingdom the record industry argued unsuccessfully that the sale of the Amstrad twin-tape cassette machine was an incitement to infringe copyright (see *Amstrad Consumer Electronics plc* v *The British Phonograph Industry*

Ltd [1986] FSR 159, and *CBS Songs Ltd* v *Amstrad Consumer Electronics plc* [1988] 2 WLR 1191). The way these machines were advertised did nothing to reassure the industry, using phrases such as 'you can even make a copy of your favourite cassettes', and it is true that most purchasers of such machines would use them to make unauthorised copies of music tapes and computer software, especially computer games on cassette tape. In the first Amstrad case above, it was held that supplying machines which would be likely to be used to unlawfully copy pre-recorded cassettes subject to copyright protection was insufficient to make the manufacturer or supplier an infringer of copyright. Neither could Amstrad be said to be authorising infringement of copyright because it had no control over the way its machines were used once sold. In the latter case, it was held that a claim that Amstrad, by its advertising literature, was inciting others to infringe copyright gave no legal remedies in civil law to the relevant copyright owner. In any case, Amstrad had printed a small warning about infringing copyright in its literature.

These two cases illustrate the difficulties in reconciling two distinct objectives – that is, encouraging technical innovation and making it available to the public on the one hand and protecting the interests of those willing to invest in music, films, computer software, etc. on the other hand.

Incitement is a common law offence and, with the exception of incitement to commit murder, is not to be found in Acts of Parliament. This gives the courts some flexibility in applying and interpreting this area of law. Although Amstrad, because of the use of a warning against copyright infringement, was not guilty of incitement, there may be other situations where a conviction might be more likely. For example, in the case of devices and computer software specifically designed to circumvent copy protection, the makers and sellers of such gadgets and software cannot point to legitimate uses unlike the Amstrad and similar twin-tape machines. They are designed to enable persons to make copies of software packages clearly against the wishes of the owners of the copyright in such packages. Indeed, as has been noted in Chapter 4, the Copyright, Designs and Patents Act 1988 specifically provides that civil law remedies should be available against persons responsible for the sale and distribution of such methods of overcoming copy-protection. It would appear that the criminal law offence of incitement also may be available against such persons.

A pirate who copies or imports copied software with a view to selling it may commit other offences apart from those under copyright law, depending on the circumstances. The Forgery and Counterfeiting Act 1981, the Trade Descriptions Act 1968 and section 25 of the Theft Act 1968 may be relevant. The pirate can also be pursued through the civil courts and the decision to pursue civil or criminal remedies, or both, will depend on the nature and scale of the infringement, the pirate's knowledge of the existence of copyright in the work and whether the pirate has any funds available to pay damages.

The Copyright, Designs and Patents Act 1988 has been used increasingly to prosecute computer software pirates and magistrates and judges are at last taking this form of crime seriously, using custodial sentences in some cases. For example, an Oxford computer dealer was imprisoned for six months and fined £5000 for making unauthorised copies of a popular word processing package with the intention of selling them (*Computing*, 11 August 1994, p 3). A few weeks earlier, a brother and sister pleaded guilty to 23 counts of software piracy and offences under the Trade Descriptions Act 1968 and were sentenced to 200 and 100 hours' community service respectively (*Computing*, 23 June 1994, p 14).

Forgery and Counterfeiting Act 1981

Section 1 of this Act states that:

A person is guilty of forgery if he makes a false instrument, with the intention that he or another shall use it to induce somebody to accept it as genuine, and by reason of so accepting it to do or not to do some act to his own or any other person's prejudice.

We have seen that the application of this offence to computer hacking has been a failure. If a computer software pirate makes copies of a popular package, however, dressing up the copies to look like the original and then selling them, he may be guilty of the offence contained in section 1 of the Act. It may seem strange to talk in terms of a 'false instrument' in relation to computer software, but section 8 of the Act describes a false instrument as including:

... any disc, tape, sound track or other device on or in which information is recorded or stored by mechanical, electronic or other means.

It would seem that every form or method of storing computer software will fall within this definition.

It could be argued that the person who buys a pirate copy of computer software will not be deceived and that he will know that, in the circumstances, the software he is purchasing is an unauthorised copy, especially if the price is considerably lower than usual, but this does not matter. The Act requires that the pirate intends the customer to accept the copy as being genuine and in one sense the copy will be genuine as it will be a direct copy of the computer programs. The programs themselves are the genuine programs. Section 1 requires that someone should accept the false instrument as genuine resulting in that person or another being prejudiced. Therefore, it does not matter if the person buying the copy is not prejudiced – after all he will have obtained a copy which works as well as the genuine article – it is sufficient that someone else has been prejudiced. That someone else is the owner of the copyright subsisting in the programs who will have been prejudiced because he has lost a potential sale as a result of the pirate's activities. If the customer himself believes that the software is genuine, then the pirate can be charged with the offence of obtaining by deception (Theft Act 1968, section 15) which carries a maximum of ten years' imprisonment, the same as under section 1 of the Forgery and Counterfeiting Act 1981. The choice between these two offences will have to be carefully considered in the light of the actual circumstances. In April 1991, a computer dealer was found guilty of obtaining by deception for selling pirate copies of software at the full retail price. He was sentenced to nine months' imprisonment, suspended for two years (*Computing*, 18 April 1992, p 3).

Trade Descriptions Act 1968

By section 1 of the Trade Descriptions Act 1968, any person who, in the course of a trade or business, applies a false trade description to any goods or supplies or offers to supply goods to which a false trade description has been applied, is guilty of an offence. A 'trade description' includes an indication as to the person by whom the goods are manufactured. Therefore, if a computer software pirate makes copies of a software package, without the permission of the copyright owner, in such a way that the copies look like the genuine article, then the offence is committed. A person who sells or offers such copies for sale will also be guilty of the offence. The rationale behind these provisions is to protect the public from being deceived into buying inferior goods rather than protecting the interests of copyright owners. Prosecution is normally undertaken by trading standards officers and the offence carries a maximum of two years' imprisonment and/or a fine if tried in the Crown Court or a fine not exceeding £5000 if the offender is convicted in a Magistrates' Court. The utility of this offence is that it is appropriate to pirated goods, including computer software, video cassettes, etc. sold in markets, often in the unofficial Sunday markets or car boot sales, which will be monitored by trading standards officers.

The offence can only apply if the copy carries the name or mark of the genuine maker, or a name or mark which is similar (false to a material degree). So a pirate can avoid the consequences of this legislation if he takes care to use a different name for the software and its maker and uses packaging which is different.

If the maker of computer software uses a registered trade mark (many of the names of popular software packages and the names of the makers of the packages are registered trade marks), someone who, without consent, applies a mark which is identical to or likely to be mistaken for the registered mark or sells or offers for sale, etc. goods which bear that applied mark, is guilty of an offence under section 92 of the Trade Marks Act 1994 if he does so with a view to gain for himself or another or with intent to cause loss to another.

This also applies to such use of the mark on labels, packaging, business papers and advertisements and, with the requisite knowledge (knowing or having reason to believe), also to making or adapting articles to make copies of the trade mark or to be in possession of such an article. The penalties for this offence are relatively severe, reflecting the problems of imported counterfeit goods, ranging from pedal cycles to T-shirts to spare parts for vehicles to pharmaceuticals to computer software. On conviction on indictment the maximum term of imprisonment is ten years and/or a fine, while on summary conviction the maximum is six months' imprisonment and/or a fine not exceeding £5000. Computer software pirates would be well advised not to use a registered trade mark or anything remotely resembling a registered trade mark in connection with their pirated copies of software.

The offences mentioned in this chapter are not limited to computer software and could, just as easily, apply to hardware. For example, a person selling counterfeit computer equipment to which he has attached a registered trade mark without authorisation could be found guilty of both of the above offences.

Section 25 of the Theft Act 1968

Consider a software pirate travelling by car to a car boot sale with a quantity of pirated software. He is stopped on the way by the police and the pirate copies are noticed. Has he committed an offence? He has not yet sold or offered any of the copies for sale. By section 25 of the Theft Act 1968, he may be guilty of 'going equipped to cheat' and 'cheat' means the same as obtaining by deception (section 15). Therefore, if the pirate intends to sell the software as genuine to obtain payment, he is guilty of the offence. The maximum penalty is three years' imprisonment. It must be noted, however, that the software must look like the genuine article and it must be packaged to look like the real thing so that potential customers will be deceived.

Pornography

There has been considerable publicity about the availability of pornographic material on the Internet and it is clear that the courts treat this form of computer abuse seriously. The law is reasonably well provided with relevant offences though there may be difficulties in deciding whether something is obscene. Under section 1 of the Obscene Publications Act 1959, an article shall be deemed to be obscene if its effect is such as to tend to deprave and corrupt persons who are likely, having regard to all relevant circumstances, to read, see or hear the matter contained or embodied in it. By section 2, any person who, whether for gain or not, publishes an obscene article or who has an obscene article for publication for gain (whether gain to himself or another) commits an offence. There may be some difficulty with the requirement for an article but this is defined as any description of article containing or embodying matter to be read or looked at or both, any sound record, and any film or other record of a picture or pictures. There is no reason to doubt that it will include a magnetic disk or other form of electronic storage media.

Apart from the Obscene Publications Acts of 1959 and 1964, section 1 of the Protection of Children Act 1978 makes it an offence to take or permit to be taken any indecent photograph of a child or to distribute or show such a photograph or to have it in possession with an intention to distribute or show it. Indecent photographs are defined as including data stored on a computer disk or by other electronic means which is capable of conversion to a photograph (section 7 as amended by the Criminal Justice and Public Order Act 1994).

In *R v Fellows* (1997) 1 Cr App R 244, Fellows was a computer specialist from Birmingham University who used a University computer to store indecent pictures of children and he printed copies. He also made the data available on the Internet. The Court of Appeal rejected the accused's argument that the computer data did not comprise a photograph for the purposes of the Protection of Children Act 1978. It was claimed that Parliament could not have envisaged data being stored on computer so as to reproduce photographs which could be transmitted anywhere in the world when the relevant legislation was enacted. However, the Court of Appeal held that the images held in digital form were copies of photographs for the purposes of section 1 of the 1978 Act. The authority of an earlier case was accepted in which the court accepted that a video cassette was an article for the purposes of section 1(2) of the Obscene Publications Act 1959; *Attorney-General's Reference (No. 5 of 1980)* (1980) 72 Cr App R 71. In that case, the court found the accused guilty notwithstanding that it was accepted that Parliament probably had not envisaged that video cassettes would become widely available and provide a means of distributing obscene material.

In *Fellows*, Lord Justice Evans said that a computer disk was not a photograph but was a copy of a photograph which made the original photograph or a copy of it available for viewing by a person with access to the disk. Furthermore, under section 7 of the Protection of Children Act 1978, there was no restriction on the form of the copy of an indecent photograph and later, contemporary copies were included. Fellows' appeal, and that of a person who received material from Fellows' archive, were dismissed. Fellows had been sentenced to three years' imprisonment, demonstrating the seriousness with which such activities are regarded by the courts.

Section 1 of the Protection of Children Act 1978 also applies to pseudo-photographs (as does section 160 of the Criminal Justice Act 1988 – offence of being in possession of an indecent photograph). A 'pseudo-photograph' is defined as an image, whether made by computer graphics or otherwise, which appears to be a photograph. This extends to data stored on a computer disk or by other electronic means and which is capable of conversion to a pseudo-photograph.

If distributing or downloading pornographic material by the Internet can result in criminal prosecutions for the perpetrators, what is the position of Internet Service Providers? In Germany, an Internet Service Provider manager was sentenced to two years' imprisonment, suspended, for not censoring newsgroups which were making pornographic material available on the service (*Computing*, 4 June 1998, p 4). There are clear dangers for Internet Service Providers and their managers as it is impossible for them to continually monitor what is being passed through their networks. Under English law, incitement to distribute pornography might be an appropriate offence. Incitement typically involves soliciting, encouraging, pressurising, or endeavouring to persuade another person to commit an offence. To be guilty of incitement, a person must intend that the offence will be committed though it appears that recklessness might suffice.

It would seem reasonable that, under English law, if an Internet Service Provider takes steps to prevent the use of his service to distribute pornographic material and removes it immediately if detected, he will not be guilty of incitement to commit an offence under the legislation dealing with obscenity. Some appropriate system of monitoring ought to be implemented, including the use of random checks and subscribers ought to be informed that distributing or downloading pornographic material using the service is a serious breach of the service agreement as well as attracting criminal liability.

Threatening e-mails

We have seen in Chapter 25 that sending a threatening or malicious message by a public telecommunications system, including by e-mail, can constitute an offence under the Telecommunications Act 1984. A much wider piece of legislation was brought in to deal with the problem of stalking and other antisocial behaviour such as that emanating from 'neighbours from hell'. The Protection from Harassment Act 1997 may apply where threatening messages are sent by e-mail or other forms of communication. It provides for criminal penalties as well as a civil remedy.

The relevant provisions of the Act came into force on 16 June 1997. Under section 1, pursuing a course of conduct which amounts to harassment of another, and which the person responsible knows or ought to know amounts to harassment of the other, is an offence. Whether a person 'ought to know' is an objective test based on a reasonable person in possession of the same information. If such a person would think the course of conduct amounted to harassment of the other, that is sufficient. By section 7, references to harassing a person include alarming the person or causing the person distress and a 'course of conduct' must involve conduct on at least two occasions though not necessarily the same conduct. 'Conduct' includes speech.

It can be seen that the offence can be committed relatively easily. Just sending two e-mails which objectively would cause in a reasonable person alarm or distress should be sufficient. For example, if Rodney sends two messages threatening to harm Wendy that should be an offence. The same applies if Rodney makes unwelcome sexual advances of an unpleasant nature to Wendy by e-mail. As it appears that the conduct does not have to be the same variety, Rodney could also possibly commit the offence by sending one threatening e-mail and making one telephone call to Wendy.

The threshold for the offence may be relatively low if the Lord Chancellor's view is accepted. He approved of a description favoured by Lord Russell (*Hansard*, HC Deb, 24 January 1997) to the following effect:

He said first, it [the conduct] is driving me round the bend. That is harassment. It is a continuation of the matter. Secondly it was unwelcome: that is an important criterion. He said that the activity went on and on. That makes for a course of conduct. He also said 'I did not want it'. Those are the elements of harassment.

The offence is triable in the Magistrates' Courts only and carries a maximum penalty of imprisonment for a term not exceeding six months and/or a fine not exceeding level 5 on the standard scale.

A more serious form of the offence is covered by section 4 of the Act. This is where the course of conduct causes another to fear violence on each occasion. The person pursuing the course of conduct must know or he ought to know that the other person will fear violence. Whether a person ought to know is based on an objective test – whether a reasonable person with knowledge of the same information would think it would put the victim in fear of violence. The offence is triable either way and, on conviction on indictment in the Crown Court, the maximum penalty is imprisonment for not more than five years and/or a fine.

In terms of the civil remedy, an actual or apprehended breach of section 1 is sufficient to give a right of action. The use of the word 'apprehended' makes it clear that it is the victim's perception which is important. Damages are available and there is provision also for injunctions, for example, prohibiting the person responsible from continuing the conduct.

There are some specific defences to the offence of harassment and it does not apply to a course of conduct if the person who pursued it shows that it was pursued for the purpose of preventing or detecting crime, that it was pursued under any enactment or rule of law or to comply with any condition or requirement imposed by any person under any enactment, or that in the particular circumstances the pursuit of the course of conduct was reasonable. For the section 4 offence the defences are the same except the last one which is to the effect that the conduct was reasonable for the protection of the person pursuing the conduct or another or for the protection of his or another's property. Note that the burden of proof is on the person responsible for the conduct (this will be satisfied on a balance of probabilities – the usual criminal standard of proof, beyond reasonable doubt, does not apply to defences).

Chapter 28

Computer evidence and criminal proceedings

Introduction

Criminal evidence is a complicated subject, littered with rules and exceptions to rules. One of the rules governs the admissibility of hearsay evidence; that is, a statement other than by a person giving oral evidence in the proceedings is not normally admissible or any fact or opinion contained in the statement. In relation to civil proceedings, this rule has all but been abolished but it remains firmly in place in criminal cases. The rule against hearsay evidence developed as a way of excluding evidence of which a witness did not have direct knowledge and so could not be effectively examined and cross-examined on it. The original maker of a statement is in the best position to give evidence of it. (Note that the law on the admissibility of evidence in criminal proceedings is different in Scotland and neither the relevant provisions of the Police and Criminal Justice Act 1984 nor the Criminal Justice Act 1988 apply there.)

There are many exceptions to the hearsay rule such as dying declarations, statements in public documents, depositions given before a magistrate, documentary evidence, etc. Without these exceptions, the person responsible for the statement in question must attend court and make the statement in person. In the case of computer documents there has to be some exception to the hearsay rule as, in many cases, it will not be possible to identify the person or persons who entered the information in question. The information may have passed through the hands of a chain of employees, a number of whom may have been responsible for its final form into the computer. The law of evidence has to be flexible enough to cope with the realities of the modern business world, otherwise persons committing criminal offences (particularly those involving dishonesty and fraud) would escape conviction all too easily. It must also be recognised, however, that computers are not infallible and some fundamental requirements have to be satisfied before computer documents can be admitted in evidence in criminal proceedings under an exception to the hearsay rule.

Main provisions

The relevant statutory provisions are contained in section 69 of the Police and Criminal Evidence Act 1984 and in section 24 of the Criminal Justice Act 1988 which replaces section 68 of the 1984 Act. Section 24 applies to 'business documents'. In basic terms computer-generated documents and computer printouts are admissible in evidence if created or received by a person in the course of a trade, business, profession or other occupation, or as the holder of a paid or unpaid office. Furthermore, the information contained in the document must have been supplied by a person having, or reasonably supposed to have, personal knowledge of it. An additional requirement is that the person who supplied the information cannot reasonably be expected to have any recollection of the matters contained in that information. This will obviously be the case in a large organisation where employees are dealing with many transactions each working day. If, however, the person supplying the information can be identified and does remember it, then that person can give evidence of it, in which case his evidence will not be hearsay but will be first hand and directly admissible.

Section 24 of the 1988 Act is subject to section 69 of the Police and Criminal Evidence Act 1984 which expresses that a statement produced by a computer is not evidence of any fact stated in it, unless it can be shown that there are no reasonable grounds for believing that the statement is inaccurate because of improper use of the computer and that the computer was operating properly at all material times or, if not, any failure was not such as to affect the production of the document or the accuracy of the contents.

It might be thought that a failure of a computer to operate properly would make any evidence in a statement produced from the computer completely inadmissible. If there is a problem with the computer it might reasonably be thought to cast grave doubts on the veracity of any information stored or processed by the computer. However, the wording of section 69 suggests that a computer statement may be admissible as evidence notwithstanding some problem with the operation of the computer.

The meaning of the section was not fully explored until the House of Lords case of *Director of Public Prosecutions* v *McKeown* [1997] 1 WLR 295 in which appeals against a decision of the Queen's Bench Divisional Court quashing convictions for driving after consuming alcohol in excess of the legal limit contrary to section 5(1) of the Road Traffic Act 1988 were allowed. It was accepted that the Lion Intoximeter, a breathalyser device, was a computer for the purposes of section 69 of the Police and Criminal Evidence Act 1984. In the cases before the House of Lords, the clock on the breathalyser device was approximately one and a quarter hours slow. However, the police sergeant operating it had properly tested and calibrated it.

Lord Hoffmann said that the words in section 69 were not meant to be taken too literally. Of course, the discrepancy resulted in the accuracy of the printout being affected in that the time shown on the printout was wrong. However, the section accepts that a computer may not have been operating properly at all material times but the evidence may still be admissible if that was not such as to affect the production of the document or the accuracy of its contents. An example of a fault which caused the document to be printed in lower case when it should have been in upper case was given by Lord Hoffmann who thought a rule which excluded such a document would be totally irrational. The purpose of the rule had to be considered to give effect to what Parliament had intended. He thought the purpose of section 69 was a relatively modest one and did not require the prosecution to show that the statement was likely to be true. That was a question for the jury. All the section requires is that there is positive evidence that the computer had properly processed, stored and reproduced whatever information it received. If the information it received was wrong, that did not make the evidence inadmissible. In other words, the processing accuracy of the computer was the critical factor. As the old adage goes, garbage in – garbage out. The production of garbage by a computer does not mean to say it has not been operating properly.

During the trial in the Magistrates' Court, the justices had a statement from the police sergeant identifying the document and describing the manner in which it was produced, giving particulars of any device involved in the production of the document and dealing with matters mentioned in section 69(1), that is, to the best of his belief that there were no reasonable grounds for believing that the statement was inaccurate because of improper use of the computer and that it was at all material times operating properly or, if not, was not such as to affect the production of the document or the accuracy of its contents (PACE, Schedule 3, paragraph 8).

Lord Hoffmann said that a computer is a device for storing, processing and retrieving information. An error in clock display would not have anything to do with whether the computer itself was operating properly and, in any case, he doubted that the clock mechanism itself would constitute part of the computer for the purposes of section 69(1). Instead it was likely to be something which supplies information to the computer.

Where computer evidence is involved, it is an attractive proposition to attack the admissibility of computer evidence, particularly if that evidence has significant probative value from the prosecution's point of view. However, following *DPP* v *McKeown*, the courts seem to be taking a more robust view and are more prepared to admit computer evidence. In *Reid* v *Director of Public Prosecutions, The Times*, 6 March 1998, minor typographical errors in a printout produced by a breathalyser device did not alter the validity of the results of the analysis of the breath specimen produced by the machine when it had been properly calibrated and was functioning properly. The errors were the omission of the second half of the first character and second character in every line and, in one version, the top line was printed in smaller font than the rest of the printout. The evidence was admissible under section 69 and the court referred to the outcome in *DPP* v *McKeown* [1997] 1 WLR 295, making it more difficult for unmeritorious and unattractive claims to succeed. The printer malfunction did not alter the way in which the machine processed, stored or retrieved information used to generate the statement. 'Getting off on a technicality' no longer seems possible where computer evidence is involved.

Evidence to show that it is safe to rely on the documents produced by a computer may be tendered in two ways. One way is by a certificate which must be signed by someone who was qualified so as to be in a position to give reliable evidence of the operation of the computer – in other words, a computer expert. The other way is by oral evidence given by a person familiar with the operation of the computer who can give evidence of its reliability. So it was held in *R* v *Shephard* [1993] AC 380 by the House of Lords. In that case, a woman had been convicted of theft for shoplifting. Various goods had been found in her car. She did not have any receipts, claiming that she never kept receipts anyway. However, the store detective from the shop where she claimed to have bought the goods went through the till rolls (produced by cash tills connected to a central computer) but found no record of any sale of the goods in question. The till rolls had been submitted in evidence. It was clear that the store detective was familiar with the workings of the tills and computer though not an expert. The House of Lords in upholding the conviction confirmed that it would rarely be necessary to call expert witnesses and, in most cases, the requirement in section 69 could be satisfied by calling a witness who was familiar with the computer and who knew what it did and who could confirm that it was operating properly at the relevant time.

If oral evidence is given by someone familiar with the computer in question, it must be so as to confirm that the computer was operating properly and not simply to confirm what the computer did. Convictions for carrying excess weight in lorries were quashed by the Queen's Bench Division in *East West Transport Ltd* v *Crown Prosecution Service* (unreported) 15 February 1995. Here a weighbridge had been used to measure the axle load of the lorries but the weighbridge operators gave oral evidence only about the function performed by the computer, nothing else. At the trial in the Magistrates' Court, the magistrates had erred by considering that the evidence from the computer was admissible without proof of accuracy, in the absence of evidence that the machine was not functioning properly. In another weighbridge case, *Connolly* v *Lancashire County Council* [1994] RTR 79, evidence that the weighbridge (being a computer for the purposes of section 69) had been tested regularly and was found to be working properly before and after the date on which the offences were alleged to have been committed was deemed to be sufficient. The judge confirmed that in most cases a certificate will be submitted and in other cases oral evidence will suffice. He went on to say that in some cases circumstantial evidence would lead to a legitimate inference.

Section 25 of the Criminal Justice Act 1988 gives the court a discretion to refuse to admit hearsay evidence, including computer documents, if the court is of the opinion that the statement ought not to be admitted in the interests of justice.

The application of the provisions relating to the admissibility of computer documents has not proved easy for the courts and, in the case of *R v Harper* [1989] 1 WLR 441, the Court of Appeal laid down some guidelines. This case involved the interpretation of section 68 of the Police and Criminal Evidence Act 1984 which has now been replaced by section 24 of the Criminal Justice Act 1988, but the principles should be the same. If anything, section 24 is a less stringent provision. The guidelines suggest the following approach:

1 Section 24 of the Criminal Justice Act 1988 and section 69 of the Police and Criminal Evidence Act 1984 are not independent tests but should both be satisfied notwithstanding that section 69 applies to all computer documents whereas section 24 is more limited as was confirmed in *R v Shephard*.
2 Although the 'personal knowledge' requirement of section 24 might prove difficult to show in practice because it might not be possible to identify the exact persons involved in a large organisation, circumstantial evidence of the usual habit or routine regarding the use of the computer might suffice, based on a presumption of regularity. The same applies to the requirement that the person who supplied the information cannot reasonably be expected to have any recollection of the matters contained in the information concerned.
3 The trial judge should critically examine any suggestions that any prior malfunction of the computer or its software has any relevance to the reliability of the particular computer records submitted in evidence.
4 If the judge decides that the computer evidence is admissible, he should direct the jury that the weight to be attached to such evidence is a matter for the jury to assess.

These provisions are not notable for their clarity and the flowchart in Fig. 28.1 will help to explain them. It is based on the assumption that both section 24 and section 69 apply. Some computer printouts may be admitted as direct evidence and not subject to section 24 such as where the computer simply keeps a record of some physical characteristic such as air temperature.

An example might also help to clarify the position. Joe Smith alters his building society passbook to show a balance of £1000, when he should only have a balance of £100, and this is the figure recorded on the computer along with a record of transactions on his account. Joe is prosecuted for forgery and attempting to obtain property by deception after he tries to withdraw £500 from the building society. The prosecution wishes to submit, in evidence, a computer printout showing details of his account and the transactions on it.

Referring to the flowchart, the first test is easily satisfied because the building society is acting in the course of business. The second test is more difficult

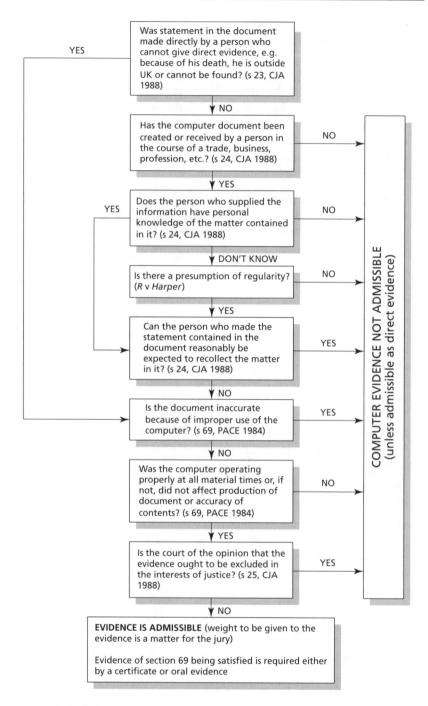

Fig. 28.1 Admissibility of computer evidence in criminal proceedings

because the employees of the building society who supplied details of the transactions entered into the computer system cannot be identified with any certainty. It can be presumed, however, from the regular business of the building society (that is, the third test) that staff supplying the details would have personal knowledge, at the time, of those details, so this provides sufficient circumstantial evidence. The fourth test, concerned with the recollection of the matters in the information, can be answered in the negative for it is self-evident that the persons who made the statement would not in the normal way be able to remember the information. If, however, there was something very unusual about it these individuals would be able to be identified and so could give evidence directly.

The sixth and seventh stages of the flowchart concern the use and operation of the computer system. Say that in the example concerning Joe Smith there have been problems with the computer software which resulted in errors in the recording of certain transactions, but there is evidence that the problems were quickly overcome and that Joe Smith's account was not in use at the time of the problems. Furthermore, a computer hacker has penetrated the computer system but it is claimed that the system is now secure and, again, Joe Smith's account was not affected. On the basis of the foregoing, it is likely that the trial judge would allow the computer printout to be admitted in evidence, but he would direct the jury that the weight to be attached to this evidence was a matter for them to assess in the light of the problems experienced with the computer system.

Once more, the importance of maintaining a secure computer system can be seen. If a jury is satisfied that the computer system has been professionally operated and maintained, it is more likely to believe that the computer printout is accurate and truly reflects what happened. It is vital that nothing should detract from the admissibility or weight to be attached to computer evidence in view of the now widespread use of computers to handle and record information. The ability of hackers to penetrate a computer system coupled with poor hardware and software monitoring and maintenance procedures is likely to destroy the admissibility of computer evidence or, at the very least, reduce its credibility.

A hacker or fraudster can make his subsequent prosecution and conviction more difficult by altering or destroying programs or data stored in a computer system. The insertion of a computer virus would be especially effective. The best way to prevent or nullify this is to keep back-up copies of the programs and data and, preferably, several copies providing an historical record of the state of programs and data. Of course, by modifying the contents of the computer, offences under section 3 of the Computer Misuse Act 1990 would also be committed.

Section 23 of the Criminal Justice Act 1988 also provides for the admissibility of computer evidence in criminal proceedings applying where the statement in the document has been made directly by the person concerned.

An example might be where a person writes some notes concerning an assault he has witnessed, using a word processor, and that person cannot give direct evidence for any one of the following reasons:

(a) the person has subsequently died or is unfit to give evidence because of his bodily or mental condition;
(b) the person is no longer in the United Kingdom and it is not reasonably practicable for him to attend as a witness; or
(c) the person cannot be found, after taking reasonable steps to find him.

Section 23 is also subject to the provisos in section 69 of the Police and Criminal Evidence Act 1984; that is, that the document is accurate because there has been no improper use of the computer and the computer has been operating properly at all material times. Section 25 also gives the judge a discretion to exclude evidence which is admissible under section 23.

Section 69 of the Police and Criminal Evidence Act 1985 also applies to extradition hearings. In R v *Governor of Brixton Prison, ex parte Levin* [1997] 3 All ER 289 Levin was alleged to have used a computer terminal in St Petersburg, Russia to gain unauthorised access to a computerised funds transfer service at a bank in New Jersey, USA in order to make fraudulent transfers of funds from the bank to accounts which his associates controlled. He was charged before a Federal District Court in the USA and arrested in the United Kingdom. There followed an application to extradite him from the United States government which submitted evidence that included computer printouts. Levin argued that section 69 did not apply to extradition proceedings and, consequently, the printouts were inadmissible as evidence.

The House of Lords held that for the purposes of the Police and Criminal Evidence Act 1984, extradition proceedings were criminal proceedings on the basis of section 9(2) of and paragraph 6(1) of Schedule 1 to the Extradition Act 1989 which required extradition proceedings to be conducted as nearly as may be as if they were committal proceedings before magistrates. Therefore, the normal rules of evidence and procedure applied to extradition proceedings. In any event the printouts were not hearsay as they were tendered to prove the transfers of funds which they recorded and did not assert that the transfers took place. They were direct evidence.

As technology moves on, apart from issues of admissibility of computer evidence, the complexity of the evidence itself may be lost on a jury. For example, in R v *Adams (No. 2), The Times*, 3 November 1998, the defence led evidence expressed in mathematical probability and the jury were invited by the defence to pay attention to Bayes Theorem. This is a method of combining a number of independent observations or results to derive an overall probability of a given hypothesis, a technique regarded by some as controversial. The Court of Appeal ruled that, in the absence of special cases, such evidence was a recipe for confusion and misunderstanding and misjudgment, possibly among counsel, probably among judges and almost certainly among jurors.

Reform of hearsay rule

The Law Commission has investigated the requirement to prove, in effect, the infallibility of computers in court before evidence produced or stored in them can be admitted. The Commission cited one case where 20 hours were spent trying to prove that four computers were working properly. There is a suggestion that some lawyers have been using section 69 of the Police and Criminal Evidence Act 1984 as a device to obstruct the course of justice. The Law Commission recommended, therefore, that section 69 be repealed (*Computing*, 13 July 1995, p 2). In view of the fact that a growing number of jury members are likely to have some experience in the use of computers, this would be a sensible move, and a jury should be left to make its own mind up about the weight to be given to computer evidence. If there have been problems with the computer, or if there is a suspicion that this is the case, it should be up to the defence to put this to the judge who could then rule whether or not the evidence should be admissible and, if so, give an appropriate warning to the jury.

Chapter 29

Computer crime – concluding remarks

Suggestions to prevent or minimise criminal activities

There are several things which the owner or operator of a computer system can do to prevent or minimise the possibility of criminal activities being successfully perpetrated against the computer system or the data or software stored therein. The main principle is to avoid complacency; it would be a very brave IT manager who considers his system so secure that it is safe against criminals and malicious employees. To some extent, strong security can foster complacency and can even present the would-be criminal with an enjoyable challenge. However, the golden thread running through the suggestions below is that security is a most important means of protection and great care must be taken to develop a strong, yet workable system of passwords and hierarchical access. Persons using the computer system should only be able to obtain access to those parts of the system which they will use. Different modes of access might be appropriate for different operators. For example, if the computer system contains a database, some users will only need to view and inspect the data, while some will be allowed to add to the data; yet others may be entitled to delete or edit the data or parts of the data. The scope of access granted to various people should reflect their responsibilities and be no more than is necessary for them to carry out their duties. Access will be by way of passwords and passwords which are easy to guess such as car registration numbers, spouse's names, etc. should be avoided. Passwords need to be changed frequently and the use of a two-password system, one password or identifier unique to each user and another for his level of access, should be considered.

A log of access to the computer system must be kept which notes user identification and times of ingress and egress, and these must be checked with users periodically. Furthermore, it must be made as difficult as possible for ordinary users to enter the computer's operating system. It is wise to invest some time and effort in making computer systems secure, appointing specialist staff or consultants for this purpose. Although this will require financial commitment it should be remembered that the consequences of poor security can be dire, not just in terms of direct costs but also in relation to the costs associated with detection and prosecution and in validating that a system is now free from viruses. For example, in the Audit Commission Survey of 1990, the average cost of detection and prosecution was £3468 per single incident.

With this general advice in mind, some more suggestions, related to specific criminal threats, are described below.

Fraud and theft

The largest threat is from within – that is, from employees. Therefore, employees' attention needs to be drawn to the fact that security is taken seriously and incidents will be reported to the police. This must be reinforced by the operation of a system of audits and spot checks and systems for double-checking (including manual systems). These systems should be varied from time to time as variety is the criminal's greatest enemy and someone considering using the computer to commit a fraud will usually do so only after they have become cognisant of the systems in operation. Changes will frustrate attempts to do this. Spot checks should be carried out on accounts chosen at random and on any unusual transactions – for example, sudden movement in an account that has been dormant for some time.

As regards supplier/sub-contractor accounts and wages systems, it must be ensured that any new accounts are genuine and that they have performed the work for which they are being paid. A data processing manager must learn to behave like an external auditor with his own computer systems and to use a high profile when it comes to checking that everything is as it should be.

Hacking

Obviously, security is very important here too. The location of passwords must be carefully considered: are they in a text file stored on the computer which can be easily inspected by a person working in the operating system? Some form of code for any passwords which must, of necessity, be stored on the computer system should be considered. If a computer system is being installed or expanded, the need for linking that system with a telecommunications system must be carefully considered. Is it essential to have remote access to the system? Would it be feasible to have computers at branch offices which are updated by being sent new copies of the data on disk or tape from time to time? Security needs to be made a high-profile matter at branch offices.

Educating employees should be seen as a priority. The need to take care of their passwords and change them frequently should be stressed. It may be better if the software is designed so that password changes are forced on employees after a period of time. Employees should be made aware of the dangers of accessing software they are not entitled to access and they should be given express instructions as to what they can and cannot access and what they are allowed to do where they have access.

Unauthorised modification (including time-bombs and viruses)

The danger here can come from hackers, employees, freelance programmers and sub-contractors. Employees who have been dismissed or have been given notice of termination of their employment represent a significant threat of damage to a computer system for such a person may seek revenge. If an employee has been given notice to leave his employment, or has been dismissed, that employee should be denied access to the computer system and should perhaps be given salary in lieu of notice. Passwords and security generally will need to be reviewed and changed depending on the employee's familiarity with the computer system. It should be borne in mind that the employee may have found out a considerable amount about the computer system during his employment – perhaps more than he should know for the purpose of performing his duties. It is worthwhile keeping a separate set of back-up copies of important programs and data in write-protected form. For example, when a new software package has been obtained the original disks need to be write-protected immediately and duplicates made which can be used as working copies.

Again, it needs to be clear that security is taken seriously and that the computer system is constantly being monitored. A potential source of computer viruses is pirated software which is to be avoided at all costs as should any software of doubtful pedigree. If a computer is attended to by a maintenance engineer, his diagnostic disks should be checked to ensure that they are write-protected for, if not, he may have collected a virus on his rounds which could be passed on to any computer. The acquisition of suitable 'anti-virus' software is a must and should be updated as new versions are available in an effort to keep up with the ever increasing number of viruses. Executable files must not be downloaded by remote access, especially on the Internet, unless they are known, positively and absolutely, to be free from viruses. Particular caution should be exercised with unsolicited e-mails.

Intellectual property offences

So far as these offences are concerned, little can be done in terms of prevention apart from pursuing the pirates ruthlessly and using the full weight of the civil law as well as the criminal law. Copy-protection can be counter-productive. Users should be educated about the important benefits of using genuine software such as support and the availability of updates. Care must be taken to prevent employees copying software and distributing it as this could breach the terms of the employer's licence agreement, allowing the licensor to revoke the licence and claim damages.

Evidence

Sloppy computer management could result in vital evidence of criminal activity being declared inadmissible. IT managers should be aware of the requirements for admissibility and they should ensure that there is a detailed record of the computer's operation. Some months or even years into the future, the IT manager may have to sign a certificate confirming that the computer was operating properly at the material time or, if not, that any failure was not such as to affect the accuracy of the document in question. Even ordinary computer operators, or at least their managers, should note in their desk diaries changes to software (for example, installation of an updated operating system), virus checks and audits and the results of these as well as anything untoward. It is important to build up a picture of the computer's operation. Historical back-up copies of programs and data should also be kept together with a record of when they were made. The fact that computer files are normally dated when they were last altered is very useful but only if the computer's clock is accurate. This includes taking account of British Summer Time. In one case, an argument that a printout from a breathalyser device should not be admitted as evidence because the time was incorrectly set was accepted and a conviction for 'drunk driving' was quashed (*Gerrard Jones* v *Director of Public Prosecutions* [1995] Crim LR 69). However, this was overturned on appeal to the House of Lords, as discussed in the preceding chapter in the case of *DPP* v *McKeown*.

Audit Commission recommendations

The Audit Commission reports, *Ghost in the Machine: An Analysis of IT Fraud and Abuse* (Audit Commission Publications, 1998) and *Opportunity Makes a Thief: An Analysis of Computer Abuse* (HMSO, 1994), contain many recommendations to improve security on the basis that prevention is better than cure. All persons having responsibility for the management of computer installations of whatever size would do well to read the reports. The reports identify a number of characteristics as being important in terms of an IT security policy; these are summarised below:

- an IT security which fits in with business strategy;
- a clear statement by management of the importance it places on IT security;
- a statement of staff responsibilities to protect the investment in IT and in respect of the computer data they use;
- a statement of the relevant legislation confirming that it will be enforced (this applies not only in terms of computer crime but also software piracy and data protection law);
- a statement indicating the steps taken by management to encourage and enforce high security standards;

- the steps taken to minimise computer abuse (adequate division of duties, secure password systems, etc.);
- the procedures relating to the acquisition of new hardware and software to ensure completeness and accuracy of data processing;
- the internal control mechanisms for monitoring that the policy is working and being adhered to; and
- the role of internal audit and other monitoring agencies in the organisation.

The reports recommend the use of codes of practices such as the British Standard for Information Security Management (BS 7799). The British Standard proposes ten key controls over information, including having an information security document, education and training, allocating responsibilities as to security, reporting incidents, having virus controls in place, controls over copying software, data protection and complying with security policy. The latest report goes on to suggest a checklist of questions that should be asked by management, which include questions as to 'all risks', fraud, viruses, sabotage, private work, theft of data and software, the Internet, hacking, illicit software and misuse of personal data. The questions include individual issues such as whether:

- management has issued an IT security policy and, if so, whether this is known to all staff,
- regular audit and security reviews are carried out of all key systems,
- staff are instructed not to use externally acquired disks,
- procedures are clear when disgruntled employees resign,
- risks posed by the Internet have been reviewed and steps taken to prevent access to the Internet for unauthorised and improper purposes,
- records of Internet sites visited are regularly reviewed,
- attempts at password guessing are monitored,
- staff are aware of the Data Protection Act and have been warned against misusing personal data.

The seriousness of computer misuse cannot be overstated and the consequences of poor controls and procedures can be very costly. As more reliance is placed on IT systems, it is vital that effective and workable security policies are established and reviewed regularly and implemented in an effective manner. The importance of good security can be put into perspective when one reflects on the annual UK budget for information technology spending, which is in the order of a staggering £26 billion (Audit Commission, *Ghost in the Machine: An Analysis of IT Fraud and Abuse*, Audit Commission Publications, 1998, p 3).

Organisations should develop their own code of practice and ensure that it filters down to all departments. Probably the most important aspect is raising staff awareness and obtaining the commitment and support of staff at all levels in developing and maintaining secure computer systems. Good security will come from delegation of responsibilities and developing an ethos of mutual commitment rather than by the imposition from on high of time-consuming and awkward procedures with little explanation of their importance and rationale.

Summary

It has been shown that a wide variety of criminal offences can be committed using or involving computer technology. Other offences may also be carried out. For example, murder or manslaughter can be committed by interfering with a 'safety-critical system' such as an air traffic control computer or a hospital computer monitoring the treatment of patients. Of course, some offences are not relevant to computer technology and it would be difficult to envisage a situation where rape could be carried out using a computer. However, given the ingenuity of the criminal mind, there are certain to be other forms of crime which will be attempted in the future.

The criminal law is now quite strong in relation to all forms of computer crime following the enactment of the Computer Misuse Act 1990 and computer programs and data are relatively well protected by the criminal law. On the whole, the legal environment in the United Kingdom has struck a reasonable balance between the interests of industry and commerce and the private individual. At least we do not execute computer hackers as happened in China a few years ago. Although the Computer Misuse Act has been welcomed by many in the computer industry and financial institutions, the presence of stronger laws should not be seen as a substitute for strong security measures and effective systems of auditing. Those organisations which store confidential information concerning individual members of the public or which have safety-critical systems have a moral duty (and in some circumstances a legal duty) to protect their computer systems from criminal activities, whether perpetrated from outside the organisation or within it.

Finally, the fact is that only the minority of offences result in prosecutions. Of the 537 reported incidents in the Audit Commission report published in 1994 only 58 of the culprits were prosecuted. There were 510 incidents reported in the 1998 report from 900 organisations. In terms of all IT fraud and abuse around 20 per cent resulted in dismissal and/or prosecution. As regards computer fraud over 40 per cent of detected incidents led to prosecutions. One welcome sign is that judges seem to be more prepared to take computer crime seriously and a number of offenders have been imprisoned. This now seems to be the most likely outcome where fraud, large-scale piracy or a serious case of hacking is involved. Other penalties imposed include large fines, suspended sentences and community service orders.

Table 29.1 gives a summary of offences together with their maximum penalties and some comment concerning their scope. It should be noted that, in most cases, a fine is also possible in addition to a prison sentence. Of course, subject to the maximum penalty, the courts have a full range of other disposals available to them such as probation orders, community sentences and absolute or conditional discharges.

Table 29.1 Summary of offences

Offence	Description	Maximum penalty	Comment
Fraud/theft related			
s 15 Theft Act 1968	Obtaining property by deception	10 years	Difficulty with respect to machine being deceived (requires a human to be deceived)
s 15A Theft Act 1968	Obtaining a money transfer by deception	10 years	Designed for, but not restricted to, 'mortgage frauds'; applies to electronic funds transfers as well as cheques
s 1 Theft Act 1968	Theft	7 years	Will cover most cases involving computer 'fraud'
ss 17–20 Theft Act 1968	False accounting, etc.	7 years	No particular difficulties with computer technology
s 2 Computer Misuse Act 1990	Basic hacking plus ulterior intent	5 years	Useful for attempts and not restricted to fraud
Conspiracy	Common law	10 years	2 or more persons
Cheating	Common law	Imprisonment and/or fine without limit	Only available for Inland Revenue and VAT frauds
Hacking and damage			
s 1 Computer Misuse Act 1990	Basic hacking offence	6 months	Triable only in MC. Search warrants available from circuit judge
s 13 Theft Act 1968	Abstracting electricity	5 years	May be difficulty with respect to 'knowledge'

Table 29.1 cont.

Offence	Description	Maximum penalty	Comment
s 1 Interception of Communications Act 1985	Interception of communication during its transmission through a public telecommunications system	2 years	Suitable for computer 'eaves-dropping'. If tried in MC, max. is a fine of £5000
s 43 Telecommunications Act 1984	The transmission of grossly offensive, indecent obscene or menacing messages	Fine max. £1000 summary trial only	Can only be tried in MC. Must be by public telecommunications system
s 3 Computer Misuse Act 1990	Unauthorised modification of computer material	5 years	Replaces criminal damage in relation to programs and data
s 21 Theft Act 1968	Blackmail	14 years	Unwarranted demand with menaces. Triable in CC only
Intellectual property related s 107 Copyright, Designs & Patents Act 1988	Secondary infringement generally making pirate copies for sale or 'dealing' with pirate copies		See Table 27.1 for penalties
s 1 Forgery and Counterfeiting Act 1981	Making a false instrument	10 years	Requires someone to believe it to be genuine
s 1 Trade Descriptions Act 1968	Applying false trade description, etc.	2 years	Trade description includes an indication of the manufacturer of the goods
s 92 Trade Marks Act 1994	Applying a registered trade mark, etc. without consent	10 years	It is a defence if the person concerned reasonably believed that the use did not infringe
s 25 Theft Act 1968	Going equipped to cheat	3 years	'Cheat' has same meaning as 'obtaining by deception'

Continued overleaf

Table 29.1 cont.

Offence	Description	Maximum penalty	Comment
Other s 21 Data Protection Act 1998	Processing personal data without having notified	Unlimited fine	Strict liability; failure to notify changes is also an offence subject to a due diligence defence
s 55 Data Protection Act 1998	Obtaining, disclosing or procuring the disclosure of personal data without the consent of the data controller	Unlimited fine	Some defences apply. Selling such data is an offence. For further offences under the Data Protection Act, see Part Four of this book
Obscene Publication Acts 1959 & 1964 (s 2 of the 1959 Act as amended)	Publishing obscene article or having obscene article for publication for gain	3 years and/or a fine	Would apply with respect to a computer disk containing pornographic images or information but some doubt about transmission over network
s 1 Protection of Children Act 1978	Taking, or permitting to be taken, an indecent photograph of a child, distributing, showing or being in possession with intent to distribute or show such a photograph	3 years	Possession of an indecent photograph without intent is triable in the MC only and subject to a fine not exceeding level 5 on the standard scale (s 160 Criminal Justice Act 1988)
s 84 Criminal Justice and Public Order Act 1994	Obscene and indecent photographs of children extended to 'pseudo-photographs'	3 years	'Pseudo-photograph' covers computer graphics images and covers data stored on disk or electronically
s 1 Protection from Harassment Act 1997	Pursuing a course of conduct which causes alarm or distress on at least two occasions	6 months and/or a fine not exceeding level 5 on the standard scale	A course of conduct (more than one occasion); could include sending threatening e-mails
s 4 Protection from Harassment Act 1997	Pursuing a course of conduct causing another to fear violence on at least two occasions	5 years and/or a fine	Course of conduct as for s 1 offence

Table 29.1 cont

Offence	Description	Maximum penalty	Comment
Incitement	Encouraging, persuading, suggesting, proposing to someone to commit a criminal offence	At the court's discretion if tried in CC	Could apply particularly to material posted on the Internet, for example, describing how to make a bomb, how to write a computer virus

Note: CC = Crown Court, MC = Magistrates' Court.

Unless otherwise indicated, offences can be tried in either a Magistrates' Court or in the Crown Court and, if tried in a Magistrates' Court, the maximum penalty available is 6 months' imprisonment and/or a fine not exceeding £5000.

PART FOUR

Data protection

Computer technology heightened fears about a society of the kind portrayed in George Orwell's *1984*, because of the power of computers in terms of information processing. Even now, there remains a popular feeling that computers undermine human skills and that the growth of computer technology heralds the dawn of an austere and coldly logical society. Certainly, the power of computers can be misused and there needs to be a system of checks and balances to prevent abuse of this power. In particular, computers raise concerns about individuals and their privacy.

There is no general right to privacy in English law although some legal remedies may be available in some circumstances. For example, disclosure of confidential information may be actionable as will be the publication of defamatory material. There are rights of privacy in relation to certain photographs or films made for private and domestic circumstances under copyright law. Other examples exist where a right to privacy may be affected indirectly. The absence of a general right to privacy has been criticised but English law has striven to strike a balance between individual interests and freedom of speech.

We are now entering a new era in terms of protecting rights to privacy. The Data Protection Act 1984 made a start but this only applied to personal data which were processed automatically. However, two major developments occurred in 1998. The first was the passing of the Data Protection Act 1998 which will replace the 1984 Act. The importance of this Act should not be underestimated. It marks a watershed in relation to privacy and personal data and gives individuals much greater rights than they had under the previous Act. It is also important in that it extends data protection law much more than before to manual files. The second development has been the passing of the Human Rights Act 1998. This incorporates the European Convention on Human Rights into United Kingdom law. Of particular interest is Article 8 of the Convention which states that everyone has the right to respect for his private and family life, his home and his correspondence. At the time of writing, the Data Protection Act 1998 is not yet in force (apart from some provisions dealing with definitions and the like). The Government has announced that it will come into force on 1 March 2000. The Human Rights Act 1998 looks a little further away at this stage but it should be implemented in the next year or so.

This Part of the book focuses on the Data Protection Act 1998, with comparisons to the equivalent provisions under the 1984 Act where appropriate. The next chapter looks at the background to the Act, the main definitions in it, the data protection principles, which are central to data protection law, and the role of the Data Protection Commissioner (the new name for the Data Protection Registrar) and the Working Party set up under the 'Data Protection Directive'. The following chapter looks at the Act from the perspective of the person who processed personal data, the data controller. There is then a chapter on the Act from a data user's point of view, followed by a chapter on the parallel legislation in the telecommunications field and the United Kingdom implementation of the 'Privacy in Telecommunications Directive'. Appendix 2 to this book contains a summary of data protection law under the 1984 Act for reference.

Note: Unless otherwise mentioned, all statutory references in this Part are to the Data Protection Act 1998.

Chapter 30

Introduction and background to the Data Protection Act 1998

Introduction

Data protection law affects everybody. Most persons process information about individuals, even if it is simply name, address and telephone number. Many do this by computer and only those who use a computer for little more than straightforward word processing will fail to be regulated under data protection law. A great many people have manual filing systems containing information relating to individuals. These may be in the form of a card index system or even a simple address book. Until now, data protection law has not covered manual systems but, with the advent of the new law, this is about to change. Even if we do not process personal information, the chances are others process information relating to us. Indeed, there can be very few persons who are not affected by data protection law as being the subject of data processed by others. Data protection law, therefore, has two main impacts. First, those who process information concerning individuals are subject to regulation and constraint. Second, as individuals we all have rights under data protection law. As this area of law is changing, the rights of individuals are given more prominence and a key phrase is 'transparency of processing'. Individuals should be better informed as to who is processing data relating to them, what the purpose of the processing is and what other processing activities are involved. They also have a right to more information than before in response to a request for access and greater rights to control processing activity.

There are many horror stories about people who have had information wrongly attributed to them and stored on computer. For example, a man with an impeccable character and without any convictions at all was arrested and charged with driving while disqualified because of incorrect information stored on the police national computer. Details about the disqualification had been entered against his name by mistake. He lost his job and had his car impounded. It took him four months to trace the man to whom the previous conviction related and who had a very similar name before he could clear his name (*The Times*, 8 May 1990, p 4). Another problem has been the lack of control of organisations who pass on personal information to others, resulting in many people having been inundated with unsolicited mail. A more sinister aspect of computer-stored information is a direct result of the powerful processing capacity of computers and the ability to use computers to target certain groups of individuals. The dangers of permitting the use of sensitive information stored on computers to continue unchecked are manifold.

As computer technology becomes progressively powerful and more use is made of computers, the dangers are set to increase. Numerous concerns have been expressed in the past by the Data Protection Registrar and others. For example, some data may be very sensitive and may cause considerable harm if its use is not strictly controlled such as data relating to genetic information or illnesses and diseases. Other concerns flow from the use of 'white data' showing that a person has a good credit record and the activities of private investigators has caused concern in the past. Other issues relate to the balance between freedom of speech and individuals' right to privacy, two areas of apparently diametrically opposed interests always very difficult to reconcile. Nor is computer technology the only threat. The Economic League was an organisation which retained details of individuals who had been active trade unionists or members of the Communist Party. All this data was kept on paper. The Data Protection Act 1984 had no effect upon such data processing – it had to be by automatic means. Structured manual files can pose just as many problems as automated processing activities.

The Data Protection Act 1984 received the Royal Assent at an appropriate time in Orwellian terms. It was designed to control the storage and use of information about individuals stored and processed by computer. Control of processing was provided for by a system of registration with penalties for failing to register and for acting beyond the scope of the registration. Additionally, the Act introduced a set of *Data Protection Principles* which must be followed by persons who store or process information, using computers, about living persons. Computer bureaux providing services to those who process such information were also controlled and were required to register under the 1984 Act. Individuals, about whom information is stored on computer, were given rights of access and a right to have inaccurate records corrected or deleted. Under certain circumstances, individuals had a right to compensation.

The history leading up to the 1984 Act was relatively long and there were several Parliamentary Bills, Reports and White Papers concerning privacy and data protection. The Lindop Report (*Report of the Committee on Data Protection*, Cmnd 7341, HMSO, 1978) was important in respect of moves towards legislation. In the late 1970s several countries introduced data protection laws, in particular the United States of America, Sweden and Germany. The final impetus was provided by the Council of Europe's Convention on Data Protection which was signed by the United Kingdom in 1981. The convention included principles for data protection and proposed a common set of standards. In 1982, a White Paper was published, outlining the Government's intentions (Cmnd 8539) and following this a Bill was introduced in the House of Lords. However, this failed to become law because of the general election of 1983 and a new Bill was introduced after the election and eventually received the Royal Assent in July 1984. The Data Protection Act 1984 was implemented in stages, the last of which mainly concerned individuals' rights of access and which came into effect on 11 November 1987.

In this chapter, following a brief discussion of the Data Protection Directive, the background to the Data Protection Act 1998 is described. Next the *Data Protection Principles* are stated and there follows a look at the definitions contained in the Act. The work of the Data Protection Commissioner is then considered, followed by material on the Data Protection Tribunal and the Working Party set up under the Data Protection Directive.

The Data Protection Directive

In the context of a Single European Market, it is essential that there should be no barriers to the transfer of information between member states. The principle of freedom of movement of goods and services has been largely achieved and it would be unthinkable if, in this age of information technology, the same freedom of movement did not apply to computer data. However, not all the member states complied with the European Convention on Data Protection. Being conscious of the possibility that member states of the European Community could erect barriers to the flows of computer data on the basis of insufficient protection for individuals in other member states, the Commission worked towards a Directive laying down a basic framework for the protection of personal data while stressing the freedom of movement of personal data. The argument is that, if all member states adhere to the minimum standard of protection, there should be no barriers to the movement of personal data within the Community.

A proposal for a Directive on the protection of individuals in relation to the processing of personal data was published in 1990 (COM(90) 314 final – SYN 287, OJ [1990] C277/3) and provided a complex system differentiating between the public and private sector as was then the position in some countries such as the Netherlands. A further proposal was published in 1992 (COM(92) 24 final – SYN 393, OJ [1992] C311/38). The distinction between the public and private sector disappeared but this particular proposal was perceived by data users as being unduly restrictive and extremely onerous to comply with. Particular concerns were directed at the extension of data protection law to manual files, the requirements to inform data subjects and, in some cases, the need to seek data subjects' consent to processing. A survey carried out for the Home Office in the United Kingdom indicated that compliance would cost the 625 organisations included in the survey at least £2 billion (*Costs of implementing the Data Protection Directive: Paper by the United Kingdom,* Home Office (1994)) while the Department of Health estimated that it would be necessary to inform every member of the population that it held personal data concerning them and that this would cost over £1 billion (*Draft EC proposed Directive on data protection: analysis of costs*, Department of Health (1994)).

The Commission responded to some of the concerns of data users and changes were made to reduce the financial burden while retaining the principle of protecting the individuals' rights of privacy. Furthermore, a survey carried out for the Commission by the author of this book and a number of colleagues at Aston University and the University of Leiden indicated that the above costs were exaggerated. Eventually, the Directive was adopted in July 1995 although the United Kingdom abstained in the vote. The full title of the Directive is Directive 95/46/EC of the European Parliament and of the Council on the protection of personal data with regard to the processing of personal data and of the free movement of such data (OJ [1995] L281/31). In this and the remaining chapters in this Part of the book it will simply be referred to as the 'Data Protection Directive'.

Model of data protection under the Directive

The Directive has, by Article 1, twin aims which at first sight appear to be incompatible. It states:

1 **In accordance with this Directive Member States shall protect the fundamental rights and freedoms of natural persons, and in particular their right of privacy, with respect to the processing of personal data.**
2 **Member States shall neither restrict nor prohibit the free flow of personal data between Member States for reasons connected with the protection afforded under paragraph 1.**

In other words, providing member states have complied with the requirements of the Directive there must be freedom of movement of personal data throughout the Community.

Although the Directive marks a significant change in data protection law, it has at its heart data protection principles in Article 6. These derive from the European Convention on data protection and provide a common link between the new law and that under the 1984 Act. Thus, fair and lawful processing must be ensured, personal data must be processed only for specified purposes, the data must be adequate, relevant and not excessive, they must be accurate and up to date and not kept in a form which permits identification of the data subject for longer than necessary. Nevertheless, and reflecting the changes to data protection law, the mechanism of protection under the Directive is, it is fair to say, more complex than that under the Data Protection Act 1984. It is shown in Figure 30.1.

Although the definitions used in the Directive and the Data Protection Act 1998 are described below, for the purposes of understanding the diagram, suffice it to say that the data controller is the person who decides the pur-

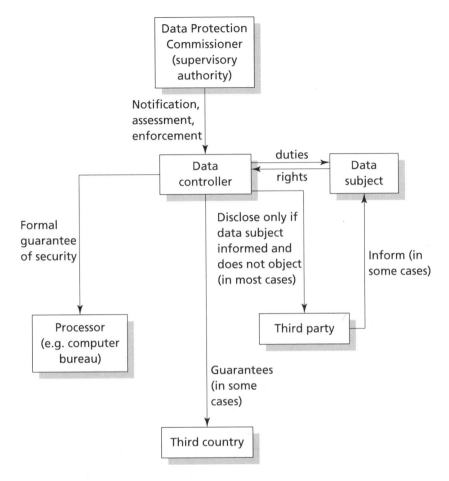

Fig. 30.1 Model of data protection under the Data Protection Directive

poses and manner of processing, the processor is a person who processes personal data on behalf of the data controller, the data subject is the individual to whom the personal data in question relate, a third country is a country outside the European Economic Area (the EEA comprises the EC member states plus Iceland, Liechtenstein and Norway). The Data Protection Commissioner is responsible, among other things, for supervising compliance with the Act and a third party is any person other than a data controller, processor or employee or agent of either.

Data controllers are required to notify their processing activities to the supervisory authority (the Data Protection Commissioner in the United Kingdom). Where the processing in question is likely to pose specific risks to rights and freedoms, the processing operation must be examined before it can commence. The Directive permits exemption from or simplification of notification where the processing is unlikely to affect the rights and freedoms of data subjects or where an 'in-house' data protection official is appointed under national law. Data controllers can only process personal data if they fall within one of a number of conditions. One of a further number of conditions must be satisfied where the personal data are 'sensitive', for example, relating to racial or ethnic origin, health, political or religious beliefs. Further duties are imposed on data controllers to inform data subjects and, in some cases, to seek their consent. Data subjects are given rights of access and rights to object to processing and to prevent processing in some cases. They are also given certain additional rights in respect of automated decision taking and rights of rectification, erasure or blocking of data the processing of which does not comply with the Directive.

Security obligations are imposed on a data controller and, where a data controller engages a processor, such as a computer bureau or a company to provide IT facilities management services, equivalent security obligations must be imposed on the processor. This must be by contractual means or by some other legal act and be in writing or equivalent form. Transfers to countries outside the European Economic Area may be prohibited or allowed only under certain conditions if the country in question does not have adequate protection for personal data.

The Directive also applies to structured manual files which, because of their structure, make it easy to access personal data belonging to a particular individual. However, there are a number of important derogations and options provided for in the Directive which allow for its impact to be lessened somewhat. Particularly important are the derogations allowing member states to delay the implementation of the Directive to processing already under way at 24 October 1998 (the date the Directive should have been implemented into domestic law) and to further delay the impact of certain parts of the Directive on manual processing.

A feature of the Directive is that the definitions used are fairly wide. For example, it is clear that personal data can include image data or sound data. The definition of processing is breathtakingly wide, including:

... collection, recording, organisation, storage, adaptation or alteration, retrieval, consultation, use, disclosure by transmission, dissemination or otherwise making available, alignment or combination, blocking, erasure or destruction.

The presence of the word 'storage' indicates that simply being in possession of personal data is processing for the purposes of the Directive.

To summarise, issues flowing from the Directive which caused particular concern were:

- the extension of data protection law to some manual files,
- the requirement to inform data subjects on collection of data or otherwise,

- the possibility of data subjects objecting to processing,
- having to seek data subjects' consent to processing in some cases,
- the introduction of conditions for processing to proceed,
- possible constraints over transfers of personal data to third countries (outside the EEA),
- security of processing of personal data, and
- controls over automated decision making.

In the remainder of this chapter and the following two chapters, the provisions of the Data Protection Act 1998 will be examined. Where appropriate, the provisions of the Directive will be discussed though, generally, it must be noted that the 1998 Act appears to be a reasonably faithful implementation of the Directive. The United Kingdom has taken advantage of many (though not all) of the derogations and options available in the Directive. Of course, mention will also be made of the 1984 Act where appropriate and particularly where the new law is significantly different. The data protection cases mentioned were, of course, decided under the 1984 Act but remain. Some are no longer relevant: for example, *R* v *Brown* [1996] 1 AC 543, an unsatisfactory decision under the 1984 Act by the House of Lords which has been overtaken by the wider definition of processing. But others remain very valuable in determining the scope of the new law: for example, *Innovations (Mail Order) Ltd* v *Data Protection Registrar* (unreported) 29 September 1993, concerning the provision of information to data subjects in the context of fair processing.

The Data Protection Act 1998

The Data Protection Bill was introduced in the House of Lords in January 1998. During its passage through the Lords and, later, through the House of Commons, it underwent many changes. For example, as first printed, the Bill had no specific provisions for transitional arrangements and there was no control over enforced subject access. The Act finally received the Royal Assent on 16 July 1998. Some provisions came into force immediately, being primarily concerned with the definitions under the Act and the arrangements to make regulations under the Act. A number of regulations must be made before the bulk of the Act can come into force. For example, there must be regulations to deal with the fine detail of the notification requirements.

Before looking at the Data Protection Principles, the definitions and other provisions of the Act, it must be noted that the Act is not the only source of constraints and controls on the collection, processing and use of personal data. Other areas of law may be highly relevant. For example, a person holding personal data may have an obligation of confidence not to disclose the data or a fiduciary duty in relation to them. Disclosure may be allowed only in a limited number of situations as is the case in banking where rules concerning when personal data may be disclosed were laid down in *Tournier* v *National Provincial* [1924] 1 KB 461. In that case, it was held that disclosure of confidential information could proceed where the interests of the bank required disclosure. However, it is an old case and it is arguable whether it would be applied in the present climate of greater respect for individuals' rights and freedoms. Disclosure may otherwise be lawful if the individual consents or where the disclosure is in the public interest or where it is required by law. The laws of copyright and defamation may also restrict the use and disclosure of information relating to individuals.

The Data Protection Principles

The Data Protection Principles are at the root of data protection law and they are contained in Part I of Schedule 1 to the Act. Part II of the Schedule provides interpretation of the Principles. The Principles appear much as before although there are some important differences. They are as follows.

1 Personal data shall be processed fairly and lawfully and, in particular, shall not be processed unless –
   (a) at least one of the conditions in Schedule 2 is met, and
   (b) in the case of sensitive personal data, at least one of the conditions in Schedule 3 is also met.
2 Personal data shall be obtained only for one or more specified and lawful purposes and shall not be further processed in any manner incompatible with that purpose or those purposes.
3 Personal data shall be adequate, relevant and not excessive in relation to the purpose or purposes for which they are processed.
4 Personal data shall be accurate and, where necessary, kept up to date.
5 Personal data processed for any purpose or purposes shall not be kept for longer than is necessary for that purpose or those purposes.
6 Personal data shall be processed in accordance with the rights of data subjects under this Act.
7 Appropriate technical and organisational measures shall be taken against unauthorised or unlawful processing of personal data and against accidental loss or destruction of, or damage to, personal data.
8 Personal data shall not be transferred to a country or territory outside the European Economic Area unless that country or territory ensures an adequate level of protection for the rights and freedoms of data subjects in relation to the processing of personal data.

While these are very similar to those under the 1984 Act, Principle 8 is new and reflects concerns about transfers of personal data to countries which do not have adequate protection. Furthermore, the first Principle now refers to conditions for processing. Again this is new. Of course, the first Principle is without a doubt the most important – that processing shall be fair and lawful – and it could be said that the rest of data protection law merely fleshes this out and provides the detail of just what fair and lawful processing is.

There have been a number of cases on the Data Protection Principles under the 1984 Act, particularly in respect of the first Principle and these are discussed in depth in the next chapter. Some of the other Principles have also exercised the Registrar who was quite active at the time of the introduction of the Community Charge ('poll tax') following concerns that a number of local authorities were collecting unnecessary information about persons and that the information was excessive in terms of that required for the purposes of the Community Charge. In *Rhondda BC* v *Data Protection Registrar* (unreported) 11 October 1991, the Tribunal upheld the Registrar's interpretation of the fourth principle (third principle under the 1998 Act) and confirmed the enforcement notice issued against the officers in charge of collecting information. They had been asking for individuals' dates of birth. In *CCRO of Runneymede BC* v *Data Protection Registrar* (unreported) 1990, Data Protection Tribunal, information relating to the type of property in which the poll tax payer resided was deemed excessive.

The seventh Principle is concerned with security (it was the eighth Principle under the 1984 Act) and, following a number of thefts of computers from doctors' surgeries, the Data Protection Registrar warned general practitioners to review their security arrangements otherwise they could be in breach of that Principle (*The Times*, 2 December 1992, at p 3). The worry here was that the information stored could be used to blackmail individuals. One criticism of the 1984 Act (and the same applies to the 1998 Act) is that there was no express requirement to report the 'theft' of data and a spate of 20 such thefts over a six-month period could be just the tip of the iceberg.

The Principles and their interpretation will be discussed in greater depth in the following chapters. It is considered to be useful, however, to let readers have sight of them now and to stress that it is the Principles which underpin the new law, as they did the previous law under the 1984 Act.

Definitions

The definitions are very significant and they set out the scope of the new law. The most important definitions are contained in section 1 of the Act. Some are similar to those under the 1984 Act, though others are much wider. First, the definition of data is given.

'*data*' means information which–
(a) is being processed by means of equipment operating automatically in response to instructions given for that purpose,

(b) is recorded with the intention that it should be processed by means of such equipment,

(c) is recorded as part of a relevant filing system or with the intention that it should form part of a relevant filing system, or

(d) does not fall within paragraph (a), (b) or (c) but forms part of an accessible record as defined by section 68.

Data within (a) and (b) above are those which are being or are to be processed by automatic means; in other words, computer data. Data within (c) are those in structured manual filing systems ('relevant filing system' is defined below). These are the data to which data protection law will now extend. The inclusion of such data was seen as one of the most costly provisions in the new law to implement.

Accessible records within (d) above are health records and certain educational and local authority records, which are caught by the new law even if they are processed manually and are not structured within the meaning required for a relevant filing system. The inclusion of such data is to incorporate the effect of the Access to Personal Files Act 1987 within the new law. This Act gave a right of access to certain local authority files such as social services files and housing files and is repealed in full. Access to health records which was covered by the Access to Health Records Act 1990 is also included in the new law. Where local authority files or health records are processed by computer, they are treated in the same way as other data under the 1998 Act.

Automatically processed data are treated somewhat differently than data in relevant filing systems within (c) above and accessible records within (d) above. In particular, only automatic processing need be notified (although in rare cases, manual processing may be subject to a preliminary assessment before processing can proceed). There are also provisions delaying parts of the new law specifically directed towards manual processing.

'personal data' means data which relate to a living individual who can be identified–

(a) from those data, or

(b) from those data and other information which is in the possession of, or likely to come into the possession of, the data controller,

and includes any expression of opinion about the individual and any indication of the intentions of the data controller or any other person in respect of the individual.

There is some doubt as to whether the Directive intended to restrict personal data to living individuals but the 1998 Act puts this beyond doubt. The definition confirms that it is not necessary for all the identifying data to be subject to the processing activity. It is enough for there to be further information which the person processing the data has or will obtain and which, together with the data being processed, provides identification. For example, a computer database may not include names but might, instead, operate on individuals' national insurance numbers. If the person processing the data also has a card index which contains national insurance numbers and the names of the individuals to whom they belong, that is sufficient for the data being processing by computer to be classified as personal data.

Personal data now include expressions of opinion and any indication of intentions. The latter was expressly excluded from the meaning of personal data under the 1984 Act. However, some of the exemptions from the subject access provisions will compensate for this change. In any case, it might be difficult to distinguish between an expression of opinion and a statement of intention. 'The performance of Joe Bloggs as a sale executive indicates that it is unlikely that he will be promoted in the near future' is an example.

'relevant filing system' means any set of information relating to individuals to the extent that, although the information is not processed by means of equipment operating automatically in response to instructions given for that purpose, the set is structured, either by reference to individuals or by reference to criteria relating to individuals, in such a way that specific information relating to a particular individual is readily accessible.

The requirement is that personal data are easily accessible because of the structure, such as in the case of a *pro forma* application form. This is confirmed in the Directive and its recital 15, which emphasises ease of access by virtue of structure. Clearly a card index system where each card bears an individual's name on the top, the cards being stored in name order, will be a relevant filing system. It would appear that a file relating to a specific individual containing, for example, only correspondence to and from that individual will not be deemed to be a relevant filing system. The Home Office view was that some internal structure also is required. However, it is possible that a simple address book set out in alphabetical order is caught by the new law. If this contains name, address, telephone number and e-mail address it is at least arguable that it is a relevant filing system as it enables ease of access to information relating to any particular individual. Furthermore, it probably will have some form of internal structure: for example, it may have two columns, the left hand column containing a name followed below by an address; the right hand column might have telephone numbers and the like. Fortunately, if a simple address book is a relevant filing system, as such it does not have to be the subject of formal notification to the Data Protection Commissioner, as we shall see. Note that accessible records in the definition of data are caught by the new law whether or not the data are in structured files.

'data controller' means ... a person who (either alone or jointly or in common with other persons) determines the purposes for which and the manner in which any personal data are, or are to be, processed.

Data controllers are the equivalent to 'data users' under the 1984 Act. Note that there may be two or more data controllers in respect of a single collection of personal data: for example, where an association of builders mutually share and are responsible for a central database of sub-contractors and suppliers. The significance of the phrase 'jointly or in common with other persons' is that if two or more data controllers agree between themselves as to the purposes and manner of processing, then they determine these matters jointly. However, if two or more data controllers have access to a central database, say a data warehouse, but they each have their own individual purposes and manner of processing, then they determine these matters in common. For example, Company A has a data warehouse (a massive collection of data relating to individuals where the information has been obtained from a number of sources). Company A uses this to extract information relating to creditworthiness of its customers. Company A also allows Company B to access the data warehouse. Company B has its own computer programs which are used to identify potential customers for a marketing campaign and to print out envelopes with the selected persons' names and addresses.

As before, under the 1984 Act, a *data subject* is simply an individual who is the subject of personal data. He is the person to whom the personal data relate or refer.

'Processing' is very widely defined (much more than under the 1984 Act) and, in relation to information or data, means:

> obtaining, recording or holding the information or data or carrying out any operation or set of operations on the information or data, including–
> (a) organisation, adaptation or alteration of the information or data,
> (b) retrieval, consultation or use of the information or data,
> (c) disclosure of the information or data by transmission, dissemination or otherwise making available, or
> (d) alignment, combination, blocking, erasure or destruction of the information or data.

Obtaining, recording, using or disclosing data extends to the information contained within the data and it is immaterial if the processing or inclusion in a relevant filing system takes place outside the European Economic Area (EEA).

The definition extends to holding personal data (the Directive uses the term 'storage' instead). This means that simply being in possession of personal data will be processing for the purposes of the Act. Even if the data are stored in structured paper files kept as archive material in a dusty basement, the person responsible will be processing those data. Under section 1 of the 1984 Act, a data user was defined by being a person who holds personal data. Holding data was then defined in terms of the data being part of a collection processed or intended to be processed by automatic means and the person holding the data alone or jointly or in common with others controlled the contents and use of the data. The definition also extended to data which were not at the time in a form ready for processing. Although 'holding' is not defined in the 1998 Act, one view is that, if the data are in a store and not subject to current processing activity, there must be an intention to process the data in the future. Given the very wide definition of processing, there would be little point in keeping data without having such an intention.

The definition of processing covers every conceivable use of data and its width is enhanced because the operations referred to are not intended to be exhaustive because of the insertion of the word 'including'. The House of Lords case of *R v Brown* [1996] 1 AC 543, heard under the 1984 Act, shows the importance of having a wide definition of 'processing'. In that case, a police officer worked in his spare time with a friend in their debt collection agency. The agency was engaged by a third party to recover a debt. The police officer used the police national computer to obtain information concerning the debtor. He denied that he had used the computer for non-police purposes and said that he accessed the data because he had noticed that the debtor's car was without a tax disc. Furthermore, he claimed that he had only accessed the data and had not 'used' it subsequently. He was convicted at first instance for an offence under section 5(2)(b) of the Data Protection Act 1984 which made it an offence to hold or use personal data for a purpose which had not been registered.

The police officer's conviction was quashed by the Court of Appeal and this was confirmed in the House of Lords, which dismissed the appeal by the Crown by a 3:2 majority. The majority confirmed that the word 'use' must be given its ordinary dictionary meaning and simply retrieving the information in computer readable form from the database was not using the information so recorded. The minority judges thought that the word 'use' should be liberally interpreted so as to achieve the purpose of the Act otherwise there would be a serious gap in the law.

The definition of 'processing' takes on special significance when we look at the meaning of a '*data processor*' which is:

any person (other than an employee of the data controller) who processes data on behalf of the data controller.

A computer bureau, processing data on behalf of a data controller, will certainly be a data processor. However, unlike the old law, computer bureaux do not have to register under the 1998 Act. But, as the meaning of processing is very wide, it is worth considering the types of persons who will be classed as processors under the new law. There follow some examples (it is assumed that the persons involved are not employees of the data controller – they may be self-employed, freelances or independent organisations):

• persons collecting data, such as market researchers accosting individuals in a shopping precinct,

- mail order catalogue agents,
- a small IT company providing data entry services,
- a company providing disaster recovery services or other back-up services,
- a company engaged to carry out database quality control by verifying, checking and, where necessary, correcting inaccurate information,
- a person engaged to prepare reports for a client, using the client's database,
- an Internet Service Provider which provides Web pages or e-mail services to a client who includes personal data on those Web pages or e-mails,
- a company providing IT facilities management services to a client who has 'outsourced' his IT function,
- a company engaged to remove and destroy old computer printout or archived files containing personal data.

The significance of being classified as a processor is that they must be subject to security obligations which are in writing.

Further definitions are contained in sections 2 and 3 and elsewhere in the Act. A very important definition is that of *sensitive personal data* which are, by virtue of section 2 of the Data Protection Act 1998, personal data consisting of information as to:

(a) the racial or ethnic origin of the data subject,
(b) his political opinions,
(c) his religious or other beliefs of a similar nature,
(d) whether he is a member of a trade union ...,
(e) his physical or mental health or condition,
(f) his sexual life,
(g) the commission or alleged commission by him of any offence, or
(h) any proceedings for any offence committed or alleged to have been committed by him, the disposal of such proceedings or the sentence of any court in such proceedings.

Sensitive data are treated somewhat differently from other personal data. As far as all personal data are concerned, they can only be processed if one of a list of conditions in Schedule 2 to the Act is present. For sensitive personal data, there must also be present a condition from a list of further conditions in Schedule 3. These are considered further in the following chapter.

The Act contains comprehensive provisions aimed at protecting freedom of speech. There is an obvious tension between this and the powers of the Data Protection Commissioner which are severely constrained where processing is for the special purposes, defined in section 3 as any one or more of the following:

(a) the purposes of journalism,
(b) artistic purposes, and
(c) literary purposes.

Further definitions are buried away in section 70. They include:

> *'recipient'*, in relation to any personal data, means any person to whom the data are disclosed, including any person (such as an employee or agent of the data controller, a data processor or an employee or agent of a data processor) to whom they are disclosed in the course of processing the data for the data controller, but does not include any person to whom disclosure is or may be made as a result of, or with a view to, a particular inquiry by or on behalf of that person made in the exercise of any power conferred by law.

This is relevant in terms of notification of processing activity as recipients must be described in the particulars notified to the Data Protection Commissioner. Note that employees and agents of the data controller and any data processor must be mentioned. The latter part of the definition is intended to excuse the notification of recipients who cannot easily be predicted but to whom personal data may be required to be disclosed to by law. A particular example is where a government department makes a particular one-off enquiry to a local authority where the person concerned is based.

> *'third party'*, in relation to personal data, means any person other than–
> (a) the data subject,
> (b) the data controller, or
> (c) any data processor or other person authorised to process data for the data controller or processor.

The relevance of the identity of third parties is that, under certain circumstances, where data are disclosed to a third party, there is an obligation to inform data subjects of this. For example, where data controller A sells a copy of his customer list to data controller B, he should inform all the data subjects concerned unless they are already aware that this would happen.

Now that the main definitions have been introduced, it is useful to reflect on the identity of the various persons involved in data processing and this is set out in Fig. 30.2.

Application of the Act

The Data Protection Act 1998 applies to the United Kingdom and extends to Northern Ireland. By section 5, except as otherwise provided for by or under section 54 (which concerns the Commissioner carrying out designated functions to enable the government to give effect to any international obligations of the United Kingdom), the Act applies to a data controller in respect of any data only if:

> (a) the data controller is established in the United Kingdom and the data are processed in the context of that establishment, or

375

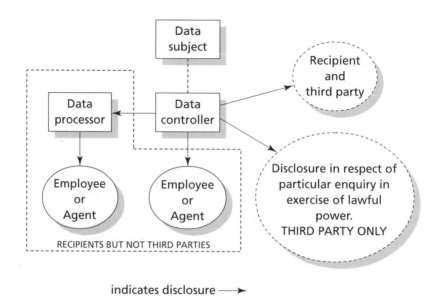

indicates disclosure ——➤

Fig. 30.2 Persons involved in processing activity

(b) the data controller is established neither in the United Kingdom nor in any EEA State but uses equipment in the United Kingdom for processing the data otherwise than for transit through the United Kingdom.

In the last case, the data controller must nominate a representative established in the United Kingdom. Thus, an English company processing data in connection with its business operations is subject to the 1998 Act. A Spanish company which engages a French company to process personal data on its behalf will be subject to the Spanish implementation of the Data Protection Directive under Spanish law. An Australian company using the services of a computer bureau situated in Scotland and using equipment situated there will be subject to the United Kingdom Act and must nominate a representative in the United Kingdom. In this case, it can be expected that it will be the Scottish company which will be the representative. Of course, in the latter case, the Australian company must notify the Data Protection Commissioner of the processing activity carried out in Scotland. If a Brazilian company transfers personal data to Japan via a computer situated in the United Kingdom, the United Kingdom Act will not apply unless the data are processed in the United Kingdom for any purpose other than the purpose of transit to Japan. This latter point is particularly important in terms of transmission via public telecommunications systems including by e-mail and the Internet. It obviates the need for the data controller to notify in all the member states of the EEA if the data is likely to pass through any or all of them (which it is by the nature of transmission over the Internet).

Role of the Data Protection Commissioner

The Data Protection Registrar under the 1984 Act is presently Elizabeth France. She will be the first Data Protection Commissioner under the new law. The Commissioner is required to act in an independent manner and is appointed by Her Majesty by Letters Patent. The role of the Commissioner can be seen as being concerned with the following major functions:

- consultation and dissemination of information,
- investigation,
- intervention,
- enforcement, and
- co-operation.

Consultation and dissemination of information

As required by the Data Protection Directive, the Commissioner must be consulted as regards administrative measures and regulations relating to the protection of individuals' rights and freedoms with regard to the processing of personal data. Thus, under section 67 of the Data Protection Act 1998, the Secretary of State shall consult the Commissioner before making an order under the Act (except for an order bringing parts of the Act into force) or before making any regulations under the Act except for the notification regulations.

Under the 1984 Act, the Data Protection Registrar was very active in the dissemination of information concerning the Act and compliance with it. This included advertising and the publication of an excellent set of Guidelines, written in plain English. Anyone interested in seeing these and various other reports and other information should visit the Registrar's Website at http://www.open.gov.uk/dpr/dprhome.htm which also gives access to the register and is well worth the time taken to visit. Under the 1998 Act, the responsibility for the Commissioner to disseminate information continues and is extended.

As before, the Commissioner is given general duties to promote good practice by data controllers and to promote observance of the Act. This includes the dissemination of information about good practice and about other matters within the Commissioner's functions under the Act. The Commissioner may give advice to any person as to any of those matters.

As before, there is a duty to lay a report before Parliament annually. Other reports may be placed before Parliament as must be codes of practice ordered to be prepared by the Secretary of State who may direct the Commissioner to draw up and disseminate codes of practice after consultation with trade associations, data subjects or persons representing data subjects. The order will describe the personal data or processing to which the code is to relate and may also describe the persons or classes of persons to whom it is to relate. The

Commissioner may also draw up codes of practice where she considers it appropriate.

A new function is that the Commissioner will disseminate Community findings as regards the adequacy of protection for personal data in third countries (countries or territories outside the EEA) and decisions under Article 31(2) of the Directive made for the purposes of Article 26(3) or (4) as regards measures to be taken in respect of adequacy of protection in third countries and contractual clauses considered to offer sufficient safeguards and such other information relating to processing of personal data outside the EEA.

Investigation

The Commissioner has wide-ranging powers of investigation aimed at determining that processing complies with the Data Protection Principles and whether there has been otherwise any contravention of the Act. The powers of investigation are exercised through:

- information notices,
- special information notices, or
- powers of entry and inspection.

Before looking at these individually, it should be noted that any individual who considers that he is directly affected by any processing may, under section 42, apply to the Commissioner for an assessment as to whether or not it is likely that the processing has been or is being carried out in compliance with the Act. The Commissioner must, upon receipt of such a request, make such assessment, providing she has been furnished with sufficient information to identify the person making the request and the processing in question. The Commissioner may take into account the following factors to determine the manner of the assessment:

- the extent to which the request appears to the Commissioner to raise a matter of substance,
- any undue delay in making the request, and
- whether the person making the request is entitled to make a subject access request.

The Commissioner shall notify the person whether an assessment has been made as a result of the request and any view formed or action to be taken, having regard in particular to any exemption from subject access enjoyed by the data controller. In particular, a request for an assessment may cause the Commissioner to serve an information notice.

Information notices

An information notice may be served as a result of a request for assessment from an individual or if the Commissioner has reasonable grounds for suspecting that the data controller has contravened or is contravening any of the Principles. The notice requires the data controller to furnish the Commissioner with information relating to the request within the specified time and in such form as may be specified. The notice must include a statement that the notice has been served in response to a request from an individual if that is the case or, otherwise, with a statement that the information requested is regarded to be relevant in determining whether the data controller has complied or is complying with the Principles, together with reasons why the information is regarded as relevant. The notice must also contain particulars of appeal.

Normally, the time to reply should not be less than the time during which an appeal may be brought (not specified in the new Act but likely to be 28 days as under the 1984 Act) except where the Commissioner considers that the information is required as a matter of urgency where the time limit can be seven days. The Commissioner must state the reasons why the information is required as a matter of urgency. The data controller is excused from providing information which is privileged or would reveal evidence of an offence other than an offence under the Act.

Information notices may not be served on a data controller in respect of processing for the special purposes (journalism, artistic or literary expression) unless a determination has been made and has taken effect under section 45 where it appears to the Commissioner that the personal data are not being processed only for the special purposes or are not being processed with a view to publication by any person of any journalistic, literary or artistic material which has not previously been published by the data controller. This provision is intended to prevent undue interference with freedom of speech. Figure 30.3 shows when an information notice may be served by the Commissioner.

Section 45 determinations are important also in respect of special information notices and enforcement notices, as described later. The Commissioner must serve on the data controller notice of the determination which must include particulars of the right to appeal and must not take effect until the end of the period for an appeal or, if an appeal is pending, until the appeal has been determined or withdrawn. Thus, if processing is for the special purposes only or with a view to publication, the Commissioner's powers are curtailed until a determination has taken effect. Note that publication can be by any person; presumably this includes the data controller, and of any personal data not previously having been published by the data controller. Thus, if the data controller has already published material including the personal data in question, he cannot rely on the restrictions to the Commissioner's powers if he is now processing the data with an intention that he should re-publish it or that another should now publish it. Even so, the Commissioner would still need to make a determination under section 45.

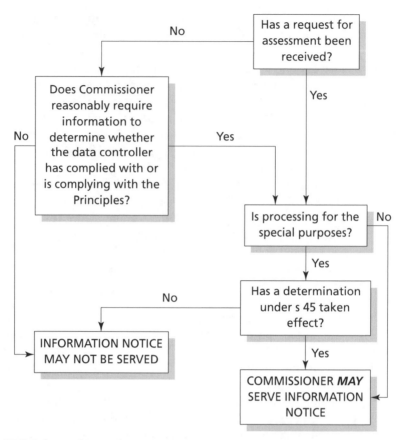

Fig 30.3 Information notice

Special information notices

These notices relate to processing for the special purposes (journalism, literary and artistic purposes). These provisions are, in many respects, similar to those for information notices. Under section 44, the notice may be served if the Commissioner has received a request for assessment from an individual under section 42 (the Act is silent on whether there must be, on its face, an issue in the request relating to the special purposes) or if the Commissioner has reasonable grounds for suspecting that, in a case where proceedings have been stayed under section 32, the data are not being processed only for the special purposes or with a view to publication for the first time by the data controller.

A stay under section 32 may be ordered by the court where the data controller claims that the processing is only for the special purposes and with view to publication by any person of any journalistic, literary or artistic material which, at the time 24 hours immediately before the time of the claim, had not previously been published by the data controller.

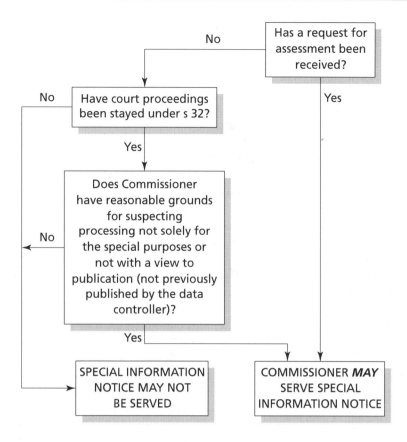

Fig. 30.4 Special information notice

The proceedings referred to in section 32 are in relation to subject access, processing likely to cause damage or distress, automated decision taking or rights in relation to inaccurate data. The stay applies until the Commissioner makes a determination under section 45 or the data controller withdraws the claim.

Unless the notice is sent after a request for assessment is made, the notice may only be sent where a data controller has used the exemption under section 32 (special purposes) as a shield in any proceedings to obtain a stay. The purpose of the notice is to obtain information to determine whether the exemption for the special purposes does indeed apply. Figure 30.4 shows when a special information notice may be served.

Entry and inspection

The Commissioner has powers of entry and inspection, which are very similar to those under the 1984 Act. The powers are contained in Schedule 9 to the Data Protection Act 1998 and can be exercised by her after obtaining a warrant from a circuit judge who will grant the warrant if he is satisfied by information supplied by the Commissioner on oath that there are reasonable grounds for suspecting that a data controller has contravened or is contravening any of the Data Protection Principles or that an offence under the Act has been or is being committed. If the processing is for the special purposes, a warrant must not be issued until a determination under section 45 has taken effect. The warrant must be executed within seven days of the date of its issue.

A judge must not issue a warrant (except if satisfied that the case is urgent as discussed below) unless he is satisfied that the Commissioner has given the occupier of the premises in question seven days' notice in writing demanding access and such access was demanded at a reasonable time and was unreasonably refused or although entry was granted the occupier unreasonably refused to comply with a request to permit the Commissioner or her officers or staff to do anything within the powers of entry and inspection, and the occupier, after such refusal, has been notified of the intended application for a warrant and has had the opportunity to be heard by the judge concerned. However, where the case is urgent and the judge is also satisfied that to comply with the above provisions would defeat the object of entry, he may issue a warrant without those preconditions being present.

A warrant will permit the Commissioner or her officers or staff executing the warrant to use such force as is reasonably necessary to enter and search the premises within seven days, to inspect, examine and operate any test respecting any data processing equipment on the premises and to inspect and seize any documents or other materials (presumably including items such as magnetic disks and tapes) which may be evidence of an offence or contravention of the Data Protection Principles. Warrants are not available in the case of personal data which are exempt from any provisions of the Act under the national security provisions under section 28.

Intervention

The Data Protection Directive requires that the supervisory authority shall have effective powers of intervention. This requires the Commissioner to carry out a preliminary assessment of processing operations likely to pose specific risks to the rights and freedoms of individuals. The types of operations concerned will be specified by the Secretary of State and such processing must not proceed until the Commissioner has made the assessment to ensure that the processing will comply with the Act: section 22. In the normal course of events, the Commissioner should inform the data controller of the results within 28 days of notification by the data controller. The period can be extended for a further period not exceeding 14 days.

It is unlikely that a preliminary assessment will be required in many cases. Indeed, the Directive states in recital 54 that the amount of processing likely to pose specific risks should be very limited. The Home Office has indicated that it might apply in the case of genetic data, data matching (that is, where personal data from different sources are matched to find any discrepancies which might indicate that the person concerned is involved in fraudulent applications for credit) and processing by private investigators. The key should be whether the particular description of processing is likely to cause substantial damage or substantial distress to data subjects or to otherwise significantly prejudice the rights and freedoms of data subjects. Processing may not proceed until the 28 days (as extended, if applicable) has expired or the data controller has received a notice from the Commissioner permitting processing.

Another form of intervention is that the Commissioner may require a data controller to rectify, block, erase or destroy inaccurate data as part of an enforcement notice and the Commissioner may also require the data controller to inform third parties to whom the data have been disclosed, having regard, in particular, to the number of persons who would have to be notified.

Enforcement

The Commissioner has two ways of enforcing the new data protection law. One is through enforcement notices, the second is by bringing a prosecution under the Act. In England and Wales and Northern Ireland, prosecutions normally will be brought by the Commissioner. Otherwise a prosecution may be brought by or with the consent of the Director of Public Prosecutions (or Director of Public Prosecutions for Northern Ireland). Presumably, in Scotland, prosecutions are brought by or with the leave of the Procurator Fiscal. The offences, of which there a several, are set out in the following chapter.

Under section 40, if the Commissioner is satisfied that the data controller has contravened or is contravening any of the Data Protection Principles, she may serve a notice requiring the data controller to take or refrain from taking specified steps within a specified time and/or refrain from processing after a specified time:

- any personal data,
- personal data of a specified description, or
- for a specified purpose or purposes or in a specified manner.

As mentioned above, where an enforcement notice relates to a breach of the fourth Data Protection Principle (in that the data are inaccurate), the Commissioner may, if reasonably practicable, require the data controller to notify third parties to whom the data have been disclosed. Regard is to be had to the number of persons who would have to be notified. The court also has similar powers in respect of inaccurate data that record accurately information provided by the data subject or a third party.

383

In deciding whether to serve the notice, the Commissioner is to consider whether the contravention has or is likely to cause any person damage or distress. The provisions as to the service of enforcement notices are subject to restrictions as regards processing for the special purposes (journalism, literary and artistic purposes). Here, the provisions envisage that a court must give leave to serve the notice. In particular, the notice shall not be served unless a determination under section 45 has taken effect and the court has granted leave for the notice to be served. Such leave will only be granted if the Commissioner has reason to suspect a contravention of substantial public interest and, except in cases of urgency, the data controller has been given notice in accordance with the rules of court for the application to the court for leave to serve the notice. Figure 30.5 shows when an enforcement notice may be served.

Enforcement notices cannot take effect until the period for appeal has expired (expected to be 28 days) or pending an appeal unless the case is a matter of urgency, in which case the time for compliance is seven days. An enforcement notice may be cancelled or varied by the Commissioner. This may be done on the Commissioner's own initiative or following a written

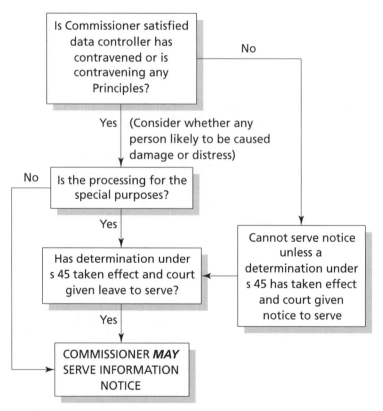

Fig. 30.5 Enforcement notice

application by the data controller after the period for appeal has expired where he can show by reason of a change in circumstances some or all of the provisions of the notice need not be complied with to ensure compliance with the data protection principles: section 41.

Under the 1984 Act, in *British Gas Trading Ltd* v *Data Protection Registrar* (unreported) 24 March 1998, the Data Protection Tribunal held that the Registrar was right to serve an enforcement notice under the 1984 Act rather than accept an undertaking from British Gas Trading Ltd. Under the 1984 Act, there were other forms of enforcement, by de-registration notices and transfer prohibition notices. These find no direct equivalent under the new Act. The Data Protection Registrar had developed a preliminary notice with the approval of the Data Protection Tribunal. It is likely that an informal preliminary notice system might be used under the new law, where it can operate as a useful 'Yellow Card' system, except where processing is, or is alleged to be, for the special purposes.

Co-operation

All the supervisory authorities in the EEA are required to co-operate with each other in respect of exchanging all useful information and to the extent necessary for the performance of their duties. Furthermore, each member state shall designate a representative of its supervisory authority (or a joint representative if the member state has more than one supervisory authority, unlike the United Kingdom) to be a member of the Working Party set up under the Data Protection Directive, discussed later in this chapter.

Co-operation is also implicit in the drawing up of codes of practice, which may be required by the Secretary of State or may be developed as a result of the Commissioner's own initiative. Another provision is that the Commissioner can, with the consent of the data controller, assess processing for the observance of good practice. The Commissioner may, with the consent of the Secretary of State, charge for this service. This is not to be confused with requests for preliminary assessments which will be required in specified cases posing risks to rights and freedoms of data subjects before processing can commence.

Where an individual is an actual or prospective party to proceedings under one of a number of provisions, being in respect of:

- a failure to comply with a subject access request,
- a failure to cease processing likely to cause substantial damage or substantial distress,
- a failure to comply with the provisions on automated decision taking,
- an application to have inaccurate data rectified, erased, blocked or destroyed, or
- the compensation provisions,

385

that individual can apply to the Commissioner for assistance where the processing relates to processing for the special purposes (that is, journalism, artistic or literary expression). The Commissioner shall provide assistance where it appears to her to involve a matter of substantial public interest under section 53. The assistance provided may be in the form of legal advice or assistance from a solicitor or counsel or assistance during proceedings. The Commissioner has a first charge on any costs or award in respect of the expenses in providing assistance.

The Commissioner will continue to be the designated authority for the purposes of Article 13 of the European Data Protection Convention 1981 and will be the supervisory authority for the purposes of the Data Protection Directive. Orders may be made for the Commissioner to co-operate with the European Commission and supervisory authorities in other EEA states and to carry out data functions to enable the government to give effect to international obligations in the United Kingdom.

The Tribunal and appeals

The Data Protection Tribunal is the first line of appeal from notices served by the Commissioner or a determination by the Commissioner under section 45. The Tribunal is made up of:

- a chairman appointed by the Lord Chancellor after consulting the Lord Advocate (being a lawyer of at least seven years' standing),
- such number of deputy chairmen as determined by the Lord Chancellor (also being lawyers of at least seven years' standing), and
- such number of other members appointed by the Secretary of State (being persons representing the interests of data subjects or persons representing the interests of data controllers).

Under section 48, a person may appeal to the Tribunal on grounds related to the following:

- enforcement, information or special information notices,
- a refusal by the Commissioner to cancel or vary an enforcement notice,
- where a notice contains a statement that the notice must be complied with as a matter of urgency within seven days, the Commissioner's decision to include the statement or the effect of the inclusion of the statement as regards any part of the notice, or
- a determination under section 45.

The Tribunal may:

- allow the appeal,
- substitute another notice if it considers that the notice is not in accordance with the law,

- where it involved an exercise of discretion by the Commissioner, rule that the discretion ought to have been exercised differently,
- cancel or vary a notice,
- rule on a statement made by the Commissioner that compliance is required as a matter of urgency,
- cancel a determination of the Commissioner.

The rules of procedure will be made under powers in Schedule 6 to the Act (replacing the Data Tribunal Rules 1985) which also deals with the constitution of the Tribunal (a chairman or deputy chairman plus an equal number of persons representing the interests of data subjects and the interests of data controllers), *ex parte* proceedings in cases involving certificates in relation to national security, and the power to remit to the High Court for contempt. The Tribunal may review any determination of fact on which the notice in question was based. Appeals from the Tribunal on a point of law go to the High Court in England or Wales.

The Working Party

A Working Party on the Protection of Individuals with regard to the Processing of Personal Data ('the Working Party') was established under the Data Protection Directive. It is an independent body with an advisory status. The Working Party is composed of a representative from the supervisory authority of each member state. Where a member state has more than one supervisory authority (for example, where one looks after the public sector and another looks after the private sector), a joint representative is nominated. A representative of the authority or authorities established for the Community institutions and bodies and a representative of the Commission are also members of the Working Party. A chair is elected every two years and decisions are taken by a simple majority of representatives of supervisory authorities. The Working Party considers items placed on its agenda by the chairman, either on his own initiative or at the request of a representative of the supervisory authorities or at the request of the European Commission.

The brief of the Working Party is set out in Article 30 of the Directive and is to:

- examine any questions covering the application of national measures implementing the Directive so as to contribute to the uniform application of such measures,
- give the Commission an opinion on the level of protection afforded in the Community and in third countries,
- advise the Commission on any proposed amendment to the Directive, on any additional or specific measures to safeguard rights and freedoms with

regard to the processing of personal data and to advise on any other proposed Community measures affecting such rights and freedoms,

- give opinions on codes of practice drawn up at Community level.

Furthermore, the Working Party must inform the Commission if it finds disparity between the laws of member states in respect of the protection of individuals with regard to the processing personal data. It may, on its own initiative, make recommendations on all data protection matters. An annual report, which will be made public, is to be drawn up dealing with the protection of natural persons with regard to the processing of personal data within the Community and in third countries. The Commission must inform the Working Party of the action it takes in response to its opinions and recommendations. This is to be done in a report forwarded to the European Parliament and the Council and will also be made public.

The Fourteenth Annual Report of the Data Protection Registrar (The Stationery Office, 1998) contains in Appendix 10 some of the documents and recommendations of the Working Party. There is a working document on assessing adequacy of protection in third countries, and another setting out preliminary views on the use of contractual provisions in the context of transfers of personal data to third countries. These transfers are a minefield and, at the time of writing, there are important discussions between the United States and the Commission trying to solve the problem that the United States has a different approach to data protection, being based on a more fragmented, self-regulatory system. There is also a working paper on whether self-regulation makes a meaningful contribution to the level of data protection in third countries and a recommendation on airline computerised reservation systems. In relation to the latter, recommendations include providing consumers with clear information about processing, obtaining express consent where the data are sensitive (for example, disability, status or religion), responding quickly to subject access requests, archiving data off-line no more than 72 hours after completion of the journey and destroying the data within three years (during this period, the data can only be consulted for billing dispute reasons; the data can be kept longer if needed in a particular case to settle a claim for damages or if necessary to comply with a legal obligation – for example, for tax or accounting purposes).

Chapter 31

Data controllers and the Data Protection Act 1998

Introduction

It is upon the data controllers, those who process personal data, that the main burden of data protection legislation falls. In spite of some changes to the text of the 1992 proposed Directive and the significant use by the United Kingdom of derogations permitted by the Directive, costs of implementing the new law are still likely to be substantial. The financial memorandum to the Data Protection Bill put the figures as shown in Table 31.1.

Table 31.1 Financial impact of the new law

Sector	Start-up costs (£ m)	Annual recurring costs (£ m)
Central government	90	46
Local government	104	29
Private sector	836	630
Voluntary sector	120	37

Although these figures are worryingly high, there is a lot data controllers can do to ease the burden of complying with the new law. By understanding data protection law, data controllers are in a much better position to develop systems and procedures to minimise the financial impact of compliance.

The purpose of this chapter is to explore the model of data protection law under the 1998 Act from the perspective of the data controller. The discussion will involve further consideration of the Data Protection Principles which, with their interpretative provisions, are very important. Some of these latter provisions contain some of the most important and potentially onerous elements of the Directive. First, the notification requirements will be described. From a data controller's point of view, this is arguably of most immediate impact. This will include a look at the requirements to provide data subjects with information when data are obtained from them and in other cases. Following this, the constraints on processing activity are discussed. These include the conditions for processing which cannot proceed unless one of the conditions applies for normal data and, in the case of sensitive data, a further condition also is satisfied. These conditions are a new departure for the United Kingdom except in so far as processing was required to be fair under the 1984 Act.

The security provisions are, to some extent, similar to those under the 1984 Act but there are important requirements where data processors are engaged. Following the discussion of security, the exemptions are described. Although a number of exemptions are similar, on the whole, there are considerable differences to those under the 1984 Act, some of which disappear including the 'word processing' exemption and those relating to unincorporated members' clubs and mailing lists. Next there is a brief look at enforcement from the data controller's viewpoint. This builds up on the description of the Data Protection Commissioner's functions in the previous chapter. The offences under the Act are then described in summary, as many will have been dealt with previously. Finally, the complex, though important, transitional provisions are discussed. One advantage of studying these is that some aspects of the transitional arrangements show how the new law differs from that under the 1984 Act.

Notification and informing data subjects

The Data Protection Act 1998 exempts from notification all manual processing of data, that is data that are part of a relevant filing system or accessible record as defined in section 1. Unless exempt, all automated processing must be notified. However, even if required to be notified, processing may still be subject to a preliminary assessment where it poses specific risks and the Secretary of State has made the appropriate order requiring such assessment before processing can commence. Exemption from formal notification to the Data Protection Commissioner is not all good news as the data controller must still furnish information to any person making a written request, as we shall see later. Further exemption from notification is possible by order of the Secretary of State. This may be possible in the future for payroll, personnel and work planning, purchase and sales administration, general administration, unincorporated members' clubs and certain non-profit-seeking bodies.

Under section 4(4) a duty is placed on every data controller, unless exempt, to comply with the Data Protection Principles. This applies whether or not he has notified his processing activities. Section 19 states that personal data must not be processed until registered, except in the case of manual processing which is not subject to a preliminary assessment (which will usually be the case) or if the processing is of a particular description to be exempted by notification regulations or if the sole purpose of the processing is the maintenance of a public register – for example, the electoral roll. Unless exempt from the notification requirements, section 18 requires data controllers to notify the 'registrable particulars' together with a general description of security measures. The information to be contained in the registrable particulars is set out in section 16(1), being in relation to a data controller:

(a) his name and address,
(b) if he has nominated a representative, the name and address of the representative,
(c) a description of personal data being or to be processed by or on behalf of the data controller and of the category or categories of data subject to which they relate,
(d) a description of the purpose or purposes for which the data are being or are to be processed,
(e) a description of any recipient or recipients to whom the data controller intends or may wish to disclose the data,
(f) the names, or a description of, any countries or territories outside the European Economic Area to which the data controller directly or indirectly transfers, or intends or may wish directly or indirectly to transfer, the data.

As regards security measures, one possible approach might be for data controllers to signify their adherence to BS7799, Information Security Standard and Certification Scheme.

Where relevant, a statement must also be included of the fact that the notification does not extend to personal data being processed, or intended to be processed, but not subject to notification. This will apply to manual processing exempt from notification where the data controller has not chosen to notify such processing. For example, if a data controller has a computer database containing personal data, he must notify that. If he also has a card index system processed manually, that is likely to be exempt from the notification requirements. The data controller may choose not to notify his card index system and, if he so chooses, he must include a statement in his notification of his automatic processing that he also processes personal data not subject to notification. This simply flags the fact that there is other processing being carried on and a person alerted to that fact may wish to obtain further information from the data controller in respect of such processing, as discussed below. Alternatively, the data controller may decide to notify his manual processing also, in which case he need not provide a supplementary statement. The rationale is that of transparency of processing. Individuals should be able to see what processing is being carried out by consulting the register and, if alerted to the fact that there is non-notifiable processing also going on, he can find out what that is also.

The Act states that notification will last for 12 months, although the mechanism is included to modify this period. Under the 1984 Act, the period of registration was three years.

Under the 1984 Act, the Registrar could refuse to register anyone as a data user if it appeared that the processing would contravene the Data Protection Principles or insufficient information had been furnished to allow the Registrar to determine this. Furthermore, the Registrar could issue a de-registration notice if satisfied that the processing has contravened or is contravening any of the Data Protection Principles. This link between registration and policing has disappeared under the 1998 Act and it appears that, providing the applicant has provided the registrable particulars and a general description of security measures and tendered the fee (to be announced) the Commissioner must enter the relevant details on the register. Of course, if it appeared that the processing did contravene the Data Protection Principles, the Commissioner could then exercise her enforcement powers under the Act or bring a prosecution, as appropriate. The only proviso to this apparent removal of checking the registrable particulars for compliance is that notification regulations, yet to be made at the time of writing, may make some provision for checking though there appears to be no specific power for this under the Act. One exception is that, in relation to processing of a description or descriptions to be specified by the Secretary of State, a preliminary assessment by the Commissioner to ensure compliance with the Act will be required before processing can proceed.

Under section 19, the Commissioner will maintain a register of data controllers, available for public inspection free of charge. Certified copies may be obtained for a prescribed fee, expected to be £2. The general description of security measures is not available to the public. The existing register under the 1984 Act is available through the Data Protection Registrar's Website at

http://www.open.gov.uk/dpr/dprhome.htm

and it is expected that the register under the 1998 Act will also be available in this useful form. One significant difference is that, under the 1984 Act, data users could have more than one register entry. The 1998 Act only allows one entry per data controller. This could ease the task of individuals carrying out subject access requests.

Failure to notify is an offence of strict liability. Even if the person processing personal data had never heard of data protection law, he will be guilty of the offence. There is a further duty on the data controller to notify changes in the registrable particulars by virtue of section 20. However, failure to notify any changes is a criminal offence which is subject to a due diligence defence.

The basis of a due diligence defence is that, generally, liability is strict unless the accused makes out a defence. Such a statutory defence presumes that the fault is the responsibility of another person and that the accused has exercised due diligence to prevent the wrongful act from occurring. One way a data controller may prove that he has exercised due diligence is to show that he had installed systems or procedures aimed at preventing the wrong occurring. This might be by training employees or agents as to the importance of data protection law and providing them with clear information as to what the scope of their duties was. In terms of failing to notify changes, a data controller might escape liability if he can show that clear instructions had been given to an employee responsible for data protection within the data controller's business.

Under the transitional provisions contained in Schedule 14 to the Act, existing registrations under the Data Protection Act 1984 continue to be effective until they expire, providing they expire before 24 October 2001.

Requirement to provide information to any person on request

Where a data controller has not notified his processing activity because he is not required to do so and has chosen not to do so, he must still be in a position to supply information equivalent to the registrable particulars (as per (a) to (f) above) to any person who submits a written request for such information. The information must be provided within 21 days of the written request otherwise the data controller commits an offence, subject to a due diligence defence under section 24. No charge can be made for providing this information and the person making the request does not have to be a data subject in relation to the data controller. Specific exemption from this requirement may be made by notification regulations.

The main implication of this provision is that it may suit a data controller to notify processing which he is not required to. A further point is that, if a data controller has not notified all his processing which is within the scope of the Act, he ought to consider implementing a procedure for dealing with such requests although, for many data controllers, they are likely to be quite rare.

Preliminary assessment (prior checking)

In cases, to be specified by the Secretary of State, processing will be subject to a preliminary assessment by the Commissioner (known as 'prior checking' in the Directive) and the processing must not proceed until the Commissioner has made a preliminary assessment to ensure that it will comply with the Act: section 22. Where a preliminary assessment is required, in the normal course of events, the Commissioner should inform the data controller of his assessment within 28 days of notification by the data controller. The period can be extended for a further period not exceeding 14 days. No distinction is made between automatic and manual processing for a preliminary assessment. The Secretary of State will, by order, detail the descriptions of processing for which preliminary assessment is required. It is likely to be required in relatively few cases where it appears to the Secretary of State that a particular description of processing is likely to cause substantial damage or substantial distress to data subjects or to otherwise significantly prejudice the rights and freedoms of data subjects. Processing genetic data, data matching, endangered life databases and other sensitive processing operations are likely to be caught. Processing may not proceed until the 28 days (as extended, if applicable) has expired or the data controller has received a notice from the

Commissioner permitting processing. Otherwise a criminal offence of strict liability is committed.

The preliminary assessment provisions contain no power for the Commissioner to prohibit processing. The intention is that they enable the Commissioner to give a view on whether the processing is likely to comply. It will then be up to the data controller to decide whether or not to proceed. Of course, if the Commissioner considers the processing unlikely to comply with the Act, she may use her powers of enforcement if the data controller decides to go ahead.

Data protection supervisors

In some member states, a system of internal data protection supervisors is in place. In-house officials oversee compliance with data protection law. The Directive provided the opportunity for other member states to adopt such a system which should permit the exemption or simplification of notification and allow internal preliminary assessments to be made, reducing the time delay in introducing new forms of sensitive processing. Data protection supervisors will not come in with the first wave of the new law but the Act contains the mechanism to introduce them at a later date. Under section 23 of the Data Protection Act 1998, the Secretary of State is given the power to make orders providing for personal data supervisors. They are to be responsible in particular for monitoring, in an independent manner, the data controller's compliance with the Act. There are likely to be duties imposed on personal data supervisors owed to the Commissioner who may be given functions in respect of them. It may be some time before we see data protection supervisors in the United Kingdom. Perhaps the first place they may be allowed is in the public sector.

Informing data subjects on collection and in other cases

The provisions on interpretation of the Data Protection Principles require that, for the first principle, the method of obtaining the data and whether the person from whom they were obtained was deceived or misled as to the purpose or purposes of processing are factors in determining whether the processing is fair (although data obtained or supplied under statutory authorisation is automatically deemed to be fairly obtained). Transparency is obviously important here and the individual should know what personal data relating to him are to be used for. This principle of openness is developed further in the interpretative provisions which place further duties on data controllers to provide specific information to an individual on collection of personal data and in other cases, especially where the data are disclosed to a third party.

These obligations to inform data subjects are derived from Articles 10 and 11 of the Data Protection Directive and have no equivalent under the 1984

Act, except as developed by case law such as in *Innovations (Mail Order) Ltd v Data Protection Registrar*, 29 September 1993, Data Protection Tribunal. In that case, Innovations operated a large mail-order business, advertised through catalogues, newspapers and television. It also had a lucrative business selling its customer lists to other retailers and service providers (an activity known as 'list trading'). Customers ordering goods from Innovations were not told of the list trading activity at the time they placed their orders. It was only when they received a written acknowledgement of their orders that they were informed by way of a notice on the rear of the acknowledgement form. The notice informed customers that they could have their names removed from the lists if they applied formally, sending in details of their name and address.

The Data Protection Registrar took the view that this was a breach of the first Data Protection Principle as the data were not being obtained fairly because customers ought to have been informed at the time the data were collected and not later. An enforcement notice was served on Innovations which appealed to the Tribunal. The Tribunal agreed with the Registrar and said that the question as to whether data had been fairly obtained related to the time of the obtaining and not a later time. If a purpose for which the data are intended to be used is not obvious at the time of obtaining the data, the data subject must be told of that non-obvious purpose at *that* time. If the data user does not inform the data subject at the time of collection of the data, the data subject's express consent must be sought before any non-obvious processing can be commenced.

This approach was adopted again by the Tribunal in *British Gas Trading Ltd v Data Protection Registrar*, 24 March 1998. British Gas Trading had inherited a large number of its customers from the previous bodies which made and supplied gas. When it wanted to send marketing material to all its customers, British Gas Trading inserted a note to that effect when it sent out gas bills and statements. The note informed customers that they could opt out of receiving such marketing material by writing in. The Tribunal held that this was not fair processing. A number of factors in the case are important and instructive:

- at least some of the marketing material related to services or products that were not directly related to gas or gas appliances (for example, the 'Goldfish' credit card),
- customers should be able to object without having to perform a positive act like writing in – they should be able to signify consent or otherwise at the time data were collected from them, 'there and then',
- new customers could be informed and given an opportunity to object when completing a contract form, for example by ticking the 'opt-out' box.

Some other submissions by the Registrar that the processing was also unlawful, for example, by being in breach of confidence or contract, were rejected by the Tribunal. This and the *Innovations* case show that, although there was no specific duty to inform individuals of non-obvious uses at the time the data were collected, the duty arose as a direct consequence of the requirement that processing must be fair. However, the duty under the 1998 Act is much more extensive.

Inform on collection

Part II of Schedule 1 to the Data Protection Act 1998 requires that, where the data are obtained from the data subject, the data controller must ensure, so far as is practicable, that the data subject has or is provided with the 'relevant information' or *has made it readily available to him*. The relevant information to be provided is:

- the identity of the data controller (and representative, if any),
- the purpose or purposes of the processing (but see below on the second Data Protection Principle),
- any further information, having regard to the circumstances in which the data are or are to be processed to enable such processing in respect of the data subject to be fair.

The White Paper, *Data Protection: The Government's Proposals* (Home Office, Cm 3725, 1997) which preceded the Bill suggested that it would be the controller who would decide whether further information was required to be given, though the Act is silent on this point. The second Data Protection Principle requires that data shall be obtained only for one or more specified and lawful purposes and not further processed in an incompatible manner. The interpretation on this allows the purpose to be specified either by notification to the Commissioner or in a notice given to the data subject for the purpose of informing him, as above. This means that, where the data controller has notified his processing to the Commissioner (which he must do in the case of automatic processing, unless exempt), the data controller will not have to separately provide this information to the data subject. As the purposes of processing are among the registrable particulars, this information will be publicly available where processing is notified. Thus, the data subject can, by consulting the data protection register, find this information out himself.

Unless further information is deemed to be required to ensure fair processing, all the data controller will have to do is to identify himself to the data subject, unless a non-obvious use is envisaged or disclosure to a third party is possible. *Innovations* and *British Gas Trading* are likely to remain good law under the 1998 Act. Certainly, if the data are to be used for marketing purposes, this is likely to be a situation where further information must be given. However, it should be noted that the Tribunal in *British Gas Trading* accepted that what is or is not obvious may change over time as consumers become more aware of diversification of business activity carried out by a company or group of companies.

Inform in other cases

Other cases will cover the situation where the data have not been obtained directly from the individual concerned. For example, it might be that the data are disclosed by the data controller who obtained the data from the data subject in the first place and now chooses to disclose them to a second data controller. Another example is where a data controller generates for himself data relating to the data subject.

In cases other than where the data are being obtained directly from the data subject, the data controller must ensure so far as practicable that, *before the 'relevant time' or as soon as practicable thereafter*, the data subject has or is provided with the relevant information or *has it made readily available* to him. The requirement to provide information does not apply where its provision would involve a disproportionate effort or where the recording or disclosure is necessary to comply with a legal obligation to which the data controller is subject (other than a contractual obligation) together with such further conditions as may be prescribed by regulations. Although many data controllers will be tempted to claim 'disproportionate effort' it will probably apply in limited circumstances only. It might apply where a large number of individuals would have to be informed and the processing is non-sensitive. It probably will not apply where the proposed use to be made of the data could trigger one of the rights of data subjects to object to processing – for example, where the purpose is direct marketing or involved automated decision taking.

It should be noted that the exception to providing information where a disproportionate effort is involved does not apply to the situation where data are being obtained from the data subject. An example of where the recording or disclosure is required by law is in the field of employment law, especially in the context of official returns and disclosures to the Inland Revenue and Department of Social Security.

The information to be provided is exactly as applies in relation to obtaining data from the data subject. The 'relevant time' is when the controller first processes the data or, where disclosure to a third party within a reasonable period is envisaged:

- if it is in fact disclosed to such a person within that period, the time of disclosure,
- if during that period the data controller becomes or ought to become aware that the data are unlikely to be disclosed to such a person within that period, the time he does become or ought to become so aware, or
- in any other case at the end of that period.

Presumably, the disclosure referred to must be envisaged by both the data controller and the data subject. If it is not envisaged by the data subject, the provision of information in the second and third times would seem fairly pointless.

The need to provide information on first processing could apply where data have been disclosed to a third party and the third party now processes the data (bearing in mind the very wide definition of 'processing'). As in all cases, the data controller is excused where the data subject already has the information or has it made *readily* available to him. It would seem that, in the latter case, it may be permissible to require the data subject to perform some positive task such as making a request for the information though it must be *readily* available. Where data are disclosed to a third party, it may be that the first data controller is in a position to inform the data subject that this will happen. If he does inform the data subject of the identity (at least) of the third party, then the third party may be excused because the data subject already has the requisite information.

For example, consider two data controllers, Andrew and Barbara. Andrew obtained data from Clarence and, at the time, provided information as required. If disclosure to a third party within a reasonable period was envisaged, when Andrew discloses the data to Barbara, Andrew must inform Clarence no later than that time that the data have been disclosed. When Barbara first processes the data, she must inform Clarence of her identity (at least), unless to do so would involve a disproportionate effort or where the recording or disclosure is required by law. However, if Andrew previously informed Clarence that the data would be disclosed to Barbara, then Barbara is excused providing this information and any further information which might be required if Andrew previously informed Clarence of it. Figure 31.1 shows the working of these provisions. It assumes that disclosure by Andrew within a reasonable period was envisaged and that the disclosure does in fact take place.

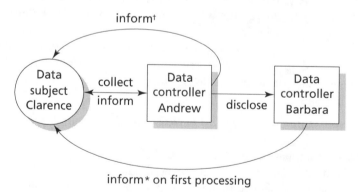

inform* on first processing

†Unless Clarence (data subject) already has information or has it readily available

*Unless Clarence already has information or has it readily available or where required by law (but not contractual obligation) or where it would involve a disproportionate effort

Fig 31.1 Informing data subjects

The Secretary of State may by order impose conditions as to the processing of any general identifier (for example, an identity number) should, of course, such an identifier be introduced in the United Kingdom. This may be include further obligations to inform data subjects.

Constraints on processing

The Data Protection Act 1984 imposed relatively few constraints on the processing of personal data providing that the Data Protection Principles were not contravened. As long as the data user had registered under the Act and kept his processing within the scope of his registration, he would be able to process without undue interference. One reason for this was that the Data Protection Registrar would only register a data user if he had supplied sufficient information to enable the Registrar to be satisfied that the proposed processing would be within the Data Protection Principles. At first sight, the new law appears far more restrictive. Apart from the spectre of individuals exercising their new found right to object to processing and prevent it in some cases, processing can only be carried out if it meets one of the conditions for processing or, in the case of sensitive data, two conditions.

The requirement for processing to be allowed only if it meets a particular condition is new and data controllers have to ensure that their processing falls within one or more of the specified conditions. The conditions are central to the controls over processing contained in the Data Protection Directive (Articles 7 and 8). The 1998 Act includes the conditions from the Directive in Schedules 2 and 3 to the Act which are an extension of the first Data Protection Principle, fair and lawful processing, which is expressed as:

1 Personal data shall be processed fairly and lawfully and, in particular, shall not be processed unless –
   (a) at least one of the conditions in Schedule 2 is met, and
   (b) in the case of sensitive personal data, at least one of the conditions in Schedule 3 is also met.

The conditions are examined further below.

Conditions for processing 'normal' data

'Normal' personal data are those not defined as sensitive personal data in section 2 of the Act. The conditions in Schedule 2 are:

1 The data subject has given his consent to the processing.
2 The processing is necessary for the performance of a contract to which the data subject is a party or for taking steps at the data subject's request for entering into a contract.

3 The processing is necessary for compliance with any legal obligation to which the data controller is subject, other than a contractual obligation.

4 The processing is necessary to protect the vital interests of the data subject.

5 The processing is necessary for the administration of justice, for the exercise of functions conferred on any person under any enactment, for the exercise of any function of the Crown, a Minister of the Crown or government department, or for the exercise of any other functions of a public nature exercised in the public interest by any person.

6 (1) The processing is necessary for the purposes of the legitimate interests pursued by the data controller or by the third party or parties to whom the data are disclosed, except where the processing is unwarranted in any particular case by reason of prejudice to the rights and freedoms or legitimate interests of the data subject.

(2) The Secretary of State may by order specify particular circumstances in which this condition is, or is not, to be taken to be satisfied.

If the data controller cannot fit within any of these conditions, then he may not process the data unless otherwise exempt.

A number of points can be made about these conditions:

- the data subject's consent is not stated to be express or explicit (unlike the case with sensitive data) and it would seem reasonable that it may be implied or result from failing to object, having been given the opportunity, for example, by failing to tick a box on a form;

- the word 'necessary' appears in all the other conditions – this is unlikely to be taken in a strict sense such as it being absolutely essential: although somewhat of a contradiction, it should be taken to mean 'reasonably necessary' – there is authority for this in a registered design case where the word 'dictated' was not taken in a strong sense by the House of Lords: *Amp Inc* v *Utilux Pty Ltd* [1972] RPC 103;

- an example of the vital interests of the data subject could be where his present address is disclosed to an appropriate authority after it has been discovered that he has been in contact with someone with a contagious disease or where he is using a defective and dangerous implement;

- the fifth condition will apply to a great deal of processing in the public sector, including but not restricted to central and local government;

- most commercial organisations will be able to rely on the second or sixth condition (although the data subject's consent may still be required to ensure processing is fair generally): there is, however, a slight difference to the language used in the Directive which speaks of the legitimate interests being 'overridden by the interests for fundamental rights and freedoms of the data subject which require protection under Article 1(1)' (being in particular the right to privacy in relation to processing of personal data) – the Data Protection Act 1998 seems slightly more restrictive;

- it is a little difficult to say just what 'legitimate interests' are – one view is that they cover any activity that is lawful while another, perhaps better view, is that they cover activities within the organisation's powers, that is, the organisation is acting *intra vires* (within its powers);
- some flexibility is introduced by empowering the Secretary of State (the Home Secretary in this context) to specify what is or is not within the 'legitimate interests' form of processing – although this power is not mentioned in the Directive it could be important as the requirement for conditions is new to the United Kingdom and the practical application of the sixth condition may be unpredictable.

In most cases data controllers should find that they satisfy at least one of the above conditions and, in practice, this requirement will not prove restrictive. It is difficult to think of a form of processing that falls outside all the conditions and would yet be deemed to be fair and lawful. Where the personal data are sensitive, the data controller must satisfy one of the conditions in Schedule 2 above as well as one of the conditions in Schedule 3, discussed below.

Conditions for processing 'sensitive' data

'Sensitive' personal data are defined in section 2 of the Data Protection Act 1998 and include data relating to racial or ethnic origin, political opinions, religious or other similar beliefs, trade union membership, physical or mental health or condition, sexual life and data relating to offences (including proceedings, disposal of such proceedings or the sentence of any court).

The conditions contained in Schedule 3 are as follows.

1 The data subject has given his explicit consent to the processing.
2 The processing is necessary for employment law rights or obligations (subject to potential modification by the Secretary of State).
3 The processing is necessary to protect the vital interests of the data subject or another where consent cannot be given by or on behalf of the data subject or the data controller cannot reasonably be expected to obtain the consent of the data subject or the processing is necessary to protect vital interests of another person in a case where consent by or on behalf of the data subject has been unreasonably withheld.
4 The processing is carried out subject to appropriate safeguards by a non-profit-making body or association which exists for political, philosophical, religious or trade-union purposes – processing must be carried out with appropriate safeguards for the rights and freedoms of data subjects and relate only to individuals who are members or have regular contact in connection with the body's or association's purposes and which does not involve disclosure to a third party without the consent of the data subject.

5 The information contained in the data has been deliberately made public by the data subject.

6 The processing is necessary in respect of legal proceedings, legal advice and legal rights.

7 The processing is necessary for the administration of justice, the exercise of functions conferred by or under any enactment, the exercise of any functions of the Crown, a Minister of the Crown or a government department (the Secretary of State may exclude this condition in specified cases or require further conditions to be satisfied).

8 The processing is necessary for medical purposes (includes preventative medicine, medical diagnosis, medical research, provision of care and treatment and management of healthcare services) and is undertaken by a health professional or a person under a duty of confidentiality equivalent to that owed by a health professional.

9 The processing of sensitive personal data consisting of information as to racial or ethnic origin when it is necessary for the purpose of identifying or keeping under review the existence or absence of equality of opportunity or treatment between persons of different racial or ethnic origins, with a view to enabling such equality to be promoted or maintained, and is carried out with appropriate safeguards for the rights and freedoms of data subjects.

10 The Secretary of State may by order allow sensitive data to be processed in other circumstances.

A 'health professional' is defined in section 69 and includes, *inter alia*, registered practitioners such as doctors, dentists, opticians, pharmaceutical chemists, nurses, midwives or health visitors, chiropractors, clinical psychologists, child psychotherapists or speech therapists, music therapists employed by a health service body or a scientist employed as head of department of such a body.

These conditions are fairly extensive and the following points can be made in respect of them:

- where the data subject's consent is relied upon it has to be explicit and it should be informed consent – failing to tick a box on a form will not be good enough;
- what has been said above in relation to the word 'necessary' ought also to apply here;
- vital interests in this context will include situations where an individual is unconscious and disclosure of his blood group is required so that he can be given a life-saving blood transfusion;
- certain types of non-profit-making bodies are included as much of the personal data such bodies will be processing will fall within the definition of sensitive data and it is plainly important for them to process such data belonging to their own members or others having regular contact (note

that the condition does not necessarily relate to charities): disclosure requires the consent of the data subjects and it is likely that express consent should be obtained;

- conditions relating to legal proceedings and justice, legally imposed functions and government functions are as expected but note that the Secretary of State has the power to exclude some of these in particular cases or require further conditions – he is not empowered to add to the list;

- processing for racial or ethnic monitoring is not specifically mentioned in the Directive but it does allow member states to include other conditions allowing processing where there is substantial public interest subject to satisfactory safeguards;

- there is no sweeping condition allowing processing of personal data relating to criminal offences such that, for example, commercial organisations which grant credit can process such data – unless exempt (there is a limited exemption for the purposes of crime and taxation but this is unlikely to apply in such cases – this is discussed later in the chapter): such processing generally can only be done under legally conferred functions or for the administration of justice. However, the government has indicated that it will allow processing of data relating to offences and convictions for the purpose of preventing or detecting fraud and other offences by financial institutions and some voluntary organisations, subject to suitable safeguards. This will require an order to be made by the Secretary of State.

Data controllers who intend to process sensitive data must ensure that they fall within one of the conditions above. In some cases, to be specified, the intended processing may fall within the requirement to have a preliminary assessment carried out by the Data Protection Commissioner and, in other cases, where the data controller is unsure, he could consider approaching the Commissioner for guidance or consulting a representative body such as a trade association. It may be that appropriate Codes of Practice will have been published to further assist the data controller in deciding whether he can process the sensitive data in question. Furthermore, the Commissioner may, with the consent of the data controller, individually assess the processing for good practice. This service is likely to be charged for if the Secretary of State so provides.

Data subjects and their exercise of rights to prevent processing

Although data subjects are given some new rights under the Data Protection Act 1998 and the rights they enjoyed previously have been enhanced, in the past individuals have not generally exercised their rights to any great extent directly against the data controller. Of course, it is impossible to verify precisely how frequently data subjects made use of their rights (for example, no figures are published on how many data subjects sought to gain access to personal data relating to them); it is reasonable to assume that a much larger proportion of individuals complained to the Data Protection Registrar in preference to bringing a personal action before a civil court against a data controller ('data user' under the old law). Under the 1984 Act, the total number of complaints made to the Data Protection Registrar was 4137 for the year to 1 April 1998. The peak was 4590 for the year to 1 June 1993. The largest numbers of complaints typically relate to consumer credit.

Subject access requests, with some exceptions, do not seem to be made in large volumes (this may be because it was possible to charge the data subject up to a maximum £10 in respect of the request). One exception is in relation to data held by credit reference agencies which, under the old law, was dealt with under section 158 of the Consumer Credit Act 1974. As regards individuals, these requests have been brought within the scope of the Data Protection Act 1998 although the right to have wrong information corrected is still dealt with under the 1974 Act.

In most cases, where a data controller is processing safely within the Data Protection Principles and the processing activities carried on are not particularly sensitive, the data controller should not experience a great deal of activity from data subjects exercising their rights. That being so, the basic rights are stated briefly below but they are described in more detail in the following chapter which focuses on data subjects.

The following rights, which existed under the 1984 Act, are enhanced or improved:

- right to subject access (more information should be given now),
- right to compensation available in respect of damage or distress caused by *any* contravention of the new law,
- rights of rectification and erasure (extended to blocking and destruction and somewhat widened in scope).

Of course, the rights are considerably expanded when one takes into account that the new law extends also to certain manual files (relevant filing systems and accessible records).

The new rights granted to data subjects are:

- rights to be informed, as discussed above,
- a right to prevent processing likely to cause substantial damage or substantial distress,
- a right to prevent processing for purposes of direct marketing, and
- rights in relation to automated decision taking.

Apart from the concerns about the requirement to inform data subjects (although in some cases, this was a requirement under the previous law, as in the *Innovations* case), data controllers expressed some anxiety about the possibility of data subjects objecting to certain forms of processing and being able, in some cases, to require the data controller to stop processing personal data relating to them. The reality is unlikely to be less burdensome. In particular, fair and lawful processing will rarely cause substantial damage or substantial distress; the mailing preference scheme already exists as a way of preventing (or at least reducing the amount of marketing material an individual receives) and the rights in the context of automated decision taking are considerably reduced in a contractual situation or where authorised or provided for by legislation.

Transfers to third countries

Of more immediate concern to data controllers are the provisions in the Act which apply where personal data are being transferred to a country outside the European Economic Area (EEA). As mentioned earlier, the rationale behind the Data Protection Directive is that, by providing a level playing field in terms of effective protection for rights and freedoms of individuals, particularly with respect to their right of privacy in relation to processing personal data, there can be no barriers to freedom of movement of personal data throughout the EEA. However, problems may occur where a data controller wishes, as many do, to have his data processed elsewhere and the country to which he wants to transfer the personal data for processing has no specific data protection laws or, if such laws exist, they fail to meet the European standards and safeguards.

The eighth Data Protection Principle requires that personal data must not be transferred to a country or territory outside the EEA unless it ensures an adequate level of protection for the rights and freedoms of data subjects in relation to the processing of personal data. The interpretative provisions in Part II of Schedule 1 state that an adequate level of protection is one which is adequate in all the circumstances of the case, having regard in particular to:

(a) the nature of the data,
(b) the country or territory of origin of the information contained in the data,
(c) the country or territory of final destination of that information,
(d) the purposes for which and period during which the data are intended to be processed,
(e) the law in force in the country or territory in question,
(f) the international obligations of that country or territory,
(g) any relevant codes of conduct or other rules which are enforceable in that country or territory (whether generally or by arrangement in particular cases) and

(h) any security measures taken in respect of the data in that country or territory.

Thus, adequacy depends on a number of factors and it will not be possible to say that a particular country does not have an adequate level of protection in all cases. It might be possible to say the opposite, however, where a country embraces a model of data protection law which is, to all intents and purposes, a mirror image of that in Europe. Such a country may be described as a 'white' country.

Even if a particular country or territory does not have an adequate level of protection in terms of the particular transfer envisaged, it may still be possible to make that transfer. The European Community legislators have at least adopted a sense of reality and accepted that there may be good reasons why a data controller might validly wish to transfer data to such a country. The approach taken is to allow the transfer subject to a condition being satisfied; the purpose of the conditions is to try to overcome the danger of inadequate protection. Thus, the eighth Data Protection Principle does not apply to data within Schedule 4 (except by order of the Secretary of State), being where any one of the following conditions is present:

1 The data subject has given consent to transfer.
2 The transfer is necessary for the performance of a contract between the data subject and data controller or for taking steps at the request of the data subject with a view to his entering into such a contract.
3 The transfer is necessary for the conclusion of a contract between the data controller and a third person entered into at the request of the data subject or in his interests, or is necessary for the performance of the contract.
4 The transfer is necessary for reasons of substantial public interest (the Secretary of State may specify circumstances in which a transfer is or is not covered by this).
5 The transfer is necessary with respect to legal proceedings, legal rights or obtaining legal advice.
6 The transfer is necessary to protect the vital interests of the data subject.
7 The transfer is of part of the personal data on a public register and any conditions subject to which the register is open to inspection are complied with by any person to whom the data are or may be disclosed after the transfer.
8 The transfer is made on terms of a kind approved by the Commissioner as ensuring adequate safeguards for the rights and freedoms of data subjects.
9 The transfer has been authorised by the Commissioner as being made in such a manner as to ensure adequate safeguards for the rights and freedoms of data subjects.

In relation to the eighth condition above, the Commissioner may approve kinds of terms which ensure adequate safeguards or authorise transfer as being made so as to ensure adequate safeguards. In any proceedings under the new law, questions as to whether the eighth Principle has been met are to be determined in accordance with any finding made by the European Commission under Article 31(2) of the Directive as to transfers of the kind in question. In the main, safeguards are likely to come from approved contractual terms. There are obligations to inform the Commission to the European Communities as to authorisations granted and the Commission may decide certain standard contractual clauses offer sufficient safeguards and member states are required to comply with such decisions. At the time of writing, it appears likely that contractual safeguards will require the recipient in the third country, as appropriate, to abide by the European model of data protection and to be under a contractual obligation to do so.

Security

The seventh Data Protection Principle requires that appropriate technical and organisational measures are taken against unauthorised or unlawful processing of personal data and against accidental loss or destruction of, or damage to, personal data. Security was an important aspect of data protection law under the 1984 Act and is continued under the new law with additional emphasis on the relationship between the data controller and a processor (under the 1984 Act, computer bureaux also had to comply with the security requirements). Factors influencing the level of security include the state of technological development, the cost of implementation, the potential harm of unauthorised processing or accidental loss, destruction or damage and the nature of the data. That being so, a prudent data controller will continually review his security arrangements and monitor technological improvements to security measures available.

Data controllers must take reasonable steps to ensure the reliability of staff having access to personal data. They must choose processors who provide sufficient guarantees as regards technical and organisational measures and take reasonable steps to ensure compliance with those measures. Where a processor is engaged, the processing must be carried out under a contract made or evidenced in writing under which the processor is to act only on the instructions of the data controller and which imposes equivalent security obligations on the processor. Although processors do not have to notify the processing they perform on behalf of others, this mechanism is designed to make sure that they are aware of the importance of security and, in the event of a failure on the part of the processor, he will be liable for breach of contract.

Exemptions

The Data Protection Act 1998, in common with the previous legislation, contains a large number of exemptions from parts of the Act. However, there are significant differences and some of the exemptions under the 1984 Act find no room in the new law. Reference to the section on the transitional provisions illustrates the differences in this respect as specific provision has to be made to cater for these differences.

First, it should be noted that there are some multiple exemptions from the 'subject information provisions' and the 'non-disclosure provisions', as follows:

- 'subject information provisions' meaning the first Principle, in as much as it requires compliance with Part II, paragraph 2 of Schedule 1 (providing information to the data subject on collection or in other cases) and section 7 (subject access),
- 'non-disclosure provisions' meaning the first Data Protection Principle (but not with respect to the requirement that one of the conditions in Schedule 2 is met and, for sensitive data, one of the conditions in Schedule 3 is also met), the second to the fifth Data Protection Principles, section 10 (the right to prevent processing likely to cause damage or distress) and section 14(1) to (3) (right of rectification, etc. in relation to inaccurate data) *to the extent that they are inconsistent with the disclosure in question.*

Except as provided for in the exemptions, the subject access provisions are unaffected by any enactment or rule of law prohibiting or restricting the disclosure, or authorising the withholding of information.

The exemptions, some of which are set out in Schedule 7, are numerous. The Secretary of State is given the power to make further exemptions to the subject information provisions and the non-disclosure provisions if he considers further exemption is necessary to safeguard the interests of data subjects or the rights and freedoms of any other individual. This is a basis for exemption in the Directive. Some of the exemptions are outwith the scope of the Directive in any case, such as those relating to national security or processing by an individual for a purely personal or household activity: Article 3(2).

It should be noted that a general principle is that exemption from the relevant provisions of the Act is available only in as much as compliance would prejudice the purpose governed by the exemption or if the particular exemption is required for the purpose concerned. For example, exemption is granted from the subject access provisions for the purposes of the prevention or detection of crime. However, if subject access can be granted without prejudicing these purposes (or other exempted purposes), then it must be granted. The exemptions are not generally blanket exemptions and require a value-judgement by the data controller as to whether an exemption is available in a particular circumstance.

All the exemptions are listed in Table 31.2, later, but first a selection of some of the exemptions, which are considered in more depth.

National security

This exemption is provided under section 28 and applies if it is necessary for the purpose of safeguarding national security. The exemption is very wide-ranging and is from all the principles, the rights of data subjects, notification and enforcement. Furthermore, the offences in section 55 in respect of unlawful obtaining, etc. do not apply if this exemption applies. A certificate signed by a Minister of the Crown who is a member of the Cabinet, the Attorney-General or Lord Advocate is conclusive evidence that the exemption is required. The need for this exemption is plain but the certification arrangements mean that there is little control over the scope and application of this exemption. However, there is provision for an appeal against a certificate to the Data Protection Tribunal. Any appeal will be held before the Chairman and/or deputy chairmen as designated by the Lord Chancellor and proceedings will be held *ex parte*, that is, without hearing the person appealing against the certificate.

Crime and taxation

This applies if the personal data are held for the purpose of the prevention or detection of crime, the apprehension or prosecution of offenders or the assessment or collection of any tax or duty or imposition of a similar nature. Under section 29, the exemption is from the first Data Protection Principle and the subject access provisions. However, the conditions for processing under the first Principle (in Schedules 2 and/or 3) still apply. The exemption applies only in as much as the provision in question would be likely to prejudice any of the purposes covered by the exemption.

The exemption also applies to anyone discharging a statutory function who has obtained the data from a person who held the data for any of the above purposes but here the exemption is from the subject information provisions. An example might be personal data held by the police which has been given to the Crown Prosecution Service which is considering whether to prosecute the individual concerned. As a judgment has to be made by the data controller as to whether any of the purposes covered would be prejudiced by compliance, a subjective and qualitative element is brought into the practical application of the exemption. This can be criticised as it will be the data controller who decides this, subject only to a challenge by an aggrieved person. Further exemption is granted, from the non-disclosure provisions where the disclosure is for any of the above purposes and where compliance would prejudice any of those matters.

An example of the latter is where a local authority, empowered under section 163 of the Criminal Justice and Public Order Act 1994 and section 111 of the Local Government Act 1972 to use video surveillance in order to promote the prevention of crime, discloses copies of a video to the media in order to facilitate this purpose. In *R v Brentwood Borough Council, ex parte Peck, The Times*, 18 December 1997, an applicant for judicial review complained when the local authority disclosed a video showing him walking down the High Street, Brentwood, with a knife. He later attempted suicide by slashing his wrists but this was not caught on video. He was not charged by the police. The video was shown on television and some of the applicant's friends and neighbours recognised him. The application was dismissed, Mr Justice Harrison confirming that the statutory provisions above empowered the local authority to take the actions it had. Furthermore, it had not acted irrationally and had not known of the objection until the video had been broadcast.

Under the 1998 Act, personal data can extend to visual data (this is confirmed by the Directive) and a local authority acting as Brentwood Borough Council did would rely on the crime and taxation exemption. The exemption which applies where disclosure is required by law, discussed later, would not seem to be appropriate as the local authority was empowered to carry out the video surveillance and make the disclosure. It was not required to do so.

Where the data controller is a lawful authority (government department, local authority or other authority administering housing benefit or council tax benefit) and the personal data consist of a classification of the data subject as part of a risk assessment system, exemption from the subject access provisions is granted. This applies only with respect to the purposes of assessment of tax, duty or similar imposition or the prevention or detection or crime, apprehension of offenders or where the offence concerned involves any unlawful claim for payment out of, or any unlawful application of, public funds where the processing is for any of those purposes.

Under the 1984 Act, the Data Protection Registrar had a long-running dispute over the scope of the equivalent exemption with the Halifax Building Society. It all started when an individual complained to the Registrar that he had not received all the information he was entitled to in pursuance of a subject access request. The Society had withheld data which it considered to be 'system security data' on the basis that the crime prevention exemption applied to the data. The Data Protection Registrar issued an enforcement notice and the Society appealed to the Tribunal. After many meetings and discussions and the issue of a preliminary notice in respect of the complainant (with which the Society complied), an agreement was reached between the Halifax Building Society and the Registrar.

The Society had been concerned about the secrecy of its customers' accounts and the need to restrict knowledge to only a few of its own staff. The agreement was to the effect that the Society would not normally give details of transactions on the data subject's account, card number, computer terminal and location of the automated teller machine. However, as part of the agreement (*Agreement in the Enforcement Action against the Halifax Building Society*, 6 January 1992), the Society agreed to inform any person making a subject access request of this fact and that all other information had been made available: for example, details of address, financial circumstances, balance and the Society's views (if appropriate). The data subject would also be informed that the Society would consider requests for other information if there was a genuine need for the data subject to see it. Finally, the Society agreed to inform data subjects that they are entitled to complain to the Data Protection Registrar if not satisfied with the Society's response.

Health, education and social work

Similar to the 1984 Act, section 30 of the Data Protection Act 1998 empowers the Secretary of State to make orders concerning exemptions from subject access. At the time of writing no orders have been made but it is likely that orders similar to those made under the 1984 Act may be made, in addition to an order relating to education. Orders made under the 1984 Act were the Data Protection (Subject Access Modification) (Health) Order 1987 and Data Protection (Subject Access Modification) (Social Work) Order 1987. They applied to personal data relating to the physical or mental health of a data subject (health data) or held in connection with social services functions (social data). Similar orders are likely to be made under the 1998 Act.

With respect to health data, the exemption from subject access under the 1984 Act applied if the data were held by a health professional or any other person (so long as the information constituting the data was first recorded by a health professional). The data user could withhold data from the data subject if giving access to the data subject would be likely to cause serious harm to the physical or mental health of the data subject, or lead the data subject to identify another person (other than the health professional involved in the care of the data subject) who has not consented to the disclosure of his or her identity.

The Department of Health made it clear that this exemption should be relied on only in exceptional circumstances. An example might be where a doctor has diagnosed a fatal illness and considers that it would be in the data subject's best interests for him not to discover this. It was apparent that there was no common law right of subject access in such circumstances to override or supplement that under the Data Protection Act 1984 or complementary legislation such as the Access to Health Records Act 1990 which gave a right of subject access to information concerning physical or mental health held by health professionals. However, by section 5(1) of the 1990 Act there was exemption from subject access if there was a likelihood of causing serious harm to the physical or mental health of the patient or any other individual – a very similar exemption to that provided under the Data Protection Act 1984.

The basis of such exemptions can be seen in the House of Lords case of *Sidaway* v *Board of Governors of the Bethlem Royal Hospital* [1985] AC 871 which made it clear that a doctor's duty, as with the health authority, was to act at all times in the best interests of the patient and this could, in some circumstances, permit the withholding of information. In *R* v *Mid-Glamorgan Family Health Services, ex parte Martin* (unreported) 29 July 1994, a patient had been refused access to his health records going back to before 1990 on the basis that it would be detrimental for the patient to see those records directly. An offer was made to disclose the records conditionally to a medical expert appointed by the patient but was not accepted. The patient claimed that there was a right of access at common law. However, the Court of Appeal refused to grant access on the 'best interests' principle, denying that there was such a common law right.

The social work exemption under the 1984 Act applied to bodies such as local authorities, the probation service and local education authorities, etc. The body concerned could withhold data if access would be likely to prejudice the carrying out of social work by causing serious harm to the physical or mental health or emotional condition of the data subject or any other person, or to lead the data subject or any other person who is likely to obtain access to the data to identify another individual (other than someone involved professionally in social work) who has not consented to the disclosure of his or her identity. The problems caused by such an exemption could be seen in the case of *Gaskin* v *United Kingdom* (1990) 12 EHRR 36 before the European Court of Human Rights, discussed in the following chapter.

As regards the new provisions allowing exemption from subject access in the case of education, the Secretary of State may make exemption where the data controller is a proprietor or teacher at a school and the personal data consists of information relating to persons who are or have been pupils at the school or in relation to education authorities in Scotland.

Regulatory activity

This exemption from the subject information provisions covers a wide range of regulatory activities in order to protect the public from dishonesty, malpractice and the like by persons involved with financial services, carrying on any profession or other activity or in relation to charities. It also extends to health and safety at work. A complete list is given in Table 31.2. Under section 31, the function is one conferred by or under any enactment, any function of the Crown or a Minister of the Crown or a government department or any other function of a public nature which is exercised in the public interest. This latter category is potentially very wide ranging.

Further exemption is available from the subject information provisions in respect of statutory functions of the Parliamentary Commissioner for Administration, the Commission for Local Administration, the Health Service

Commission and other public bodies. The exemption also applies to certain functions of the Director General of Fair Trading.

In all cases, the exemption is only available where the application of the subject information provisions would be likely to prejudice the proper discharge of the relevant function. The purpose of the exemption is to prevent, for example, a person under investigation by the Charity Commissioners for the misapplication of the property of a charity discovering that his activities are being investigated. He could find out by carrying out a subject access request or because, under normal circumstances, he is required to be informed of the disclosure of personal data relating to him to the Charity Commissioners.

Journalism, literature and art

This is an important and wide-ranging exemption protecting freedom of speech. Under section 32, exemption is from all the Data Protection Principles (except the seventh on security measures), and most of the rights of data subjects including subject access. We have seen in the previous chapter how the Data Protection Commissioner's powers are severely constrained in relation to the purposes of journalism and artistic and literary purposes (the special purposes). Indeed, in a court action in relation to the data subjects' rights or compensation, a claim by the data controller that he is processing only for the special purposes with a view to publication of material not previously published by him at a time 24 hours before he makes that claim, proceedings must be stayed until the Commissioner makes a determination under section 45 as to whether the special purposes do apply or the claim is withdrawn. The same applies if it appears to the court that the special purposes apply.

For the exemption to apply, the processing must be undertaken with a view to publication of any journalistic, literary or artistic material and the data controller must reasonably believe that publication is in the public interest, having regard in particular to the special importance of the public interest in freedom of expression. Furthermore, the data controller must reasonably believe that compliance with the exemption in question is incompatible with the special purposes. In making a determination as to the data controller's belief that publication is in the public interest, regard may be had to his compliance with any relevant code of practice designated by the Secretary of State for this purpose. As noted previously, the Secretary of State can order the Commissioner to prepare and disseminate codes of practice after consultation with trade associations and data subjects or persons representing data subjects.

Research, history and statistics

In many cases, data processed for statistical or research purposes only will not be within data protection law as the data will be anonymous and, therefore, not personal data within the meaning in section 1(1). However, where the data remain personal data because they contain identifiers or the data controller has or may obtain other data which, together with the research data, allow individuals to be identified, section 33 allows some useful exemptions. These apply where the relevant conditions are present, being that the data are not processed to support measures or decisions with respect to particular individuals and are not processed so as to cause, or be likely to cause, substantial damage or substantial distress to any data subject. These conditions will usually be easily satisfied. If the data are being used to support measures or decisions affecting particular individuals, it may be that other exemptions are relevant – for example, in the case of research data relating to health which are now being processed to identify persons who have been exposed to some virus in the past and are now in need of an urgent inoculation.

The first exemption is simply to the effect that further processing only for research purposes is not to be regarded as incompatible with the purposes for which they were obtained, otherwise this could be a breach of the second Data Protection Principle. The fifth Principle requires that personal data are not kept for longer than is necessary and exemption from that requirement is granted in that data processed only for research purposes can be kept indefinitely. A further exemption is from the subject access provisions but only if the results of any research or any resulting statistics are not made available in a form identifying any data subject.

The exemptions are not lost merely because the data are disclosed to any person for research purposes only, to the data subject or a person acting on his behalf or at the request of, or with the consent of, the data subject or a person acting on his behalf. Nor are the exemptions lost if the person making the disclosure has reasonable grounds for believing any of these apply in the circumstances.

Information available to the public

This applies where the data consist of information which the data controller is required to make available to the public, whether by publication or making it available for inspection or otherwise and whether or not a fee is charged. The exemption is from the subject information provisions, the fourth Data Protection Principle (accuracy and kept up to date), the right of rectification within section 14(1) to (3) and the non-disclosure provisions. Clearly where information has to be made available, full application of these provisions would be unnecessary. The type of information that will be within this exemption includes the electoral roll, copies of birth, marriage and death certificates and copies of specifications for patents.

Disclosures required by law or in connection with legal proceedings, etc.

Other exemptions in the main body of the Act are disclosures required by law or made in connection with legal proceedings or for the purpose of obtaining legal advice or otherwise necessary for the purposes of establishing, exercising or defending legal rights: section 35. A related exemption is in Schedule 7, paragraph 10, being exemption from the subject information provisions on the basis of legal professional privilege. Thus, there can be no barrier to disclosing personal information in connection with legal proceedings. For example, Andrew, who is a self-employed accountant, wishes to sue Brenda (one of his clients) for non-payment of accountancy fees. Andrew has a meeting with his solicitor, Carolyn, and provides her with information about Brenda and the work he did for her. Andrew is a data controller under the Act. Naturally, his notification does not mention such a disclosure but section 35 grants him exemption. As the meeting between Andrew and Carolyn is privileged, neither has to give Brenda any information about it. For example, there is no need to inform Brenda that Carolyn now has personal data relating to Brenda and, of course, any subject access request made by Brenda to Carolyn can be ignored with impunity.

Under the 1984 Act, the question of disclosure of data where the data user was exempt from registration came up for consideration in *Rowley* v *Liverpool City Council* (unreported) 24 October 1989. The judgment amply demonstrates the complexity of that Act (the new Act is no less complex), and Lord Justice Woolf in the Court of Appeal said of the 1984 Act:

> ... it is right to say straightaway that the act is a complex enactment in which it is difficult to find your way about unless you are very familiar with it indeed.

In that case, the plaintiff brought an action against her former employer for personal injury and she had made an application for discovery (disclosure to a party in legal proceedings) of information including details of three 'comparative earners'. She wanted details of payments made to three persons employed in a similar capacity to help work out what she would have been paid had she not had to stop working because of her injury. The defendant refused claiming that such disclosure was prohibited by the Data Protection Act 1984.

The defendant was exempt from registration because the data related to payroll and accounts (this exemption disappears under the 1998 Act but is available until 24 October 2001 under the transitional provisions). Section 32(2) of the 1984 Act made it a condition of the exemption that the data are not disclosed except in limited circumstances relating to payroll and accounts. However, section 34(5) of the 1984 Act, in similar though not identical lines to the equivalent provision in the 1998 Act, allowed disclosure if required by law or in the course of legal proceedings and, therefore, the disclosure requested did not contravene the Act. Disclosure was allowed in two ways: first, because it was in the course of legal proceedings in which the defendant was a party and, second, in compliance with an order of the court.

Domestic purposes

The Data Protection Directive does not apply to processing by a natural person in the course of a purely personal or household activity. Thus, section 36 of the Act exempts from all the Data Protection Principles the rights of data subjects and the requirements as to notification of personal data processed by an individual for that individual's personal, family or household affairs. This also extends to recreational purposes. The Commissioner may still exercise her powers of enforcement in the context of such processing if it is believed that the individual concerned is processing in such a manner as to exceed the scope of this exemption. If this is so, then the exemption will be lost to that extent. In particular, an individual who is otherwise employed but who carries on some private work in his spare time may be required to notify.

Schedule 7 exemptions

For no particular reason, a further set of exemptions is tucked away in a Schedule to the Act. All of these exemptions are listed in Table 31.2, but the following are notable and discussed in more detail.

Confidential references

This exemption is from the subject access provisions only and is given under paragraph 1 of the Schedule. It applies where the reference is given or to be given by the data controller for the purposes of the education, training or employment (actual or prospective) of the data subject or the appointment or prospective appointment of the data subject to any office or the provision or prospective provision by the data subject of any service. The reference must be given or be intended to be given in confidence. There is no distinction between the person by whom the reference is given and the person who receives it. Both will be data controllers for the purpose of this provision *if and only if* the personal data are within the scope of the Act.

To take an example, consider Harold, an employee of the Peak Accountancy Practice who now seeks employment with Flaky Financial Services. Flaky has requested a reference from Peak, which is in the form of letter hand written by Paul, Peak's managing director. This letter is unlikely to be within the meaning of data for the purposes of the Act. It is not automatically processed nor intended so to be and is not a relevant filing system. Both Peak and Flaky can refuse Harold access to it. However, if the letter is produced on a word processor by Paul, it will be within the Act but Peak can refuse

Harold access to it providing it is given in confidence. Flaky is under no obligation to grant access, whether it is confidential or not, because Flaky is not processing the data automatically. If the reference is made out on a *pro forma* document, then both Peak and Flaky must provide access (unless it was given in confidence) providing the reference is recorded as part of or with the intention that it should form part of a relevant filing system. This will be so if Peak and Flaky keep a file of references given or received.

Management forecasts and negotiations

These two distinct exemptions are discussed together here as they may overlap and often both will apply in the context of business planning and strategy and relationships with employees. Both exemptions are from the subject information provisions. In both cases, the exemption only applies if and to the extent that compliance would be likely to prejudice the activity or negotiations, as appropriate. Both of these exemptions are new and the 1984 Act had no direct equivalent.

The first applies to personal data processed for the purposes of management forecasting or management planning to assist the data controller in the conduct of any business or other activity: paragraph 5. No further guidance is given but this could apply, for example, where a company is carrying out a feasibility study on some new proposed venture. It might involve personal data relating to present and potential employees and other individuals such as investors. The company may wish to gather information on individuals who are candidates for 'head-hunting' to lead the new venture. Alternatively, a company may be considering closing down some of its activities which, if carried out, will affect numerous employees. Fulfilling a subject access request could destroy the secrecy of such forecasting or planning and cause serious prejudice.

Paragraph 7 deals with negotiations with the data subject and records of intentions in respect of such negotiations by the data controller. Under the 1984 Act, statements of intentions in respect of individuals were outside the definition of personal data and, therefore, outwith the scope of the Act. This is not so under the Directive and statements of intention are personal data, providing the other requirements are met. It was thought important to grant exemption from the subject information provisions – after all, an intention is not a reality until it is carried out and the data controller may change his mind. The sort of things covered will include an intention to promote an employee or provide some person with a particular service. The exemption is not limited to negotiations between employers and employees and can apply in any context.

Examination marks and examination scripts

The exemption for examination marks is similar to that under the 1984 Act and gives exemption from the subject access provisions though it can only act to delay subject access. Under paragraph 8 of Schedule 7, the marks or other information must be held for the purpose of determining the results of an academic, professional or other examination or enabling such determination or in consequence of the determination of any such results. In the case of an undergraduate, such information might include the marks he obtained in each subject by examination (including assessed coursework) and the details of the degree classification to be awarded to the student. 'Examination' includes a process for determining the knowledge, intelligence, skill or ability of a candidate by reference to his performance in any test, work or other activity. The normal period for responding to a subject access request is 40 days though this may be changed under the 1998 Act. Where the period of 40 days is used below, it is to be taken to be 40 days or such other period as may be prescribed.

Normally, a data controller must comply with a data subject request within 40 days but, in respect of examination marks, the data controller does not have to respond until either the end of five months after the request has been received or 40 days after the day the results are announced (published or made available or communicated to candidates), whichever is the earlier. If the request is complied with more than 40 days after it was made, the response by the data user must include all the information held at the time of the request *and* subsequently.

The following dates provide an example of the workings of these provisions:

1	Student sits examination	4 June 1999
2	Marks entered on a computer	28 June 1999
3	Student makes subject access request	2 July 1999
4	Results published	23 July 1999

Normally, the request must be complied with within 40 days from the request at the latest; that is, within 40 days of 2 July, which gives 11 August as being the latest date for compliance. However, in the case of examination marks, the request must be complied with by the earlier of five months after the request (3 December 1999) or 40 days after publication (1 September 1999). Therefore, the data controller must supply the data by 2 September. But, unlike other subject access requests which may take account of amendments, in this case the information supplied must include that held on 3 July (the request date) *and* must also include any subsequent amendments up to the date of reply. Consequently, a data controller holding examination marks must be careful to make sure that he retains copies of the personal data prior to any amendments or deletions so that he can provide all this information. For example, if the student's degree classification is changed, perhaps from a lower second honours degree to an upper second honours degree after mistakes have been found in the marking, the response must show this fact indicating the marks before and after correction. This requirement could prove very embarrassing to the data controller.

The exemption that applies to examination scripts is new and is granted in respect of the subject access provisions. The meaning of 'examination' is as above and the exemption relates to personal data consisting of information recorded by candidates during an academic, professional or other examination. As the 1984 Act only applied to automatically processed personal data, there was no real need for such an exemption under that Act as most examinations were handwritten, though this is changing rapidly: for example, by the use of multiple-choice tests performed on computers. Of course, the last thing most students want is access to their examination scripts.

Power to make further exemptions

It should be noted that, under section 38, the Secretary of State is empowered to add to the list of exemptions from the subject information provisions and exemptions from the non-disclosure provisions. In both cases the exemption must be necessary for safeguarding the interests of the data subject or the rights and freedoms of any other individual. In the case of the subject information provisions, it must relate to a situation where disclosure is prohibited or restricted by or under any enactment.

An example of an order made under equivalent powers under the 1984 Act was the Data Protection (Miscellaneous Subject Access Exemptions) Order 1987. The Order applied to information contained in adoption records and with respect to the special educational needs of children. Also, the Human Fertilisation and Embryology Act 1990 inserted section 35A into the Data Protection Act 1984 and exempted personal data showing that an identifiable individual was or might have been born as a result of treatment regulated under the 1990 Act. An equivalent provision is likely to be made under section 38 of the Data Protection Act 1998. Section 12 of the Charities Act 1993 provided for the making of an Order exempting certain functions of the Charity Commissioners from the subject access provisions. This section was repealed by the 1998 Act.

The exemptions are set out in Table 31.2. In particular, it should be noted that the exemptions under the 1984 Act relating to payroll and accounts, unincorporated members' clubs, mailing lists and back-up data find no place among the exemptions under the 1998 Act. Nor is there any specific exemption relating to word processing (this was outside the scope of the 1984 Act, providing the data were not used for anything else). The transitional provisions deal with these changes to the exemptions.

Table 31.2 Exemptions under the Data Protection Act 1998

Description	Exemption provided from	Notes
National security, s 28	• all the Principles • Parts II, III and V (rights of data subjects, notification, enforcement) • s 55 (offence of unlawful obtaining etc. of personal data – see later)	The exemption must be required for the purpose of safeguarding national security but a certificate signed by a Minister of the Crown to that effect is conclusive (as it was under the 1984 Act) – there are provisions for any person affected to appeal to the Tribunal In Schedule 6, para 6 the Tribunal's jurisdiction shall be exercised *ex parte* by the Chairman or a Deputy Chairman – subject to rules made under para 7 for regulating the exercise of the right of appeal
Crime and taxation, s 29	• 1st Principle (except to the extent which it requires compliance with conditions in Schedules 2 and 3 – thus the conditions still apply) • s 7 (subject access) • all only to the extent to which application of those provisions would be likely to prejudice matters in s 29(1)	Only for purposes of prevention/detection of crime, apprehension/prosecution of offenders or assessment/collection of any tax or duty or any imposition of a similar nature (s 29(1)) Data processed for purpose of discharging statutory function where information obtained for any purpose mentioned above are exempt from subject information provisions to the same extent Data disclosed for purposes of crime or taxation are exempt from non-disclosure provisions if those provisions would be likely to prejudice those purposes Where the data controller is a government department, local authority or other authority administering housing or council tax benefit, data are exempt from s 7 (subject access) if the exemption is required in the interests of a system of risk assessment for taxation or crime where the offence involves unlawful application for or claim in respect of public funds
Health, education and social work, s 30	• exemptions from subject information provisions will be implemented by SIs	Leaves it to the Secretary of State to make orders – but not to confer exemptions likely to prejudice the carrying out of social work – may cover situation where, for example, a doctor does not want to allow a patient access to his file if it shows the patient is terminally ill and the doctor considers this knowledge would be harmful to the patient

Table 31.2 cont.

Description	Exemption provided from	Notes
Regulatory activity, s 31	• subject information provisions	If likely to prejudice proper discharge of function covered (to protect public, charities, persons at work (as appropriate)) functions are: • financial loss resulting from dishonesty, malpractice, unfitness, incompetence of persons concerned in banking, insurance, investment or other financial services or management of bodies corporate • financial loss resulting from the conduct of a bankrupt • dishonesty etc. by professional persons • misconduct or mismanagement in administration of charities • in respect of protecting property of charities • in relation to health and safety at work Exemption is extended to others such as the Parliamentary Commissioner for Administration, Health Service Commissioner, Director General of Fair Trading, etc.
Journalism, literature and art, s 32	• all the Principles (except 7th – security measures) • s 7 (subject access) • s 10 (right to prevent processing likely to cause damage or distress) • s 12 (automated decision taking) • s 14(1)–(3) (rectification etc.)	An important exemption protecting freedom of speech Where personal data are processed for the special purposes the exemption applies if: (a) processing is with a view to publication by any person of journalistic, literary or artistic material, (b) the data controller reasonably believes it is in the public interest, having regard to the special importance of freedom of expression, (c) the data controller reasonably believes, in all the circumstances, that compliance with the provision is incompatible with the special purposes Codes of practice may be designated by the Secretary of State which will be taken into account in determining reasonableness of public interest belief Provision for the court to stay certain types of proceedings if data controller makes a claim that special purposes exist and he has not published the material in the preceding 24 hours – the stay is subject to the claim being withdrawn or the coming into effect of a determination by the Commissioner under s 45

Continued overleaf

Table 31.2 cont.

Description	Exemption provided from	Notes
Research, history, statistics, s 33	• such further processing not incompatible with Principle 2 (purpose for which obtained) • may be kept indefinitely notwithstanding principle 5 • s 7 (subject access) – if processed in accordance with relevant conditions and results not made available in any form identifying any data subject	Research purposes includes statistical or historical purposes 'Relevant conditions' are: (a) the data are not processed to support measures or decisions with respect to particular individuals, and (b) are not processed in such a way that substantial damage or substantial distress is or is likely to be caused to any data subject Personal data will still be treated as processed for research purposes where disclosure is to any person for research purposes, to the data subject or person acting on his behalf, at the request or with consent of data subject or person acting on his behalf or where person making disclosure has reasonable grounds for believing any of the above disclosures apply
Information available to public by or under any enactment, s 34	• subject information provisions • 4th Principle • s 14(1) – (3) (rectification etc.) • non-disclosure provisions	If the data controller is obliged to make the information available to the public whether by publicising it, making it available for inspection or otherwise, whether on payment of a fee or not
Disclosures required by law or in connection with legal proceedings etc., s 35	• non-disclosure provisions	Where disclosure required by or under any enactment, rule of law or by court order or if necessary for legal proceedings, obtaining legal advice or establishing, exercising or defending a legal right
Domestic purposes, s 36	• all the Principles • Parts II & III (rights of data subjects and notification)	Processed by an individual only for that individual's personal, family or household affairs (including recreational purposes)
Miscellaneous exceptions in Schedule 7		
Confidential references by data controller, para 1	• s 7 (subject access)	Applies to references in respect of education, employment or appointment of data subject to any office (actual or prospective) or the provisions of services by the data subject (actual or prospective)
Armed forces, para 2	• subject information provisions	If likely to prejudice the combat effectiveness of any of the armed forces of the Crown
Judicial appointments, honours, para 3	• subject information provisions	To assess suitability for judicial office or as a QC or conferring honours by the Crown

Table 31.2 cont.

Description	Exemption provided from	Notes
Crown employment etc., para 4	• subject access provisions (by order of Secretary of State)	Processing to assess any person's suitability for: (a) employment by/under Crown, (b) any office to which appointments are made by Her Majesty, by a Minister of the Crown or Northern Ireland Department
Management forecasts, para 5	• subject information provisions	For purposes of management forecasting or planning to assist the data controller in the conduct of any business or other activity where complying would be likely to prejudice that conduct
Corporate finance, para 6	• subject information provisions	Underwriting in respect of issues, advice to undertakings on capital structure, industrial strategy and related matters, advice and services in relation to mergers and acquisitions of undertakings and underwriting such matters
		Where compliance could affect the price of an instrument in relation to investment services or if exemption required to safeguard important economic or financial interest of UK
		Secretary of State may specify by order circumstances in which exemption is or is not taken to be required or matters to be taken into account in determining whether required for safeguarding important economic or financial interest of UK
Negotiations, para 7	• subject information provisions (to extent would prejudice negotiations)	Records of intentions in relation to any negotiations with the data subject if likely to prejudice those negotiations
Examination marks, para 8	• s 7 (subject access)	Simply postpones the time for compliance in cases where application made before examination results are announced
		Time for compliance is 5 months after request or 40 days after results announced, whichever is the earlier
		If based on the 5-month period, there is a duty to supply details at the time the request was made together with subsequent versions

Continued overleaf

Table 31.2 cont.

Description	Exemption provided from	Notes
Examination scripts, para 9	• s 7 (subject access)	Personal data recorded by candidates during academic, professional or other examination
Legal professional privilege, para 10	• subject information provisions	Information in respect of which legal professional privilege could be maintained in legal proceedings
Self-incrimination, para 11	• s 7 (subject access)	But not in respect of offences under this Act, though such information is not admissible in criminal proceedings

Enforcement

The Commissioner's powers of enforcement have been described in the previous chapter. It should be noted here that a person on whom an enforcement notice has been served may, under section 41(2), at any time after the time for appeal against the notice has expired (expected to be 28 days) apply in writing to the Commissioner asking for the notice to be cancelled or varied on the basis that, because of a change in circumstances, all or part of the notice need not be complied with. This might be relevant where a data controller, on whom an enforcement notice has been served because the Commissioner is satisfied that there has been or is a contravention of the Data Protection Principles, has modified his processing activity to prevent a particular contravention or has changed his procedures to prevent the reoccurrence of a past contravention. An enforcement notice may also be cancelled or varied on the Commissioner's own initiative.

Appeals against notices and certain decisions and determinations by the Commissioner go to the Data Protection Tribunal. Under section 48, appeals may be lodged in respect of:

- enforcement, information or special information notices,
- a refusal by the Commissioner to cancel or vary an enforcement notice,
- where a notice contains a statement that the notice must be complied with as a matter of urgency within seven days, the Commissioner's decision to include the statement or the effect of the inclusion of the statement as regards any part of the notice, or
- a determination under section 45.

The Tribunal may allow the appeal, substitute another notice if it considers that the notice is not in accordance with the law or, where it involved an exercise of discretion by the Commissioner, if that discretion ought to have been exercised differently, may cancel or vary a notice, make statements ineffective regarding compliance as a matter of urgency in respect of the whole or part of a notice, or cancel a determination of the Commissioner, as appropriate.

The rules of procedure will be made under powers in Schedule 6 to the Act which also deals with the constitution of the Tribunal, *ex parte* proceedings in cases involving certificates in relation to national security and the power to remit to the High Court for contempt. The Tribunal may review any determination of fact on which the notice in question was based. Appeals from decisions of the Tribunal on a point of law go to the High Court in England or Wales (in Scotland, the Court of Session and, in Northern Ireland, the High Court of Justice in Northern Ireland). The volume of enforcement and other notices served under the 1984 Act was relatively small. The Registrar under that Act developed a system of preliminary notices and this continues under the new law as far as enforcement notices are concerned. Under the old law, enforcement notices, de-registration notices and transfer prohibition notices were available but only the enforcement notice has survived the changes, to be supplemented by the information notice and special information notice. Table 31.3 shows how many notices were served under the 1984 Act from the period 1994 to 1998. The years are from 1 April to 31 March. No de-registration notices were served during the period covered in the Table but notices under section 7 of the 1984 Act whereby the Registrar gives reasons for refusing to accept an application to register are listed in the table. These 'notices' are not notices in the normal sense of supervisory notices under the 1984 Act. It can be seen from the Table that relatively few notices were served.

Table 31.3 Supervisory notices served by the Data Protection Registrar 1994–8

Form of notice served	1994/95	1995/96	1996/97	1997/98
preliminary enforcement notice	4	5	6	19
enforcement notice	2	3	2	5
preliminary transfer prohibition notice	0	1	0	0
transfer prohibition notice	0	0	0	0
preliminary registration refusal notice	9	1	0	0
registration refusal notice	32	31	0	0
Totals	**47**	**41**	**8**	**24**

Source: The Data Protection Registrar, *The Fourteenth Annual Report*, The Stationery Office, 1998.

Offences

There are some changes to the data protection offences. In particular, some new offences are brought in to reflect differences in the new law and some of the offences under the 1984 Act relating to processing outwith the scope of the register entry, which were contained in section 5(2) of that Act, have disappeared. In practice, under the old law, the majority of prosecutions were for failing to register.

The offences in section 55(1) – without the consent of the data controller, obtaining or disclosing personal data or procuring the disclosure to another person and the associated offences relating to selling or offering to sell data obtained in contravention of section 55(4) and (5) – are the equivalent to those inserted into the 1984 Act by section 161 of the Criminal Justice and Public Order Act 1994. Section 55 is, however, wider and is not restricted to procuring, selling and offering to sell. The 'procuring' offences only came into force on 3 February 1995 but there have been a number of successful convictions in respect of them. For example, in July 1998, a father and son were found guilty at Horseferry Magistrates Court of a number of offences under the 1984 Act. The father operated a private investigation company and his son, who worked for the National Westminster Bank, passed on details of individuals from the bank's database to his father. The son was convicted of two charges of unauthorised disclosure and fined £500 for each. The father's company was charged with being an unregistered data user and with two charges of unlawful procuring of personal data and two charges of unlawful sale of personal data, and was fined a total of £5000. The father was convicted of four charges of consenting or conniving with the offences committed by his company and was fined £500 for each.

The utility of the unlawful obtaining, disclosure, procuring and selling offences is clear. Apart from widening the ambit of them, there is also a change to the state of mind required of the accused (known as the *mens rea* to lawyers) as, before, it was 'knowing or having reason to believe' whereas now, for the offences in section 55(1), it is 'knowingly or recklessly'. A person behaves 'recklessly' if the risk of the relevant act or omission transpiring would be obvious to a reasonable man, whether or not the person responsible for the act or omission thought about the possibility of the risk. It is, therefore, an objective test. The seriousness of the risk is not a factor to be taken into account. There are two leading cases on the meaning of recklessness, both decided in the House of Lords on the same day. In the first, *R v Caldwell* [1982] AC 341, a case on criminal damage, Lord Diplock described the test of recklessness in terms of a real risk of the relevant harmful consequences which would be apparent to the ordinary prudent individual. The accused would be reckless if he gave some thought about the risk and decided to ignore it or if he failed to give any thought to it at all. However, in *R v Lawrence* [1982] AC 510, a case of reckless driving (this offence no longer exists and has been replaced by dangerous driving), Lord Diplock spoke of *serious* harmful consequences.

The fine distinction between these two judgments (that is, the inclusion of the word 'serious' in *Lawrence*) has exercised the mind of many law students ever since. In the case of *Data Protection Registrar* v *Amnesty International (British Section)* (unreported) 8 November 1994, Amnesty International was charged with offences under section 5(2)(b) and (d) of the Act after exchanging its mailing lists with another charitable body. The offences were holding data for purposes other than those mentioned in the register entry and disclosing data to a person not described in the register entry (there are no offences directly equivalent to these under the 1998 Act). One of the subscribers to Amnesty International complained after receiving a request for money from the other charity. The exchange of the list was outside the scope of Amnesty's registration. There had been no fee charged for the list and the stipendiary magistrate accepted that Amnesty International honestly believed it was acting in accordance with its registration. The stipendiary found that Amnesty International had not been reckless because the disclosure of the list did not cause a serious harmful consequence, relying on Lord Diplock's judgment in *Lawrence,* and dismissed the case. The Data Protection Registrar appealed by way of case stated on a point of law.

The Divisional Court of the Queen's Bench Division allowed the appeal, confirming that, taking the two speeches of Lord Diplock together, it is not a prerequisite of recklessness that serious harm should result. Lord Justice Rose said that in order to prove recklessness for the purposes of section 5(2) of the Data Protection Act 1984:

(a) there must be something in the circumstances that would draw the attention of the ordinary prudent individual to the possibility that his act was capable of causing the kind of mischief that section 5(2) is intended to prevent and the risk of that mischief occurring was not so slight that an ordinary prudent individual would feel justified as treating it as negligible, and

(b) before doing the act, the accused either failed to give any thought to the possibility of there being such a risk or having recognised that there was such a risk, he nevertheless went on to do it.

Although the offences involved are not in the 1998 Act, this case is important authority for the meaning of recklessness for the offences in the 1998 Act, for which recklessness will suffice for the mental element of the offence.

The offences under the 1998 Act are summarised in Table 31.4. The Table contains the section number and a description of the offence, the state of mind required of the accused and whether there are any specific defences. Note that many of the offences are strict liability, that is to say that ignorance of the offence will not excuse.

Table 31.4 Offences under the Data Protection Act 1998

Section	Description	State of mind (mens rea)	Defences
21(1)	Processing personal data without having notified where this is required under s 17	Strict liability	None
21(2)	Failing in the duty to notify changes in the registrable particulars or in the measures taken to comply with the security requirements under the seventh principle	Strict liability	Where the person charged can show that he exercised all due diligence to comply with the duty
22(6)	Carrying on assessable processing unless notification has been received from the Commissioner	Strict liability	None
24(4)	In a case where processing has not been notified (because it was not required and the data controller has chosen not to notify), failing to provide relevant particulars to any person on request within 21 days	Strict liability	Where the person charged can show that he exercised all due diligence to comply with the duty
47(1)	Failing to comply with an enforcement, information or special information notice	Strict liability	Where the person charged can show that he exercised all due diligence to comply with the duty
47(2)	In purported compliance with an information notice or special information notice, making a statement which is false in a material respect	Knowing that the statement is false in a material respect or recklessly making such a statement	None
55(1) & (3)	Without the consent of the data controller – (a) obtaining or disclosing personal data or the information contained in personal data, or (b) procuring the disclosure to another person of the information contained in personal data	Knowledge or recklessness required	Does not apply where the person shows: (a) that the obtaining, disclosing or procuring – (i) was necessary for the purposes of preventing or detecting crime, or (ii) was required or authorised by or under any enactment, by any rule of law or by the order of a court,

Table 31.4 cont.

Section	Description	State of mind (mens rea)	Defences
55(1) & (3) (cont.)			(b) that he acted in the reasonable belief that he had in law the right to obtain or disclose the data or information or, as the case may be, to procure the disclosure of the information to the other person, (c) that he acted in the reasonable belief that he would have had the consent of the data controller if the data controller had known of the obtaining, disclosing or procuring and the circumstances of it, or (d) that in the particular circumstances the obtaining, disclosing or procuring was justified as being in the public interest
55(4)	Selling personal data by a person who has obtained the data in contravention of s 55(1)	Strict liability	None
55(5)	Offering to sell personal data if: (a) the person has obtained the data in contravention of s 55(1), or (b) he subsequently obtains the data in contravention of s 55(1) Note: offering to sell includes an advertisement indicating that personal data are or may be for sale 55 (7) Section 1(2) does not apply for the purposes of this section; and for the purposes of this and the above offence (s 55(4)), 'personal data' includes information extracted from personal data		The defences that apply to the s 55(1) & (3) offences do not apply to this offence

Continued overleaf

Table 31.4 cont.

Section	Description	State of mind (mens rea)	Defences
56(5)	Requiring a person to supply a relevant record (enforced subject access) in connection with: (a) the recruitment of another person as an employee, (b) the continued employment of another person, or (c) any contract for the provision of services to him by another person or Requiring a person to supply a relevant record as a condition of providing or offering to provide goods, facilities or services A relevant record is one relating to convictions or cautions or in relation to certain types of benefit	Strict liability	But not where required or authorised by or under any enactment, rules of law or by court order, or where the requirement is justified as being in the public interest
59(3)	The disclosure of information obtained or furnished under the Act which relates to a living individual or business and has not previously been available to the public from other sources by a present or past Data Protection Commissioner, member of the Commissioner's staff or an agent of the Commissioner	Knowledge or recklessness as to the contravention	None
61(1)	Where an offence under this Act has been committed by a body corporate and is proved to have been committed by or with the consent of, connivance of, or to be attributable to any neglect on the part of any director, manager, secretary or similar officer of the body corporate or any person who was purporting to act in any such capacity, he as well as the body corporate shall be guilty of an offence and be liable to be proceeded against and punished accordingly	Consent, connivance or neglect (the latter would seem to be based on an objective test)	None

Table 31.4 cont.

Section	Description	State of mind (mens rea)	Defences
Schedule 9, para 12	Intentionally obstructing a person in the execution of a warrant issued under this Schedule, or failing without reasonable excuse to give any person executing such a warrant such assistance as he may reasonably require for the execution of the warrant	Intention or not having reasonable excuse as the case may be	None

All the offences, apart from those relating to warrants in Schedule 9, are triable either way: that is, either on indictment in the Crown Court or summarily in a Magistrates' Court. They are punishable on conviction on indictment by a fine or, on summary conviction, by a fine not exceeding the statutory maximum: section 60. Offences in relation to warrants are summary only and punishable on conviction with a fine not exceeding level 5 on the standard scale. There are also provisions for forfeiture, destruction or erasure of documents or other material, subject to persons other than the offender being heard as to why the order should not be made.

Section 61 applies the usual provisions with respect to offences committed by a body corporate where it is proved that the offence was committed with the consent or connivance or was attributable to any neglect on the part of any director, manager, secretary or similar officer or person purporting to act in such a capacity. If this is so, that person as well as the body corporate is liable to prosecution. This also applies where the affairs of the body corporate are managed by its members. They are treated as directors for the purposes of this provision.

In England and Wales, no proceedings for an offence under the Act can be brought except by the Commissioner or by or with the consent of the Director of Public Prosecutions: section 60.

Figure 31.2 shows the numbers of prosecutions leading to convictions under the 1984 Act from 1995 to 1998. It will be seen that the majority of prosecutions relate to a failure to register. Offences under section 5(6) and (7) of the 1984 Act, which were inserted by the Criminal Justice and Public Order Act 1994 (the 'procuring and selling' offences), find their equivalent in section 55 of the 1998 Act. During the year 1997/98, there were six convictions each for these offences. Most convictions resulted in fines being imposed. The range of fines in 1997/98 was from £50 to £2500. The maximum fine ever imposed for an offence under the 1984 Act was £3000, imposed in the year to 1 April 1997. In 1997/98, five convictions resulted in discharges, either absolute or conditional. In one case a clerk to the justices was prosecuted and he received only an absolute discharge!

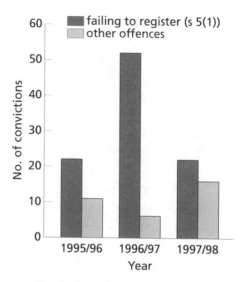

Fig. 31.2 Offences under the Data Protection Act 1984

Transitional provisions

Because the new law marks such a sea change in the regulation of processing of personal data, there is need for comprehensive transitional provisions. Additionally, these make full use of the derogations permitted in the Directive, allowing the application of the law to pre-existing processing to be delayed for up to three years for automatic processing and up to 12 years for manual processing.

Schedule 8 to the Data Protection Act 1998 contains the main transitional provisions. There are two transitional periods as follows:

'the first transitional period' means the period beginning with the commencement of this Schedule and ending with 23rd October 2001; and

'the second transitional period' means the period beginning with 24th October 2001 and ending with 23rd October 2007.

The first period applies to automated processing already underway and also deals with the exemptions under the 1984 Act which are no longer available. The second period relates only to manual files (relevant filing systems and accessible records). Processing for historical research already underway, whether automated or not, is separately provided for and there is no time limit for such processing.

To understand the scope of the transitional provisions, it is vital to look at the meaning of processing already underway. A particular issue is whether automatically processed personal data which were subject to processing on 23 October 1998 lose the advantage of the exemptions if new personal data are added subsequently. Three possibilities exist.

1 The collection of personal data as a whole continues to be able to take advantage of the transitional provisions.
2 The collection of personal data as a whole is now caught by the new law and the exemption is lost.
3 The new personal data must comply with the new law in all respects but the pre-existing data do not have to.

The Directive is somewhat ambiguous on the point and is couched in terms of 'processing already under way'. However, the Data Protection Act 1998 seems clearer but, potentially, less generous to data controllers. The exemptions in the Act under the transitional provisions are expressed primarily in terms of 'eligible data'. These are defined in the following terms (emphasis added): 'personal data are "eligible data" at any time *if, and to the extent that,* they are at any time subject to processing which was already under way immediately before 24th October 1998'. Eligible automated data are eligible data processed or to be processed by automatic means and eligible manual data are simply eligible data which are not eligible automated data. Two points can be made about the definition of eligible data.

1 There is no express requirement that the data are being processed by or on behalf of the data controller. Simply the fact that they are subject to processing by any data controller should suffice; that is, data that exist before 24 October 1998 are eligible data.
2 The phrase 'if, and to the extent that,' implies that data created on or after 24 October 1998 are not eligible data and subject immediately to the new law. This suggests that the third alternative interpretation above is the correct one. However, if this is so, the scope of some of the transitional provisions is seriously prejudiced.

Another unresolved issue is what the effect is of commencing some new processing activity in respect of pre-existing personal data. If a strict interpretation is taken of the definition of eligible data, it would appear, at least to that extent, that the personal data will no longer be eligible data.

The two transitional periods will now be examined in greater depth together with other transitional provisions relating to research data and the requirement for a preliminary assessment.

The first transitional period

This applies to automated processing and manual processing until 24 October 2001. The provisions differ for automatic data and manual data.

Manual data

Eligible manual data, other than data forming part of an accessible record, are exempt from the data protection principles and Parts II and III of this Act during the first transitional period. Parts II and III contain the rights of data subjects and the notification requirements respectively. However, if the manual data consist of information relevant to the financial standing of the data subject and the data controller is a credit reference agency, the exemption is limited. It does not extend to the right of access of data subjects (section 7 as modified by section 9) and there is a right to rectification, erasure, blocking or destruction of inaccurate or incomplete data and a right to require the data controller to cease holding exempt manual data in a manner incompatible with the data controller's legitimate interests (it is the data controller's legitimate interests that are relevant, not those of the data subject). These latter rights are provided by section 12A of the Act which is inserted until 24 October 2007.

Where the data are part of an accessible record, whether eligible data or not, the exemptions are largely subject to the same rights of data subjects as applies to credit reference agencies. Thus, pre-existing and new data contained in accessible records such as health records, educational and certain local authority records have exemption from the Principles (except in so far as the sixth principle in as much as it relates to subject access under sections 7 and 12A), other rights of data subjects (such as the rights to prevent processing) and the notification requirements. The complexity of this can be explained by the fact that the 1998 Act has incorporated some provisions of other legislation allowing access to personal data such as the Consumer Credit Act 1974 (access to credit reference agencies data) and the Access to Personal Files Act 1987, which is repealed in its entirety by the Data Protection Act 1998.

Eligible automated data – general exemption

The new data protection law is significantly different to that under the 1984 Act. As well as applying the possibility in the Directive not to make processing already under way subject to the new law for three years, the transitional provisions have to cope with a number of differences between the new and old law, particularly in respect to a number of exemptions under the 1984 Act that are no longer available.

Paragraph 13 of Schedule 8 to the Act gives general exemption to all eligible automated data and is intended generally to place such data in the same position as applied under the 1984 Act. The exemptions are as set out below (bearing in mind that, nevertheless, the Principles under the 1984 Act still apply to such processing).

- The data controller does not have to provide data subjects with information when data are obtained from him and in other cases.

- There is no need for any of the conditions for processing in Schedule 2 to be present nor, in the case of sensitive data, any of those in Schedule 3.
- There is no obligation to impose security obligations on processors in writing or evidenced in writing.
- The new provisions controlling transfers of personal data to third countries not having an adequate level of protection do not apply.
- The requirement to give additional information in response to a data subject request compared to that required under the 1984 Act (such as a description of the data, the purposes of processing, and recipients) does not apply.
- The data controller is exempt from the right of data subjects to prevent processing causing or likely to cause substantial damage or substantial distress, the right to prevent processing for the purposes of direct marketing and the rights of data subjects in respect of automated decision taking.
- The enhanced rights of data subjects to compensation do not apply and are restricted to those under the 1984 Act.

The above exemptions are helpful in showing how the new law differs from the old law in relation to automatic processing.

Eligible automated data – particular exemptions

Other exemptions for automated processing are needed because some of the exemptions under the 1984 Act disappear. For the purposes of the Data Protection Act 1984, processing had to be by reference to the data subject. An express exception was where processing was performed only for the purpose of preparing the text of documents (the 'word processing' exception). Paragraph 5 of Schedule 8 extends the benefit of this exemption for a further three years for eligible automated data.

An important exemption under the 1984 Act which disappears and which was relied on by many data users under the 1984 Act was in respect of processing for payroll and accounts. The exemption was not total but was from the registration requirements and the rights of data subjects. This is continued for a further three years until 24 October 2001. Eligible automated data processed for payroll or accounts are exempt from the Data Protection Principles and Parts II and III (data subjects' rights and notification) during the first transitional period. However, the data must not be processed for any other purpose, although the exemption will not be lost by any processing for any other purpose if the data controller can show that he had taken such care to prevent it as in all the circumstances was reasonably required. The burden of proof to show this is so is imposed on the data controller.

Certain disclosures are also permitted, such as to any person by whom the remuneration or pensions are payable; for the purpose of obtaining actuarial advice; or for the purpose of giving information as to the person in any employment office; or for use in medical research into the health of, or

435

injuries suffered by, persons engaged in particular occupations or working in particular places or areas. The data subject (or a person acting on his behalf) may also request or consent to the disclosure either generally or in the circumstances in which the disclosure in question is made. The exemption still applies if the person making the disclosure has reasonable grounds for believing that the data subject requested or consented to the disclosure. Further disclosures are permitted which include the purpose of audit or for the purpose only of giving information about the data controller's financial affairs.

The problem is – what if new data, perhaps relating to a new employee, are added to a database or other collection of data which existed prior to 24 October 1998? If the meaning of eligible automated data does not extend to newly added personal data, the exemption is lost. This could be quite serious because the data controller is unlikely to realise that this is so and, if he does not notify his processing for payroll and accounts, he could commit an offence of strict liability under the 1998 Act. The same applies in relation to unincorporated members' lists and mailing lists which also had an exemption under the 1984 Act. The transitional provisions again attempt to extend this for a further three years. The exemption is, as before, from the Data Protection Principles and Parts II and III of the Act, but again it may not be safe to rely on the exemption where new data are created and added to the pre-existing data. The conditions which applied to unincorporated members' clubs and mailing lists under the 1984 Act, such as the requirement to ask data subjects whether they object to the processing of personal data relating to them, still apply during the transitional period.

A further exemption under the 1984 Act was from the subject access provisions where the data were solely for back-up purposes, for example to replace data on a computer in the event that they were accidentally erased or corrupted in some way. This is continued until 24 October 2001.

The second transitional period

The second period applies only to manual processing and is a partial derogation for 12 years, until 24 October 2007, and applies to eligible manual data and accessible records, whether eligible or not. It does not apply to eligible manual data processed only for the purposes of historical research for which there is separate provision. The exemption is from the first Data Protection Principle (except to the extent to which it requires compliance with the requirements to inform data subjects when the data are obtained from the data subject or in other cases), the second, third, fourth and fifth Data Protection Principles, and section 14(1) to (3) which contains the basic rights to rectification, blocking, erasure and destruction. Of course, there is no requirement generally to notify manual processing (except where the processing is assessable). Data subjects still have a right of access to such data and a right to be informed in accordance with the first Principle. Although exemption is granted in respect of some of the rights of rectification under section 14(1) to (3), this is of little consequence as the processing is subject to section 12A instead which grants similar rights in addition to a right in relation to processing not in accordance with the legitimate interests of the data controller.

Even though the new law will not fully affect manual records until 24 October 2007, some data controllers could still find it difficult and expensive to comply fully after that date. This is a particular problem where an organisation has a significant amount of archived data which it wants to retain, for example, for future research purposes or for defending legal claims. During the lead up to the Directive, the Council and Commission made a joint statement to the effect that, in certain circumstances:

> at the end of the 12 year transitional period, controllers must take all reasonable steps relating to the requirements of Articles 6, 7 and 8, which do not prove impossible or involve a disproportionate effort in terms of cost.

The manual data exemption does not prevent individuals exercising their right of subject access, their right to prevent processing and their rights to compensation. The security obligations also apply and data controllers need to review this aspect in relation to manual files. For example, are manual files kept in secure locations and is access to them restricted to those having a genuine need to use or access them?

Processing for historical research (partial derogation)

This exemption is indefinite in time. After 23 October 2001, eligible manual data processed only for the purpose of historical research in compliance with the 'relevant conditions' and relevant automated data which are processed only for the purpose of historical research, in compliance with the relevant conditions, and otherwise than by reference to the data subject, are exempt from the first Data Protection Principle (but not as regards informing data subjects), the second, third, fourth and fifth Data Protection Principles, and the rights of rectification, blocking, erasure and destruction under section 14(1) to (3).

The relevant conditions are those specified in section 33 and are that the data are not processed to support measures or decisions with respect to particular individuals and that they are not processed in such a way that substantial damage or substantial distress is, or is likely to be, caused to any data subject.

Other eligible automated data processed only for the purpose of historical research in compliance with the relevant conditions are exempt from the first Data Protection Principle to the extent to which it requires compliance with the conditions in Schedules 2 and 3 (the conditions for processing). This more limited exemption applies where, in spite of the other conditions being present, the data are processed by reference to the data subject.

In respect of these exemptions, personal data are not to be treated as processed otherwise than for the purpose of historical research merely because the data are disclosed:

(a) to any person, for the purpose of historical research only,
(b) to the data subject or a person acting on his behalf,
(c) at the request, or with the consent, of the data subject or a person acting on his behalf, or
(d) in circumstances in which the person making the disclosure has reasonable grounds for believing that the disclosure falls within paragraph (a), (b) or (c).

Section 12A does not apply to eligible manual data processed for historical research.

If the relevant conditions are not met, the exemption for eligible automated data is of the more restricted variety and applies only in respect of the first Data Protection Principle but subject to the conditions for processing.

Assessable processing

Where, by its nature, processing activity is likely to cause substantial damage or substantial distress to data subjects or is likely otherwise to significantly prejudice the rights and freedoms of data subjects, section 22 of the 1998 Act provides that the processing will be subject to a preliminary assessment by the Data Protection Commissioner before processing can proceed. The types of processing affected will be specified by order of the Secretary of State and is likely to be relatively limited covering processing of genetic data, data matching and processing by private investigators. However, by virtue of paragraph 19 of Schedule 8, processing which was already under way immediately before 24 October 1998 is not assessable processing for these purposes. This applies to both the manual and automated data.

Chapter 32

Data subjects' rights

Introduction

This chapter looks at the Data Protection Act 1998 from the perspective of data subjects. We have seen how the Act impacts upon data controllers, and many individuals as well as organisations in the public and private sectors (ranging from central government departments to sole traders) will be classed as data controllers, even if they do not possess a computer. But we are all data subjects. There can be very few, if any, persons in respect of whom someone, somewhere, is not processing personal data relating to them in a manner within the new law. As information processing becomes more powerful, there is a growing need to protect the rights of individuals in that context, because of the threats to privacy and freedom. The 1984 Act contained a number of rights given to data subjects; the new law empowers data individuals to a much greater extent by granting them some new rights whilst strengthening pre-existing rights. Although data controllers may feel some concern about how these new and enhanced rights will be exercised, individuals will welcome the additional control they provide over processing activity, particularly where it is in contravention of the 1998 Act.

In addition to the rights of subject access, rectification and right to compensation for damage and distress caused by inaccurate data or loss, unauthorised destruction or disclosure under the 1984 Act, data subjects have a right to be informed on the obtaining of personal data from them and in other circumstances such as on disclosure to third parties as described in the previous chapter. This alone should increase transparency of processing and enable individuals to know more about who is processing data relating to them and for what purposes. Enforced subject access – for example, where a prospective employer requires a person to carry out a subject access request to show whether that person has any previous convictions or cautions – is made a criminal offence in some cases. Further important new rights granted to data subjects are:

- a right to prevent processing likely to cause substantial damage or substantial distress,
- a right to prevent processing for purposes of direct marketing, and
- rights in relation to automated decision taking.

These new rights have no direct equivalent under the old law. Of course, in some cases, a data subject may have been able to put a stop to a processing activity covered by these new rights by complaining to the Data Protection Registrar (now named Data Protection Commissioner) who, if the activity was in contravention of the Data Protection Principles or within the scope of the criminal offences, may have decided to use her powers of enforcement or bring a prosecution. A good proportion of the criminal prosecutions in the past appear to have come about as a result, initially, of a complaint by an individual. For example, in *Data Protection Registrar* v *Amnesty International (British Section)* (unreported) 8 November 1994, Queen's Bench Divisional Court, a subscriber to Amnesty International complained to the Registrar when she received a mailing from another charity to which Amnesty International had passed on details of its subscribers. This was held to be an offence as Amnesty International's registration under the 1984 Act at the time of the disclosure did not permit such disclosures.

Under the 1998 Act, data subjects may still approach the Data Protection Commissioner. They may ask for an assessment and, in some cases, ask for assistance such as the payment of legal fees. As far as enforcing their rights, data subjects may apply to a court for compensation or to ask the court to order the data controller to do something required, such as comply with a subject access request, or to refrain from doing something – for example, to

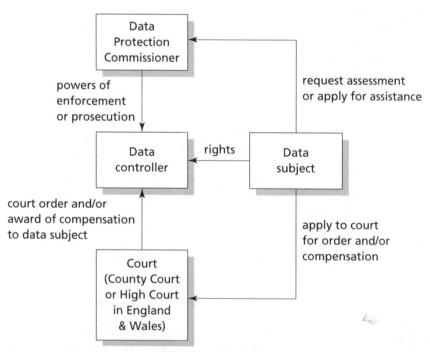

Fig. 32.1 Relationship between the data subject, Commissioner and court in respect of data subjects' rights

comply with a notice from a data subject requiring the data controller to cease processing which is causing substantial damage to the data subject or another person. Figure 32.1 shows the relationship between the data subject, the Commissioner and the courts.

Before looking at the new rights provided for by the 1998 Act, the pre-existing rights are described and the changes made to them highlighted. Reference should be made to the previous chapter for a description of the general right to receive information from the data controller as this does not require any act from the data subject to initiate the right to information and is more in the way of a general obligation placed on the data controller.

Right of access

The data subject's right of access is fundamental to the policing of data protection law by individuals. By seeing what personal data relating to a particular individual a data controller is processing, that person may, with the knowledge of other factors such as the purposes of the processing, take a view on whether the processing is fair and lawful or otherwise within the Data Protection Principles. In particular, individuals are likely to be concerned to satisfy themselves that their personal data are correct and not excessive. This may be important where the granting of credit or obtaining employment or services could depend on the data and considerable damage can be done if it is incorrect – for example, by falsely indicating that a person has a criminal record, has a county court judgment against him for debt, is an active member of an extreme political group and so on.

A statutory right of access is essential as there is no common law right to access. In R v Mid-Glamorgan Family Health Services, ex parte Martin (unreported) 29 July 1994, a patient had been refused access to his health records going back to before 1990 on the basis that it would be detrimental for the patient to see those records directly. An offer was made to disclose the records conditionally to a medical expert appointed by the patient but this was not accepted. The patient claimed that there was a right of access at common law. However, the Court of Appeal refused to grant access denying that there was a right of access under common law.

There may be a right of access under the European Convention on Human Rights, in particular as a result of Article 8 which provides that everyone has the right to respect for his private and family life, his home and his correspondence. The Convention will be brought into law in the United Kingdom under the auspices of the Human Rights Act 1998 which is due to come into force in 2000. In McGinley & Egan v United Kingdom (unreported) 9 June 1998, European Court of Human Rights, two ex-soldiers had witnessed nuclear testing carried out by the United Kingdom in 1957 and 1958 at Christmas Island in the Pacific Ocean. They later suffered health problems which they thought were caused by their exposure to radiation and they lodged claims for war pensions. These were turned down and the government did not disclose documents indicating the radiation levels at the time.

The Court held that access to the documents would have either allayed their fears or allowed them to assess the danger to which they had been exposed and this raised an issue under Article 8. Although Article 8 was primarily a negative undertaking by, for example, protecting a person against arbitrary interference by public authorities, it went beyond that and could give rise to positive obligations (also recognised in *Gaskin* v *United Kingdom*: see later). Those obligations required a balance between the interests of individuals and the general interest of the community. Where a government was engaged in a hazardous activity which might have adverse consequences on the health of those involved, Article 8 required that an accessible and effective procedure was in place to enable such persons to seek all relevant and appropriate information. However, there was no breach of Article 8 in the present case as the ex-soldiers had failed to avail themselves of an appeal under rule 6 of the Pensions Appeals Tribunals (Scotland) Rules 1981 which would have allowed them to apply for an order for disclosure of the relevant documents. The existence of that procedure meant that the United Kingdom had fulfilled its obligations under Article 8.

Article 8 may well be relevant in the future where no procedure exists for an appeal against a refusal to disclose personal data to the individual to whom it relates. It is noteworthy that the European Court of Human Rights interprets Article 8 as imposing a positive obligation to do something, at least in certain circumstances. It must be said, however, at this stage, that its application in the United Kingdom is likely to be somewhat unpredictable at first. One possible area of conflict involving Article 8 may be in connection with the exemptions from subject access provided for in the 1998 Act – for example if a data controller is relying on the exemption from subject access on the basis that the data are being processed for the purposes of national security.

A right of access was available under the 1984 Act but was limited simply to a statement from the data user (now data controller) as to whether he was processing data relating to the applicant and, if so, to access the data. Various rules existed to deal with the situation where access to the data would reveal information relating to another identifiable individual and a similar basic mechanism continues under the 1998 Act but with some significant improvements and other changes.

Sections 7 to 9 of the Data Protection Act 1998 deal with data subjects' right of access. The information to be given to the data subject is:

whether any data relating to the data subject are being processed by or on behalf of the data controller and, if so, the data controller must give:

- a description of the personal data,
- the purposes for which they are being or are to be processed, and

- the recipients or classes of recipients to whom they are or may be disclosed,
- communication to the data subject in an intelligible form – accompanied with an explanation if necessary, of:
  - the information constituting the personal data (a copy in permanent form unless this is not possible or would require a disproportionate effort or if the data subject agrees otherwise),
  - any available information as to the source of the data, and
- where the processing is within the provisions relating to automatic decision taking, a description of the logic involved in that automated decision taking.

Thus, far more information is required than under the 1984 Act, although much of this additional information would be available to a data subject who examined the register entry, except for the description of the logic involved in any automated decision taking. Of course, from the data subject's point of view, it is much easier if the data controller provides all this information directly. As individuals may not realise that they are entitled to more information than was the case previously, the Act allows the Secretary of State to make regulations in particular cases so that a request for any of the above information is to be treated as a request for all the other information required to be given.

To overcome the problem of 'nuisance' subject access requests, made at frequent intervals by the same person, the data controller can refuse to comply with a subsequent identical or similar request by a particular individual unless a reasonable interval has elapsed. In determining what a reasonable interval is, regard should be given to the nature of the data, the purposes of the processing and the frequency with which the data are altered. So, for example, where data are being updated and modified on an ongoing basis, fairly frequent requests may be deemed reasonable. The information to be given must be as it was when the request was received apart from deletions or amendments which would have been made notwithstanding the request. Therefore, if the data are inaccurate and in breach of the fourth Data Protection Principle, the data controller must not deliberately correct the data because a subject access request has been made. However, if the data controller systematically checks the validity of the personal data as part of the management of his processing activity and, as a result of such checking, an inaccuracy is detected and corrected between the time the subject access request is made and the time when it is complied with, then the data controller need give access to the data as corrected only. As noted in the exemptions in the previous chapter, if the data are evidence that the data controller has committed an offence other than one under the Act, he is excused compliance with the subject access request to the extent that such evidence would be revealed.

Where the processing is by automatic means and has constituted or is likely to constitute the sole basis for any decision significantly affecting him, in evaluating matters relating to the data subject such as his performance at work, creditworthiness, reliability or conduct, the data subject has the right to be informed of the logic involved in that decision taking but not if, or to the extent that, the information constitutes a trade secret. 'Trade secret' is not defined but it would seem sensible to apply the meaning used in the law of breach of confidence, although it is not particularly clearly defined there. Perhaps it would be reasonable to consider a 'trade secret' here to be information the disclosure of which would harm the data controller's legitimate interests, be of benefit to a competitor or expose the data controller to a serious risk of fraud.

The provisions dealing with the situation when compliance with a subject access request would disclose information relating to another identifiable individual have been somewhat modified, partly as a result of a case before the European Court of Human Rights, *Gaskin* v *United Kingdom* (1990) 12 EHRR 36. The applicant for subject access claimed he had been ill-treated while a child in care of the local authority. He sought access to confidential records concerning him and his care from Liverpool City Council, which was required to keep such records. The City Council decided to give Gaskin access provided the persons who contributed to his file consented. Only 19 out of 46 of the contributors gave their consent and the relevant documents were released to him. However, the remainder, where the contributors refused consent or could not be traced, were not disclosed to him. It was held by the European Court of Human Rights that this was a breach of his right to respect for his private and family life under Article 8 of the European Convention on Human Rights. Although the United Kingdom could not be said to have interfered with his private life, there could be circumstances where an inherent positive obligation arose in respect for private life. Whether such an obligation arose in a particular case was a matter of balance and, on the basis of proportionality, required that an independent authority decided whether access should be granted or denied if a contributor to such records withheld consent or did not answer. That had not happened in *Gaskin*, hence the breach of Article 8.

Now, under the 1998 Act, to comply with the request, the data controller must be satisfied that the other person has consented to the disclosure of his personal data to the person making the request. Otherwise, and this is the new provision, access can be given where it is reasonable in all the circumstances to comply without the consent of the other. In determining whether it is reasonable in all the circumstances to comply without the consent of the other, factors that may be taken into account are any duty of confidentiality owed to the other, any steps taken by the data controller to gain the consent of the other, whether the other is capable of giving consent and any express refusal of consent by the other individual.

444

In other cases such as where it would not be reasonable to comply, lack of consent does not excuse a data controller altogether where he can provide the access to the applicant's data without disclosing the identity of the other individual – for example, by omitting the name or other identifying particulars. This may be done by suppressing the identifying information from a computer printout which is handed to the person making the subject access request or, in the case of manual files caught by the new law, by masking the relevant information when making a photocopy to give to the person making the request.

Further provisions deal with the time in which the data controller has to comply and the need for the data subject to make a written request providing sufficient information and paying the required fee. The basic time period will be 40 days (this may be altered by regulations) and the maximum fee will be set out in regulations. Under the 1984 Act, the maximum fee was £10. For applications to credit reference agencies under section 158 of the Consumer Credit Act 1974 the fee was raised to £2. Different time periods and fees may be prescribed in different cases. As applications under the latter Act will be dealt with under the Data Protection Act 1998, this differential is likely to continue. It will be interesting to see whether a higher maximum fee will be permitted for subject access to manual files as compliance could be potentially more expensive in some cases in respect of such files. Any failure to comply with a subject access request may result in a court ordering compliance.

Credit reference agencies

Under section 9 of the Data Protection Act 1998, an application to a credit reference agency is taken to be limited to financial information relating to the data subject unless a contrary intention is expressed. The data controller must include a statement of the data subject's rights under section 159 of the Consumer Credit Act 1974 (a right to have wrong information corrected), to the extent required as prescribed. Section 62 of the Data Protection Act 1998 modifies section 158 of the Consumer Credit Act 1974 and the right under that section to obtain a copy of a file applies only in relation to partnerships. For other individuals the right to a copy of the file is under section 9 of the 1998 Act, although the right of correction of wrong information remains under section 159 of the 1974 Act.

Enforced subject access

Enforced subject access has long been perceived as objectionable by the Data Protection Registrar. This occurs where, for example, a potential employee requires a job applicant to provide a copy of his police file showing whether the data subject has been convicted or cautioned in relation to any offences.

The dangers of leaving enforced subject access uncontrolled were clearly seen in *R v Chief Constable of 'B', ex parte R* (unreported) 24 November 1997, Queen's Bench Division.

R, who was 29 years old at the time, wanted to travel to a foreign country to teach English to adults and, to do so, he had to apply for a visa. He was required by the Consulate General of the country concerned to provide a certificate of his prosecution and conviction history. Unfortunately, R had a conviction for a minor offence of theft committed when he was 19 years old for which he received a conditional discharge and was ordered to pay compensation. However, the conviction was a 'spent conviction' under the Rehabilitation of Offenders Act 1974, the effect being that by virtue of section 4 of that Act, he was treated in law as a person who had not committed or been charged with or prosecuted for or sentenced for the offence. The purpose is that a person who has 'lived down' the offence and not reoffended will not be prejudiced by an unwarranted disclosure of the fact of the offence to a third party. The Chief Constable to whom R applied for subject access provided a statement to the effect that R had 'no citeable convictions' but this was not on the standard form issued under the Data Protection Act 1984 and as required by the Consulate General. This form would show R's spent conviction.

The Code of Practice for Data Protection used by the Association of Chief Police Officers generally requires 'reportable' offences to be retained for 20 years, even though they may be spent convictions. However, the Data Protection Act 1984 contained no discretion to exclude some information from being provided under a subject access request and, according to Lord Justice Laws, section 21 of that Act clearly required all the information constituting the personal data to be supplied. Any conflict with the Rehabilitation of Offenders Act 1974 was removed by section 26(4) of the 1984 Act which stated that the subject access provisions apply notwithstanding any enactment or rule of law prohibiting or restricting disclosure or withholding information. The judge expressed sympathy for R whom he described as having lived down his conviction, gaining a series of academic and professional qualifications and generally leading an exemplary and productive life. The judge said it was little comfort to R that enforced subject access under the new law is intended to obviate the problems he had encountered but it came too late for R. Of course, in other situations, enforced subject access can be important such as where a person applies for employment in a position of trust or authority where children or other vulnerable persons are involved.

In a late amendment to the Bill, provisions were added to prevent enforced subject access, in specified cases. Section 56 of the Act sets out the situations where enforced subject access is prohibited, being in relation to:

• the recruitment of another as an employee,

- the continued employment of another person,
- any contract for the provision of services *by another person*, or
- the provision of goods, facilities or services *to any person* (this extends also to the supply of a relevant record by a third party).

The prohibition applies in relation to 'relevant records', being those showing convictions and cautions where the data controller is a chief officer of police or the Secretary of State. Also included are details of the detention of young persons for long periods of time for grave crimes under section 53 of the Children and Young Persons Act 1933, the Secretary of State's functions under the Prison Act 1952, under the Social Security Contributions and Benefits Act 1992, the Social Security Administration Act 1992, the Jobseekers Act 1995 or in relation to certificates of criminal records under Part V of the Police Act 1997 (with necessary amendments for Scotland and Northern Ireland). Even if the record simply states that the data controller is not processing data relating to a particular matter, this is still to be taken as relating to that matter. For example, if the information provided under the subject access request states that the person concerned has no convictions or cautions, this will still be deemed to be within the prohibition.

Contravention of the enforced subject access provisions is a criminal offence of strict liability. However, this does not apply where the access is authorised or required by law or court order or justified as being in the public interest. However, the latter does not include the ground that it would assist in the prevention or detection of crime – there must be some other public interest involved.

Enforced subject access in relation to health records is also controlled but not by way of imposing criminal liability. Rather, it is a matter of making any such requirement void in contractual terms. Under section 57, any term or condition in a contract is void in as much as it purports to require the supply of, or producing to another person of, a record, copy or part of a record consisting of information contained in any health record as defined in section 68(2), which is a record consisting of information relating to the physical or mental health or condition of an individual made by or on behalf of a health professional in connection with the care of that individual. 'Health professional' is widely defined in section 69.

Right to prevent processing likely to cause substantial damage or substantial distress

This is a new right as such under the 1998 Act without a direct equivalent under the 1984 Act, although processing which had the potential to cause damage or distress might have been caught by the first Data Protection Principle in particular and dealt with by the Registrar's powers of enforcement. However, processing that could cause damage or distress to an individual might otherwise have been in accordance with the Principles and within the register entry, leaving the individual and the Registrar powerless to act to prevent it. An example might be where sensitive data were lawfully disclosed to a person known to the data subject. Enforced subject access, not unlawful under the 1984 Act, was a good example. This new right is a considerable improvement to the rights of the data subject in that it empowers individuals to require the data controller to stop or not commence processing that has certain consequences for the individual concerned or another. This right is backed by the power of the court to order compliance.

A data subject can require the data controller to cease or not to begin processing for a specified purpose or in a specified manner on the ground that, for specified reasons, it is unwarranted as causing or being likely to cause substantial damage or substantial distress to him or another: section 10(1). However, a limitation is that this right does not apply to processing under conditions 1 to 4 in Schedule 2, being processing where the data subject has given consent, where it is necessary in relation to a contract, where it is necessary for compliance with a legal obligation or where it is to protect the vital interests of the data subject. The Secretary of State may add further exceptions to the right. It can apply to the other conditions for processing 'normal' data (such as processing necessary for the legitimate interests of the data controller or a third party to whom the data are disclosed) and to all the conditions for processing of 'sensitive' data in Schedule 3.

The data subject has to give notice in writing to the data controller, specifying the purpose or manner of processing objected to and the reasons why he or another is likely to be caused substantial damage or substantial distress. Within 21 days, the data controller must give a written notice stating that he has complied with the data subject's notice or intends to do so or stating why he considers the notice unjustified to any extent and the extent, if any, to which he has complied or intends to comply.

If the data controller does not comply with the data subject's notice in whole or in part, the data subject may apply to a court for an order requiring the data controller to comply with the notice. The order will be granted if the court considers the notice justified to any extent and the data controller has failed to comply to that extent. An application to the court might include a claim for compensation under section 13, discussed later.

Right to prevent processing for purposes of direct marketing

Direct marketing, otherwise known as 'junk mail' was perceived as a particular problem by the European Commission. It was decided that an individual ought to be able to prevent it in a case where the marketing material is addressed specifically to the individual. Anonymous advertising material – that is, material which is not addressed to specific persons, such as advertising inserts in newspapers and magazines or which is simply pushed through letterboxes in a blanket mailing – is not affected by data protection law. For one thing, advertising campaigns of that nature do not require the processing of personal data of the recipients.

The Directive gives individuals an absolute right to prevent processing for the purposes of direct marketing and it also requires that member states ensure that individuals are aware of this right. Thus, under section 11 of the Data Protection Act 1998, a data subject has a right, by giving written notice, to require a data controller to cease within a reasonable time in the circumstances or not to begin processing his personal data for the purposes of direct marketing. 'Direct marketing' is defined in the Act as meaning the communication by any means of any advertising or marketing material which is directed at particular individuals. The data controller must give the data subject a written notice within 21 days of receipt of the data subject's notice stating what steps he has taken or will take to comply. Again, the court has the power to order the data controller to comply, following an application by the data subject and if satisfied that the data controller has failed to comply with the data subject's notice.

In the United Kingdom, the presence of the mailing preference system (MOPS) already allows individuals to indicate that they do not wish to receive marketing material. Organisations which send out marketing material are informed from time to time of persons who do not wish to receive such material. Furthermore, if individuals are careful to make sure that they always tick the ubiquitous 'no marketing' box on forms and the like, this should prevent a great deal of marketing material being sent to them. However, neither doing this nor MOPS is foolproof and this additional right may be useful to prevent mailings from a particular data controller. Of course, it does require the data subject to be proactive.

If a data subject does not exercise the right to prevent processing for the purposes of direct marketing nor the right to prevent processing likely to cause substantial damage or substantial distress, this does not affect his other rights under Part II of the Act (the Part dealing with data subjects' rights).

Automated decision taking

Another concern in the lead up to the Directive was automated decision taking where the decisions had or could have significant impacts on data subjects. There are obvious dangers where decisions are taken dogmatically on the basis of a number of factors without any discretion that could be used in particular cases. We have already seen the apparent unfairness of decisions

449

to grant credit being influenced on the credit record of the previous occupant of the house or flat presently occupied by the applicant for credit in *Equifax Europe Ltd* v *Data Protection Registrar* (unreported) 28 February 1992, Data Protection Tribunal. In that case, a credit reference agency was using personal data relating to the financial status of individuals by reference to the current or previous address of the data subject together with financial information relating to *any other individual who had been recorded as residing at any time at the same or a similar address*. The use of such third party data was deemed to be unfair by the Data Protection Registrar although, in the event, the Tribunal did not revoke the enforcement notice but substituted its own on much narrower terms: for example, allowing the use of such third party data if there appeared to be a financial relationship or dependence between the applicant and the third party.

A mechanical and predetermined decision-making process can bring unsatisfactory decisions. It could be because a factor which is a good statistical predictor is built into the logic of the decision process. The data subject's postal code is a good example but says nothing about any particular data subject. Another example is where the data subject has a foreign-sounding name. The controls over automated decision taking are aimed at overcoming decisions that are unfair in a particular case. The Directive took a fairly severe approach and permitted such decision taking only in the context of contracts or, subject to safeguards, where national legislation specifically allowed it.

Section 12 of the Data Protection Act 1998 deals with automated decision taking and takes advantage of the Directive permitting it in cases other than contract. The provisions are targeted at decision taking which significantly affects an individual and which is:

> based solely on the processing by automatic means of personal data in respect of which that individual is the data subject for the purposes of evaluating matters relating to him such as, for example, his performance of work, his creditworthiness, his reliability or his conduct (section 12(1)).

Note that the definition is not exhaustive. Decisions in the context of contract or specifically permitted under legislation (known as 'exempt decisions') are treated somewhat differently to other forms of automated decision taking. In the latter case, the data subject has the right to prevent automated decisions being taken in respect of him or to require a data controller to reconsider such a decision. In terms of 'exempt decisions', the data controller must take steps to safeguard the legitimate interests of the data subject.

Exempt decisions

The precise meaning of 'exempt decisions' is given in section 12(4) to (7), being where:

- the decision is taken in the course of steps taken to consider whether to enter into a contract with the data subject or with a view to entering into such a contract or in the course of performing such a contract, or is authorised or required by or under any enactment, and
- the effect of the decision is to grant a request of the data subject or steps have been taken to safeguard his legitimate interests (for example, allowing him to make representations).

These may be added to by the Secretary of State. However, the conditions that either the data subject's request is granted or steps have been taken to safeguard the data subject's legitimate interests do not automatically apply to any further types of decision added by the Secretary of State although, of course, any regulations adding to the list of exempt decisions may make specific provisions for safeguards.

As an example of an exempt decision, consider an individual, Herbert, who has applied for hire purchase to buy a used car. The hire-purchase company, Grabbitt & Co Ltd, use an automated decision system on a computer which is based on a credit scoring formula. If Grabbitt & Co accepts Herbert's application and a hire-purchase contract is duly executed, there is no further requirement under these provisions. (Of course, if Grabbitt & Co want to disclose personal data relating to Herbert to another company, say for marketing purposes, Herbert should be told this, preferably by having a 'tick box' on the hire-purchase application form.) However, if Grabbitt & Co turn down Herbert's application, his legitimate interests must be safeguarded and, as the Act suggests, this will probably be by allowing him to make representations, that is, to respond to the failure to be granted credit. It may be that some years ago Herbert had a court judgment against him for debt and he has been open about this when completing the application form (or Grabbitt & Co have found out from a credit reference agency that he has been in default of a loan). Herbert might now want to say to Grabbitt & Co that he is a much better credit risk nowadays and that his default was at a time when he lost his job and he has since repaid the amount outstanding in full.

The Act is silent on what, if anything, the data controller should do in response to representations made by a data subject but a reasonable data controller ought seriously to consider any representations made by an individual and, in appropriate circumstances, reconsider the decision, perhaps by personal review rather than by automated decision taking.

Non-exempt decisions

As mentioned above, where the decision itself is not an exempt one, data subjects have far greater rights and can even prevent automated decision taking in respect of them where the decisions, based solely on automated decision taking, significantly affect them and are for the purpose of evaluating matters such as performance at work, creditworthiness, reliability or conduct. Probably the greatest proportion of automated decision taking within section 12 of the Data Protection Act 1998 will be in respect of contracts and will be exempt decisions. Other exempt decisions may be specifically authorised by or required by legislation. An example might be an automated system to determine social security payments.

It is not an easy matter to think of examples of automated decision taking which will be outside the realms of contract. One possible hypothetical candidate is where a doctor in a local NHS Trust hospital uses an automated system to decide on priority for operations where there is a long waiting list. Being an NHS Trust hospital, there is no contract between the patient and the hospital, or for that matter, between the patient and the doctor. Indeed, there are probably several other potential areas where the public sector confers benefits on individuals outwith contract. Some, such as the social security example quoted above, may be specifically provided for by legislation and thus become exempt decisions.

In respect of automated decision taking which is not exempt, under section 12(1) the data subject is given a right to prevent such decisions by serving a written notice on the data controller. There is no mention of any time limit for the notice to take effect nor that it has to be reasonable. It would seem that the intention is for the notice to take immediate effect. As with direct marketing, this right is absolute but does not, of course, apply to exempt decisions.

Where no notice has been served by the data subject, further safeguards are provided. Under section 12(2), the data controller is required to notify the data subject that the decision was taken on the basis of automated decision taking as soon as reasonably practicable. The data subject then has the opportunity to ask the data controller, by written notice, to reconsider the decision or take a new decision by other means within 21 days of receipt of the notice. Within that period, the data controller must serve a written notice on the data subject stating what steps he intends to take to comply with the data subject's notice. These rights of data subjects are backed by court powers to order compliance by the 'responsible person', being the person taking the decision in respect of the data subject. The use of the term 'responsible person' presumably is used to include the situation where the decision taking is actually carried out on behalf of a data controller by a processor, such as a computer bureau. Any court order does not affect the rights of any person other than the data subject or the responsible person.

A final point is to note that these provisions apply only where the decision is based *solely* on processing by automatic means. The word 'solely' should not be taken in a strong sense. For example, simply having the person operating the automated decision-taking software confirm or ratify the decision in an unquestioning way will not take the decision taking outside the controls on automated decision taking. Simply 'rubber-stamping' the result is not enough to escape the provisions. It would be different, however, if some aspects of the decision were actively reviewed by a human being.

Compensation

Individuals are entitled to compensation from the data controller for damage resulting from a contravention of *any* of the requirements in the Act. Although similar in operation, this is much wider than under the 1984 Act as it extends to any contravention of the Act, whereas before it was available only in respect of inaccurate data, loss of data, unauthorised destruction of data or unauthorised disclosure of or access to the data. Now, under section 13 of the 1998 Act, compensation is available for any contravention causing damage to the data subject. Under the 1984 Act compensation was also available for distress suffered by the data subject but it appeared that this applied only where the data subject had also sustained damage. Under the 1998 Act, compensation for distress is available generally where there is also damage or where the contravention concerns processing for the 'special purposes' (journalism, artistic or literary expression).

Examples of situations where the data subject should be able to claim compensation for damage and/or distress under the 1998 Act are given below.

Andrew has been turned down for employment because a reference given by a former employer taken from Andrew's personnel file contained a statement that Andrew had been subject to disciplinary action for dishonesty when, in actual fact, Andrew had been cleared of the charge following an appeal within the company's disciplinary procedures. He may now have a claim for compensation for damage and, possibly, depending on the circumstances, for distress.

Brenda is a famous singer who had an illegitimate child some years before she became famous. A local newspaper published details of this last week, including the identity of the child (who was unaware of the identity of Brenda or even that he was adopted), and today the newspaper has sold the story to a national television company which intends to broadcast details in a documentary on single mothers. Brenda (and her son) may have a claim for distress as such processing may not be able to rely on the exemptions for the special purposes. The publication and broadcast would be permissible only if the data controller reasonably believes that it is in the public interest: see section 32. If this is not so, and it may not be so because the information published probably goes beyond what is required in the public interest, the exemption from fair processing under the first Data Protection Principle will be lost.

Colin is a self-employed management consultant. He recently submitted a quotation to carry out an in-depth management analysis for Fizkin plc, a large manufacturing company. However, the managing director of Fizkin has spoken to the company secretary of Pipkin Trading Ltd who told him that Colin used to be a member of the Communist Party. Colin used to carry out consulting work for Pipkin. Fizkin turns down Colin's quotation and tells him that the company has discovered from Pipkin that he has a dubious political background. Colin made a data subject access request to Pipkin and the printout from the computer file indeed shows that Colin was a member of the Communist Party when he was a student many years ago. Colin should have a claim for compensation for damage because, although the information is correct, it is probably in breach of the third Data Protection Principle in that the data relating to him held by Pipkin are excessive in relation to the purposes for processing (keeping information about consultants, their work, payments to them, etc.).

Deborah recently went into hospital to have a toe amputated. Her details were sent to the hospital from her general practitioner and the hospital added further information. Her general practitioner failed to note that, in the last year or so, Brenda has developed an allergy to a certain type of anaesthetic. The information was kept in a structured paper file (a 'relevant filing system'). Unfortunately, the junior doctor entering information into her file made a mistake and this was not spotted by the surgeon. The wrong toe was amputated and, as a result, Brenda is more severely disabled physically than she would have been had the correct toe been amputated in the first place. She has also suffered minor brain damage as a result of being given an anaesthetic to which she is allergic. Brenda should have a claim to compensation for damage and possibly also for distress because the data were in breach of the fourth Data Protection Principle in that that they were inaccurate and not kept up to date (the allergy was not mentioned). Of course, Brenda will also have a claim for damages on account of negligence, apart from data protection law, and it is most likely that this will be her main claim. However, there is nothing in the Data Protection Act to suggest that full compensation cannot be given for the breaches of duty imposed by the Act.

The right to compensation is tempered by the existence of a defence similar to that under the 1984 Act, being where the data controller can prove that he took such care as was in all the circumstances reasonably required to comply with the requirement which has been contravened. Of course, compensation can only be awarded to an individual who goes to court. There are no powers for the Data Protection Commissioner to award compensation. A data subject seeking compensation has to go to either the county court or High Court (in England and Wales). Choice of court will depend, to some extent, on the amount of compensation sought.

Rights in relation to inaccurate data

Fundamentally, the rights of data subjects in respect of personal data that are inaccurate are similar to those under the 1984 Act. However, there are some changes and the scope of the right is widened somewhat. There is also the possibility now that any court order may require that third parties to whom the data have been disclosed are informed of the inaccuracy. Another change is that, under the 1984 Act, the rights related to rectification or erasure. Under the 1998 Act, reflecting the fact this Act also covers certain types of manual data, rights relating to blocking and destruction are added. 'Blocking' is defined neither in the Act nor in the Directive but it would seem reasonable to assume that it means suppressing the data without erasing them. For example, in a computer database, data may be suppressed from a particular form of processing or a 'flag' may be set indicating that data relating to a particular person are no longer to be processed even though they are not deleted permanently. 'Destruction' clearly is applicable in relation to manual data.

Under section 70(2), data are inaccurate if they are incorrect or misleading as to any matter of fact. This is an identical definition to that under the 1984 Act. There are two forms of control in the 1998 Act, contained in section 14. The first relates to data that are inaccurate. The second relates to serious contraventions of the Act causing damage to the data subject. As with compensation, the data subject must apply to the court for an appropriate order for rectification, blocking, erasure or destruction. However, it should be noted that the Commissioner may also require rectification, blocking, erasure or destruction of inaccurate data as part of an enforcement notice.

Inaccurate data

Inaccurate data may be ordered by a court, on application by the data subject, to be rectified, blocked, erased or destroyed, if the court is satisfied that they are inaccurate. This extends to other data which contain an expression of opinion about the data subject which is based upon such inaccurate data: section 14(1). Paragraph 7 of Part II of Schedule 1 (interpretation of the Data Protection Principles) states that it is not a contravention of the fourth Principle (data shall be accurate and, where necessary, kept up to date) if the data accurately record information given by the data subject or a third party where:

- having regard to the purpose or purposes for which the data were obtained and further processed, the data controller has taken reasonable steps in the circumstances to ensure the accuracy of the data, and
- if notified by the data subject of his view that the data are inaccurate, the data indicate that fact.

Thus, where this is the case, the court may instead of ordering rectification, etc. require a supplementary statement of the true facts. If data accurately record information received or obtained from the data subject or a third party but paragraph 7 of Part II of Schedule 1 does not apply (for example, where the data controller has *failed* to take reasonable steps to ensure accuracy), the court may instead of ordering rectification, etc., make an order to secure compliance with or without a further order for a supplementary statement of the true facts.

The court may also order the data controller to inform third parties to whom the inaccurate data have been disclosed of the rectification, blocking, erasure or destruction.

Any contravention of the Act

The court has a general power to order rectification, blocking, erasure or destruction of data where the data subject has suffered damage in circumstances which entitle him to compensation under the Act and where there is a substantial risk of further contravention in respect of those data in such circumstances. This could apply, for example, where data are accurate but excessive in breach of the third Data Protection Principle. The equivalent provision to this under the 1984 Act was limited to unauthorised disclosures of or access to personal data and only permitted the court to order erasure.

In addition to the order above and as with inaccurate data, a court may, where it considers it to be reasonably practicable, order the data controller to notify third parties to whom the data have been disclosed of the rectification, blocking, erasure or disclosure. Regard is to be had, in particular, to the number of persons involved. In the Directive third parties are required to be notified unless it proves impossible or involves a disproportionate effort. This provision also applies in relation to inaccurate data described above. To some extent, the ease with which third parties can be notified will be a reflection of how well the data controller keeps records of disclosures. With the use of electronic mail and a good audit trail of disclosures, notifying third parties could be quite an easy matter even if there are a large number to be informed. This could be important from the point of view of third parties as, until they have rectified, blocked, erased or destroyed, third parties will probably be in breach of the Data Protection Act 1998 and vulnerable to an action for compensation.

Jurisdiction and procedure

Under section 15, jurisdiction is conferred, in England and Wales, on the High Court or a county court. In Scotland, it is the Court of Session or the sheriff court. Where there is an issue as to whether a data subject is entitled to subject access under section 7 (including information as to the logic in any automated decision taking), the data subject or his representative will not have access to the information unless and until the court determines the matter of right of access in favour of the data subject. If this were not so, the ordinary rules of discovery in court proceedings could defeat the subject access exemptions where litigation is under way.

Summary

We have seen that the rights of data subjects have been significantly improved by the Data Protection Act 1998. However, rights are only any good if the persons to whom they are given are aware of them and prepared to exercise them. There are no statistics to indicate how much use has been made of the rights under the 1984 Act but it is unlikely that many persons have been prepared to go to the expense and worry of a court action. For the aggrieved data subject, there is an alternative route to obtain a data controller's compliance with the Act and that is by approaching the Data Protection Commissioner. Under the 1984 Act, the number of complaints made to the Data Protection Registrar ran into thousands, peaking at 4590 in the year 1992/93 (this peak was probably the result of a television advertising campaign by the Registrar). In the latest year for which figures are available (1998/99), there were 3653 complaints received by the Registrar of which 48 per cent were investigated (Data Protection Registrar, *Fifteenth Annual Report of the Data Protection Registrar*, The Stationery Office, 1999). The Registrar under the 1984 Act was very effective in raising awareness about data protection law, both by data users and data subjects. This is likely to continue under the 1998 Act; indeed, it is one of the Commissioner's duties to do so.

The complaints procedure has been changed slightly under the 1998 Act, partly reflecting changes to the Commissioner's powers of enforcement, and any individual who considers that he is directly affected by any processing may, under section 42, apply to the Commissioner for an assessment as to whether or not it is likely that the processing has been or is being carried out in compliance with the Act. This is described in more detail in Chapter 30 in the context of the Commissioner's powers as also is the right of an individual to apply to the Commissioner for assistance where the processing relates to processing for the special purposes.

It is unlikely that we will see a sudden increase in the exercise of data subjects' rights with the introduction of the new law. As before, individuals generally will not use their right to access to personal data unless something appears wrong: for example, where they have been denied credit. The fact that the data controller can charge a fee, up to a prescribed maximum, will deter all but the most curious from carrying out subject access requests simply for the sake of it. The right to prevent processing for the purposes of direct marketing is the right likely to be used the most, if it is properly publicised, but the other rights are very important in the minority of cases where there are problems. However, it must be noted that the rights of data subjects are tempered by the large number of exemptions from the subject information provisions, described in the previous chapter. Unless a data subject knows who is processing personal data relating to him and/or can exercise a subject access request, the other rights will be difficult if not impossible to enforce. In such circumstances, it would seem that a request for an assessment made to the Commissioner may be the only effective way for an individual to proceed.

Chapter 33

Privacy in telecommunications

Introduction

The advent of new technological developments in the telecommunications sector, such as the ability to capture information such as a caller's telephone number or to see the number from which an incoming call is made before deciding whether to answer, has brought concerns about privacy. Another issue is the growing use of telephones and facsimile machines ('faxes') for marketing purposes. There is nothing more irritating than seeing your fax machine churning out unsolicited advertising material, tying up the machine and using your paper. Other concerns relate to the use and storage of personal data relating to customers of telecommunication service providers, automatic call forwarding and information made available in directories, whether in paper or software form. Security and the prevention of unlawful eavesdropping are other privacy issues.

In part, these issues are already addressed in the United Kingdom, for example, by the Interception of Communications Act 1985. Other control is by self-regulation in the public telecommunications sector: for example, where a customer of a service provider can request that his name does not appear in the published directory of subscribers ('ex-directory'). Another possibility is to contact the Telephone Preference Service in the hope of reducing the number of unsolicited marketing calls received ('cold-calling') or, for fax machines, the Fax Preference Service. Once again, however, the stimulus for change and greater protection for individuals' rights to privacy comes about by way of a European initiative. Directive 97/66/EC of the European Parliament and of the Council concerning the processing of personal data and the protection of privacy in the telecommunications sector (OJ [1998] L 24/1) was adopted on 15 December 1997 (the 'Telecomms Directive').

In many respects, the Telecomms Directive supplements the Data Protection Directive set in the context of telecommunications. The latter applies to the protection of fundamental rights and freedoms which are not specifically covered by the Telecomms Directive and, generally, to non-public telecommunications networks. Both Directives required compliance by 24 October 1998. It has already been noted that, at the time of writing, the new data protection law should be brought into force imminently. Part of the Telecomms Directive came into force on 1 May 1999 by virtue of the Telecommunications (Data Protection and Privacy) (Direct Marketing) Regulations 1998. A feature of the Regulations is that rights are given to corporate subscribers in addition to individual subscribers. This chapter examines the Telecomms Directive first and then looks at the Regulations.

The Telecomms Directive

The recitals to the Directive indicate that the need for it arises from the introduction of new public digital telecommunications networks and new telecommunications services. The successful cross-border development of such services including video-on-demand and interactive television is, to some extent, claimed to be reliant upon the confidence that users have in respect to their privacy. Integrated Services Digital Networks (ISDN) and digital mobile networks are also highlighted as specific examples. The adoption of appropriate and harmonised legal, regulatory and technical measures is seen as important in the development of new telecommunications services and networks between and across member states. There is a danger that this development could be hindered without some degree of harmonisation. The main provisions of the Directive deal with:

- security and confidentiality
- traffic and billing data
- calling line and connected line information
- unsolicited calls and automatic call forwarding
- directories
- technical features and standardisation.

Scope and definitions

In line with the Data Protection Directive, the Telecomms Directive provides for the freedom of movement of personal data by requiring a harmonised level of protection of personal data: Article 1(1). It also extends to the free movement of telecommunications equipment. However, unlike the Data Protection Directive, some provisions also extend to legal persons as well as natural persons and the legitimate interests of subscribers who are legal persons, such as corporations, are protected.

The definitions contained in Article 2 supplement those in the Data Protection Directive and are set out below:

(a) 'subscriber' is any natural or legal person, being a party to a contract for the supply of services in relation to publicly available telecommunications services;

(b) 'user' is a natural person using such a service for private or business purposes, without necessarily being a subscriber to that service – thus, an employee of a corporate subscriber is a user if he uses the telecommunications service subscribed to his or her employer;

(c) 'public telecommunications network' is a transmission system which permits the conveyance between defined termination points used in whole or in part for the provision of publicly available telecommunications services – this includes switching systems and other resources and extends to transmission by wire, radio, optical or other electromagnetic means;

(d) 'telecommunications service' consists wholly or partly in transmitting and routing signals on telecommunications networks but this does not include radio or television broadcasting.

The Telecomms Directive applies to processing personal data in connection with the provision of publicly available telecommunications services (PATS) in public telecommunications networks (PTNs): Article 3. ISDN and public digital mobile networks are singled out as particular examples.

Security and confidentiality

The provider of a PATS must take appropriate technical and organisational security measures, if necessary, in conjunction with the provider of the PTN: Article 4. Factors to be taken into account are the state of the art, cost of implementation and the risk. Where there is a particular risk of a breach of security, the provider of a PATS must inform subscribers of this risk and any possible remedies including the costs involved.

Confidentiality of communications by means of PTNs must be ensured by national regulations under Article 5. Listening, tapping, storage or other kinds of interception or surveillance must be prohibited except where authorised by law in order to safeguard national security, defence and public security, or for the prevention, investigation, detection and prosecution of criminal offences, or where covered by the exemptions under the Data Protection Directive. The Interception of Communications Act 1985 already prohibits some forms of tapping and surveillance to some extent. However, recording of communications in the course of lawful business practice for the purpose of providing evidence of commercial transactions or other business communications which are legally authorised are unaffected. This could apply, for example, where an individual takes out car insurance over the telephone.

Traffic and billing data

Providers of PTNs and PATS need to process data relating to calls for the purpose of billing their customers. A considerable amount of information may be collected by the service provider and will include the subscriber's number, the number called, the date, start time, finish time, duration of the call, the call rate and the charge cost. Other information may be involved such as the data volume, the tariff class and data identifying the telephone exchange.

By virtue of Article 6, providers of PTNs and PATS may process personal data for billing and interconnection payments and, with the consent of subscribers, process for marketing their own services. Where the processing is for the purpose of billing and interconnection disputes, it is only allowed until the end of the period during which the bill may lawfully be challenged or payment may be pursued. This should be the limitation period (normally six years) under the Limitation Act 1980. The type of data that can be processed is restricted and is set out in the Annex to the Directive as data containing:

- the number or identification of the subscriber station,
- the address of the subscriber and the type of station,
- the total number of units to be charged for the accounting period,
- the called subscriber number,
- the type, starting time and duration of calls made and/or the data volume transmitted,
- the date of the call/service,
- other information concerning payments such as advance payment, payments by instalments, disconnection and reminders.

The processing must be restricted to persons acting under the authority of the provider of the service or network, as the case may be, handling billing or traffic management, customer enquiries, fraud detection and marketing the provider's own services. Furthermore, the processing must be restricted to that necessary for the purposes of such activities.

Apart from such processing, the general rule is that data relating to subscribers and users processed to establish calls which are stored by the provider must be erased or made anonymous upon termination of the call. However, these restrictions are without prejudice to the possibility of national authorities being informed of billing or traffic data under applicable legislation for settling disputes – in particular, disputes relating to interconnection or billing. In the United Kingdom this would, for example, allow for the disclosure of billing or traffic data to Oftel (the Office of Telecommunications).

Subscribers are given a right to receive non-itemised bills under Article 7. Where itemised bills are sent out, this could conflict with the right of privacy of calling users and called subscribers (outlined below). To reconcile this problem member states must, by national provisions, for example, ensure that 'sufficient alternative modalities for communications or payments are available to such users and subscribers'. The clue to this resides in the recitals to the Directive. One solution suggested is to delete a certain number of digits from the called numbers in itemised bills.

Calling and connected line identification

Articles 8, 9 and 10 concern calling line and connected line identification and automatic call forwarding. These Articles apply to subscriber lines connected to digital exchanges and, where it is technically possible and does not require a disproportionate economic effort, to subscriber lines connected to analogue exchanges. Any cases exempted on the basis of technical impossibility or because it would require a disproportionate investment must be notified to the Commission by member states.

Article 8 contains various provisions relating to the suppression of calling-line identification (CLI), where this is offered. The provisions are that:

- a calling user must be able, simply and free of charge, to prevent the presentation of CLI on a per-call basis and a calling subscriber must be able to do this on a per-line basis,
- a called subscriber must be able, simply and free of charge, to prevent the presentation of CLI on incoming calls (why a subscriber would want to do this is unclear although it could be relevant where the subscriber is a company and it wants to prevent employees selectively declining to answer calls from, for example, awkward customers),
- where CLI is presented prior to the call being established (that is, prior to connection) a called subscriber must be able by simple means to reject any incoming call for which CLI has been suppressed (an individual called at home late in the evening would probably prefer not to answer a call where CLI has been suppressed),
- a called subscriber must be able, simply and free of charge, to eliminate the presentation of CLI to the calling user (this would prevent the automatic capture of the subscriber's telephone number, say, by a commercial organisation),
- the elimination of the presentation of calling-line identification by a calling user or calling subscriber must also apply to calls to third countries and the other provisions must also apply in respect of calls coming from third countries (that is, from outside the European Community).

Member states are obliged to ensure that providers of PATS publicise the possibility of the ability to suppress CLI and to reject calls in respect of which CLI has been suppressed.

As complete suppression of CLI could hinder the tracing of persons making malicious or threatening calls, providers of PTNs and PATS may override the elimination of presentation of CLI in two cases: Article 9. First, on a temporary basis at the request of a subscriber wishing to trace malicious or nuisance calls. This will allow the storage of the CLI relating to the calling user and the making available of such information. The second case applies to the police and emergency services and like organisations. This will operate on a per-call basis. The overriding of the elimination of presentation of CLI must be by transparent procedures. In other words, the public must know about it or, at least, be able to find out. It appears that CLI relating to a first malicious call will not be stored. It is only in response to a request from the subscriber that the CLI will be stored. Such a request will usually come only after a first malicious call has been made. This is in line with the Protection from Harassment Act 1997 which requires a course of conduct which means there must be more than one occasion or incident. The Directive, as is usual, does not apply to activities outside Community law, which include activities of the state in areas of criminal law.

Unsolicited calls and automatic call forwarding

Most people find unsolicited calls from organisations trying to sell something intrusive and a nuisance. It can be very irritating to go and answer the telephone while in the middle of cooking a meal, reading a book or performing some other enjoyable activity only to find that it is someone 'cold-calling', trying to get you to buy double glazing, financial services or whatever. By subscribing to the Telephone Preference System, these cold-calls can be reduced to a minimum, if not eliminated altogether. Another way to reduce them is to be 'ex-directory', though this defeats the usefulness of telephone directories as a source of information and may prevent a welcome telephone contact.

As far as unsolicited calls are concerned, there are two forms of control provided for in Article 12 of the Directive. In the context of automatic calling machines which operate without human intervention and fax machines, direct marketing may only be pursued by the prior consent of the subscribers. For unsolicited calls for purposes of direct marketing by other means, member states have two choices. They may either require the consent of subscribers or use a system like the Telephone Preference System whereby subscribers make known that they do not wish to receive such calls. The prevention of such calls by subscribers must be free of charge.

The basic rights in respect of unsolicited calls are given to natural persons. However, there must also be provisions to give sufficient protection to the legitimate interests of persons other than natural persons (that is, artificial legal persons such as limited companies) with regard to unsolicited calls for purposes of direct marketing. Under Article 10, every subscriber has a right to prevent automatic call forwarding by a third party to his terminal by simple means and without charge.

Directories

Telephone directories may seem innocuous enough but may still contain information that can threaten privacy or even safety. The information may indicate the sex of the subscriber by the appropriate title or may indicate some calling or profession such as where the title is Rev. or Dr. It may indicate that the subscriber possibly lives alone, such as where the title 'Miss' is used. Under Article 11, personal data contained in directories of subscribers, whether in printed or electronic form and which are made available to the public or obtainable through directory enquiry services shall be limited to those necessary to identify a particular subscriber. If they wish, subscribers may consent to the publication of additional data providing such consent is unambiguous; in other words, it should be express and informed consent. Subscribers can request, generally without charge (but see below), that:

- they are omitted from the directory,
- his or her personal data are not used for direct marketing,
- his or her address is omitted in part,
- there is no reference to his or her sex 'where this is linguistically applicable' – for example, by requesting that titles such as Mr or Mrs are not used.

Member states may allow subscribers wishing to be ex-directory to be charged for this providing the sum does not exceed the actual costs incurred by the operator of the service and such a charge does not act as a disincentive to the exercise of this right. The rights apply to natural persons but member states must also extend the rights in regard to entries to other subscribers such that their legitimate interests are sufficiently protected, within the framework of Community law and applicable national legislation. For example, organisations of a type which may be a target for extremist groups should be able to prevent the publication of their addresses in the directory. An example could be an organisation legitimately performing research into genetic engineering.

Technical features and standardisation

If different member states adopt different technical features to comply with the Directive, this will work against the common market by impeding the placing of equipment on the market and the free circulation of telecommunications equipment. The basic rule, expressed in Article 13, is that there shall be no mandatory requirements for specific technical features imposed on terminals and other telecommunications equipment by member states in their implementation of the Directive which would distort the single market. However, where the provisions of the Directive can only be implemented by requiring specific technical features applied to terminals or other telecommunications equipment, member states shall inform the Commission accordingly. Where required, the Commission will ensure the drawing up of common European standards in respect of such technical features in accordance with Council Decision 87/95/EEC on standardisation in the field of information technology and telecommunications (OJ [1987] L36/31).

Other provisions

Some of the provisions of the Data Protection Directive are extended to the subject matter of the Telecomms Directive. For example, Chapter III of the former Directive (judicial remedies, liabilities and sanctions) apply here also and the Working Party on data protection will also have within its brief the protection of fundamental rights and freedoms (natural persons) and of the legitimate interests (artificial legal persons) in the telecommunications sector.

Although the date for implementation of the Telecomms Directive is not later than 24 October 1998, Article 5 on confidentiality of communications can be delayed until 24 October 2000. A provider of a PATS already processing personal data as at the time the Directive is implemented by national law for the purpose of marketing its own telecommunications services may continue so to do without the consent of the subscribers. However, the subscribers must be informed of such processing and not object within a period of time to be determined by the member state in question. The provisions in Article 11 concerning directories of subscribers do not apply in the case of directories already published by the time the Directive is implemented by national law.

The Direct Marketing Regulations

The Telecommunications (Data Protection and Privacy) (Direct Marketing) Regulations 1998 (the 'Regulations') came into force on 1 May 1999 and implement those parts of the Telecomms Directive dealing with direct marketing. Controls are provided in respect of:

- automated calling systems for direct marketing,
- unsolicited fax communications for direct marketing, and
- other unsolicited calls for direct marketing purposes.

The first two apply to corporate subscribers but the last one applies only in respect of individuals, who, in England and Wales, include unincorporated bodies of individuals such as partnerships. Partnerships in Scotland are treated as corporate subscribers.

There are requirements for telecommunications service providers, producers of directories of subscribers and persons providing information to directory producers to notify the Director General of Communications of subscribers who have indicated that they do not wish to receive unsolicited fax communications or other unsolicited calls. The Director General maintains a record of such subscribers as under the Telephone Preference System and the Fax Preference System. Any person suffering damage as a result of any contravention of the requirements of the Regulations is entitled to compensation from the person responsible.

All the controls relate to the use of publicly available telecommunications services for direct marketing purposes, being the communication of any advertising or marketing material on a particular line. A 'line' is the telephone or other line through which the communication is made or, if made wholly or partly other than by line – for example, in the case of a mobile telephone – any reference to a line in the Regulations is to what functionally corresponds to a line. The powers of the Data Protection Registrar are enlarged to enable the use of enforcement notices and entry and inspection under the Data Protection Act 1984. The appeal system under that Act is also available. Presumably, as the main provisions of the Data Protection Act 1998 are brought into force, the Regulations will be amended to relate to the Data Protection Commissioner and the equivalent provisions dealing with enforcement notices and entry and inspection under that Act.

In all cases, it is the person who uses or instigates the use of a publicly available telecommunications system or permits his line to be used for marketing purposes who is controlled and, where applicable, has been notified of the called subscriber's consent to the marketing.

Automatic calling systems

An automatic calling system is, under regulation 6, a system which, when activated, makes calls without human intervention. Such systems are strictly controlled and marketing by this method is allowed only where the subscriber, whether an individual subscriber or corporate subscriber, has previously notified the person calling of his consent. Note that it is the person calling who must have been notified so that, where a subscriber has allowed a third party to use his line, it is the third party to whom the called subscriber must have notified his or its consent.

Unsolicited fax communications

There is a slight difference in these provisions, contained in regulation 7, depending on whether the called subscriber is an individual subscriber or a corporate subscriber. However, in both cases, an unsolicited fax communication for marketing purposes cannot be made if the record kept by the Director General of Telecommunications indicates that the subscriber does not for the time being wish to receive such communications. Nor may it be sent if the called line is that of a subscriber who has previously notified the person concerned that such communications should not be sent on that line. However, a fax communication is not deemed to be unsolicited if the subscriber has notified the caller that he does not object to receiving faxes for direct marketing purposes on that line from that caller.

Individual subscribers have a further form of control in that their prior consent to the communication is required under regulation 8.

Other unsolicited calls

Other unsolicited calls for marketing purposes are those which are not via automatic calling systems or by facsimile transmission. Thus, under regulation 9, this control applies to cold-calling where a person trying to sell something telephones other persons, perhaps working their way through a database of subscribers or telephone directory. These provisions only apply to individual subscribers and they may not be called if they have either had their objection to receiving such calls placed on the record kept by the Director General of Telecommunications or if they have notified the person concerned of their objection to such calls being made on that line. However, a call is not deemed to be unsolicited if the subscriber has notified the caller that he does not object to receiving calls for direct marketing purposes on that line made by or at the instigation of that caller.

As regards the availability of compensation under regulation 12, it is a defence to show that the person concerned had taken such care as in all the circumstances was reasonably required to comply with the requirement concerned. Of course, in most cases, the amount of compensation to be awarded is unlikely to be substantial. That being so, few subscribers are likely to apply to a court for compensation and are more likely instead to complain to the Data Protection Registrar (Commissioner).

Chapter 34

Summary of data protection law

The Data Protection Act 1984 attempted to reconcile the rights and interests of individuals with the need of others to process personal data. The right to be able to process personal data is essential for many organisations and, for others, considerable difficulties would be experienced if they were prevented from processing personal data at all or if it were to be over-regulated. It is fair to say that the balance achieved by the 1984 Act favoured the data processor rather than the individual data subject. Although compliance with the data protection principles was required, in most cases, data protection law meant little more than the imposition of a triennial chore of registering under the Act. Furthermore, the experiences of enforcement of data protection law including criminal prosecutions under the 1984 Act suggested that this data protection law had relatively little impact on data users, as they were known under the old law, and computer bureaux.

All of this is set to change with the Data Protection Act 1998. It makes sweeping changes to data protection law even though, as before, it has at its heart the Data Protection Principles which are derived from the European Convention on data protection. Not only are the rights of individuals significantly improved, they have several important new rights. A basic premise of the new law is that of transparency of processing. Individuals should be able to find out who is processing personal data relating to them and for what purposes much more easily than before. Serious concerns were expressed about the new law and its restrictive nature and the extension of data protection law to certain types of structured manual files. It is probable that initial estimates of the likely costs of compliance were exaggerated and, when the new law has had time to settle down, most persons and organisations processing personal data will find that it is not as onerous as first was thought. Nevertheless, it must be recognised that the new law does go much further than before and those involved in processing personal data must be aware of the changes and give serious consideration to how compliance can be achieved in as painless a way as possible.

Those who process personal data (data controllers and processors) would do well to develop a data protection policy (or modify their existing policy). In particular, they should:

- allocate responsibilities among staff for compliance with data protection law: the IT manager will have a central role to play in the development of the policy and in assuming responsibility for compliance and should be fully conversant with the new law and how it impacts on the organisation's activities; extensive training and updating of knowledge is desirable for IT managers as is the need for them to keep senior management informed of procedures and changes to them and developments in data protection law,

- educate and train staff: make sure that they know how data protection law impacts on their work and they know the importance of data protection law; in particular, employees must be informed of what they can and cannot do with the personal data they will process (for example, by stressing the consequences of disclosing personal data without the employer's consent),

- check and, if necessary, modify forms and other documentation, for example, to ensure compliance with new requirements to provide individuals with information and in relation to obtaining the data subject's consent (in some cases, the simple tick box approach, where failure to tick the box indicates consent, will probably not suffice and express consent may be required),

- review responses to subject access requests in the light of the new law and procedures put in place to comply with requests for the equivalent of the registrable particulars in respect of processing that does not need to be, and has not been, notified,

- set up procedures to deal with the new and enhanced rights of individuals; for example, in relation to automatic decision taking, it may be important to provide the individual with a right to be heard if his request is not complied with or if he requires the decision to be taken again or taken by other means,

- ensure that contracts with processors (bearing in mind the very wide definition of processing) contain written guarantees of data security and integrity and stress their security obligations which have to be in line with those imposed on the data controller,

- be aware that transfers of personal data to some countries outside the European Economic Area may be permitted only in certain circumstances such as where there are contractual guarantees as to adequacy of data protection or where the individuals to whom the data relate have consented to the transfer; watch out for approved contractual clauses which may be used to permit transfers to countries outside the European Economic Area that do not have adequate protection for personal data,

- regularly review security arrangements and regularly monitor technological developments in security measures with a view to implementing them,

- watch for relevant codes of practice for data protection being published and look for guidance on the new law published by the Data Protection Commissioner; in particular, regularly check the Commissioner's Website available through www.open.gov.uk (go to the organisational index and look for Data Protection Commissioner, although at the time of writing, it is still down as the Data Protection Registrar).

Although the new law is very welcome for individuals, with its emphasis on protecting rights and freedoms, in particular, with respect to privacy of personal data, there are still a number of worrying aspects. Data protection law, like many laws, looks fairly ineffective when faced with controlling the Internet and much work needs to be done in this area. Other issues include the processing of genetic data, disclosures of financial information relating to persons who have a good credit record (white data) and the operations of private investigation agencies. The new Act allows for preliminary assessment of processing where it is likely to pose specific risks and this is certainly so with respect to genetic data. The Secretary of State will make an order listing forms of processing which will be subject to a preliminary assessment. However, the Commissioner has no power to prevent such processing (apart from using her enforcement powers or by bringing prosecutions under the Act if the data controller decides to process after receiving an adverse Commissioner's assessment). The idea is that preliminary assessment gives the Commissioner an opportunity to inform the data controller whether she thinks it is likely to comply with the Act.

Other forms of processing which may give concern are:

- data matching, where personal data from different sources relating to a particular individual are compared, for example, in order to try to detect a possible fraudster if the information is contradictory,
- the use of an 'impaired life' database by insurance companies,
- lifestyle databases where data is collected, often from different sources, to build up a picture of a person's lifestyle; this can be extremely useful in targeting marketing material or providing a 'better' service to consumers, for example, when booking accommodation through a travel agent who has a record that the person concerned likes golf and is a vegetarian non-smoker,
- data warehousing, where massive amounts of data are collected from numerous sources with all the inherent dangers of inaccuracies,
- health data of a sensitive nature.

With the new law, and the implementation of the Telecomms Directive, the United Kingdom has gone along the path of formal regulation, unlike the approach in some countries, particularly the United States where self-regulation is favoured in most sectors. This difference in approach is already causing problems and tensions as it could be thought that countries with no or few data protection laws do not have sufficient protection to allow transfers of personal data to them.

In the meantime, the new law will take some time to bed down and much remains to be done. There are provisions for numerous regulations to be made under the Act by the Secretary of State. Already, it is being suggested that a particular exemption will be made allowing financial institutions and the like to process personal data relating to criminal convictions to assist such data controllers in avoiding being victims of widespread fraud.

General

Gringras, C, *The Laws of the Internet*, Butterworths, 1997.
Knight, P and Fitzsimons, J, *The Legal Environment of Computing*, Addison-Wesley, 1990.
Lloyd, I J, *Information Technology Law*, 2nd edn, Butterworths, 1997.
Reed, C (ed), *Computer Law*, 3rd edn, Blackstone, 1996.
Tapper, C, *Computer Law*, 4th edn, Longman, 1990.

Computers and intellectual property

Bainbridge, D I, *Intellectual Property*, 4th edn, FT Pitman Publishing (Pearson Education), 1999.
Bainbridge, D I, *Software Copyright Law*, 4th edn, Butterworths, 1999.
Coleman, A, *The Legal Protection of Trade Secrets*, Sweet and Maxwell, 1992.
Cornish, W R, *Intellectual Property: Patents, Copyright, Trade Marks and Allied Rights*, 3rd edn, Sweet and Maxwell, 1996.
Dworkin, G and Taylor, R D, *Copyright, Designs and Patents Act 1988*, Blackstone, 1989.
Saxby, S (ed), *Encyclopedia of Information Technology Law*, Sweet and Maxwell, 1990.

Computer contracts

Bainbridge, D I, *Software Licensing*, 2nd edn, Central Law Publishing, 1999.
Chissick, M and Kelman, A, *Electronic Commerce: Law and Practice*, Sweet and Maxwell, 1999.
Henry, M, *Publishing and Multimedia Law*, Butterworths, 1994.
Institute of Purchasing and Supply, *Standard Form Contracts* (various), available from the Institute at Easton House, Easton on the Hill, Stamford PE9 3NZ.
Klinger, P and Burnett, R, *Drafting and Negotiating Computer Contracts*, Butterworths, 1994.
Michele Rennie, M T, *Computer Contracts*, Sweet and Maxwell, 1994.
Morgan, R and Steadman, G, *Computer Contracts*, 5th edn, Longman, 1995.
Pearson, H E, *Computer Contracts: An International Guide to Agreements and Software Protection*, Financial Training Publications, 1984.
Walden, I (ed), *EDI and the Law*, Blenheim Online, 1989.

Computers and crime

Audit Commission, *Ghost in the Machine: An Analysis of IT Fraud and Abuse*, Audit Commission Publications, 1998.

Audit Commission, *Opportunity Makes a Thief: An Analysis of Computer Abuse*, HMSO, 1994.

Audit Commission, *Survey of Computer Fraud and Abuse 1987*, HMSO, 1988.

Audit Commission, *Survey of Computer Fraud and Abuse 1990*, HMSO, 1991.

Law Commission, *Computer Misuse* (Working Paper No. 110), HMSO, 1988.

Law Commission, *Criminal Law: Computer Misuse* (Law Com. No. 186), Cm 819, HMSO, 1989.

National Audit Office, *IT Security in Government Departments*, HMSO, 1995.

Wasik, M, *Crime and the Computer*, Clarendon Press, 1991.

Data protection

Bainbridge, D I, *The EC Data Protection Directive*, Butterworths, 1996.

Charlton S, Gaskill S and Sterling, J A L, *Encyclopedia of Data Protection*, Sweet and Maxwell, 1988.

Cornwell, R and Staunton, M, *Data Protection: Putting the Record Straight*, National Council for Civil Liberties, 1985.

Data Protection Registrar, *Fourteenth Annual Report of the Data Protection Registrar*, The Stationery Office, 1998 (and previous reports).

Data Protection Registrar, *The Guidelines*. Available free of charge from the Office of the Data Protection Registrar, Wycliffe House, Water Lane, Wilmslow, Cheshire SK9 5AF or through the Registrar's Website (http://www.open.gov.uk/dpr/dprhome.htm).

Evans, A, *Data Protection Policies and Practice*, Institute of Personnel Management, 1987.

Gulleford, K, *Data Protection in Practice*, Butterworths, 1986.

Niblett, B, *Data Protection Act 1984*, Oyez, 1984.

Report of the Committee on Data Protection, *The Lindop Report*, Cmnd 7341, HMSO, December 1978.

Savage, N and Edwards, C, *Guide to the Data Protection Act*, 2nd edn, Blackstone, 1988.

Index

Database of Summaries of Computer Law Cases and Software Copyright Legislation

A computer database of summaries of important computer law cases is available from the author. The database usefully supplements this book and contains summaries of many of the cases referred to. The database comprises summaries of over 80 cases including some of the most recent ones. The database is provided complete with an easy to use computer program having retrieval and editing facilities. Also included is a database of legislation relating to software copyright which includes extracts from the Copyright, Designs and Patents Act 1988, as amended, and from the Copyright and Rights in Databases Regulations 1997. The extracts, which are Crown copyright, are annotated by the author of this book and published under the terms of Crown Copyright Policy Guidance issued by HMSO. The author updates the databases on a continuing basis.

The databases may be modified and added to and new databases can be created. The databases are in dBase III+ format and also may be used with most WINDOWS database packages including MICROSOFT ACCESS, LOTUS APPROACH and dBASE for WINDOWS, allowing users to design their own forms and reports (you will need to have some familiarity with these packages to take full advantage of their powerful facilities). For users of MICROSOFT ACCESS Version 7 for WINDOWS 95, at no extra cost, a special version of the databases is available as an alternative with built-in menus, forms and queries. If you want both the DOS and ACCESS versions, please make this clear and add £2.00 to your order.

The databases are available on a 3½ inch disk (1.44MB) suitable for an IBM personal computer or equivalent running DOS with a 1.44MB capacity disk drive. A hard disk is desirable. The system can be run from DOS or it can be run from the Windows environment (as a DOS program) or used with the database packages mentioned above.

The databases are available for the price of £9.99 for students and academics or £15.99 for practitioners. If you want the Access Version 7 for Windows 95 version of the database, please specify ACCESS on your order. Send payment (cheque or postal order payable to David Bainbridge) to the address below quoting reference **CL4**. Every effort will be made to deliver more quickly but please allow 21 days. Prices include post and packing for UK only.

> **Dr David Bainbridge**
> **Aston Business School**
> **Aston University**
> **Aston Triangle**
> **Birmingham B4 7ET**

Note: if entering new materials to the database or creating new databases, please take care to avoid infringing copyright (see Chapters 6 and 7 of this book). All trade marks are acknowledged.